Yamaha
XJR1200 & 1300
Service and Repair Manual

by Matthew Coombs

Models covered

(3981 - 272)

XJR1200. 1188cc. 1995 to 1998
XJR1300. 1250cc. 1999 to 2003
XJR1300SP. 1250cc. 2000 and 2001

ABCDE
FGHIJ   Printed in the USA
KLMNO
PQRS

© Haynes Publishing 2003

Haynes Publishing
Sparkford, Yeovil, Somerset BA22 7JJ, England

A book in the Haynes Service and Repair Manual Series

Haynes North America, Inc
861 Lawrence Drive, Newbury Park, California 91320, USA

All rights reserved. No part of this book may be reproduced or transmitted in any form or by any means, electronic or mechanical, including photocopying, recording or by any information storage or retrieval system, without permission in writing from the copyright holder.

Editions Haynes
4, Rue de l'Abreuvoir
92415 COURBEVOIE CEDEX, France

ISBN 1 85960 981 3

Haynes Publishing Nordiska AB
Box 1504, 751 45 UPPSALA, Sweden

British Library Cataloguing in Publication Data
A catalogue record for this book is available from the British Library.

Contents

LIVING WITH YOUR YAMAHA XJR

Introduction

Yamaha – Musical instruments to Motorcycles	Page	0•4
Acknowledgements	Page	0•8
About this manual	Page	0•8
Safety first!	Page	0•9
Model development	Page	0•10
Performance data	Page	0•10
Bike spec	Page	0•11
Identification numbers	Page	0•12
Buying spare parts	Page	0•12

Daily (pre-ride) checks

Engine/transmission oil level check	Page	0•13
Brake fluid level checks	Page	0•14
Clutch fluid level check	Page	0•15
Tyre checks	Page	0•16
Suspension, steering and final drive checks	Page	0•16
Legal and safety checks	Page	0•16

MAINTENANCE

Routine maintenance and servicing

Specifications	Page	1•2
Recommended lubricants and fluids	Page	1•2
Maintenance schedule	Page	1•3
Component locations	Page	1•5
Maintenance procedures	Page	1•7

Contents

REPAIRS AND OVERHAUL

Engine, transmission and associated systems

Engine, clutch and transmission	Page	2•1
Fuel and exhaust systems	Page	3•1
Ignition system	Page	4•1

Chassis and bodywork components

Frame, suspension and final drive	Page	5•1
Brakes, wheels and tyres	Page	6•1
Bodywork	Page	7•1

Electrical system
Page 8•1

Wiring diagrams
Page 8•26

REFERENCE

Tools and Workshop Tips	Page	REF•2
Security	Page	REF•20
Lubricants and fluids	Page	REF•23
Conversion Factors	Page	REF•26
MOT test checks	Page	REF•27
Storage	Page	REF•32
Fault finding	Page	REF•35
Fault finding equipment	Page	REF•44
Technical terms explained	Page	REF•48

Index
Page REF•52

Introduction

Yamaha
Musical instruments to motorcycles

**The FS1E -
first bike of many sixteen year olds in the UK**

The Yamaha Motor Company

The Yamaha name can be traced back to 1889, when Torakusu Yamaha founded the Yamaha Organ Manufacturing Company. Such was the success of the company, that in 1897 it became Nippon Gakki Limited and manufactured a wide range of reed organs and pianos.

During World War II, Nippon Gakki's manufacturing base was utilised by the Japanese authorities to produce propellers and fuel tanks for their aviation industry. The end of the war brought about a huge public demand for low cost transport and many firms decided to utilise their obsolete aircraft tooling for the production of motorcycles. Nippon Gakki's first motorcycle went on sale in February 1955 and was named the 125 YA-1 Red Dragonfly. This machine was a copy of the German DKW RT125 motorcycle, featuring a single cylinder two-stroke engine with a four-speed gearbox. Due to the outstanding success of this model the motorcycle operation was separated from Nippon Gakki in July 1955 and the Yamaha Motor Company was formed.

The YA-1 also received acclaim by winning two of Japan's biggest road races, the Mount Fuji Climbing race and the Asama Volcano race. The high level of public demand for the YA-1 led to the development of a whole series of two-stroke singles and twins.

Having made a large impact on their home market, Yamahas were exported to the USA in 1958 and to the UK in 1962. In the UK the signing of an Anglo-Japanese trade

Introduction

agreement during 1962 enabled the sale of Japanese lightweight motorcycles and scooters in Britain. At that time, competition between the many motorcycle producers in Japan had reduced numbers significantly and by the end of the sixties, only the big-four which are familiar with today remained.

Yamaha Europe was founded in 1968 and based in Holland. Although originally set up to market marine products, the Dutch base is now the official European Headquarters and distribution centre. Yamaha motorcycles are built at factories in Holland, Denmark, Norway, Italy, France, Spain and Portugal. Yamahas are imported into the UK by Yamaha Motor UK Ltd, formerly Mitsui Machinery Sales (UK) Ltd. Mitsui and Co. were originally a trading house, handling the shipping, distribution and marketing of Japanese products into western countries. Ultimately Mitsui Machinery Sales was formed to handle Yamaha motorcycles and outboard motors.

Based on the technology derived from its motorcycle operation, Yamaha have produced many other products, such as automobile and lightweight aircraft engines, marine engines and boats, generators, pumps, ATVs, snowmobiles, golf cars, industrial robots, lawnmowers, swimming pools and archery equipment.

Two-strokes first

Part of Yamaha's success was a whole string of innovations in the two-stroke world. Autolube engine lubrication, torque induction, multi-ported engines, reed valves and power valves kept their two-strokes at the forefront of technology. Many advances were achieved with the use of racing as a development laboratory. They went to the USA in the late 1950s with an air-cooled 250cc twin but didn't hit the GPs until the early 1960s when Fumio Ito scored a hat-trick of sixth places in the Isle of Man TT, the Dutch TT and the Belgian GP. This experiment gave rise to the idea of the over-the-counter racer, an idea that became reality in the TD1, the first in an unmatched series of two-stroke racers that were the standard issue for privateers at national and international level for years and helped Yamaha develop their road engines. While privateers raced the twins, Yamaha built the outrageously complicated vee-four 250 for Phil Read and followed it with a vee-four 125 that Bill Ivy lapped the Isle of Man on at over 100mph! When the FIM regulations were changed to limit the smaller GP classes to two cylinders, these exotic bikes died but set the scene for an unparalleled dynasty of mass-produced racers based on the same technology as the road bikes.

In the 1960s and 70s the two-stroke engined YAS3 125, YDS1 to YDS7 250 and YR5 350 formed the core of Yamaha's range. By the mid-70s they had been superseded by the RD (Race-Developed) 125, 250, and 350 range of two-stroke twins, featuring improved 7-port engines with reed valve induction. Braking was improved by the use of an hydraulic brake on the front wheel of DX models, instead of the drum arrangement used previously, and cast alloy wheels were available as an option on later RD models. The RD350 was replaced by the RD400 in 1976.

Running parallel with the RD twins was a range of single-cylinder two-strokes. Used in a variety of chassis types, the engine was used in the popular 50 cc FS1-E moped, the V50 to 90 step-thrus, RS100 and 125, YB100 and the DT trail range.

The TD racers got water-cooling in 1973 to become the TZs, the most successful and numerous over-the-counter racers ever built. That same year, Jarno Saarinen became the first rider to win a 500cc GP on a four-cylinder two-stroke on the new in-line four which was effectively a pair of TZs side-by-side. TZs won everywhere – including the Daytona 200 and 500 races when overbored to 351cc. A 700cc TZ also appeared, one year later taken out to 750cc. Steve Baker won the first Formula 750 world title – one of the precursors of Superbike – on one in 1977. The following year Kenny Roberts won Yamaha's first world 500 title and would be succeeded by Wayne Rainey and Eddie Lawson before Mick Doohan and the NSR500 took over.

The air-cooled single and twin cylinder RD road bikes were eventually replaced by the LC series in 1980, featuring liquid-cooled engines, radical new styling, spiral pattern cast wheels and cantilever rear suspension (Yamaha's Monoshock). Of all the LC models, the RD350LC, or RD350R as it was later known, has made the most impact in the market. Later models had YPVS (Yamaha Power Valve System) engines, another first for Yamaha – this was essentially a valve located in the exhaust ports which was electronically operated to alter port timing to achieve maximum power output. The RD500LC was the largest two-stroke made by Yamaha and differed from the other LCs by the use of its vee-four cylinder engine.

With the exception of the RD350R, now manufactured in Brazil, the LC range has been discontinued. Two-stroke engined models have given way to environmental pressure, and thus with a few exceptions, such as the TZR125 and TZR250, are used only in scooters and small capacity bikes.

The distinctive paintwork and trim of the RD models

0•6 Introduction

The Four-strokes

Yamaha concentrated solely on two-stroke models until 1970 when the XS1 was produced, their first four-stroke motorcycle. It was perhaps Yamaha's success with two-strokes that postponed an earlier move into the four-stroke motorcycle market, although their work with Toyota during the 1960s had given them a sound base in four-stroke technology.

The XS1 had a 650 cc twin-cylinder SOHC engine and was later to become known as the XS650, appearing also in the popular SE custom form. Yamaha introduced a three cylinder 750 cc engine in 1976, fitted in a sport-tourer frame and called the XS750, TX750 in the USA. The XS750 established itself well in the sport tourer class and remained in production with very few changes until uprated to 850 cc in 1980.

Other four-strokes followed in 1976, with the introduction of the XS250/360/400 series twins. The XS range was strengthened in 1978 by the four-cylinder XS1100.

The 1980s saw a new family of four-strokes, the XJ550, 650, 750 and 900 Fours. Improvements over the XS range amounted to a slimmer DOHC engine unit due to the relocation of the alternator behind the cylinders, electronic ignition and uprated braking and suspension systems. Models were available mainly in standard trim, although custom-styled Maxims were produced especially for the US market. The XJ650T was the first model from Yamaha to have a turbo-charged engine. Although these early XJ models have now been discontinued, their roots live on in the XJ600S and XJ900S Diversion (Seca II) models.

The FZR prefix encompasses the pure sports Yamaha models. With the exception of the 16-valve FZR400 and FZR600 models, the FZ/FZR750 and FZR1000 used 20-valve engines, two exhaust valves and three inlet

The XS650 led the way for Yamaha's four-stroke range

Yamaha's XS750 was produced from 1976 to 1982 and then uprated to 850 cc

Introduction 0•7

valves per cylinder. This concept was called Genesis and gave improved gas flow to the combustion chambers. Other features of the new engine were the use of down-draught carburetors and the engine's inclined angle in the frame, plus the change to liquid-cooling. Lightweight Deltabox design aluminium frames and uprated suspension improved the bikes's handling. The Genesis engine lives on in the YZF750 and 1000 models.

The Genesis concept was the basis of Yamaha's foray into four-stroke racing, first with a bike known simply as 'The Genesis', an FZ750 motor in a TT Formula 1 bike with which the factory attempted to steal the Honda RVF750's thunder at important events like the Suzuka 8 Hours and the Bol d'Or although they never fielded it for a whole World Championship season. That had to wait for the advent of the World Superbike Championship, although there was no full works team until 1995, instead it was left to individual importers to support teams. It was the Australian Dealer Team Yamaha which scored the factory's first World Superbike win in the series debut year of 1988. The rider? Mick Doohan. Slightly, embarrassingly, it was the steel framed FZ750 rather than the FZR homologation special that won races. The OW01 was a race winner, mainly in the hands of Fabrizio Pirovano, the factory's most successful Superbike racer with ten victories, but national success in the UK, Japan, and in the Daytona 200 has not been translated into World Championships for any of Yamaha's 750s.

The vee-twin engine has been the mainstay of the XV Virago range. Since 1981 XVs have been produced in 535, 700, 750, 920, 1000 and 1100 engine sizes, all using the same basic air-cooled sohc vee-twin engine. Other uses of vee engines have been in the XZ550 of the early 1980s, the XVZ12 Venture and the mighty VMX-12 V-Max.

A new family of four-strokes was released in 1980 with the introduction of the XJ range

Yamaha has always been a sporting-orientated company whose motto could be 'Racing Improves the Breed', so it's no surprise that the latest generation of lightweight sportsters are at the cutting edge of performance on and off the track. The R6 won more races than any other machine in the inaugural year of the World Supersports Championship, the R7 won a race in its debut year in World Superbike in the hands of the mercurial Noriyuki Haga, and the mighty 1000cc R1 ended Honda's domination of the Isle of Man F1 TT when David Jefferies won three races in a week in 1999.

In Grand Prix racing, the factory took several years to get over the shock of Wayne Rainey's crippling accident. and first 500cc win since the American's enforced retirement didn't come until 1998 when Simon Crafar won at Donington Park. For 1999, Yamaha refocussed their ambitions and signed Italian superstar Max Biaggi plus Spanish trier Carlos Checa for the works team, while dashing young Frenchman Regis Laconi and tough little Aussie Gary McCoy rode for the WCM satellite team. Both teams got a win in the '99 season and with a new TZ250 being developed for 2000 it looks as if Yamaha's spirit of competition will go on unabated into the new Millenium.

The XV535 Virago vee-twin

Introduction

The XJRs

Most of the modern bikes saddled with the 'retro' label aren't. They are modern bikes with the expensive glass fibre taken off - naked sportsters. The Suzuki Bandit more or less invented the class and everyone else followed suit. When the Yamaha XJR1200 appeared in 1995 it was the genuine article – a retro design. Check out the spec: no water cooling, no aluminium frame, no upside-down multi-adjustable front forks, no six-pot brake calipers, no rising-rate rear suspension – in fact not even a monoshock, just good old twin shock absorbers. Reads like the spec sheet of something from 20 years ago, doesn't it? You could say that about some other bikes that usually carry the retro tag but the Yamaha carries things further by using an air-cooled motor that can trace its ancestry back to Yamaha's first four-cylinder four stroke, the XS1100 that first appeared back in 1977.

The original design got a serious update for the seminal FJ1100/1200, one of the most accomplished bikes of the 1980s but the close-pitched finning of the XJR's cylinders bears a close family relationship to the old bikes. The 1200 and its 1300 cc brother both make around 100 bhp thus enabling Yamaha to make one model for all markets – an important cost consideration for what is, compared to something like an R7, a low-volume product.

That doesn't mean the motor isn't fun. Great gobs of torque, just under 70 ft -lb from the 1200, come in below 4000 rpm and stay there till just before 8000. Torque curves don't get much flatter, which makes for a lazy ride during which gear changing becomes almost irrelevant. The steel tube chassis is another throwback but the big beefy aluminium swinging arm doesn't look out of place, after all it's the sort of thing an '80s superbike race would have worn. The '80s theme is carried through to pillion comfort as well – this is as good a bike as you can get for two-up riding – assuming you aren't in GoldWing territory. And then there are the looks – very musclebike (there's an '80s term if ever there was one) with just enough chrome to keep the Sunday morning polishers happy.

It's a good package provided you don't push it too hard. If you do, both the chassis and the brakes are capable of finding out the bike's weakness – the suspension, and particularly the spindly looking and adjustment-free 43 mm front forks. Yamaha have taken flack for saving pennies in the suspension department on other models and the XJR meant they took some more.

As you'd expect from a low-volume model of this type, it was hardly changed throughout its life; it got a handlebar-mounted choke in '96, a new starter-motor clutch in '97 and lever span adjusters in '98, and that's it! In 1999 the XJR got 2 mm bigger bores and became the XJR1300. The new engine now made 106 bhp and 74 ft-lb torque. Criticisms of the bikes forks were partially answered by giving them adjustable spring preload and calipers off the R1 completed the list of mechanical modifications. Just like the 1200, the new bike has remained virtually unmodified through its life: heated carbs came in for 2002 and that's it.

Now of all the bikes you could bring to mind the XJR is not one you'd associate with the race track, so the French invented a race series for them. This Gallic lunacy gave rise to an SP (for Sports Production) version of the 1300. For about £500 over the stock bike's price you got a new seat, extra badging, racy paint, trick Öhlins rear shocks complete with yellow springs, and a gold anodised chain. On the road, the difference between the stock bike and the SP were hardly noticeable. Which didn't stop everyone wanting the racy looking paint and ostentatious Swedish shocks. Some markets got the mother of all Yamaha paint schemes, the old Yamaha USA black-and-yellow as worn by Kenny Roberts.

Acknowledgements

Our thanks are due to GT Motorcycles of Yeovil and Taylors Motorcycles of Misterton, Crewkerne, who supplied the machines featured in the illustrations throughout this manual. We would also like to thank Mitsui Machinery Sales (UK) Ltd for permission to reproduce certain illustrations used in the manual and for supplying the cover photographs, also NGK Spark Plugs (UK) Ltd for supplying the colour spark plug condition photographs, the Avon Rubber Company for supplying information on tyre fitting and Draper Tools Ltd for some of the workshop tools shown.

Thanks are also due to Julian Ryder who wrote the introduction 'Musical Instruments to Motorcycles'.

About this manual

The aim of this manual is to help you get the best value from your motorcycle. It can do so in several ways. It can help you decide what work must be done, even if you choose to have it done by a dealer; it provides information and procedures for routine maintenance and servicing; and it offers diagnostic and repair procedures to follow when trouble occurs.

We hope you use the manual to tackle the work yourself. For many simpler jobs, doing it yourself may be quicker than arranging an appointment to get the motorcycle into a dealer and making the trips to leave it and pick it up. More importantly, a lot of money can be saved by avoiding the expense the shop must pass on to you to cover its labour and overhead costs. An added benefit is the sense of satisfaction and accomplishment that you feel after doing the job yourself.

References to the left or right side of the motorcycle assume you are sitting on the seat, facing forward.

We take great pride in the accuracy of information given in this manual, but motorcycle manufacturers make alterations and design changes during the production run of a particular motorcycle of which they do not inform us. No liability can be accepted by the authors or publishers for loss, damage or injury caused by any errors in, or omissions from, the information given.

The 1999 XJR1300

The 2000 XJR1300SP

Safety first! 0•9

Professional mechanics are trained in safe working procedures. However enthusiastic you may be about getting on with the job at hand, take the time to ensure that your safety is not put at risk. A moment's lack of attention can result in an accident, as can failure to observe simple precautions.

There will always be new ways of having accidents, and the following is not a comprehensive list of all dangers; it is intended rather to make you aware of the risks and to encourage a safe approach to all work you carry out on your bike.

Asbestos

● Certain friction, insulating, sealing and other products - such as brake pads, clutch linings, gaskets, etc. - contain asbestos. Extreme care must be taken to avoid inhalation of dust from such products since it is hazardous to health. If in doubt, assume that they do contain asbestos.

Fire

● Remember at all times that petrol is highly flammable. Never smoke or have any kind of naked flame around, when working on the vehicle. But the risk does not end there - a spark caused by an electrical short-circuit, by two metal surfaces contacting each other, by careless use of tools, or even by static electricity built up in your body under certain conditions, can ignite petrol vapour, which in a confined space is highly explosive. Never use petrol as a cleaning solvent. Use an approved safety solvent.

● Always disconnect the battery earth terminal before working on any part of the fuel or electrical system, and never risk spilling fuel on to a hot engine or exhaust.

● It is recommended that a fire extinguisher of a type suitable for fuel and electrical fires is kept handy in the garage or workplace at all times. Never try to extinguish a fuel or electrical fire with water.

Fumes

● Certain fumes are highly toxic and can quickly cause unconsciousness and even death if inhaled to any extent. Petrol vapour comes into this category, as do the vapours from certain solvents such as trichloro-ethylene. Any draining or pouring of such volatile fluids should be done in a well ventilated area.

● When using cleaning fluids and solvents, read the instructions carefully. Never use materials from unmarked containers - they may give off poisonous vapours.

● Never run the engine of a motor vehicle in an enclosed space such as a garage. Exhaust fumes contain carbon monoxide which is extremely poisonous; if you need to run the engine, always do so in the open air or at least have the rear of the vehicle outside the workplace.

The battery

● Never cause a spark, or allow a naked light near the vehicle's battery. It will normally be giving off a certain amount of hydrogen gas, which is highly explosive.

● Always disconnect the battery ground (earth) terminal before working on the fuel or electrical systems (except where noted).

● If possible, loosen the filler plugs or cover when charging the battery from an external source. Do not charge at an excessive rate or the battery may burst.

● Take care when topping up, cleaning or carrying the battery. The acid electrolyte, evenwhen diluted, is very corrosive and should not be allowed to contact the eyes or skin. Always wear rubber gloves and goggles or a face shield. If you ever need to prepare electrolyte yourself, always add the acid slowly to the water; never add the water to the acid.

Electricity

● When using an electric power tool, inspection light etc., always ensure that the appliance is correctly connected to its plug and that, where necessary, it is properly grounded (earthed). Do not use such appliances in damp conditions and, again, beware of creating a spark or applying excessive heat in the vicinity of fuel or fuel vapour. Also ensure that the appliances meet national safety standards.

● A severe electric shock can result from touching certain parts of the electrical system, such as the spark plug wires (HT leads), when the engine is running or being cranked, particularly if components are damp or the insulation is defective. Where an electronic ignition system is used, the secondary (HT) voltage is much higher and could prove fatal.

Remember...

✗ **Don't** start the engine without first ascertaining that the transmission is in neutral.

✗ **Don't** suddenly remove the pressure cap from a hot cooling system - cover it with a cloth and release the pressure gradually first, or you may get scalded by escaping coolant.

✗ **Don't** attempt to drain oil until you are sure it has cooled sufficiently to avoid scalding you.

✗ **Don't** grasp any part of the engine or exhaust system without first ascertaining that it is cool enough not to burn you.

✗ **Don't** allow brake fluid or antifreeze to contact the machine's paintwork or plastic components.

✗ **Don't** siphon toxic liquids such as fuel, hydraulic fluid or antifreeze by mouth, or allow them to remain on your skin.

✗ **Don't** inhale dust - it may be injurious to health (see Asbestos heading).

✗ **Don't** allow any spilled oil or grease to remain on the floor - wipe it up right away, before someone slips on it.

✗ **Don't** use ill-fitting spanners or other tools which may slip and cause injury.

✗ **Don't** lift a heavy component which may be beyond your capability - get assistance.

✗ **Don't** rush to finish a job or take unverified short cuts.

✗ **Don't** allow children or animals in or around an unattended vehicle.

✗ **Don't** inflate a tyre above the recommended pressure. Apart from overstressing the carcass, in extreme cases the tyre may blow off forcibly.

✔ **Do** ensure that the machine is supported securely at all times. This is especially important when the machine is blocked up to aid wheel or fork removal.

✔ **Do** take care when attempting to loosen a stubborn nut or bolt. It is generally better to pull on a spanner, rather than push, so that if you slip, you fall away from the machine rather than onto it.

✔ **Do** wear eye protection when using power tools such as drill, sander, bench grinder etc.

✔ **Do** use a barrier cream on your hands prior to undertaking dirty jobs - it will protect your skin from infection as well as making the dirt easier to remove afterwards; but make sure your hands aren't left slippery. Note that long-term contact with used engine oil can be a health hazard.

✔ **Do** keep loose clothing (cuffs, ties etc. and long hair) well out of the way of moving mechanical parts.

✔ **Do** remove rings, wristwatch etc., before working on the vehicle - especially the electrical system.

✔ **Do** keep your work area tidy - it is only too easy to fall over articles left lying around.

✔ **Do** exercise caution when compressing springs for removal or installation. Ensure that the tension is applied and released in a controlled manner, using suitable tools which preclude the possibility of the spring escaping violently.

✔ **Do** ensure that any lifting tackle used has a safe working load rating adequate for the job.

✔ **Do** get someone to check periodically that all is well, when working alone on the vehicle.

✔ **Do** carry out work in a logical sequence and check that everything is correctly assembled and tightened afterwards.

✔ **Do** remember that your vehicle's safety affects that of yourself and others. If in doubt on any point, get professional advice.

● If in spite of following these precautions, you are unfortunate enough to injure yourself, seek medical attention as soon as possible.

Model development and Performance data

Model development

XJR1200 (1995 model year)
Introduced in 1995 as a 'naked retro muscle-bike', with an in-line four cylinder engine derived from the FJ1200.

The engine was primarily air-cooled, though it had a radiator-type oil cooler to assist. The double overhead camshafts were chain driven off the crankshaft and operated four valves per cylinder. Power was transmitted through a diaphragm-sprung wet multi-plate clutch to a 5-speed constant mesh gearbox, and then to the rear wheel by chain and sprockets. The engine was fed by four 36 mm CV carburettors, with ignition by a digital electronic system.

The engine was mounted in a duplex cradle-type tubular steel frame. Suspension was provided by conventional 43 mm oil-damped telescopic forks at the front, and a box-section aluminium swingarm acting on twin shock absorbers with piggyback reservoirs at the rear. The shock absorbers were adjustable for spring pre-load. Braking was by twin disc and twin opposed-piston calipers at the front and by a disc and single opposed-piston caliper at the rear.

The XJR1200 was available in dark red and black.

XJR1200 (1996 model year)
The only significant change was to the choke, which was previously operated using a knob on the carburettors, but now operated by a lever incorporated in the handlebar switchgear via a cable. As a result new handlebar switchgear was fitted. Available in dark red and black.

XJR1200 (1997 model year)
The starter clutch was modified and used sprags instead of rollers. Available in red, black, and blue/black.

XJR1200 (1998 model year)
With the exception of handlebar levers which incorporated span adjusters, the bike was unchanged. Available in black and metallic grey.

XJR1300 (1999 model year)
The most significant change to the XJR was the larger engine capacity, achieved by increasing the bore size by 2 mm. The cylinder block was of all-aluminium construction with plated bore surfaces. The front forks were adjustable for spring pre-load. Different front brake calipers, taken from the YZF-R1, were fitted. The side panels, tail light lens and tail light cover were modified. Available in black and metallic cyan.

XJR1300 (2000 model year)
There were no significant changes for 2000. Available in black and metallic silver.

XJR1300SP (2000 model year)
The XJR-SP was basically the same bike as the standard XJR, but had additional emblems on the fuel tank and tail light cover, and a new low-slip design seat. It also featured Öhlins rear shock absorbers with distinctive yellow springs and gold sideplates on the final drive chain. Available in red and metallic purplish blue.

XJR1300 (2001 model year)
There were no significant changes for 2001. Available in black and metallic silver.

XJR1300SP (2001 model year)
There were no significant changes for 2001. Available in yellow and metallic purplish blue.

XJR1300 (2002 model year)
The carburettors were modified to incorporate electric heater elements, and their bore size was increased to 37 mm. The camshafts were modified. Öhlins rear shock replaced the previous stock items. Available in black, metallic purplish blue, and bluish silver.

XJR1300 (2003 model year)
There were no significant changes for 2003. Available in blue, midnight black and yellow.

Performance data

XJR1200

Maximum power
Claimed .... 98 bhp @ 8000 rpm

Maximum torque
Claimed .... 67 lbf ft (91 Nm) @ 6000 rpm

Top speed
Estimated .... 144 mph (230 km/h)

Acceleration
Time taken to cover a 1/4 mile from a standing start ...... 11.7 secs
Terminal speed after 1/4 mile .... 115 mph (185 km/h)

Average fuel consumption
Miles per Imp gal, miles per litre,
  litres per 100 km .... 42 mpg, 9.2 mpl, 6.7 l/100 km

Fuel tank range
Based on average fuel consumption rate .... 194 miles (312 km)

XJR1300

Maximum power
Claimed .... 106 bhp @ 8000 rpm

Maximum torque
Claimed .... 74 lbf ft (100 Nm) @ 6000 rpm

Top speed
Estimated .... 141 mph (226 km/h)

Acceleration
Time taken to cover a 1/4 mile from a standing start ...... 11.1 secs
Terminal speed after 1/4 mile .... 117 mph (188 km/h)

Average fuel consumption
Miles per Imp gal, miles per litre,
  litres per 100 km .... 42 mpg, 9.2 mpl, 6.7 l/100 km

Fuel tank range
Based on average fuel consumption rate .... 194 miles (312 km)

Performance data sourced from Motor Cycle News road test features. See the MCN website for up-to-date biking news.

MCN www.motorcyclenews.com

Bike spec

Bike spec

Dimensions and weights
XJR1200
  Overall length . . . . .2255 mm
  Overall width . . . . .765 mm
  Overall height . . . . .1120 mm
  Wheelbase . . . . .1500 mm
  Seat height . . . . .790 mm
  Ground clearance . . . . .135 mm
  Weight (dry) . . . . .232 kg
  Weight (wet) . . . . .255 kg
XJR1300
  Overall length . . . . .2175 mm
  Overall width . . . . .775 mm
  Overall height . . . . .1115 mm
  Wheelbase . . . . .1500 mm
  Seat height . . . . .790 mm
  Ground clearance . . . . .120 mm
  Weight (dry) . . . . .230 kg
  Weight (wet) . . . . .253 kg

Engine
Type . . . . .Four-stroke in-line four cylinder, air-cooled,
                                                     four valves per cylinder
Capacity
  XJR1200 . . . . .1188 cc
  XJR1300 . . . . .1250 cc
Bore and stroke
  XJR1200 . . . . .77.0 x 63.8 mm
  XJR1300 . . . . .79.0 x 63.8 mm
Compression ratio 9.7:1
Camshafts . . . . .DOHC, chain-driven

Engine (continued)
Lubrication . . . . .Wet sump, pump-fed
Carburettors
  XJR1200 and XJR1300 up to 2001 . . . . . .4 x Mikuni BS36, CV type
  XJR1300 from 2002 . . . . .4 x Mikuni BSR37, CV type
Ignition system . . . . .Transistorized with electronic advance
Clutch . . . .Wet multi-plate, diaphragm-sprung, hydraulically operated
Gearbox . . . . .5-speed constant mesh
Final drive . . . . .Chain and sprockets

Chassis
Frame type . . . . .Duplex cradle, tubular steel
Rake and trail
  XJR1200 . . . . .25.5°, 103 mm
  XJR1300 . . . . .25.5°, 100 mm
Fuel tank capacity . . . . .21 litres (inc. reserve of 4.5 litres)
Front suspension
  Type . . . . .43 mm oil-damped telescopic forks
  Travel . . . . .130 mm
Rear suspension
  Type . . . . .Twin shock absorbers with piggyback reservoirs,
                                                box section aluminium swingarm
  Travel (at wheel) . . . . .110 mm
  Adjustment . . . . .Spring pre-load
Wheels . . . . .17 inch cast aluminium-alloy
Tyres
  XJR1200 . . . . .130/70ZR17 front, 170/60ZR17 rear
  XJR1300 . . . . .120/70ZR17 (58W) front, 180/55ZR17 (73W) rear
Front brake . .Sumitomo twin opposed-piston calipers, 320 mm discs
Rear brake . . . . .Sumitomo opposed-piston caliper, 267 mm disc

0•12 Identification numbers

Frame and engine numbers

The frame number is stamped into the right-hand side of the steering head. The engine number is stamped into the top of the crankcase on the right-hand side of the engine. These numbers should be recorded and kept in a safe place so they can be furnished to law enforcement officials in the event of a theft. There is also a carburettor identification number on the intake side of each carburettor body, and a model code label on the frame under the seat.

The frame serial number, engine serial number, carburettor identification number and model code should be recorded and kept in a handy place (such as with your driver's licence) so that they are always available when purchasing or ordering parts for your machine.

The procedures in this manual identify the bikes by year and model (e.g. 1998 XJR1200). The model codes for all years and models covered are tabled below.

Buying spare parts

Once you have found all the identification numbers, record them for reference when buying parts. Since the manufacturers change specifications, parts and vendors (companies that manufacture various components on the machine), providing the ID numbers is the only way to be reasonably sure that you are buying the correct parts.

Whenever possible, take the worn part to the dealer so direct comparison with the new component can be made. Along the trail from the manufacturer to the parts shelf there are numerous places that the part can end up with the wrong number or be listed incorrectly.

The two places to purchase new parts for your motorcycle – the accessory store and the franchised dealer – differ in the type of parts they carry. While dealers can obtain virtually every part for your motorcycle, the accessory dealer is usually limited to normal high wear items such as shock absorbers, tune-up parts, various engine gaskets, cables, chains, brake parts, etc. Rarely will an accessory outlet have major suspension components, cylinders, transmission gears, or cases.

Used parts can be obtained from breakers yards for roughly half the price of new ones, but you can't always be sure of what you're getting. Once again, take your worn part to the breaker for direct comparison, or when ordering by mail order make sure that you can return it if you are not happy.

Whether buying new, used or rebuilt parts, the best course is to deal directly with someone who specialises in your particular make.

Model	Year	Model code for European models
XJR1200	1995	4PU1 (4PU2 Spain, 4RB1 Switzerland/Austria)
XJR1200	1996	4PU3 (4PU4 Spain, 4RB2 Switzerland/Austria)
XJR1200	1997	4PU7 (4PU8 Spain, 4RB4 Switzerland/Austria)
XJR1200	1998	4PU9 (4PUA Spain, 4RB5 Switzerland/Austria)
XJR1300	1999	5EA3 (5EA2 Austria and Finland)
XJR1300	2000	5EAB (5EAA Austria and Finland)
XJR1300SP	2000	5EAE (5EAD Austria and Finland)
XJR1300	2001	5EAJ (5EAH Austria and Finland)
XJR1300SP	2001	5EAM (5EAL Austria and Finland)
XJR1300	2002/3	5EAT/W

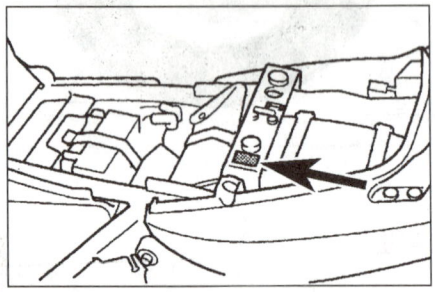

Model code label location on the rear of the frame

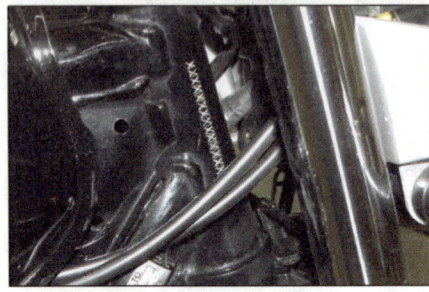

The frame number is stamped into the right-hand side of the steering head

The engine number is stamped into the crankcase on the right-hand side of the engine

Daily (pre-ride) checks 0•13

Engine/transmission oil level check

Before you start:
✔ Take the motorcycle on a short run to allow it to reach normal operating temperature.
Caution: Do not run the engine in an enclosed space such as a garage or workshop.
✔ Stop the engine and support the motorcycle on its centrestand. Make sure it is on level ground. Allow it to stand undisturbed for a few minutes to allow the oil level to stabilise.

Bike care:
● If you have to add oil frequently, you should check whether you have any oil leaks. If there is no sign of oil leakage from the joints and gaskets the engine could be burning oil (see *Fault Finding*).

The correct oil
● Modern, high-revving engines place great demands on their oil. It is very important that the correct oil for your bike is used.
● Always top up with a good quality oil of the specified type and viscosity and do not overfill the engine.
Caution: Do not use oil additives or motor oils which contain anti-friction additives, often labelled ENERGY CONSERVING II. Such additives or oils could cause clutch and starter clutch slip.

Oil type	API grade SE, SF, SG or higher
Oil viscosity	SAE 10W/30, 10W/40, SAE 15W/40, SAE 20W/40 or SAE 20W/50*

*Refer to the viscosity table to select the oil best suited to your conditions.

1 The oil level inspection window is located on the right-hand side of the engine – wipe it so that it is clean if necessary. With the motorcycle vertical, the oil level should lie between the maximum and minimum levels on the window (arrowed).

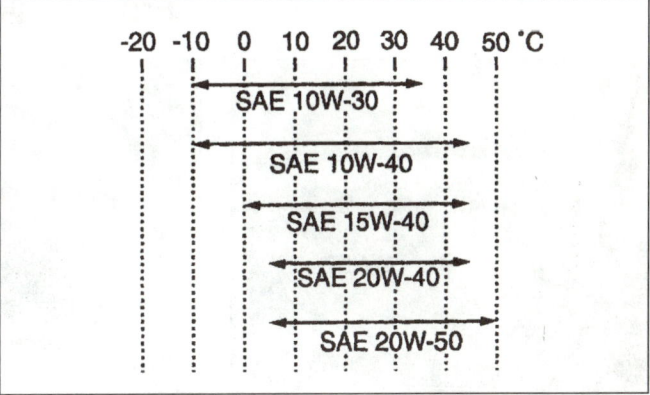

Oil viscosity table; select the oil best suited to the conditions

2 If the level is below the minimum line, remove the filler cap from the top of the clutch cover.

3 Top the engine up with the recommended grade and type of oil, to bring the level up to the maximum level on the window. Install the filler cap.

0•14 Daily (pre-ride) checks

Brake fluid level checks

> **Warning:** Hydraulic fluid can harm your eyes and damage painted surfaces, so use extreme caution when handling and pouring it and cover surrounding surfaces with rag. Do not use fluid that has been standing open for some time, as it absorbs moisture from the air which can cause a dangerous loss of braking effectiveness.

Before you start:

✔ The front master cylinder reservoir is on the right-hand handlebar. The rear master cylinder reservoir is located behind the right-hand side panel – remove the panel to access it (see Chapter 7).
✔ Support the motorcycle on its centrestand. Make sure it is on level ground. Turn the handlebars until the top of the front master cylinder is level.
✔ Make sure you have the correct hydraulic fluid. DOT 4 is recommended.
✔ Wrap a rag around the reservoir being worked on to ensure that any spillage does not come into contact with painted surfaces.

Bike care:

● The fluid in the front and rear brake master cylinder reservoirs will drop slightly as the brake pads wear down (refer to Chapter 1 to check the amount of wear in the pads if required).
● If either fluid reservoir requires repeated topping-up there could be a leak somewhere in the system which should be investigated immediately.
● Check for signs of hydraulic fluid leakage from the hoses and brake system components – if found, rectify immediately (see Chapter 6).
● Check the operation of both brakes before taking the machine on the road; if there is evidence of air in the system (spongy feel to lever or pedal), it must be bled (see Chapter 6).

Front brake fluid level

1 The front brake fluid level is visible through the window in the reservoir body – it must be above the LOWER level line.

2 If the level is below the LOWER line, undo the two reservoir cover screws and remove the cover, diaphragm plate and diaphragm.

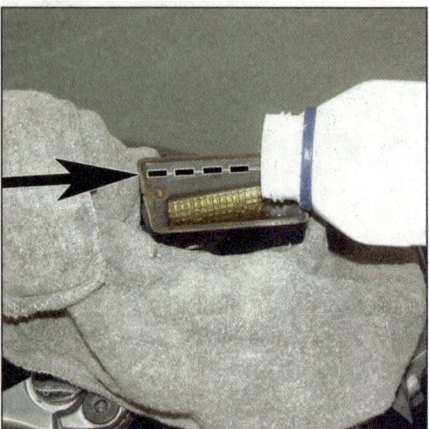

3 Top up with fluid of the recommended type until the level is up to the ridge along the inside of the front wall of the reservoir (arrowed). Do not overfill.

4 Ensure that the diaphragm is correctly seated before installing the plate and cover. Tighten the cover screws securely.

Rear brake fluid

5 The rear brake fluid level is visible through the reservoir body – it must be above the LOWER level line.

6 If it is below the LOWER level line, undo the reservoir mounting screw and displace the reservoir.

Daily (pre-ride) checks   0•15

7 Unscrew the reservoir cap and remove the diaphragm plate and the diaphragm.

8 Top up with new clean DOT 4 hydraulic fluid, until the level is above the line. Take care to avoid spills (see **Warning** above). Do not overfill.

9 Ensure that the diaphragm is correctly seated before installing the plate and cap. Tighten the cap securely. Remount the reservoir.

Clutch fluid level checks

> ⚠ **Warning: Hydraulic fluid can harm your eyes and damage painted surfaces, so use extreme caution when handling and pouring it and cover surrounding surfaces with rag. Do not use fluid that has been standing open for some time, as it absorbs moisture from the air which can cause a loss of clutch effectiveness.**

Before you start:
✔ The clutch master cylinder reservoir is on the left-hand end of the handlebars.
✔ Support the motorcycle on its centrestand. Make sure it is on level ground. Turn the handlebars until the top of the clutch master cylinder is level.
✔ Make sure you have the correct hydraulic fluid. DOT 4 is recommended.
✔ Wrap a rag around the reservoir being worked on to ensure that any spillage does not come into contact with painted surfaces.

Bike care:
● The fluid in the clutch master cylinder reservoir will drop slightly as the clutch plates wear down.
● If the fluid reservoir requires repeated topping-up there could be an hydraulic leak somewhere in the system, which should be investigated immediately.
● Check for signs of fluid leakage from the hydraulic hoses and clutch release system components – if found, rectify immediately (see Chapter 2).
● Check the operation of the clutch before taking the machine on the road; if there is evidence of air in the system (spongy feel to the lever, difficulty in engaging gear, drag when in gear), it must be bled as described in Chapter 2.

1 The clutch fluid level is visible through the window in the reservoir body – it must be above the LOWER level line.

2 If the level is below the LOWER line, undo the two reservoir cover screws and remove the cover, diaphragm plate and diaphragm.

3 Top up with fluid of the recommended type until the level is up to the ridge along the inside of the front wall of the reservoir (arrowed). Do not overfill.

4 Ensure that the diaphragm is correctly seated before installing the plate and cover. Tighten the cover screws securely.

0•16 Daily (pre-ride) checks

Tyre checks

The correct pressures:
- The tyres must be checked when **cold**, not immediately after riding. Note that low tyre pressures may cause the tyre to slip on the rim or come off. High tyre pressures will cause abnormal tread wear and unsafe handling.
- Use an accurate pressure gauge. Many garage forecourt gauges are wildly inaccurate. If you buy your own, spend as much as you can justify on a quality gauge.
- Correct air pressure will increase tyre life and provide maximum stability, handling capability and ride comfort.

Tyre care:
- Check the tyres carefully for cuts, tears, embedded nails or other sharp objects and excessive wear. Operation of the motorcycle with excessively worn tyres is extremely hazardous, as traction and handling are directly affected.
- Check the condition of the tyre valve and ensure the dust cap is in place.
- Pick out any stones or nails which may have become embedded in the tyre tread. If left, they will eventually penetrate through the casing and cause a puncture.
- If tyre damage is apparent, or unexplained loss of pressure is experienced, seek the advice of a tyre fitting specialist without delay.

Tyre tread depth:
- At the time of writing UK law requires that tread depth must be at least 1 mm over 3/4 of the tread breadth all the way around the tyre, with no bald patches. Many riders, however, consider 2 mm tread depth minimum to be a safer limit. Yamaha recommend a minimum of 1.6 mm.
- Many tyres now incorporate wear indicators in the tread. Identify the triangular pointer or TWI mark on the tyre sidewall to locate the indicator bar and renew the tyre if the tread has worn down to the bar.

Loading/speed	Front	Rear
Rider only	36 psi (2.50 Bar)	36 psi (2.50 Bar)
Rider only – high speed riding	36 psi (2.50 Bar)	42 psi (2.90 Bar)
Rider and passenger	36 psi (2.50 Bar)	42 psi (2.90 Bar)

1 Check the tyre pressures when the tyres are **cold** and keep them properly inflated.

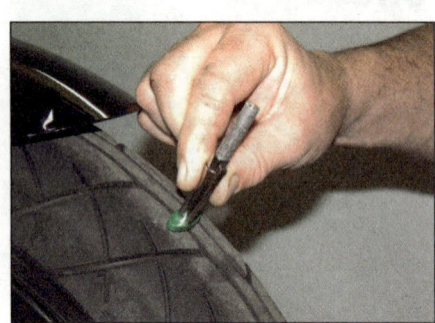

2 Measure tread depth at the centre of the tyre using a tread depth gauge.

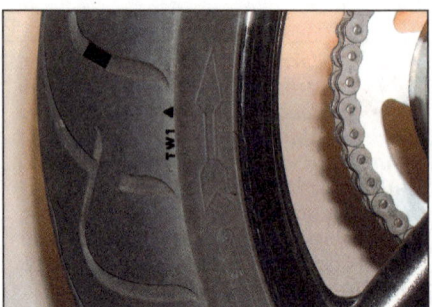

3 Tyre tread wear indicator bar and its location marking (usually either an arrow, a triangle or the letters TWI) on the sidewall.

Suspension, steering and final drive checks

Suspension and steering:
- Check that the front and rear suspension operates smoothly without binding (see Chapter 1).
- Check that the suspension is adjusted as required (see Chapter 5).

- Check that the steering moves smoothly from lock-to-lock.

Drive chain:
- Check that the chain isn't too loose or too tight, and adjust it if necessary (see Chapter 1).
- If the chain looks dry, lubricate it (see Chapter 1).

Legal and safety checks

Lighting and signalling:
- Take a minute to check that the sidelight, headlight, tail light, brake light, instrument lights and turn signals all work correctly.
- Check that the horn sounds when the switch is operated.
- A working speedometer graduated in mph is a statutory requirement in the UK.

Safety:
- Check that the throttle grip rotates smoothly and snaps shut when released, in all steering positions. Also check for the correct amount of freeplay (see Chapter 1).
- Check that the engine shuts off when the kill switch is operated.
- Check that sidestand and centrestand return springs hold the stands up securely when retracted.

Fuel:
- This may seem obvious, but check that you have enough fuel to complete your journey. If you notice signs of fuel leakage – rectify the cause immediately.
- Ensure you use the correct grade fuel – see Chapter 3 Specifications.

Chapter 1
Routine maintenance and servicing

Contents

Air filter – cleaning and renewal 5	Engine oil level check .... .see Daily (pre-ride) checks
Alternator brushes – renewal 24	Front forks – oil renewal 32
Battery – charging .... see Chapter 8	Fuel hoses – renewal 31
Battery – check 11	Fuel system and air induction system (AIS) – check 6
Battery – removal, installation, inspection and	Headlight aim – check and adjustment 28
maintenance .... see Chapter 8	Idle speed – check and adjustment 3
Brake and clutch fluid – renewal 26	Nuts and bolts – tightness check 15
Brake and clutch hoses – renewal 27	Sidestand and centrestand – check 14
Brake and clutch hydraulic seals – renewal 25	Spark plugs – check 2
Brake fluid level check .... .see Daily (pre-ride) checks	Stands, lever pivots and cables – lubrication 17
Brake pads – check 8	Steering head bearings – check and adjustment 19
Brake system – check 9	Steering head bearings – re-greasing 22
Carburettors – synchronisation 4	Suspension – check 18
Clutch – check 10	Swingarm bearings – re-greasing 21
Clutch fluid change 26	Throttle and choke – check and adjustment 16
Cylinder compression – check 29	Tyre pressure and tread depth .... .see Daily (pre-ride) checks
Drive chain and sprockets – check, adjustment and lubrication 1	Valve clearances – check and adjustment 23
Engine oil pressure – check 30	Wheel bearings – check 13
Engine oil and filter – renewal 20	Wheels and tyres – general check 12
Engine oil – renewal 7	

Degrees of difficulty

| Easy, suitable for novice with little experience  | Fairly easy, suitable for beginner with some experience | Fairly difficult, suitable for competent DIY mechanic | Difficult, suitable for experienced DIY mechanic  | Very difficult, suitable for expert DIY or professional 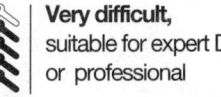 |

Specifications

Engine

Spark plugs
   Type .... NGK DPR8EA-9 or Nippondenso X24EPR-U9
   Electrode gap .... 0.8 to 0.9 mm
Engine idle speed
   1995 to 2001 models .... 1000 to 1100 rpm
   2002 models .... 950 to 1150 rpm
Cylinder identification .... numbered 1 to 4 from left to right
Carburettor synchronisation – intake vacuum at idle .... 235 mmHg
Carburettor synchronisation – max. difference between carburettors .. 10 mmHg
Valve clearances (COLD engine)
   Intake valves .... 0.11 to 0.15 mm
   Exhaust valves .... 0.16 to 0.20 mm
Cylinder compression @ 400 rpm
   Standard .... 152 psi (10.5 Bar)
   Maximum .... 174 psi (12.0 Bar)
   Minimum .... 130 psi (9.0 Bar)
   Max. difference between cylinders .... 14.5 psi (1.0 Bar)
Engine oil pressure .... 11.5 psi (0.8 Bar) @ 1000 rpm, oil at 70 to 80°C

Cycle parts

Drive chain slack (freeplay) .... 20 to 30 mm
Chain stretch limit (see text)
   XJR1200 .... 154 mm
   XJR1300 .... 150 mm
Rear brake pedal height (see text) .... 45 mm
Throttle cable freeplay (see text) .... 3 to 5 mm
Tyre pressures (cold) .... see *Daily (pre-ride) checks*

Recommended lubricants and fluids

Engine/transmission oil type .... see *Daily (pre-ride) checks*
Engine/transmission oil capacity
   Oil change .... 3.0 litres
   Oil and filter change .... 3.35 litres
   Following engine overhaul – dry engine, new filter .... 4.2 litres
Brake/clutch fluid .... DOT 4
Drive chain .... Chain lubricant suitable for O-ring chains
Steering head bearings .... Lithium-based multi-purpose grease
Swingarm pivot components and bearings .... Molybdenum disulphide grease
Wheel bearing seal lips .... Lithium-based multi-purpose grease
Gearchange lever/clutch lever/front brake lever/
   rear brake pedal/sidestand pivots .... Lithium-based multi-purpose grease
Cables .... 10W40 motor oil or cable lubricant
Throttle grip .... Lithium-based multi-purpose grease or dry film lubricant

Torque wrench settings

Brake torque arm nut .... 23 Nm
Fork clamp bolts (top yoke) .... 30 Nm
Oil drain plug .... 43 Nm
Oil filter bolt .... 15 Nm
Oil gallery plug .... 12 Nm
Rear axle nut .... 150 Nm
Spark plugs .... 18 Nm
Steering head bearing adjuster nut
   Initial setting .... 52 Nm
   Final setting .... 18 Nm
Steering stem nut .... 110 Nm
Timing rotor/pick-up coil cover screws .... 7 Nm

Maintenance schedule - 1995 to 1999 models

Note: *The daily (pre-ride) checks outlined in the owner's manual covers those items which should be inspected on a daily basis. Always perform the pre-ride inspection at every maintenance interval (in addition to the procedures listed). The intervals listed below are the intervals recommended by the manufacturer for each particular operation during the model years covered in this manual. Your owner's manual may have different intervals for your model.*

Daily (pre-ride)
☐ See *Daily (pre-ride) checks* at the beginning of this manual.

After the initial 600 miles (1000 km)
Note: *This first service is performed by a Yamaha dealer after 600 miles (1000 km) from new. Thereafter, maintenance is carried out according to the following intervals of the schedule. If your motorcycle is still within its warranty period, check the warranty conditions before performing your own service work as you could invalidate it.*

Every 300 miles (500 km)
☐ Check, adjust, clean and lubricate the drive chain (Section 1)

Every 4000 miles (6000 km) or 6 months (whichever comes sooner)
☐ Check the spark plug gaps (Section 2)
☐ Check and adjust the idle speed (Section 3)
☐ Check/adjust the carburettor synchronisation (Section 4)
☐ Clean and check the air filter element (Section 5)
☐ Check the fuel system (Section 6)
☐ Renew the engine/transmission oil (Section 7)
☐ Check the brake pads (Section 8)
☐ Check the brake system and brake light switch operation (Section 9)
☐ Check the clutch (Section 10)
☐ Check the battery (Section 11)
☐ Check the condition of the wheels and tyres (Section 12)
☐ Check the wheel bearings (Section 13)
☐ Check the sidestand and centrestand (Section 14)
☐ Check the tightness of all nuts, bolts and fasteners (Section 15)
☐ Check throttle and choke action and adjust cable(s) (Section 16)
☐ Lubricate the clutch/gearchange/brake lever/brake pedal/stand pivots and the throttle/choke cables (Section 17)
☐ Check the suspension (Section 18)

Every 8000 miles (12,000 km) or 12 months (whichever comes sooner)
Carry out all the items under the 4000 mile (6000 km) check, plus the following
☐ Renew the spark plugs (Section 2)
☐ Check and adjust the steering head bearings (Section 19)
☐ Renew the engine/transmission oil and filter (Section 20)

Every 16,000 miles (24,000 km) or two years (whichever comes sooner)
Carry out all the items under the 8000 mile (12,000 km) check, plus the following
☐ Re-grease the swingarm bearings (Section 21)
☐ Re-grease the steering head bearings (Section 22)
☐ Check and adjust the valve clearances (Section 23)

Every 62,000 miles (100,000 km) or two years (whichever comes sooner)
☐ Renew the alternator brushes (Section 24)

Every two years
☐ Renew the brake and clutch master cylinder and caliper/release cylinder seals (Section 25)
☐ Renew the brake and clutch fluid (Section 26)

Every four years
☐ Renew the brake and clutch hoses (Section 27)

Non-scheduled maintenance
☐ Check and adjust the headlight aim (Section 28)
☐ Check the cylinder compression (Section 29)
☐ Check the engine oil pressure (Section 30)
☐ Renew the fuel hoses (Section 31)
☐ Renew the front fork oil (Section 32)

Maintenance schedule - 2000-on models

Note: *The daily (pre-ride) checks outlined in the owner's manual covers those items which should be inspected on a daily basis. Always perform the pre-ride inspection at every maintenance interval (in addition to the procedures listed). The intervals listed below are the intervals recommended by the manufacturer for each particular operation during the model years covered in this manual. Your owner's manual may have different intervals for your model.*

Daily (pre-ride)
- [ ] See *Daily (pre-ride) checks* at the beginning of this manual.

After the initial 600 miles (1000 km)
Note: *This first service is performed by a Yamaha dealer after 600 miles (1000 km) from new. Thereafter, maintenance is carried out according to the following intervals of the schedule. If your motorcycle is still within its warranty period, check the warranty conditions before performing your own service work as you could invalidate it.*

Every 600 miles (1000 km)
- [ ] Check, adjust, clean and lubricate the drive chain (Section 1)

Every 6000 miles (10,000 km) or 6 months (whichever comes sooner)
- [ ] Check the spark plug gaps (Section 2)
- [ ] Check and adjust the idle speed (Section 3)
- [ ] Check/adjust the carburettor synchronisation (Section 4)
- [ ] Clean and check the air filter element (Section 5)
- [ ] Check the fuel system (Section 6)
- [ ] Renew the engine/transmission oil (Section 7)
- [ ] Check the brake pads (Section 8)
- [ ] Check the brake system and brake light switch operation (Section 9)
- [ ] Check the clutch (Section 10)
- [ ] Check the battery (Section 11)
- [ ] Check the condition of the wheels and tyres (Section 12)
- [ ] Check the wheel bearings (Section 13)
- [ ] Check the sidestand and centrestand (Section 14)
- [ ] Check the tightness of all nuts, bolts and fasteners (Section 15)
- [ ] Check throttle and choke action and adjust cable(s) (Section 16)
- [ ] Lubricate the clutch/gearchange/brake lever/brake pedal/stand pivots and the throttle/choke cables (Section 17)
- [ ] Check the suspension (Section 18)

Every 12,000 miles (20,000 km) or 12 months (whichever comes sooner)
Carry out all the items under the 6000 mile (10,000 km) check, plus the following
- [ ] Renew the spark plugs (Section 2)
- [ ] Renew the air filter element (Section 5)
- [ ] Check and adjust the steering head bearings (Section 19)
- [ ] Renew the engine/transmission oil and filter (Section 20)
- [ ] Re-grease the steering head bearings (Section 22)
- [ ] Check and adjust the valve clearances (Section 23)

Every 30,000 miles (50,000 km) or two years (whichever comes sooner)
Carry out all the items under the 6000 mile (10,000 km) check, plus the following
- [ ] Re-grease the swingarm bearings (Section 21)

Every 62,000 miles (100,000 km) or two years (whichever comes sooner)
- [ ] Renew the alternator brushes (Section 24)

Every two years
- [ ] Renew the brake and clutch master cylinder and caliper/release cylinder seals (Section 25)
- [ ] Renew the brake and clutch fluid (Section 26)

Every four years
- [ ] Renew the brake and clutch hoses (Section 27)

Non-scheduled maintenance
- [ ] Check and adjust the headlight aim (Section 28)
- [ ] Check the cylinder compression (Section 29)
- [ ] Check the engine oil pressure (Section 30)
- [ ] Renew the fuel hoses (Section 31)
- [ ] Renew the front fork oil (Section 32)

Component locations 1•5

Component locations on the right-hand side

1 Rear brake fluid reservoir
2 Air filter
3 In-line fuel filter (XJR1300 only)
4 Front brake fluid reservoir
5 Throttle cable upper adjuster
6 Fork seals
7 Oil delivery check bolt
8 Oil filler cap
9 Oil level inspection window
10 Rear brake light switch
11 Rear brake pedal height adjuster

1•6 Component locations

Component locations on the left-hand side

1 Steering head bearing adjuster
2 Clutch fluid reservoir
3 Air induction system valve
4 Fuel tap strainer
5 Idle speed adjuster
6 Battery
7 Drive chain adjusters
8 Alternator brushes
9 Oil filter
10 Oil drain plug
11 Main oil gallery plug

Introduction 1•7

1 This Chapter is designed to help the home mechanic maintain his/her motorcycle for safety, economy, long life and peak performance.
2 Deciding where to start or plug into the routine maintenance schedule depends on several factors. If your motorcycle has been maintained according to the warranty standards and has just come out of warranty, start routine maintenance as it coincides with the next mileage or calendar interval. If you have owned the machine for some time but have never performed any maintenance on it, start at the nearest interval and include some additional procedures to ensure that nothing important is overlooked. If you have just had a major engine overhaul, then start the maintenance routine from the beginning. If you have a used machine and have no knowledge of its history or maintenance record, combine all the checks into one large service initially and then settle into the specified maintenance schedule.
3 Before beginning any maintenance or repair, the machine should be cleaned thoroughly, especially around the oil filter, spark plugs, valve covers, body panels, carburettors, etc. Cleaning will help ensure that dirt does not contaminate the engine and will allow you to detect wear and damage that could otherwise easily go unnoticed.
4 Certain maintenance information is sometimes printed on labels attached to the motorcycle. If the information on the labels differs from that included here, use the information on the label.

Maintenance procedures

1 Drive chain and sprockets – check, adjustment and lubrication

Every 300 miles (500 km) – 1995 to 1999 models

Every 600 miles (1000 km) – 2000-on models

Check

1 The chain stretches with wear, so periodic adjustment is necessary to maintain the correct tension. A neglected drive chain won't last long and can quickly damage the sprockets. Routine chain adjustment and lubrication isn't difficult and will ensure maximum chain and sprocket life.
2 To check the chain, support the bike on the centrestand, and shift the transmission into neutral.
3 Push up on the bottom run of the chain and measure the slack (freeplay) midway between the two sprockets **(see illustration)**. Compare your measurement to that listed in this Chapter's Specifications. Since the chain will rarely wear evenly, resulting in a tight spot, turn the rear wheel so that another section of chain can be checked; do this several times to check the entire length of chain. Any adjustment should be based upon the measurement taken at the tightest point. Adjust the chain if required as described below.
4 Every so often, and especially as the chain gets older, measure the amount of chain stretch as follows and compare the result to the stretch limit specified at the beginning of the Chapter. Following the procedure in Steps 10 to 12 below, turn the adjuster bolts out evenly until the slack is removed but not so much that the chain is taut. Measure along the bottom run the length of 11 pins (from the centre of the 1st pin to the centre of the 11th pin) and compare the result with the service limit specified at the beginning of the Chapter **(see illustration)**. Rotate the rear wheel so that several sections of the chain are measured, then calculate the average. If the chain stretch measurement exceeds the service limit it must be renewed (see Chapter 5). **Note:** *Never install a new chain on old sprockets, and never use the old chain if you install new sprockets – renew the chain and sprockets as a set.* If the chain is good, reset the adjusters so that there is the correct amount of freeplay, then tighten the axle nut and the brake torque arm nut to the specified torque settings. On XJR1200 models fit a new split pin into the torque arm bolt and bend its ends securely.
5 In some cases where lubrication has been neglected, corrosion and galling may cause the links to bind and kink, which effectively shortens the chain's length. Any such links should be thoroughly cleaned and worked free. If the chain is tight between the sprockets, rusty or kinked, it's time to renew it. If you find a tight area, mark it with felt pen or paint, and repeat the measurement after the bike has been ridden. If the chain is still tight in the same area, it may be damaged or worn. Because a tight or kinked chain can damage the transmission output shaft bearings, it's a good idea to renew it (see Chapter 5).
6 Check the entire length of the chain for damaged rollers, loose links and pins, and missing O-rings and renew it if damage is found.
7 Remove the front sprocket cover (see Chapter 5, Section 16). Check the teeth on the engine sprocket and the rear wheel sprocket for wear **(see illustration)**.
8 Inspect the drive chain slider on the swingarm for excessive wear and renew it if worn (see Chapter 5).
Note: *You should never install a new chain on old sprockets, and never use the old chain if you install new sprockets – renew the chain and sprockets as a set.*

Adjustment

9 Support the bike on its centrestand. Rotate the rear wheel until the chain is positioned with the tightest point at the centre of its bottom run.
10 Slacken the nut on the bolt securing the brake torque arm to the rear brake caliper, on

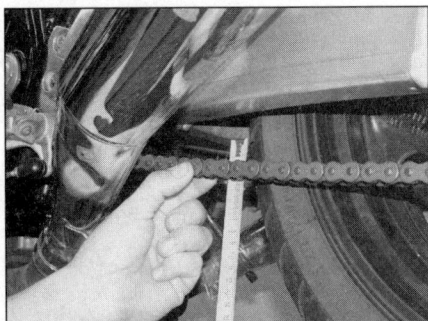

1.3 Push up on the chain and measure the slack

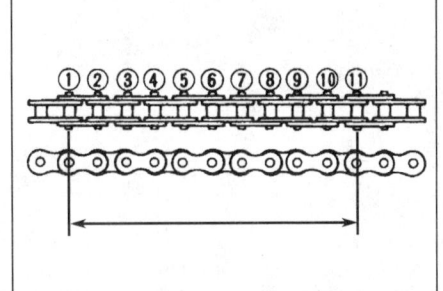

1.4 Check the amount of stretch with the chain taut by measuring as shown

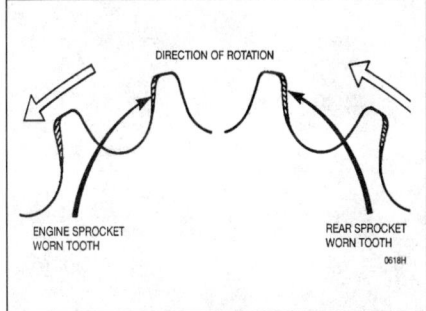

1.7 Check the sprockets in the areas indicated to see if they are worn excessively

1•8 Routine Maintenance and Servicing

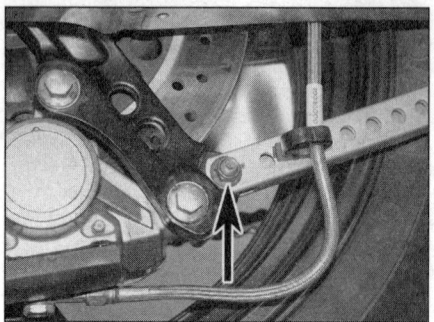

1.10 Remove the split pin where fitted, then slacken the nut (arrowed)

1.11 Slacken the rear axle nut (arrowed)

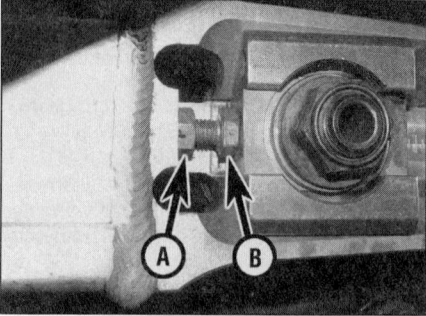

1.12a Slacken the locknut (A) and turn the adjuster (B) as required

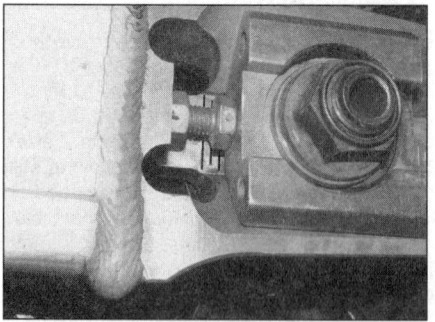

1.12b Check the relative position of the front edge . . .

1.12c . . . or back edge of the adjustment marker with the marks on the swingarm. On this bike you would use the front edge as the rear edge has not yet reached the alignment marks

1.14 Tighten the axle nut to the specified torque

XJR1200 models having first removed the split pin **(see illustration)**.

11 Slacken the axle nut **(see illustration)**.

12 Slacken the adjuster locknut on each side of the swingarm, then turn the adjusters evenly until the amount of freeplay specified at the beginning of the Chapter is obtained at the centre of the bottom run of the chain **(see illustration)**. Following chain adjustment, check that either the front or back edge (according to the current amount of chain wear) of each chain adjustment marker is in the same position in relation to the marks on the swingarm **(see illustrations)**. It is important each adjuster aligns with the same mark; if not, the rear wheel will be out of alignment with the front. Also check that there is no clearance between the adjuster bolt and the front of the adjustment marker – push or kick the wheel forwards to eliminate any freeplay (but make sure you don't rock the bike off its stand!).

> **HAYNES HiNT** Refer to Chapter 6 for information on checking wheel alignment.

13 If there is a discrepancy in the chain adjuster positions, adjust one of them so that its position is exactly the same as the other. Check the chain freeplay as described above and readjust if necessary.

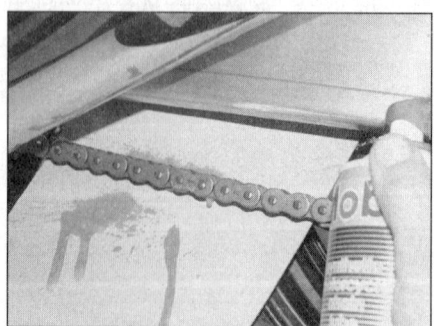

1.16 Apply the lubricant to the overlap between the sideplates. Note the use of a piece of card to prevent lubricant contacting the tyre

14 Tighten the axle nut to the torque setting specified at the beginning of the Chapter, then tighten the adjuster locknuts securely **(see illustration and 1.12a)**. Recheck the chain adjustment. Tighten the brake torque arm nut to the specified torque, then on XJR1200 models fit a new split pin through the bolt and bend its ends securely **(see illustration 1.10)**.

Lubrication

15 If required, wash the chain in paraffin (kerosene) or a suitable non-flammable or high flash-point solvent that will not damage the O-rings, using a soft brush to work any dirt out if necessary. Wipe the cleaner off the chain and allow it to dry, using compressed air if available. If the chain is excessively dirty it should be removed from the machine and allowed to soak in the paraffin or solvent (see Chapter 5).

Caution: Don't use petrol (gasoline), solvent or other cleaning fluids which might damage the internal sealing properties of the chain. Don't use high-pressure water or steam cleaners. The entire process shouldn't take longer than ten minutes – if it does, the O-rings in the chain rollers could be damaged.

16 For routine lubrication, the best time to lubricate the chain is after the motorcycle has been ridden. When the chain is warm, the lubricant will penetrate the joints between the side plates better than when cold. **Note:** *Use a chain lube that is specifically for O-ring chains; do not use any other chain lubricants – the solvents could damage the chain's sealing rings.* Apply the lubricant to the area where the side plates overlap – not the middle of the rollers **(see illustration)**.

> **HAYNES HiNT** *Apply the lubricant to the top of the lower chain run, so centrifugal force will work it into the chain when the bike is moving. After applying the lubricant, let it soak in a few minutes before wiping off any excess.*

Routine Maintenance and Servicing

2.3 Pull the cap off the spark plug

2.4 Unscrewing the spark plug using the Yamaha tool

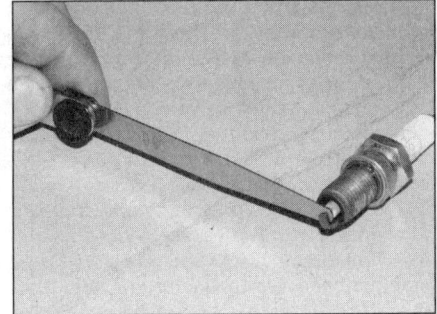

2.8a Using a feeler gauge to measure the spark plug electrode gap

2 Spark plugs – check

Every 4000 miles (6000 km) – 1995 to 1999 models

Every 6000 miles (10,000 km) – 2000-on models

1 Make sure your spark plug socket is the correct size before attempting to remove the plugs – a suitable one is supplied in the motorcycle's tool kit which is stored under the seat.
2 Remove the fuel tank (see Chapter 3).
3 Work on one plug at a time. Pull the cap off the spark plug **(see illustration)**. Using compressed air if available, clean the area around the base of the plug to prevent any dirt falling into the engine when the plug is removed.
4 Using either the plug removing tool supplied in the bike's toolkit or a deep socket type wrench, unscrew the plugs from the cylinder head **(see illustration)**.
5 Inspect their electrodes for wear. Both the centre and side electrodes should have square edges and the side electrode should be of uniform thickness – if not, they are worn. Look for excessive deposits and evidence of a cracked or chipped insulator around the centre electrode. Check the colour of the plug then refer to the chart at the end of this manual to determine whether there are any carburation or ignition problems. Check the threads, the washer and the ceramic insulator body for cracks and other damage.
6 If the electrodes are not excessively worn, if no cracks or chips are visible in the insulator, and if the deposits can be easily removed with a wire brush, the plugs can be re-gapped and re-used. If in doubt concerning the condition of the plugs, renew them as the expense is minimal.
7 You can clean spark plugs by sandblasting them, provided you blow out the plugs with compressed air and clean them with a high flash-point solvent afterwards. Alternatively the plugs can be cleaned with a wire brush.
8 Before installing the plugs, make sure they are the correct type and heat range and check the gap between the electrodes **(see illustrations)**. Compare the gap to that specified and adjust as necessary. If the gap must be adjusted, bend the side electrode only and be very careful not to chip or crack the insulator nose **(see illustration)**. Make sure the washer is in place before installing each plug.
9 Fit the plug into the end of the tool, then use the tool to insert the plug **(see illustration)**. Since the cylinder head is made of aluminium, which is soft and easily damaged, thread the plug as far as possible into the head turning the tool by hand. Once the plug is finger-tight, finish the job using a spanner on the tool supplied or a socket drive.

If a torque wrench can be applied, tighten the spark plug to the torque setting specified at the beginning of the Chapter. Otherwise, tighten it according the instructions on the box – generally if new plugs are being used, tighten them by 1/2 a turn after the washer has seated, and if the old plugs are being reused, tighten them by 1/8 to 1/4 turn after they have seated. Do not over-tighten them.
10 Fit the cap back onto the spark plug. Install the fuel tank (see Chapter 3).

> **HAYNES HINT** *Stripped plug threads in the cylinder head can be repaired with a Heli-Coil thread insert – see 'Tools and Workshop Tips' in the Reference section.*

3 Idle speed – check and adjustment

Every 4000 miles (6000 km) – 1995 to 1999 models

Every 6000 miles (10,000 km) – 2000-on models

1 The idle speed should be checked and adjusted before and after the carburettors are synchronised (balanced), and when it is obviously too high or too low. Before

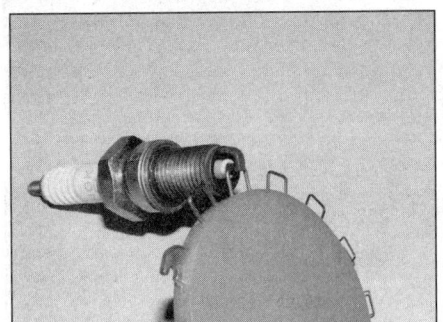

2.8b Using a wire type gauge to measure the spark plug electrode gap

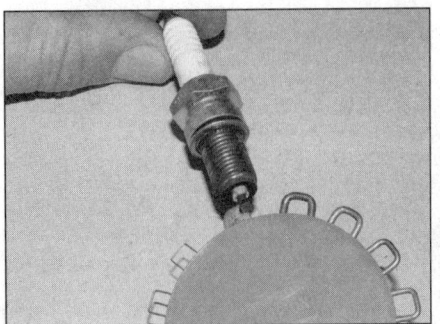

2.8c Adjust the electrode gap by bending the side electrode only

2.9 Thread the plug as far as possible turning the tool by hand

1•10 Routine Maintenance and Servicing

adjusting the idle speed, turn the handlebars from side-to-side and check the idle speed does not change as you do. If it does, the throttle cables may not be adjusted or routed correctly, or may be worn out. This is a dangerous condition that can cause loss of control of the bike. Be sure to correct this problem before proceeding.

2 The engine should be at normal operating temperature, which is usually reached after 10 to 15 minutes of stop-and-go riding. Make sure the transmission is in neutral, and place the motorcycle on its centrestand.

3 The idle speed adjuster is located on the left-hand end of the bank of carburettors (see illustration). With the engine idling, turn the adjuster until the speed listed in this Chapter's Specifications is obtained. Turn the knob clockwise to increase idle speed, and anti-clockwise to decrease it.

4 Snap the throttle open and shut a few times, then recheck the idle speed. If necessary, repeat the adjustment procedure.

5 If a smooth, steady idle can't be achieved, the fuel/air mixture may be incorrect (check the pilot screw settings – see Chapter 3) or the carburettors may need synchronising (see Section 4). Also check the intake manifold rubbers for cracks which will cause an air leak, resulting in a weak mixture.

4 Carburettors – synchronisation

Every 4000 miles (6000 km) – 1995 to 1999 models
Every 6000 miles (10,000 km) – 2000-on models

> **Warning:** Petrol (gasoline) is extremely flammable, so take extra precautions when you work on any part of the fuel system. Don't smoke or allow open flames or bare light bulbs near the work area, and don't work in a garage where a natural gas-type appliance is present. If you spill any fuel on your skin, rinse it off immediately with soap and water. When you perform any kind of work on the fuel system, wear safety glasses and have a fire extinguisher suitable for a Class B type fire (flammable liquids) on hand.

> **Warning:** Take great care not to burn your hand on the hot engine unit when accessing the gauge take-off points on the intake manifolds. Do not allow exhaust gases to build up in the work area; either perform the check outside or use an exhaust gas extraction system.

1 Synchronising or balancing the carburettors is simply the process of adjusting the throttle linkage setting so each carburettor passes the same amount of fuel/air mixture to each cylinder. This is done by measuring the vacuum produced in each cylinder. Carburettors that are out of synchronisation will result in increased fuel consumption, increased engine temperature, less than ideal throttle response and higher vibration levels. If you are also checking the valve clearances as part of a major service, do that before synchronising the carburettors. If the clearances have been checked recently, there should be no reason for them to need readjusting. Make sure the idle speed is correct (see Section 3).

2 To properly synchronise the carburettors you will need a set of vacuum gauges or a manometer. These instruments measure engine vacuum, and can be obtained from motorcycle dealers or mail order parts suppliers. The equipment used should be suitable for a four cylinder engine and come complete with the necessary adapters and hoses to fit the take off points. **Note:** *Because of the nature of the synchronisation procedure and the need for special instruments, most owners leave the task to a Yamaha dealer.*

3.3 Idle speed adjuster (arrowed)

4.4a Remove the blanking caps ...

4.4b ... and hose(s) from the take-off points ...

4.4c ... and attach the gauge hoses to them

Routine Maintenance and Servicing 1•11

4.7 Carburettor synchronisation set-up

4.8a Left-hand synchronising screw (A) ...

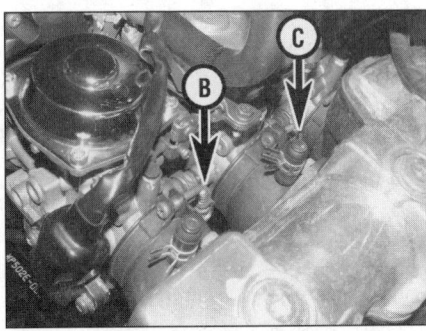

4.8b ... right-hand synchronising screw (B), and centre synchronising screw (C)

3 The engine should be at normal operating temperature, which is usually reached after 10 to 15 minutes of stop-and-go riding. Place the machine on its centrestand on level ground. Remove the fuel tank (see Chapter 3).

4 Release the clamps and detach the blanking caps and the hose(s) from the vacuum take-off unions on the intake manifolds **(see illustrations)**. Attach the gauge or manometer hoses to the unions **(see illustration)**. Make sure the No. 1 (left-hand) gauge is attached to the No. 1 (left-hand) union, and so on.

5 Arrange a temporary fuel supply using an auxiliary tank and some hosing (see **Tool Tip**).

6 Start the engine and let it idle. If the gauges are fitted with damping adjustment, set this so that the needle flutter is just eliminated but so that they can still respond to small changes in pressure.

7 The vacuum readings for all cylinders should be the same **(see illustration)**. If the vacuum readings differ, proceed as follows.

8 Identify the synchronising screws situated in-between each carburettor, in the throttle linkage, then obtain a suitable screwdriver with which to turn them **(see illustrations)**. **Note:** *Do not press down on the screws whilst adjusting them, otherwise a false reading will be obtained.* First synchronise No. 1 carburettor to No. 2 using the left-hand synchronising screw until the readings are the same. Then synchronise No. 3 carburettor to No. 4 using the right-hand screw. Finally synchronise Nos. 1 and 2 carburettors to

An auxiliary fuel tank can be made using an empty gear oil container (or any container of a suitable material that has a nozzle cap to which a hose can be attached). Simply fill it with fuel, attach one end of a suitable hose to the cap nozzle and the other to the fuel hose on the bike, then invert the container and hang or support it so that it is safe. Alternatively obtain a two-stroke motorcycle oil tank from a breaker and attach a hose between the union on its base and the fuel hose.

Nos. 3 and 4 using the centre screw. When all the carburettors are synchronised, open and close the throttle quickly to settle the linkage, and recheck the gauge readings, readjusting if necessary.

9 When the adjustment is complete, recheck the vacuum readings, then adjust the idle speed (see Section 3), and check the throttle cable freeplay (see Section 16). Detach the temporary fuel supply and install the fuel tank (see Chapter 3). Remove the gauges and refit the blanking caps and hose(s) – on all models attach the fuel tap vacuum hose to the No. 2 cylinder take-off union **(see illustration 4.4b)**. On 2002 models onwards attach the AIS (air induction system) hose to the No. 3 cylinder take-off union. Fit the blanking caps to the other unions **(see illustration 4.4a)**. Make sure they are all secured by their clamps.

5 Air filter – cleaning and renewal

Every 4000 miles (6000 km) – 1995 to 1999 models

Every 6000 miles (10,000 km) – 2000-on models

1 Remove the right-hand side panel (see Chapter 7).

2 Undo the screws securing the air filter cover to the filter housing, then remove the cover and withdraw the filter element from the housing **(see illustrations)**. Check the condition of the rubber seal in the cover and renew it if it is damaged, deformed or deteriorated.

3 Tap the element on a hard surface to dislodge any large particles of dirt. If compressed air is available, use it to clean the

5.2a Undo the screws (arrowed) ...

5.2b ... then remove the cover ...

5.2c ... and withdraw the element

1•12 Routine Maintenance and Servicing

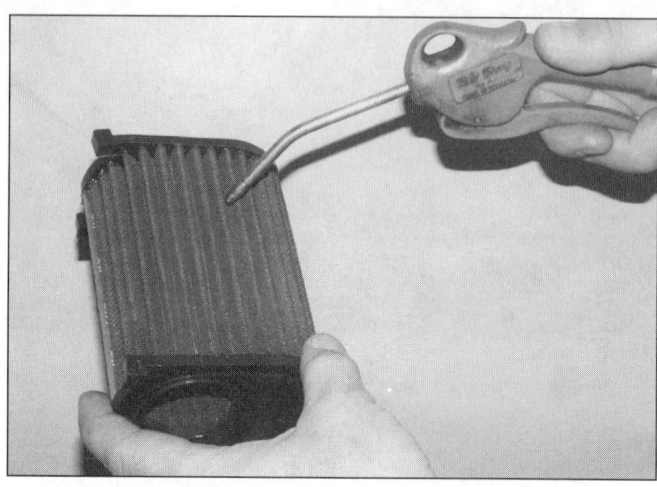

5.3 Direct the air in the opposite direction to normal airflow

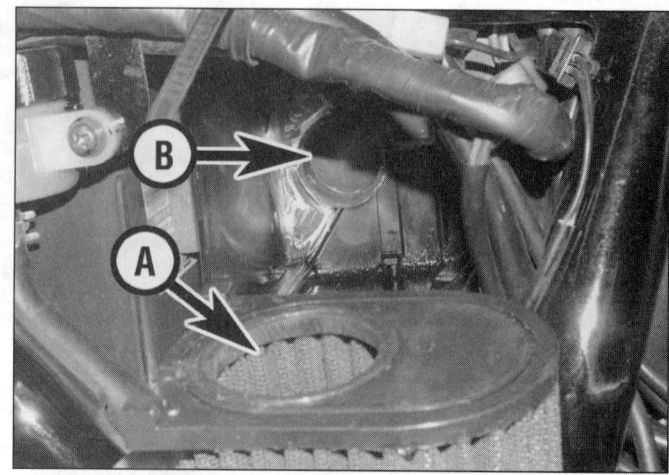

5.5 Locate the open end of the element (A) over the rim (B)

element, directing the air in the opposite direction of normal airflow (see illustration).

> **HAYNES HINT** *If using compressed air to clean the element, place either your hand, a rag, or a piece of card on the inside of the element to prevent any dust and debris being blown from one side of the element into the other.*

Caution: *If the machine is continually ridden in dusty conditions, the filter should be cleaned more frequently.*

4 Check the element for signs of damage. If the element is torn or cannot be cleaned, or is obviously beyond further use it must be renewed.

5 Install the filter element, making sure it locates correctly (see illustration). Fit the air filter cover, making sure the rubber seal is in place in the rim and the cover seals properly (see illustration 5.2b). Install the right-hand side panel (see Chapter 7).

6 Check that the collector in the air filter housing drain hose has not become blocked, and drain it if necessary – the hose comes out of the front left side of the housing (see illustration).

7 Check the crankcase breather hose between the engine and the front of the air filter housing for loose connections, cracks and deterioration, and renew it if necessary (see illustration).

6 Fuel system and air induction system (AIS) – check

Every 4000 miles (6000 km) – 1995 to 1999 models

Every 6000 miles (10,000 km) – 2000-on models

> ⚠ **Warning:** *Petrol (gasoline) is extremely flammable, so take extra precautions when you work on any part of the fuel system. Don't smoke or allow open flames or bare light bulbs near the work area, and don't work in a garage where a natural gas-type appliance is present. If you spill any fuel on your skin, rinse it off immediately with soap and water. When you perform any kind of work on the fuel system, wear safety glasses and have a fire extinguisher suitable for a Class B type fire (flammable liquids) on hand.*

Fuel system

1 Remove the fuel tank (see Chapter 3) and check the tank, the fuel tap and the fuel hoses for signs of leakage, deterioration or damage; in particular check that there is no leakage from the fuel hoses. Renew any hoses which are cracked or have deteriorated (see Section 31).

2 If the fuel tap is leaking, tighten the assembly screws and/or mounting screws, depending on the site of the leak (see

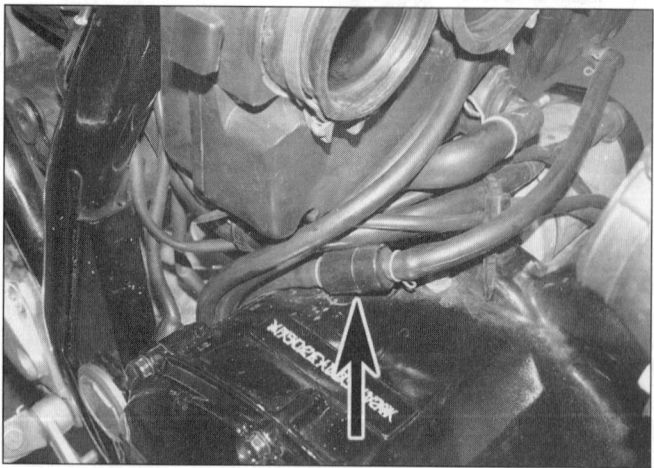

5.6 Check the collector (arrowed) . . .

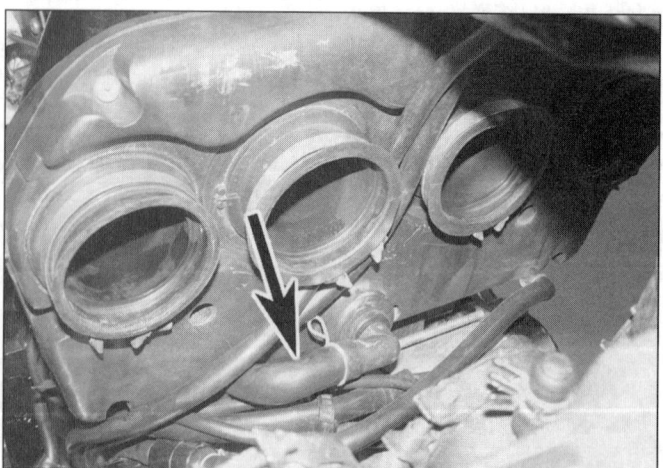

5.7 . . . and the breather hose (arrowed) as described

Routine Maintenance and Servicing 1•13

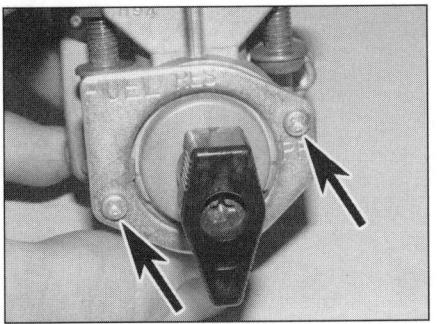
6.2a Tighten the front assembly screws (arrowed) . . .

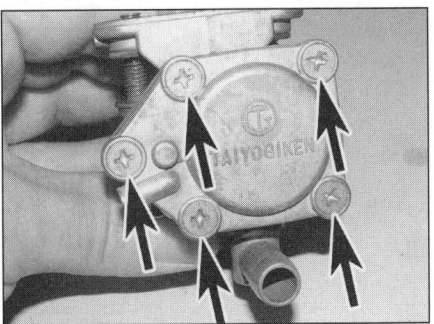
6.2b . . . the rear assembly screws (arrowed) . . .

6.2c . . . or the mounting screws as required to stem any leaks

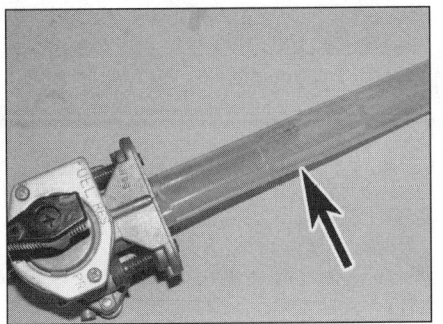
6.4 Fuel strainer (arrowed)

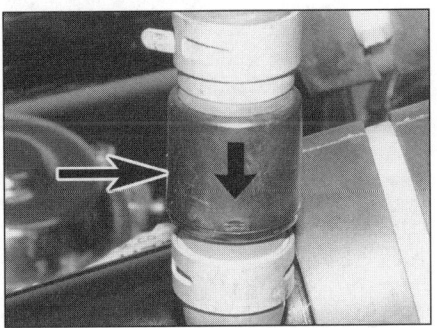
6.5 In-line fuel filter (arrowed). Note the directional arrow marked on the body

6.6 Check the AIS valve assembly (arrowed), hoses and pipes as described

illustrations). If leakage persists remove the tap and disassemble it, noting how the components fit (see Chapter 3). Inspect all components for wear and damage. Renew the seal and O-ring.

3 If the carburettor gaskets are leaking, disassemble the carburettors and rebuild them using new gaskets and seals (see Chapter 3).

4 A fuel strainer is mounted in the tank and is integral with the fuel tap. Remove the fuel tank and the fuel tap (see Chapter 3). Clean the gauze strainer to remove all traces of dirt and fuel sediment **(see illustration)**. Check the gauze for holes. If any are found, a new tap should be fitted – the strainer is not available separately. If the strainer is dirty, check the condition of the inside of your tank – if there is evidence of rust, drain and clean the tank (see Chapter 3).

5 On XJR1300 models an in-line filter is fitted in the fuel hose between the tap and the carburettors **(see illustration)**. Renewal of the strainer is advised after a high mileage has been covered. It is also necessary if fuel starvation is suspected. Remove the fuel tank (see Chapter 3). Release the clamps securing the hoses to the filter and detach them. Fit the new filter, noting that the directional arrow on the body must point in the direction of fuel flow. Make sure the clamps are in good condition and are secure.

Air induction system (AIS) – 2002 models onwards

6 Remove the fuel tank (see Chapter 3). Check the air cut-off valve and the reed valve assembly above the engine for signs of physical damage and renew it if necessary **(see illustration)** (see Chapter 3).

7 Check the AIS hoses and pipes for signs of deterioration or damage, and check that they are all securely connected with the hoses clamped at each end. Renew any hoses which are cracked or deteriorated (see Chapter 3).

8 If the valves clearances are all correct and the carburettors have been synchronised, and have no other faults, and the idle speed cannot be set properly, it is possible the AIS is faulty. Further information and checks on the system are in Chapter 3.

7 Engine oil change

Every 4000 miles (6000 km) – 1995 to 1999 models

Every 6000 miles (10,000 km) – 2000-on models

 Warning: Be careful when draining the oil, as the exhaust pipes, the engine, and the oil itself can cause severe burns.

1 Consistent routine oil and filter changes are the single most important maintenance procedure you can perform on a motorcycle. The oil not only lubricates the internal parts of the engine, transmission and clutch, but it also acts as a coolant, a cleaner, a sealant, and a protector. Because of these demands, the oil takes a terrific amount of abuse and should be changed often with new oil of the recommended grade and type. Saving a little money on the difference in cost between a good oil and a cheap oil won't pay off if the engine is damaged. The oil filter should be changed with every second oil change (see Section 20).

2 Before changing the oil, warm up the engine so the oil will drain easily.

3 Position a clean drain tray below the engine. Unscrew the oil filler cap from the clutch cover to vent it and to act as a reminder that there is no oil in the engine **(see illustration)**.

4 Unscrew the oil drain plug from the underside of the engine and allow the oil to

7.3 Remove the oil filler cap from the clutch cover

1•14 Routine Maintenance and Servicing

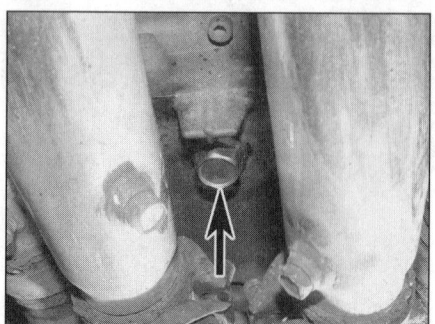

7.4a Unscrew the engine oil drain plug . . .

7.4b . . . and allow the oil to drain

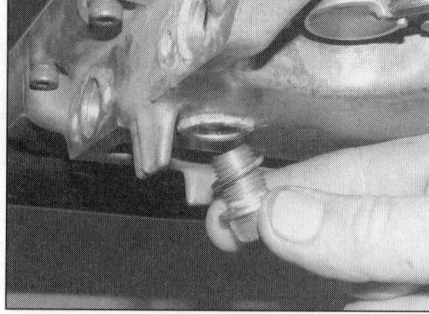

7.5 Install the drain plug using a new sealing washer

flow into the drain tray **(see illustrations)**. Check the condition of the sealing washer on the drain plug and discard it if it is damaged or worn – you will probably have to cut the old one off using pliers. It is best to use a new one whatever the condition of the old one.

5 When the oil has completely drained, fit the plug into the crankcase, preferably using a new sealing washer, and tighten it to the torque setting specified at the beginning of the Chapter **(see illustration)**. Avoid overtightening, as you will damage the sump.

6 Refill the engine to the proper level using the recommended type and amount of oil (see *Daily (pre-ride) checks*). With the motorcycle vertical, the oil level should lie between the maximum and minimum level lines on the inspection window (see *Daily (pre-ride) checks*). Install the filler cap **(see illustration 7.3)**. Start the engine and let it run for two or three minutes. Stop the engine, wait a few minutes, then check the oil level. If necessary, add more oil to bring the level up to the maximum level line on the window. Check that there are no leaks around the drain plug.

7 Every so often, and especially as Yamaha do not fit an oil pressure switch and warning light (the system fitted uses an oil level sensor), it is advisable to perform an oil pressure check (see Section 30).

8 The old oil drained from the engine cannot be re-used and should be disposed of properly. Check with your local refuse disposal company, disposal facility or environmental agency to see whether they will accept the used oil for recycling. Don't pour used oil into drains or onto the ground.

> **HAYNES HINT**
> *Check the old oil carefully – if it is very metallic coloured, then the engine is experiencing wear from break-in (new engine) or from insufficient lubrication. If there are flakes or chips of metal in the oil, then something is drastically wrong internally and the engine will have to be disassembled for inspection and repair. If there are pieces of fibre-like material in the oil, the clutch is experiencing excessive wear and should be checked.*

Note: It is antisocial and illegal to dump oil down the drain. To find the location of your nearest oil recycling bank in the UK, call this number free. In the USA, note that any oil supplier must accept used oil for recycling.

8 Brake pads – check

Every 4000 miles (6000 km) – 1995 to 1999 models

Every 6000 miles (10,000 km) – 2000-on models

1 Each brake pad has wear indicators that can be viewed without removing the pads from the caliper.

2 The turned-in corners of the brake pad backing material form the wear indicators – when they are almost contacting the disc itself the pads must be renewed **(see illustration)**. The indicators are visible by looking at the exposed corner of the pads **(see illustrations)**. Note: *Some after-market pads may use different indicators (such as a groove cut into the friction material); the pad is worn when the groove is no longer visible.*

Caution: Do not allow the pads to wear to the extent that the indicators contact the disc itself as the disc will be damaged.

3 If the pads are worn to the indicators, new ones must be installed. If the pads are dirty or if you are in doubt as to the amount of friction material remaining, remove them for inspection (see Chapter 6). If required, measure the amount of friction material remaining – the absolute minimum is 0.5 mm.

4 Refer to Chapter 6 for details of pad renewal.

9 Brake system – check

Every 4000 miles (6000 km) – 1995 to 1999 models

Every 6000 miles (10,000 km) – 2000-on models

1 A routine general check of the brake system will ensure that any problems are discovered

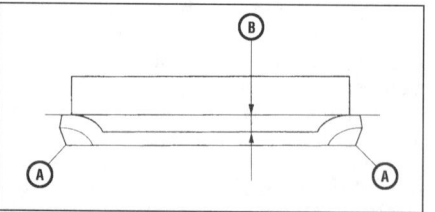

8.2a Brake pad wear indicators (A) and minimum thickness (B)

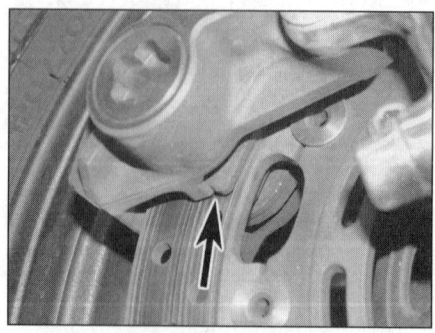

8.2b Front brake pad wear indicator (arrowed)

8.2c Rear brake pad wear indicator (arrowed)

Routine Maintenance and Servicing 1•15

9.3 Flex the brake hose and check for cracks, bulges and leaking fluid

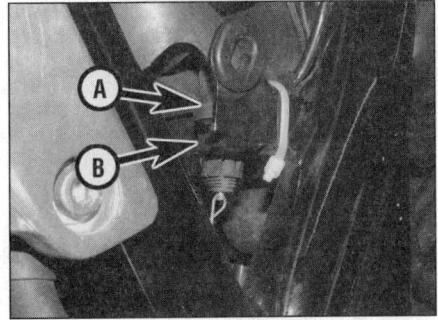

9.5 Hold the rear brake light switch (A) and turn the adjuster nut (B)

9.6 Adjusting the front brake lever span

and remedied before the rider's safety is jeopardised.

2 Check the brake lever and pedal for looseness, improper or rough action, excessive play, bends, and other damage. Renew any damaged parts (see Chapter 6). Clean and lubricate the lever and pedal pivots if their action is stiff or rough (see Section 17).

3 Make sure all brake fasteners are tight. Check the brake pads for wear (see Section 8) and make sure the fluid level in the reservoirs is correct (see *Daily (pre-ride) checks*). Look for leaks at the hose connections and check for cracks in the hoses themselves **(see illustration)**. If the lever or pedal action is spongy bleed the brakes (see Chapter 6). The brake fluid should be changed every two years (see Section 26) and the hoses renewed if they deteriorate, or every four years irrespective of their condition (see Section 27). The master cylinder and caliper seals should be renewed every two years, or if leakage from them is evident (see Section 25).

4 Make sure the brake light operates when the front brake lever is pulled in. The front brake light switch, mounted on the underside of the master cylinder, is not adjustable. If it fails to operate properly, check it (see Chapter 8).

5 Make sure the brake light is activated just before the rear brake takes effect. If adjustment is necessary, hold the switch and turn the adjuster nut on the switch body until the brake light is activated when required **(see illustration)**. If the brake light comes on too late, turn the nut clockwise. If the brake light comes on too soon or is permanently on, turn the nut anti-clockwise. If the switch doesn't operate the brake light, check it (see Chapter 8).

6 On 1998-on models the front brake lever has a span adjuster which alters the distance of the lever from the handlebar. Each setting is identified by a number on the adjuster which aligns with the arrow on the lever bracket. Pull the lever away from the handlebar and turn the adjuster ring until the setting which best suits the rider is obtained **(see illustration)**. When making adjustment ensure that the pin set in the lever bracket is engaged in its detent in the adjuster.

7 Check the position of the brake pedal. Yamaha recommend the distance between the top of the brake pedal and the top of the

9.7a Measure the distance between the top of the footrest and the top of the brake pedal as shown

rider's footrest should be as specified at the beginning of the Chapter **(see illustration)**. If the pedal height is incorrect, or if the rider's preference is different, slacken the clevis locknut on the master cylinder pushrod, then turn the pushrod using a spanner on the hex at the top of the rod until the pedal is at the correct or desired height **(see illustration)**. After adjustment check that the pushrod end is still visible in the hole in the clevis. On completion tighten the locknut securely. Adjust the rear brake light switch after adjusting the pedal height (see Step 5).

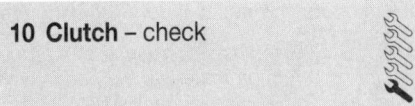

10 Clutch – check

Every 4000 miles (6000 km) – 1995 to 1999 models

Every 6000 miles (10,000 km) – 2000-on models

1 All models are fitted with an hydraulic clutch, for which there is no method of adjustment.

2 Check the fluid level in the reservoir (see *Daily (pre-ride) checks*).

3 Inspect the hose and its connections for signs of fluid leakage, cracking, deterioration and wear. The clutch fluid should be changed every two years (see Section 26), and the hose renewed if damaged or deteriorated, or every four years irrespective of condition (see

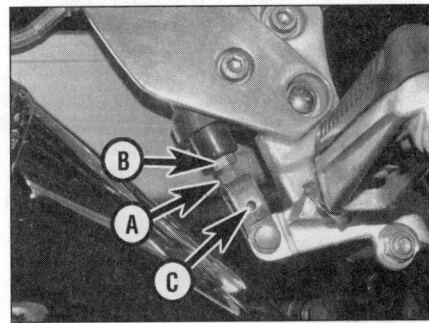

9.7b Slacken the locknut (A) and turn the pushrod using the hex (B) making sure the rod end is still visible in the hole (C)

Section 27). The master and release cylinder seals should be changed every two years, or if leakage from them is evident (see Section 25).

4 Check the operation of the clutch. If there is evidence of air in the system (spongy feel to the lever, difficulty in engaging gear, drag when in gear), bleed the clutch (see Chapter 2). If the lever feels stiff or sticky, overhaul the release mechanism (see Chapter 2).

5 On 1998-on models the clutch lever has a span adjuster which alters the distance of the lever from the handlebar. Each setting is identified by a number on the adjuster which aligns with the arrow on the lever bracket. Pull the lever away from the handlebar and turn the adjuster ring until the setting which best suits the rider is obtained **(see illustration)**. When making adjustment ensure that the pin set in the lever bracket is engaged in its detent in the adjuster.

10.5 Adjusting the clutch lever span

1•16 Routine Maintenance and Servicing

11 Battery – check

Every 4000 miles (6000 km) – 1995 to 1999 models

Every 6000 miles (10,000 km) – 2000-on models

1 All models are fitted with a sealed (maintenance-free) battery which requires no maintenance. **Note:** *Do not attempt to remove the battery caps to check the electrolyte level or battery specific gravity. Removal will damage the caps, resulting in electrolyte leakage and battery damage.*
2 All that should be done is to check that the terminals are clean and tight and that the casing is not damaged or leaking. See Chapter 8 for further details.
Caution: Be extremely careful when handling or working around the battery. The electrolyte is very caustic and an explosive gas (hydrogen) is given off when the battery is charging.
3 If the machine is not in regular use, disconnect the battery and give it a refresher charge every month to six weeks (see Chapter 8).

12 Wheels and tyres – general check

Every 4000 miles (6000 km) – 1995 to 1999 models

Every 6000 miles (10,000 km) – 2000-on models

Tyres
1 Check the tyre condition and tread depth thoroughly – see *Daily (pre-ride) checks*.

Wheels
2 Cast wheels are virtually maintenance free, but they should be kept clean and checked periodically for cracks and other damage. Also check the wheel runout and alignment (see Chapter 6). Never attempt to repair

damaged cast wheels; they must be renewed. Check the valve rubber for signs of damage or deterioration and have it renewed if necessary. Also, make sure the valve cap is in place and tight.

13 Wheel bearings – check

Every 4000 miles (6000 km) – 1995 to 1999 models

Every 6000 miles (10,000 km) – 2000-on models

1 Wheel bearings will wear over a period of time and result in handling problems.
2 Place the motorcycle on its centrestand. Check for any play in the bearings by pushing and pulling the wheel against the hub **(see illustration)**. Also rotate the wheel and check that it rotates smoothly.
3 If any play is detected in the hub, or if the wheel does not rotate smoothly (and this is not due to brake or transmission drag), the wheel bearings must be removed and inspected for wear or damage (see Chapter 6).

14 Sidestand and centrestand – check

Every 4000 miles (6000 km) – 1995 to 1999 models

Every 6000 miles (10,000 km) – 2000-on models

1 Check the stand springs for damage and distortion. The springs must be capable of retracting the stands fully and holding them retracted when the motorcycle is in use. If a spring is sagged or broken it must be renewed.
2 Lubricate the stand pivots regularly (see Section 17).
3 Check the stands and their mounts for bends and cracks. Stands can often be repaired by welding.
4 The sidestand switch forms part of the ignition cut-off system. Place the motorcycle on its centrestand and check the system as described below.
5 Check the operation of the starter interlock circuit by trying to start the engine with the sidestand down – the engine should not start. Retract the stand and now try to start the engine when it is in gear – it should only start with the clutch lever pulled in. Shift the transmission into neutral and start the engine. Pull in the clutch lever and select a gear. Extend the sidestand. The engine should stop as the sidestand is extended. If the sidestand switch does not operate as described, check its circuit (see Chapter 8).

15 Nuts and bolts – tightness check

Every 4000 miles (6000 km) – 1995 to 1999 models

Every 6000 miles (10,000 km) – 2000-on models

1 Since vibration of the machine tends to loosen fasteners, all nuts, bolts, screws, etc. should be periodically checked for proper tightness.
2 Pay particular attention to the following:
  Spark plugs
  Engine oil drain plug
  Gearchange lever, brake and clutch lever, and brake pedal bolts/nuts
  Footrest and stand bolts
  Engine mounting bolts
  Shock absorber bolts and swingarm pivot bolt nut
  Handlebar clamp bolts
  Front axle bolt and axle clamp bolt
  Front fork clamp bolts (top and bottom yoke)
  Rear axle nut
  Brake caliper mounting bolts
  Brake hose banjo bolts and caliper bleed valves
  Brake disc bolts
  Exhaust system bolts/nuts
3 If a torque wrench is available, use it along with the torque specifications at the beginning of this and other Chapters.

16 Throttle and choke – check and adjustment

Every 4000 miles (6000 km) – 1995 to 1999 models

Every 6000 miles (10,000 km) – 2000-on models

Note: *At the carburettor end of the cables, on 1995 to 2001 models the accelerator (opening cable) fits into the front holder on the cable bracket and the decelerator (closing) cable fits into the rear holder, and the choke cable routes between the two throttle cables. From 2002 the throttle cables are the other way round in the bracket, and the choke cable routes in front of both of them.*

Throttle
1 Make sure the throttle grip rotates easily from fully closed to fully open with the handlebars turned at various angles. The grip should return automatically from fully open to fully closed when released.
2 If the throttle sticks, this is probably due to a cable fault. Remove the cables (see Chapter 3) and lubricate them (see Section 17). Check that the inner cables slide freely and

13.2 Checking for play in the wheel bearings

Routine Maintenance and Servicing 1•17

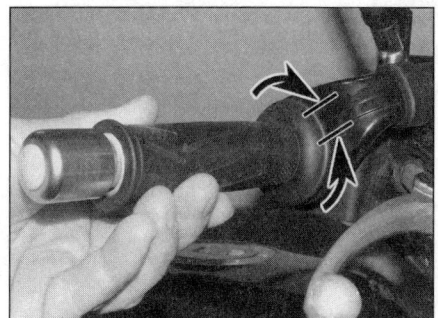

16.3 Measure the amount of freeplay in the throttle as shown

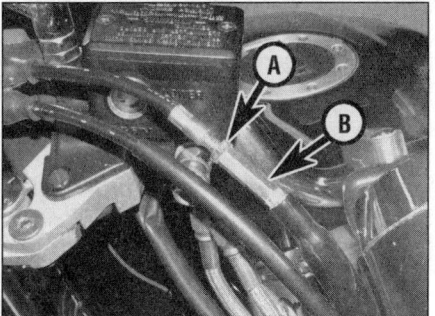

16.4 Throttle cable adjuster locknut (A) and adjuster (B).

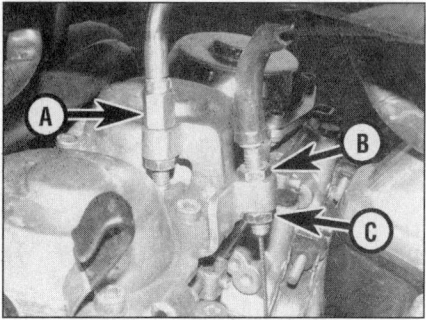

16.6a Make sure the decelerator cable (A) is tight against the bracket. Accelerator cable top nut (B) and bottom nut (C)

easily in the outer cables. If not, renew the cables. With the cables removed, make sure the throttle twistgrip rotates freely on the handlebar. Install the cables, making sure they are correctly routed. If this fails to improve the operation of the throttle, the cables must be renewed. Note that in very rare cases the fault could lie in the carburettors rather than the cables, necessitating their removal and inspection (see Chapter 3).

3 With the throttle operating smoothly, check for a small amount of freeplay in the cables, measured in terms of the amount of twistgrip rotation before the throttle opens, and compare the amount to that listed in this Chapter's Specifications **(see illustration)**. If it's incorrect, adjust the cables to correct it as follows.

4 Freeplay adjustments can be made at the throttle twistgrip end of the cable. Loosen the locknut on the adjuster **(see illustration)**. Turn the adjuster until the specified amount of freeplay is obtained (see this Chapter's Specifications), then retighten the locknut. Turn the adjuster in to increase freeplay and out to reduce it.

5 If the adjuster has reached its limit of adjustment, reset it so that the freeplay is at a maximum, then adjust the cable at the carburettor end as follows. Remove the fuel tank (see Chapter 3).

6 First check that the decelerator cable is tightened fully down onto the bracket **(see illustration)**. Now slacken the accelerator (opening) cable top nut and slide the cable down in the bracket until the bottom nut is clear of the lug, then thread the bottom nut up or down as required – thread it down to reduce freeplay, and thread it up to increase it **(see illustration)**. Draw the cable up into the bracket so the bottom nut becomes captive against the lug, then tighten the top nut down onto the bracket **(see illustration)**. Further adjustments can now be made using the adjuster at the throttle end (see Step 4). If the cable cannot be adjusted as specified, renew the cable (see Chapter 3).

 Warning: Turn the handlebars all the way through their travel with the engine idling. Idle speed should not change. If it does, the cable may be routed incorrectly. Correct this condition before riding the bike.

7 Check that the throttle twistgrip operates smoothly and snaps shut quickly when released. Install the fuel tank (see Chapter 3).

Choke

Note: *On 1995 models the choke is operated by a control knob on the carburettor body. On all later models the choke is operated by a lever on the left handlebar via a cable.*

8 On 1995 models, if the choke does not operate smoothly, remove the carburettors and inspect the choke plungers (see Chapter 3). Also check that the choke knob shaft is not bent. No adjustment is possible.

9 On 1996-on models, if the choke does not operate smoothly this is probably due to a cable fault. Remove the cable (see Chapter 3) and lubricate it (see Section 17). If the inner cable still does not run smoothly in the outer cable, renew it. If this fails to improve the operation of the choke, check that the lever is not binding in the switch housing. If the lever action is OK, the fault could lie in the carburettors rather than the cable, necessitating their removal and inspection of the choke plungers (see Chapter 3). Make sure there is a small amount of freeplay in the cable before the plungers move. If there isn't, check that the cable is seating correctly at the carburettor end – remove the fuel tank (see Chapter 3) for access. You can create some freeplay in the cable by slackening the locknut on the cable adjuster then turning the adjuster until a small amount of freeplay is created – turn the adjuster in to increase freeplay and out to reduce it, then tighten the locknut against the adjuster **(see illustration)**. Otherwise, renew the cable.

17 Stand, lever pivots and cables – lubrication

Every 4000 miles (6000 km) – 1995 to 1999 models

Every 6000 miles (10,000 km) – 2000-on models

1 Since the controls, cables and various other components of a motorcycle are exposed to the elements, they should be lubricated

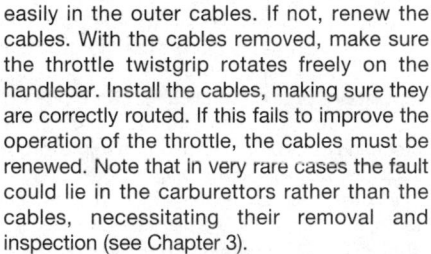

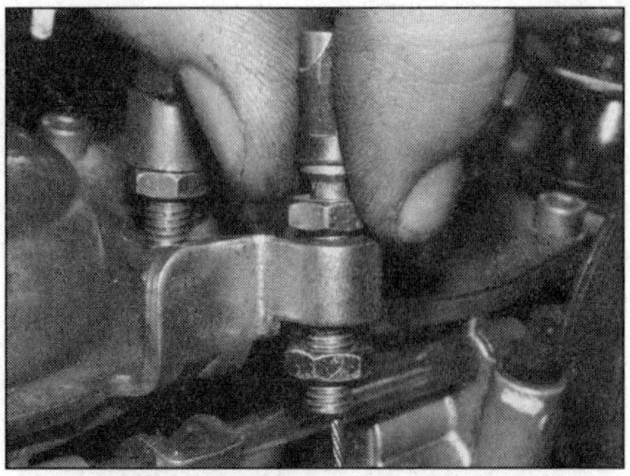

16.6b Slacken the top nut, move the cable down in the bracket and adjust the position of the bottom nut as required

16.6c Draw the cable up so the bottom nut is captive against the bracket, then tighten the top nut

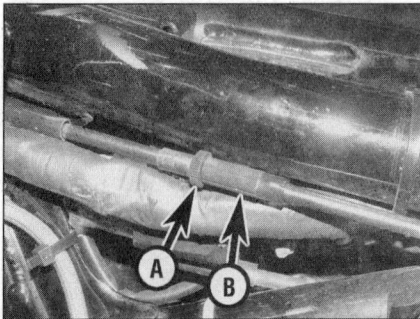

16.9 Choke cable adjuster locknut (A) and adjuster (B)

1•18 Routine Maintenance and Servicing

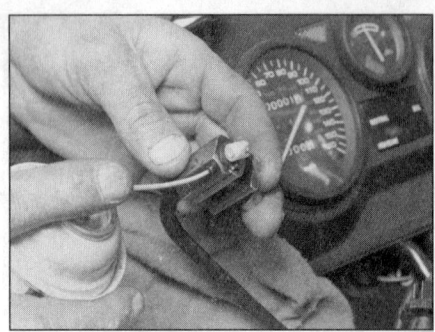

17.3a Lubricating a cable with a pressure lubricator. Make sure the tool seals around the outer cable

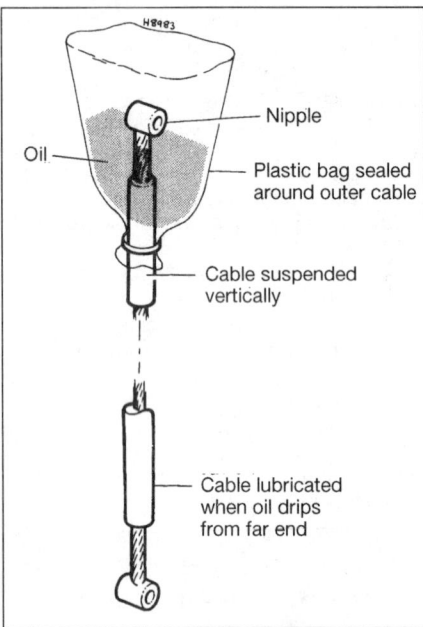

17.3b Lubricating a cable with a makeshift funnel and motor oil

periodically to ensure safe and trouble-free operation.

2 The footrests, clutch and brake levers, brake pedal, gearchange lever linkage and sidestand and centrestand pivots should be lubricated frequently. In order for the lubricant to be applied where it will do the most good, the component should be disassembled. However, if an aerosol cable lubricant is being used, it can be applied to the pivot joint gaps and will usually work its way into the areas where friction occurs. If motor oil or light grease is being used, apply it sparingly as it may attract dirt (which could cause the controls to bind or wear at an accelerated rate). **Note:** *One of the best lubricants for the control lever pivots is a dry-film lubricant (available from many sources by different names).*

3 To lubricate the throttle and choke cables, disconnect the relevant cable at its upper end, then lubricate the cable with a pressure adapter, or if one is not available, using the set-up shown **(see illustrations)**. See Chapter 3 for the throttle and choke cable removal procedures.

18 Suspension – check

Every 4000 miles (6000 km) – 1995 to 1999 models

Every 6000 miles (10,000 km) – 2000-on models

1 The suspension components must be maintained in top operating condition to ensure rider safety. Loose, worn or damaged suspension parts decrease the motorcycle's stability and control.

Front suspension

2 While standing alongside the motorcycle, apply the front brake and push on the handlebars to compress the forks several times. See if they move up-and-down smoothly without binding. If binding is felt, the forks should be disassembled and inspected (see Chapter 5).

3 Inspect the area around the dust seal for signs of oil leakage, then carefully lever up the seal using a flat-bladed screwdriver and inspect the area around the fork seal **(see illustration)**. If leakage is evident, the seals must be renewed (see Chapter 5). Also check for corrosion and pitting which could cause a seal to leak; the only remedy for this is to renew the tubes (see Chapter 5).

4 Check the tightness of all suspension nuts and bolts to be sure none have worked loose, applying the torque settings at the beginning of Chapter 5.

Rear suspension

5 Inspect the rear shock absorbers for fluid leakage and tightness of their mountings. If leakage is found, the shock absorber(s) must be renewed (see Chapter 5).

6 With the aid of an assistant to support the bike, compress the rear suspension several times. It should move up and down freely without binding. If any binding is felt, the worn or faulty component must be identified and renewed. The problem could be due to either the shock absorbers or the swingarm components.

7 Support the motorcycle on its centrestand. Grab the swingarm and rock it from side to side – there should be no discernible movement at the rear **(see illustration)**. If there's a little movement or a slight clicking can be heard, inspect the tightness of all the rear suspension mounting bolts and nuts, referring to the torque settings specified at the beginning of Chapter 5, and re-check for movement. Next, grasp the top of the rear wheel and pull it upwards – there should be no discernible freeplay before the shock absorbers begin to compress **(see illustration)**. Any freeplay felt in either check indicates worn bearings in the swingarm, or worn shock absorber mountings. The worn components must be renewed (see Chapter 5).

8 To make an accurate assessment of the swingarm bearings, remove the rear wheel (see Chapter 6) and the bolts securing the shock absorbers to the swingarm (see Chapter 5). Grasp the rear of the swingarm with one hand and place your other hand at the junction of the swingarm and the frame. Try to move the rear of the swingarm from side-to-side. Any wear (play) in the bearings should be felt as movement between the swingarm and the frame at the front. If there is any play the swingarm will be felt to move forward and backward at the front (not from side-to-side). Next, move the swingarm up and down through its full travel. It should move freely, without any binding or rough spots. If any play in the swingarm is noted or if the swingarm does not move freely, the swingarm must be removed for inspection of the bearings (see Chapter 5).

18.3 Check for oil leakage, scratches, corrosion, and pitting on the fork tube

18.7a Checking for play in the swingarm bearings

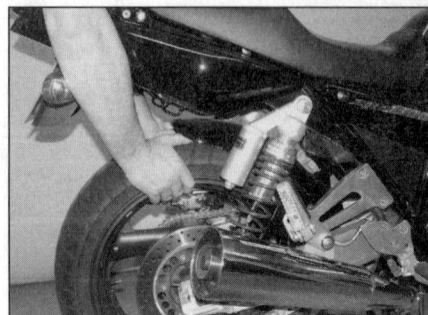

18.7b Checking for play in the suspension mountings and swingarm bearings

Routine Maintenance and Servicing 1•19

19.4 Checking for play in the steering head bearings

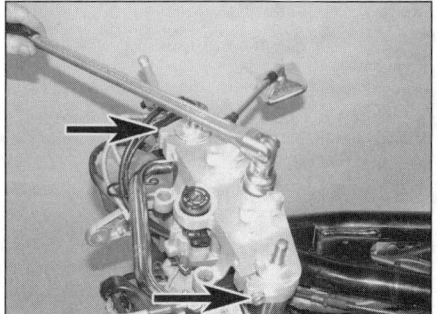

19.7 Slacken the fork clamp bolts (arrowed), then unscrew the steering stem nut

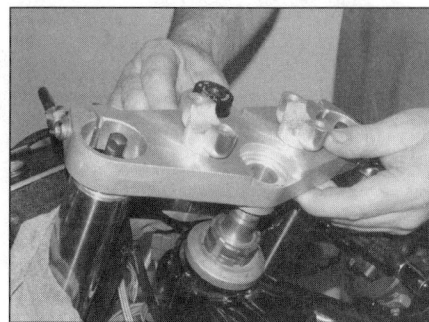

19.9 Ease the top yoke up off the steering stem and forks

19 Steering head bearings – check and adjustment

Every 8000 miles (12,000 km) – 1995 to 1999 models

Every 12,000 miles (20,000 km) – 2000-on models

1 This motorcycle is equipped with caged ball steering head bearings which can become dented, rough or loose during normal use of the machine. In extreme cases, worn or loose steering head bearings can cause steering wobble – a condition that is potentially dangerous.

Check

2 Support the motorcycle on its centrestand, making sure it is on level ground. Raise the front wheel off the ground either by having an assistant push down on the rear, or by placing a support under the engine.
3 Point the front wheel straight-ahead and slowly move the handlebars from side-to-side. Any dents or roughness in the bearing races will be felt and the bars will not move smoothly and freely.
4 Next, grasp the fork sliders and try to pull and push them forward and backward **(see illustration)**. Any looseness in the steering head bearings will be felt as front-to-rear movement of the forks. If play is felt in the bearings, adjust the steering head as follows.

 *Freeplay in the fork due to worn fork bushes can be misinterpreted as steering head bearing play – do not confuse the two.*

Adjustment

5 Support the motorcycle on its centrestand, making sure it is on level ground. Raise the front wheel off the ground either by having an assistant push down on the rear, or by placing a support under the engine. Remove the fuel tank (see Chapter 3) and the instrument cluster (see Chapter 8). **Note:** *Although it is not strictly necessary to remove the fuel tank,*

doing so will prevent the possibility of damage should a tool slip.
6 Displace the handlebars from the top yoke and lay them on some rag across the frame behind the steering head (see Chapter 5).
7 Slacken the fork clamp bolts in the top yoke **(see illustration)**.
8 Unscrew the steering stem nut, and on 1997-on models remove the washer – the washer sits in a recess in the yoke and needs to be eased out with a small screwdriver or a magnet, or alternatively tip it out of the yoke after it has been lifted off **(see illustration 19.7)**.
9 Gently ease the top yoke up and off the steering stem and fork tubes and position it clear, using a rag to protect the tank or other components **(see illustration)**.
10 Remove the tabbed lockwasher, noting how it fits, then unscrew and remove the locknut, if required using either a C-spanner, a

19.10a Remove the tabbed lockwasher

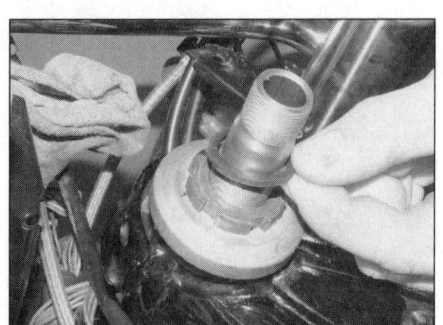

19.10c . . . and the rubber washer

peg spanner or a drift located in one of the notches, though it should only be finger-tight **(see illustrations)**. Remove the rubber washer **(see illustration)**.
11 To adjust the bearings as specified by Yamaha, a special service tool (Pt. No. 90890-01403) and a torque wrench are required. If the tool is available, first slacken the adjuster nut, then tighten it to the initial torque setting specified at the beginning of the Chapter, making sure the torque wrench handle is at right-angles (90°) to the line between the adjuster nut and the wrench socket in the special tool **(see illustration)**. Now slacken the nut so that it is loose, then tighten it to the final torque setting specified. Check that the steering is still able to move freely from side to side, but that all freeplay is eliminated.
12 If the Yamaha tool is not available, using either a C-spanner, a peg spanner or a drift

19.10b . . . the locknut, which should only be finger-tight . . .

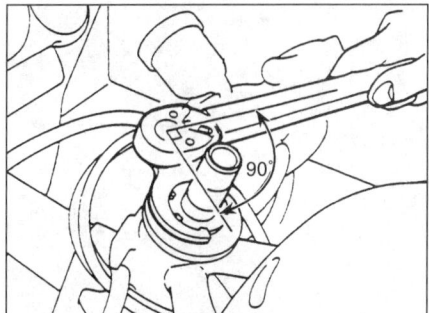

19.11 Make sure the torque wrench arm is at right-angles (90°) to the tool

Routine Maintenance and Servicing

19.12 If the tool is not available, adjust the bearings as described – here a C-spanner is being used

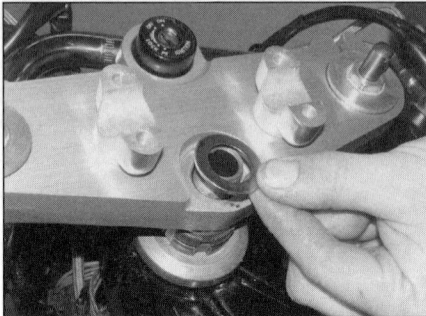

19.14a Install the washer (1997-on models) . . .

19.14b . . . and the steering stem nut . . .

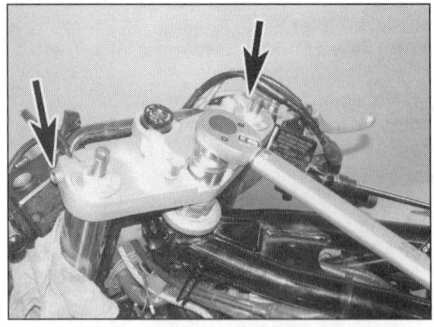

19.14c . . . then tighten the nut to the specified torque setting, followed by the clamp bolts (arrowed)

located in one of the notches, slacken the adjuster nut slightly until pressure is just released, then tighten it until all freeplay is removed, then tighten it a little more **(see illustration)**. This pre-loads the bearings. Now slacken the nut, then tighten it again, setting it so that all freeplay is just removed yet the steering is able to move freely from side to side. To do this tighten the nut only a little at a time, and after each tightening repeat the checks outlined above (Steps 3 and 4) until the bearings are correctly set. The object is to set the adjuster nut so that the bearings are under a very light loading, just enough to remove any freeplay.

Caution: Take great care not to apply excessive pressure because this will cause premature failure of the bearings.

13 With the bearings correctly adjusted, install the rubber washer and the locknut. Tighten the locknut finger-tight, then tighten it further until its notches align with those in the adjuster nut, but make sure it is not so tight that the rubber washer starts to be squeezed out the side. Install the tabbed lockwasher so that the tabs fit into the notches in both the locknut and adjuster nut **(see illustration 19.10a)**.

14 Fit the top yoke onto the steering stem, then install the washer (where fitted) and the steering stem nut and tighten the nut to the torque setting specified at the beginning of the Chapter **(see illustrations)**. Now tighten both the fork clamp bolts to the specified torque setting.

15 Fit the handlebars onto the top yoke (see Chapter 5).

16 Install the fuel tank (see Chapter 3) and the instrument cluster (see Chapter 8).

17 Re-check the bearing adjustment as described above and re-adjust if necessary.

20 Engine oil and filter change

Every 8000 miles (12,000 km) – 1995 to 1999 models

Every 12,000 miles (20,000 km) – 2000-on models

> **Warning: Be careful when draining the oil, as the exhaust pipes, the engine, and the oil itself can cause severe burns.**

1 Drain the engine oil as described in Section 7, Steps 2 to 5.

2 Now place the drain tray below the oil filter, which is on the left-hand side of the engine. If on your model the clutch hose is not clear of the filter cover (i.e. someone has omitted the spacer), displace the clutch release cylinder (see Chapter 2) – there is no need to detach the hose.

3 Unscrew the large bolt in the centre of the cover and remove the cover and filter assembly **(see illustrations)**. Withdraw the filter from the cover, noting the washer and spring, and tip any residual oil into the drain tray **(see illustration)**. If the washer is not in the cover it will be stuck to the end of the filter. Wipe any oil out of the cover and clean it. Discard the cover O-ring as a new one must be used.

4 Check the action of the bypass valve in the filter bolt by levering against it with a screwdriver. If it doesn't move, renew the bolt **(see illustration)**.

20.3a Unscrew the bolt . . .

20.3b . . . and remove the filter assembly

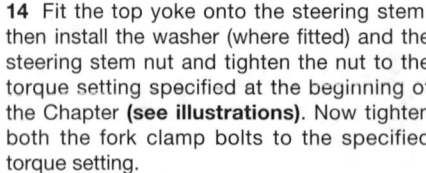

20.3c Remove the filter and tip the oil into the tray

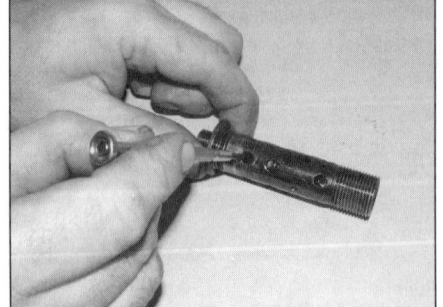

20.4 Check the bypass valve action as described

Routine Maintenance and Servicing 1•21

5 Fit a new O-ring onto the bolt **(see illustration)**. Fit the large bolt into the cover, then fit the spring, washer and new filter over the bolt **(see illustrations)**.

6 Fit a new O-ring smeared with grease onto the cover, then install the cover and filter assembly, aligning the projection on the cover with the indent on the crankcase **(see illustrations)**. Tighten the bolt to the torque setting specified at the beginning of the Chapter **(see illustration)**.

7 If displaced, install the clutch release cylinder (see Chapter 2). Replenish the engine oil to the proper level as described in Section 7, Step 6. See also the notes concerning the disposal of used engine oil in Section 7 – the used oil filter element should also be taken to the disposal site.

21 Swingarm bearings – re-greasing

Every 16,000 miles (24,000 km) – 1995 to 1999 models

Every 30,000 miles (50,000 km) – 2000-on models

1 Over a period of time the grease will harden and dirt will penetrate the bearings.
2 The swingarm is not equipped with grease nipples. Remove the swingarm as described in Chapter 5 for greasing of the bearings.

22 Steering head bearings – re-greasing

Every 16,000 miles (24,000 km) – 1995 to 1999 models

Every 12,000 miles (20,000 km) – 2000-on models

1 Over a period of time the grease will harden or may be washed out of the bearings by incorrect use of jet washes.
2 Disassemble the steering head for re-greasing of the bearings. Refer to Chapter 5 for details.

23 Valve clearances – check and adjustment

Every 16,000 miles (24,000 km) – 1995 to 1999 models

Every 12,000 miles (20,000 km) – 2000-on models

1 The engine must be completely cool for this maintenance procedure, so let the machine sit overnight before beginning.
2 Remove the valve cover (see Chapter 2), and the spark plugs (see Section 2). Each

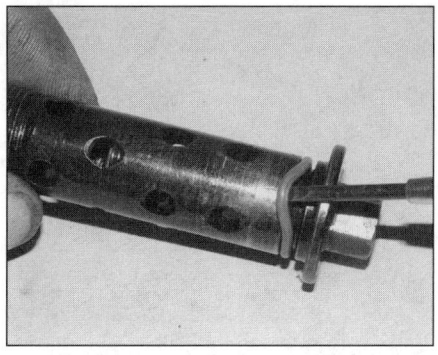

20.5a Fit a new O-ring onto the bolt

20.5b Insert the bolt . . .

20.5c . . . then fit the spring . . .

20.5d . . . the washer . . .

20.5e . . . and the new filter

20.6a Fit the greased O-ring into the groove . . .

20.6b . . . then install the filter assembly . . .

20.6c . . . and tighten the bolt

1•22 Routine Maintenance and Servicing

23.4 Undo the screws (arrowed) and remove the cover and the gasket

23.5a Turn the engine anti-clockwise . . .

cylinder is referred to by a number – 1 to 4 from left to right.

3 Make a chart or sketch of all valve positions so that a note of each clearance can be made against the relevant valve.

4 Undo the screws securing the timing rotor/pick-up coil cover on the left-hand side of the engine and remove the cover **(see illustration)**. Discard the gasket as a new one must be used.

5 Turn the engine using a spanner or socket on the timing rotor bolt, turning it in an anti-clockwise direction only, until the 'T' mark faces back and aligns with the static timing mark which is a horizontal line on the pick-up coil, and the camshaft lobes for the No. 1 (left-hand) cylinder face away from each other **(see illustrations)**. If the cam lobes are facing towards each other, turn the engine anti-clockwise 360° (one full turn) so that the 'T' mark again aligns with the static timing mark. The camshaft lobes will now be facing away from each other, meaning the No. 1 cylinder is at TDC (top dead centre) on the compression stroke.

6 With No. 1 cylinder at TDC on the compression stroke, check the clearances on the No. 1 cylinder intake and exhaust valves. Insert a feeler gauge of the same thickness as the correct valve clearance (see Specifications) between the base of the camshaft lobe and the shim on each valve and check that it is a firm sliding fit – you should feel a slight drag when the you pull the gauge out **(see illustration)**. If not, use the feeler gauges to obtain the exact clearance. Record the measured clearance on the chart.

7 Now turn the engine anti-clockwise 180° (half a turn) so that the 'T' mark faces forward and the camshaft lobes for the No. 2 cylinder are facing away from each other. The No. 2 cylinder is now at TDC on the compression stroke. Measure the clearances of the No. 2 cylinder valves using the method described in Step 6.

8 Now turn the engine anti-clockwise 180° (half a turn) so that the 'T' mark faces back and aligns with the static timing mark and the camshaft lobes for the No. 4 cylinder are facing away from each other. The No. 4 cylinder is now at TDC on the compression stroke. Measure the clearances of the No. 4 cylinder valves using the method described in Step 6.

9 Now turn the engine anti-clockwise 180° (half a turn) so that the 'T' mark faces forward and the camshaft lobes for the No. 3 cylinder are facing away from each other. The No. 3 cylinder is now at TDC on the compression stroke. Measure the clearances of the No. 3 cylinder valves using the method described in Step 6.

10 When all clearances have been measured and charted, identify whether the clearance on any valve falls outside that specified. If it does, the shim in the top of the cam follower must be replaced with one of a thickness which will restore the correct clearance.

11 Shim replacement requires the use of a Yamaha special tool (Pt. No.90890-04110). This is readily available from dealers and should not be expensive. It is also possible to obtain an after-market tool from a good accessory shop or mail-order parts specialist,

23.5b . . . until the T mark aligns with the static mark on the pick-up coil . . .

23.5c . . . and the No. 1 cylinder cam lobes face away from each other

Routine Maintenance and Servicing 1•23

23.6 Insert the feeler gauge between the cam and the follower

23.12 Position the slot (arrowed) as described

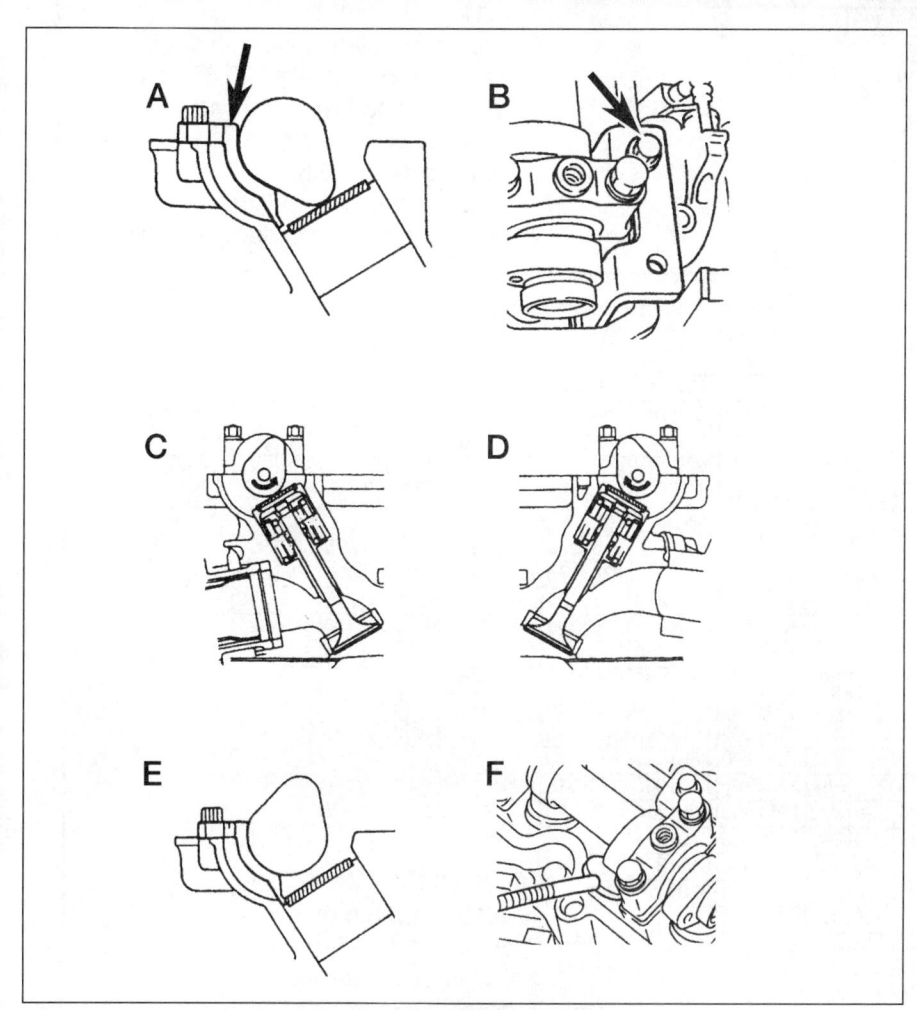

23.13 Shim removal procedure

A – Locate the tool (arrowed) against the follower and not the shim
B – Secure the tool to the cylinder head using a suitable bolt (arrowed)
C – Turn the engine anti-clockwise when doing an exhaust valve
D – Turn the engine clockwise when doing an intake valve
E – The lobe moves off the shim and the follower is held down by the tool
F – Removing the shim

but make sure you get the correct one as many are available.

12 Position the cam follower of the valve in question so that its shim removing slot faces backwards (exhaust valve) or forwards (inlet valve) **(see illustration)**. Turn the engine anticlockwise until the valve is fully open, i.e. the follower is fully depressed by the camshaft lobe.

13 Fit the tool, making sure it contacts only the follower and not the shim, and secure it in place using a suitable bolt **(see illustration)**.

14 Rotate the crankshaft, turning it clockwise if working on an inlet valve and anti-clockwise if working on an exhaust valve so that the cam lobe moves off the follower and away from the tool, leaving the follower held down by the tool.

Caution: Turn the crankshaft so the camshaft lobe moves away from the tool. Do not allow the lobe to contact the tool or serious damage to the camshaft or the cylinder head could result.

15 Prise the shim out of the follower using a small screwdriver inserted in its slot, and remove it using a pair of pliers or a magnet **(see illustration 23.12)**.

16 A size mark should be stamped on one face of the shim **(see illustration)**. A shim size of 250 denotes a thickness of 2.5 mm, 245 is 2.45 mm. If the mark is not visible the shim

23.16 Size marking is stamped on one side of the shim

1•24 Routine Maintenance and Servicing

MEASURED CLEARANCE	INSTALLED PAD NUMBER
	200 205 210 215 220 225 230 235 240 245 250 255 260 265 270 275 280 285 290 295 300 305 310 315 320
0.00 ~ 0.05	200 205 210 215 220 225 230 235 240 245 250 255 260 265 270 275 280 285 290 295 300 305 310
0.06 ~ 0.10	200 205 210 215 220 225 230 235 240 245 250 255 260 265 270 275 280 285 290 295 300 305 310 315
0.11 ~ 0.15	STANDARD CLEARANCE
0.16 ~ 0.20	205 210 215 220 225 230 235 240 245 250 255 260 265 270 275 280 285 290 295 300 305 310 315 320
0.21 ~ 0.25	210 215 220 225 230 235 240 245 250 255 260 265 270 275 280 285 290 295 300 305 310 315 320
0.26 ~ 0.30	215 220 225 230 235 240 245 250 255 260 265 270 275 280 285 290 295 300 305 310 315 320
0.31 ~ 0.35	220 225 230 235 240 245 250 255 260 265 270 275 280 285 290 295 300 305 310 315 320
0.36 ~ 0.40	225 230 235 240 245 250 255 260 265 270 275 280 285 290 295 300 305 310 315 320
0.41 ~ 0.45	230 235 240 245 250 255 260 265 270 275 280 285 290 295 300 305 310 315 320
0.46 ~ 0.50	235 240 245 250 255 260 265 270 275 280 285 290 295 300 305 310 315 320
0.51 ~ 0.55	240 245 250 255 260 265 270 275 280 285 290 295 300 305 310 315 320
0.56 ~ 0.60	245 250 255 260 265 270 275 280 285 290 295 300 305 310 315 320
0.61 ~ 0.65	250 255 260 265 270 275 280 285 290 295 300 305 310 315 320
0.66 ~ 0.70	255 260 265 270 275 280 285 290 295 300 305 310 315 320
0.71 ~ 0.75	260 265 270 275 280 285 290 295 300 305 310 315 320
0.76 ~ 0.80	265 270 275 280 285 290 295 300 305 310 315 320
0.81 ~ 0.85	270 275 280 285 290 295 300 305 310 315 320
0.86 ~ 0.90	275 280 285 290 295 300 305 310 315 320
0.91 ~ 0.95	280 285 290 295 300 305 310 315 320
0.96 ~ 1.00	285 290 295 300 305 310 315 320
1.01 ~ 1.05	290 295 300 305 310 315 320
1.06 ~ 1.10	295 300 305 310 315 320
1.11 ~ 1.15	300 305 310 315 320
1.16 ~ 1.20	305 310 315 320
1.21 ~ 1.25	310 315 320
1.26 ~ 1.30	315 320
1.31 ~ 1.35	320

VALVE CLEARANCE (cold):
 0.11 ~ 0.15 mm
Example: Installed is 250
 Measured clearance is 0.23 mm
Replace 250 pad with 260 pad
 Pad number: (example)
 Pad No. 250 = 2.50 mm
 Pad No. 260 = 2.60 mm
Always install pad with number down.

23.17a Shim selection chart – intake camshaft

MEASURED CLEARANCE	INSTALLED PAD NUMBER
	200 205 210 215 220 225 230 235 240 245 250 255 260 265 270 275 280 285 290 295 300 305 310 315 320
0.00 ~ 0.05	200 205 210 215 220 225 230 255 240 245 250 255 260 265 270 275 280 285 290 295 300 305
0.06 ~ 0.10	200 205 210 215 220 225 230 235 240 245 250 255 260 265 270 275 280 285 290 295 300 305 310
0.11 ~ 0.15	200 205 210 215 220 225 230 235 240 245 250 255 260 265 270 275 280 285 290 295 300 305 310 315
0.16 ~ 0.20	STANDARD CLEARANCE
0.21 ~ 0.25	205 210 215 220 225 230 235 240 245 250 255 260 265 270 275 280 285 290 295 300 305 310 315 320
0.26 ~ 0.30	210 215 220 225 230 235 240 245 250 255 260 265 270 275 280 285 290 295 300 305 310 315 320
0.31 ~ 0.35	215 220 225 230 235 240 245 250 255 260 265 270 275 280 285 290 295 300 305 310 315 320
0.36 ~ 0.40	220 225 230 235 240 245 250 255 260 265 270 275 280 285 290 295 300 305 310 315 320
0.41 ~ 0.45	225 230 235 240 245 250 255 260 265 270 275 280 285 290 295 300 305 310 315 320
0.46 ~ 0.50	230 235 240 245 250 255 260 265 270 275 280 285 290 295 300 305 310 315 320
0.51 ~ 0.55	235 240 245 250 255 260 265 270 275 280 285 290 295 300 305 310 315 320
0.56 ~ 0.60	240 245 250 255 260 265 270 275 280 285 290 295 300 305 310 315 320
0.61 ~ 0.65	245 250 255 260 265 270 275 280 285 290 295 300 305 310 315 320
0.66 ~ 0.70	250 255 260 265 270 275 280 285 290 295 300 305 310 315 320
0.71 ~ 0.75	255 260 265 270 275 280 285 290 295 300 305 310 315 320
0.76 ~ 0.80	260 265 270 275 280 285 290 295 300 305 310 315 320
0.81 ~ 0.85	265 270 275 280 285 290 295 300 305 310 315 320
0.86 ~ 0.90	270 275 280 285 290 295 300 305 310 315 320
0.91 ~ 0.95	275 280 285 290 295 300 305 310 315 320
0.96 ~ 1.00	280 285 290 295 300 305 310 315 320
1.01 ~ 1.05	285 290 295 300 305 310 315 320
1.06 ~ 1.10	290 295 300 305 310 315 320
1.11 ~ 1.15	295 300 305 310 315 320
1.16 ~ 1.20	300 305 310 315 320
1.21 ~ 1.25	305 310 315 320
1.26 ~ 1.30	310 315 320
1.31 ~ 1.35	315 320
1.36 ~ 1.40	320

VALVE CLEARANCE (cold):
 0.16 ~ 0.20 mm
Example: Instaled is 250
 Measured clearance is 0.32 mm
Replace 250 pad with 265 pad
 Pad number: (example)
 Pad No. 250 = 2.50 mm
 Pad No. 265 = 2.65 mm
Always install pad with number down.

23.17b Shim selection chart – exhaust camshaft

Routine Maintenance and Servicing 1•25

23.21a Fit a new gasket...

23.21b ...and install the cover

24.1a Unscrew the bolts (arrowed)...

thickness will have to be measured. It is recommended that the shim is measured anyway to check that it has not worn. Shims are available in 0.05 mm increments from 2.00 to 3.20 mm.

17 Using the appropriate shim selection chart, find where the measured valve clearance and existing shim thickness values intersect and read off the shim size required **(see illustrations)**. **Note:** *If the existing shim is marked with a number not ending in 0 or 5, round it up or down as appropriate to the nearest number ending in 0 or 5 so that the chart can be used.* Shims are available in 0.05 mm increments from 2.00 to 3.20 mm. **Note:** *If the required replacement shim is greater than 3.20 mm (the largest available), the valve is probably not seating correctly due to a build-up of carbon deposits and should be checked and cleaned or resurfaced as required (see Chapter 2).*

18 Obtain the replacement shim, then lubricate it with molybdenum disulphide oil (a 50/50 mixture of molybdenum disulphide grease and engine oil) and fit it into its recess in the top of the follower, with the size mark facing down. Make sure the shim is correctly seated.

19 Rotate the crankshaft in the opposite direction to that described in Step 14 so that the cam lobe moves back onto the follower then remove the shim replacement tool.
20 Rotate the crankshaft several turns to seat the new shim(s), then check the clearances again.
21 Install the timing rotor/pick-up coil cover using a new gasket, and tighten the screws to the torque setting specified at the beginning of the Chapter **(see illustrations)**. Install the valve cover (see Chapter 2), and the spark plugs (see Section 2).

24 Alternator brushes – renewal

Every 62,000 miles (100,000 km) – all models

1 Disconnect the battery negative (-ve) lead. Unscrew the alternator cover bolts and remove the cover **(see illustrations)**.
2 Undo the screws securing the brush holder, noting the lead secured by the bottom screw,

24.1b ...and remove the alternator cover

and remove the holder, noting how it fits **(see illustrations)**. The brushes, holder and rubber cover come as an assembly, so discard the old one.
3 Clean the rotor slip rings with a rag moistened with solvent. If they are badly marked, tidy them up with very fine emery cloth.
4 Fit the new brush holder assembly, making sure the brushes locate correctly against the slip rings, and tighten the screws securely, not forgetting to secure the wiring connector with the bottom screw.

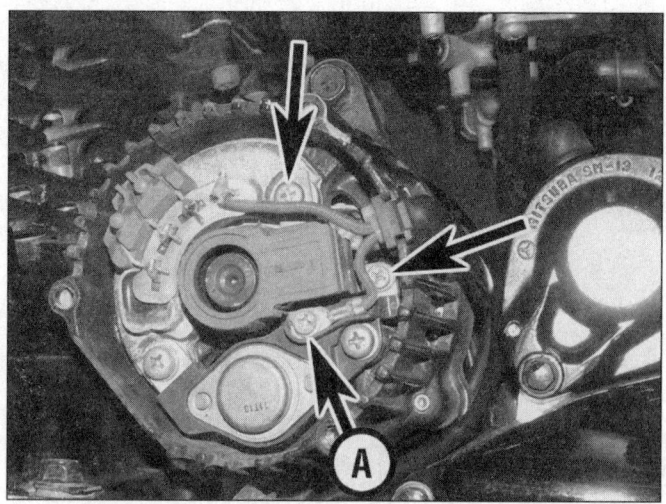

24.2a Undo the screws (arrowed), noting the wiring connector (A)...

24.2b ...and remove the brush holder

1•26 Routine Maintenance and Servicing

5 Install the cover and tighten its screws securely. Reconnect the battery negative lead.

25 Brake and clutch hydraulic seals – renewal

Every two years – all models

1 The seals in the brake calipers and master cylinders, and in the clutch release cylinder and master cylinder, will deteriorate over a period of time and lose their effectiveness, leading to sticky operation or fluid loss, or allowing the ingress of air and dirt. Refer to Chapter 6 for the brake master cylinders and calipers and Chapter 2 for the clutch master and release cylinders.

26 Brakes and clutch fluid – renewal

Every two years – all models

1 The brake and clutch fluid should be renewed every two years or whenever a master cylinder or caliper/release cylinder overhaul is carried out. Refer to Chapter 6 (brake) and the Chapter 2 (clutch) for the fluid renewal procedures.

27 Brake and clutch hoses – renewal

Every four years – all models

1 The hoses will deteriorate with age and should be renewed every four years regardless of their apparent condition.
2 Refer to Chapter 6 (brakes) and Chapter 2 (clutch) and disconnect the hoses from the master cylinders and calipers or release cylinder; take careful note of the hose routing as a guide to installation. Always renew the banjo union sealing washers.

Non-scheduled maintenance

28 Headlight aim – check and adjustment

Note: *An improperly adjusted headlight may cause problems for oncoming traffic or provide poor, unsafe illumination of the road ahead. Before adjusting the headlight aim, be sure to consult with local traffic laws and regulations – for UK models refer to MOT Test Checks in the Reference section.*

1 The headlight beam can adjusted both horizontally and vertically. Before making any adjustment, check that the tyre pressures are correct and the suspension is adjusted as required. Make any adjustments to the headlight aim with the machine on level ground, with the fuel tank half full and with an assistant sitting on the seat. If the bike is usually ridden with a passenger, have a second assistant to do this.
2 Vertical adjustment is made by turning the adjuster screw on the bottom of the headlight unit using a screwdriver **(see illustration)**. Turn it clockwise to raise the beam and anti-clockwise to lower it.
3 Horizontal adjustment is made by turning the adjuster screw on the right-hand side of the headlight **(see illustration)**. Turn it clockwise to move the beam to the right and anti-clockwise to move it to the left.

29 Cylinder compression – check

1 Among other things, poor engine performance may be caused by leaking valves, incorrect valve clearances, a leaking head gasket, or worn pistons, rings and/or cylinder walls. A cylinder compression check will help pinpoint these conditions and can also indicate the presence of excessive carbon deposits in the cylinder head.
2 A compression gauge with a threaded adaptor to fit the spark plug hole threads in the cylinder head will be required. Depending on the outcome of the initial test, a squirt-type oil can may also be needed.
3 Make sure the valve clearances are correctly set (see Section 23) and that the cylinder head nuts are tightened to the correct torque setting (see Chapter 2).
4 Refer to *Fault Finding Equipment* in the Reference section for details of the compression test. Refer to the specifications at the beginning of this Chapter for compression figures.

30 Engine oil pressure – check

1 The XJR models are fitted with an oil level sensor and warning light (see Chapter 8 for further information). If a lubrication problem is suspected, first check the oil level (see *Daily (pre-ride) checks*).
2 If the oil level is correct, an oil pressure check must be carried out. The check provides useful information about the condition of the engine's lubrication system.
3 To check the oil pressure, a suitable gauge and adapter (which screws into the

28.2 Vertical adjuster (arrowed)

28.3 Horizontal adjuster (arrowed)

Routine Maintenance and Servicing 1•27

crankcase) will be needed. Yamaha provide the components (Pt. Nos. 90890-03153 (gauge) and 90890-03124 (adapter)) for this purpose, or a gauge can be obtained commercially, but make sure it comes with the correct adapter, otherwise this will have to be purchased separately from Yamaha. You will also need a container and some rags to catch and mop up any oil that gets lost in between removing the main oil gallery plug and installing the gauge. Check the engine oil level after installing the gauge and replenish if necessary *(see Daily (pre-ride) checks)*.

4 Unscrew the main oil gallery plug, located on the left-hand side of the engine just below the timing rotor/pick-up coil cover, and swiftly screw the gauge assembly in its place **(see illustration)**.

5 Warm the engine up to normal operating temperature).

6 With the engine speed at 1000 rpm the oil pressure should be similar to that given in the Specifications at the start of this Chapter. Stop the engine.

7 Fit a new O-ring onto the main oil gallery plug. Unscrew the gauge assembly and immediately install the plug, tightening it to the torque setting specified at the beginning of the Chapter.

8 Check the oil level (see *Daily (pre-ride) checks*) and replenish if necessary.

9 If a gauge is unobtainable, or if you just want to check that oil is circulating after an engine rebuild, slacken the oil gallery check bolt in the front of the right-hand side of the cylinder head – there is no need to remove it **(see illustration)**. Remove the spark plugs (see Section 2) and fit them back into their caps, then lay the plugs against the cylinder head with their threads contacting it. Check that the kill switch is in the 'RUN' position and the transmission is in neutral, then turn the ignition switch ON and turn the engine over on the starter motor. Oil should begin to seep out of the oil check bolt. Do not operate the

30.4 Main oil gallery plug (arrowed)

starter motor for an excessive period of time. Turn the ignition OFF, refit the spark plugs and tighten the check bolt securely.

10 If the pressure is significantly lower than the standard, either the pressure relief valve is stuck open, the oil pump or its drive mechanism is worn, the oil strainer or filter is blocked, or there is other engine damage. Also make sure the correct grade oil is being used. Begin diagnosis by checking the oil filter, strainer and relief valve, then the oil pump (see Chapter 2). If those items check out okay, chances are the bearing oil clearances are excessive and the engine needs to be overhauled.

11 If the pressure is too high, either an oil passage is clogged, the relief valve is stuck closed or the wrong grade of oil is being used.

31 Fuel hoses – renewal

Warning: Petrol (gasoline) is extremely flammable, so take extra precautions when you work on any part of the fuel system. Don't smoke or allow open flames or bare light bulbs near the work area, and

30.9 Oil gallery check bolt (arrowed)

don't work in a garage where a natural gas-type appliance is present. If you spill any fuel on your skin, rinse it off immediately with soap and water. When you perform any kind of work on the fuel system, wear safety glasses and have a fire extinguisher suitable for a Class B type fire (flammable liquids) on hand.

1 The fuel delivery hoses should be renewed after a few years regardless of their condition.

2 Remove the fuel tank (see Chapter 3). Disconnect the fuel hoses from the carburettors, noting their routing (see Chapter 3 if required). It is advisable to make a sketch to ensure correct installation.

3 Secure the new hoses to the unions using new clamps. Run the engine and check for leaks before taking the machine out on the road.

32 Front forks – oil renewal

1 Fork oil degrades over a period of time and loses its damping qualities. Refer to the fork oil renewal procedure in Chapter 5. The forks do not need to be completely disassembled, though they must be removed.

Notes

Chapter 2
Engine, clutch and transmission

Contents

Alternator – check, removal and installation . . . . .see Chapter 8	Main and connecting rod bearings – general information 27
Alternator drive shaft, starter clutch and idle/reduction gear – check and overhaul 28	Major engine repair – general information 4
	Neutral switch – check, removal and installation . . . . . . .see Chapter 8
Cam chain tensioner – removal, inspection and installation 9	Oil and filter – renewal . . . . .see Chapter 1
Cam chain, tensioner blade and guides – removal, inspection and installation 10	Oil cooler – removal, inspection and installation 7
Camshafts and followers – removal, inspection and installation 11	Oil level – check . . . . .see Daily (pre-ride) checks
Clutch hydraulic release system – bleeding and fluid renewal 21	Oil level sensor and relay – check and renewal . . . . .see Chapter 8
Clutch – check . . . . .see Chapter 1	Oil pressure – check . . . . .see Chapter 1
Clutch master cylinder – removal, overhaul and installation 19	Oil pump – check, removal, inspection and installation 23
Clutch release cylinder – removal, overhaul and installation 20	Oil sump, oil strainer and pressure relief valves – removal, inspection and installation 24
Clutch – removal, inspection and installation 18	Operations possible with the engine in the frame 2
Connecting rods – removal, inspection and installation 30	Operations requiring engine removal 3
Crankcase halves – inspection and servicing 26	Pick-up coil assembly – removal and installation . . . . . .see Chapter 4
Crankcase halves – separation and reassembly 25	Piston rings – inspection and installation 17
Crankshaft and main bearings – removal, inspection and installation 29	Pistons – removal, inspection and installation 16
Cylinder block – removal, inspection and installation 15	Recommended running-in procedure 35
Cylinder head and valves – disassembly, inspection and reassembly 14	Selector drum and forks – removal, inspection and installation 33
	Spark plugs – check and adjustment . . . . .see Chapter 1
Cylinder head – removal and installation 12	Starter clutch and idle/reduction gear – removal, inspection and installation 28
Engine disassembly and reassembly – general information 6	Starter motor – removal and installation . . . . .see Chapter 8
Engine – compression check . . . . .see Chapter 1	Transmission shafts – disassembly, inspection and reassembly . . . 32
Engine – removal and installation 5	Transmission shafts – removal and installation 31
Gearchange mechanism – removal, inspection and installation 22	Valve clearances – check and adjustment . . . . .see Chapter 1
General information 1	Valve cover – removal and installation 8
Idle speed – check and adjustment . . . . .see Chapter 1	Valves/valve seats/valve guides – servicing 13
Initial start-up after overhaul 34	

Degrees of difficulty

| Easy, suitable for novice with little experience | Fairly easy, suitable for beginner with some experience | Fairly difficult, suitable for competent DIY mechanic | Difficult, suitable for experienced DIY mechanic | Very difficult, suitable for expert DIY or professional |

Specifications

General
Type	Four-stroke in-line four, air cooled
Capacity	
XJR1200	1188 cc
XJR1300	1250 cc
Bore	
XJR1200	77.0 mm
XJR1300	79.0 mm
Stroke	63.8 mm
Compression ratio	9.7 to 1
Cylinder numbering	1 to 4 from left to right
Clutch	Wet multi-plate
Transmission	Five-speed constant mesh
Final drive	Chain

Camshafts
Intake lobe height	
Standard	35.95 to 36.05 mm
Service limit (min)	35.85 mm
Exhaust lobe height	
Standard	35.95 to 36.05 mm
Service limit (min)	35.85 mm
Journal diameter	24.967 to 24.980 mm
Holder diameter	25.000 to 25.021 mm
Journal oil clearance	0.020 to 0.054 mm
Runout (max)	0.03 mm

Cylinder head
Warpage (max)	
XJR1200	0.03 mm
XJR1300	0.1 mm

Cylinder bores
Bore diameter	
XJR1200	
Standard	76.96 to 77.02 mm
Service limit (max)	77.1 mm
XJR1300	
Standard	79.00 to 79.01 mm
Service limit (max)	79.1 mm
Ovality (out-of-round) (max)	0.05 mm
Taper (max)	0.05 mm
Cylinder compression	see Chapter 1

Pistons
Piston diameter	
XJR1200	
Measuring point	2 mm up from skirt, at 90° to piston pin axis
Standard	76.920 to 76.980 mm
Oversize	+ 0.50 mm
XJR1300	
Measuring point	
1999 to 2001 models	3 mm up from skirt, at 90° to piston pin axis
2002-on models	5 mm up from skirt, at 90° to piston pin axis
Standard	78.970 to 78.985 mm
Oversize	none
Piston-to-bore clearance	
XJR1200	
Standard	0.03 to 0.05 mm
Service limit (max)	0.1 mm
XJR1300	
Standard	0.015 to 0.040 mm
Service limit (max)	0.15 mm
Piston pin diameter	17.991 to 18.000 mm
Piston pin bore diameter in piston	18.004 to 18.015 mm
Piston pin-to-pin bore clearance	0.004 to 0.024 mm

Engine, clutch and transmission 2•3

Piston rings
Top ring
  Type .... Barrel
  Ring width .... 3.05 mm
  Ring thickness .... 1.0 mm

	Standard	Maximum
Ring end gap (installed)	0.20 to 0.35 mm	0.60 mm
Piston ring-to-groove clearance	0.04 to 0.08 mm	0.1 mm

2nd ring
  Type .... Taper
  Ring width .... 3.0 mm
  Ring thickness .... 1.2 mm
  Ring end gap (installed)

	Standard	Maximum
XJR1200	0.20 to 0.35 mm	0.60 mm
XJR1300	0.35 to 0.50 mm	0.75 mm
Piston ring-to-groove clearance	0.03 to 0.07 mm	0.1 mm

Oil ring
  XJR1200
    Ring width .... 2.8 mm
    Ring thickness .... 2.5 mm
    Side-rail end gap (installed) .... 0.2 to 0.8 mm
    Piston ring-to-groove clearance .... 0.0 to 0.025 mm
  XJR1300
    Ring width .... 2.9 mm
    Ring thickness .... 2.5 mm
    Side-rail end gap (installed) .... 0.2 to 0.5 mm
    Piston ring-to-groove clearance .... 0.050 to 0.155 mm

Valves, guides and springs
Valve clearances .... see Chapter 1
Intake valve
  Stem diameter
    Standard .... 5.475 to 5.490 mm
    Service limit (min) .... 5.445 mm
  Guide bore diameter
    Standard .... 5.500 to 5.512 mm
    Service limit (max) .... 5.55 mm
  Stem-to-guide clearance
    Standard .... 0.010 to 0.037 mm
    Service limit (max) .... 0.08 mm
  Head diameter .... 28.9 to 29.1 mm
  Face width .... 1.98 to 2.55 mm
  Seat width .... 0.9 to 1.1 mm
  Margin thickness .... 0.8 to 1.2 mm
  Stem runout (max) .... 0.01 mm
Exhaust valve
  Stem diameter
    Standard .... 5.460 to 5.475 mm
    Service limit (min) .... 5.430 mm
  Guide bore diameter
    Standard .... 5.500 to 5.512 mm
    Service limit (max) .... 5.552 mm
  Stem-to-guide clearance
    Standard .... 0.025 to 0.052 mm
    Service limit (max) .... 0.1 mm
  Head diameter .... 24.9 to 25.1 mm
  Face width .... 1.98 to 2.55 mm
  Seat width .... 0.9 to 1.1 mm
  Margin thickness .... 0.8 to 1.2 mm
  Stem runout (max) .... 0.01 mm
Valve springs
  Free length – inner spring
    Standard .... 39.65 mm
    Minimum .... 37.5 mm
  Free length – outer spring
    Standard .... 41.1 mm
    Minimum .... 39.0 mm
  Spring bend (max)
    Intake .... 1.7 mm
    Exhaust .... 1.7 mm

Clutch
Friction plates
- Quantity 8
- Thickness
  - Standard ..... 2.9 to 3.1 mm
  - Service limit (min) ..... 2.8 mm

Plain plates
- Quantity 7
- Thickness ..... 1.9 to 2.1 mm
- Warpage (max) ..... 0.1 mm

Pushrod bend limit ..... 0.3 mm
Diaphragm spring free height (minimum) ..... 6.0 mm
Diaphragm spring warp limit ..... 0.1 mm

Lubrication system
Oil pressure ..... see Chapter 1
Relief valve opening pressure ..... 70 to 84 psi (4.80 to 5.8 Bar)
By-pass valve setting pressure ..... 26 to 32 psi (1.80 to 2.2 Bar)
Oil pump
- Inner rotor tip-to-outer rotor clearance
  - Standard ..... 0.12 to 0.17 mm
  - Service limit (max) ..... 0.2 mm
- Outer rotor-to-body clearance
  - Standard ..... 0.03 to 0.08 mm
  - Service limit (max) ..... 0.15 mm
- Rotor end-float
  - Standard ..... 0.03 to 0.08 mm
  - Service limit (max) ..... 0.15 mm

Crankshaft and bearings
Main bearing oil clearance
- Standard ..... 0.030 to 0.064 mm
- Service limit (max) ..... 0.09 mm

Runout (max)
- XJR1200 ..... 0.03 mm
- XJR1300 ..... 0.02 mm

Connecting rods
Big-end side clearance
- Standard ..... 0.160 to 0.262 mm
- Service limit (max) ..... 0.5 mm

Big-end oil clearance
- Standard ..... 0.017 to 0.040 mm
- Service limit (max) ..... 0.08 mm

Transmission
Gear ratios (no. of teeth)
- Primary reduction ..... 1.750 to 1 (98/56T)
- Final reduction
  - 1995 to 2001 models ..... 2.235 to 1 (38/17T)
  - 2002-on models ..... 2.167 to 1 (39/18T)
- 1st gear ..... 2.857 to 1 (40/14T)
- 2nd gear ..... 2.000 to 1 (36/18T)
- 3rd gear ..... 1.571 to 1 (33/21T)
- 4th gear ..... 1.292 to 1 (31/24T)
- 5th gear ..... 1.115 to 1 (29/26T)

Shaft runout (max)
- XJR1200 ..... 0.08 mm
- XJR1300 ..... 0.06 mm

Selector drum and forks
Selector fork shaft runout (max) ..... 0.1 mm

Torque wrench settings
Alternator drive shaft bearing retainer/seal housing screws ..... 10 Nm
Cam chain tensioner blade bolt ..... 10 Nm
Cam chain tensioner cap bolt ..... 20 Nm
Cam chain tensioner mounting bolts ..... 10 Nm

Engine, clutch and transmission 2•5

Torque wrench settings (continued)

Camshaft holder bolts	12 Nm
Camshaft sprocket bolts	20 Nm
Clutch cover bolts	10 Nm
Clutch diaphragm spring bolts	8 Nm
Clutch hose banjo bolts	30 Nm
Clutch master cylinder clamp bolts	10 Nm
Clutch nut	70 Nm
Clutch release cylinder bleed valve	6 Nm
Clutch release cylinder bolts	10 Nm
Connecting rod cap nuts	
Initial setting (see Text)	20 Nm
Final setting	36 Nm
Crankcase 6 mm bolts	12 Nm
Crankcase 8 mm bolts	24 Nm
Crankcase 10 mm bolts	35 Nm
Cylinder block nut	20 Nm
Cylinder head nuts	
Domed nuts	35 Nm
Plain nuts	10 Nm
Engine mounting bolts	
Upper rear mounting brackets, lower frame bolts	88 Nm
Upper rear mounting brackets, upper frame bolts	48 Nm
Upper rear engine bolt nut	55 Nm
Front mounting brackets, frame bolts	30 Nm
Front engine bolt nut	64 Nm
Torque link bracket nuts	64 Nm
Exhaust collector box bracket bolts	20 Nm
Frame cradle bolts	26 Nm
Footrest bracket bolts	28 Nm
Gearchange shaft centralising spring locating pin	22 Nm
Idle/reduction gear shaft retainer bolt	7 Nm
Oil cooler hose bolts	10 Nm
Oil cooler mounting bolts	10 Nm
Oil pump assembly screws	10 Nm
Oil pump mounting bolts	10 Nm
Oil strainer bolts	10 Nm
Oil sump bolts	10 Nm
Pick-up coil baseplate screws	4 Nm
Pick-up coil cover screws	7 Nm
Sprocket cover bolts	10 Nm
Starter clutch bolts (1995 and 1996 models)	25 Nm
Stopper arm bolt	10 Nm
Timing rotor bolt	45 Nm
Timing rotor/pick-up coil cover bolts	7 Nm
Transmission input shaft bearing retainer plate screws	10 Nm
Valve cover bolts	10 Nm

1 General information

The engine/transmission unit is an air-cooled in-line four cylinder with four valves per cylinder. The valves are operated by double overhead camshafts which are chain driven off the crankshaft. The engine/transmission assembly is constructed from aluminium alloy. The crankcase is divided horizontally.

The crankcase incorporates a wet sump, pressure-fed lubrication system which uses a gear-driven, dual-rotor oil pump (one set of rotors for the engine and the other for the oil cooler), an oil filter, relief valves and an oil level switch

A Hy-Vo chain running off the crankshaft drives a shaft which has the alternator on its left-hand end and the starter clutch on its right-hand end.

Power from the crankshaft is routed to the transmission via the clutch. The clutch is of the wet, multi-plate type and is gear-driven off the crankshaft. The transmission is a five-speed constant-mesh unit. Final drive to the rear wheel is by chain and sprockets.

2 Operations possible with the engine in the frame

The components and assemblies listed below can be removed without having to remove the engine/transmission assembly from the frame. If however, a number of areas require attention at the same time, removal of the engine is recommended.

    Valve cover
    Camshafts
    Cam chain
    Cylinder head*
    Cylinder block, pistons and piston rings
    Clutch and starter clutch
    Gearchange mechanism (external
      components)
    Alternator
    Starter motor
    Pick-up coil assembly
    Oil filter and cooler
    Oil sump, oil strainer and oil pressure relief
      valves
    Oil pump
*see Note at beginning of Section 12.

2•6 Engine, clutch and transmission

3 Operations requiring engine removal

It is necessary to remove the engine/transmission assembly from the frame to gain access to the following components.
Crankshaft and bearings
Connecting rods and bearings
Transmission shafts
Selector drum and forks
Alternator drive shaft, starter clutch and idle/reduction gear

4 Major engine repair – general information

1 It is not always easy to determine when or if an engine should be completely overhauled, as a number of factors must be considered.
2 High mileage is not necessarily an indication that an overhaul is needed, while low mileage, on the other hand, does not preclude the need for an overhaul. Frequency of servicing is probably the single most important consideration. An engine that has regular and frequent oil and filter changes, as well as other required maintenance, will most likely give many miles of reliable service. Conversely, a neglected engine, or one which has not been run in properly, may require an overhaul very early in its life.

3 Exhaust smoke and excessive oil consumption are both indications that piston rings and/or valve guides are in need of attention, although make sure that the fault is not due to oil leakage.
4 If the engine is making obvious knocking or rumbling noises, the connecting rods and/or main bearings are probably at fault.
5 Loss of power, rough running, excessive valve train noise and high fuel consumption may also point to the need for an overhaul, especially if they are all present at the same time. If a complete tune-up does not remedy the situation, major mechanical work is the only solution.
6 An engine overhaul generally involves restoring the internal parts to the specifications of a new engine. The piston rings and main and connecting rod bearings are usually renewed and the cylinder walls honed or, if necessary, re-bored (oversize pistons are available for 1200 models only), during a major overhaul. Generally the valve seats are re-ground, since they are usually in less than perfect condition at this point. The end result should be a like new engine that will give as many trouble-free miles as the original.
7 Before beginning the engine overhaul, read through the related procedures to familiarise yourself with the scope and requirements of the job. Overhauling an engine is not all that difficult, but it is time consuming. Plan on the motorcycle being tied up for a minimum of two weeks. Check on the availability of parts and make sure that any necessary special tools, equipment and supplies are obtained in advance.
8 Most work can be done with typical workshop hand tools, although a number of precision measuring tools are required for inspecting parts to determine if they must be renewed. Often a dealer will handle the inspection of parts and offer advice concerning reconditioning and renewal. As a general rule, time is the primary cost of an overhaul so it does not pay to install worn or substandard parts.
9 As a final note, to ensure maximum life and minimum trouble from a rebuilt engine, everything must be assembled with care in a spotlessly clean environment.

5 Engine – removal and installation

Caution: The engine is very heavy. Engine removal and installation should be carried out with the aid of at least one assistant. Personal injury or damage could occur if the engine falls or is dropped. An hydraulic or mechanical floor jack should be used to support and lower or raise the engine if possible.

Removal

1 Support the motorcycle on its centrestand. Work can be made easier by raising the machine to a suitable working height on an hydraulic ramp or a suitable platform. Make sure the motorcycle is secure and will not topple over (see Section 1 of *Tools and Workshop Tips* in the Reference section). When disconnecting any wiring, cables and hoses, it is advisable to mark or tag them as a reminder to where they connect, and to make a note of their routing.
2 If the engine is dirty, particularly around its mountings, wash it thoroughly before starting any major dismantling work. This will make work much easier and rule out the possibility of caked-on lumps of dirt falling into some vital component.
3 Remove the seat and side panels (see Chapter 7).
4 Remove the fuel tank and the exhaust system (see Chapter 3).
5 Drain the engine oil (see Chapter 1). Remove the oil cooler with its feed and return pipes (see Section 7). Unscrew the nuts securing the cooler hose bracket and remove the bracket **(see illustration)**.
6 Undo each air duct screw and remove the ducts, noting how the pegs locate in the grommets **(see illustrations)**. Note that each duct is marked with an L or R to denote its side.
7 Disconnect the negative (–ve) lead from the battery, then disconnect the positive (+ve) lead (see Chapter 8). Unscrew the bolt securing the negative cable to the back of the

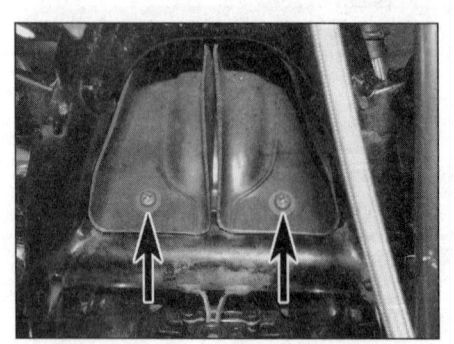

5.5 Unscrew the lower nuts (arrowed) and remove the bracket

5.6a Undo the screws (arrowed) . . .

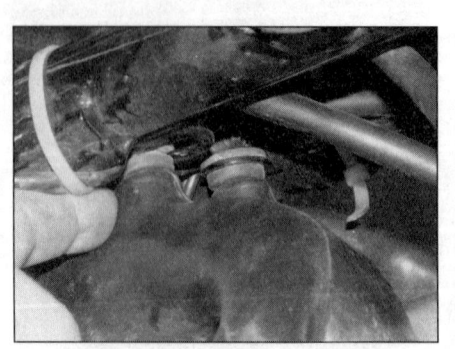

5.6b . . . release the pegs from the grommets . . .

5.6c . . . and remove the air ducts

Engine, clutch and transmission 2•7

5.7 Pull back the rubber boot, then unscrew the bolt (arrowed) and detach the lead

5.11a Detach the crankcase breather hose . . .

5.11b . . . and draw the hoses (arrowed) out of their guide

engine and detach the cable **(see illustration)**. Replace the bolt afterwards.
8 Remove the carburettors (see Chapter 3). Plug the intake manifolds with clean rag.
9 Displace the clutch release cylinder (see Section 20). There is no need to disconnect the hydraulic hose from the cylinder, but release it from its guides on the left-hand frame downtube then remove the guides from the frame as it is easy for them to be knocked and damaged when manoeuvring the engine out. After the left-hand front mounting bracket has been removed slip the hose out from between the engine and frame and secure the release cylinder clear. **Note:** *Don't operate the clutch lever while the release cylinder is removed or the piston will be forced out.*

> **HAYNES HINT** *Wrap some cable ties around the piston and through the mounting bolt holes to prevent the piston creeping out, or from being displaced should the lever be accidentally pulled in*

10 Remove the front sprocket (see Chapter 5).
11 Disconnect the breather hose from the crankcase **(see illustration)**. Draw the air filter housing drain hose and the fuel tank drain and breather hoses out of the guide on the back of the engine **(see illustration)**.
12 Unscrew the bolts securing the exhaust collector box bracket and remove it, noting how it fits **(see illustration)**.

13 Trace the wiring from the alternator and disconnect it at the connector **(see illustration)**. Release the wiring from any clips or ties as necessary, noting its routing, and coil it so that it does not impede engine removal.
14 Trace the wiring from the ignition pick-up coil on the left-hand side of the engine and disconnect it at the connector **(see illustration)**. Release the wiring from any clips or ties as necessary, noting its routing, and coil it so that it does not impede engine removal.
15 Trace the wiring from the neutral switch and oil level sensor and disconnect it at the connector. Release the wiring from any clips or ties as necessary (there is no need to release the wiring from the engine mounted clamps), noting its routing, and coil it so that it does not impede engine removal.

16 Trace the wiring from the sidestand switch and disconnect it at the connector. Release the wiring from any clips or ties, noting its routing, and feed it down to the switch.
17 Pull the spark plug caps off the spark plugs and secure them clear of the engine **(see illustration)**.
18 Pull back the rubber cover on the starter motor terminal, then unscrew the nut and detach the lead **(see illustration)**. Secure it clear of the engine.
19 At this point, position an hydraulic or mechanical jack under the engine with a block of wood between the jack head and crankcase. Make sure the jack is centrally positioned so the engine will not topple in any direction when the last mounting bolt is removed. Take the weight of the engine on the jack. It is also advisable to place a block of wood between

5.12 Unscrew the bolts (arrowed) and remove the bracket

5.13 Disconnect the alternator wiring connector

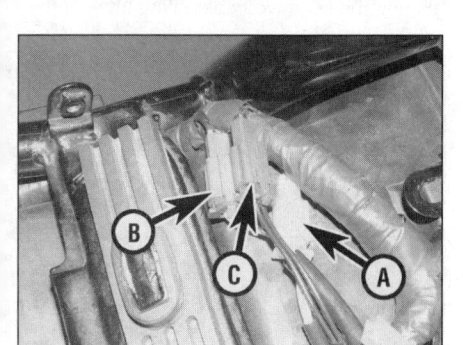

5.14 Disconnect the pick-up coil (A), neutral/oil level sensor (B) and sidestand switch (C) wiring connectors

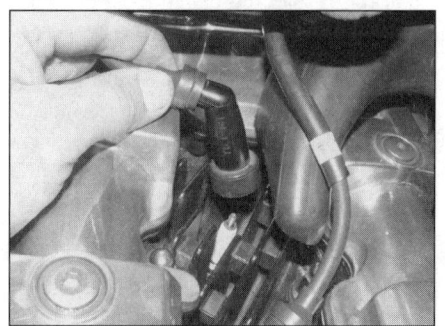

5.17 Pull the caps off the spark plugs

5.18 Unscrew the nut and detach the lead from the starter motor

2•8 Engine, clutch and transmission

5.20a Unhook the brake light switch spring (arrowed) . . .

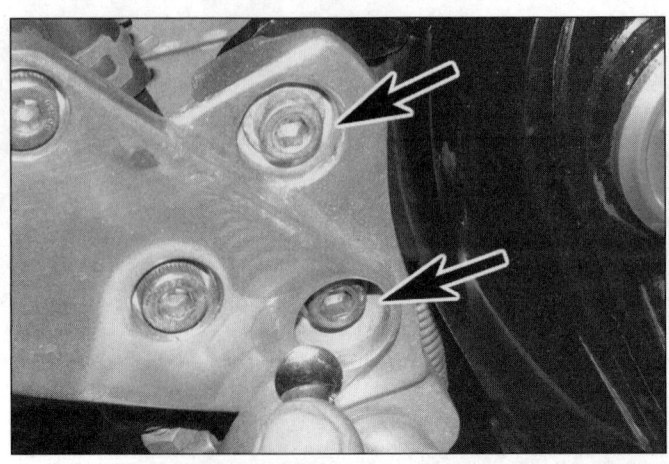

5.20b . . . then remove the blanking caps and unscrew the bolts (arrowed)

5.21a Unscrew the bolts securing each front bracket to the frame (arrows) - note the engine protection bars shown are not fitted as standard

5.21b Slip the hydraulic hose out from between the engine and frame

the rear wheel and the ground, or under the swingarm, in case the bike tilts back onto the rear wheel when the engine is removed. Check around the engine and frame to make sure that all wiring, cables and hoses that need to be disconnected have been disconnected, and that any remaining connected to the engine are not retained by any clips, guides or brackets connected to the frame. Check that any protruding mounting brackets will not get in the way and remove them if necessary.

20 Unhook the rear brake light switch spring from the brake pedal **(see illustration)**. Remove the blanking caps from the rider's right-hand footrest bracket bolts, then unscrew the bolts and displace the bracket **(see illustration)**. Tie it to the frame making sure no strain is placed on the brake hose.
21 Unscrew the bolts securing the engine front mounting bolt brackets to the frame and remove them, noting how they fit **(see illustration)**. Slip the clutch hose out from between the engine and frame. Unscrew the nut on the right-hand end of the bolt and remove the bracket, then withdraw the bolt with the left-hand bracket and remove the sleeve **(see illustrations)**. Note that it's common for the bolt to become corroded in the sleeve, in which case the bolt will bring the sleeve and left-hand mounting rubber with it.
22 Unscrew the bolts securing the right-hand frame cradle and remove it **(see illustration)**.
23 Unscrew the nuts and withdraw the bolts

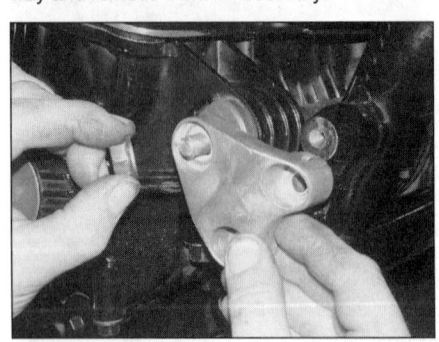

5.21c Unscrew the nut and remove the bracket . . .

5.21d . . . then withdraw the front mounting bolt and remove the sleeve

5.22 Unscrew the four bolts and remove the frame cradle section

Engine, clutch and transmission 2•9

5.23a Unscrew the torque link bracket bolt nuts . . .

5.23b . . . then withdraw the bolts . . .

5.23c . . . and remove the bracket

securing the torque link bracket to the engine and frame and remove it, noting how it fits **(see illustrations)**. Remove the sleeve from the bearing in the engine for safekeeping **(see illustration)**.
24 Make sure the engine is properly supported on the jack, and have an assistant support it as well. Unscrew the nut on the upper rear mounting bolt and withdraw the bolt **(see illustrations)**.
25 Unscrew the bolts securing the right-hand upper rear mounting bracket to the frame and remove it, noting how it fits **(see illustration)**. Note the spacer in the upper frame bolt bore

(see illustration). Also note the R marking which denotes this as the right-hand bracket.
26 Wrap some rags around the vulnerable parts of the frame to prevent damage if the engine contacts it **(see illustration)**. Carefully manoeuvre the engine out from the right-hand side, noting that it is very heavy. Note the damping rubbers in the front mounts and remove them for safekeeping if loose **(see illustration)**.
27 If required unscrew the bolts securing the left-hand upper rear mounting bracket to the frame and remove it, noting how it fits **(see**

5.23d Withdraw the sleeve from the bearing in the engine

5.24a Unscrew the nut (arrowed) . . .

5.24b . . . and withdraw the upper rear bolt

5.25a Unscrew the bolts and remove the bracket, noting how it fits

5.25b Note the spacer and bearing in the upper frame bolt bore

5.26a Protect vulnerable parts of the frame with rag, then carefully remove the engine from the right-hand side

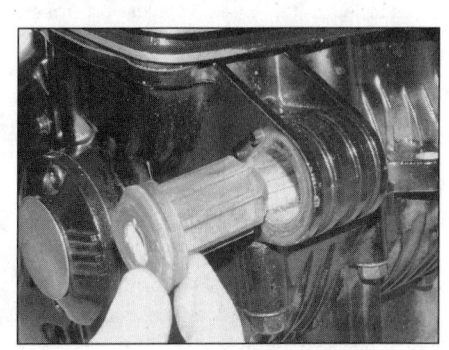

5.26b Remove the damping rubbers if loose

2•10 Engine, clutch and transmission

5.27a If required, unscrew the bolts . . .

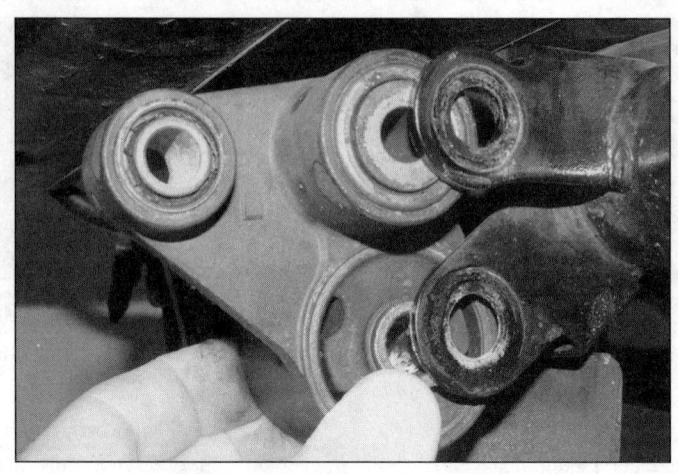

5.27b . . . and remove the bracket

illustrations). Note the spacer in the upper frame bolt bore **(see illustration 5.25b)**. Also note the L marking which denotes this as the left-hand bracket.

Installation

28 Installation is the reverse of removal, noting the following points:
- Check the condition of the front mounting rubber dampers and renew them if damaged, deformed or deteriorated **(see illustration 5.26b)**.
- Check the condition of the bearings and bushes for the upper rear mounting brackets and renew the brackets if necessary **(see illustration 5.25b)** – the bushes and bearing are not listed as being separately available. On the model shown water had penetrated the bearings which had consequently become rusted and gritty, though they did clean up with rust remover and solvent. Grease the bearings before installing the brackets. Note that the left-hand bracket (marked with an L) must be fitted before the engine is installed, but leave the frame bolts loose until all other mountings are installed. Similarly check the bearing in the engine mount for the torque link bracket – this bearing is available separately, but the bush in the bracket for the frame mount is not.
- Make sure no wires, cables or hoses become trapped between the engine and the frame when installing the engine.
- Feed the clutch hose between the engine and frame before installing the left-hand front mounting bracket **(see illustration 5.21b)**.
- Many of the engine mounting bolts are of different size and length. Make sure the correct bolt is installed in its correct location, with its washer if fitted. Install the bolts and nuts finger-tight only until they are all located, then tighten them in the order below to the torque settings specified at the beginning of the Chapter. Do not forget to fit the sleeve for the front mounting bolt, and smear the bolt with grease to deter corrosion **(see illustration 5.21d)**.

- First tighten the lower frame bolt on each upper rear mounting bracket, then tighten the upper frame bolts, and finally the nut on the upper rear bolt. Now tighten the front mounting bracket frame bolts, followed by the nut on the front engine bolt. Finally tighten the nuts on the torque link bracket. Also tighten the frame cradle bolts, the footrest bracket bolts and the exhaust collector box bracket bolts to the specified torque settings. Note that if engine protection bars are fitted (as on the model shown) you will have to tighten the frame cradle bolts before locating the right-hand front mounting bracket bolts as the bars will get in the way.
- Make sure all wires, cables and hoses are correctly routed and connected, and secured by any clips or ties.
- Refill the engine with the specified quantity oil and check the level (see Chapter 1).
- Adjust the throttle cable freeplay and engine idle speed (see Chapter 1).
- Adjust the drive chain slack (see Chapter 1).
- Start the engine and check that there are no oil leaks.

6 Engine disassembly and reassembly – general information

Disassembly

1 Before disassembling the engine, thoroughly clean and degrease its external surfaces. This will prevent contamination of the engine internals, and will also make working a lot easier and cleaner. A high flash-point solvent, such as paraffin (kerosene) can be used, or better still, a proprietary engine degreaser such as Gunk. Use old paintbrushes and toothbrushes to work the solvent into the various recesses of the casings. Take care to exclude solvent or water from the electrical components and intake and exhaust ports.

⚠ *Warning: The use of petrol (gasoline) as a cleaning agent should be avoided because of the risk of fire.*

2 When clean and dry, position the engine on the workbench, leaving suitable clear area for working. Gather a selection of small containers, plastic bags and some labels so that parts can be grouped together in an easily identifiable manner. Also get some paper and a pen so that notes can be taken. You will also need a supply of clean rag, which should be as absorbent as possible.

3 Before commencing work, read through the appropriate section so that some idea of the necessary procedure can be gained. When removing components note that great force is seldom required, unless specified (checking the specified torque setting of the particular bolt being removed will indicate how tight it is, and therefore how much force should be needed). In many cases, a component's reluctance to be removed is indicative of an incorrect approach or removal method, or the use of inappropriate tools – if in any doubt, re-check with the text.

4 An engine support stand can be made from short lengths of 2 x 4 inch wood bolted together into a rectangle to help support the engine if required **(see illustration)**. The perimeter of the mount should be just big

6.4 An engine support made from pieces of 2 x 4 inch wood

Engine, clutch and transmission 2•11

enough to accommodate the sump within it so that the engine rests on its crankcase. Alternatively use individual blocks of wood wedged between the engine and the work surface.

5 When disassembling the engine, keep 'mated' parts together (including, pistons, connecting rods, valves, gears etc. that have been in contact with each other during engine operation).

6 A complete engine/transmission disassembly should be done in the following general order with reference to the appropriate Sections.
   Remove the valve cover
   Remove the camshafts
   Remove the cylinder head
   Remove the cylinder block and pistons
   Remove the clutch
   Remove the pick-up coil assembly (see Chapter 4)
   Remove the alternator (see Chapter 8)
   Remove the starter motor (see Chapter 8)
   Remove the gearchange mechanism external components
   Remove the oil sump
   Remove the oil pump
   Separate the crankcase halves
   Remove the crankshaft
   Remove the connecting rods
   Remove the transmission shafts
   Remove the selector drum and forks
   Remove the alternator driveshaft, starter clutch and idle reduction gear

Reassembly

7 Reassembly is accomplished by reversing the general disassembly sequence.

7 Oil cooler – removal, inspection and installation

Note: *The oil cooler can be removed with the engine in the frame. If the engine has been removed, ignore the steps which do not apply.*

Removal

1 The cooler is located on the front of the engine. Drain the engine oil (see Chapter 1). For best and easiest access to the hose union bolts on the sump remove the exhaust system (see Chapter 3), but this is only really necessary if you do not have the appropriate tools to access the bolts.

2 To remove the cooler without its feed and return pipes, unscrew the bolts securing the hose unions to the cooler and detach the hoses **(see illustration)**. Unscrew the cooler mounting bolts and lift it out of its bottom mounting grommet, noting how the lug locates **(see illustrations)**. Discard the hose union O-rings as new ones must be used.

3 To remove the cooler with its feed and return pipes, unscrew the bolt securing the pipe holder bracket **(see illustration)**. Unscrew the bolts securing each pipe union to the sump and detach the pipes **(see illustration)**. Unscrew the cooler mounting bolts and lift it out of its bottom mounting grommet, noting how the lug locates. Discard the pipe union O-rings as new ones must be used **(see illustration)**.

4 To remove the pipes but leave the cooler in place, unscrew the bolt securing the pipe holder bracket **(see illustration 7.3a)**. Unscrew the bolts securing each pipe union to the sump and detach them **(see illustration 7.3b)**. Unscrew the bolts securing the pipe unions to the cooler and detach them **(see illustration 7.2a)**. Discard the hose and pipe union O-rings as new ones must be used **(see illustration 7.3c)**.

Inspection

5 Check the cooler fins for mud, dirt and insects, which may impede the flow of air through the radiator. If the fins are dirty, clean the cooler using water or low pressure compressed air directed through the fins from the rear of the radiator. If the fins are bent or

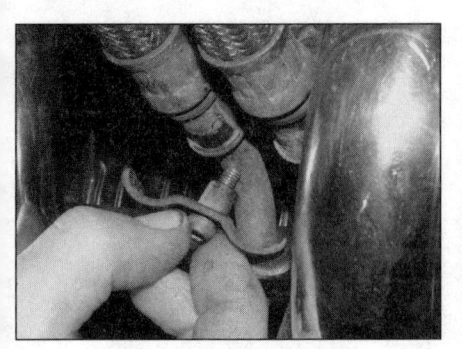

7.2a Unscrew the bolts (arrowed) on each side and detach the hoses from the cooler

7.2b Unscrew the cooler mounting bolts . . .

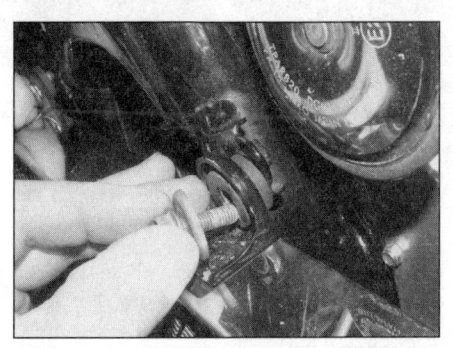

7.2c . . . noting the washers, collars and grommets . . .

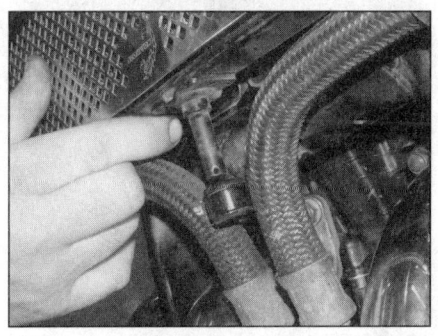

7.2d . . . and lift the cooler lug out of its grommet

7.3a Unscrew the bolt and remove the pipe holder

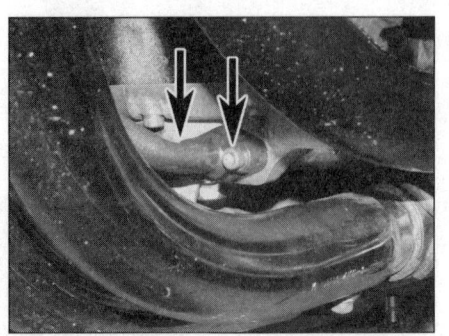

7.3b Unscrew the bolts (arrowed) on each side and detach the pipes from the sump

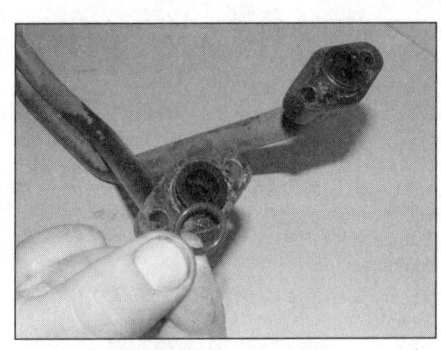

7.3c Discard the O-rings and fit new ones on installation

2•12 Engine, clutch and transmission

8.5a Unscrew the bolts (arrowed) . . .

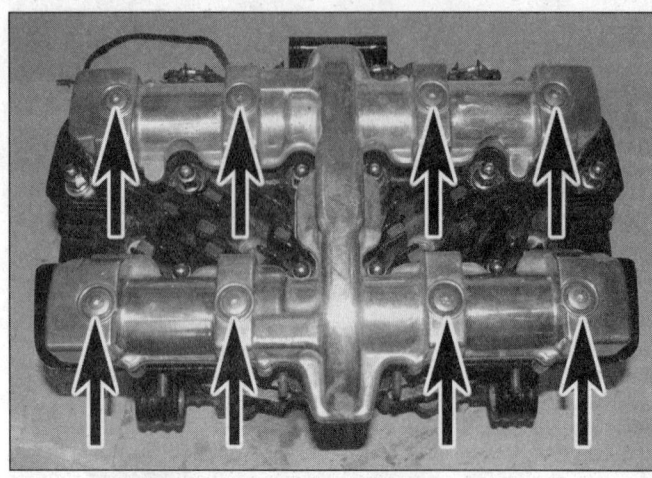

8.5b . . . and lift the valve cover off the engine

distorted, straighten them carefully with a screwdriver. If the air flow is restricted by bent or damaged fins over more than 20% of the cooler's surface area, renew the cooler.

Installation

6 Installation is the reverse of removal, noting the following:
● Always use new O-rings on the hose and pipe unions and smear them with grease.
● Check the condition of the cooler mounting grommets and renew them if they are damaged or deteriorated.
● Fill the engine with the specified quantity of oil and check the level (see Chapter 1).

8 Valve cover –
removal and installation

Note: *The valve cover can be removed with the engine in the frame. If the engine has been removed, ignore the steps which do not apply.*

Removal

1 Remove the fuel tank (see Chapter 3). On 2002 models onwards, remove the air induction system (AIS) (see Chapter 3).

2 Unscrew the oil cooler mounting bolts and tilt the cooler forward **(see illustrations 7.2b and c)**. Use a long screwdriver to access the air duct screws, otherwise you may have to lift the cooler out of its bottom mount, in which case unscrew the pipe holder bolt to give some freeplay **(see illustration 7.3a)**.
3 Undo each air duct screw and remove the ducts, noting how the pegs locate in the grommets **(see illustrations 5.6a, b and c)**. Note that each duct is marked with an L or R to denote its side.
4 Pull the spark plug caps off the spark plugs and position them clear of the valve cover **(see illustration 5.17)**.
5 Unscrew the bolts securing the valve cover and remove it **(see illustrations)**. If the cover is stuck, do not try to lever it off with a screwdriver. Tap it gently around the sides with a rubber hammer or block of wood to dislodge it.

Installation

6 Examine the valve cover gasket for signs of damage or deterioration and obtain a new one if necessary. Similarly check the rubber washers on the cover bolts for cracks, hardening and deterioration.

7 Clean the mating surfaces of the cylinder head and the valve cover.
8 Fit the gasket into the valve cover, making sure it locates correctly into the groove **(see illustration)**. Use a few dabs of grease to keep the gasket in place while the cover is fitted.
9 Apply a suitable sealant to the cut-outs in the cylinder head where the gasket half-circles fit **(see illustration)**. Position the valve cover on the cylinder head, making sure the gasket stays in place. Install the cover bolts with their rubber washers and tighten them to the torque setting specified at the beginning of the Chapter **(see illustration)**.
10 Install the remaining components in the reverse order of removal.

9 Cam chain tensioner –
removal, inspection and installation

Note: *The cam chain tensioner can be removed with the engine in the frame.*

Removal

1 For best access, remove the carburettors (see Chapter 3).

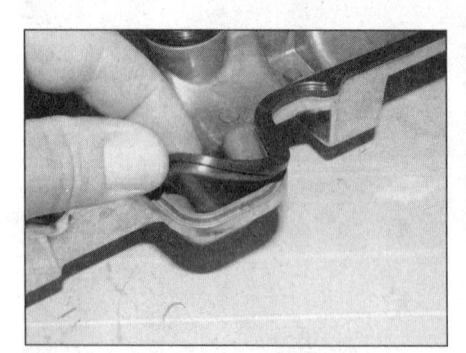

8.8 Fit the gasket into the groove in the cover

8.9a Apply the sealant to each cutout in the head (arrow)

8.9b Fit the bolts with their washers

Engine, clutch and transmission 2•13

9.2 Unscrew the cap bolt (arrowed) and withdraw the springs (one fits inside the other)

9.3 Unscrew the bolts (arrowed) and remove the tensioner

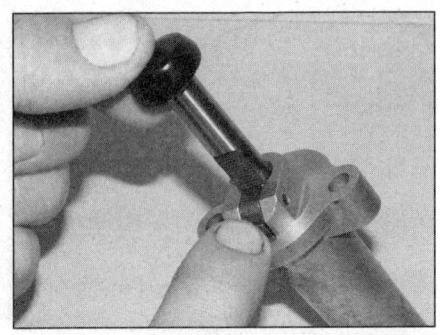

9.6 Release the ratchet mechanism to free the plunger

2 Unscrew the tensioner cap bolt and withdraw the springs from the tensioner body **(see illustration)**.

3 Unscrew the two tensioner mounting bolts and withdraw the tensioner from the back of the cylinder block, noting which way up it fits **(see illustration)**.

4 Remove the gasket and discard it as a new one must be used.

Inspection

5 Examine the tensioner components for signs of wear or damage.

6 Release the ratchet mechanism and check that the plunger moves freely in and out of the tensioner body **(see illustration)**.

7 If the tensioner or any of its components are worn or damaged, or if the plunger is seized in the body, the tensioner must be renewed. Individual internal components are not available.

Installation

8 Release the ratchet mechanism and press the tensioner plunger all the way into the tensioner body **(see illustration 9.6)**.

9 Fit a new gasket onto the tensioner body, then fit the tensioner into the engine, making sure the ratchet release lever is on the bottom **(see illustration)**. Tighten the bolts to the torque setting specified at the beginning of the Chapter.

10 Check the condition of the sealing washer on the cap bolt and renew it if it is worn or damaged. Install the springs and cap bolt and tighten the bolt to the specified torque setting **(see illustrations)**.

11 Unscrew the bolts securing the timing rotor/pick-up coil cover on the left-hand side of the engine and remove the cover **(see illustration 11.2)**. Discard the gasket as a new one must be used. Turn the crankshaft anti-clockwise through two full turns using a socket on the rotor bolt **(see illustration 11.3a)**. This will allow the tensioner to set itself properly. Install the cover using a new gasket, and tighten the screws to the torque setting specified at the beginning of the Chapter **(see illustrations 11.33a and b)**.

12 It is advisable to remove the valve cover (see Section 8) and check that the cam chain is tensioned and all the timing marks are in alignment (see Section 11). If the chain is slack, the tensioner plunger did not release when the spring and cap bolt were installed. Remove the tensioner again and re-check it. Again check the timing marks (see Section 11), then install the valve cover (see Section 8).

13 Install the carburettors (see Chapter 3).

9.9 Install the tensioner using a new gasket

10 Cam chain, tensioner blade and guides – removal, inspection and installation

Note: *The tensioner blade and guides can be removed with the engine in the frame. The engine must be removed and the crankcases separated to remove the cam chain.*

Cam chain

Removal

1 Remove the engine (see Section 5).

9.10a Install the springs . . .

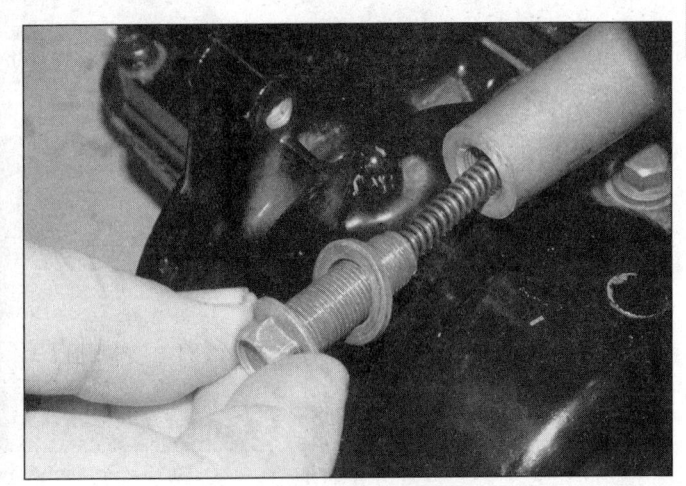

9.10b . . . then fit the cap bolt with its washer

2•14 Engine, clutch and transmission

10.8 Unscrew the bolts (arrowed) and remove the cam chain top guide

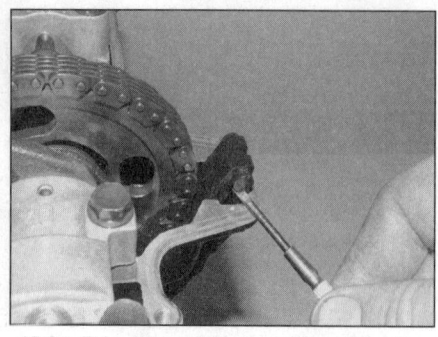

10.9a Prise the guide out, noting how the lugs locate . . .

10.9b . . . and withdraw it from the engine

2 Separate the crankcase halves (see Section 25).
3 Remove the crankshaft (see Section 29).
4 Remove the cam chain from the crankshaft.

Inspection

5 Check the chain for binding, kinks and any obvious damage and renew it if necessary. Check the camshaft and crankshaft sprocket teeth for wear and renew the cam chain, camshaft sprockets and crankshaft sprocket as a set if necessary.

Installation

6 Loop the chain around the crankshaft, then install the crankshaft (see Section 29).

Tensioner blade and guides

Removal

7 Remove the valve cover (see Section 8).

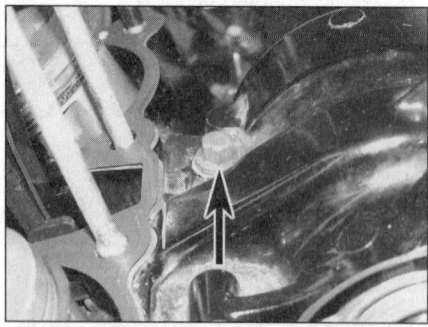

8 To remove the cam chain top guide, unscrew the four bolts securing it to the cylinder head and remove it, noting which way round it fits – there should be an arrow pointing to the front, but if not mark your own as the guide should be installed the same way round **(see illustration)**.
9 To remove the cam chain front guide, prise it up out of the cutout in the cylinder head and withdraw it from the engine, noting which way round it fits and how it locates **(see illustrations)**. Note that the blade could be difficult to remove as it is a tight fit with the exhaust camshaft in place. If you experience difficulty removing the guide and are likely to damage it, remove the exhaust camshaft first (see Section 11).
10 To remove the cam chain tensioner blade, first remove the cylinder block (see Section 15), but leave the gasket in place.

Unscrew the tensioner blade pivot pin bolt and remove the washer, then withdraw the spring and rod **(see illustrations)**. Lift the tensioner blade out, noting how it fits **(see illustration)**. Discard the washer if it is damaged or deformed. Now remove the base gasket. Discard it as a new one must be used.

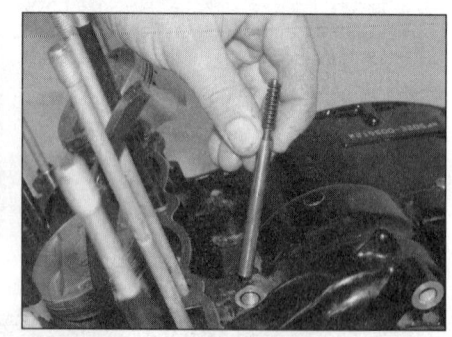

Inspection

11 Check the sliding surfaces of the blade and guides for excessive wear, deep grooves, cracking and other obvious damage, and renew them if necessary.

Installation

12 Apply some clean engine oil to the chain and the faces of the blade and guides before installing them.
13 Before installing the tensioner blade fit a new base gasket (see Section 15). Install the tensioner blade **(see illustration 10.10c)**, making sure its base locates correctly in the seat **(see illustration)**. Install the rod and the spring, making sure the rod locates correctly onto the blade pivot **(see illustration 10.10b)**. Fit the bolt using a new sealing washer if necessary and tighten it to the torque setting specified at the beginning of the Chapter **(see illustration)**. Install the cylinder block (see Section 15).
14 Slide the front guide blade into the front of the cam chain tunnel **(see illustration 10.9b)**, making sure it locates correctly onto its seat

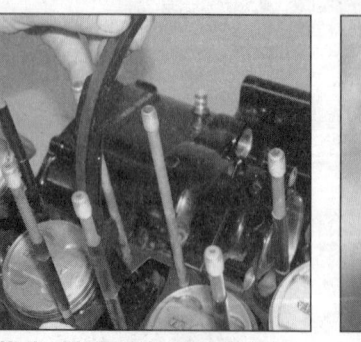

10.10a Unscrew the bolt (arrowed) . . .

10.10b . . . and withdraw the spring and rod

10.10c Lift the blade out of the engine

10.13a Tensioner blade seat (arrowed)

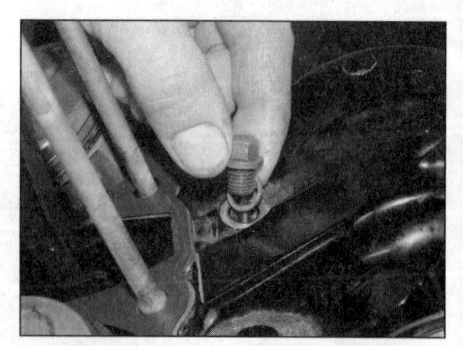

10.13b Install the bolt with its washer and tighten it to the specified torque

Engine, clutch and transmission 2•15

10.14 Make sure the lugs locate in the cutouts (arrowed)

10.15 Fit the top guide with the arrow pointing forwards

and its lugs locate in their cutouts **(see illustration)**.
15 Fit the top guide onto the cylinder head with the arrow pointing to the front and tighten the bolts securely **(see illustration)**.
16 Install the valve cover (see Section 8).

11 Camshafts and followers – removal, inspection and installation

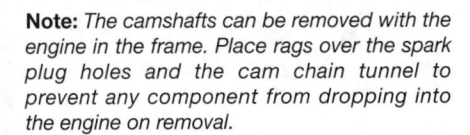

Note: *The camshafts can be removed with the engine in the frame. Place rags over the spark plug holes and the cam chain tunnel to prevent any component from dropping into the engine on removal.*

Removal

1 Remove the valve cover (see Section 8).
2 Undo the screws securing the timing rotor/pick-up coil cover on the left-hand side of the engine and remove the cover **(see illustration)**. Discard the gasket as a new one must be used.
3 Turn the engine using a spanner or socket on the timing rotor bolt, turning it in an anti-clockwise direction only, until the 'T' mark faces back and aligns with the static timing mark on the pick-up coil baseplate **(see illustrations)**, and the camshaft lobes for the No. 1 (left-hand) cylinder face away from each other, and the dot on each camshaft (adjacent to the sprocket) is visible via the holes in the camshaft caps **(see illustrations)**. If the cam lobes are facing towards each other and the dots are facing down, turn the engine anti-clockwise 360° (one full turn) so that the 'T' mark again aligns with the static timing mark. The camshaft lobes will now be facing away from each other, and the dots will be visible, meaning the No. 1 cylinder is at TDC (top dead centre) on the compression stroke.
4 Before disturbing the camshafts, make a note of the timing markings described above and how they align. If you are in any doubt as to the alignment of the markings, or if they are not visible for some reason, make your own alignment marks between all components, before disturbing them. These markings ensure that the valve timing can be correctly set up on assembly without difficulty.
5 Remove the cam chain tensioner (see Section 9).
6 Remove the cam chain top and front guides (see Section 10).
7 Before removing the camshaft holders, make a note of which fits where. Each holder is marked with a letter and a number to denote its location – 'I' denotes that the holder is for the intake camshaft at the back, 'E' denotes it is for the exhaust camshaft at the front **(see illustration)**. The number denotes the cylinder above which it fits, i.e. 1 to 4 from left to right. If the marks are not visible, make your own before disturbing them – it is essential they are returned to their original locations on installation. Note that the arrow or triangular pointer on each holder points to the right-hand side of the engine.
8 Unscrew the holder bolts for the camshaft being worked on evenly and a little at a time in a criss-cross sequence, slackening the bolts above any lobes that are pressing onto a valve last in the sequence so that the pressure

11.2 Undo the screws (arrowed) and remove the cover and the gasket

11.3a Turn the engine anti-clockwise ...

11.3b ... until the T mark aligns with the static mark on the pick-up coil ...

11.3c ... the No. 1 cylinder cam lobes face away from each other ...

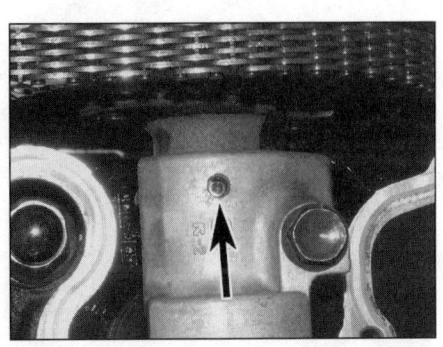

11.3d ... and the dot on each camshaft is visible in the hole in the cap (arrowed)

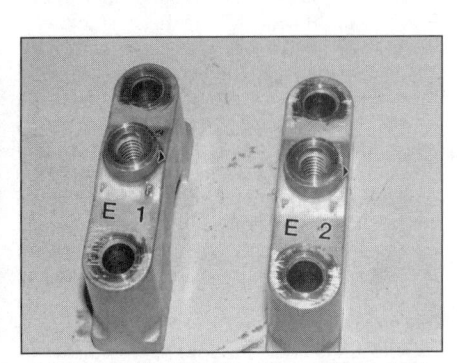

11.7 Note the identification marks which denote the location of each holder

2•16 Engine, clutch and transmission

11.8 Unscrew the camshaft holder bolts (arrowed) as described

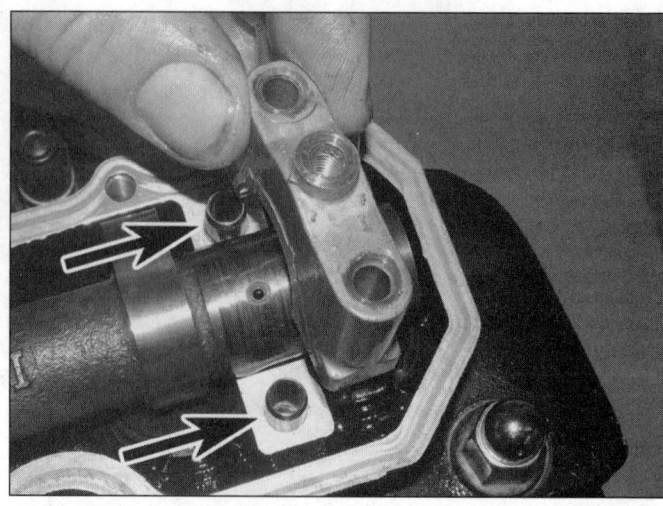

11.9a Lift the holder off and remove the dowels (arrowed) if loose

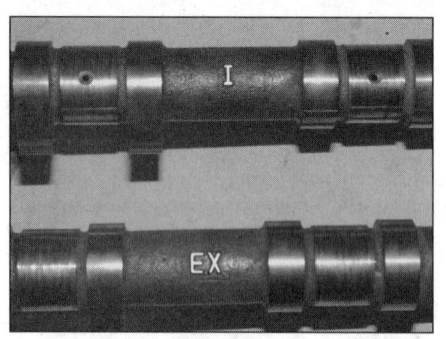

11.9b Note the identification marking on each camshaft

from the open valves cannot cause the camshaft to bend **(see illustration)**.
Caution: A camshaft could break if the holder bolts are not slackened as described and the pressure from a depressed valve causes the shaft to bend. Also, if the holder does not come squarely away from the head, the holder is likely to break. If this happens the cylinder head must be renewed; the holders are matched to the head and cannot be renewed separately.

9 Remove the bolts, then lift off the camshaft holders, noting how they fit **(see illustration)**. Retrieve the dowels from either the holder or the cylinder head if they are loose. Remove the intake camshaft first, then the exhaust, rotating them towards the centre of the engine as you do so. Keep all mated parts together. While the camshafts are out, don't allow the cam chain to go slack and do not rotate the crankshaft – the chain may drop down and bind between the crankshaft and crankcase, which could damage these components. Wire the chain to another component or secure it using a rod of some sort to prevent it from dropping. Note that the intake camshaft is marked I, and the exhaust EX **(see illustration)**.

10 If the followers and shims are being removed from the cylinder head, obtain a container which is divided into sixteen compartments, and label each compartment with the location of a valve in the cylinder head, i.e. mark the cylinder number, whether it is the left-hand or right-hand valve for that cylinder, and whether it belongs with an intake or an exhaust valve. If a container is not available, use labelled plastic bags (egg cartons also work very well). Remove the cam follower of the valve in question, leaving the shim in place in the top of the follower **(see illustration)**. The shims can be removed if required, but make sure each mated shim and follower are stored together otherwise the valve clearances will be incorrect on reassembly.

11 Cover the top of the cylinder head with a rag to prevent foreign objects from falling into the engine.

Inspection

12 Inspect the bearing surfaces of the cylinder head and holders and the corresponding journals on the camshaft. Look for score marks, deep scratches and evidence of spalling (a pitted appearance). If damage is noted or wear is excessive, renew the cylinder head and holders as a set – individual holders are not available.

13 Check the camshaft lobes for heat discoloration (blue appearance), score marks, chipped areas, flat spots and spalling. Measure the height of each lobe with a micrometer **(see illustration)** and compare the results to the minimum lobe height listed in this Chapter's Specifications. If damage is noted or wear is excessive, the camshaft must be renewed. Also, be sure to check the condition of the followers.

14 Check the amount of camshaft runout by supporting each end of the camshaft on V-blocks, and measuring any runout using a dial gauge. If the runout exceeds the specified limit the camshaft must be renewed.

> **HAYNES HiNT** *Refer to Tools and Workshop Tips (Section 3) in the Reference section for details of how to read a micrometer and dial gauge.*

15 Next, check the camshaft journal oil clearances. Check each camshaft in turn rather than at the same time – the exhaust camshaft is identifiable by its EX mark, and the intake camshaft by its I mark **(see illustration 11.9b)**. Clean the camshaft, the bearing surfaces in the cylinder head and camshaft holders with a clean lint-free cloth,

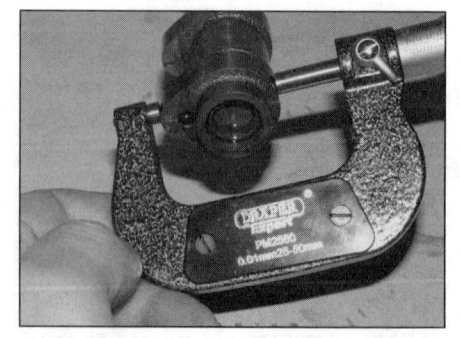

11.10 Lift out the follower using a magnet or valve lapping tool if necessary

11.13 Measure the height of the camshaft lobes with a micrometer

Engine, clutch and transmission 2•17

11.18 Measure the cam bearing journals with a micrometer

11.20a Sprocket bolts (arrowed)

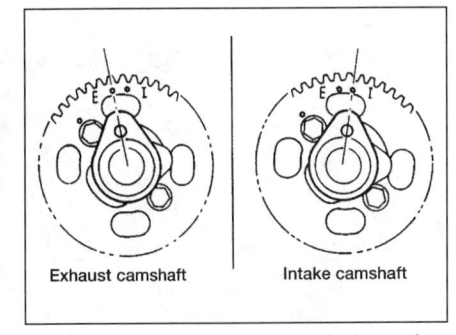

11.20b Make sure the camshafts and sprockets are aligned as shown

then lay the camshaft in place in the head, position it so that the lobes for No. 1 cylinder face forwards (exhaust camshaft) or rearwards (intake camshaft); the punch mark on the camshaft should be facing upwards.

16 Cut some strips of Plastigauge and lay one piece on each journal, parallel with the camshaft centreline. Make sure the camshaft holder dowels are installed **(see illustration 11.9a)**. Lay the holders in their correct place in the head with the arrows pointing to the right-hand side of the engine (see Step 7). When fitting the large holder locate the cutout on the inner end over the thin raised section with the punch mark. Fit the bolts and tighten them evenly and a little at a time in a criss-cross sequence to the torque setting specified at the beginning of the Chapter, starting with the bolts that are above valves that will be pushed open when the camshaft is tightened down. Whilst tightening the bolts, make sure the holders are being pulled squarely down and are not binding on the dowels. While doing this, don't let the camshaft rotate.

17 Now unscrew the bolts evenly and a little at a time in a criss-cross sequence, slackening the bolts above any lobes that are pressing onto a valve last in the sequence so that the pressure from the open valves cannot cause the camshaft to bend.

18 To determine the oil clearance, compare the crushed Plastigauge (at its widest point) on each journal to the scale printed on the Plastigauge container. Compare the results to this Chapter's Specifications. If the oil clearance is greater than specified, measure the diameter of the camshaft journal with a micrometer **(see illustration)**. If the journal diameter is less than the specified limit, renew the camshaft and recheck the clearance. If the clearance is still too great, or if the camshaft journal is within its limit, renew the cylinder head and holders as a set – individual holders are not available. If required the holder/cylinder head bore sizes can be measured with the camshafts removed and the holders tightened down, using a small bore gauge and micrometer, comparing the results to the specifications.

> **HAYNES HINT** *Before renewing the camshafts, cylinder head or holders because of damage, check with local machine shops specialising in motorcycle engine work. In the case of the camshafts, it may be possible for cam lobes to be welded, reground and hardened, at a cost far lower than that of a new camshaft. If the bearing surfaces in the head or holders are damaged, it may be possible for them to be bored out to accept bearing inserts. Due to the cost of new components it is recommended that all options are explored!*

19 Except in cases of oil starvation, the cam chain wears very little. If the chain has stretched excessively, which makes it difficult to maintain proper tension, or if it is stiff or the links are binding or kinking, renew it (see Section 10).

20 Check the sprockets for wear, cracks and other damage. If the sprockets are worn, the cam chain is also worn, and so is the sprocket on the crankshaft. If severe wear is apparent, the entire engine should be disassembled for inspection. If necessary, make a note of the alignment of the sprocket on the camshaft, then unscrew the bolts and remove the sprocket **(see illustration)**. Fit the new sprocket, aligning it as shown, and tighten the bolts to the torque setting specified at the beginning of the Chapter **(see illustration)**.

21 Inspect the cam chain guides and tensioner blade (see Section 10).

22 Inspect the outer surfaces of the cam followers for evidence of scoring or other damage **(see illustration)**. If a follower is in poor condition, it is probable that the bore in which it works is also damaged. Check for clearance between the followers and their bores. Whilst no specifications are given, if slack is excessive, renew the followers. If the bores are seriously out-of-round or tapered, renew the cylinder head/holders and the followers.

Installation

23 If removed, lubricate each shim and its follower with molybdenum disulphide oil (a 50/50 mixture of molybdenum disulphide grease and engine oil) and fit each shim into its recess in the top of the follower, with the size marking on each shim facing down. Make sure each shim is correctly seated, then install each follower, making sure it fits squarely in its bore **(see illustration)**. **Note:** *It is most important that the shims and followers are returned to their original valves otherwise the valve clearances will be inaccurate.*

24 Make sure the bearing surfaces on the camshafts and in the cylinder head are clean, then apply molybdenum disulphide oil (a 50/50 mixture of molybdenum disulphide grease and engine oil) to each of them. Also apply it to the camshaft lobes.

25 Check that the 'T' mark on the rotor still aligns with the static timing mark (see Step 3) **(see illustration 11.3b)**.

26 Fit the exhaust camshaft, identifiable by its EX mark **(see illustration 11.9b)**, through

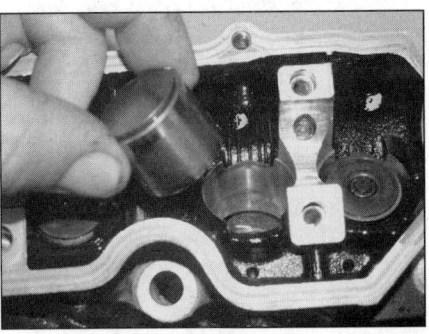

11.22 Check the followers and bores as described

11.23 Fit the shim into the follower, then fit the follower into its bore and onto the valve

2•18 Engine, clutch and transmission

11.26a Fit the exhaust camshaft through the chain and onto the head . . .

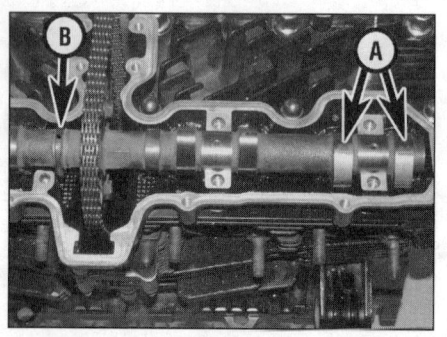

11.26b . . . making sure the No. 1 lobes (A) point forwards and the punch mark (B) faces up

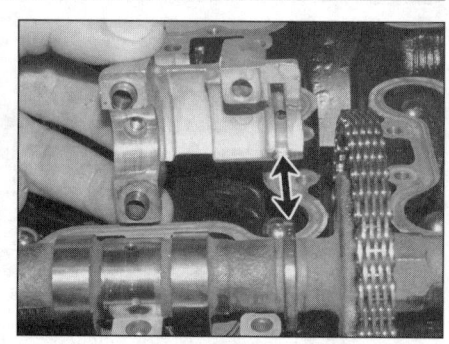

11.27 Locate the cutout over the raised section (arrows)

the cam chain and onto the front of the head, making sure the No. 1 (left-hand) cylinder lobes are facing forwards and the punch mark on the camshaft is facing up **(see illustrations)**. Fit the cam chain around the sprocket, pulling up on the front run to remove all slack from it.

27 Fit the exhaust camshaft holder dowels into the cylinder head or holders **(see illustration 11.9a)**. Make sure the bearing surfaces in the holders are clean, then apply molybdenum disulphide oil (a 50/50 mixture of molybdenum disulphide grease and engine oil) to them. Lay the holders in their correct place in the head with the arrows pointing to the right-hand side of the engine (see Step 7). When fitting the large holder locate the cutout on the inner end over the thin raised section with the punch mark **(see illustration)**. Install the bolts in the holders and tighten them evenly and a little at a time in a criss-cross pattern to the torque setting specified at the beginning of the Chapter, starting with the bolts that are above valves that will be pushed open when the camshaft is tightened down. Whilst tightening the bolts, make sure the holders are being pulled squarely down and are not binding on the dowels. At this stage check that the timing marks relevant to the exhaust camshaft still align (see Step 3). If not, slip the chain off the sprocket and turn the camshaft as required using a suitable spanner on the hex adjacent to the sprocket, then refit the chain. Remember that the chain must be tight between the crankshaft and exhaust camshaft.

Caution: The camshaft is likely to break if it is tightened down onto the closed valves before the open valves. The holders are likely to break if they are not tightened down evenly and squarely.

28 Now fit the intake camshaft, identifiable by its IN mark **(see illustration 11.9b)**, through the cam chain and onto the back of the head, making sure the No. 1 cylinder lobes are facing back and the punch mark on the camshaft is facing up **(see illustrations)**. Fit the cam chain around the intake sprocket, pulling it tight between the two camshaft sprockets – any slack in the chain must lie in the rear run so that it is taken up by the tensioner. Fit the intake camshaft holders as described in Step 27.

11.28a Fit the intake camshaft through the chain and onto the head . . .

29 Using a piece of wooden dowel, press on the back of the cam chain tensioner blade via the tensioner bore in the crankcase to ensure that any slack in the cam chain between the crankshaft and the intake camshaft, and between the two camshafts, is taken up and transferred to the rear run of the chain (where it will later be taken up by the tensioner). At this point check that all the timing marks are still in **exact** alignment as described in Step 3. Note that it is easy to be slightly out (one tooth on the sprocket) without the marks appearing drastically out of alignment. If the marks are out, verify which sprocket is misaligned, then unscrew its bolts and slide it off the camshaft, then disengage it from the chain **(see illustration 11.20a)**. Move the camshaft round as required, then fit the sprocket back into the chain and onto the camshaft, and check the marks again. With everything correctly aligned, tighten the sprocket bolts to

11.28b . . . making sure the No. 1 lobes (A) point backwards and the punch mark (B) faces up

the torque setting specified at the beginning of the Chapter.

Caution: If the marks are not aligned exactly as described, the valve timing will be incorrect and the valves may strike the pistons, causing extensive damage to the engine.

30 Install the cam chain front and top guides (see Section 10).

31 Install the cam chain tensioner (see Section 9). Turn the engine anti-clockwise through two full turns and check again that all the timing marks still align (see Step 3).

32 Check the valve clearances and adjust them if necessary (see Chapter 1).

33 Install the timing rotor/pick-up coil cover using a new gasket, and tighten the screws to the torque setting specified at the beginning of the Chapter **(see illustrations)**.

34 Install the valve cover (see Section 8).

11.33a Fit a new gasket . . .

11.33b . . . and install the cover

Engine, clutch and transmission 2•19

12 Cylinder head – removal and installation

Caution: *The engine must be completely cool before beginning this procedure or the cylinder head may become warped.*

Note: *The cylinder head can be removed with the engine in the frame although due to the limited clearance available in the frame, it may be necessary to remove the engine mountings and tilt the engine forwards to enable cylinder head removal. Refer to Sectin 5 for details of the engine mounting points and ensure that the engine is well supported under the crankcase before removing the mounting bolts.*

Removal

1 Remove the carburettors and exhaust system (see Chapter 3).

2 Remove the valve cover (see Section 8) and the camshafts and followers (see Section 11).

3 The cylinder head is secured by sixteen nuts. First unscrew and remove the plain nuts and washers on the studs at the front and back of the cylinder head **(see illustrations)**. Now slacken the domed nuts evenly and a little at a time in a **reverse** of the numerical tightening sequence shown, until they are all slack, then remove the nuts and their washers **(see illustration)** – be careful not to let them fall into the cam chain tunnel. Use either a magnet, a screwdriver, or a piece of wire hooked over at the end to lift the washers out where necessary. Note that the two washers on the right-hand end are copper, while the rest are steel **(see illustration)**. The copper washers must be installed in the same place. If they are damaged or deformed, renew them.

4 Pull the cylinder head up off the cylinder block studs. If it is stuck, tap around the joint faces of the head with a soft-faced mallet to free it. Do not attempt to free the head by inserting a screwdriver between it and the block – you'll damage the sealing surfaces. It is best to have an assistant on hand to pass the cam chain through the head and to then secure it to the engine rather than letting it drop down the tunnel. Remove the old cylinder head gasket and discard it as a new one must be used. Plug the cam chain tunnel with some clean rag.

5 Remove the two O-rings from around the two dowels on the right-hand end of the cylinder block and discard them **(see illustration 12.8b)**. If they are loose, remove the four dowels from the cylinder block **(see illustration 12.8a)**. If they appear to be missing they are probably stuck in the underside of the cylinder head.

6 Check the cylinder head gasket and the mating surfaces on the cylinder head and block for signs of leakage, which could

12.3a Unscrew the nuts (arrowed) on the front . . .

12.3b . . . and on the back of the head

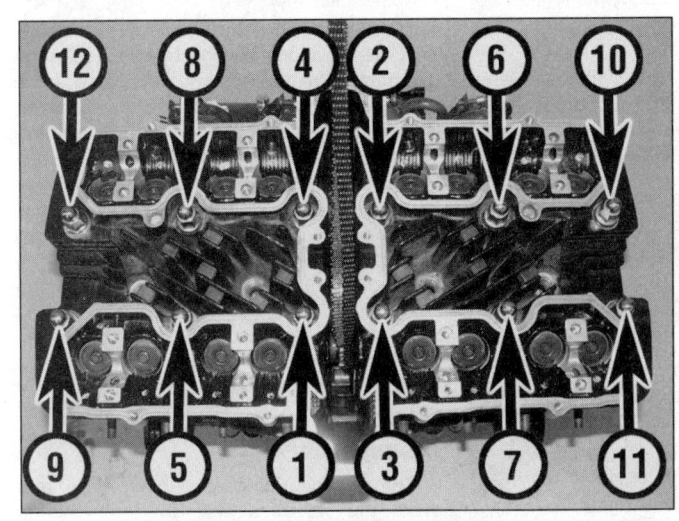

12.3c Cylinder head nut TIGHTENING sequence – slacken the nuts in reverse order

12.3d Note the location of the two copper washers (arrowed)

2•20 Engine, clutch and transmission

12.8a Fit the dowels (arrowed) ...

12.8b ... and the two O-rings around the end dowels

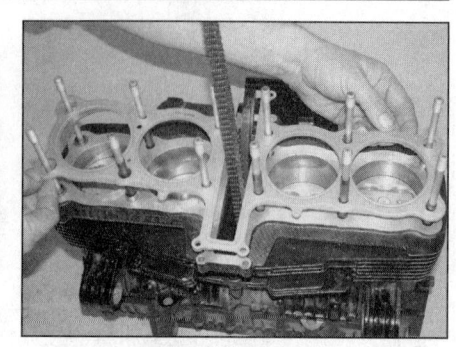

12.8c Lay the new gasket over the dowels and onto the head

indicate warpage. Refer to Section 14 and check the flatness of the cylinder head.

Installation

7 Clean all traces of old gasket material from the cylinder head and block. If a scraper is used, take care not to scratch or gouge the soft aluminium. Be careful not to let any of the gasket material fall into the crankcase, the cylinder bores or the oil passages.

> **HAYNES HiNT** *Refer to Tools and Workshop Tips (Section 7) for details of gasket removal methods.*

8 Ensure both cylinder head and block mating surfaces are clean. If removed, fit the dowels into the cylinder block, then fit two new O-rings over the dowels on the right-hand end **(see illustrations)**. Remove the rag from the cam chain tunnel. Lay the new head gasket in place, aligning it so the larger stud holes locate over the dowels **(see illustration)**. Never re-use the old gasket, and do not use any gasket sealant.

9 Carefully fit the cylinder head over the studs and onto the cylinder block, making sure it locates correctly onto the dowels. You may need to press the tensioner blade in so it doesn't catch on the underside of the head. Have an assistant pass the cam chain up through the head as you lower it – using a piece of wire to hook it up is the best way, then use the piece of wire to secure the chain and prevent it from dropping back down.

12.10a Install the nuts with their washers ...

12.10b ... and tighten them as described to the specified torque setting

10 Lubricate the threads and seating surfaces of the cylinder head nuts with clean engine oil. Install the nuts and washers, taking care not to let them fall into the cam chain tunnel **(see illustration)**; make sure the two copper washers are on the right-hand end **(see illustration 12.3d)** (use new ones if necessary), and tighten them finger-tight. Now tighten the nuts evenly and a little at a time, in the correct numerical sequence shown **(see illustration 12.3c)**, to the torque setting specified at the beginning of the Chapter **(see illustration)**.

11 Now install the plain nuts with their washers onto the studs at the front and rear of the head, again lubricating them with oil, and tighten them to the specified torque setting.

12 Install the remaining components in a reverse of their removal sequence, referring to the relevant Sections or Chapters (see Steps 1 and 2).

13 Valves/valve seats/valve guides – servicing

1 Because of the complex nature of this job and the special tools and equipment required, most owners leave servicing of the valves, valve seats and valve guides to a professional. However, you can make an initial assessment of whether the valves are seating correctly, and therefore sealing, by pouring a small amount of solvent into each of the valve ports.

If the solvent leaks past any valve into the combustion chamber area the valve is not seating correctly and sealing.

2 You can also remove the valves from the cylinder head, clean the components, check them for wear to assess the extent of the work needed, and, unless a valve service is required, grind in the valves (see Section 14). The head can then be reassembled.

3 A dealer service department will remove the valves and springs, renew the valves and guides, re-cut the valve seats, check and renew the valve springs, spring retainers and collets (as necessary), renew the valve stem seals and reassemble the valve components.

4 After the valve service has been performed, the head will be in like-new condition. When the head is returned, be sure to clean it again very thoroughly before installation on the engine to remove any metal particles or abrasive grit that may still be present from the valve service operations. Use compressed air, if available, to blow out all the holes and passages.

14 Cylinder head and valves – disassembly, inspection and reassembly

1 As mentioned in the previous section, valve overhaul should be left to a Yamaha dealer or cylinder head specialist. However, disassembly, cleaning and inspection of the valves and related components can be done (if the necessary special tools are available) by the home mechanic. This way no expense is incurred if the inspection reveals that overhaul is not required at this time.

2 To disassemble the valve components without the risk of damaging them, a valve spring compressor is absolutely essential. Make sure it is suitable for motorcycle work and comes with the correct adapters for your valve size.

Disassembly

3 Before proceeding, arrange to label and store the valves along with their related components in such a way that they can be returned to their original locations without

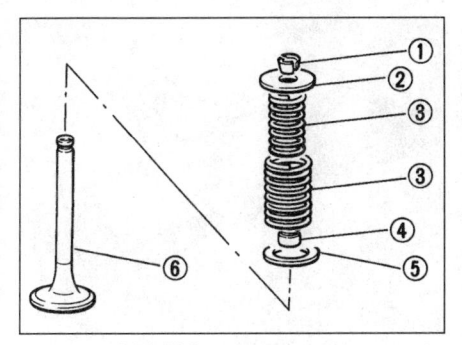

Engine, clutch and transmission 2•21

14.3 Valve components

1 Collets
2 Spring retainer
3 Valve springs
4 Valve stem oil seal
5 Spring seat
6 Valve

14.5a Compressing the valve springs using a valve spring compressor

14.5b Make sure the compressor is a good fit both on the top . . .

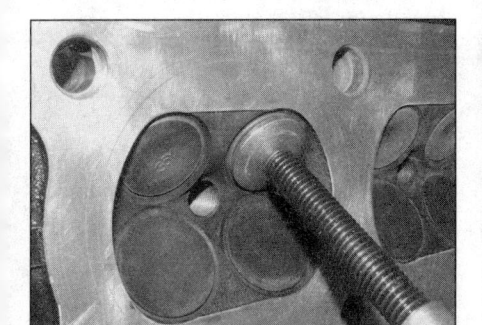

14.5c . . . and the bottom of the valve assembly

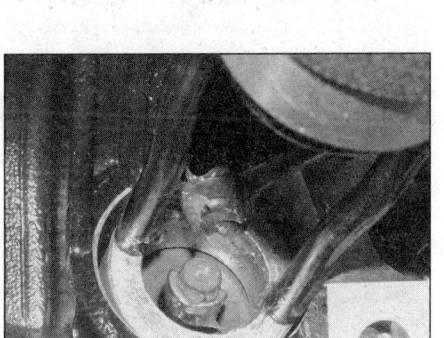

14.6a Remove the collets with needle-nose pliers, tweezers, a magnet or a screwdriver with a dab of grease on it

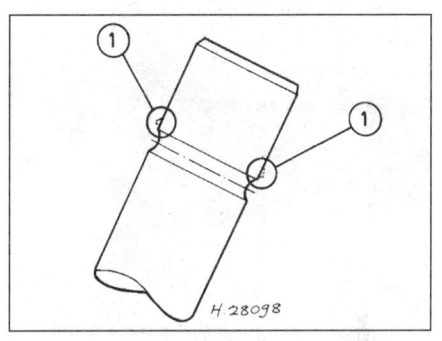

14.6b If the valve stem won't pull through the guide, deburr the area above the collet groove (1)

getting mixed up **(see illustration)**. A good way to do this is to obtain a container which is divided into sixteen compartments, and label each compartment with the location of a valve in the cylinder head, i.e. mark the cylinder number, whether it is the left-hand or right-hand valve for that cylinder, and whether it belongs with an intake or an exhaust valve. If a container is not available, use labelled plastic bags (egg cartons also work very well!). The easy alternative is to use the same container(s) in which the followers and shims are stored.

4 Clean all traces of old gasket material from the cylinder head. If a scraper is used, take care not to scratch or gouge the soft aluminium.

> **HAYNES HiNT** *Refer to Tools and Workshop Tips for details of gasket removal methods.*

5 First locate the valve spring compressor on each end of the valve assembly, making sure it is the correct size **(see illustration)**. On the top of the valve the adaptor needs to be about the same size as the spring retainer – if it is too big it will contact the follower bore and mark it, and if it is too small it will be difficult to remove and install the collets **(see illustration)**. On the underside of the head make sure the plate on the compressor only contacts the valve and not the soft aluminium of the head – if the plate is too big for the valve, use a spacer between them **(see illustration)**.

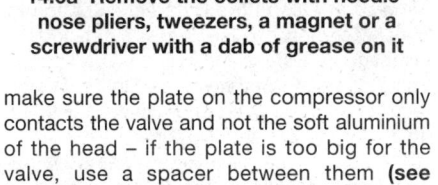

6 Compress the valve springs on the first valve – do not compress the springs any more than is absolutely necessary. Remove the collets, using either needle-nose pliers, tweezers, a magnet or a screwdriver with a dab of grease on it **(see illustration)**. Carefully release the valve spring compressor and remove it. Remove the spring retainer, noting which way up it fits **(see illustration 14.30c)**. Remove the springs, noting that the closer wound coils are at the bottom **(see illustrations 14.30b and a)**. Press down on the top of the valve stem and draw the valve out from the underside of the head **(see illustration 14.29)**. If the valve binds in the guide (won't pull through), push it back into the head and deburr the area around the collet groove with a very fine file or whetstone **(see illustration)**.

7 Once the valve has been removed and labelled, pull the valve stem oil seal off the top of the valve guide and discard it (the old seals should never be reused) **(see illustration)**. Now remove the spring seat **(see illustration)**. If the seat is difficult to get hold of, either use a small magnet or turn the head upside down and tip it out.

8 Repeat the procedure for the remaining valves. Remember to keep the parts for each valve together and in order so they can be reinstalled in the same location.

14.7a Pull the seal off the valve stem . . .

14.7b . . . then remove the spring seat

2•22 Engine, clutch and transmission

14.15a Measure the valve stem diameter with a micrometer

14.15b Insert a small hole gauge into the valve guide and expand it so there's a slight drag when it's pulled out

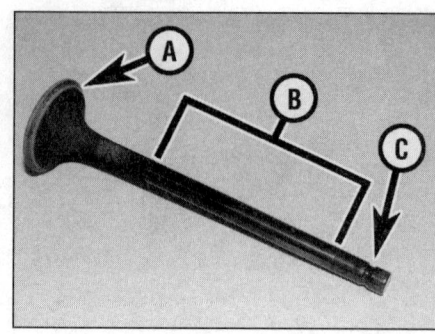

14.16a Check the valve face (A), stem (B) and collet groove (C) for signs of wear and damage

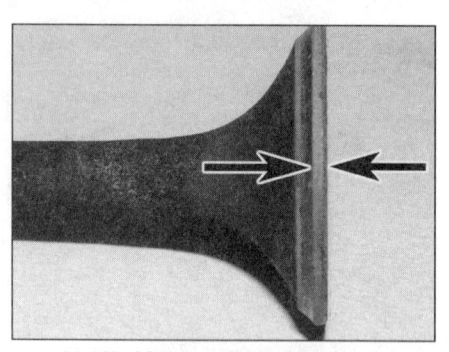

14.16b Measure the valve margin thickness as shown

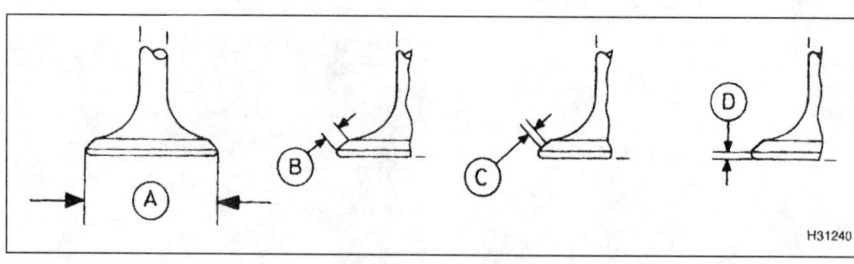

14.16c Valve head measurement points

A Head diameter   B Face width   C Seat width   D Margin thickness

9 Next, clean the cylinder head with solvent and dry it thoroughly. Compressed air will speed the drying process and ensure that all holes and recessed areas are reached.

10 Clean all of the valve springs, collets, retainers and spring seats with solvent and dry them thoroughly. Do the parts from one valve at a time so they don't get mixed up.

11 Scrape off any deposits that may have formed on the valve, then use a motorised wire brush to remove deposits from the valve heads and stems. Again, make sure the valves do not get mixed up.

Inspection

12 Inspect the head very carefully for cracks and other damage. If cracks are found, a new head will be required. Check the camshaft bearing surfaces for wear and evidence of seizure. Check the camshafts and holders for wear as well (see Section 11).

13 Inspect the outer surfaces of the cam followers for evidence of scoring or other damage **(see illustration 11.22)**. If a follower is in poor condition, it is probable that the bore in which it works is also damaged. Check for clearance between the followers and their bores. Whilst no specifications are given, if slack is excessive, renew the followers. If the bores are seriously out-of-round or tapered, the cylinder head and the followers must be renewed.

14 Using a precision straight-edge and a feeler gauge set to the warpage limit listed in the specifications at the beginning of the Chapter, check the head gasket mating surface for warpage. Refer to *Tools and Workshop Tips* in the Reference section for details of how to use the straight-edge. If warpage is evident, the cylinder head can be resurfaced by rotating it in a figure of eight pattern on a surface paper covered with 400 to 600 grade wet and dry paper.

15 Measure the valve stem diameter **(see illustration)**. Clean the valve guides to remove any carbon build-up, then measure the inside diameters of the guides (at both ends and the centre of the guide) with a small hole gauge and micrometer **(see illustration)**. Measure the guides at the ends and at the centre to determine if they are worn in a bell-mouth pattern (more wear at the ends). Subtract the stem diameter from the valve guide diameter to obtain the valve stem-to-guide clearance. If the stem-to-guide clearance is greater than listed in this Chapter's Specifications, renew whichever components are worn beyond their specification limits. If the valve guide is within specifications, but is worn unevenly, it should be renewed.

16 Carefully inspect each valve face, stem and collet groove area for cracks, pits and burned spots **(see illustration)**. Measure the valve margin thickness and compare it to the specifications **(see illustration)**. The margin is the portion of the valve head which is below the valve seat. Also measure the valve head diameter, face width and seat width **(see illustration)**.

17 Examine the valve seats in each of the combustion chambers. If they are pitted, cracked or burned, the head will require valve service that's beyond the scope of the home mechanic. Measure the valve seat width **(see illustration)** and compare it to this Chapter's Specifications. If it is not within the specified range, or if it varies around its circumference, valve service work is required.

18 Rotate the valve and check for any obvious indication that it is bent. Using V-blocks and a dial gauge if available, measure the valve stem runout and compare the results to the specifications **(see**

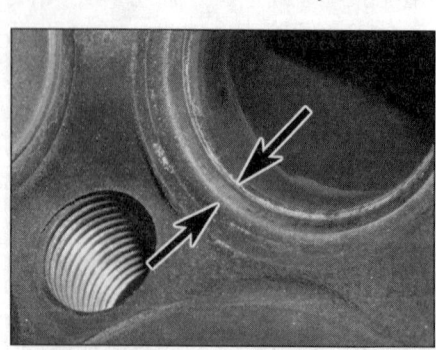

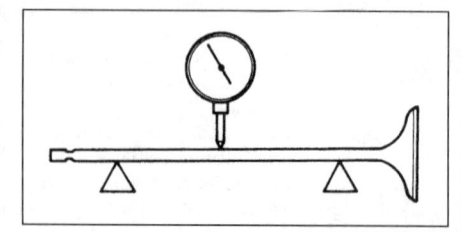

14.17 Measure the valve seat width as shown

14.18 Check the valve stem for runout using V-blocks and a dial gauge

14.19a Measure the free length of the valve springs

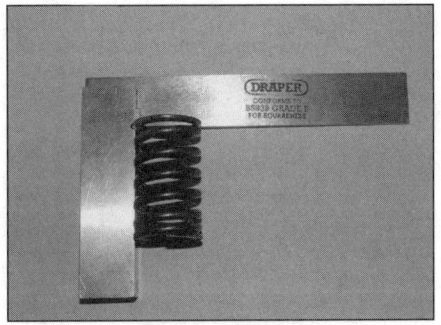

14.19b Check the valve springs for squareness

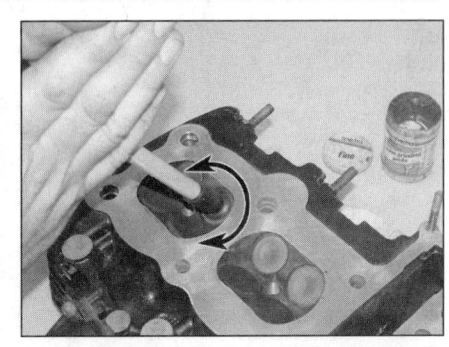

14.24a Rotate the valve grinding tool back and forth between the palms of your hands

illustration). If the measurement exceeds the service limit specified, the valve must be renewed. Check the end of the stem for pitting and excessive wear. The presence of any of the above conditions indicates the need for valve servicing.

19 Check the end of each valve spring for wear and pitting. Measure the spring free length and compare it to that listed in the specifications (see illustration). If any spring is shorter than specified it has sagged and must be renewed. Also place the spring upright on a flat surface and check it for bend by placing a ruler against it (see illustration). If the bend in any spring exceeds the specified limit, it must be renewed.

20 Check the spring seats, retainers and collets for obvious wear and cracks. Any questionable parts should not be reused, as extensive damage will occur in the event of failure during engine operation.

21 If the inspection indicates that no overhaul work is required, the valve components can be reinstalled in the head.

Reassembly

22 Unless a valve service has been performed, before installing the valves in the head they should be ground in (lapped) to ensure a positive seal between the valves and seats. This procedure requires coarse and fine valve grinding compound and a valve grinding tool. If a grinding tool is not available, a piece of rubber or plastic hose can be slipped over the valve stem (after the valve has been installed in the guide) and used to turn the valve.

23 Apply a small amount of coarse grinding compound to the valve face, and some molybdenum disulphide oil (a 50/50 mixture of molybdenum disulphide grease and engine oil) to the valve stem, then slip the valve into the guide (see illustration 14.29). Note: *Make sure each valve is installed in its correct guide and be careful not to get any grinding compound on the valve stem.*

24 Attach the grinding tool (or hose) to the valve and rotate the tool between the palms of your hands. Use a back-and-forth motion (as though rubbing your hands together) rather than a circular motion (i.e. so that the valve rotates alternately clockwise and anti-clockwise rather than in one direction only) (see illustration). Lift the valve off the seat and turn it at regular intervals to distribute the grinding compound properly. Continue the grinding procedure until the valve face and seat contact area is of uniform and correct width, and unbroken around the entire circumference (see illustration and 14.17).

25 Carefully remove the valve from the guide and wipe off all traces of grinding compound, making sure none gets in the guide. Use solvent to clean the valve and wipe the seat area thoroughly with a solvent soaked cloth.

26 Repeat the procedure with fine valve grinding compound, then repeat the entire procedure for the remaining valves.

27 Working on one valve at a time, lay the spring seat in place in the cylinder head,

14.24b The valve face and seat should show a uniform unbroken ring

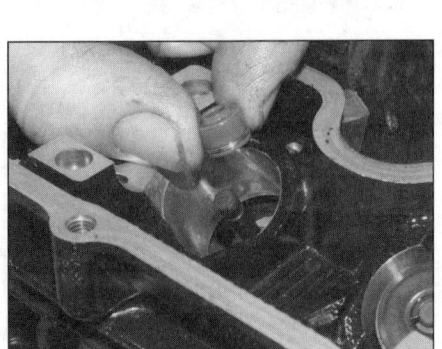

14.28a Fit a new valve stem seal . . .

making sure the shouldered side faces up – sliding the seat down a rod or screwdriver shaft helps to locate it around the top of the guide and prevents it getting skewed (see illustration).

28 Fit a new valve stem seal onto the guide. Usually finger pressure is sufficient to get it to clip into place, otherwise use a stem seal fitting tool or an appropriate size deep socket to push the seal over the end of the valve guide until it is felt to clip into place (see illustrations). Don't twist or cock the seal, or it will not seal properly against the valve stem. Also, don't remove it again or it will be damaged.

29 Coat the valve stem with molybdenum disulphide oil (a 50/50 mixture of molybdenum disulphide grease and engine oil), then install it into its guide, rotating it slowly to avoid

14.27 Lay the spring seat over the top of the guide and onto the head

14.28b . . . using a suitable deep socket to press it on if necessary

2•24 Engine, clutch and transmission

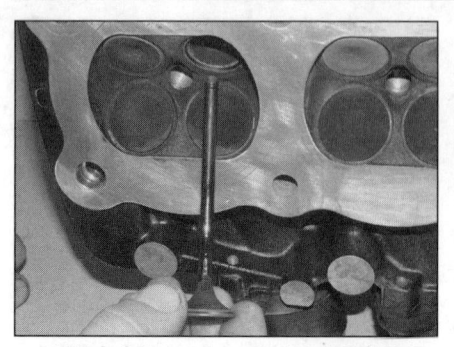

14.29 Lubricate the stem and slide the valve into its correct location

14.30a Fit the inner valve spring with its closer wound coils facing down . . .

14.30b . . . then fit the outer spring in the same way . . .

14.30c . . . then fit the spring retainer

14.31a Locate the collets . . .

14.31b . . . making sure they stay in place

damaging the seal **(see illustration)**. Check that the valve moves up and down freely in the guide.

30 Next, install the inner and outer springs, with the closer-wound coils facing down into the cylinder head **(see illustrations)**. Fit the spring retainer, with its shouldered side facing down so that it fits into the top of the springs **(see illustration)**.

31 Compress the valve spring with a spring compressor, making sure it is correctly located onto each end of the valve assembly (see Step 5) **(see illustrations 14.5a, b and c)**. Do not compress the springs any more than is necessary to slip the collets into place. Apply a small amount of grease to the collets to help hold them in place. Locate each collet in turn into the groove in the valve stem **(see illustrations)**, then carefully release the compressor, making sure the collets seat and lock as you do. Check that the collets are

securely locked in the retaining groove **(see illustration)**.

32 Support the cylinder head on blocks so the valves can't contact the workbench top, then tap the top of the valve stem with a brass drift **(see illustration)**. This will help seat the collets in the groove. If you don't have a brass drift, use a soft-faced hammer.

HAYNES HiNT *Check for proper sealing of the valves by pouring a small amount of solvent into each of the valve ports. If the solvent leaks past any valve into the combustion chamber area the valve grinding operation on that valve should be repeated.*

33 Repeat the procedure for the remaining valves. Remember to keep the parts for each

valve together, and separate from the other valves, so they can be reinstalled in the same location. After the cylinder head and camshafts have been installed, check the valve clearances and adjust as required (see Chapter 1).

15 Cylinder block – removal, inspection and installation

Note: *The block can be removed with the engine in the frame. If the engine has been removed, ignore the steps that don't apply.*

Removal

1 Remove the cylinder head (see Section 12).
2 Unscrew the cylinder block nut **(see illustration)**.
3 Hold the cam chain up and pull the cylinder

14.31c Check that the collets are correctly seated . . .

14.32 . . . then tap the valve stem end to make sure

15.2 Unscrew the nut (arrowed)

Engine, clutch and transmission 2•25

15.11a Using a telescoping bore gauge . . .

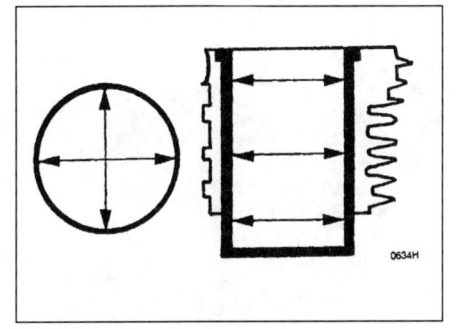

15.11b . . . measure the cylinder bore in the directions shown, then measure the gauge with a micrometer

block up off the crankcase, taking care not to allow the connecting rods to knock against the crankcase once the pistons are free, then pass the cam chain down through the tunnel and drape it over the engine (see illustration 15.24). Do not let the chain fall into the crankcase – secure it with a piece of wire or metal bar to prevent it from doing so. If the block is stuck, tap around the base of it with a soft-faced mallet. Do not try to free it by inserting a screwdriver between the block and crankcase – you'll damage the surfaces. After the block has been removed, stuff clean rags around the pistons and in the cam chain tunnel to prevent anything falling into the crankcase.

4 Remove the cam chain tensioner blade (see Section 10). Remove the old base gasket and discard it. On XJR1200 models remove the O-ring from around the base of each cylinder and discard them as new ones must be used.
5 If they are loose, remove the two dowels from the cylinder block or crankcase (see illustration 15.22a).
6 Check the base gasket and the mating surfaces on the cylinder head and block for signs of leakage, which could indicate warpage.
7 Clean all traces of old gasket material from the cylinder block and crankcase. If a scraper is used, take care not to scratch or gouge the soft aluminium. Be careful not to let any of the gasket material drop into the crankcase or the oil passages.

Inspection – XJR1200 models

8 Steel liners are fitted in the aluminium cylinder block – do not attempt to separate the liners from the block.
9 Check the cylinder walls carefully for scratches and score marks.
10 No service limit is given for cylinder block warpage, but the cylinder head warpage limit check can be used as a guide – see Section 14 for details.
11 Using a telescoping bore gauge and a micrometer (see Tools and Workshop Tips), check the dimensions of each cylinder to assess the amount of wear, taper and ovality. Measure near the top (but below the level of the top piston ring at TDC), centre and bottom (but above the level of the oil ring at BDC) of the bore, both parallel to and across the crankshaft axis (see illustrations). Compare the results to the specifications at the beginning of the Chapter. If the cylinders are worn, oval or tapered beyond the service limit they can be rebored, and an oversize (+ 0.50) set of pistons and rings are available from Yamaha. Note that the person carrying out the rebore must be aware of the piston-to-bore clearance for the oversize piston (see Specifications).
12 If the precision measuring tools are not available, take the block to a Yamaha dealer or specialist motorcycle repair shop for assessment and advice.
13 If the cylinder bores are in good condition and the piston-to-bore clearance is within specifications (see Section 16), the bores should be honed (de-glazed). To perform this operation you will need the proper size flexible hone with fine stones, or a bottle-brush type hone, plenty of light oil or honing oil, some clean rags and an electric drill motor.
14 Hold the block sideways (so that the bores are horizontal rather than vertical) in a vice with soft jaws or cushioned with wooden blocks. Thoroughly lubricate the cylinder walls. Mount the hone in the drill motor, compress the stones and insert the hone into the bore. Turn on the drill and move the hone up and down in the bore at a pace which produces a fine cross-hatch pattern on the cylinder wall with the lines intersecting at an angle of approximately 60°. Be sure to use plenty of lubricant and do not take off any more material than is necessary to produce the desired effect. Do not withdraw the hone from the cylinder while it is still turning. Switch off the drill and continue to move it up and down in the cylinder until it has stopped turning, then compress the stones and withdraw the hone. Wipe the oil from the cylinder and repeat the procedure on the others. Remember, do not take too much material from the cylinder walls.
15 Wash the bores thoroughly with warm soapy water to remove all traces of the abrasive grit produced during the honing operation. Be sure to run a brush through the oil passages and stud holes and flush them with running water. After rinsing, dry the cylinders thoroughly and apply a thin coat of light, rust-preventative oil to all machined surfaces.
16 If you do not have the equipment or desire to perform the honing operation, take the cylinders to a Yamaha dealer or specialist motorcycle repair shop.

Inspection – XJR1300 models

17 The cylinder block is of all-aluminium construction with chrome-composite plating on the cylinder bores. The surface plating has a high resistance to wear and should last the life of the engine.
18 The cylinder block surface can be checked for warpage and the bore surface examined and measured as described above in steps 9 to 12, although any damage or wear can only be rectified by fitting a new cylinder block. Reboring and honing are not possible.

Installation

19 Check that the mating surfaces of the cylinder block and crankcase are free from oil or pieces of old gasket.
20 On XJR1200 models fit a new O-ring around the base of each cylinder.
21 If removed, fit the dowels into the crankcase or into the block, and push them firmly home (see illustration 15.22a).
22 Remove the rags from around the pistons and the cam chain tunnel, taking care not to let the connecting rods fall against the crankcase. Lay the new base gasket in place with the UP mark facing up, locating it over the dowels (if they are in the crankcase) (see illustrations). Never re-use the old gasket,

15.22a Make sure there is a dowel (arrowed) at each front corner, then fit the gasket . . .

15.22b . . . making sure the UP mark reads correctly

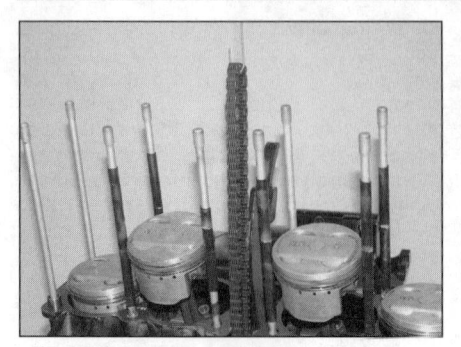

2•26 Engine, clutch and transmission

15.23 Turn the crankshaft so the centre pistons are at their highest point

15.24 Carefully lower the block onto the pistons, keeping the tensioner blade clear

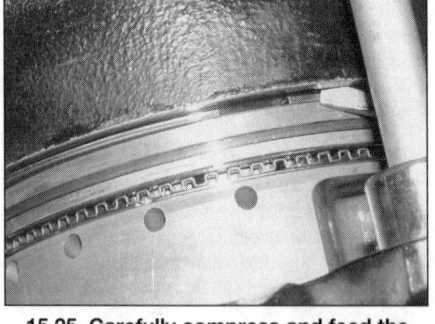

15.25 Carefully compress and feed the rings in using a screwdriver and/or fingernails

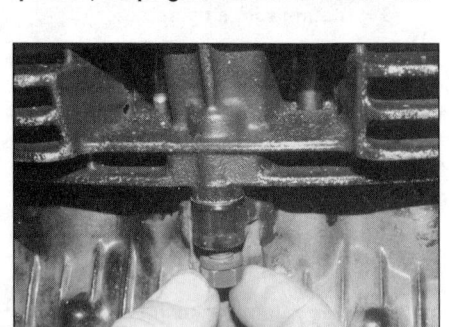

15.28 Fit the nut with its washer

and do not use any gasket sealant. Install the cam chain tensioner blade (see Section 10).
23 Rotate the crankshaft so that the Nos. 2 and 3 pistons are at their highest point (top dead centre) **(see illustration)**. It is useful to place a support under the pistons so that they remain at TDC while the block is fitted, otherwise the downward pressure will turn the crankshaft and the pistons will drop. Lubricate the cylinder bores, pistons and piston rings with clean engine oil. Check that the piston ring end gaps are correctly spaced **(see illustration 17.14)**.
24 Carefully lower the block until the piston crowns fit into the bore, feeding the cam chain up the tunnel as you do **(see illustration)**. You may need to press the tensioner blade in so it doesn't snag the bottom of the block. It is helpful to have an assistant to pass the chain up and slip a piece of wire through it to prevent it falling back into the engine. Keep the chain taut to prevent it becoming disengaged from the crankshaft sprocket.
25 Gently push the cylinder block down, holding the underside of the pistons if you are not using a support to prevent them dropping, and making sure they enter the bore squarely and do not get cocked sideways. Carefully compress and feed each ring into the bore as the cylinder is lowered **(see illustration)** – take care not to break the piston rings. If necessary gently tap the block down, but do not use force if it appears to be stuck as the piston and/or rings will be damaged. Support the block so that its weight does not rest on the piston rings.
26 Lower the block until pistons 1 and 4 enter their bores. If necessary, rotate the crankshaft slightly to raise the pistons, allowing more room to work, but make sure that pistons 2 and 3 do not exit their bores. Fit the pistons and rings into the bores as above.
27 When the piston crown and rings are correctly installed in the bore, remove the support if used then press the cylinder down onto the base gasket, making sure the dowels locate.
28 Fit the cylinder block nut with its washer and tighten it to the torque setting specified at the beginning of the Chapter **(see illustration)**.
29 Holding the cam chain to prevent it bunching, turn the crankshaft and check that the pistons move smoothly in their bores.
30 Install the cylinder head (see Section 12).

16 Pistons – removal, inspection and installation

Note: *The pistons can be removed with the engine in the frame.*

Removal

1 Remove the cylinder block (see Section 15). After the block has been removed, and if not already done, stuff clean rags around the pistons and in the cam chain tunnel to prevent anything falling into the crankcase.
2 Before removing the pistons from the connecting rods, use a sharp scriber or felt marker pen to write the cylinder identity on the crown of each piston (or on the inside of the skirt if the piston is dirty and going to be cleaned). Each piston crown should already have a triangular mark or arrow on the crown that points to the front of the cylinder, though it is likely to be indistinct until the piston is cleaned **(see illustration)**.
3 Work on one piston at a time. Carefully prise out the circlip on one side of the piston using needle-nose pliers or a small flat-bladed screwdriver inserted into the notch **(see illustration)**. Push the piston pin out from the other side to free the piston from the connecting rod **(see illustration)**. Remove the other circlip and discard them both as new ones must be used. When the piston has been removed, slide its pin back into its bore so that related parts do not get mixed up.

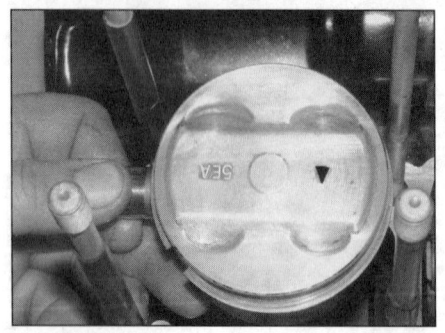

16.2 Note the mark on the piston which must point forwards

16.3a Prise out the circlip ...

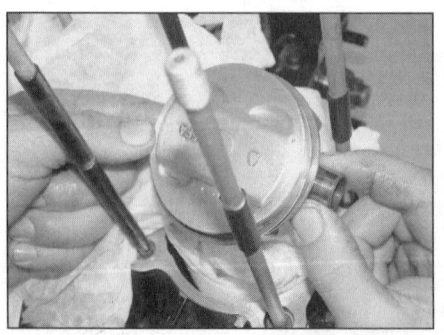

16.3b ... then push out the pin and remove the piston

Engine, clutch and transmission 2•27

> **HAYNES HINT**: If a piston pin is a tight fit in the piston bosses, soak a rag in boiling water then wring it out and wrap it around the piston – this will expand the alloy piston sufficiently to release its grip on the pin. If the piston pin is particularly stubborn, extract it using a drawbolt tool, but be careful to protect the piston's working surfaces.

Inspection

4 Work on one piston at a time. Using your thumbs or a piston ring removal and installation tool, carefully remove the rings from the piston **(see illustration)**. Do not nick or gouge the piston in the process. Carefully note which way up each ring fits and in which groove as they must be installed in their original positions if being re-used. The upper surface of the second (middle) ring should be marked with the letter R at one end, and this mark must face up. There may be a mark on the top ring, which must also face up. The top and middle rings can also be identified by their different profiles and thickness **(see illustration 17.12a)**.

5 Scrape all traces of carbon from the top of the piston. A hand-held wire brush or a piece of fine emery cloth can be used once most of the deposits have been scraped away. Do not, under any circumstances, use a wire brush mounted in a drill motor to remove deposits from the piston; the piston material is soft and will be eroded away by the wire brush.

6 Use a piston ring groove cleaning tool to remove any carbon deposits from the ring grooves. If a tool is not available, a piece broken off an old ring will do the job. Be very careful to remove only the carbon deposits. Do not remove any metal and do not nick or gouge the sides of the ring grooves.

7 Once the deposits have been removed, clean the pistons with solvent and dry them thoroughly. If the cylinder identification previously marked on the piston is cleaned off, be sure to re-mark it with the correct identity. Make sure the oil return holes below the oil ring groove are clear.

8 Carefully inspect the piston for cracks around the skirt, at the pin bosses and at the

16.4 Remove the rings carefully - they break easily

ring lands. Normal piston wear appears as even, vertical wear on the thrust surfaces of the piston and slight looseness of the top ring in its groove. If the skirt is scored or scuffed, the engine may have been suffering from overheating and/or abnormal combustion, which caused excessively high operating temperatures. The oil pump should be checked thoroughly. Also check that the circlip grooves are not damaged.

9 A hole in the piston crown, an extreme to be sure, is an indication that abnormal combustion (pre-ignition) was occurring. Burned areas at the edge of the piston crown are usually evidence of spark knock (detonation). If any of the above problems exist, the causes must be corrected or the damage will occur again.

10 Measure the piston ring-to-groove clearance, either by laying each piston ring in its groove and slipping a feeler gauge in beside it, or by measuring the thickness of the ring and the width of the groove and subtracting one from the other. Make sure you have the correct ring for the groove (see Step 4). Check the clearance at three or four locations around the groove. If the clearance is greater than specified, renew both the piston and rings as a set. If new rings are being used anyway, measure the clearance using the new rings. If the clearance is greater than that specified, the piston is worn and must be renewed.

11 Check the piston-to-bore clearance by measuring the bore (see Section 15) and the piston diameter. Make sure each piston is

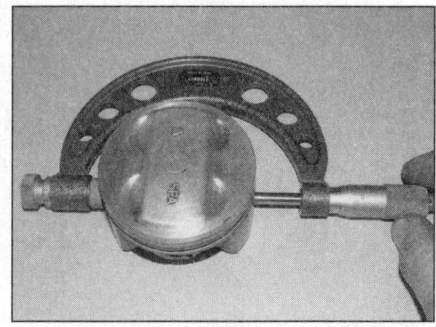

16.11 Measure the piston diameter with a micrometer at the specified distance from the bottom of the skirt

matched to its correct cylinder. Measure the piston the specified distance up from the bottom of the skirt and at 90° to the piston pin axis – refer to the Specifications at the beginning of the Chapter **(see illustration)**. Subtract the piston diameter from the bore diameter to obtain the clearance. If it is greater than the specified figure, and if not already done, check the cylinder for wear (see Section 15). If the cylinder is good but the piston is worn, renew the piston. On XJR1200 models, if the cylinders are worn, oval or tapered beyond the service limit they can be rebored, and an oversize (+ 0.50) set of pistons and rings are available from Yamaha. Note that the person carrying out the rebore must be aware of the piston-to-bore clearance for the oversize piston (see Specifications). On XJR1300 models a new block will have to be fitted – reboring is not possible.

12 Apply clean engine oil to the piston pin, insert it into the piston and check for any freeplay between the two **(see illustration)**. Measure the pin external diameter and the pin bore in the piston **(see illustrations)**. Calculate the difference to obtain the piston pin-to-piston pin bore clearance. Compare the result to the specifications at the beginning of the Chapter. If the clearance is greater than specified, renew the components that are worn beyond their specified limits. If not already done (see Section 30), repeat the measurements between the pin and the connecting rod small-end.

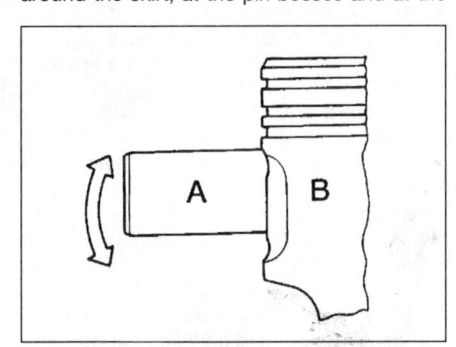

16.12a Slip the pin (A) into the piston (B) and try to rock it back and forth. If it's loose, renew the piston and pin

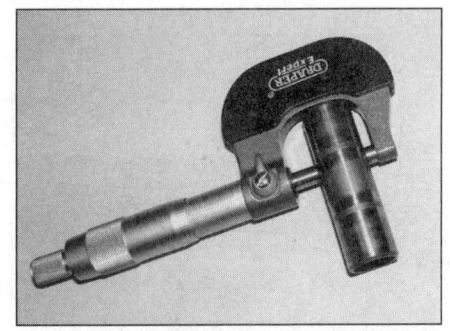

16.12b Measure the external diameter of the pin ...

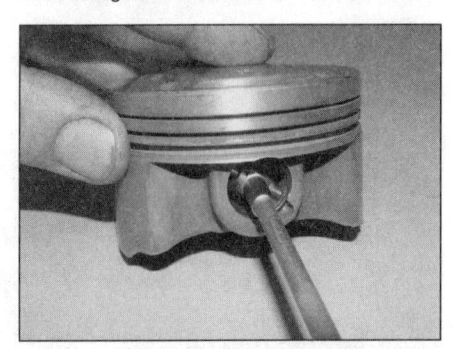

16.12c ... and the internal diameter of the bore in the piston

2•28 Engine, clutch and transmission

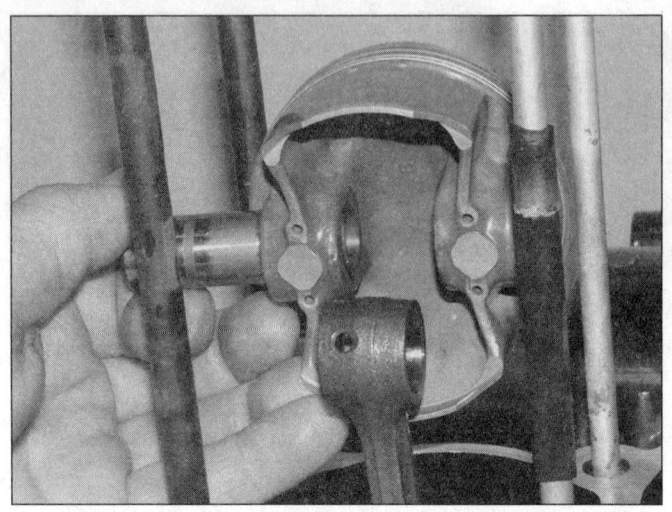

16.16a Align the piston on its rod and slide the pin through

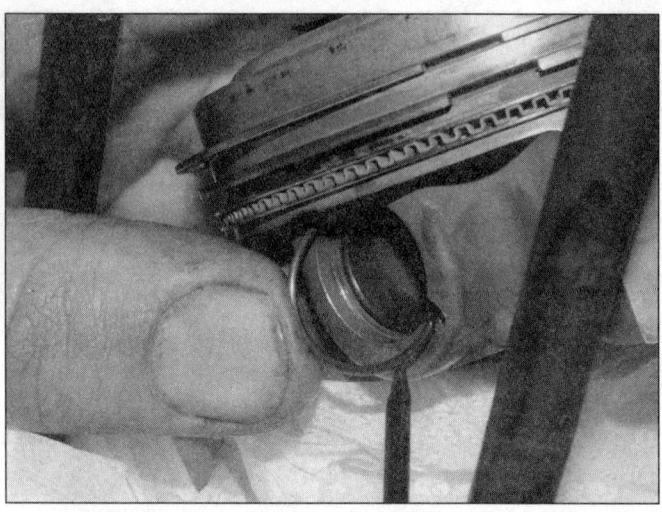

16.16b Do not over-compress the circlip and make sure it seats in the groove

Installation

13 Inspect and install the piston rings (see Section 17).
14 Lubricate the piston pin, the piston pin bore and the connecting rod small-end bore with molybdenum disulphide oil (a 50/50 mixture of molybdenum disulphide grease and clean engine oil).
15 When installing the pistons onto the connecting rods, make sure you have the correct piston for the cylinder being worked on and the arrow on the piston crown points to the front of the engine **(see illustration 16.2)**.
16 Fit a *new* circlip in the side of the piston that faces the centre of the engine – do not re-use old circlips. Line up the piston on its correct connecting rod, and insert the piston pin from the opposite side to the installed circlip **(see illustration)**. Secure the pin with the other *new* circlip **(see illustration)**. When installing the circlips, compress them only just enough to fit them in the piston, and make sure they are properly seated in their grooves with the open end away from the removal notch.
17 Install the cylinder block (see Section 15).

17 Piston rings – inspection and installation

1 If not already done, measure the piston ring-to-groove clearance (see Section 16, Step 10).
2 It is good practice to renew the piston rings when an engine is being overhauled. Before installing the rings (new or old), check the installed end gaps of the top and second (middle) rings and the oil ring side rails as follows.
3 If new rings are being used, lay out each piston with a new ring set and keep them together so the rings will be matched with the same piston and bore during the end gap measurement procedure and engine assembly. If the old rings are being reused, make sure they are matched with their correct piston and cylinder.
4 To measure the installed ring end gap, insert the ring into the top of the bore and square it up with the bore walls by pushing it in with the top of the piston. The ring should be about 20 mm below the top edge of the bore. Slip a feeler gauge between the ends of the ring and measure the gap **(see illustration)**. Compare the measurements to the specifications at the beginning of the Chapter.
5 If the gap is larger or smaller than specified, double check to make sure that you have the correct rings before proceeding.
6 If the gap is too small, the ring ends may come in contact with each other during engine operation, which can cause serious damage.
7 Excess end gap is not critical unless it exceeds the service limit. Again, double-check to make sure you have the correct rings for your engine and check that the bore is not worn (see Section 15).
8 Repeat the procedure for the other rings. Remember to keep the rings, pistons and bores matched up.
9 Once the ring end gaps have been checked, the rings can be installed on the pistons.
10 Install the oil control ring (lowest on the piston) first. It is composed of three separate components, namely the expander and the upper and lower side rails. Slip the expander into the groove, making sure the ends don't overlap, then install the lower side rail **(see illustrations)**. Do not use a piston ring installation tool on the side rails as they may be damaged. Instead, place one end of the side rail into the groove between the expander and the ring land. Hold it firmly in place and slide a finger around the piston while pushing the rail into the groove. Next, install the upper side rail in the same manner **(see illustration)**. Check that the ends of the expander have not overlapped.
11 After the three oil ring components have been installed, check to make sure that both the upper and lower side rails can be turned smoothly in the ring groove.
12 Install the second (middle) ring next – its upper surface should be marked with the letter R at one end. The top and middle rings can also be identified by their different profiles

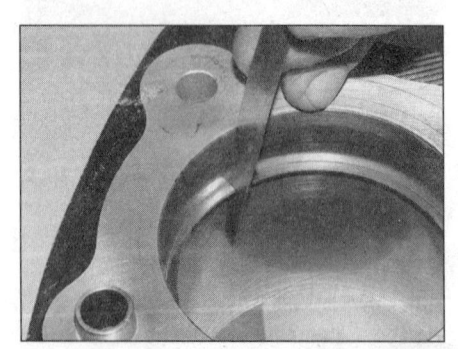

17.4 Measuring piston ring installed end gap

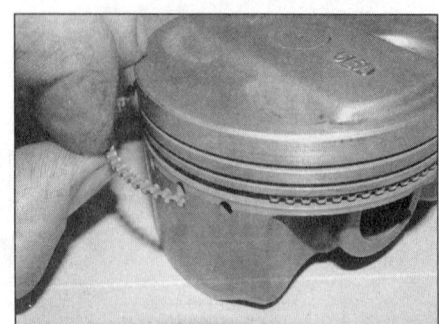

17.10a Install the oil ring expander in its groove . . .

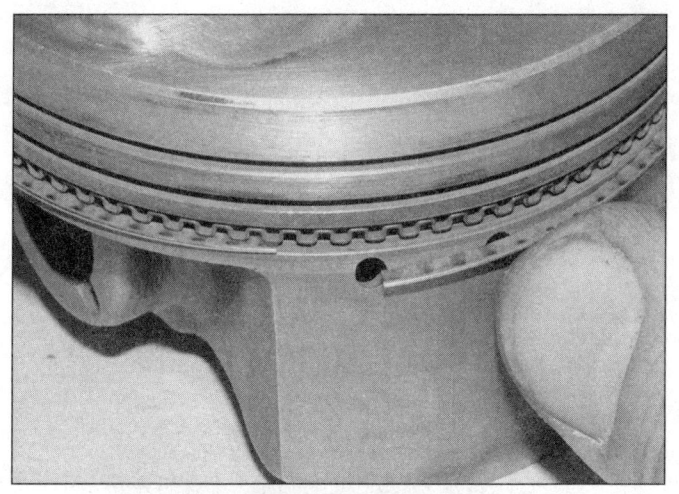

Engine, clutch and transmission 2•29

17.10b ... then fit the lower side rail ...

17.10c ... and the upper side rail

and thickness **(see illustration)**. Make sure that the letter is facing up, and the wider edge is at the bottom, as shown in the illustration of the profile. Fit the second ring into the middle groove in the piston. Do not expand the ring any more than is necessary to slide it into place. To avoid breaking the ring, use a piston ring installation tool, or alternatively a feeler gauge blade can be used as shown **(see illustration)**.

13 Finally, install the top ring in the same manner into the top groove in the piston **(see illustration)**. Make sure any identification mark or letter near the end gap is facing up.

14 Once the rings are correctly installed, check they move freely without snagging and stagger their end gaps as shown **(see illustration)**.

18 Clutch – removal, inspection and installation

Note: *The clutch can be removed with the engine in the frame. If the engine has been removed, ignore the steps which don't apply.*

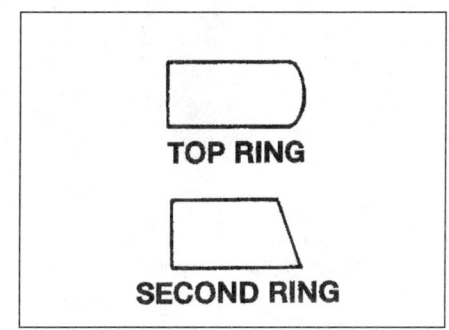

17.12a The rings can be identified by their different profiles

Removal

1 Drain the engine oil (see Chapter 1).
2 Working evenly in a criss-cross pattern, unscrew the clutch cover bolts **(see illustration)**. Remove the cover, being prepared to catch any residual oil.
3 Remove the gasket and discard it. Note the

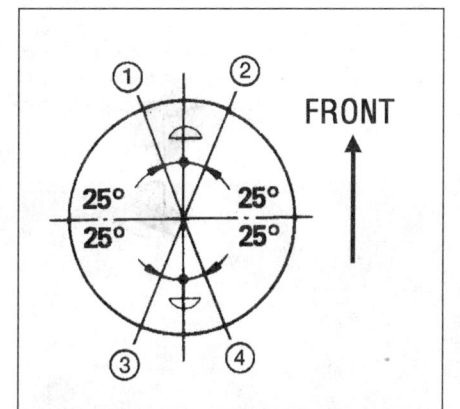

17.14 Stagger the ring end gaps as shown
1 Top ring
2 Oil ring lower side rail
3 Oil ring upper side rail
4 Second (middle) ring

17.12b Old pieces of feeler gauge blade can be used to guide the ring over the piston

positions of the two locating dowels and remove them for safe-keeping if they are loose – they could be in either the cover or the crankcase.

4 Working in a criss-cross pattern, gradually slacken the clutch diaphragm spring retainer bolts until spring pressure is released **(see**

17.13 Finally fit the top ring

18.2 Unscrew the bolts (arrowed) and remove the cover

2•30 Engine, clutch and transmission

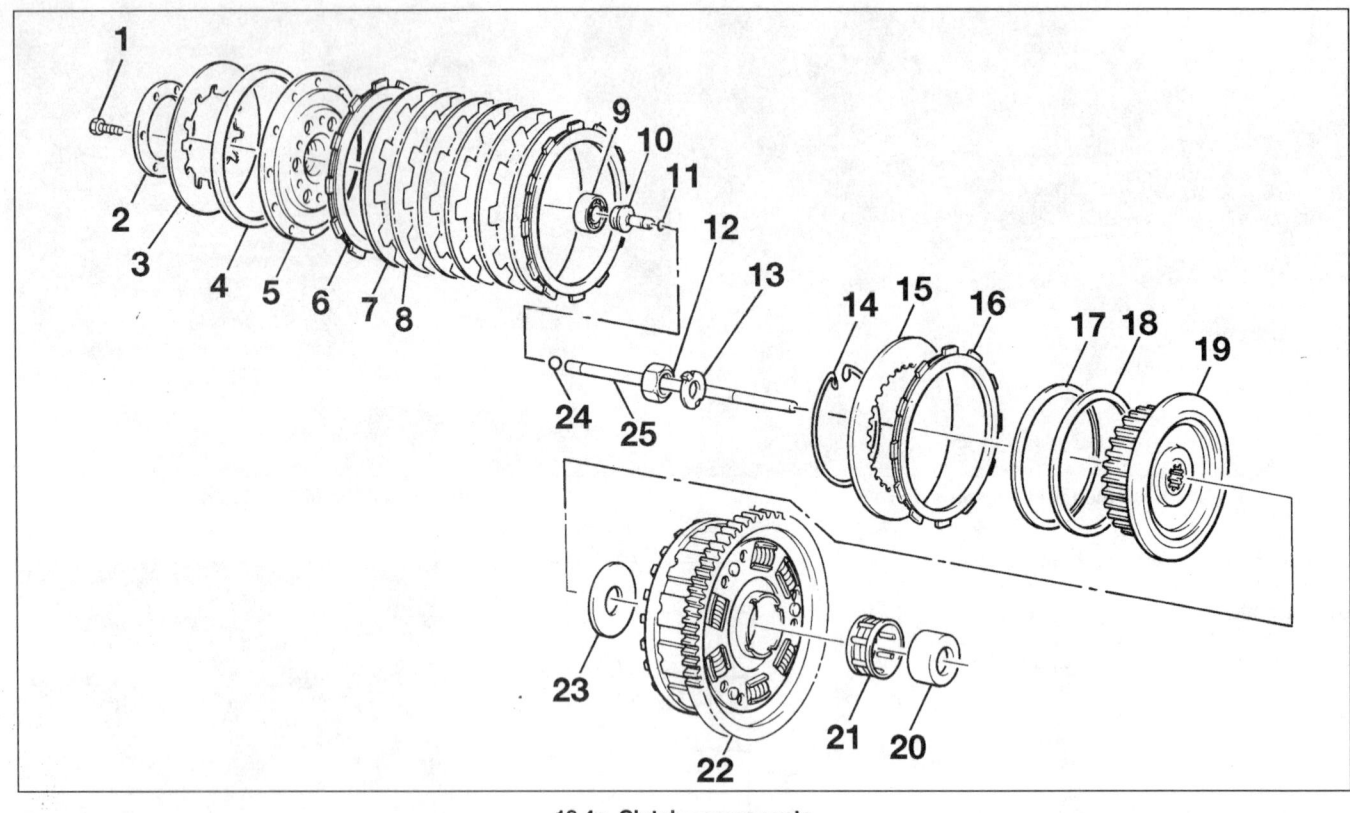

18.4a Clutch components

1 Spring retainer bolts
2 Spring retainer
3 Diaphragm spring
4 Spring seat
5 Pressure plate
6 Narrow friction plate
7 Plain plates
8 Wide friction plates
9 Pressure plate bearing
10 Short pushrod
11 O-ring
12 Clutch nut
13 Lockwasher
14 Wire retainer
15 Plain plate
16 Narrow friction plate
17 Anti-judder spring
18 Spring seat
19 Clutch centre
20 Collar
21 Needle bearing
22 Clutch housing
23 Thrust washer
24 Ball bearing
25 Long pushrod

illustrations). Counter-hold the clutch housing to prevent it turning. Remove the bolts, retainer, diaphragm spring and spring seat, then remove the clutch pressure plate **(see illustrations 18.28e, d, c and b)**.

5 Remove the short pushrod and steel ball **(see illustrations 18.27b and a)**. There is another, longer pushrod behind the steel ball which can be removed for inspection after removing the release cylinder (see Section 20).

6 Grasp the complete set of clutch plates and remove them as a pack **(see illustration)**. Unless the plates are being renewed, keep them in their original order – note that the outermost friction plate has a slightly larger internal diameter to the rest, and must be installed in its correct position. Do not yet remove the inner plain and friction plates that are part of the anti-judder assembly.

7 Bend back the tabs on the clutch nut lockwasher **(see illustration)**. To remove the clutch nut the transmission input shaft must be locked. This can be done in several ways. If the engine is in the frame, engage 5th gear and have an assistant hold the rear brake on hard with the rear tyre in firm contact with the ground. Alternatively, the Yamaha service tool (Pt. No. 90890-04086) can be used to stop the clutch centre from turning whilst the nut is

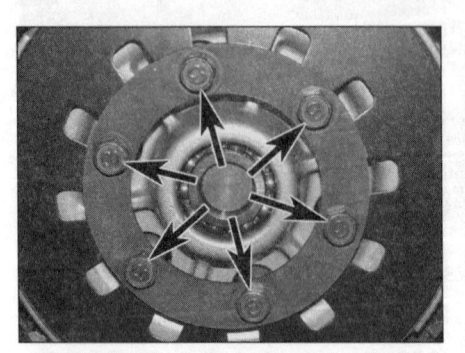

18.4b Diaphragm spring retainer bolts (arrowed)

18.6 Draw off the clutch plates as a pack

18.7a Bend back the lockwasher tabs

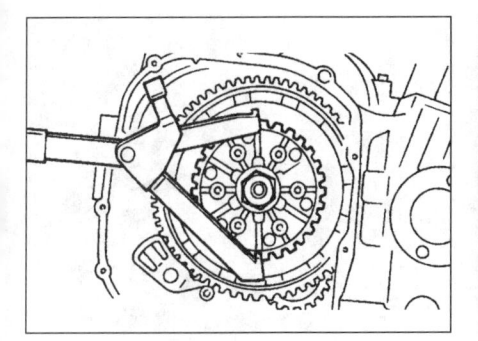

Engine, clutch and transmission 2•31

18.7b Using the Yamaha tool to hold the clutch centre

18.7c Locate the tool on the sprocket and lock it tightly in place . . .

18.7d . . . then unscrew the clutch nut

slackened **(see illustration)**. It is also possible to use a commercially available holding tool, though due to the fact the clutch centre is recessed in the crankcases it must be located on the front sprocket instead as shown **(see illustration)**. It was found that because the tool is short the amount of counter-leverage is small making the tool difficult to hold by hand, so place a block of wood against the engine as a stopper and rest the tool against the wood **(see illustration)**. Unscrew the nut and remove the lockwasher from the input shaft, noting how it fits. Discard the lockwasher as a new one must be used on installation.

8 Slide the clutch centre and the thrust washer off the shaft **(see illustrations 18.25a and 24)**.

9 Slide a pair of 6 mm bolts into the collar in the centre of the clutch housing – clutch cover bolts should work, but if it's stuck, you may need longer bolts for a better grip. Support the clutch housing, then squeeze the bolt ends together so they grip the collar and pull the collar out, then remove the bearing and the clutch housing **(see illustration and 18.23c and b)**.

10 Remove the wire retainer from the clutch centre and slide off the inner plain plate and friction plate, the anti-judder spring and spring seat **(see illustrations 18.21g, d, c, b and a)**. Keep all components in order and the correct way round – note that the friction plate has a slightly larger internal diameter like the

18.9 Use a pair of bolts as described to draw the collar out

outermost plate so it can fit over the anti-judder spring and seat.

11 If required, remove the oil pump drive gear, the collar and the washer **(see illustrations 18.22c, b and a)**. Note the bearing in the sprocket.

Inspection

12 After an extended period of service the clutch friction plates will wear and cause clutch slip. Measure the thickness of each friction plate using a vernier caliper **(see illustration)**. If any plate has worn to or beyond the service limit given in the Specifications at the beginning of the Chapter, the friction plates must be renewed as a set. Also, if any of the plates smell burnt or are glazed, they must be renewed as a set.

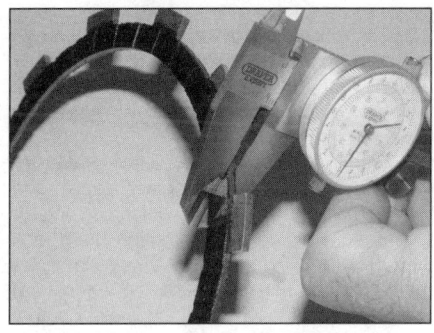

18.12 Measure the clutch friction plate thickness

13 Lay the plain (metal) plates, one at a time, on a perfectly flat surface (such as a piece of plate glass) and check for warpage by trying to slip a gauge between the flat surface and the plate **(see illustration)**. The feeler gauge should be the same thickness as the warpage limit listed in this Chapter's Specifications. Do this at several places around the plate's circumference. If the feeler gauge can be slipped under the plate, it is warped. The plates should not show any signs of excess heating (bluing).

14 Check the clutch diaphragm spring and spring seat for wear, damage or deformation and renew them if necessary. Place the spring on the bench and measure its height at the centre rim **(see illustration)**. If it is less than the minimum specified at the beginning of the

18.13 Check the plain plates for warpage

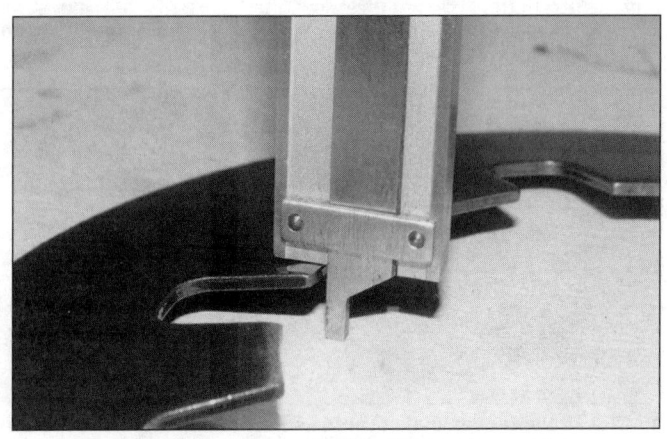

18.14 Measure the free height of the spring as shown

2•32 Engine, clutch and transmission

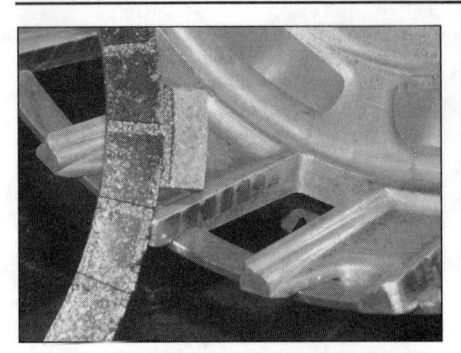

18.15a Check the friction plate tabs and clutch housing slots as described

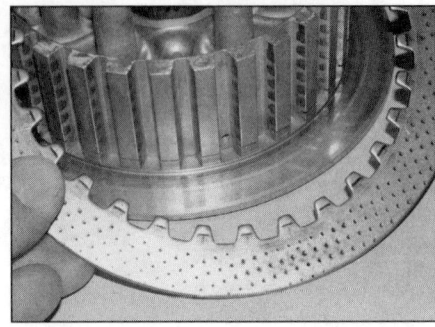

18.15b Check the plain plate tongues and the clutch centre slots as described

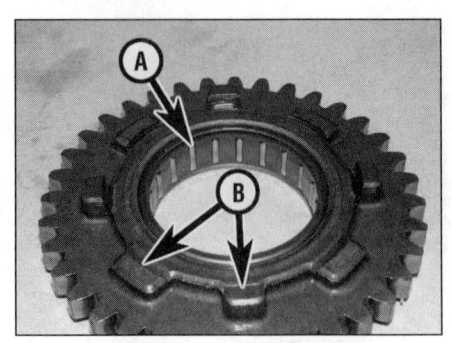

18.16 Check the oil pump drive gear bearing (A) and dogs (B)

Chapter, renew the spring. Check for warpage of the spring using a flat surface and feeler gauges. If it exceeds the maximum permissible amount of warpage, renew the spring.

15 Check the tabs on the friction plates for excessive wear and mushroomed edges, and the edges of the slots in the clutch housing for indentations made by the friction plate tabs **(see illustration)**. If the indentations are deep, the plates and housing should be renewed. If the indentations can be removed easily with a file, the life of the housing can be prolonged to an extent. Similarly check for wear between the inner tongues of the plain plates and the slots in the clutch centre **(see illustration)**. Wear of this nature will cause clutch drag and slow disengagement during gear changes as the plates will snag when the pressure plate is lifted.

16 Inspect the needle roller bearing and the clutch housing's internal bearing surface. If there are any signs of wear, pitting or other damage the affected parts must be renewed. Inspect the slots in the back of the clutch housing and the drive dogs on the oil pump drive gear and renew any worn or damaged parts **(see illustration)**. If you removed the oil pump gear, inspect its bearing and renew it if worn or damaged.

17 Check the pressure plate and its bearing for signs of wear or damage and roughness **(see illustration)**. Renew any parts as necessary.

18 Check the anti-judder spring and seat for wear, damage and deformation. If any is found, or the clutch has been juddering, renew them. Check the plain and friction plates incorporated in the anti-judder assembly as described above. Check the wire retainer ring for deformation.

19 Check the short pushrod and steel ball for wear or damage and renew them if defects are visible. Fit a new O-ring onto the pushrod. If you removed the long pushrod, make sure it isn't bent (roll it on a perfectly flat surface or use V-blocks and a dial gauge).

Installation

20 Remove all traces of old gasket from the crankcase and clutch cover surfaces.

21 Fit the anti-judder spring seat and spring onto the clutch centre, with the OUTSIDE mark on the spring facing out **(see illustrations)**. Fit the innermost friction plate

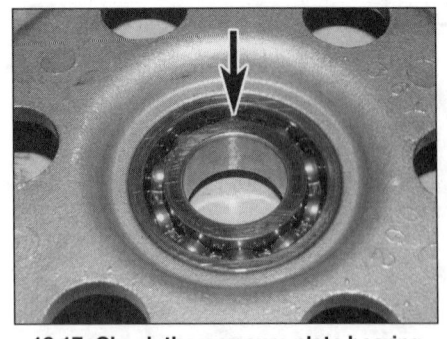

18.17 Check the pressure plate bearing (arrowed)

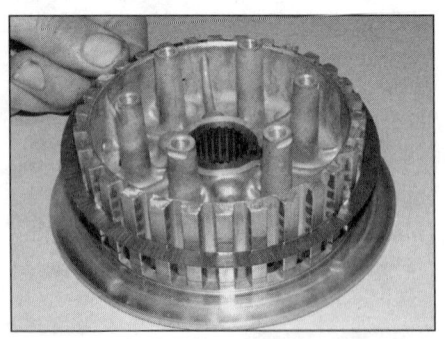

18.21a Lay the spring seat onto the clutch centre . . .

18.21b . . . followed by the anti-judder spring, with the OUTSIDE mark facing out

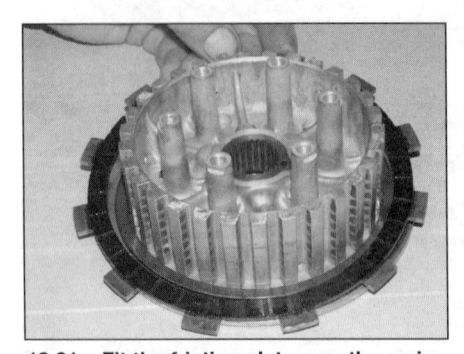

18.21c Fit the friction plate over the spring and seat . . .

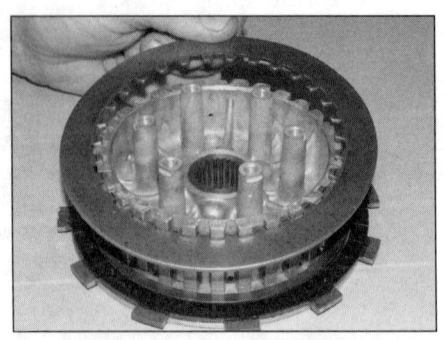

18.21d . . . then fit the plain plate

18.21e Push one end of the wire retainer into the hole . . .

Engine, clutch and transmission 2•33

18.21f ... then feed the retainer round, locating it in the groove ...

18.21g ... and push the other end into the hole

18.22a Slide the washer ...

18.22b ... the collar ...

18.22c ... and the oil pump drive gear onto the shaft

18.23a The dogs must locate in the slots

(identifiable by its larger internal diameter over the spring and spring seat, then fit the plain plate **(see illustrations)**. Secure the assembly with the wire retainer ring, making sure it locates properly in its groove **(see illustrations)**.

22 If removed, slide the washer, collar and the oil pump drive gear onto the shaft, making sure the engagement dogs on the gear are on the outside **(see illustrations)**.

23 Lubricate the clutch housing needle roller bearing with clean engine oil. Install the housing, making sure the primary drive and driven gears engage correctly, and that the dogs on the oil pump drive gear locate into the slots in the back of the housing. Fit the bearing and the collar into the centre of the housing **(see illustrations)**.

24 Lubricate the thrust washer with clean engine oil and fit it onto the shaft **(see illustration)**.

25 Slide the clutch centre onto the shaft splines, then fit the new lockwasher **(see**

18.23b Position the housing over the shaft ...

18.23c ... then fit the bearing and collar into its centre

illustrations). Install the clutch nut and, using the method employed on removal to lock the input shaft (see Step 7), tighten the nut to the torque setting specified at the beginning of

18.24 Slide the thrust washer onto the shaft

18.25a Slide the clutch centre onto the shaft ...

18.25b ... then fit the new lockwasher ...

2

2•34 Engine, clutch and transmission

18.25c ... and the nut

18.25d Tighten the nut to the specified torque setting ...

18.25e ... then bend up the lockwasher tabs

18.26a Fit a friction plate ...

18.26b ... then a plain plate and so on ...

18.26c ... finishing with the narrow friction plate

18.27a Insert the ball bearing ...

the Chapter **(see illustrations)**. **Note:** *Check that the clutch housing rotates freely after tightening.* Bend up the tabs of the lockwasher to secure the nut **(see illustration)**.

26 Coat each plain and friction plate with engine oil prior to installation. Build up the plates as follows: first fit a friction plate, then a plain plate, then alternate friction and plain plates until all are installed, making sure the outermost friction plate with the narrow friction area is on the outside **(see illustrations)**.

27 Fit a new O-ring onto the short pushrod.

Lubricate the steel ball and the short pushrod with molybdenum disulphide oil (a 50/50 mixture of molybdenum disulphide grease and engine oil). Push the steel ball into the shaft then slide the short pushrod in **(see illustrations)**.

28 Lubricate the bearing in the pressure plate with some clean oil **(see illustration 18.17)**. Fit the pressure plate onto the clutch, making sure it seats correctly with its inner rim castellations locating in the slots in the clutch centre – if there is any clearance between the clutch plates as you push on the pressure plate then it has not located properly **(see illustrations)**. Fit

18.27b ... and the short pushrod

18.28a Align the castellations on the plate with the slots in the centre ...

Engine, clutch and transmission 2•35

18.28b ... then fit the pressure plate

18.28c Fit the spring seat ...

18.28d ... the diaphragm spring ...

18.28e ... and the retainer

18.29a Locate the new gasket onto the dowels (arrowed) ...

18.29b ... then install the cover

the spring seat, diaphragm spring and spring retainer **(see illustrations)**. Install the retainer bolts and tighten them evenly and a little at a time in a criss-cross sequence to the specified torque setting **(see illustration 18.4b)**. Counter-hold the clutch housing to prevent it turning when tightening the spring bolts.
29 Fit the dowels into the crankcase, then install the clutch cover using a new gasket and tighten its bolts evenly in a criss-cross sequence to the specified torque setting **(see illustrations)**.
30 Refill the engine with the specified quantity and type of oil (see Chapter 1).

19 Clutch master cylinder – removal, overhaul and installation

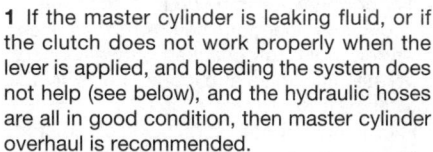

1 If the master cylinder is leaking fluid, or if the clutch does not work properly when the lever is applied, and bleeding the system does not help (see below), and the hydraulic hoses are all in good condition, then master cylinder overhaul is recommended.
2 Before disassembling the master cylinder, read through the entire procedure and make sure that you have the correct rebuild kit **(see illustration)**. Also, you will need some new

DOT 4 hydraulic brake and clutch fluid, some clean rags and internal circlip pliers.
Caution: Brake/clutch fluid will damage paint. To prevent damage from spilled fluid, always cover the fuel tank and any painted surfaces when working on the master cylinder. Wipe up any spills immediately and wash the area with soap and water.
Caution: Disassembly, overhaul and reassembly of the master cylinder must be done in a spotlessly clean work area to avoid contamination and possible failure of the hydraulic system components.

Removal

Note: If the master cylinder is being displaced from the handlebar and not being removed completely or overhauled, follow Steps 4 and 7 only.
3 Support the motorcycle on its centrestand. Slacken the reservoir cover screws, then lightly tighten them again **(see illustration)**.

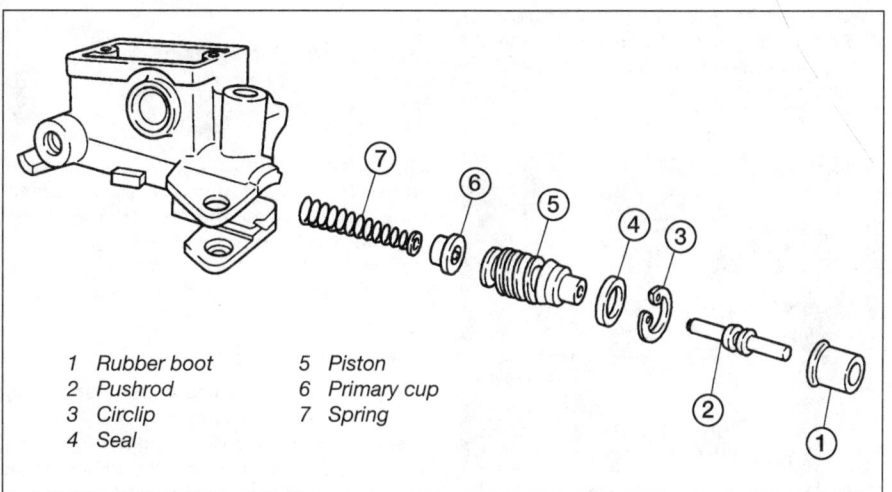

1 Rubber boot
2 Pushrod
3 Circlip
4 Seal
5 Piston
6 Primary cup
7 Spring

19.2 Clutch master cylinder components

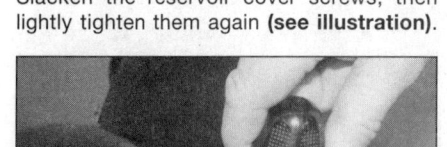

19.3 Slacken the reservoir cover screws

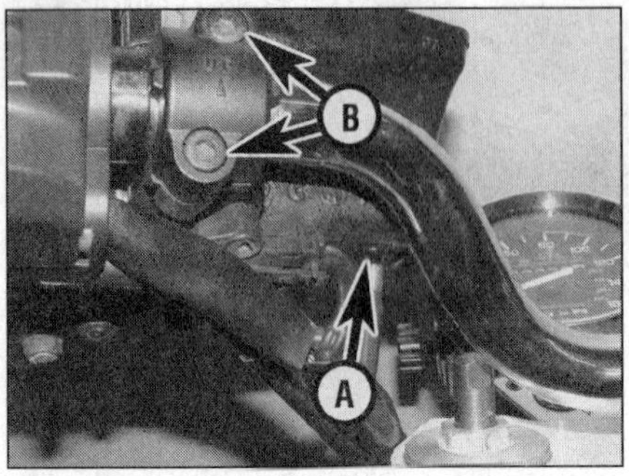

2•36 Engine, clutch and transmission

19.4 Disconnect the clutch switch wiring connector (A). Master cylinder clamp bolts (B)

19.6 Clutch hose banjo bolt (arrowed)

Turn the handlebars as required so that the top of the reservoir is level.

4 Disconnect the clutch switch wiring connector **(see illustration)**. If required, remove the clutch switch (see Chapter 8).

5 If the master cylinder is being overhauled, remove the clutch lever (see Chapter 5). If it is just being displaced it can remain in situ.

6 If the master cylinder is being completely removed or overhauled, unscrew the clutch hose banjo bolt and separate the hose from the master cylinder, noting its alignment **(see illustration)**. Discard the sealing washers as they must be renewed. Either plug the hose using another suitable short piece of hose fitted through the eye of the banjo bolt (it must be a tight fit to seal it properly), clamp it using a hose clamp, or wrap a plastic bag tightly around it to minimise fluid loss and prevent dirt entering the system. If the master cylinder is just being displaced and not completely removed or overhauled, do not disconnect the hose.

7 Unscrew the master cylinder clamp bolts, noting how the UP mark faces up and the top mating surfaces of the clamp align with the punch mark on the handlebar, then lift the master cylinder away **(see illustration 19.4)**.

Overhaul

8 Remove the reservoir cover and lift off the diaphragm plate and the rubber diaphragm. Drain the brake fluid from the reservoir into a suitable container. Wipe any remaining fluid out of the reservoir with a clean rag.

9 Draw the pushrod out of the master cylinder, noting how it locates in the rubber boot – the boot may come away with the pushrod **(see illustration 19.2)**.

10 If it didn't come with the pushrod, remove the rubber boot from the end of the piston in the cylinder.

11 Using circlip pliers, remove the circlip, then slide out the seal, piston, primary cup and spring, noting how they fit. Lay the parts out in the proper order and way round to prevent confusion during reassembly.

12 Clean all parts with clean brake/clutch fluid. If compressed air is available, use it to dry the parts thoroughly (make sure it's filtered and unlubricated).

Caution: Do not, under any circumstances, use a petroleum-based solvent to clean the parts.

13 Check the master cylinder bore for corrosion, scratches, nicks and score marks. If damage or wear is evident, the master cylinder must be renewed. If the master cylinder is in poor condition, then the release cylinder should be checked as well. Check that the fluid inlet and outlet ports in the master cylinder are clear.

14 The dust boot, circlip, seal, piston, primary cup and spring are included in the rebuild kit. Use all of the new parts, regardless of the apparent condition of the old ones. Fit all components according to the layout of the old one. Lubricate the seal, piston and primary cup with clean brake/clutch fluid.

15 Fit the spring into the master cylinder so that its narrow end faces out. Slip the primary cup into the bore and locate it against the spring.

19.19 Align the clamp mating surfaces with the punch mark (arrowed)

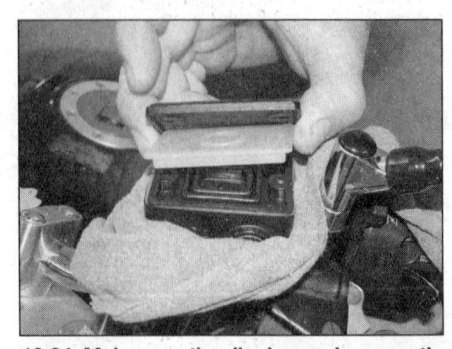

19.24 Make sure the diaphragm is correctly seated before installing the plate and cover

16 Fit the piston into the master cylinder, making sure it is the correct way round. Fit the seal onto the end of the piston. Depress the piston and install the new circlip, making sure that it locates in the groove.

17 Apply silicone grease to the inside of the rubber boot and to the pushrod. Fit the boot over the pushrod, locating the narrow rim of the boot into the groove. Install the pushrod, making sure the wide rim of the boot locates correctly in the groove in the end of the master cylinder.

18 Inspect the reservoir cover rubber diaphragm and renew it if it is damaged or deteriorated.

Installation

19 Locate the master cylinder on the handlebar and fit the clamp with its UP mark facing up, aligning the top mating surfaces of the clamp with the punch mark on the handlebar **(see illustration)**. Tighten the upper bolt first, then the lower bolt, to the torque setting specified at the beginning of the Chapter.

20 If detached, connect the clutch hose to the master cylinder, using new sealing washers on each side of the union, and aligning the hose as noted on removal **(see illustration 19.6)**. Tighten the banjo bolt to the specified torque setting.

21 If removed, install the clutch switch (see Chapter 8). Otherwise, connect the clutch switch wiring connector.

22 If removed, install the clutch lever (see Chapter 5).

23 Fill the fluid reservoir with new DOT 4 brake/clutch fluid as described in *Daily (pre-ride) checks*. Bleed the air from the system (see Section 21).

24 Fit the rubber diaphragm, making sure it is correctly seated, the diaphragm plate and the cover onto the master cylinder reservoir, and tighten the cover screws securely but not overtight **(see illustration)**.

25 Check the operation of the clutch before riding the motorcycle.

20 Clutch release cylinder – removal, overhaul and installation

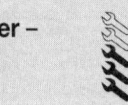

Caution: Brake/clutch fluid will damage paint. To prevent damage from spilled fluid, always cover the fuel tank and any painted surfaces when working on the master cylinder. Wipe up any spills immediately and wash the area with soap and water.

Removal

1 If the release cylinder is just being displaced and not completely removed or overhauled, do not disconnect the clutch hose. Otherwise, unscrew the clutch hose banjo bolt and separate the hose from the release cylinder, noting its alignment, and the

Engine, clutch and transmission 2•37

spacer that fits between the hose union and the release cylinder (see illustration). Discard the three sealing washers as new ones must be used on installation. Either plug the hose using another suitable short piece of hose fitted through the eye of the banjo bolt (it must be a tight fit to seal it properly), clamp it using a hose clamp, or wrap a plastic bag tightly around to minimise fluid loss and prevent dirt entering the system. **Note:** *If you're planning to overhaul the release cylinder and don't have a source of compressed air to blow out the piston, just loosen the banjo bolt at this stage and retighten it lightly. The hydraulic system can then be used to force the piston out of the body once the cylinder has been unbolted. Disconnect the hose once the piston has been sufficiently displaced.*

2 Unscrew the three bolts securing the release cylinder and remove it (see illustration 20.1). If required, withdraw the pushrod, noting which way round it fits (see illustration). Do not operate the clutch lever with the release cylinder removed.

> **HAYNES HiNT** *If the release cylinder is not being disassembled, wrap some cable ties around the piston and through the mounting bolt holes to prevent the piston creeping out, or from being displaced should the lever be accidentally pulled in.*

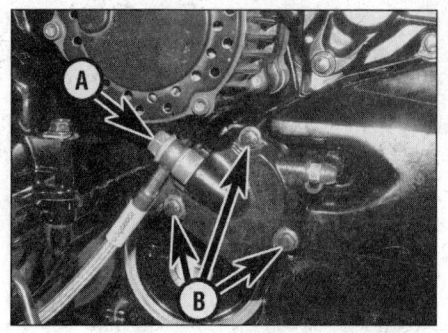

Overhaul

3 Remove the dust seal from the release cylinder (see illustration). Discard it as a new one must be used.

⚠ **Warning:** *Use only low air pressure, otherwise the piston may be forcibly expelled and cause damage or injury. Wrap the cylinder in a rag before applying the air.*

4 Have a supply of clean rags on hand, then pump the clutch lever to expel the piston under hydraulic pressure. If the hose has already been detached, use a jet of compressed air directed into the fluid inlet to expel the piston.

5 Separate the spring from the piston, noting how it fits, or withdraw it from the cylinder if it

20.1 Clutch hose banjo bolt (A), release cylinder bolts (B)

20.2 Withdraw the pushrod, noting which way round it fits

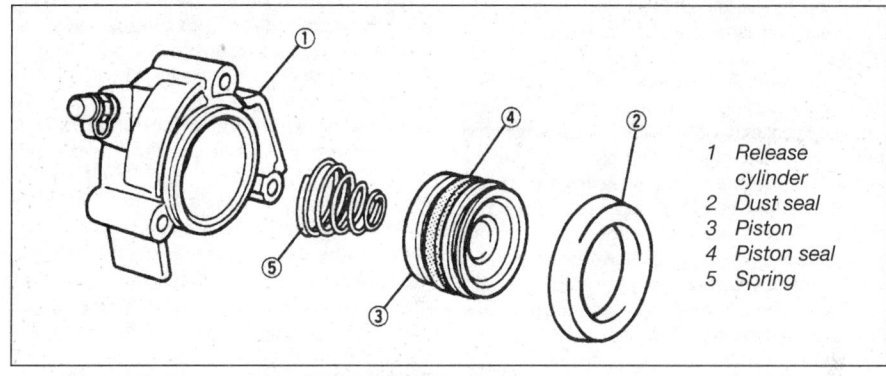

20.3 Clutch release cylinder components

1 Release cylinder
2 Dust seal
3 Piston
4 Piston seal
5 Spring

is still in there. Using a plastic or wooden tool, remove the piston seal from the groove in the piston, noting which way round it fits. Discard it as a new one must be used.

6 Clean the piston and release cylinder bore with clean hydraulic fluid.

Caution: *Do not, under any circumstances, use a petroleum-based solvent to clean hydraulic parts.*

7 Inspect the piston and release cylinder bore for signs of corrosion, nicks and burrs and loss of plating. If surface defects are found, a new piston and cylinder should be fitted. If the release cylinder is in poor condition the master cylinder should also be overhauled (see Section 19).

8 Check that the pushrod is straight by rolling it on a flat surface – if it is bent, fit a new pushrod. Remove the front sprocket cover (see Chapter 5, Section 16) and check the

pushrod oil seal in the crankcase for signs of leakage. Fit a new seal if necessary – lever out the old seal with a flat bladed screwdriver and press or drive the new one into place (see illustration). Install the front sprocket cover.

9 Lubricate the new piston seal with clean hydraulic fluid and fit it into the groove in the piston. Fit the narrow end of the spring over the lug on the inner end of the piston. Lubricate the piston and seal with clean hydraulic fluid and insert the assembly squarely into the cylinder, making sure the spring stays in place on the piston and the rim of the seal does not turn inside out. Use your thumbs to press it fully in.

10 Fit a new dust seal onto the release cylinder.

Installation

11 If removed, lubricate the pushrod with molybdenum disulphide oil (a 50/50 mixture of molybdenum disulphide grease and engine oil). Note the differences in the end sections of the clutch pushrod – the longer end section faces the left-hand side of the engine (towards the release mechanism), the shorter end section faces the right-hand side (towards the clutch). Slide the pushrod through the sprocket cover and into the engine. Wipe the outer end of the pushrod clean and smear some silicon grease onto it.

12 Remove the cable ties from the release cylinder if used, then install the cylinder and tighten the bolts to the torque setting specified at the beginning of the Chapter (see illustration).

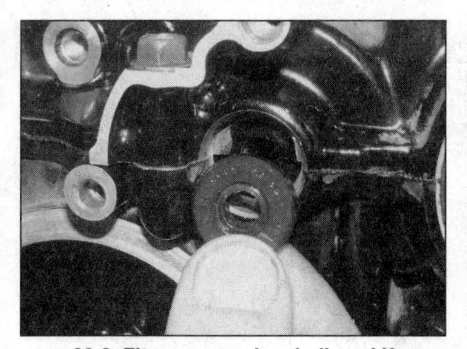

20.8 Fit a new pushrod oil seal if necessary

20.12 Install the release cylinder and tighten the bolts to the specified torque

2•38 Engine, clutch and transmission

21.5 Clutch release cylinder bleed valve (arrowed)

13 If the hydraulic hose was disconnected, fit a new sealing washer onto the banjo bolt, then fit the bolt through the hose union, fit another sealing washer, fit the spacer onto the bolt, then fit another sealing washer and thread the bolt into the release cylinder. Align the hose as noted on removal and tighten the banjo bolt to the specified torque setting **(see illustration 20.1)**.
14 Slacken the master cylinder reservoir cover screws, then remove the cover, diaphragm plate and diaphragm **(see illustration 19.3)**. Fill the reservoir with new hydraulic fluid (see *Daily (pre-ride) checks*) and bleed the system (see Section 21). Check for fluid leaks.
15 Fit the rubber diaphragm, making sure it is correctly seated, the diaphragm plate and the cover onto the master cylinder reservoir, and tighten the cover screws securely but not overtight **(see illustration 19.24)**.
16 Check the operation of the clutch before riding the motorcycle.

21 Clutch hydraulic release system – bleeding and fluid renewal

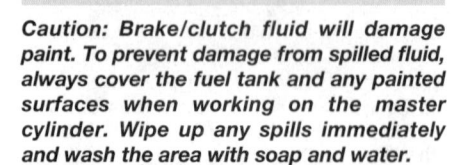

Caution: Brake/clutch fluid will damage paint. To prevent damage from spilled fluid, always cover the fuel tank and any painted surfaces when working on the master cylinder. Wipe up any spills immediately and wash the area with soap and water.

Bleeding air from the system

1 Bleeding the clutch is simply the process of removing all the air bubbles from the master cylinder, the hydraulic hose and the release cylinder. Bleeding is necessary whenever a clutch system hydraulic connection is loosened, when a component or hose is renewed, or when the master cylinder or release cylinder is overhauled. A leak in the system may also allow air to enter, but leaking clutch fluid will reveal its presence and warn you of the need for repair.
2 To bleed the clutch, you will need some new DOT 4 brake/clutch fluid, a length of clear vinyl or plastic tubing, a small container partially filled with clean fluid, a supply of clean rags and a spanner to fit the bleed valve. Note that there are commercially available bleeding kits of various sorts that enable the job to be done much more easily than the manual method described. When using such a tool, follow the manufacturer's instructions.
3 Cover the fuel tank and other painted components to prevent damage in the event that fluid is spilled.
4 Support the motorcycle on its centrestand, and turn the handlebars as required so that the top of the reservoir is level. Undo the reservoir cover screws and remove the cover, diaphragm plate and diaphragm **(see illustration 19.3)**. Slowly pump the clutch lever a few times until no air bubbles can be seen floating up from the bottom of the reservoir. Doing this bleeds air from the master cylinder end of the hose.
Caution: Do not pump the lever too quickly as fluid could spurt out of the reservoir and onto a painted component.
5 Pull the dust cap off the bleed valve on the release cylinder and attach one end of the clear tubing to the valve **(see illustration)**. Submerge the other end in the fluid in the container. Check the fluid level in the reservoir. Do not allow it to drop below the lower mark during the bleeding process.
6 Pump the clutch lever slowly three or four times and hold it in against the handlebar, then open the bleed valve. When the valve is opened, fluid will flow out of the release cylinder into the clear tubing.
7 When the fluid stops flowing, tighten the bleed valve, then release the lever gradually. Repeat the process until no air bubbles are visible in the fluid leaving the release cylinder and the clutch action feels smooth and progressive. On completion, tighten the bleed valve to the torque setting specified at the beginning of the Chapter.
8 Ensure that the reservoir level is above the lower mark (do not overfill), then fit the rubber diaphragm, making sure it is correctly seated, the diaphragm plate and the cover onto the master cylinder reservoir, and tighten the cover screws securely but not overtight **(see illustration 19.24)**. Wipe up any spilled fluid and check that there are no leaks from the system when activated. Refit the dust cap over the bleed valve.
9 Top-up the reservoir, install the diaphragm, diaphragm plate and cover, and wipe up any spilled brake fluid (see *Daily (pre-ride) checks*). Check the entire system for fluid leaks.
10 Check the operation of the clutch before riding the motorcycle.

Fluid renewal

11 Changing the clutch fluid is a similar process to bleeding and requires the same materials plus a suitable tool for siphoning the fluid out of the hydraulic reservoir. Also ensure that the container is large enough to take all the old fluid when it is flushed out of the system.
12 Cover the fuel tank, front mudguard and other painted components to prevent damage in the event that fluid is spilled.
13 Pull the dust cap off the bleed valve **(see illustration 21.5)**. Attach one end of the clear vinyl or plastic tubing to the bleed valve and submerge the other end in the fluid in the container.
14 Remove the reservoir cover, diaphragm plate and diaphragm **(see illustration 19.3)** and siphon the old fluid out of the reservoir. Fill the reservoir with new DOT 4 fluid.
15 Pump the clutch lever slowly three or four times and hold it in against the handlebar, then open the bleed valve. When the valve is opened, fluid will flow out of the release cylinder into the clear tubing.
16 When the fluid stops flowing, tighten the bleed valve, then release the lever gradually. Repeat the process until the new clean fluid can be seen emerging and no air bubbles are visible in the fluid. On completion, tighten the bleed valve to the torque setting specified at the beginning of the Chapter.

> **HAYNES HINT** *Old brake fluid is invariably much darker in colour than new fluid, making it easy to see when all old fluid has been expelled from the system.*

17 Disconnect the hose, then tighten the bleed valve to the specified torque setting and install the dust cap.
18 Top-up the reservoir, install the diaphragm, diaphragm plate and cover, and wipe up any spilled brake fluid (see *Daily (pre-ride) checks*). Check the entire system for fluid leaks.
19 Check the operation of the clutch before riding the motorcycle.

22 Gearchange mechanism – removal, inspection and installation

Note: The gearchange mechanism can be removed with the engine in the frame. If the engine has been removed, ignore the steps which don't apply.

Removal

1 Make sure the transmission is in neutral. Drain the engine oil (see Chapter 1). Remove the clutch (see Section 18).
2 Unscrew the gearchange lever linkage arm pinch bolt and slide the arm off the shaft, noting how the punch mark on the shaft aligns with that on the arm **(see illustration)**. If no

22.2 Unscrew the bolt and slide the arm off the shaft, noting the alignment punch marks

Engine, clutch and transmission 2•39

22.4 Remove the E-clip and slide the washer off the shaft

22.5 Unscrew the bolts (arrowed) and remove the plate

mark is visible, make your own before removing the arm so that it can be correctly aligned with the shaft on installation.

3 Remove the front sprocket cover (see Chapter 5, Section 16).

4 Remove the E-clip and washer from the left-hand end of the gearchange shaft **(see illustration)**.

5 Unscrew the bolts securing the oil baffle plate and remove the plate **(see illustration)**.

6 Note how the gearchange shaft centralising spring ends fit on each side of the locating pin in the crankcase, and how the pawls on the selector arm locate onto the pins on the end of the selector drum. Grasp the end of the shaft and withdraw the shaft/arm assembly **(see illustration)**. Note that there is a washer that fits between the centralising spring spacer and the crankcase – this may well stick to the crankcase, so if it is not on the shaft retrieve it and slide it back on.

7 Note how the stopper arm spring ends locate and how the roller on the arm locates in

22.6 Withdraw the shaft from the engine, noting the washer (arrowed)

the neutral detent on the selector drum. Unscrew the bolt and remove the stopper arm and spring **(see illustration)**.

Inspection

8 Check the selector arm for cracks, distortion and wear of its pawls, and check for

22.7 Unscrew the stopper arm bolt and remove the arm and spring

any corresponding wear on the selector pins on the selector drum **(see illustration)**. Also check the stopper arm roller and the detents in the selector drum for any wear or damage, and make sure the roller turns freely **(see illustration)**. Renew any components that are worn or damaged.

22.8a Check the selector arm and shaft assembly . . .

22.8b . . . and the stopper arm assembly as described

2•40 Engine, clutch and transmission

22.11a Lever out the old seal . . .

22.11b . . . and press the new one in

22.11c Renew the outer seal . . .

9 Inspect the shaft centralising spring and the stopper arm return spring for fatigue, wear or damage. If any faults are found, renew the components. Slide the centralising spring off the shaft, noting the collar. Also check that the centralising spring locating pin in the crankcase is securely tightened. If it is loose, remove it and apply a non-permanent thread locking compound to its threads, then tighten it to the torque setting specified at the beginning of the Chapter.
10 Check the gearchange shaft/arm assembly for distortion and damage to the splines. If the assembly is bent you can attempt to straighten it, but if the splines are damaged it must be renewed.
11 Check the condition of the shaft oil seal in the crankcase – if it is damaged, deteriorated or shows signs of leakage it must be renewed.

Lever out the old seal with a flat bladed screwdriver, and press or drive the new one in, with its lip facing inward, using a suitable socket **(see illustrations)**. Also check the seals and bearing in the sprocket cover **(see illustrations)**. If the bearing is damaged or does not run smoothly and freely, it must be renewed – refer to *Tools and Workshop Tips* in the Reference Section for information on bearing checks, removal and installation methods.

Installation

12 Fit the stopper arm bolt through the stopper arm, then fit the return spring **(see illustration 22.8b)**. Apply threadlock to the threads of the bolt. Install the assembly onto the crankcase, making sure the spring ends locate correctly over the stopper arm and against the crankcase, and partially tighten the bolt. Press the stopper arm down, then

fully tighten the bolt, locating the roller onto the neutral detent in the cam as they become aligned **(see illustration 22.7)**. Tighten the bolt to the specified torque setting. Afterwards make sure the arm is free to move and is returned by the pressure of the spring.
13 Make sure the centralising spring ends are correctly positioned on the selector arm and that the washer is on the shaft **(see illustration 22.8a)**. Slide the shaft/arm assembly into place, locating the selector arm pawls onto the pins on the selector drum and the centralising spring ends onto each side of the locating pin **(see illustrations)**.
14 Install the oil baffle plate **(see illustration 22.5)**.
15 Fit the washer and E-clip onto the left-hand end of the shaft, making sure the E-clip locates in its groove **(see illustrations)**.

22.11d . . . and the inner seal (arrowed) in the sprocket cover . . .

22.11e . . . and check the bearing

22.13a Slide the shaft into place as shown

22.13b The installed assembly should be as shown

22.15a Slide the washer onto the shaft . . .

22.15b . . . then fit the E-clip

Engine, clutch and transmission 2•41

16 Install the front sprocket cover (see Chapter 5).
17 Slide the gearchange lever linkage arm onto the shaft, aligning the punch marks **(see illustration 22.2)**. Tighten the pinch bolt securely.
18 Install the clutch (see Section 18).
19 Fill the engine with the specified quantity and type of new engine oil (see Chapter 1).

23 Oil pump – check, removal, inspection and installation

Note: *The oil pump can be removed with the engine in the frame. If the engine has been removed, ignore the steps which don't apply.*

Check

1 Perform an oil pressure check (see Chapter 1). If the pressure is as specified at the beginning of the Chapter then the pump is good. If the pressure is lower than it should be, and all other possible causes (as listed in Chapter 1) have been eliminated, then the pump is probably worn or faulty – remove the pump and inspect it as described below. If the pump itself is proved faulty, it must be renewed as no individual components are available.

Removal

2 Drain the engine oil (see Chapter 1).
3 Remove the clutch (see Section 18).
4 Unscrew the bolts securing the oil baffle plate and remove the plate **(see illustration 22.5)**.
5 Remove the circlip securing the oil pump driven gear, then remove the gear and the washer **(see illustrations)**.
6 Note how the arrow on the pump outer cover aligns with that on the crankcase. Unscrew the bolts securing the oil pump to the crankcase and remove the pump **(see illustration)**. Retrieve the collar and the three

23.5a Remove the circlip . . .

23.5b . . . then slide the gear off the shaft . . .

23.5c . . . and remove the washer

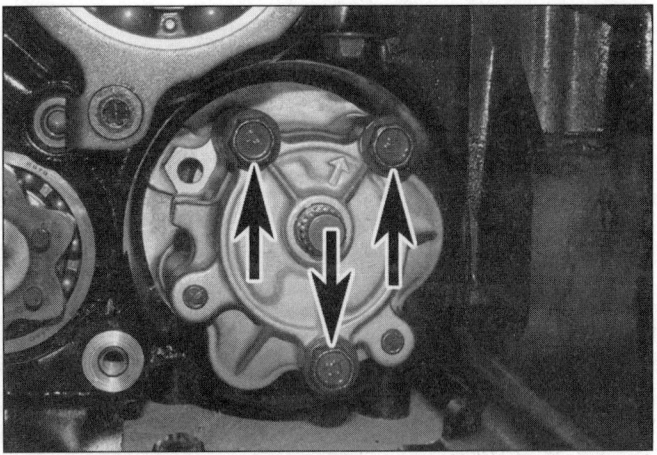

23.6a Unscrew the bolts (arrowed) and remove the pump

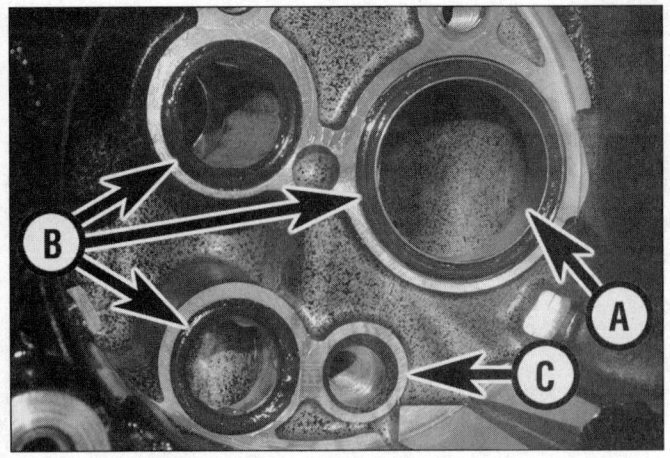

23.6b Remove the collar (A), O-rings (B), and the dowel from the crankcase (C) . . .

23.6c . . . or from the pump, as necessary

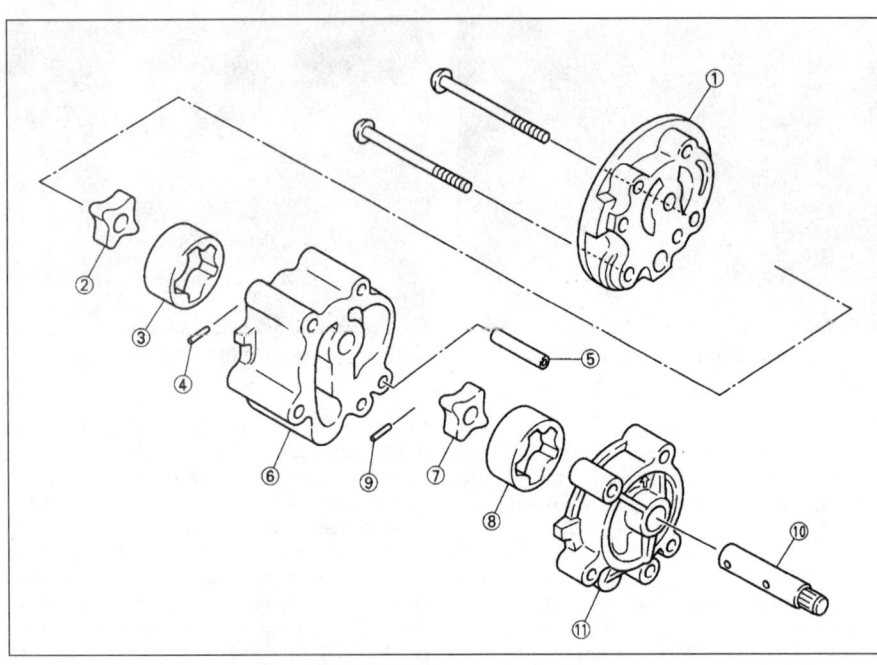

2•42 Engine, clutch and transmission

23.7 Oil pump components

1 Inner cover
2 Inner rotor (inner circuit)
3 Outer rotor (inner circuit)
4 Inner drive pin
5 Long dowel
6 Pump body
7 Inner rotor (outer circuit)
8 Outer rotor (outer circuit)
9 Outer drive pin
10 Drive shaft
11 Outer cover

O-rings, and the dowel if it is not in the pump **(see illustration)**. Discard the O-rings as new ones must be used.

Inspection

7 If required, the pump can be disassembled for cleaning and inspection **(see illustration)**.

Undo the two screws securing the end covers to the pump body **(see illustration 23.15l)**. Remove the outer cover, then remove the outer and inner rotors, noting which way round they fit and how the inner rotor cutouts locate over the drive pin ends. Remove the outer drive pin. Remove the inner cover and the long dowel. Push the drive shaft through the body and withdraw it, then remove the drive pin. Remove the inner and outer rotors from the pump body, again noting how they fit. Keep all components in order so related rotors are returned to the same side of the pump the same way round.

8 Clean all components in solvent.

9 Inspect the pump housing, covers and rotors for damage, scoring and wear. If any is evident, renew the pump.

10 Fit the rotors from the outer circuit into the outer cover and the rotors from the inner circuit into the pump body.

11 Measure the clearance between the outer rotor and the cover/body with a feeler gauge and compare it to the maximum clearance listed in the specifications at the beginning of the Chapter **(see illustration)**. If the clearance measured is greater than the maximum listed, renew the pump.

12 Measure the clearance between the inner rotor tip and the outer rotor with a feeler gauge and compare it to the maximum clearance listed in the specifications at the beginning of the Chapter **(see illustration)**. If the clearance measured is greater than the maximum listed, renew the pump.

13 Lay a straight-edge across the rotors and the pump cover/body and, using a feeler gauge, measure the rotor end-float (the gap between the rotors and the straight-edge **(see illustration)**. If the clearance measured is greater than the maximum listed, renew the pump.

14 Check the pump drive and driven gears for wear or damage, and renew them if necessary.

15 If the pump is good, make sure all the components are clean, then lubricate them with new engine oil. Fit the inner circuit outer rotor into the pump body, then fit the inner rotor into the outer rotor, with the cutouts facing out **(see illustrations)**. Slide the driveshaft into the body, then fit the inner

23.11 Measuring outer rotor to cover or body clearance

23.12 Measuring inner rotor tip to outer rotor clearance

23.13 Measuring rotor end-float

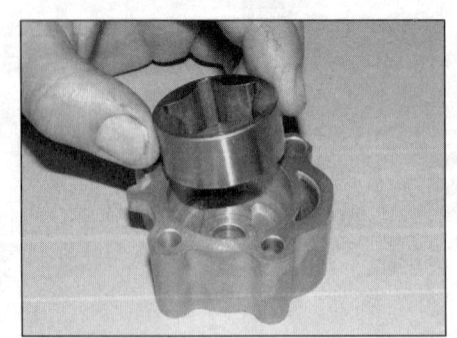

23.15a Fit the outer rotor . . .

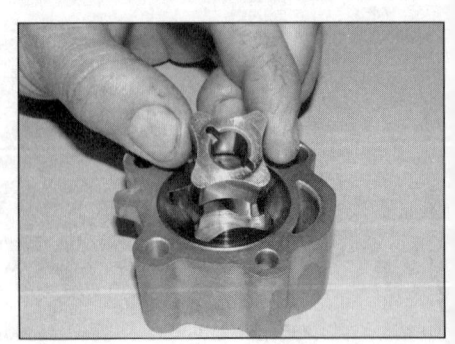

23.15b . . . and the inner rotor, with the cutouts facing out

Engine, clutch and transmission 2•43

23.15c Slide the drive shaft through . . .

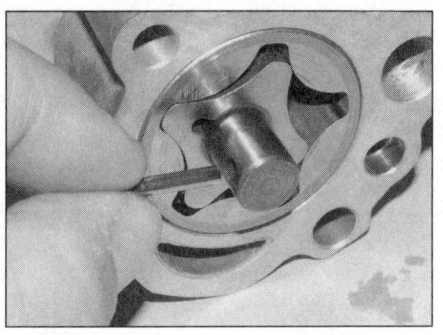

23.15d . . . then fit the drive pin . . .

23.15e . . . and locate it in the inner rotor

23.15f Fit the long dowel . . .

23.15g . . . and the inner cover

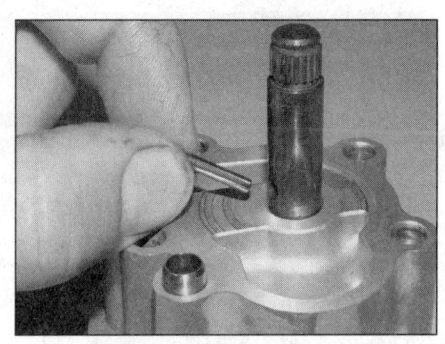

23.15h Fit the drive pin . . .

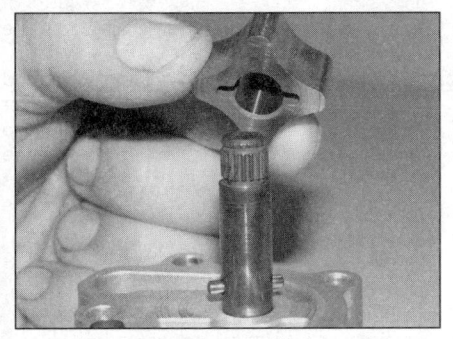

23.15i . . . then locate the inner rotor onto it . . .

23.15j . . . and fit the outer rotor over the inner rotor

23.15k Fit the outer cover . . .

23.15l . . . and secure the assembly together with the screws

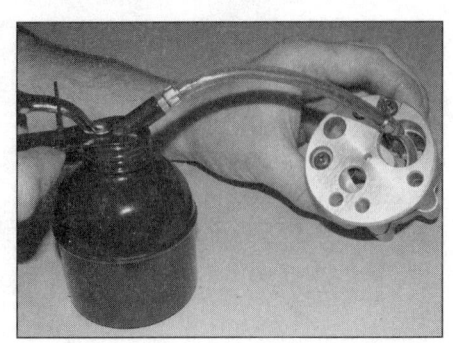

23.17 Prime the pump with oil

drive pin through the shaft and locate its ends into the cutouts in the inner rotor **(see illustrations)**. Fit the long dowel through the body, then fit the inner cover onto the body, making sure the dowel locates correctly **(see illustrations)**. Fit the outer circuit drive pin into the shaft, then fit the inner rotor, locating the cutouts over the drive pin ends **(see illustrations)**. Fit the outer rotor over the inner rotor **(see illustration)**. Fit the outer cover onto the body, then install the screws and tighten them to the torque setting specified at the beginning of the Chapter **(see illustrations)**.

16 Rotate the pump shaft by hand and check that the rotors turn smoothly and freely. If not, recheck the pump.

Installation

17 Before installing the pump, prime it by filling it with clean engine oil and rotating it a few times **(see illustration)**.

18 Fit the dowel into the pump **(see illustration 23.6c)**. Fit the collar into the

2•44 Engine, clutch and transmission

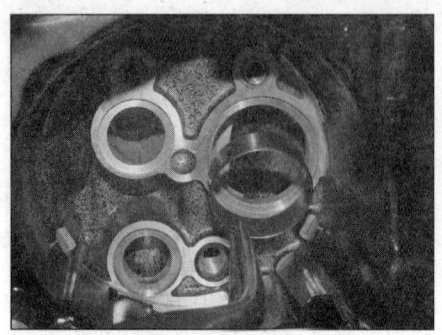

23.18 Fit the collar into its bore

23.19 Install the pump, aligning the arrow with that on the crankcase

24.2 Disconnect the wiring at the bullet connector (arrowed)

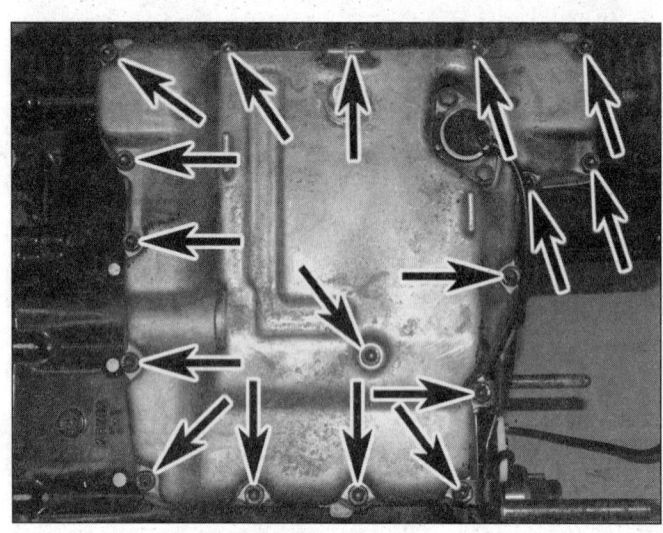

24.3a Unscrew the sump bolts (arrowed) . . .

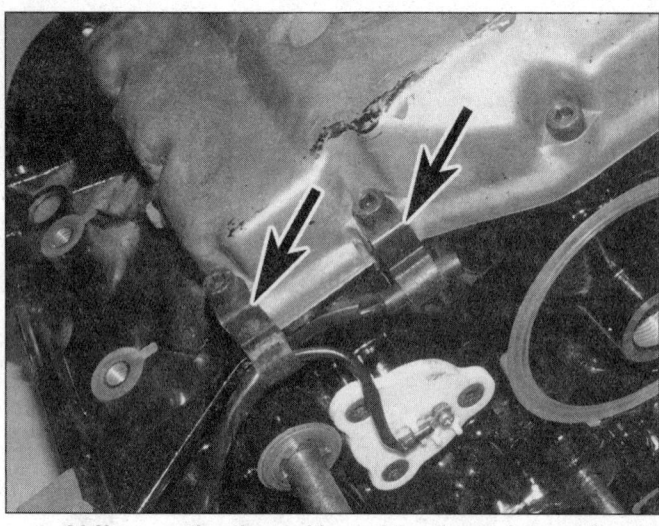

24.3b . . . noting the positions of the clamps (arrowed)

crankcase **(see illustration)**. Fit new O-rings lubricated with clean oil **(see illustration 23.6b)**.
19 Install the pump, aligning the arrow on the outer cover with that on the crankcase, and making sure the dowel and collar locate correctly **(see illustration)**. Apply a suitable non-permanent thread locking compound to the mounting bolts and tighten them to the torque setting specified at the beginning of the Chapter.
20 Fit the washer and driven gear onto the shaft and secure them with the circlip, using a new one if the old one is deformed **(see illustrations 23.5c, b and a)**.
21 Install the oil baffle plate **(see illustration 22.5)**.
22 Install the clutch (see Section 18).
23 Fill the engine with the specified quantity and type of new engine oil (see Chapter 1).

24 Oil sump, oil strainer and pressure relief valves – removal, inspection and installation

Note: *The oil sump, oil strainer and pressure relief valves can be removed with the engine in*

the frame. If the engine has been removed, ignore the steps which don't apply.

Removal

1 Remove the exhaust system (see Chapter 3).
2 Drain the engine oil (see Chapter 1). Either remove the oil level sensor if required (see Chapter 8), or trace the wire from the switch and disconnect it at the single bullet connector **(see illustration)**.
3 Unscrew the sump bolts, slackening them evenly in a criss-cross sequence to prevent distortion, and remove the sump **(see illustration)**. Note the positions of the wiring clamps **(see illustration)**. Discard the gasket, as a new one must be used. Note the positions of the dowels and remove them if they are loose. Note the copper washer fitted with the central bolt – discard it as a new one must be used.
4 Prise off the oil strainer cover, then unscrew the bolts and remove the strainer body **(see illustrations)**. Discard the gasket.

24.4a Remove the cover . . .

24.4b . . . then unscrew the bolts (arrowed) and remove the body

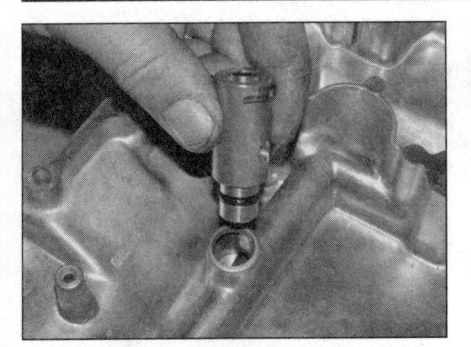

Engine, clutch and transmission 2•45

24.5a Pull the relief valves out of the sump . . .

24.5b . . . and the crankcase

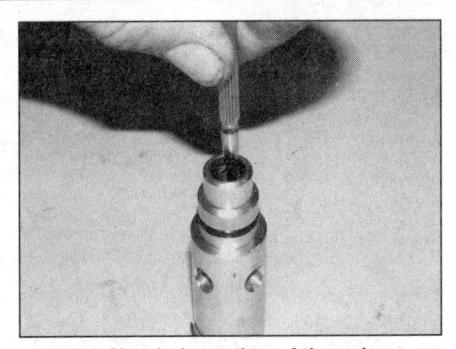

24.8a Check the action of the valve as described

5 Pull the pressure relief valves out of the sump and crankcase **(see illustrations)**. Discard the O-rings.

Inspection

6 Remove all traces of gasket from the sump and crankcase mating surfaces, and clean the inside of the sump with solvent.

7 Clean the oil strainer in solvent and remove any debris caught in the strainer mesh. Inspect the strainer for any signs of wear or damage and renew it if necessary.

8 Push the plunger on one of the relief valves into the valve body and check that it moves smoothly and freely against the spring pressure **(see illustration)**. If not, remove the split pin, pressing down on the spring seat as you do to prevent it flying out under pressure of the spring, and remove the spring seat, spring and plunger **(see illustrations)**. Clean all the components in solvent and check them for scoring, wear or damage. If any is found, renew the relief valve – individual components are not available. Otherwise, coat the inside of the valve body and the plunger with clean engine oil, then insert the plunger, spring and spring seat and secure them with a new split pin. Check the action of the valve plunger again – if it is still suspect, renew the valve. Repeat for the other valve.

Installation

9 Fit a new O-ring onto each relief valve and smear them with grease **(see illustration)**. Push the valves into their sockets in the sump and crankcase, noting that the longer valve fits into the crankcase.

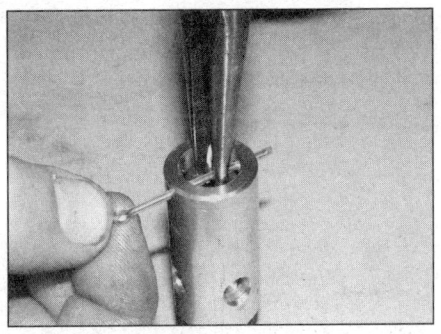

24.8b Press down on the spring seat and withdraw the split pin . . .

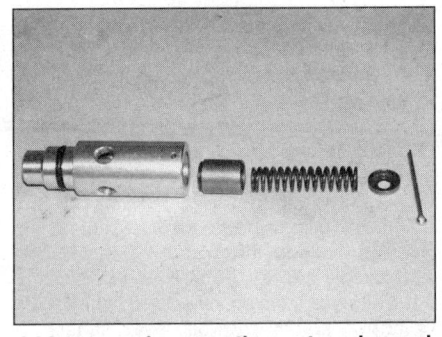

24.8c . . . and remove the seat, spring and plunger

10 Install the oil strainer body using a new gasket, making sure the arrow points to the front of the engine **(see illustrations)**. Apply a suitable non-permanent thread locking compound to the bolts and tighten them to

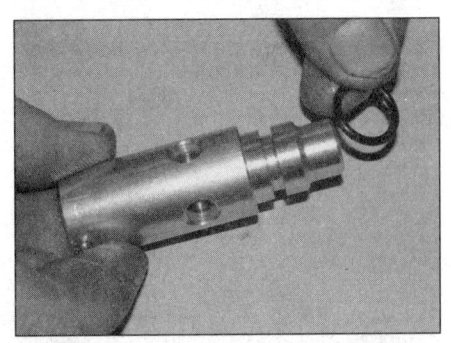

24.9 Fit a new O-ring onto each valve

24.10b . . . then install the strainer body with the arrow to the front

24.10c Fit the strainer cover with the arrow to the front

the specified torque setting. Press the strainer cover onto the body, again making sure the arrow points to the front **(see illustration)**.

11 If removed, fit the sump dowels into the crankcase **(see illustration)**. Lay a new

24.10a Fit a new gasket . . .

24.11 Fit the dowels (arrowed) and a new gasket . . .

2

2•46 Engine, clutch and transmission

24.12a ... then install the sump

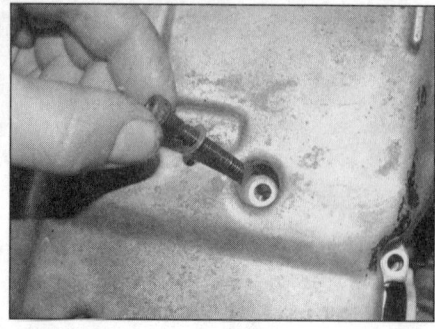

24.12b Use a new sealing washer on the central bolt

25.4 Timing rotor bolt (arrowed)

gasket onto the sump (if the engine is in the frame) or onto the crankcase (if the engine has been removed and is positioned upside down on the work surface). Make sure the holes in the gasket align correctly with the bolt holes.

12 Position the sump onto the crankcase **(see illustration)**. Install the bolts, not forgetting the wiring clamps **(see illustration 24.3b)**, and using a new copper washer on the central bolt **(see illustration)**. Tighten the bolts evenly and a little at a time in a crisscross pattern to the specified torque setting.

13 Either install the oil level sensor if removed (see Chapter 8), or connect the wire at the connector.

14 Fill the engine with the correct type and quantity of oil (see Chapter 1).

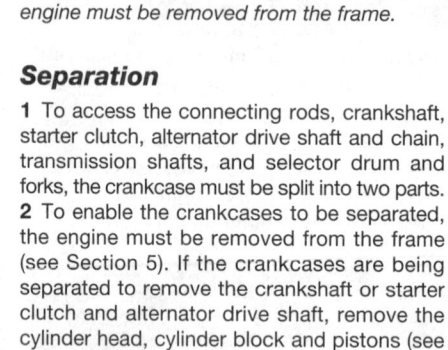

25.5 Undo the screws (arrowed) and remove the plate

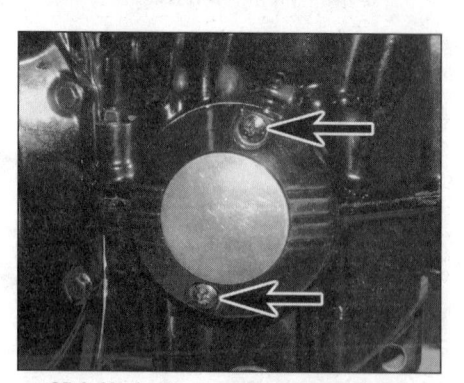

25.6 Undo the screws (arrowed) and remove the cover

15 Install the exhaust system (see Chapter 3). Start the engine and check that there are no oil leaks around the sump.

25 Crankcase halves – separation and reassembly

Note: *To separate the crankcase halves, the engine must be removed from the frame.*

Separation

1 To access the connecting rods, crankshaft, starter clutch, alternator drive shaft and chain, transmission shafts, and selector drum and forks, the crankcase must be split into two parts.

2 To enable the crankcases to be separated, the engine must be removed from the frame (see Section 5). If the crankcases are being separated to remove the crankshaft or starter clutch and alternator drive shaft, remove the cylinder head, cylinder block and pistons (see Sections 12, 15 and 16). If you are only separating the crankcase halves to remove the other components, then there is no need to disassemble the top-end. In all cases, remove the clutch (see Section 18) and the sump (see Section 24).

3 If the crankcases are being separated as part of a complete engine overhaul, remove the following components:
- Gearchange mechanism (Section 22).
- Alternator and starter motor (Chapter 8).
- Oil strainer and pressure relief valves (Section 24).
- Neutral switch and oil level sensor (Chapter 8).
- Cam chain tensioner blade (Section 10).

4 If the top-end has not been disassembled, remove the pick-up coil assembly (see Chapter 4). The timing rotor can stay in place, but if you want to remove it, undo the bolt and remove the rotor and its locating pin **(see illustration)**.

5 Undo the transmission input shaft bearing retainer plate screws and remove the plate **(see illustration)**.

6 Undo the crankshaft end-cover screws and remove the cover **(see illustration)**.

7 The crankcases are joined by a mixture of 10 mm bolts, 8 mm bolts and 6 mm bolts **(see illustration)**. All bolts are numbered according to the order in which they must be **tightened**, and the number of each bolt is cast in the crankcase adjacent to the bolt. Make a cardboard template of

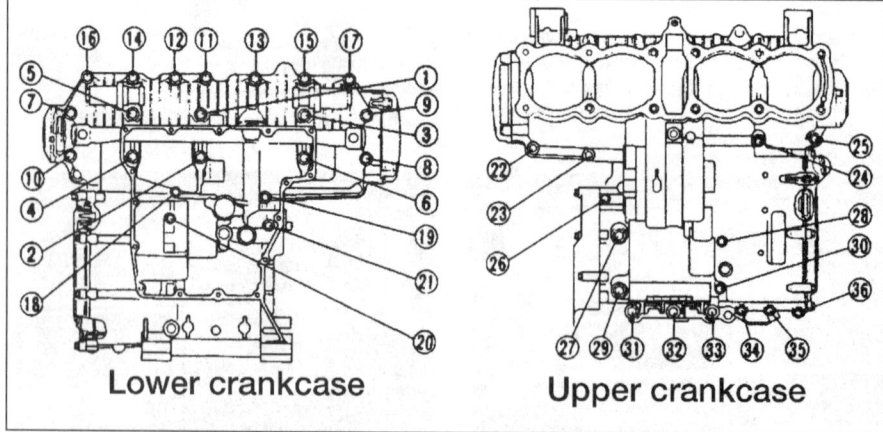

25.7 Crankcase bolt tightening sequence

On certain models, the cam chain tensioner blade bolt (see illustration 10.13b) is included in the sequence of numbers cast into the crankcase, as No. 24. In this case the final number in the sequence will be No. 37.

Engine, clutch and transmission 2•47

25.10 Carefully lift the lower half off the upper half

25.11a Remove the dowels (arrowed) ...

25.11b ... and the O-ring

the crankcase and punch a hole for each bolt location, then mark each hole with its number. This will ensure all bolts are installed correctly on reassembly – this is important as their lengths differ.

8 Unscrew the upper crankcase bolts evenly and a little at a time in a reverse of the numerical sequence marked on the crankcase until they are finger-tight, then remove them. Note any washers and wiring clamps fitted with the bolts. **Note:** *As each bolt is removed, store it in its relative position, with its washer where applicable, in the cardboard template of the crankcase halves.*

9 Turn the engine over. Unscrew the lower crankcase bolts evenly and a little at a time in a reverse of the numerical sequence marked on the crankcase until they are finger-tight, then remove them. Note any washers fitted with the bolts. **Note:** *As each bolt is removed, store it in its relative position, with its washer where applicable, in the cardboard template of the crankcase halves.*

10 Carefully lift the lower crankcase half off the upper half, using a soft-faced hammer to tap around the joint to initially separate the halves if necessary **(see illustration)**. **Note:** *If the halves do not separate easily, make sure all fasteners have been removed. Do not try and separate the halves by levering against the crankcase mating surfaces as they are easily scored and will leak oil. Tap around the joint faces with a soft-faced mallet.*

11 Remove the two locating dowels and the oil passage O-ring – they could be in either half **(see illustrations)**. Remove the crankshaft end-plug and oil seal and discard them as new ones should be used **(see illustrations 25.14b, c and d)**. Remove the transmission output shaft oil seal and discard it **(see illustration 25.14a)**.

12 Refer to Sections 26 to 33 for the removal and installation of the components housed within the crankcases.

Reassembly

13 Remove all traces of sealant from the crankcase mating surfaces. Ensure that all components and their bearings are in place in the upper and lower crankcase halves (see Section 26).

14 If not already done, fit a new oil seal onto the left-hand end of the transmission output shaft, making sure the lip on the outer rim locates into the groove in the crankcase **(see illustration)**. Fit a new crankshaft end-plug and oil seal, applying a smear of grease to their lips. **Note:** *The old-type end-plug and oil seal were lipped, the lip fitting into the groove in the crankcase* **(see illustrations)**. *These have been superseded by unlipped parts, which should be fitted flush with the crankcase walls, though as it is possible for them to become misaligned as the crankcases are joined it is best to fit them proud of the walls and to then tap them flush after the bolts are installed but before they are fully tightened. In this way they are unlikely to become too deeply set in the crankcase.*

15 Check that the selector drum is in the neutral position (see Section 33). Generously lubricate the crankshaft, transmission shafts and selector drum and forks, particularly around the bearings, with clean engine oil, then use a rag soaked in high flash-point solvent to wipe over the mating surfaces of both crankcase halves to remove all traces of oil.

16 If removed, fit the two locating dowels into the crankcase **(see illustration 25.11a)**. Fit a new O-ring onto the oil passage **(see illustration 25.11b)**.

17 Apply a small amount of suitable sealant (such as Yamaha Bond 1215) to the mating

25.14a Fit a new output shaft oil seal

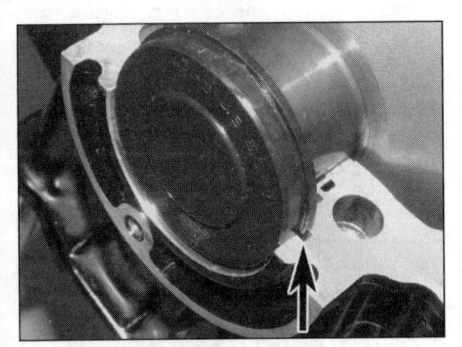

25.14b Old type lipped plug with lip locating into slot (arrow)

25.14c New type un-lipped plug

25.14d Old type lipped seal (left, unfitted), and new type un-lipped seal (right, in position)

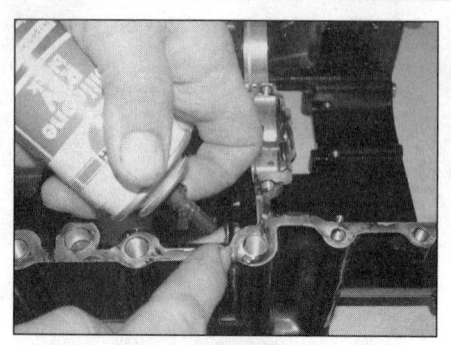

2•48 Engine, clutch and transmission

25.17 Apply the sealant to the mating surface of one crankcase half

25.18 Make sure the selector forks engage with their grooves

25.23 Use a threadlock on the retainer plate screws

surface of one crankcase half **(see illustration)**.
Caution: Do not apply an excessive amount of sealant as it will ooze out when the case halves are assembled and may obstruct oil passages. Do not apply the sealant on or too close (within 2 to 3 mm) to any of the bearing shells or surfaces.
18 Check again that all components are in position, particularly that the bearing shells are still correctly located in the lower crankcase half. Carefully fit the lower crankcase half onto the upper crankcase half **(see illustration 25.10)**, making sure the selector forks locate correctly into their grooves in the transmission shaft gears, and the dowels and bearing retainer rings locate correctly **(see illustration)**.
19 Check that the lower crankcase half is correctly seated. **Note:** *The crankcase halves should fit together without being forced. If the* casings are not correctly seated, remove the lower crankcase half and investigate the problem. Do not attempt to pull them together using the crankcase bolts as the casing will crack and be ruined. Make sure the output shaft oil seal and crankshaft end plug and oil seal are correctly seated. If the crankshaft plug and seal are non-lipped and have become misaligned, gently tap them back into position.
20 Clean the threads of the lower crankcase bolts and smear the crankshaft journal bolts (numbers 1 to 10) with new engine oil. Insert them, with their washers where fitted, in their original locations **(see illustration 25.7a)**. Secure the bolts finger-tight at first, then tighten them evenly and a little at a time in the correct numerical sequence marked on the crankcase to the torque settings specified at the beginning of the Chapter, being sure to distinguish correctly between the different bolt sizes.
21 Turn the engine over. Clean the threads of the upper crankcase bolts. Insert them, with any washers or wiring clamps where fitted, in their original locations **(see illustration 25.7a)**. Secure the bolts finger-tight at first, then tighten them evenly and a little at a time in the correct numerical sequence as marked on the crankcase to the torque settings specified at the beginning of the Chapter, being sure to distinguish correctly between the different bolt sizes.
22 With all crankcase fasteners tightened, check that the crankshaft and transmission shafts rotate smoothly and easily. Check that the transmission shafts rotate freely and independently in neutral, then rotate the selector drum by hand and select each gear in turn whilst rotating the input shaft. Check that all gears can be selected and that the shafts rotate freely in every gear. If there are any signs of undue stiffness, tight or rough spots, or of any other problem, the fault must be rectified before proceeding further.
23 Apply a suitable non-permanent thread locking compound to the threads of the transmission input shaft bearing retainer plate screws, then fit the plate and tighten the screws to the specified torque setting **(see illustration)**.
24 If removed, fit the timing rotor locating pin into the crankshaft, then fit the rotor and tighten the bolt to the specified torque setting, locking the crankshaft as on removal (see Step 4) **(see illustrations)**. Install the pick-up coil assembly (see Chapter 4), but only fit the cover if the top-end was not disassembled. Otherwise wait until the top-end has been assembled.
25 Install the crankshaft end cover **(see illustration)**.
26 Install all other removed assemblies in the reverse of the sequences given in Steps 2 and 3, according to your procedure.

26 Crankcase halves – inspection and servicing

1 After the crankcases have been separated, remove the alternator drive shaft and starter clutch, crankshaft and bearings, transmission

25.24a Insert the locating pin . . .

25.24b . . . then fit the timing rotor, locating the cutout over the pin . . .

25.24c . . . then install the bolt and tighten it to the specified torque

25.25 Install the crankshaft end cover

Engine, clutch and transmission 2•49

26.2a Main oil gallery plug (arrowed)

26.2b Note the depth of the jet (arrowed) then unscrew it

shafts, selector drum and forks, and any other components or assemblies not already removed, referring to the relevant Sections of this and other Chapters (see Steps 2 and 3 in Section 25).

2 Unscrew the oil gallery plugs **(see illustration)**. Note the depth of the oil jet in the crankcase, then unscrew it **(see illustration)**.

3 Clean the crankcases thoroughly with new solvent and dry them with compressed air. Blow out all oil passages with compressed air.

4 Remove all traces of old gasket sealant from the mating surfaces. Minor damage to the surfaces can be cleaned up with a fine sharpening stone or grindstone.

Caution: Be very careful not to nick or gouge the crankcase mating surfaces or oil leaks will result. Check both crankcase halves very carefully for cracks and other damage.

5 Small cracks or holes in aluminium castings can be repaired with an epoxy resin adhesive as a temporary measure. Permanent repairs can only be effected by argon-arc welding, and only a specialist in this process is in a position to advise on the economy or practical aspect of such a repair. If any damage is found that can't be repaired, renew the crankcase halves as a set.

6 Damaged threads can be economically reclaimed by using a diamond section wire insert, of the Heli-Coil type, which is easily fitted after drilling and re-tapping the affected thread.

7 Sheared studs or screws can be removed with stud or screw extractors, and usually succeed in dislodging the most stubborn of them.

> **HAYNES HiNT** *Refer to Tools and Workshop Tips (Section 2) for details of installing a thread insert and using screw extractors.*

8 Apply a suitable non-permanent thread locking compound to the threads of the oil gallery plugs and tighten them securely. Apply a smear of a suitable non-permanent thread locking compound to the threads of the oil jet and thread it into its bore and set it to the depth noted on removal.

9 Install the crankshaft and bearings, transmission shafts, selector drum and forks, starter clutch and alternator drive shaft and bearings, before reassembling the crankcase halves.

27 Main and connecting rod bearings – general information

1 Even though new main and connecting rod bearings are generally fitted during the engine overhaul, the old bearings should be retained for close examination as they may reveal valuable information about the condition of the engine.

2 Bearing failure occurs mainly because of lack of lubrication, the presence of dirt or other foreign particles, overloading the engine and/or corrosion. Regardless of the cause of bearing failure, it must be corrected before the engine is reassembled to prevent it from happening again.

3 When examining the bearings, remove them from their housing and lay them out on a clean surface in the same general position as their location in the crankcase or in the connecting rods. This will enable you to match any noted bearing problems with the corresponding crankshaft journal.

4 Dirt and other foreign particles get into the engine in a variety of ways. It may be left in the engine during assembly or it may pass through filters or breathers. It may get into the oil and from there into the bearings. Metal chips from machining operations and normal engine wear are often present. Abrasives are sometimes left in engine components after reconditioning operations, especially when parts are not thoroughly cleaned using the proper cleaning methods. Whatever the source, these foreign objects often end up imbedded in the soft bearing material and are easily recognised. Large particles will not imbed in the bearing and will score or gouge the bearing and journal. The best prevention for this cause of bearing failure is to clean all parts thoroughly and keep everything spotlessly clean during engine reassembly. Frequent and regular oil and filter changes are also recommended.

5 Lack of lubrication or lubrication breakdown has a number of interrelated causes. Excessive heat (which thins the oil), overloading (which squeezes the oil from the bearing face) and oil leakage or throw off (from excessive bearing clearances, worn oil pump or high engine speeds) all contribute to lubrication breakdown. Blocked oil passages will also starve a bearing and destroy it. When lack of lubrication is the cause of bearing failure, the bearing material is wiped or extruded from the steel backing of the bearing. Temperatures may increase to the point where the steel backing and the journal turn blue from overheating.

> **HAYNES HiNT** *Refer to Tools and Workshop Tips (Section 5) for bearing fault finding.*

6 Riding habits can have a definite effect on bearing life. Full throttle low speed operation, or labouring the engine, puts very high loads on bearings, which tend to squeeze out the oil film. These loads cause the bearings to flex, which produces fine cracks in the bearing face (fatigue failure). Eventually the bearing material will loosen in pieces and tear away from the steel backing. Short trip riding leads to corrosion of bearings, as insufficient engine heat is produced to drive off the condensed water and corrosive gases produced. These products collect in the engine oil, forming acid and sludge. As the oil is carried to the engine bearings, the acid attacks and corrodes the bearing material.

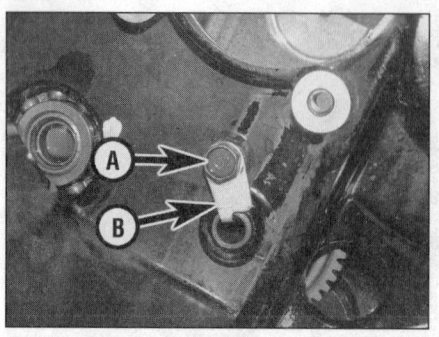

2•50 Engine, clutch and transmission

28.4a Unscrew the bolt (A) and remove the plate (B), noting how it locates

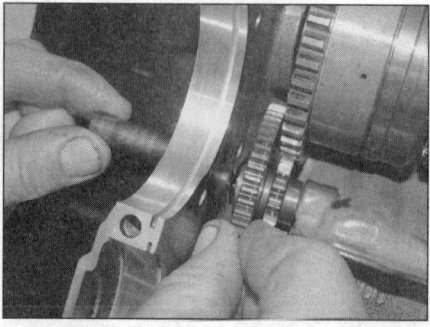

28.4b Withdraw the shaft and remove the gear

28.5 Undo the screws (arrowed) and remove the bearing retainer/seal housing

7 Incorrect bearing installation during engine assembly will lead to bearing failure as well. Tight fitting bearings which leave insufficient bearing oil clearances result in oil starvation. Dirt or foreign particles trapped behind a bearing insert result in high spots on the bearing which lead to failure.

8 To avoid bearing problems, clean all parts thoroughly before reassembly, double check all bearing clearance measurements and lubricate the new bearings with clean engine oil during installation.

28 Alternator drive shaft, starter clutch and idle/reduction gear – check and overhaul

Check

1 The operation of the starter clutch can be checked while it is in situ. Remove the starter motor (see Chapter 8). Check that the starter driven gear is able to rotate freely anti-clockwise as you look at it via the starter motor aperture, but locks when rotated clockwise. If not, the starter clutch is faulty and should be removed for inspection.

Removal

Note: *These components can only be accessed after separation of the crankcase halves.*

2 Separate the crankcase halves (see Section 25). The alternator drive shaft, starter clutch and idle/reduction gear are all located in the upper crankcase half.

28.6 Push the nozzle (arrowed) out from the inside

3 Remove the transmission input shaft (see Section 31).
4 Unscrew the idle/reduction gear shaft retaining bolt and remove the retainer plate **(see illustration)**. Support the idle/reduction gear, then withdraw the shaft and remove the gear, noting which way round it fits **(see illustration)**.
5 Undo the alternator drive shaft bearing retainer/seal housing screws and remove it from the crankcase **(see illustration)**.
6 Push the oil spray nozzle out of its recess in the crankcase noting how it locates **(see illustration)**. Discard the O-ring as a new one must be used.
7 Support the starter clutch, then withdraw the drive shaft from the crankcase **(see illustration)**. Discard the O-ring on the bearing as a new one must be used.
8 Lift the starter clutch out and disengage the Hy-Vo chain from the sprocket **(see**

28.7 Support the starter clutch and withdraw the shaft

illustration). If the Hy-Vo chain is to be removed from the crankshaft mark one of the chain side plates to indicate whether it points to the left or right side of the engine (remembering to account for the engine being upside down at this stage). This is to ensure that the chain is refitted with its direction of travel unchanged, otherwise noise and vibration can occur.
9 If required, remove the crankshaft (see Section 29) and disengage the Hy-Vo chain. Unscrew the bolts securing the chain guide to the crankcase and remove the guide, noting which way round it fits **(see illustration)**.

Inspection

10 With the starter clutch body face-down on a workbench, check that the starter driven gear rotates freely in an anti-clockwise direction and locks against the rotor in a clockwise direction **(see illustration)**. If it

28.8 Lift the starter clutch out and disengage the chain

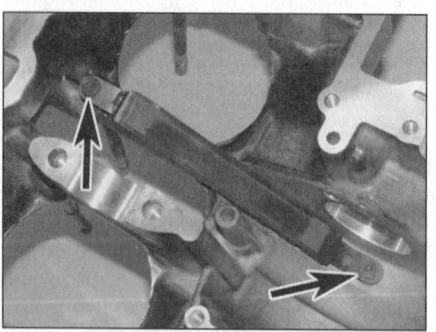

28.9 Hy-Vo chain guide bolts (arrowed)

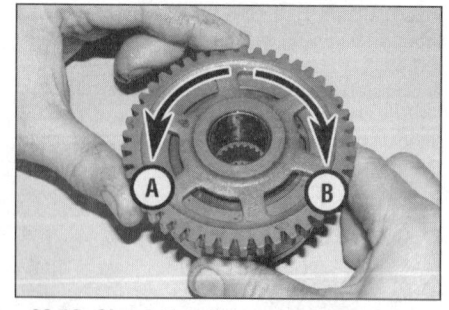

28.10 Check that the gear rotates freely when turned anti-clockwise (A) and locks when turned clockwise (B)

Engine, clutch and transmission 2•51

28.11 Withdraw the sleeve then remove the gear

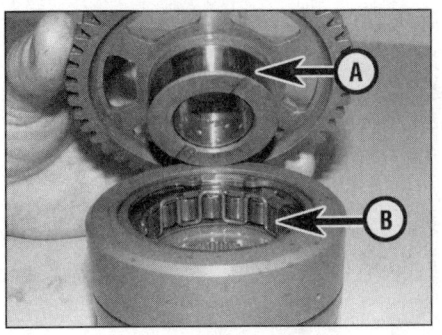

28.13a Check the hub surface (A) and the sprags (B) as described

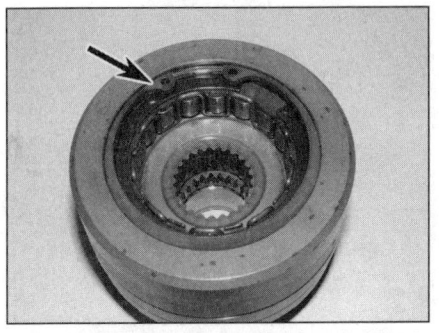

28.13b Remove the circlip (arrowed) and lift the sprag assembly out

doesn't, the starter clutch should be dismantled for further investigation.

11 Withdraw the sleeve from the starter driven gear **(see illustration)**. Remove the driven gear from the starter clutch, rotating it anti-clockwise as you do to spread the rollers/sprags.

12 On 1995 and 1996 models, inspect the bearing surface of the starter clutch gear hub and the condition of the rollers inside the clutch body. If the bearing surface shows signs of excessive wear or the rollers are damaged, marked or flattened at any point, they should be renewed. Remove the rollers and check the spring caps and springs for signs of deformation or damage. Make sure the pin moves freely in its socket. Check that the three Allen bolts securing the starter clutch assembly together are tight. If any are loose, remove the bolts and renew them. Apply a suitable non-permanent thread locking compound to the new bolts and tighten them to the torque setting specified at the beginning of the Chapter.

13 On 1997-on models inspect the bearing surface of the driven gear hub and the condition of the sprags inside the clutch body **(see illustration)**. If the bearing surface shows signs of excessive wear or the sprags are damaged, marked or flattened at any point, they should be renewed as a pair. The sprag assembly is secured in the body by a large circlip – remove this and lift the sprag assembly out, noting which way round it fits **(see illustration)**. Make sure the circlip locates correctly in its groove on installation.

14 Examine the teeth of the starter idle/reduction gear and the corresponding teeth of the driven gear and starter motor shaft. Renew the gears as a set if worn or chipped teeth are discovered.

15 Inspect the alternator drive shaft and its bearings (one on the shaft, the other in the crankcase), referring to *Tools and Workshop Tips* in the Reference Section for information on checks and renewal methods **(see illustration)**. If the shaft splines are worn or damaged the shaft must be renewed. Also check the corresponding splines in the starter clutch.

16 Drive the oil seal out of its housing using a suitable socket or driver and fit a new seal **(see illustrations)**.

17 Separate the cush drive housing from the clutch body and inspect the cush drive rubbers **(see illustrations)**. If compacted or deteriorated they should be renewed.

18 The Hy-Vo chain and its guide in the crankcase can only be inspected properly after the crankshaft has been removed (see Section 29). Check the Hy-Vo chain and the chain guide for signs of wear or damage, and renew if necessary **(see illustration 28.9)**.

Installation

19 If removed, fit the Hy-Vo chain guide in the crankcase, making sure it is the correct way round. Apply a suitable non-permanent thread locking compound to the bolts and tighten them securely **(see illustration 28.9)**. Engage the Hy-Vo chain around its sprocket on the crankshaft, making sure it is the correct way round (see Step 8). Install the crankshaft (see Section 29).

20 Insert the reassembled starter clutch in the crankcase and engage the Hy-Vo chain around the sprocket **(see illustration 28.8)**. Lay the starter clutch down in the crankcase.

21 Fit a new O-ring onto the drive shaft

28.15 Check the shaft and its bearings as described

28.16a Drive out the old seal . . .

28.16b . . . and fit a new seal

28.17a Lift the clutch body out of the cush drive housing . . .

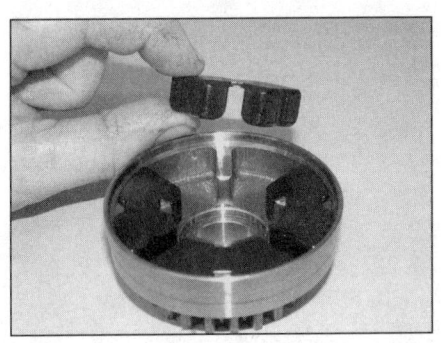

28.17b . . . and check the rubber segments

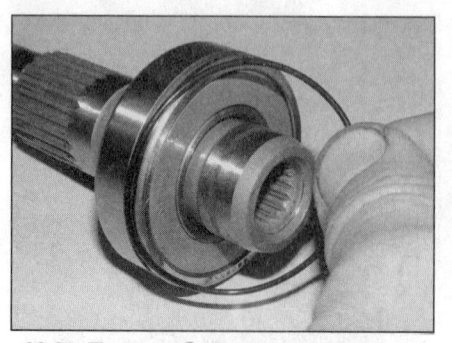

2•52 Engine, clutch and transmission

28.21 Fit a new O-ring into the groove in the bearing

28.22a Insert the oil nozzle ...

28.22b ... locating the pin in the slot (arrow)

28.23 Fit the bearing retainer/seal housing

bearing **(see illustration)**. Lubricate the rest of the alternator drive shaft, then, supporting the starter clutch, slide the shaft through from the outside of the crankcase until it seats fully into the bearing in the crankcase – you may have to turn the clutch slightly to align and engage the splines **(see illustration 28.7)**.

22 Push the oil spray nozzle into its recess in the crankcase, making sure the locating pin fits into its slot **(see illustrations)**.

23 Lubricate the lips of the oil seal, then fit the bearing retainer/seal housing, turning it as you do to ease the seal lips over the shaft end **(see illustration)**. Apply a suitable non-permanent thread-lock to the screws and tighten them to the torque setting specified at the beginning of the Chapter.

24 Position the starter idle/reduction gear in the crankcase so the smaller pinion engages with the driven gear **(see illustration 28.4b)**. Lubricate the shaft and slide it fully into place from the outside of the crankcase. Apply threadlock to the shaft retainer plate bolt, then fit the plate and tighten the bolt to the specified torque setting **(see illustration 28.4a)**.

25 Install the transmission input shaft (see Section 31) and reassemble the crankcase halves (see Section 25).

29 Crankshaft and main bearings – removal, inspection and installation

Note: To remove the crankshaft the engine must be removed from the frame and the crankcase halves separated.

Removal

1 Remove the engine from the frame (see Section 5) and separate the crankcase halves (see Section 25).

2 Remove the alternator drive shaft and starter clutch (see Section 28).

3 Mark one of the Hy-Vo chain side plates to indicate whether it points to the left or right side of the engine (remembering to account for the engine being upside down at this stage). This is to ensure that the chain is refitted with its direction of travel unchanged, otherwise noise and vibration can occur.

4 Lift the crankshaft out of the upper crankcase half **(see illustration)**. If it appears stuck, tap it gently using a soft faced mallet. Take care not to snag either the cam chain or the Hy-Vo chain when lifting the crankshaft clear. Note how the crankshaft end seal and plug fit and take care not to lose them. Disengage the chains from the crankshaft if required.

5 The main bearing shells can be removed from the crankcase halves by pushing their centres to the side, then lifting them out **(see illustration)**. Keep the bearing shells in order as they must be installed in their original positions if they are being re-used.

6 If required, separate the connecting rods from the crankshaft (see Section 30).

Inspection

7 Clean the crankshaft with solvent, using a rifle-cleaning brush to scrub out the oil passages. If available, blow the crank dry with compressed air, and also blow through the oil passages. Check the primary drive gear, cam chain and Hy-Vo chain sprockets for wear or damage **(see illustration)**. If any of the gear or sprocket teeth are excessively worn, chipped or broken, the crankshaft must be renewed. If wear or damage is found on the primary drive gear, check the driven gear on the clutch housing. Similarly check the sprockets on the camshafts and on the starter clutch assembly and the cam and Hy-Vo chains and renew them if necessary.

8 Refer to Section 27 and examine the main bearing shells. If they are scored, badly scuffed or appear to have been seized, new bearings must be installed. Always renew the main bearings as a set. If they are badly damaged, check the corresponding crankshaft journals. Evidence of extreme heat, such as discoloration, indicates that lubrication failure has occurred. Be sure to

29.4 Carefully lift the crankshaft out of the crankcase

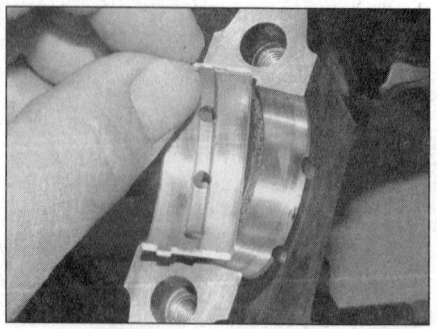

29.5 To remove a main bearing shell, push it sideways and lift it out

29.7 Check the sprockets, chains and gears as described

Engine, clutch and transmission 2•53

thoroughly check the oil pump and pressure relief valves as well as all oil holes and passages before reassembling the engine.

9 Give the crankshaft journals a close visual examination, paying particular attention where damaged bearings have been discovered. If the journals are scored or pitted in any way a new crankshaft will be required. Note that undersizes are not available, precluding the option of re-grinding the crankshaft.

10 Place the crankshaft on V-blocks and check the runout at the main bearing journals using a dial gauge. Compare the reading to the maximum specified at the beginning of the Chapter. If the runout exceeds the limit, the crankshaft must be renewed.

Oil clearance check

11 Whether new bearing shells are being fitted or the original ones are being re-used, the main bearing oil clearance should be checked before the engine is reassembled. Main bearing oil clearance is measured with a product known as Plastigauge.

12 If not already done, remove the bearing shells from the crankcase halves (see Step 5). Clean the backs of the shells and the bearing housings in both crankcase halves, and the main bearing journals on the crankshaft.

13 Press the bearing shells into their cut-outs, ensuring that the tab on each shell engages in the notch in the crankcase (see illustration 29.26). Make sure the bearings are fitted in the correct locations and take care not to touch any shell's bearing surface with your fingers.

14 Ensure the shells and crankshaft are clean and dry. Lay the crankshaft in position in the upper crankcase (see illustration 29.4).

15 Cut five lengths of the appropriate size Plastigauge (they should be slightly shorter than the width of the crankshaft journals). Place a strand of Plastigauge on each journal, making sure it will be clear of the oil holes in the shells when the lower crankcase is installed. Make sure the crankshaft is not rotated.

16 If removed, fit the dowels into the crankcase (see illustrations 25.11a). Carefully fit the lower crankcase half onto the upper half, making sure the dowel locates correctly and the Plastigauge is not disturbed (see illustration 25.10). Check that the lower crankcase half is correctly seated. Note: Do not tighten the crankcase bolts if the casing is not correctly seated.

17 Clean the threads of the lower crankcase bolts (numbers 1 to 10) and apply a smear of new engine oil to their threads. Install the bolts with their washers where fitted in their original locations, and tighten them evenly and in the correct numerical sequence to the torque setting specified at the beginning of the Chapter. Make sure that the crankshaft does not turn as the bolts are tightened.

18 Slacken each bolt in reverse sequence starting at number 10 and working backwards to number 1. Slacken each bolt 1/2 a turn at a time until they are all finger-tight, then remove the bolts. Carefully lift off the lower crankcase half, making sure the Plastigauge is not disturbed.

19 Compare the width of the crushed Plastigauge on each crankshaft journal to the scale printed on the Plastigauge envelope to obtain the main bearing oil clearance. Compare the reading to the specifications at the beginning of the Chapter.

20 On completion carefully scrape away all traces of the Plastigauge material from the crankshaft journal and bearing shells; use a fingernail or other object which is unlikely to score them.

21 If the oil clearance falls into the specified range, new shells are not required (provided they are in good condition). If the clearance is beyond the service limit, refer to the marks on the crankcase and the marks on the crankshaft and select new bearing shells (see Steps 23 and 24). Fit the new shells and check the oil clearance once again (the new shells may bring the bearing clearance within the specified range). Always renew all of the shells at the same time.

22 If the clearance is still greater than the service limit listed in this Chapter's Specifications (even with new shells), the crankshaft journal is worn and a new crankshaft should be fitted.

Main bearing shell selection

23 New bearing shells for the main bearings are supplied on a selective fit basis. Code numbers stamped on various components are used to identify the correct bearings. The crankshaft journal size numbers are stamped on the outside of the crankshaft web on the left-hand end (see illustration). The left-hand block of five numbers are for the main bearing journals (the right-hand block of four numbers are for the big-end bearing journals). The first number of the five is for the left-hand (No. 1) journal, and so on. The main bearing housing numbers are stamped into the back of the upper crankcase half (see illustration). The first number of the five is for the left-hand (No. 1) journal, and so on. Note that if there is only one number stamped into the crankcase, it means that all the journals are the same number.

24 A range of bearing shells is available. To select the correct bearing for a particular journal, subtract the main bearing journal number (stamped on the crank web) from the main bearing housing number (stamped on the crankcase), i.e. crankcase number minus crank web number. Compare the result with the table below to find the colour coding of the new bearing required. The colour is marked on the side of each bearing.

Number	Colour
1	Blue
2	Black
3	Brown
4	Green
5	Yellow

Installation

25 If not already done, remove the bearing shells from the crankcase halves (see Step 5).

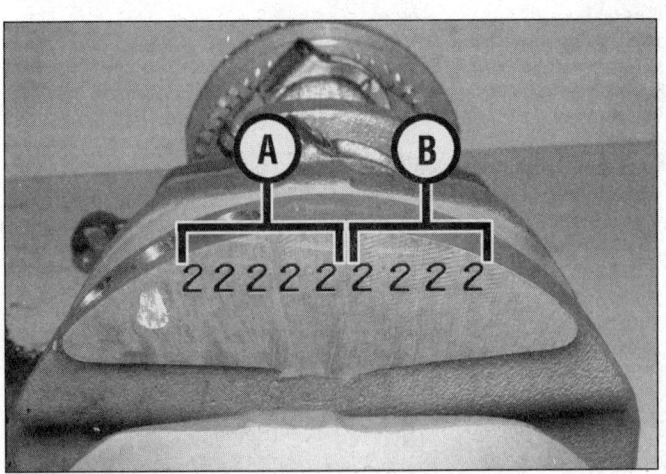

29.23a Main journal size numbers (A), big-end journal size numbers (B)

29.23b Main bearing housing numbers

2•54 Engine, clutch and transmission

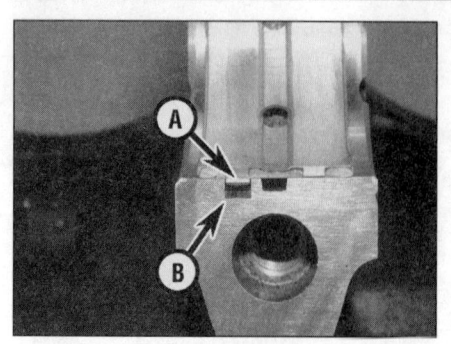

29.26 Make sure the tab (A) locates in the notch (B)

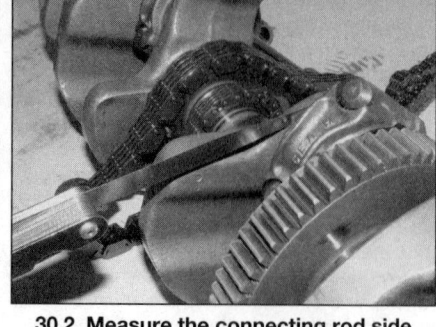

30.2 Measure the connecting rod side clearance using a feeler gauge

30.3 Note the 'Y' mark (arrowed) which must face the left-hand side of the engine

Clean the backs of the shells and the bearing housings in both crankcase halves, and the main bearing journals on the crankshaft. If new shells are being fitted, ensure that all traces of the protective grease are cleaned off using paraffin (kerosene). Wipe the shells and crankcase halves dry with a lint-free cloth. Make sure all the oil passages and holes are clear, and blow them through with compressed air if it is available.

26 Press the bearing shells into their locations. Make sure the tab on each shell engages in the notch in the casing **(see illustration)**. Make sure the bearings are fitted in the correct locations and take care not to touch any shell's bearing surface with your fingers. Lubricate each shell with clean engine oil.

27 If removed, fit the connecting rods onto the crankshaft (see Section 30).

28 Install the alternator drive shaft and starter clutch (see Section 28).

29 Engage the Hy-Vo chain (making sure it is the correct way round) (see Step 3) and the cam chain onto their sprockets on the crankshaft **(see illustration 29.7)**.

30 Lower the crankshaft into position in the upper crankcase, feeding the cam chain down through its tunnel and the Hy-Vo chain onto is guide **(see illustration 29.4)**.

31 Reassemble the crankcase halves (see Section 25).

30 Connecting rods – removal, inspection and installation

Note: *To remove the connecting rods the engine must be removed from the frame and the crankcases separated.*

Removal

1 Remove the engine from the frame (see Section 5) and separate the crankcase halves (see Section 25). Remove the crankshaft (see Section 29).

2 Before separating the rods from the crankshaft, measure the side clearance on each rod with a feeler gauge **(see illustration)**. If the clearance on any rod is greater than the service limit listed in this Chapter's Specifications, fit a new rod.

3 Using paint or a felt marker pen, mark the relevant cylinder identity on each connecting rod and cap. Mark across the cap-to-connecting rod join, and note the 'Y' mark on each connecting rod which must face to the left-hand side of the engine, to ensure that the cap and rod are fitted the correct way around on reassembly **(see illustration)**. Note that the number and letter already across the rod and cap indicate rod size and weight grade respectively, not cylinder number.

4 Unscrew the connecting rod cap nuts and separate the cap and rod from the crankpin **(see illustration)**.

5 Immediately install the relevant bearing shells (if removed) and bearing cap on its connecting rod so that they are all kept together as a matched set.

Inspection

6 Check the connecting rods for cracks and other obvious damage.

7 Apply clean engine oil to the piston pin, insert it into its connecting rod small-end and check for any freeplay between the two. If freeplay is excessive, measure the pin external diameter **(see illustration 16.12b)**. Compare the result to the specifications at the beginning of the Chapter. If the pin is worn beyond its specified limits, fit a new pin. If the pin diameter is within specifications, fit a new connecting rod. Repeat the measurements for all the rods.

8 Refer to Section 27 and examine the connecting rod bearing shells. If they are scored, badly scuffed or appear to have seized, new shells must be installed. Always renew the shells in the connecting rods as a set. If they are badly damaged, check the corresponding crankpin. Evidence of extreme heat, such as discoloration, indicates that lubrication failure has occurred. Be sure to thoroughly check the oil pump and pressure relief valves as well as all oil holes and passages before reassembling the engine.

9 Have the rods checked for twist and bend by a Yamaha dealer if you are in doubt about their straightness.

Oil clearance check

10 Whether new bearing shells are being fitted or the original ones are being re-used, the connecting rod (big-end) bearing oil clearance should be checked prior to reassembly. Check one connecting rod at a time.

11 Remove the bearing shells from the rod and cap, keeping them in order **(see illustration)**. Clean the backs of the shells and the bearing locations in both the connecting rod and cap, and the crankpin journal.

12 Press the bearing shells into their locations, ensuring that the tab on each shell engages the notch in the connecting rod/cap

30.4 Unscrew the nuts (arrowed) and remove the connecting rods

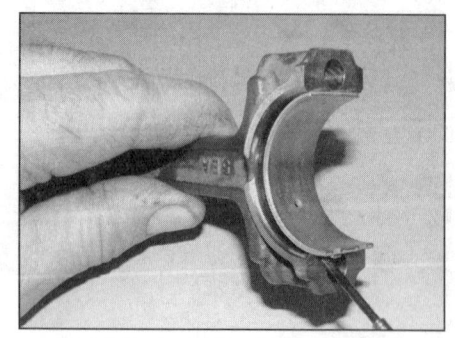

30.11 Remove the shells and clean them ...

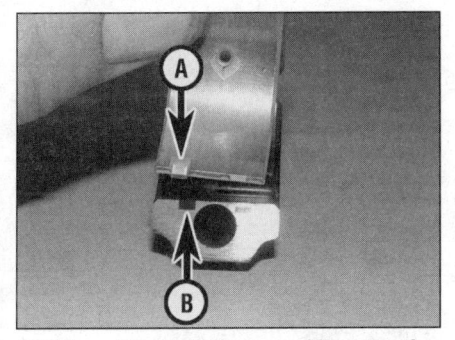

Engine, clutch and transmission 2•55

30.12 ... then refit them, making sure the tabs (A) locate in the notches (B)

30.22 The rod size number is marked across the rod and cap

(see illustration). Make sure the bearings are fitted in the correct locations and take care not to touch any shell's bearing surface with your fingers.

13 Cut a length of the appropriate size Plastigauge (it should be slightly shorter than the width of the crankpin). Place a strand of Plastigauge on the crankpin journal.

14 Apply molybdenum disulphide grease to the bolt shanks and threads and to the seats of the nuts. Fit the connecting rod and cap onto the crankshaft (see illustration 30.26a). Make sure the cap is fitted the correct way around so the previously made markings align, and that the rod is facing the correct way (see Step 3). Fit the nuts and tighten them finger-tight, making sure the connecting rod does not rotate on the crankshaft (see illustration 30.26b).

15 Tighten the cap nuts to the initial torque setting specified at the beginning of the Chapter, making sure the connecting rod does not rotate on the crankshaft (see illustration 30.27). Now tighten each nut in turn in one continuous movement to the final torque setting specified. If tightening is paused between the initial and final settings, slacken the nut to below the initial setting and repeat the procedure.

16 Slacken the cap nuts and remove the cap and rod, again taking great care not to rotate the rod or crankshaft.

17 Compare the width of the crushed Plastigauge on the crankpin to the scale printed on the Plastigauge envelope to obtain the connecting rod bearing oil clearance.

Compare the reading to the specifications at the beginning of the Chapter.

18 On completion carefully scrape away all traces of the Plastigauge material from the crankpin and bearing shells using a fingernail or other object which is unlikely to score the shells.

19 If the clearance is within the range listed in this Chapter's Specifications and the bearings are in perfect condition, they can be reused. If the clearance is beyond the service limit, fit new bearing shells (see Steps 22 and 23). Check the oil clearance once again (the new shells may be thick enough to bring bearing clearance within the specified range). Always renew all of the shells at the same time.

20 If the clearance is still greater than the service limit listed in this Chapter's Specifications, the big-end bearing journal is worn and a new crankshaft should be fitted.

21 Repeat the procedure for the remaining connecting rods.

Bearing shell selection

22 New bearing shells for the big-end bearings are supplied on a selected fit basis. Code numbers stamped on various components are used to identify the correct replacement bearings. The crankshaft journal size numbers are stamped on the outside of the crankshaft web on the left-hand end (see illustration 29.23a). The right-hand block of four numbers are for the big-end bearing journals (the left-hand block of five numbers are for the main bearing journals). The first number of the four is for the left-hand (No. 1

cylinder) journal, and so on. Each connecting rod size number is marked in ink across the flat face of the connecting rod and cap (see illustration).

23 A range of bearing shells is available. To select the correct bearing for a particular connecting rod, subtract the big-end bearing journal number (stamped on the crank web) from the connecting rod number (marked on the rod), i.e. connecting rod number minus crank web number. Compare the bearing number calculated with the table below to find the colour coding of the new bearing required. The colour is marked on the side of each bearing.

Number	Colour
1	Blue
2	Black
3	Brown
4	Green

Installation

24 Clean the backs of the bearing shells and the bearing locations in both the connecting rod and cap.

25 Press the bearing shells into their locations, making sure the tab on each shell locates in the notch in the connecting rod/cap (see illustration 30.12). Make sure the bearings are fitted in their correct locations and take care not to touch any shell's bearing surface with your fingers. Lubricate the shells with clean engine oil.

26 Apply molybdenum disulphide grease to the bolt threads and to the seats of the nuts. Assemble the connecting rod and cap on the crankpin (see illustration). Make sure the cap is fitted the correct way around so the previously made markings align, and that the rod is facing the correct way (see Step 3). Fit the nuts and tighten them finger-tight (see illustration). Check again to make sure all components have been returned to their original locations using the marks made on disassembly.

27 Tighten the cap nuts to the initial torque setting specified at the beginning of the Chapter (see illustration). Now tighten each nut in turn in one continuous movement to the final torque setting specified. If tightening is paused between the initial and final settings, slacken the nut to below the initial setting and repeat the procedure.

30.26a Assemble the rod on the crankshaft, making sure the 'Y' mark faces the left-hand end ...

30.26b ... then fit the nuts ...

30.27 ... and tighten them as described, first to the initial torque, then to the final torque

2•56 Engine, clutch and transmission

28 Check that the rods rotate smoothly and freely on the crankpin. If there are any signs of roughness or tightness, remove the rods and re-check the bearing clearance. Sometimes tapping the bottom of the connecting rod cap will relieve tightness, but if in doubt, recheck the clearances and torque settings.
29 Reassemble the crankcase halves (see Section 25).

31 Transmission shafts – removal and installation

Note: *To remove the transmission shafts the engine must be removed from the frame and the crankcase halves separated.*

Removal

1 Remove the engine from the frame (see Section 5) and separate the crankcase halves (see Section 25).
2 Lift the output shaft out of the crankcase **(see illustration)**. If it is stuck, use a soft-faced hammer and gently tap on the ends of the shaft to free it. Remove the bearing half-ring retainer from the bearing on the shaft or from the crankcase, noting how it fits **(see illustration)**.
3 Lift the input shaft out of the crankcase **(see illustration)**. If it is stuck, use a soft-faced hammer and gently tap on the ends of the shaft to free it.

Installation

4 The bearing on the left-hand end of the input shaft has a pin that locates in the hole in the bearing housing in the lower crankcase half. To make sure that the bearing is correctly positioned along the shaft in relation to the bearing retainer ring on the other end, it is best to initially fit the shaft into the lower crankcase half, locating the pin in the hole and ring in the slot, so that the distance between the pin and the ring is correct – there is very little play, but enough to cause a problem when assembling the crankcases to cause bother if not initially set **(see illustration)**. Having done that, lay the input shaft into the upper crankcase half **(see illustration 31.3)**, making sure the retainer ring on the right-hand bearing locates in its slot and the locating pin points up perpendicular to the crankcase mating surface **(see illustrations)**.
5 Smear the lips of a new output shaft oil seal with grease. Slide the seal onto the left-hand end of the shaft **(see illustration 25.14a)**.
6 Fit the output shaft bearing half-ring retainer into its slot in the bearing **(see illustration 31.2b)**. Lay the output shaft into the upper crankcase **(see illustration 31.2a)**, making sure on the right-hand end the half-ring retainer locates in the groove in the crankcase and the locating pin points up perpendicular to the crankcase mating surface **(see illustration)**, and on the left-hand end the ring locates in the groove and the pin faces back and is located against the crankcase mating surface – this pin locates in a cutout in the lower crankcase when assembled **(see illustration)**. If the oil seal

31.2a Lift the output shaft out of the crankcase . . .

31.2b . . . and remove the half-ring retainer

31.3 Lift the input shaft out of the crankcase

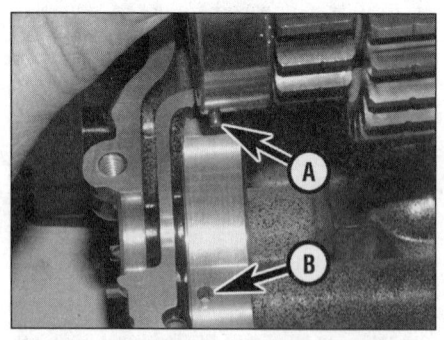

31.4a Locate the pin (A) on the bearing in the hole (B) in the lower half to set the position of the bearing

31.4b Locate the ring in its slot (arrow) . . .

31.4c . . . and make sure the pin (arrowed) points up

31.6a On the right-hand end locate the ring in the groove (A) and position the pin (B) at the top

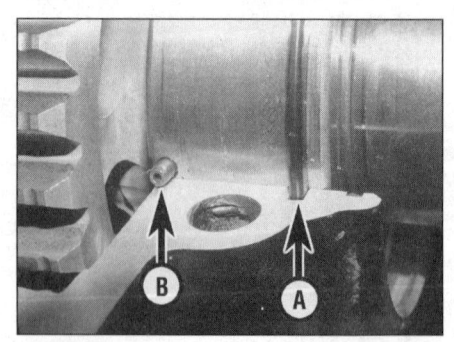

31.6b On the left-hand end locate the ring in the groove (A) and position the pin (B) against the crankcase

Engine, clutch and transmission 2•57

has a lip on the outside, make sure this locates in its groove in the crankcase.
7 Make sure both transmission shafts are correctly seated and their related pinions are correctly engaged.
Caution: If the half-ring retainer is not correctly engaged, the crankcase halves will not seat correctly.
8 Position the gears in the neutral position and check the shafts are free to rotate easily and independently (i.e. the input shaft can turn whilst the output shaft is held stationary) before proceeding further.
9 Reassemble the crankcase halves (see Section 25).

32 Transmission shafts – disassembly, inspection and reassembly

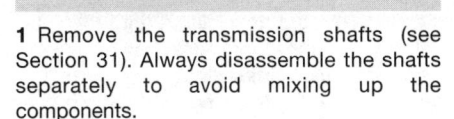

1 Remove the transmission shafts (see Section 31). Always disassemble the shafts separately to avoid mixing up the components.

Input shaft disassembly

HAYNES HiNT *When disassembling the transmission shafts, place the parts on a long rod or thread a wire through them to keep them in order and facing the proper direction.*

2 Remove the bearing from the left-hand end of the shaft (see illustration 32.20). Do not remove the bearing from the right-hand end unless it or the shaft is being renewed.
3 Remove the 2nd gear pinion from the left-hand end of the shaft using a puller. Set the puller up with the legs behind the 5th gear pinion, and draw the 2nd and 5th pinions off together **(see illustration)**. **Note:** *In some cases an hydraulic press may be needed to remove the 2nd gear pinion if it is tight on the shaft. Take the shaft to a properly equipped workshop if necessary.*
4 Remove the 5th gear pinion bush by locating a puller behind the 3rd gear pinion, and draw the bush, the thrust washer and the 3rd gear pinion off the shaft together **(see illustration)**.
5 Remove the circlip securing the 4th gear pinion, then slide the splined washer and the pinion off the shaft **(see illustrations 32.16c, b and a)**.
6 The 4th gear pinion bush and 1st gear pinion are integral with the shaft **(see illustration)**.

Input shaft inspection

7 Wash all of the components in clean solvent and dry them off.
8 Check the gear teeth for cracking, chipping, pitting and other obvious wear or damage. Any pinion that is damaged must be renewed.
9 Inspect the dogs and the dog holes in the gears for cracks, chips, and excessive wear especially in the form of rounded edges. Make sure mating gears engage properly. Renew the paired gears as a set if necessary.
10 Check for signs of scoring or bluing on the pinions, bushes and shaft. This could be caused by overheating due to inadequate lubrication. Check that all the oil holes and passages are clear. Renew any damaged pinions or bushes. Some of the bushes are a press fit.
11 Check that each mobile pinion moves freely on the shaft but without undue freeplay.
12 The shaft is unlikely to sustain damage unless the engine has seized, placing an unusually high loading on the transmission, or the machine has covered a very high mileage. Check the surface of the shaft, especially where a pinion turns on it, and renew the shaft if it has scored or picked up, or if there are any cracks. Damage of any kind can only be cured by fitting new parts. Check the shaft runout using V-blocks and a dial gauge and renew the shaft if the runout exceeds the limit specified at the beginning of the Chapter.
13 Check the washers and replace any that are bent or appear weakened or worn. Use new ones if in any doubt. New circlips should be used as a matter of course.
14 Referring to *Tools and Workshop Tips* (check Section 5) in the Reference Section, check the bearings and renew them if necessary.

Input shaft reassembly

15 During reassembly, apply molybdenum disulphide oil (a 50/50 mixture of molybdenum disulphide grease and new engine oil) to the mating surfaces of the shaft and pinions. When installing the circlips, do not expand their ends any further than is necessary. Install the stamped circlips so that their chamfered side faces the pinion it secures (see *correct fitting of a stamped circlip* illustration in Tools and Workshop Tips of the Reference section).
16 Slide the 4th gear pinion, with the pinion dog holes facing away from the integral 1st

32.3 Use a puller, or a press as shown, to remove the 2nd and 5th gear pinions

32.4 Use a puller as shown to remove the bush, washer and 3rd gear pinion

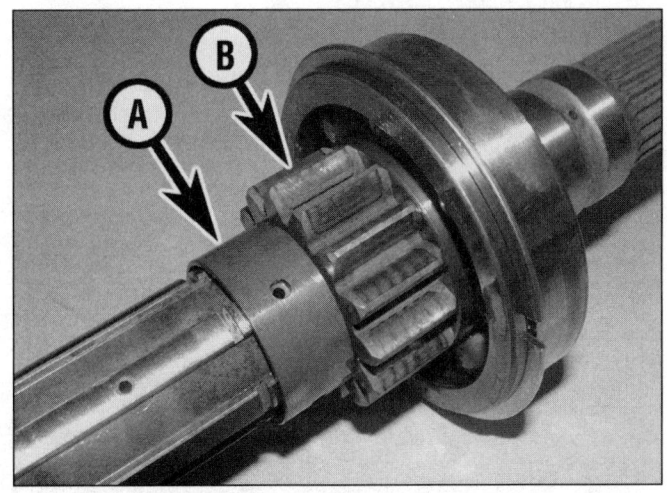

32.6 The 4th gear pinion bush (A) and 1st gear pinion (B) are integral with the shaft

2•58 Engine, clutch and transmission

32.16a Slide the 4th gear pinion . . .

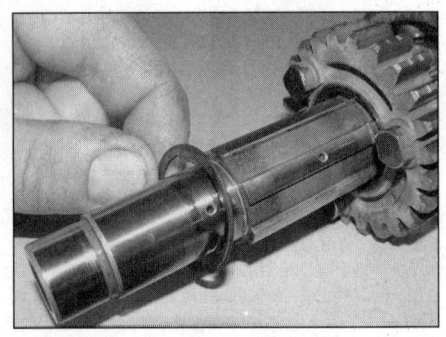

32.16b . . . and the splined washer onto the shaft . . .

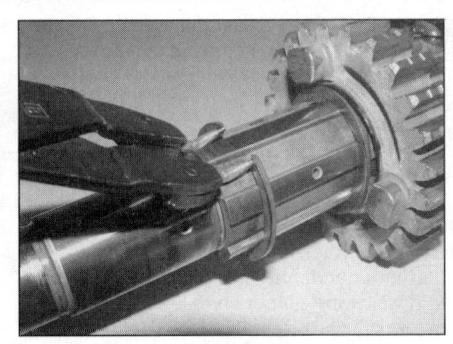

32.16c . . . then fit the circlip . . .

32.16d . . . making sure it locates correctly in the groove

32.17 Slide the 3rd gear pinion onto the shaft . . .

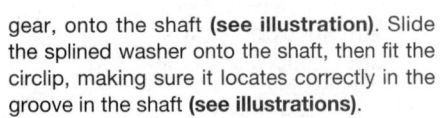

gear, onto the shaft **(see illustration)**. Slide the splined washer onto the shaft, then fit the circlip, making sure it locates correctly in the groove in the shaft **(see illustrations)**.

17 Slide the 3rd gear pinion onto the shaft with the selector fork groove facing the 4th gear pinion **(see illustration)**.

18 Slide the thrust washer and the 5th gear pinion bush onto the shaft, aligning the oil holes in the bush and shaft, then use a suitable piece of tubing or a collar and socket as shown to drive the bush on **(see illustrations)**. Slide the 5th gear pinion onto the bush **(see illustration)**.

32.18a . . . followed by the thrust washer . . .

32.18b . . . and the 5th gear pinion bush . . .

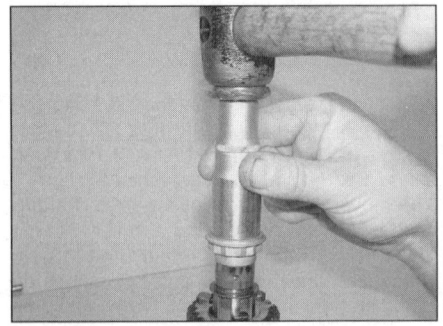

32.18c . . . driving it on as shown . . .

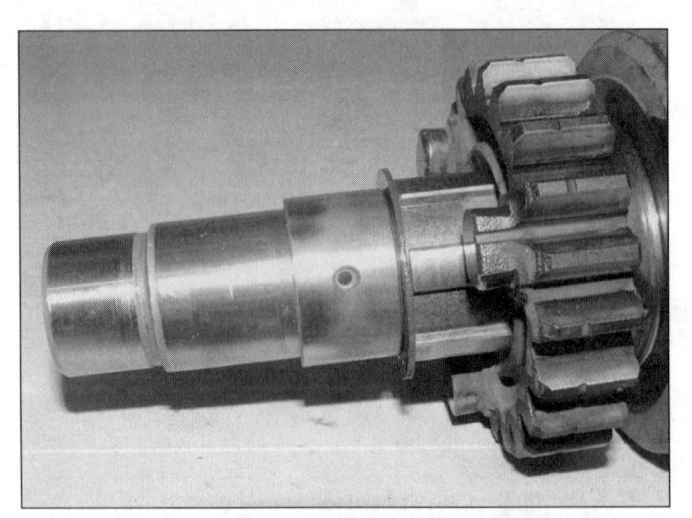

32.18d . . . making sure the oil holes align . . .

32.18e . . . then fit the 5th gear pinion onto the bush

Engine, clutch and transmission 2•59

32.19a Slide the 2nd gear pinion onto the shaft . . .

32.19b . . . then press it into place . . .

32.19c . . . setting it so the measured distance as shown is correct

32.20 Fit the bearing onto the left-hand end of the shaft

32.21 The assembled shaft should be as shown

19 Press the 2nd gear pinion onto the left-hand end of the shaft using a press or tubular drift, referring to *Tools and Workshop Tips* (Section 5) in the Reference Section if required **(see illustration)**. Set the pinion so that the distance between the outside edge of the 2nd gear pinion and the outside edge of the 1st gear pinion (which is integral with the shaft) is 114.8 mm. This equates to a distance of 132.8 mm between the outside of the 2nd gear pinion and the outside of the bearing, which is much easier to measure as shown **(see illustration)**.

20 Fit the bearing onto the left-hand end of the shaft **(see illustration)**.
21 Check that all components are correctly installed **(see illustration)**.

Output shaft disassembly

22 Remove the bearing from the right-hand end of the shaft **(see illustration 32.34c)**. Do not remove the bearing from the left-hand end unless it or the shaft are being renewed.
23 Slide the thrust washer and the 1st gear pinion off the shaft **(see illustrations 32.34b and a)**. Remove the 1st gear pinion bush by locating a puller behind the 4th gear pinion, and draw the bush, the thrust washer and the 4th gear pinion off the shaft together **(see illustration)**.
24 Remove the circlip, then slide the splined washer and the 3rd gear pinion off the shaft **(see illustrations 32.31c, b and a)**. Remove the 3rd gear pinion bush by locating a puller behind the 5th gear pinion, and draw the bush, the thrust washer and the 5th gear pinion off the shaft together **(see illustration)**.

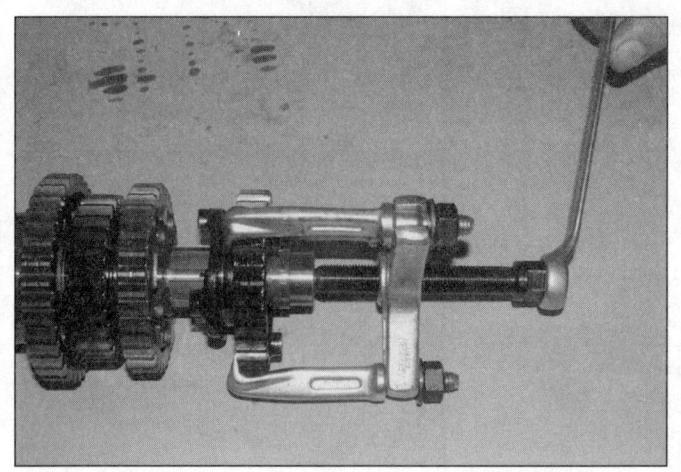

32.23 Use a puller as shown to remove the bush, washer and 4th gear pinion

32.24 Use a puller or press as shown to remove the bush, washer and 5th gear pinion

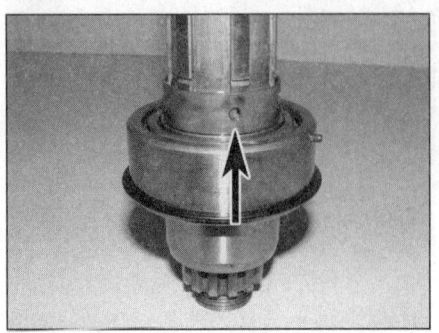

2•60 Engine, clutch and transmission

32.28a Make sure the oil holes align (arrow)

32.28b Slide the 2nd gear pinion onto the shaft . . .

32.28c . . . followed by the splined washer . . .

25 Remove the circlip securing the 2nd gear pinion, then slide the splined washer and the pinion off the shaft, then remove the bush **(see illustrations 32.28d, c and b)**.

Output shaft inspection
26 Refer to Steps 7 to 14 above.

Output shaft reassembly
27 During reassembly, apply molybdenum disulphide oil (a 50/50 mixture of molybdenum disulphide grease and new engine oil) to the mating surfaces of the shaft and pinions. When installing the circlips, do not expand their ends any further than is necessary. Install the stamped circlips so that their chamfered side faces the pinion it secures (see *correct fitting of a stamped circlip* illustration in Tools and Workshop Tips of the Reference section).
28 Fit the 2nd gear pinion bush onto the shaft, aligning the oil holes, then slide the 2nd gear pinion onto it **(see illustrations)**. Slide the splined washer onto the shaft, then fit the circlip making sure it locates correctly in its groove **(see illustrations)**.

29 Slide the 5th gear pinion onto the shaft, with the selector fork groove facing away from the 2nd gear pinion **(see illustration)**.
30 Slide the thrust washer onto the shaft, followed by the 3rd gear pinion bush, aligning the oil holes **(see illustrations)**. Set the shaft up in a vice as shown, locating a spare washer between the vice and the bush as protection, then tap the end of the shaft with a soft hammer to drive the bush into place, which is when the oil holes are aligned **(see illustrations)**. Note that this will leave a small amount of clearance between the bush and the thrust washer, leaving the washer loose. Make sure there is enough room on the other side of the bush for the splined washer before the circlip groove, otherwise the circlip will not locate properly.
31 Slide the 3rd gear pinion onto its bush, then slide the splined washer onto the shaft and

32.28d . . . then fit the circlip . . .

32.28e . . . making sure it locates correctly in the groove

32.29 Slide the 5th gear pinion onto the shaft . . .

32.30a . . . followed by the thrust washer . . .

32.30b . . . and the 3rd gear pinion bush . . .

32.30c . . . then drive the bush onto the shaft as shown . . .

32.30d . . . setting it so the oil holes align (arrow)

Engine, clutch and transmission 2•61

32.31a Slide the 3rd gear pinion onto the bush . . .

32.31b . . . followed by the splined washer . . .

32.31c . . . then fit the circlip . . .

secure them with the circlip, making sure it locates correctly in its groove **(see illustrations)**.
32 Slide the 4th gear pinion onto the shaft, with its selector fork groove facing the 3rd gear pinion **(see illustration)**.
33 Slide the thrust washer onto the shaft, followed by the 1st gear pinion bush, aligning the oil holes **(see illustrations)**. Tap the bush into place using a deep socket or piece of tubing, using a spare washer to protect the bush **(see illustration)**.
34 Slide the 1st gear pinion onto its bush, then fit the thrust washer and the bearing onto the shaft **(see illustrations)**.
35 Check that all components are correctly installed.

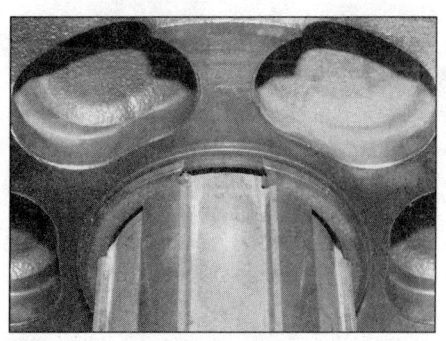

32.31d . . . making sure it locates correctly in the groove

32.32 Slide the 4th gear pinion onto the shaft . . .

32.33a . . . followed by the thrust washer

32.33b Fit the bush . . .

32.33c . . . and drive it into place

32.34a Slide the 1st gear pinion onto the bush . . .

32.34b . . . then fit the thrust washer . . .

32.34c . . . and the bearing

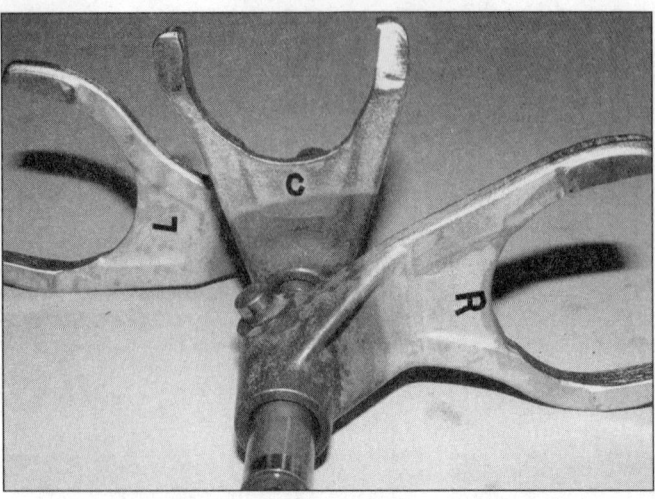

2•62 Engine, clutch and transmission

33.2 Note the letter on each fork denoting its position

33.3 Undo the screws (arrowed) and remove the plate

33 Selector drum and forks – removal, inspection and installation

Note: *To remove the selector drum and forks the engine must be removed from the frame and the crankcase halves separated.*

Removal

1 Separate the crankcase halves (see Section 25). The selector drum and forks are located in the lower half.

2 Before removing the selector forks, note that each fork is lettered for identification. The right-hand fork has an 'R', the centre fork a 'C', and the left-hand fork an 'L' **(see illustration)**. These letters face the right-hand side of the engine. If no letters are visible, mark them yourself using a felt pen. Withdraw the gear selector fork shaft from the lower crankcase half and remove the forks **(see illustrations 33.13c, b and a)**. Install the forks back on the shaft in their correct positions as a reminder for installation.

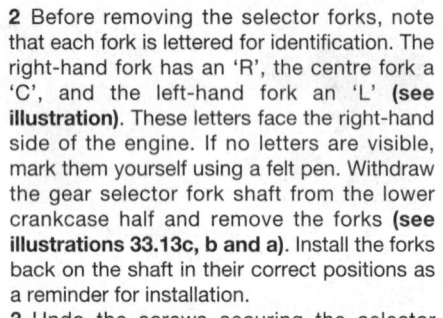

3 Undo the screws securing the selector drum bearing retainer plate and remove the plate, noting how it fits **(see illustration)**. The screws are threadlocked so you may need an impact driver.

4 Remove the neutral switch (see Chapter 8).

5 Withdraw the selector drum from the crankcase **(see illustration)**.

Inspection

6 Inspect the selector forks for any signs of wear or damage, especially around the fork ends where they engage with the groove in the pinion **(see illustration)**. Check that each fork fits correctly in its pinion groove. Check closely to see if the forks are bent. If the forks are in any way damaged they must be renewed.

7 Check that the forks fit correctly on the shaft. They should move freely with a light fit but no appreciable freeplay. Check that the fork shaft holes in the casing are not worn or damaged.

8 The selector fork shaft can be checked for trueness by rolling it along a flat surface. A bent rod will cause difficulty in selecting gears and make the gearchange action heavy. Renew the shaft if it is bent.

9 Inspect the selector drum grooves and selector fork guide pins for signs of wear or damage **(see illustration)**. If either show signs of wear or damage they must be renewed.

10 Check that the selector drum bearing rotates freely and has no signs of roughness or excessive freeplay between it and the drum or crankcase (when installed) (see *Tools and Workshop Tips* (Section 5) in the Reference Section for more information on bearings) **(see illustration)**. Renew the selector drum if necessary – the bearing is not available separately.

Installation

11 Slide the selector drum into the crankcase **(see illustration 33.5)**, aligning it so that the contact for the neutral switch points to the front of the engine and the neutral detent for the stopper arm points down **(see**

33.5 Withdraw the selector drum from the crankcase

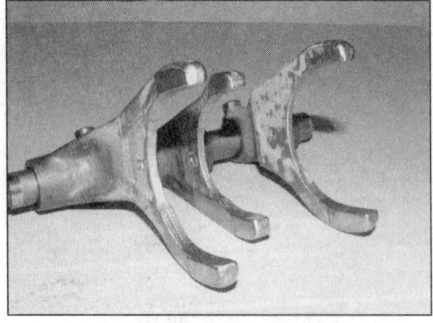

33.6 Check the fork ends and the grooves in the pinions they locate in

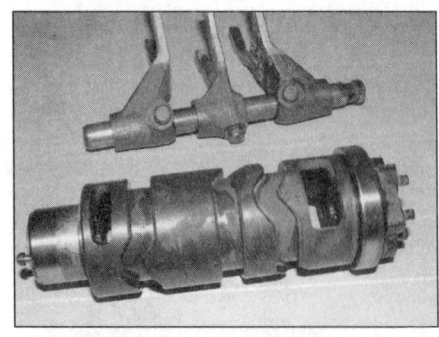

33.9 Check the fork guide pins and the grooves in the selector drum

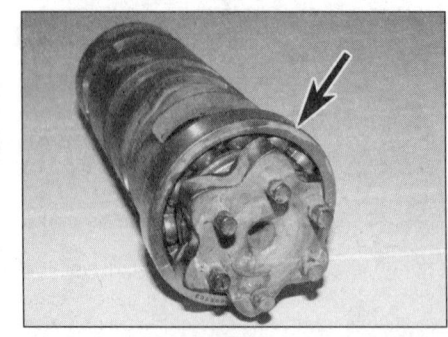

33.10 Check the bearing (arrowed) on the selector drum

Engine, clutch and transmission 2•63

33.11 Set the drum so that the neutral contact (arrowed) is positioned as shown

33.13a Slide the shaft through the R fork ...

33.13b ... the C fork ...

33.13c ... and the L fork

illustration). Fit the bearing retainer plate, then apply a suitable non-permanent threadlock to the screws and tighten them securely **(see illustration 33.3)**.
12 Install the neutral switch (see Chapter 8).
13 Refer to Step 2 for the correct location of each fork. Lubricate the selector fork shaft with clean engine oil. Slide the selector fork shaft into the crankcase and through each fork in turn, locating the guide pin on the end of each fork in its groove in the drum as you do **(see illustrations)**. Make sure the forks are positioned according to their letter (Left, Centre and Right) and with the letters facing the right-hand side of the engine.
14 Check that the selector drum and selector forks all rotate or move freely, then re-position the selector drum in the neutral position.
15 Assemble the crankcase halves (see Section 25).

34 Initial start-up after overhaul

1 Make sure the engine oil level is correct (see *Daily (pre-ride) checks*).
2 Before fitting the fuel tank, perform an oil supply check. Slacken the oil gallery check bolt in the right-hand side of the cylinder head (there is no need to remove it) **(see illustration)**. Remove the spark plugs (see Chapter 1) and fit them back into their caps, then lay the plugs against the cylinder head with their threads contacting it. Check that the kill switch is in the 'RUN' position and the transmission is in neutral, then turn the ignition switch ON and turn the engine over on the starter motor. Oil should begin to seep out of the oil check bolt. Do not operate the starter motor for an excessive period of time. Turn the ignition OFF, refit the spark plugs and tighten the check bolt securely. If no oil appeared from the check bolt, refer to Chapter 1 and perform an oil pressure check.
3 Install the fuel tank (see Chapter 3). Operate the choke and start the engine. Allow the engine to run at a moderately fast idle until it reaches operating temperature.
4 Check carefully that there are no oil leaks and make sure the transmission and controls, especially the brakes, function properly before road testing the machine. Refer to Section 35 for the recommended running-in procedure.
5 Upon completion of the road test, and after

34.2 Oil check bolt

35 Recommended running-in procedure

1 Treat the machine gently for the first few miles to make sure oil has circulated throughout the engine and any new parts installed have started to seat.

2 Even greater care is necessary if the engine has been extensively overhauled – the bike will have to be run in as when new. This means greater use of the transmission and a restraining hand on the throttle until the specified mileage has been covered. There's no point in keeping to any set speed limit – the main idea is to keep from labouring the engine and to gradually increase performance according to the table. These recommendations apply less when only a partial overhaul has been done, though it does depend to an extent on the nature of the work carried out and which components have been renewed. Experience is the best guide, since it's easy to tell when an engine is running freely. If in any doubt, consult a Yamaha dealer. The following maximum engine speed limitations, which Yamaha provide for new motorcycles, can be used as a guide.

3 If a lubrication failure is suspected, stop the engine immediately and try to find the cause. If an engine is run without oil, even for a short period of time, severe damage will occur.

4 After 600 miles (1000 km) change the engine oil and filter (see Chapter 1).

Up to 100 miles (150 km)	4000 rpm max	Vary throttle position/speed. Do not use full throttle. Stop after every hour and let engine cool for 5 to 10 minutes.
100 to 600 miles (150 to 1000 km)	4000 rpm max	Vary throttle position/speed. Do not use full throttle. Higher revs can be used for short periods, as long as the engine is not laboured
600 to 1000 miles (1000 to 1600 km)	5000 rpm max	Vary throttle position/speed. Full throttle can be used for short periods, as long as the engine is not laboured
Over 1000 miles (1600 km)		Do not exceed tachometer red line

Chapter 3
Fuel and exhaust systems

Contents

Air filter – cleaning and renewal	see Chapter 1
Air filter housing – removal and installation	4
Air induction system (AIS) – check	see Chapter 1
Air induction system (AIS) – general information, removal and information	16
Carburettor heater system – check	13
Carburettor overhaul – general information	6
Carburettor synchronisation	see Chapter 1
Carburettors – disassembly, cleaning and inspection	8
Carburettors – reassembly and float height/fuel level check	10
Carburettors – removal and installation	7
Carburettors – separation and joining	9
Choke cable – removal and installation	12
Exhaust system – removal and installation	14
Fuel gauge and level sender – check, removal and installation	15
Fuel hoses – renewal	see Chapter 1
Fuel system – check	see Chapter 1
Fuel tank – cleaning and repair	3
Fuel tank and fuel tap – removal and installation	2
General information and precautions	1
Idle fuel/air mixture adjustment – general information	5
Idle speed – check and adjustment	see Chapter 1
Throttle and choke cables – check and adjustment	see Chapter 1
Throttle cables – removal and installation	11
Throttle position sensor – check and adjustment	see Chapter 4

Degrees of difficulty

Easy, suitable for novice with little experience	**Fairly easy,** suitable for beginner with some experience	**Fairly difficult,** suitable for competent DIY mechanic	**Difficult,** suitable for experienced DIY mechanic	**Very difficult,** suitable for expert DIY or professional

Specifications

Fuel
Grade	Unleaded, minimum 91 RON (Research Octane Number)
Fuel tank capacity (including reserve)	21.0 litres
Reserve capacity	4.5 litres

Carburettors – XJR1200 models
Type	Mikuni BS36 x 4

Adjustments
Fuel level (see text)	4.5 to 5.5 mm below float chamber line
Float height	21.3 to 23.3 mm
Pilot screw setting (turns out)	3
Idle speed	see Chapter 1
Synchronisation vacuum range	see Chapter 1

Jet sizes
Main jet	95
Main air jet	45
Jet needle and clip position	5D66-3/5
Needle jet	Y-2
Pilot air jet	135
Pilot jet	40
Starter jet	32.5

Fuel and exhaust systems

Carburettors – XJR1300 1999 to 2001 models
Type .... Mikuni BS36 x 4
Adjustments
   Fuel level (see text) .... 3.5 to 4.5 mm below float chamber line
   Float height .... 21.3 to 23.3 mm
   Pilot screw setting (turns out) 1 1/2
   Idle speed .... see Chapter 1
   Synchronisation vacuum range .... see Chapter 1

Jet sizes
   Main jet 95
   Main air jet 45
   Jet needle and clip position 5D96-2
   Needle jet Y-2
   Pilot air jet 127.5
   Pilot jet 40
   Starter jet 32.5

Carburettors – XJR1300 2002-on models
Type .... Mikuni BSR37 x 4
Adjustments
   Fuel level (see text) .... 3.0 to 4.0 mm below float chamber line
   Float height .... 33 to 34 mm
   Pilot screw setting (turns out) 2
   Idle speed .... see Chapter 1
   Synchronisation vacuum range .... see Chapter 1

Jet sizes
   Main jet 107.5
   Main air jet 80
   Jet needle and clip position 5D118-53-3
   Needle jet P0-M
   Pilot air jet 140
   Pilot jet 15
   Starter jet 52.5

Carburettor heater system (2002-on models)
Heater element resistance .... 11 ohms @ 20°C

Fuel level sender
Resistance
   Full position .... 4.0 to 10 ohms @ 20°C
   Empty position .... 90 to 100 ohms @ 20°C

Torque settings
Cylinder head intake manifold bolts .... 10 Nm
Exhaust collector box bolt .... 25 Nm
Exhaust downpipe assembly flange nuts .... 25 Nm
Exhaust downpipe-to-collector box clamp bolts
   XJR1200 .... 25 Nm
   XJR1300 .... 20 Nm
Fuel level sender bolts .... 4 Nm
Fuel tank mounting bolt .... 19 Nm
Fuel tap screws .... 7 Nm
Silencer-to-collector box clamp bolts .... 20 Nm
Silencer mounting bolts
   XJR1200 .... 25 Nm
   XJR1300 .... 20 Nm

Fuel and exhaust systems 3•3

1 General information and precautions

General information

The fuel system consists of the fuel tank with internal level sender, vacuum-operated fuel tap with integral strainer, fuel hoses, carburettors and control cables. On XJR1300 models an in-line fuel filter is fitted in the supply hose to the carburettors.

The carburettors used are CV types. There is a carburettor for each cylinder. For cold starting, on 1995 models a knob is mounted on the end of the choke linkage bar on the carburettors, and on all other models a handlebar mounted lever (incorporated in the left-hand switch housing) is connected to the carburettors by a cable. On 2002 models onwards a heater is incorporated in each carburettor to prevent icing.

Air is drawn into the carburettors via an air filter which is housed under the seat.

The exhaust system is a four-into-two design.

Many of the fuel system service procedures are considered routine maintenance items and for that reason are included in Chapter 1.

Precautions

Warning: Petrol (gasoline) is extremely flammable, so take extra precautions when you work on any part of the fuel system. Don't smoke or allow open flames or bare light bulbs near the work area, and don't work in a garage where a natural gas-type appliance is present. If you spill any fuel on your skin, rinse it off immediately with soap and water. When you perform any kind of work on the fuel system, wear safety glasses and have a fire extinguisher suitable for a class B type fire (flammable liquids) on hand.

Always perform service procedures in a well-ventilated area to prevent a build-up of fumes.

Never work in a building containing a gas appliance with a pilot light, or any other form of naked flame. Ensure that there are no naked light bulbs or any sources of flame or sparks nearby.

Do not smoke (or allow anyone else to smoke) while in the vicinity of petrol or of components containing it. Remember the possible presence of vapour from these sources and move well clear before smoking.

Check all electrical equipment belonging to the house, garage or workshop where work is being undertaken (see the Safety First! section of this manual). Remember that certain electrical appliances such as drills, cutters etc create sparks in the normal course of operation and must not be used near petrol or any component containing it. Again, remember the possible presence of fumes before using electrical equipment.

Always mop up any spilt fuel and safely dispose of the rag used.

Any stored fuel that is drained off during servicing work must be kept in sealed containers that are suitable for holding petrol, and clearly marked as such; the containers themselves should be kept in a safe place. Note that this last point applies equally to the fuel tank if it is removed from the machine; also remember to keep its filler cap closed at all times.

Note that the fuel system consists of the fuel tank and tap, with its cap and related hoses.

Read the Safety first! section of this manual carefully before starting work.

2 Fuel tank and fuel tap – removal and installation

Warning: Refer to the precautions given in Section 1 before starting work.

Fuel tank

Removal

1 Make sure the fuel cap is secure and the tap is turned to ON or RES. Remove the seat and the side panels (see Chapter 7).

2 Unscrew the bolt securing the rear of the tank and remove the plate and rubber seat **(see illustrations)**. Raise the rear of the tank and place a block of wood under it to support it.

3 Disconnect the fuel level sender wiring connector **(see illustration)**.

4 Release the clamps securing the vacuum and fuel hoses to the fuel tap and detach them from their unions, being prepared to catch any residual fuel from the fuel hose with a rag **(see illustrations)**. Also detach the drain and breather hoses from their unions **(see illustration)**.

2.2a Unscrew the rear bolt (arrowed) . . .

2.2b . . . and remove the plate and rubber seat

2.3 Disconnect the level sender wiring connector

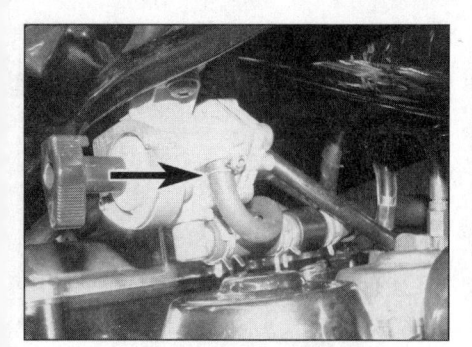

2.4a Detach the vacuum hose (arrowed) . . .

2.4b . . . the fuel hose . . .

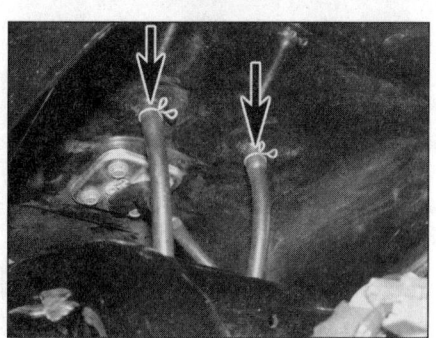

2.4c . . . and the drain and breather hoses (arrowed)

3•4 Fuel and exhaust systems

2.5 Carefully remove the tank

2.6 Release the ties and remove the rubber cover if required

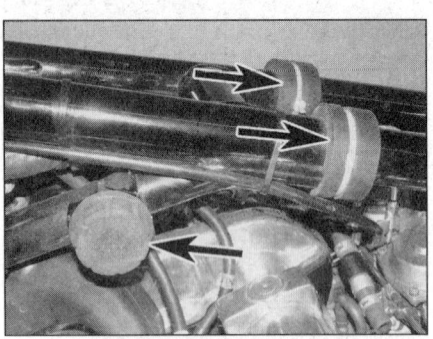

2.7 Check the rubbers (arrowed) and renew them if necessary

5 Draw the tank back off its front mounting rubbers and carefully lift it away **(see illustration)**.
6 On 2002 models onward, if required, release the cable ties securing the rubber cover to the frame and remove the cover, noting how it fits **(see illustration)**.
7 Inspect the tank mounting rubbers for signs of damage or deterioration and renew them if necessary **(see illustration)**.

Installation

8 Installation is the reverse of removal, noting the following:
● Make sure all hoses are properly attached and secured by their clamps.
● Make sure the wiring connector is securely connected.
● Tighten the mounting bolt to the torque setting specified at the beginning of the Chapter.
● Start the engine and check that there is no sign of fuel leakage.

Fuel tap

Inspection

9 If the fuel tap has been leaking, first try tightening the assembly screws and mounting bolts **(see illustrations)**. Slacken the screws and/or bolts a little first, then tighten them evenly and a little at a time to ensure the cover seats properly on the tap body. If leakage persists, the tap should be renewed, however nothing is lost by dismantling the tap for further inspection. Remove the screws on the face of the tap and disassemble it, noting how the components fit. Inspect all components for wear or damage, and renew the seal and O-ring as necessary. If any of the components are worn or damaged beyond repair a new tap must be fitted.
10 To check fuel flow, detach the hose from the carburettors and place the open end in a suitable container to catch the fuel. Set the tap in the ON or RES position and turn the engine over on the starter motor. If no fuel flows first check that the vacuum hose is secure at both ends, and that there are no splits in the hose – renew it if in any doubt. If there is still no flow, the chances are there is a split in the diaphragm. Undo the screws on the back of the tap and remove the cover and diaphragm **(see illustration 2.9b)**. Hold the diaphragm up to the light and check for any holes or splits. The diaphragm is not available separately so a new tap must be fitted if damage is found.

Removal

11 Remove the fuel tank (see above).
12 If required, connect a drain hose to the fuel outlet union on the tap and insert its end in a container suitable and large enough for storing the petrol. Turn the fuel tap to the PRI position and allow the tank to drain. When the tank has drained, turn the tap to the ON or RES position. If you don't want to drain the tank, make sure the cap is secure, then turn the tank over and lay it on a cushion of rags to protect it and soak up any fuel that may leak.
13 Undo the screws securing the tap to the tank and withdraw the tap **(see illustration 2.9c)**. Discard the rubber seal as a new one must be used.
14 Clean the gauze strainer to remove all traces of dirt and fuel sediment (see

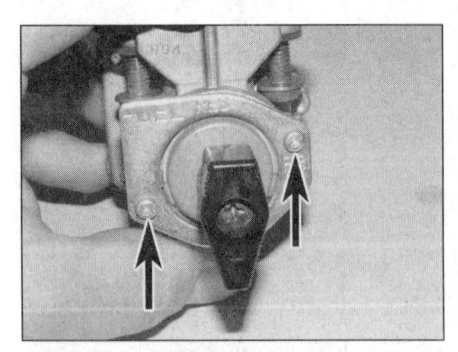

2.9a Tighten the front assembly screws (arrowed) . . .

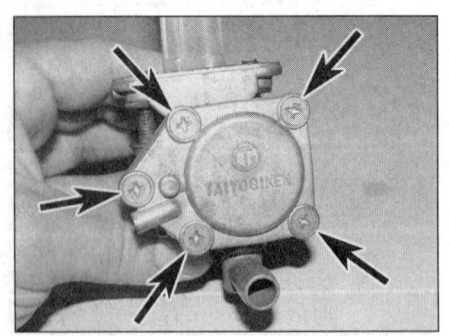

2.9b . . . the rear assembly screws (arrowed) . . .

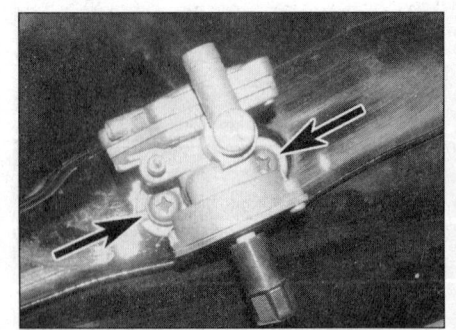

2.9c . . . or the mounting screws as required to stem any leaks

Fuel and exhaust systems 3•5

illustration). Check the gauze for holes. If any are found, a new tap should be fitted as the strainer is not available individually.

Installation

15 Installation is the reverse of removal. Use a new rubber seal and tighten the screws to the torque setting specified at the beginning of the Chapter (see illustration).

3 Fuel tank – cleaning and repair

1 All repairs to the fuel tank should be carried out by a professional who has experience in this critical and potentially dangerous work. Even after cleaning and flushing of the fuel system, explosive fumes can remain and ignite during repair of the tank.
2 If the fuel tank is removed from the bike, it should not be placed in an area where sparks or open flames could ignite the fumes coming out of the tank. Be especially careful inside garages where a natural gas-type appliance is located, because the pilot light could cause an explosion.

4 Air filter housing – removal and installation

Removal

1 Remove the engine (see Chapter 2).
2 Remove the air filter (see Chapter 1).
3 Release the clamps securing the crankcase breather hose and the drain hose, and on 2002 models onward the AIS (air induction system) hose, to the front of the air filter housing and detach them.
4 Unscrew the three bolts securing the top of the housing to the frame (see illustration).
5 Draw the housing forward and remove it.

Installation

6 Installation is the reverse of removal. Check the condition of the various hoses and their clamps and renew them if necessary.

5 Idle fuel/air mixture adjustment – general information

1 If the engine runs extremely rough at idle or continually stalls, and if a carburettor overhaul does not cure the problem (and it definitely is a carburation problem – see Section 6), the pilot screws may require adjustment. It is worth noting at this point that unless you have the experience to carry this out it is best to entrust the task to a motorcycle dealer, tuner or fuel systems specialist.
2 On 1995 to 2001 models, the pilot screws are located in the top of the carburettor bodies above the throttle shaft mechanism;

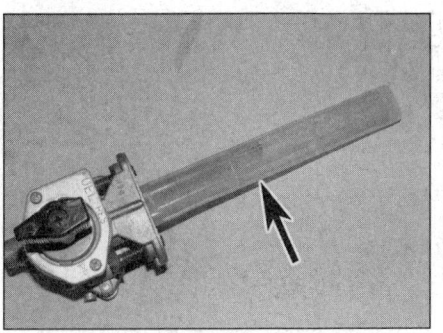

2.14 Clean and check the strainer (arrowed)

prise out the rubber blanking cap to access the screw head (see illustration 8.12). On later models (2002-on) the pilot screws are positioned underneath the carburettors, between the float bowl and the intake manifolds on the cylinder head (see illustration 8.25), and are best accessed using a purpose-made angled screwdriver with flexible drive, available from any good accessory dealer.
3 Prior to adjusting the pilot screws, make sure the valve clearances are correct and the carburettors are synchronised (see Chapter 1).
4 Warm the engine up to normal working temperature, then stop it. Screw in the pilot screw on all carburettors until they seat lightly, then back them out to the number of turns specified (see this Chapter's Specifications). This is the base position for adjustment.
3 Start the engine and reset the idle speed to the correct level (see Chapter 1). Working on one carburettor at a time, turn the pilot screw by a small amount either side of this position to find the point at which the highest consistent idle speed is obtained. When you've reached this position, reset the idle speed to the specified amount (see Chapter 1). Repeat on the other carburettors.
4 Due to the increased emphasis on controlling exhaust emissions in certain world markets, regulations have been formulated which prevent adjustment of the air/fuel mixture. On such models the pilot screw positions are pre-set at the factory and in some cases have a limiter cap fitted to prevent tampering. Where adjustment is possible, it can only be made in conjunction

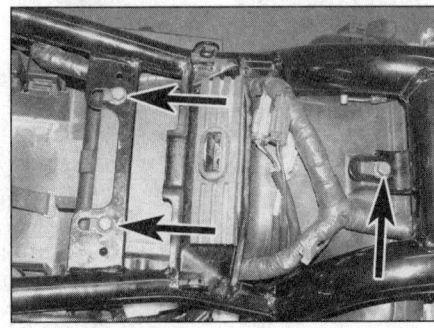

4.4 Air filter housing bolts (arrowed)

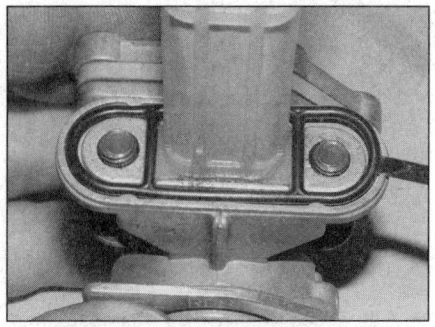

2.15 Always use a new rubber seal when installing the tap

with an exhaust gas analyser to ensure that the machine does not exceed emissions regulations.

6 Carburettor overhaul – general information

1 Poor engine performance, hesitation, hard starting, stalling, flooding and backfiring are all signs that major carburettor maintenance may be required.
2 Keep in mind that many so-called carburettor problems are really not carburettor problems at all, but mechanical problems within the engine or ignition system or other electrical malfunctions. Try to establish for certain that the carburettors are in need of maintenance before beginning a major overhaul.
3 Check the fuel tap and strainer, the fuel and vacuum hoses, the intake manifold joint clamps, the air filter, the ignition system, the spark plugs, valve clearances and carburettor synchronisation before assuming that a carburettor overhaul is required.
4 Most carburettor problems are caused by dirt particles, varnish and other deposits which build up in and block the fuel and air passages. Also, in time, gaskets and O-rings shrink or deteriorate and cause fuel and air leaks which lead to poor performance.
5 When overhauling the carburettors, disassemble them completely and clean the parts thoroughly with a carburettor cleaning solvent and dry them with filtered, unlubricated compressed air. Blow through the fuel and air passages with compressed air to force out any dirt that may have been loosened but not removed by the solvent. Once the cleaning process is complete, reassemble the carburettor using new gaskets and O-rings.
6 Before disassembling the carburettors, make sure you have all necessary O-rings and other parts, some carburettor cleaner, a supply of clean rags, some means of blowing out the carburettor passages and a clean place to work. It is recommended that only one carburettor be overhauled at a time to avoid mixing up parts.

3•6 Fuel and exhaust systems

7.2a Disconnect the throttle position sensor wiring connector – 1995 to 2001 model type shown

7.2b Throttle position sensor wiring connector (arrowed) – 2002-on models

7.2c Carburettor heater wiring connectors – 2002-on models

7 Carburettors – removal and installation

⚠️ **Warning:** *Refer to the precautions given in Section 1 before starting work.*

Removal

1 Make sure the ignition is switched OFF. Remove the battery (see Chapter 8). Remove the fuel tank (see Section 2).
2 On 1995 to 2001 models disconnect the wiring connector from the throttle position sensor, and on 2002 models onward trace the wiring from the sensor and disconnect it at the connector **(see illustrations)**. On 2002 models onward, trace the wiring from the carburettor heaters and disconnect it at the connector **(see illustration)**.
3 On 1996-on models detach the choke cable from the carburettors (see Section 12).
4 Detach the throttle cables from their bracket on the carburettors (see Section 11), but do not attempt to detach the cable ends from the throttle cam yet as it is very tricky with the carburettors in place – do it after they have been displaced.
5 Slacken the three bolts securing the top of the air filter housing to the frame **(see illustration 4.4)**.
6 Fully slacken the clamp screws or bolts securing the air intake rubbers to the carburettors – note the orientation of the clamps as they have indents which locate over tabs on the rubbers and so must be correctly positioned when tightened on installation **(see illustrations)**. On 2002 models onward draw the breather hoses out of their guides **(see illustration)**. Slide the air filter housing back off the carburettors as far as it will go **(see illustration)**.
7 Fully slacken the clamp screws or bolts securing the carburettors to the cylinder head

7.6a Air intake clamp screws (arrowed) – 1995 to 2001 models

7.6b Air intake clamp bolts (A), cylinder head manifold clamp bolts (B) – 2002-on models

7.6c Draw the breather hoses out of their guides

7.6d Draw the air filter housing back off the carburettors

Fuel and exhaust systems 3•7

7.7a Cylinder head manifold clamp screws (arrowed) – 1995 to 2001 models

7.7b Draw the carburettors back out of the manifolds . . .

7.7c . . . and slide them out to the right-hand side of the bike

manifolds, as above noting the orientation of the clamps **(see illustration or 7.6b)**. Ease the carburettors back out of the manifolds and draw them out from the right-hand side **(see illustrations)**. **Note:** *Keep the carburettors level to prevent fuel spillage from the float chambers and the possibility of the piston diaphragms being damaged.*

8 Hold the throttle cam open and detach the throttle cable ends from it, noting which fits where (see Section 11).

Caution: *Stuff clean rag into each cylinder head intake after removing the carburettors to prevent anything from falling in.*

9 Place a suitable container below the float chambers, then slacken the drain screw or bolt on each chamber in turn and drain all the fuel from the carburettors **(see illustrations)**. Tighten the drain screws or bolts securely once all the fuel has been drained.

Installation

10 Installation is the reverse of removal, noting the following.

● Check for cracks or splits in the air intake rubbers and the cylinder head manifolds, and renew them if necessary. The cylinder head manifolds are each secured by two bolts. Note the orientation of both the intake rubbers and manifolds before removing them as they must be installed in a particular way. Use new O-rings on the cylinder head manifolds and tighten the bolts to the torque setting specified at the beginning of the Chapter. The longer air intake rubbers fit into the centre holes in the air filter housing.

● Refer to Section 11 for installation of the throttle cables, which must be done before the carburettors are fully installed, and Section 12 for the choke cable (where applicable). Check the operation of the cables and adjust them as necessary (see Chapter 1).

● Make sure the carburettors are fully engaged with the cylinder head and air intake rubbers and the clamps or bolts are securely tightened.

● Do not forget to connect the heater system (2002-on models) and throttle position sensor wiring connectors.

● Make sure all hoses are correctly routed and secured and not trapped or kinked.

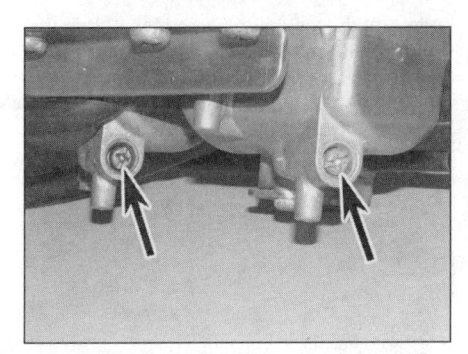

7.9a Carburettor drain screws (arrowed) – 1995 to 2001 models

● Check idle speed and carburettor synchronisation and adjust as necessary (see Chapter 1).

8 Carburettors – disassembly, cleaning and inspection

Warning: *Refer to the precautions given in Section 1 before starting work.*

Disassembly

1995 to 2001 models

1 Remove the carburettors (see Section 7). **Note:** *Do not separate the carburettors unless absolutely necessary; each carburettor can be dismantled sufficiently for all normal cleaning and adjustments while in place on the*

8.2 Top cover bolts (arrowed)

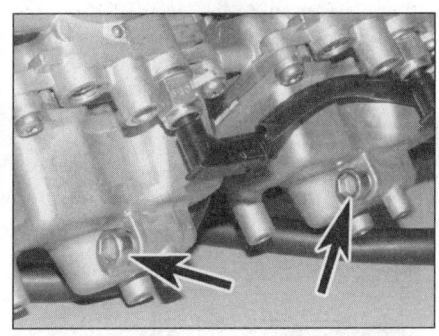

7.9b Carburettor drain bolts (arrowed) – 2002-on models

mounting brackets. Dismantle the carburettors separately to avoid interchanging parts **(see illustration 9.2)**.

2 Unscrew and remove the top cover retaining bolts – keep light finger pressure on the cover as you remove the last two as there is a spring inside which will try and push the cover up **(see illustration)**. When removing the cover on the No. 3 carburettor, note the cable holder and wiring clamp secured by the bolts. Remove the cover and withdraw the spring from the piston **(see illustrations 10.10b and a)**.

3 Carefully peel the diaphragm away from its sealing groove in the carburettor and withdraw the diaphragm and piston assembly **(see illustration)**. **Caution:** *Do not use a sharp instrument to displace the diaphragm as it is easily damaged.* Note how the tab on the diaphragm fits in the recess in the carburettor body **(see illustration 10.9b)**.

8.3 Carefully withdraw the diaphragm/piston assembly

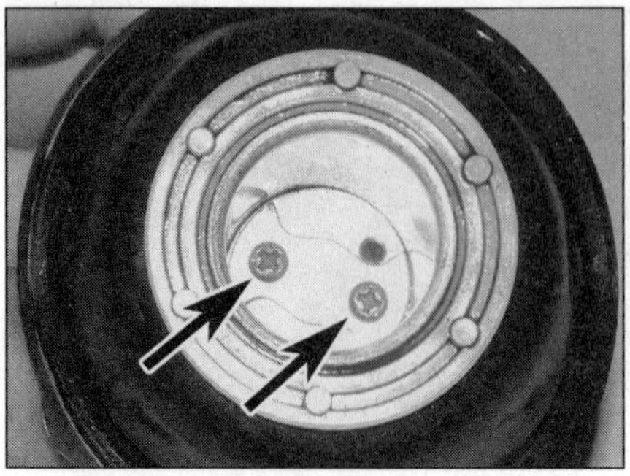

3•8 Fuel and exhaust systems

8.4a Undo the screws (arrowed) and remove the plate and spring

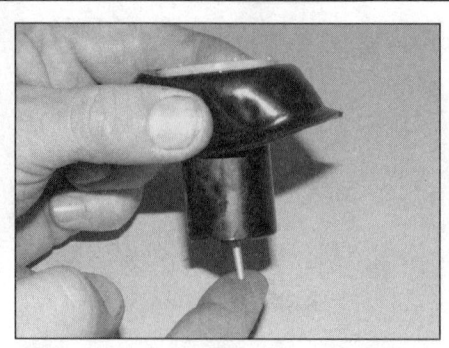

8.4b Push the needle up and withdraw it

8.5 Undo the screw (arrowed) and displace the holder

4 If necessary, undo the jet needle retainer plate screws and remove the plate and the spring, noting how they fit **(see illustration and 10.8f and e)**. Push the needle up from the bottom of the piston and withdraw it from the top **(see illustration)**. Take care not to lose the washer on the top of the needle **(see illustration 10.8c)**. There is no need to remove the E-clip and spacer from the needle **(see illustration 10.8a)**.

5 When dismantling the No. 1 carburettor, undo the screw securing the idle speed adjuster holder and displace it **(see illustration)**.

6 Undo the screws securing the float chamber to the base of the carburettor and remove the float chamber, noting how it fits **(see illustration)**. Remove the gasket and discard it as a new one must be used **(see illustration 10.7a)**.

7 Displace the float pivot pin using a small punch or a screwdriver, then withdraw the pin **(see illustration)**. Remove the float, and unhook the float needle valve, noting how it fits **(see illustrations 10.5b and a)**.

8 Undo the screw securing the float needle valve seat retaining plate and remove the plate **(see illustration)**. Draw the seat out and discard the O-ring **(see illustration 10.4b)**.

9 Unscrew and remove the pilot jet **(see illustration)**.

10 Unscrew and remove the main jet and its washer **(see illustration)**.

11 Push the needle jet up and withdraw it from the carburettor body **(see illustration)**. Note how the pin in the jet housing locates in the cut-out in the base of the jet **(see illustration 10.2b)**.

12 The pilot screw can be removed from the carburettor, but note that its setting will be disturbed (see **Haynes Hint**). Remove the blanking cap, then unscrew and remove the pilot screw along with its spring, washer and O-ring **(see illustration)**. Discard the O-ring as a new one must be used.

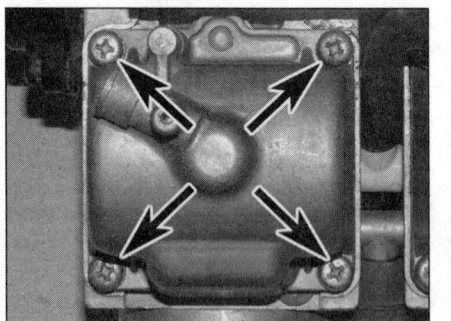

8.6 Undo the screws (arrowed) and remove the float chamber

8.7 Displace and withdraw the float pivot pin

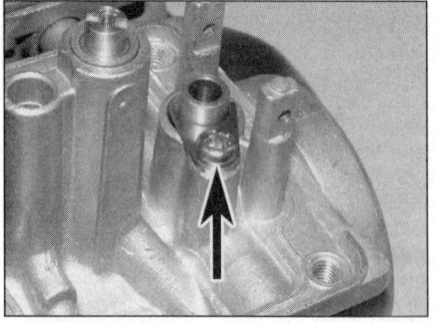

8.8 Undo the screw (arrowed) and remove the plate, then withdraw the seat

8.9 Unscrew the pilot jet (arrowed) . . .

8.10 . . . and the main jet (arrowed), noting the washer

8.11 Grasp the top of the needle jet and withdraw it

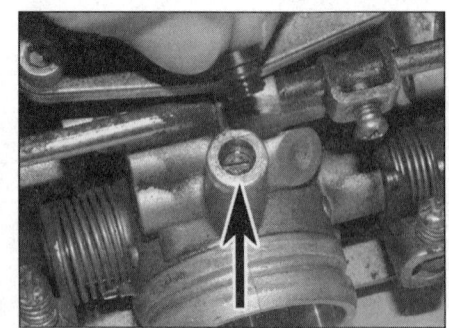

8.12 Remove the blanking cap to access the pilot screw (arrowed)

Fuel and exhaust systems 3•9

8.15 Top cover screws (arrowed)

8.16 Carefully withdraw the diaphragm/piston assembly

8.17a Remove the jet needle holder . . .

> **HAYNES HiNT** *To record the pilot screw's current setting, turn the screw in until it seats lightly, counting the number of turns necessary to achieve this, then fully unscrew it. On installation, the screw is simply backed out the number of turns you've recorded.*

13 A throttle position sensor is mounted on the outside of the right-hand carburettor. Do not remove the sensor unless absolutely necessary. Refer to Chapter 4 for details.

2002 models onward

14 Remove the carburettors (see Section 7). **Note:** *Do not separate the carburettors unless absolutely necessary; each carburettor can be dismantled sufficiently for all normal cleaning and adjustments while in place on the mounting brackets. Dismantle the carburettors separately to avoid interchanging parts* **(see illustration 9.9)**.

15 Unscrew and remove the top cover retaining screws – keep light finger pressure on the cover as you remove them as there is a spring inside which will try and push the cover up **(see illustration)**. Note that any cover screws that also secure a wiring clip or bracket are standard and there is a collar fitted in the hole in the cover, while all other screws have a collared shank and a flanged head – note what fits where. Remove the cover, noting how it fits, and withdraw the spring from the piston **(see illustrations 10.21c and b)**. Remove the air passage O-ring **(see illustration 10.21a)**.

16 Carefully peel the diaphragm away from its sealing groove in the carburettor and withdraw the diaphragm and piston assembly **(see illustration)**. **Caution: Do not use a sharp instrument to displace the diaphragm as it is easily damaged.**

17 If required, using a pair of thin-nosed pliers, carefully withdraw the jet needle holder from inside the piston – it is a press fit, held by an O-ring **(see illustration)**. Note the spring fitted into the bottom of the holder **(see illustration 10.19b)**. Push the jet needle up from the bottom of the piston and withdraw it from the top, noting the washers **(see illustration)**. There is no need to remove the E-clip and spacer from the needle **(see illustration 10.19a)**.

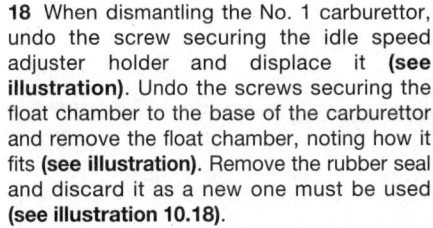

18 When dismantling the No. 1 carburettor, undo the screw securing the idle speed adjuster holder and displace it **(see illustration)**. Undo the screws securing the float chamber to the base of the carburettor and remove the float chamber, noting how it fits **(see illustration)**. Remove the rubber seal and discard it as a new one must be used **(see illustration 10.18)**.

19 Undo the screw retaining the float pivot pin **(see illustration)**. Remove the float assembly, noting how it fits **(see illustration 10.16a)**. Withdraw the pivot pin if required. Unhook the needle valve from the tab on the float, noting how it fits **(see illustration 10.5a)**.

20 Undo the screw securing the needle valve seat and draw out the seat **(see illustration)**. Discard its O-ring as a new one must be used **(see illustration 10.15a)**.

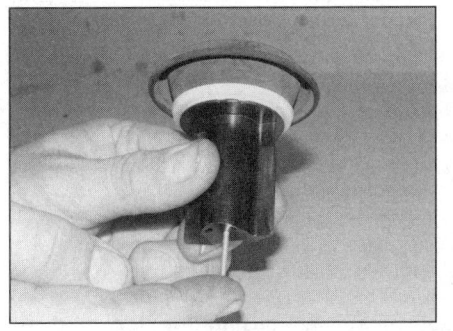

8.17b . . . then push the needle up and withdraw it

8.18a Undo the screw (arrowed) and displace the holder

8.18b Undo the screws (arrowed) and remove the float chamber

8.19 Undo the screw (arrowed) and remove the float assembly

8.20 Undo the screw (arrowed) and withdraw the seat

3•10 Fuel and exhaust systems

8.21 Unscrew the main jet (arrowed)...

8.22 ...the emulsion tube...

8.23 ...the starter jet (arrowed)...

21 Unscrew and remove the main jet **(see illustration)**.
22 Unscrew and remove the emulsion tube **(see illustration)**. The needle jet is a press fit in the body of the carburettor.
23 Unscrew and remove the starter jet, noting the collar **(see illustration)**.
24 Unscrew and remove the pilot jet **(see illustration)**.
25 The pilot screw can be removed from the carburettor, but note that its setting will be disturbed (see *Haynes Hint*). Unscrew and remove the pilot screw along with its spring, washer and O-ring **(see illustration)**. Discard the O-ring as a new one must be used.

8.24 ...and the pilot jet (arrowed)

8.25 Pilot screw (arrowed)

HAYNES HiNT *To record the pilot screw's current setting, turn the screw in until it seats lightly, counting the number of turns necessary to achieve this, then fully unscrew it. On installation, the screw is simply backed out the number of turns you've recorded.*

26 A throttle position sensor is mounted on the outside of the right-hand carburettor. Do not remove the sensor unless absolutely necessary. Refer to Chapter 4 for details.

Cleaning

Caution: Use only a petroleum based solvent for carburettor cleaning. Don't use caustic cleaners.

27 Submerge the metal components in the solvent for approximately thirty minutes (or longer, if the product directions recommend it).
28 After the carburettor has soaked long enough for the cleaner to loosen and dissolve most of the varnish and other deposits, use a nylon-bristled brush to remove the stubborn deposits. Rinse it again, then dry it with compressed air.
29 Use a jet of compressed air to blow out all of the jets and the fuel and air passages in the carburettor body. Do not forget to blow through the air jets and passages in the intake side of the carburettor.

Caution: Never clean the jets or passages with a piece of wire or a drill bit, as they will be enlarged, causing the fuel and air metering rates to be upset.

Inspection

30 Check the operation of the choke plungers by pulling on the linkage bar then letting it go. It should pull out smoothly and return home easily under spring pressure. If it doesn't move smoothly, remove the linkage bar and plungers as described below (according to model) and check all components.
31 On 1995 to 2001 models, slacken the screws securing the choke shaft to the choke plunger arms **(see illustration)**. Ease the shaft out of the arms, then remove the arms from the plungers, noting how they locate **(see illustration)**. Note the detents in the shaft which the screws locate in and serve to locate the plunger arms correctly on the shaft. Check the operation of each plunger individually **(see illustration)**. If the action on any is stiff,

8.31a Slacken the screws (arrowed)...

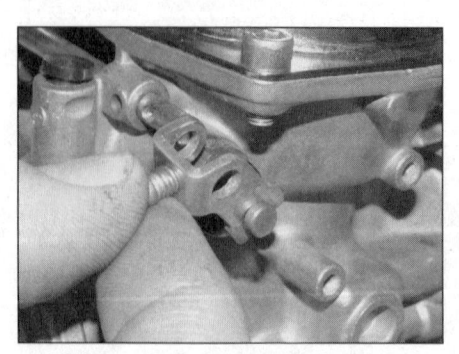

8.31b ...then withdraw the shaft and remove the arms

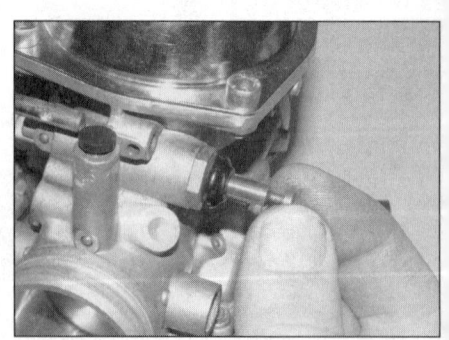

8.31c Check the action of the plunger as described

Fuel and exhaust systems 3•11

8.31d Unscrew the nut (arrowed)...

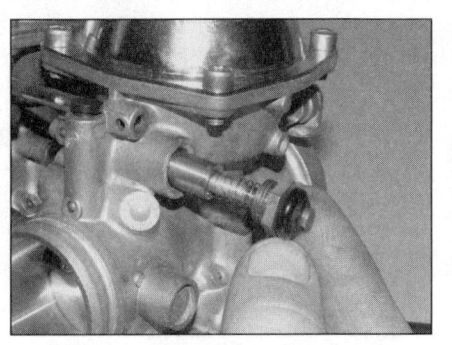

8.31e ...and withdraw the plunger assembly

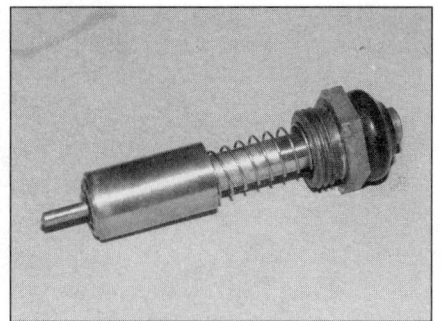

8.31f Check the plunger assembly as described

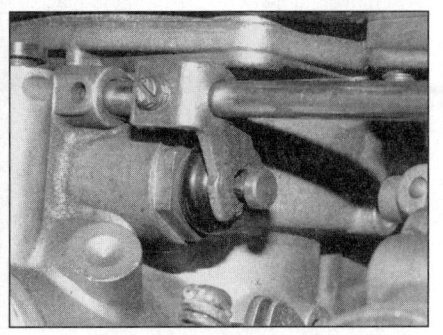

8.31g Make sure the arms locate correctly on the plungers...

8.31h ...and the shaft is aligned so the screw ends locate in the detents

unscrew the choke plunger nut, using a pair of thin nosed pliers if access is too restricted for a spanner, and withdraw the plunger assembly from the carburettor body **(see illustration)**. Inspect the needle on the end of the choke plunger, the spring and the shaft **(see illustration)**. Renew any component which is worn, damaged or bent. Note that if any plunger cannot be withdrawn with the carburettors joined, they must be separated (see Section 9). Installation of the choke assembly is the reverse of removal – make sure slots in the arms locate correctly behind the nipple on the end of each plunger, and the screw ends locate in the detents in the shaft **(see illustrations)**.

32 On 2002 models onward, unhook the choke linkage bar return spring ends and remove the spring **(see illustration)**. Undo the screws securing the linkage bar, noting the plastic washers **(see illustration)**. Lift the bar off the plungers, noting how the slots in the arms locate over the ends of the plungers. Check the operation of each plunger individually **(see illustration 8.31c)**. If the action on any is stiff, unscrew the choke plunger nut, using a pair of thin nosed pliers if access is too restricted for a spanner, and withdraw the plunger assembly from the carburettor body **(see illustrations 8.31d and e)**. Inspect the needle on the end of the choke plunger, the spring and the shaft **(see illustration 8.31f)**. Renew any component which is worn, damaged or bent. Note that if any plunger cannot be withdrawn with the carburettors joined, they must be separated (see Section 9). Installation of the choke assembly is the reverse of removal.

33 If removed from the carburettor, check the tapered portion of the pilot screw and the spring and O-ring for wear or damage. Renew them if necessary.

34 Check the carburettor body, float chamber and top cover for cracks, distorted sealing surfaces and other damage. If any defects are found, renew the faulty component, although renewal of the entire carburettor will probably be necessary (check with a Yamaha dealer on the availability of separate components).

35 Check the piston diaphragm for splits, holes and general deterioration. Holding it up to a light will help to reveal problems of this nature.

36 Insert the piston in the carburettor body and check that it moves up-and-down smoothly. Check the surface of the piston for

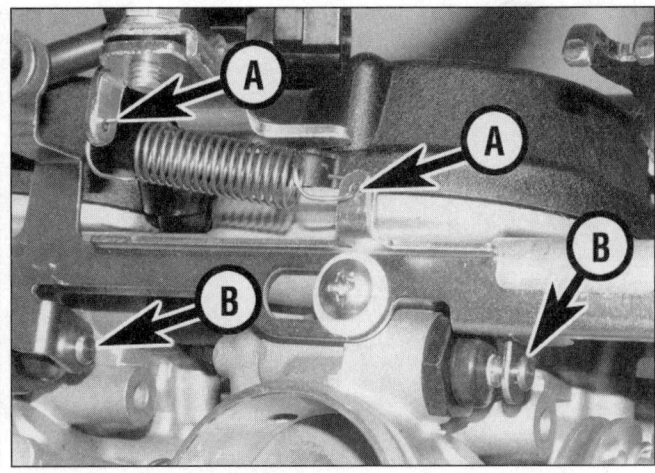

8.32a Unhook the spring ends (A). Note how the arms locate on the plungers (B)

8.32b Undo the screws (arrowed) and remove the bar

3•12 Fuel and exhaust systems

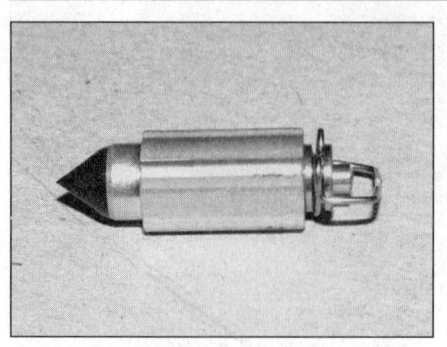

8.38 Check the needle valve as described

wear. If it's worn excessively or doesn't move smoothly in the guide, renew it.

37 Check the jet needle for straightness by rolling it on a flat surface such as a piece of glass. Renew it if it's bent or if the tip is worn.

38 Check the tip of the float needle valve and the valve seat **(see illustration)**. If either has grooves or scratches in it, or is in any way worn, they should be renewed as a set. Gently push down on the rod on the top of the needle valve then release it – if it doesn't spring back, renew the valve. Check the gauze strainer on the valve seat for holes or splits and renew it if necessary **(see illustration 10.4a)**.

39 Operate the throttle shaft to make sure the throttle butterfly valve opens and closes smoothly. If it doesn't, cleaning the throttle linkage may help. Otherwise, renew the carburettor.

40 Check the float for damage. This will usually be apparent by the presence of fuel inside the float. If the float is damaged, it must be renewed.

41 On 2002 models onward, to check the carburettor heaters and circuit, refer to Section 13.

9 Carburettors – separation and joining

⚠ *Warning: Refer to the precautions given in Section 1 before proceeding.*

Separation

1995 to 2001 models

1 The carburettors do not need to be separated for normal overhaul. If you need to separate them (to renew a carburettor body, for example), refer to the following procedure.

2 Remove the carburettors from the machine (see Section 7). Mark the body of each carburettor with its cylinder location to ensure that it is positioned correctly on reassembly **(see illustration)**.

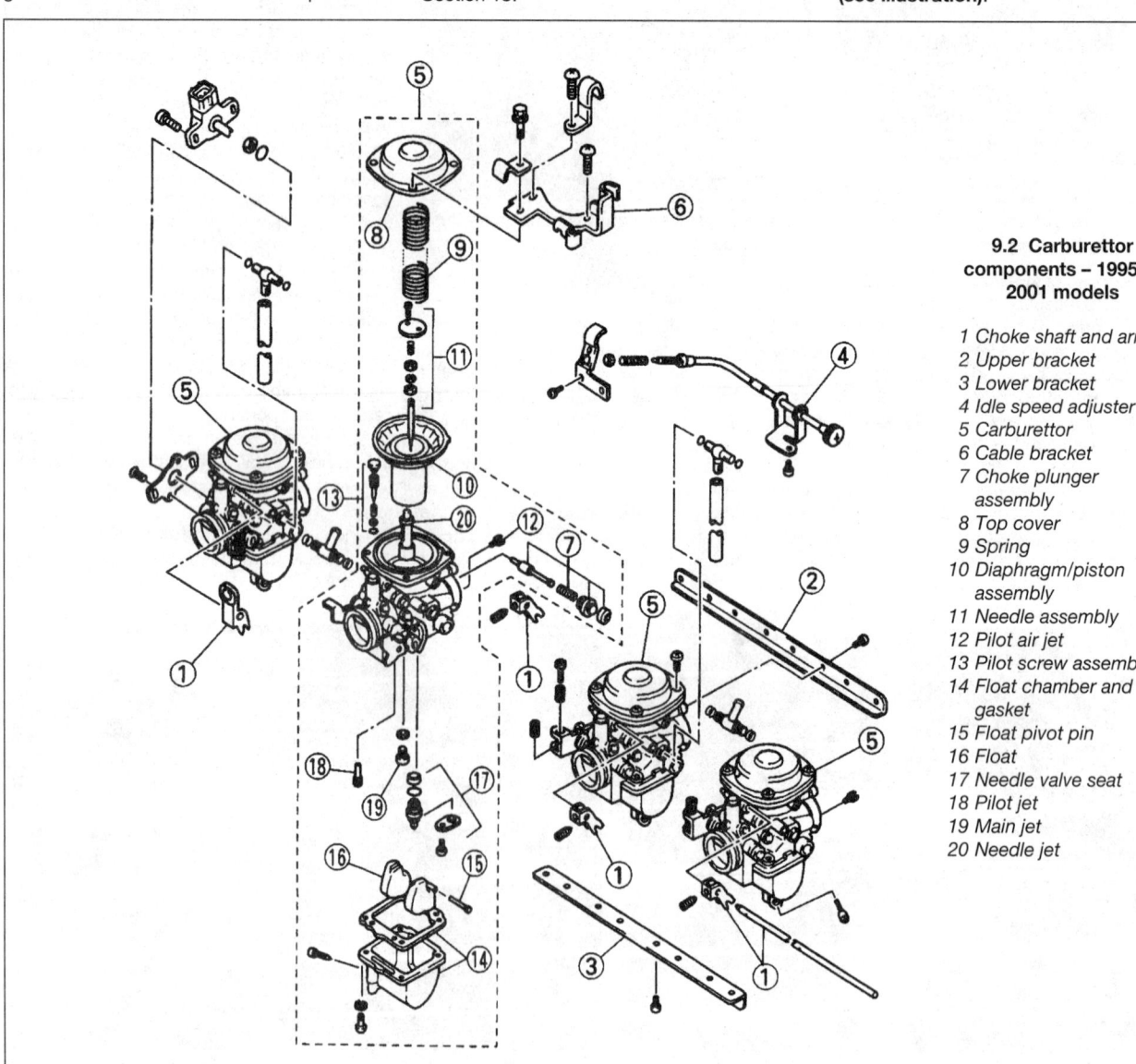

9.2 Carburettor components – 1995 to 2001 models

1 Choke shaft and arms
2 Upper bracket
3 Lower bracket
4 Idle speed adjuster
5 Carburettor
6 Cable bracket
7 Choke plunger assembly
8 Top cover
9 Spring
10 Diaphragm/piston assembly
11 Needle assembly
12 Pilot air jet
13 Pilot screw assembly
14 Float chamber and gasket
15 Float pivot pin
16 Float
17 Needle valve seat
18 Pilot jet
19 Main jet
20 Needle jet

Fuel and exhaust systems 3•13

9.3a Note the arrangement of the throttle springs . . .

9.3b . . . synchronisation springs . . .

3 Make a note of how the throttle return springs, linkage assembly and carburettor synchronisation springs are arranged to ensure that they are fitted correctly on reassembly **(see illustrations)**. Also note the arrangement of the various hoses, unions, joint pieces and collars, and of the cable brackets **(see illustrations)**.

4 Undo the screws securing the choke shaft to the choke plunger arms **(see illustration 8.31a)**. Ease the shaft out of the arms, then remove the arms from the plungers, noting how they locate **(see illustrations 8.31b)**. Note the detents in the shaft which serve to locate the plunger arms correctly on the shaft **(see illustration 8.31h)**.

5 Undo the screw securing the idle speed adjuster holder to the No. 1 carburettor float chamber and displace it **(see illustration 8.5)**.

6 Remove the screws securing the carburettors to the two mounting brackets and remove the brackets **(see illustrations)**. If it is not essential to separate all the carburettors, only release those necessary and leave the others attached to the brackets.

7 Mark the position of each carburettor and gently separate them, noting how the throttle linkage is connected, and being careful not to lose any springs or fuel and vent fittings that are present between the carburettors, noting any O-rings fitted with them.

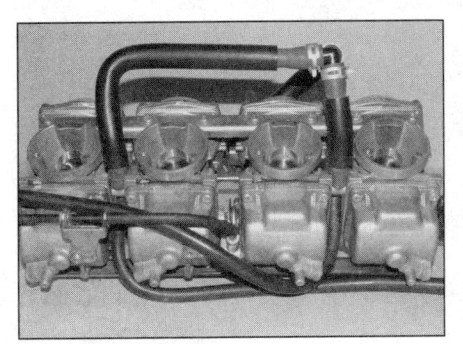

9.3c . . . hoses and unions . . .

9.3d . . . and cable brackets

2002 models onward

8 The carburettors do not need to be separated for normal overhaul. If you need to separate them (to renew a carburettor body, for example), refer to the following procedure.

9 Remove the carburettors from the machine (see Section 7). Mark the body of each

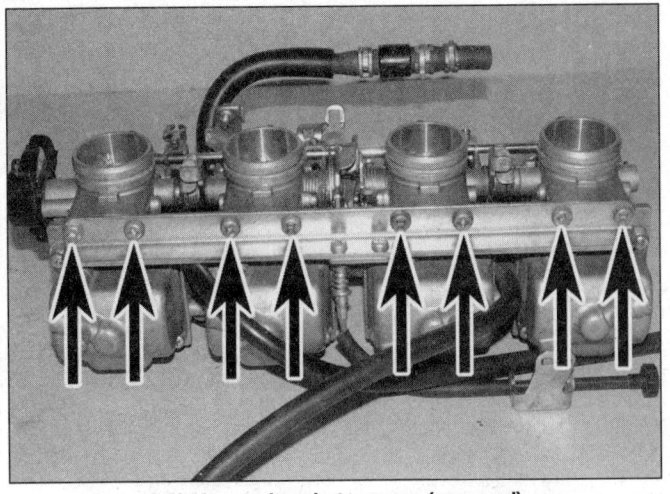

9.6b Lower bracket screws (arrowed)

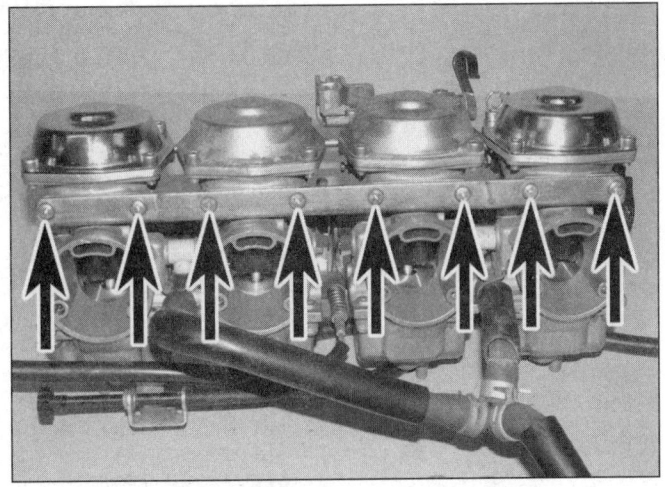

9.6a Upper bracket screws (arrowed)

3•14 Fuel and exhaust systems

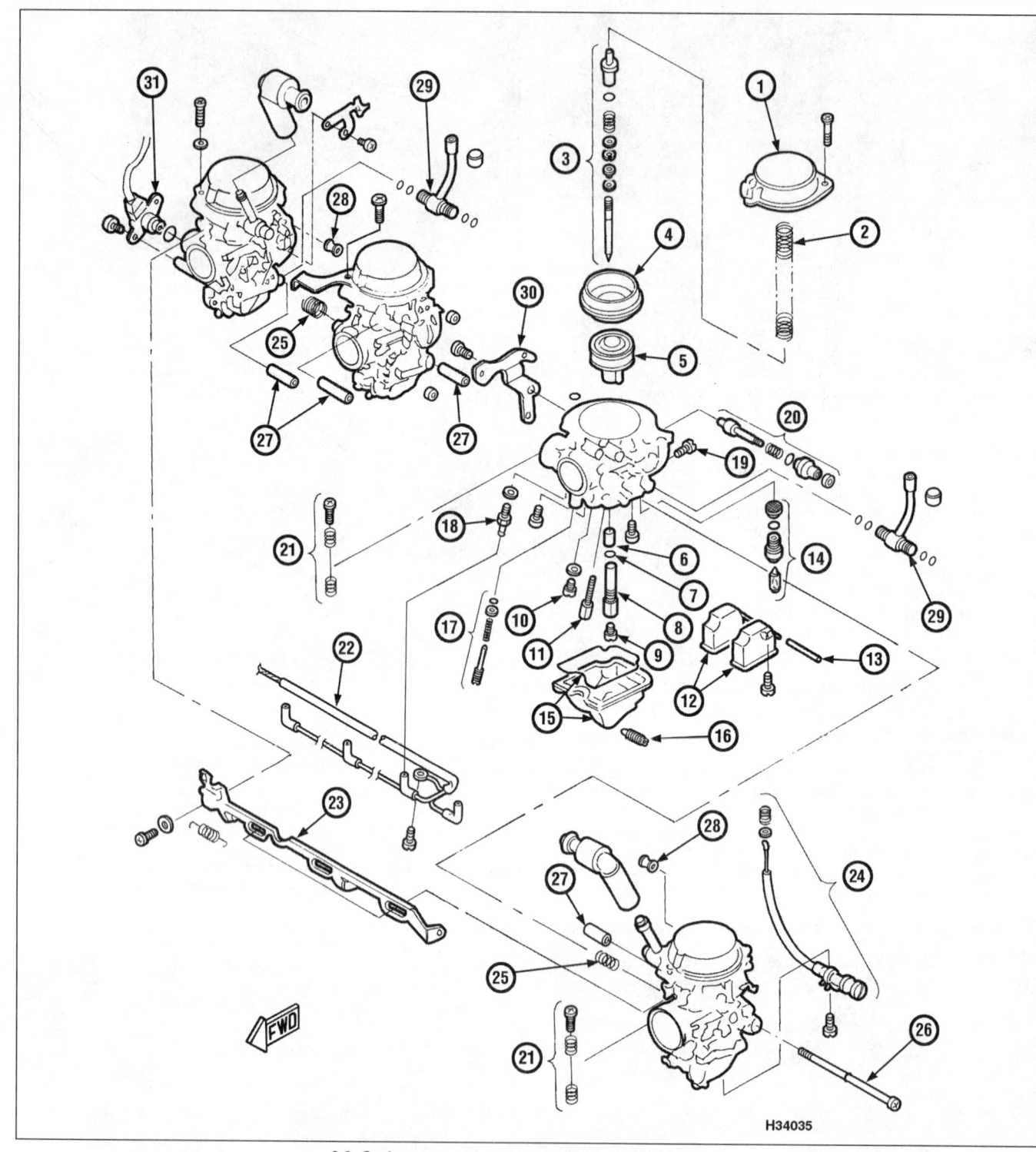

9.9 Carburettor components – 2002 models onward

1 Top cover	9 Main jet	17 Pilot screw assembly	25 Throttle shaft spring
2 Spring	10 Starter jet	18 Heater	26 Joining bolts
3 Needle assembly	11 Pilot jet	19 Air jet	27 Spacers
4 Diaphragm	12 Float	20 Choke plunger assembly	28 Connectors
5 Piston	13 Float pivot pin	21 Synchronisation screw	29 Fuel unions
6 Needle jet	14 Needle valve and seat	22 Heater sub harness	30 Throttle cable bracket
7 O-ring	15 Float chamber and gasket	23 Choke shaft	31 Throttle position sensor
8 Emulsion tube	16 Drain screw	24 Idle speed adjuster	

Fuel and exhaust systems 3•15

carburettor with its cylinder number to ensure that it is positioned correctly on reassembly **(see illustration)**.

10 Disconnect the wiring connector from each carburettor heater **(see illustration)**. Free the wiring from its cable tie and remove it.

11 Unhook the choke linkage bar return spring ends and remove the spring **(see illustration 8.32a)**. Undo the screws securing the linkage bar, noting the plastic washers **(see illustration 8.32b)**. Lift the bar off the arms, noting how it locates.

12 Make a note of how the throttle return springs, linkage assembly and carburettor synchronisation springs are arranged to ensure that they are fitted correctly on reassembly **(see illustrations)**. Also note the arrangement of the various hoses, unions, joint pieces and collars, and of the cable brackets **(see illustrations)**.

13 Unscrew the two long bolts which join the carburettors together and withdraw them. Note the spacers between each carburettor. If it is not essential to separate all the carburettors, only release those necessary and leave the others joined.

14 Mark the position of each carburettor and gently separate them, noting how the throttle linkage is connected, and being careful not to lose any spacers, springs or fuel and vent fittings that are present between the carburettors, noting any O-rings fitted with them.

Joining

15 Assembly is the reverse of the disassembly procedure, noting the following.
- Lubricate the O-rings with a light film of oil. Make sure the fuel and vent fittings are correctly and securely inserted into the carburettors.
- Install the synchronisation springs after the carburettors are joined together. Make sure they are correctly and squarely seated. Visually synchronise the throttle butterfly valves by turning the synchronising screws to equalise the clearance between the butterfly valve and throttle bore of each carburettor.

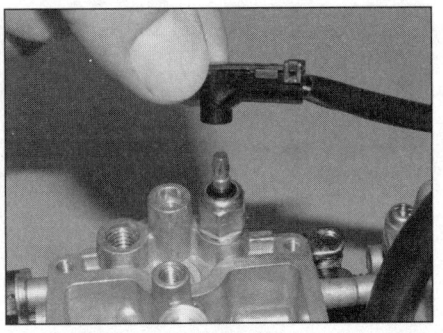

9.10 Disconnect the heater wiring connectors

9.12b ... the various unions ...

- Check the operation of both the choke and throttle linkages ensuring that both operate smoothly and return quickly under spring pressure before installing the carburettors on the machine.
- Install the carburettors (see Section 7) and check carburettor synchronisation and idle speed (see Chapter 1).

10 Carburettors – reassembly and float height/fuel level check

⚠️ *Warning: Refer to the precautions given in Section 1 before proceeding.*

Note: *When reassembling the carburettors, be sure to use the new O-rings, seals and other*

9.12a Note the arrangement of the throttle springs and synchronisation springs ...

9.12c ... and hoses

parts supplied in the rebuild kit. Do not overtighten the carburettor jets and screws as they are easily damaged.

Reassembly and float height check

1995 to 2001 models

1 Install the pilot screw (if removed) along with its spring and O-ring, turning it in until it seats lightly **(see illustration 8.12)**. Now, turn the screw out the number of turns previously recorded, or as specified at the beginning of the Chapter. Fit the blanking cap.

2 Slide the needle jet into the body of the carburettor, making sure the pin in the jet housing locates in the cut-out in the base of the jet **(see illustrations)**. Screw the main jet into the end of the needle jet, not forgetting its washer **(see illustration)**.

10.2a Slide the needle jet into its bore ...

10.2b ... locating the pin in the cutout (arrow)

10.2c Screw the main jet into the needle jet, not forgetting the washer

3•16 Fuel and exhaust systems

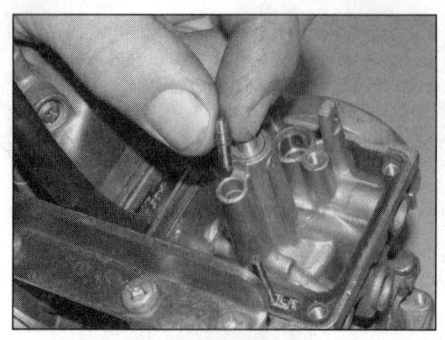

10.3 Screw the pilot jet into the carburettor

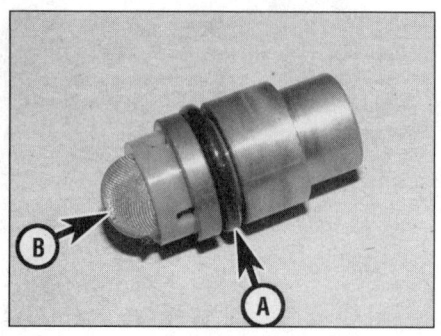

10.4a Fit a new O-ring (A) and make sure the gauze (B) is clean

10.4b Install the seat . . .

10.4c . . . and secure it with the retainer

10.5a Hook the valve onto the tab . . .

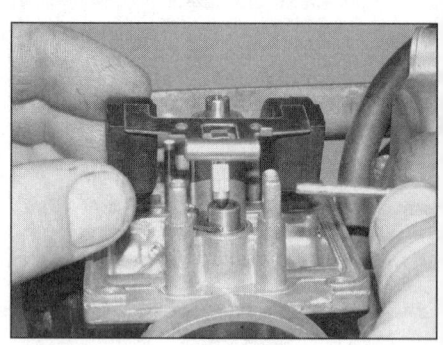

10.5b . . . then install the float assembly and pin

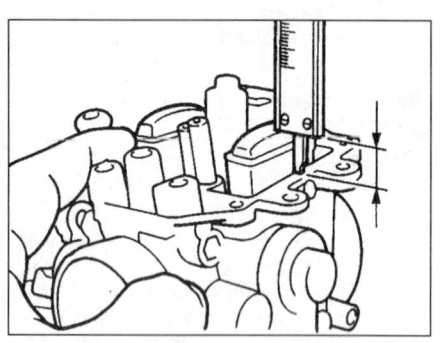

10.6 Checking float height

3 Screw the pilot jet into the carburettor **(see illustration)**.
4 Fit a new O-ring onto the needle valve seat **(see illustration)**. Make sure the strainer is clean, then press the seat into the carburettor and secure it with its retaining plate and screw **(see illustrations)**.
5 Hook the float needle valve onto the float, then position the float assembly in the carburettor and install the pivot pin, making sure it is secure **(see illustrations)**.
6 To check the float height, hold the carburettor so the float hangs down, then tilt it back until the needle valve is just seated, but not so far that the needle's spring-loaded tip is compressed. Measure the height of the float above the chamber gasket face (with the gasket removed) with an accurate ruler **(see illustration)**. The height should be as specified at the beginning of the Chapter. If not, adjust the float height by carefully bending the float tab a little at a time until the correct height is obtained. **Note:** *With the float held the same way up as it is when installed, bending the tab up increases the float height – bending it down decreases the float height.*
7 Fit a new gasket onto the carburettor then fit the float chamber and tighten its screws securely **(see illustrations)**. When assembling the No. 1 carburettor, fit the idle speed adjuster holder and secure it with its screw **(see illustration 8.5)**.

10.7a Fit a new gasket . . .

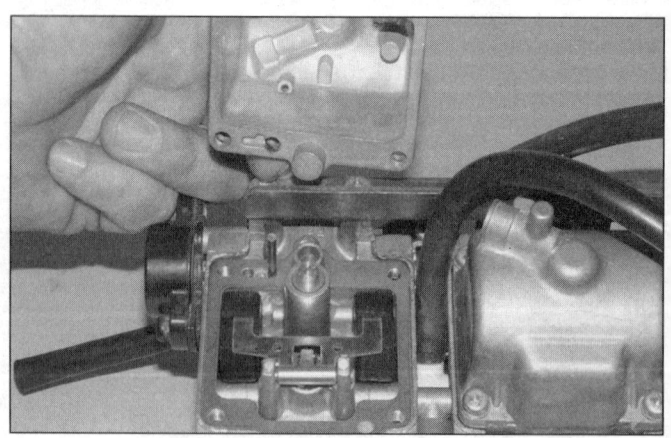

10.7b . . . then install the float chamber

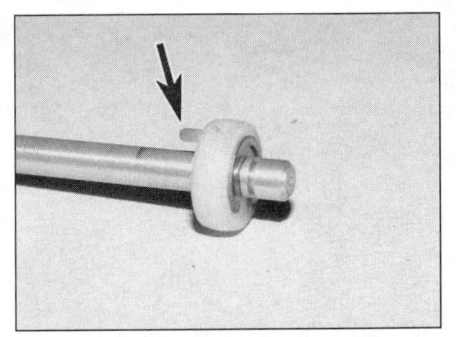

Fuel and exhaust systems 3•17

10.8a Make sure the E-clip and spacer are fitted on the needle. Note the peg (arrowed) . . .

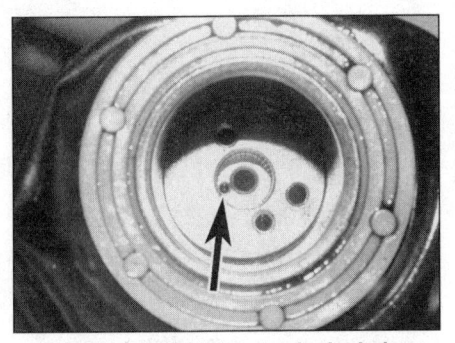

10.8b . . . which locates in the hole (arrowed) in the piston

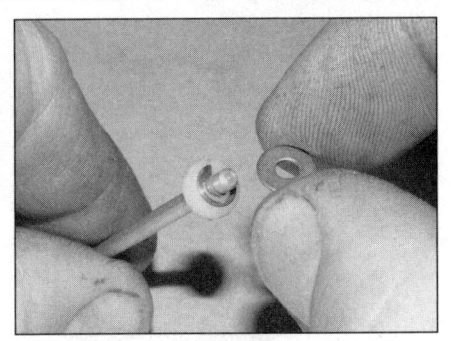

10.8c Fit the washer onto the needle

10.8d Fit the needle into the piston . . .

10.8e . . . then fit the spring onto the needle

8 Check that the spacer and E-clip are correctly installed on the jet needle, and note that the peg on the bottom of the spacer locates in the hole in the base of the piston (see illustrations). Fit the washer onto the top of the needle (see illustration). Carefully fold the piston diaphragm down, then insert the needle, making sure the peg locates in the hole (see illustration). Fit the spring over the top of the needle, then fit the retainer plate and secure it with the screws (see illustrations).

9 Insert the piston assembly into the carburettor and lightly push it down, ensuring the needle is correctly aligned with the needle jet (see illustration). Press the diaphragm rim into its groove, making sure it is correctly seated and that the tab locates in the recess (see illustration). Check the diaphragm is not creased, and that the piston moves smoothly up and down in the carburettor.

10 Fit the spring into the piston (see illustration). Fit the top cover onto the carburettor, locating the top of the spring into the recess, and tighten the screws securely (see illustration).

10.8f Fit the retainer plate . . .

10.8g . . . and secure it with the screws

10.9a Insert the piston assembly, making sure the needle enters its jet . . .

10.9b . . . then press the rim into the groove, noting the tab (arrowed)

10.10a Insert the spring . . .

10.10b . . . then install the cover

3•18 Fuel and exhaust systems

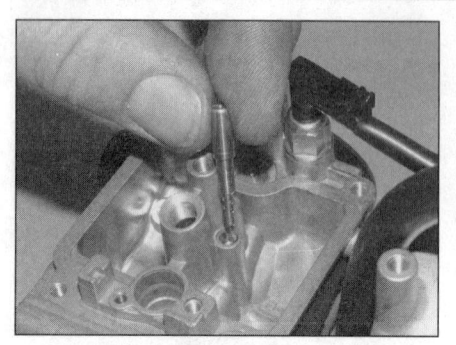

10.12 Install the pilot jet . . .

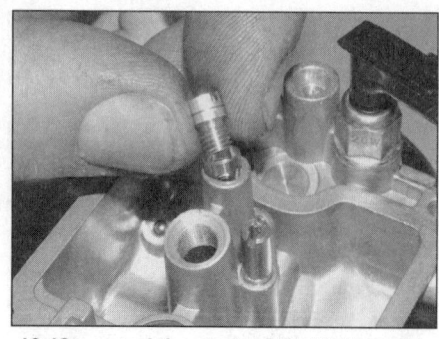

10.13 . . . and the starter jet with its collar

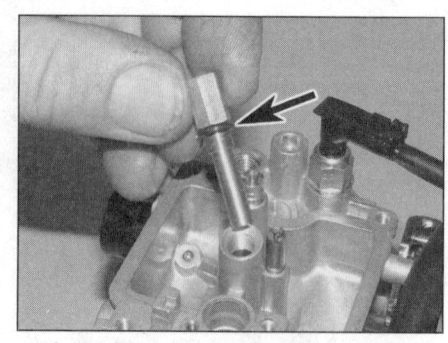

10.14a Fit a new O-ring (arrowed) then install the emulsion tube

10.14b Thread the main jet into the emulsion tube

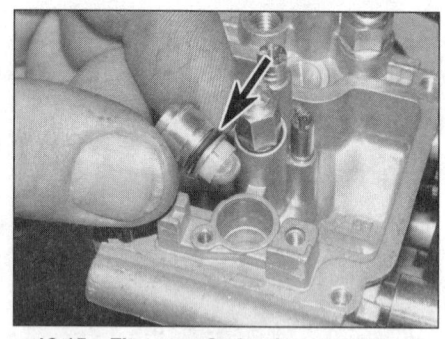

10.15a Fit a new O-ring (arrowed) then install the seat . . .

10.15b . . . and secure it with the screw

2002 models onward

Note: *When reassembling the carburettors, be sure to use the new O-rings, seals and other parts supplied in the rebuild kit. Do not overtighten the carburettor jets and screws as they are easily damaged.*

11 Install the pilot screw (if removed) along with its spring, washer and O-ring, turning it in until it seats lightly **(see illustration 8.25)**. Now, turn the screw out the number of turns previously recorded, or as specified at the beginning of the Chapter.

12 Screw the pilot jet into the carburettor **(see illustration)**.

13 Fit the starter jet with its collar and screw the jet into the carburettor **(see illustration)**.

14 If removed, press the needle jet into position in the carburettor body. Fit a new O-ring onto the emulsion tube and screw the emulsion tube into the carburettor (see illustration). Screw the main jet into the end of the emulsion tube **(see illustration)**.

15 Fit a new O-ring onto the needle valve seat. Make sure the filter is clean, then press the seat into place and secure it with the screw **(see illustrations)**.

16 Hook the float needle valve onto the tab on the float assembly **(see illustration 10.5a)**. Insert the pivot pin into the float pivot if removed. Position the float assembly onto the carburettor, making sure the needle valve locates in the seat **(see illustration)**. Install the pivot pin retaining screw **(see illustration)**.

17 To check the float height, hold the carburettor so the float hangs down, then tilt it back until the needle valve is just seated, but not so far that the needle's spring-loaded tip is compressed. Measure the height of the float above the chamber mating surface with an accurate ruler **(see illustration 10.6)**. The height should be as specified at the beginning of the Chapter. If not, adjust the float height by carefully bending the float tab a little at a time until the correct height is obtained. **Note:** *With the float held the same way up as it is when installed, bending the tab up lowers the fuel level – bending it down raises the fuel level.*

18 Fit a new rubber seal onto the float chamber, making sure it is seated properly in its groove, then fit the chamber onto the carburettor and tighten its screws securely **(see illustration)**. When assembling the No. 1 carburettor, fit the idle speed adjuster holder and secure it with its screw **(see illustration 8.18a)**.

19 Check that the spacer and E-clip are correctly installed on the jet needle, then fit the washers on top of the clip and underneath

10.16a Install the float assembly . . .

10.16b . . . and secure it with the screw

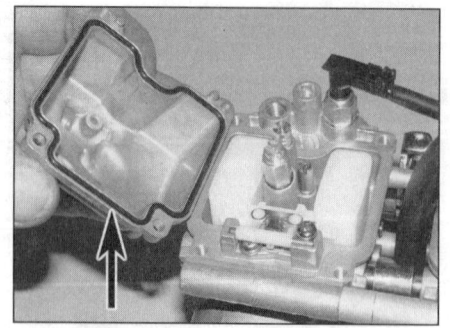

10.18 Fit a new seal (arrowed) then install the float chamber

Fuel and exhaust systems 3•19

10.19a Check that the E-clip and spacer are on the needle, then fit the washers

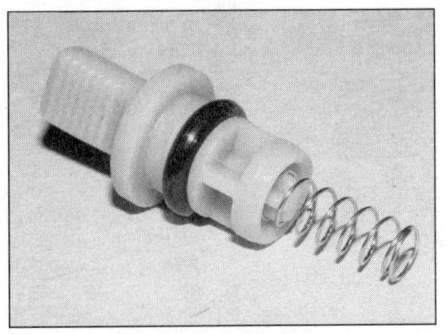

10.19b Make sure the spring is in the holder, and fit a new O-ring if necessary

10.19c Insert the needle . . .

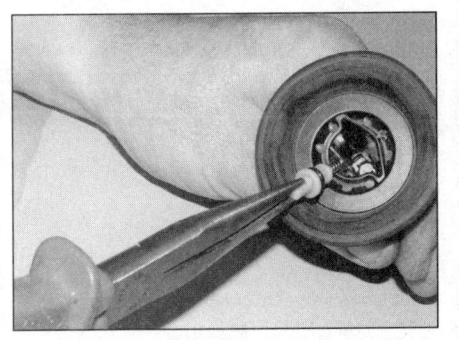

10.19d . . . and secure it with the holder

10.20 Insert the piston assembly, making sure the needle enters its jet

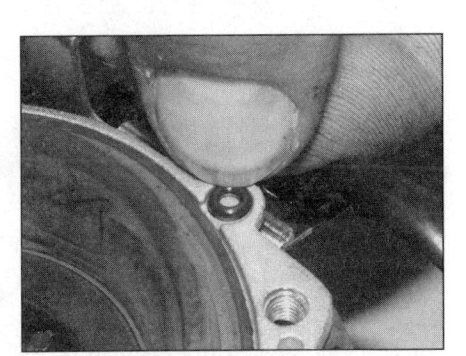

10.21a Fit the O-ring . . .

the spacer **(see illustration)**. Check that the spring and O-ring are fitted to the needle holder – use a new O-ring if necessary **(see illustration)**. Carefully fold the piston diaphragm down, then fit the needle into the piston, making sure the lower washer does not drop off by holding the piston horizontal **(see illustration)**. Fit the needle holder, locating the spring over the top of the needle, and press it gently down until it is secure **(see illustration)**.

20 Insert the piston/diaphragm assembly into the carburettor and lightly push the piston down, making sure the needle is correctly aligned with the needle jet **(see illustration)**. Press the diaphragm outer edge into its groove, making sure it is correctly seated. Check the diaphragm is not creased, and that the piston moves smoothly up and down in the carburettor.

21 Fit the air passage O-ring **(see illustration)**. Fit the spring into the piston, making sure it locates correctly onto the needle holder **(see illustration)**. Fit the top cover, locating the central peg into the top of the spring, and aligning it so the air passage locates over the O-ring and the small pegs locate in their holes, and tighten its screws securely **(see illustration)**.

Fuel level check

Note: *The fuel level is checked with the carburettors installed.*

22 To check the fuel level, position the motorcycle on level ground and support it using the centrestand so that it is vertical. Remove the fuel tank (see Section 2).

23 Arrange a temporary fuel supply, either by using a small temporary tank or by using an extra long fuel pipe to the now remote fuel tank (see **Tool Tip** in Chapter 1, Section 4). Alternatively, position the tank on a suitable base on the motorcycle, taking care not to scratch any paintwork, and making sure that the tank is safely and securely supported. Connect the fuel line to the carburettors.

24 Yamaha provide a fuel level gauge (Pt. No. 90890-01312), or alternatively a suitable length of clear plastic tubing can be used. Attach the gauge or tubing to the drain hose union on the bottom of the float chamber on the first carburettor and position its open end vertically and above the level of the carburettors **(see illustration)**.

25 If the fuel tank is being used, turn the tap to PRI. Slacken the drain screw and allow the fuel to flow into the tube. The level at which

10.21b . . . then insert the spring

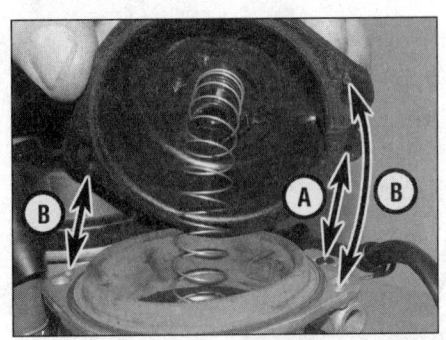

10.21c Fit the top cover, aligning the air passage with the O-ring (A) and the peg with the hole (B)

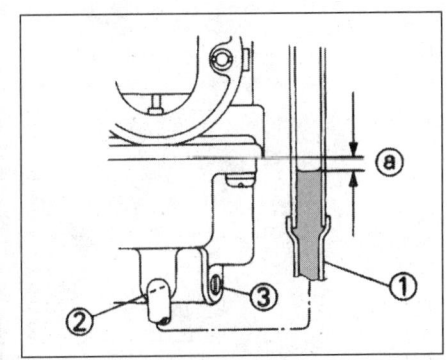

10.24 Fuel level check set-up
1 Gauge
2 Drain hose union
3 Drain screw
a Fuel level measurement

3•20 Fuel and exhaust systems

11.3a Slacken the top locknut and thread it up . . .

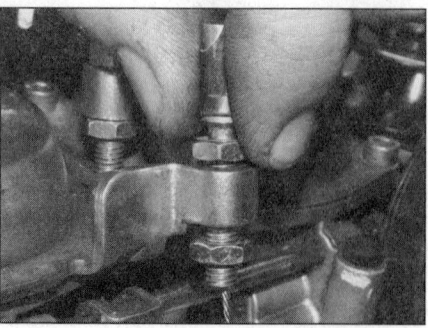

11.3b . . . then slide the cable down . . .

11.3c . . . and out of the bracket

the fuel stabilises in the tubing indicates the level of the fuel in the float chamber. Refer to the Specifications at the beginning of the Chapter and measure the level relative to the mating surface of the float chamber with the carburettor body. Tighten the drain screw, then detach the fuel supply.

26 If the level was incorrect, remove the carburettors, then remove the float from the chamber (see Section 8), and adjust the float height by carefully bending the float tab a little at a time until the correct height is obtained. Repeat the procedure for the other carburettors. **Note:** *With the float held the same way up as it is when installed, bending the tab up lowers the fuel level – bending it down raises the fuel level.*

11 Throttle cables – removal and installation

Warning: Refer to the precautions given in Section 1 before proceeding.

Note: *At the carburettor end of the cables, on 1995 to 2001 models the accelerator (opening cable) fits into the front holder on the cable bracket and the decelerator (closing) cable fits into the rear holder, and the choke cable (where fitted) routes between the two throttle cables. On 2002 models onward the throttle cables are the other way round in the bracket, and the choke cable routes in front of both of them.*

Removal

1 Remove the fuel tank (see Section 2).

2 Mark each cable according to its location at both ends. If new cables are being fitted, match them to the old cables to ensure they are correctly installed.

3 Slacken the accelerator (opening) cable top locknut and thread it up the elbow, then slide the cable down in the bracket until the bottom locknut is clear of the small lug on the bracket and slip the cable out of the bracket **(see illustrations)**.

4 Unscrew the decelerator (closing) cable hex, pulling up on it as you do so the lower nut remains captive against the lug on the bracket, thereby threading itself down **(see illustration)**. When there is enough clearance, slide the cable down in the bracket until the lower nut is clear and slip the cable out of the bracket **(see illustration)**.

5 Remove the carburettors (see Section 7), then hold the throttle cam open and detach the cable ends from it as they become accessible **(see illustrations)**.

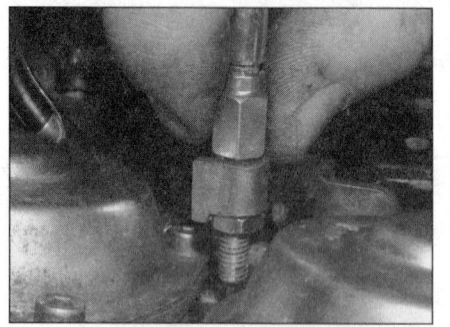

11.4a Unscrew the hex . . .

11.4b . . . and slip the cable out of the bracket

11.5a Detach the accelerator cable end from the cam . . .

11.5b . . . then the decelerator cable

Fuel and exhaust systems 3•21

11.7a Pull back the boot . . .

11.7b . . . then unscrew the bolts . . .

11.7c . . . separate the halves and detach the elbows . . .

6 Withdraw the cables from the machine noting their correct routing.

7 Pull the rubber boot back off the throttle housing on the handlebar **(see illustration)**. Unscrew the throttle housing bolts and separate the halves **(see illustration)**. Displace the cable elbows from the housing, noting how they fit, and detach the cable nipples from the pulley **(see illustrations)**. Mark each cable to ensure it is connected correctly on installation.

Installation

8 Lubricate the cable nipples with multi-purpose grease and fit them into the throttle pulley at the handlebar, making sure they are the correct way round. Fit the cable elbows into the housing, making sure they locate correctly. Join the housing halves, making sure the pin locates in the hole in the handlebar, and tighten the bolts **(see illustration)**. Fit the rubber boot.

9 Feed the cables through to the carburettors, making sure they are correctly routed (see **Note** above). The cables must not interfere with any other component and should not be kinked or bent sharply.

10 Fit the carburettors part-way between the engine and air filter housing (see Section 7). Lubricate the cable ends with multi-purpose grease. Hold the throttle cam open and fit the cable ends into their sockets, making sure they are the correct way round (see **Note**

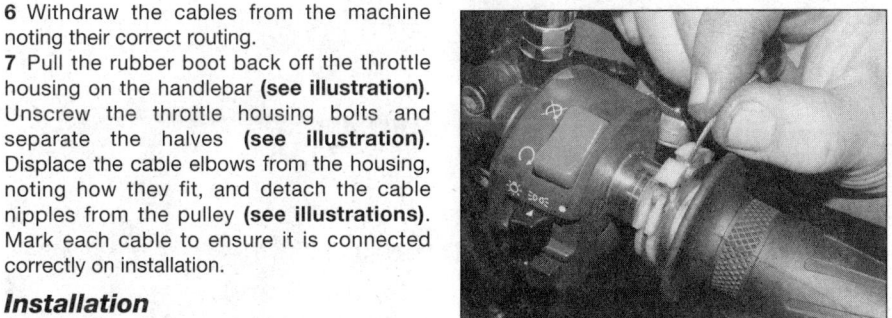

11.7d . . . and detach the cable ends

above). Install the carburettors (see Section 7).

11 Fit the decelerator cable into its holder (see **Note** above) and draw it up so that the lower nut becomes captive against the small lug. Tighten the hex down onto the bracket.

12 Fit the accelerator cable into the upper bracket and adjust is described in Chapter 1 to obtain the correct amount of freeplay.

13 Operate the throttle to check that it opens and closes freely. Turn the handlebars back and forth to make sure the cables do not cause the steering to bind.

14 Install the fuel tank (see Section 2).

15 Start the engine and check that the idle speed does not rise as the handlebars are turned. If it does, the throttle cables are

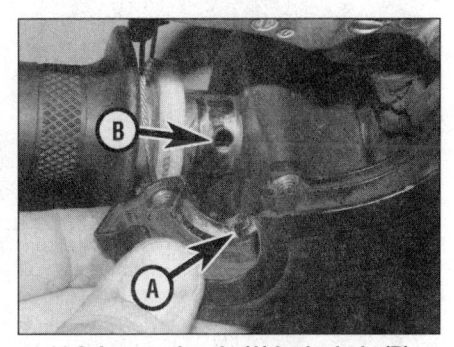

11.8 Locate the pin (A) in the hole (B)

routed incorrectly. Correct the problem before riding the motorcycle.

12 Choke cable – removal and installation

Note: *A choke cable is not fitted on 1995 models.*

Removal

1 Remove the fuel tank (see Section 2).
2 Slacken the choke outer cable holder bolt or screw and free the cable from the holder, then detach the inner cable end from its socket **(see illustrations)**.

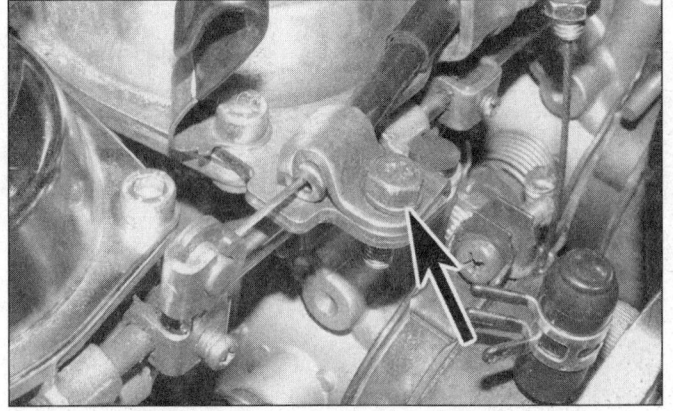

12.2a Slacken the bolt or screw (arrowed), then free the outer cable from the clamp . . .

12.2b . . . and the inner cable from its socket

3

3•22 Fuel and exhaust systems

3 Unscrew the two handlebar switch/choke lever housing screws and separate the two halves **(see illustrations)**. Lift the cable elbow and lever out of the housing, noting how they fit, and detach the cable nipple from the lever **(see illustration)**.

Installation

4 Install the cable making sure it is correctly routed. On 1996 to 2001 models the choke cable routes between the two throttle cables. On 2002 models onward the choke cable routes in front of both of them. The cable must not interfere with any other component and should not be kinked or bent sharply.

5 Lubricate the upper end of the cable with multi-purpose grease and attach it to the choke lever. Fit the lever and cable elbow into the housing, then fit the two halves of the housing onto the handlebar, making sure the lever fits correctly, and the pin in the front half of the housing locates in the hole in the front of the handlebar **(see illustration)**. Install the screws and tighten them securely.

6 Attach the lower end of the cable to its socket on the carburettor. Fit the outer cable into its bracket, making sure there is a small amount of freeplay in the inner cable, and tighten the screw.

7 Check the operation of the choke cable (see Chapter 1).

8 Install the fuel tank (see Section 2).

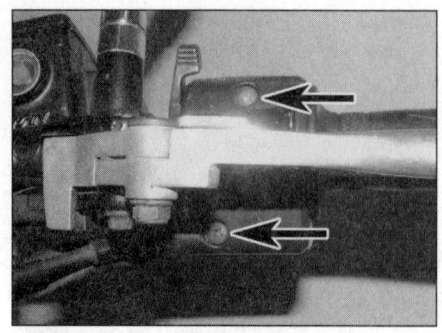

13 Carburettor heater system – check

Note: *The heater system is only fitted on 2002 models.*

> **Warning:** Refer to the precautions given in Section 1 before starting work.

1 Each carburettor has a heater unit threaded into the underside of its body. The heaters are controlled by a thermo-switch and a relay. When the ignition is ON, power from the relay is fed to the thermo switch, which when closed (temperature below 11°C) allows power to pass to the carburettor heaters. When the temperature rises above 16°C the thermo switch opens and shuts off power to the heaters. To prevent overheating of the carburettors when the engine is running at idle speed in traffic, the relay cuts off power to the thermo switch when the transmission is in neutral. Before checking the system, check the ignition circuit fuse and all the connectors, referring to the wiring diagram at the end of Chapter 8.

2 To test a heater, disconnect the wiring connector **(see illustration 9.10)**. You should be able to access all connectors and heaters with the carburettors in situ, but remove them if required (see Section 7). Using an ohmmeter or multimeter set to the ohms x 1 scale, connect the positive (+ve) probe to the tip of the heater and the negative (-ve) probe to the hex on the base of each heater. The resistance of each heater should be as specified at the beginning of the Chapter. If not, renew the heater. Note that depending on the tools available, access to some of the heaters is restricted and may necessitate removal of the carburettors (see Section 7).

3 To check the relay, remove the seat (see Chapter 8). Displace the relay from its mount and disconnect its wiring connector **(see illustration)**. Using an ohmmeter or continuity tester, connect the positive (+ve) probe to the relay's red/white wire terminal, and the negative (–ve) probe to the relay's black wire terminal. There should be continuity. Leaving the meter connected, now connect a fully charged 12 volt battery using two insulated jumper wires, connecting the positive (+ve) terminal of the battery to the relay's brown terminal, and the negative (–ve) terminal of the battery to the relay's light blue wire terminal. No continuity should be shown. If the relay does not behave as described, renew it.

4 To check the thermo switch, remove the

12.3a Undo the screws (arrowed) . . .

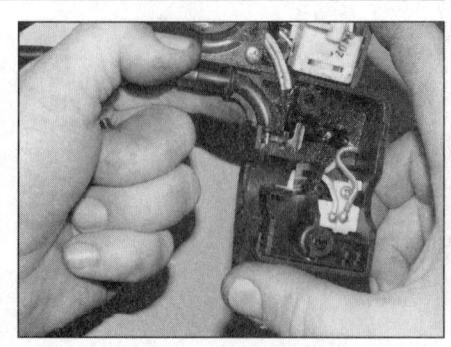

12.3b . . . then separate the halves and lift the lever and cable elbow out

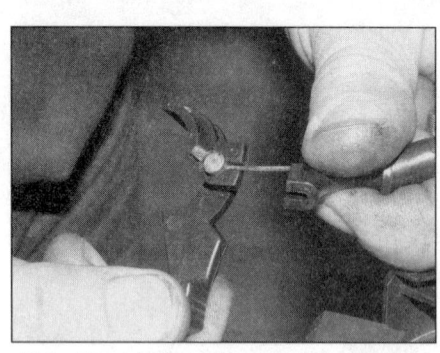

12.3c Detach the cable end from the lever

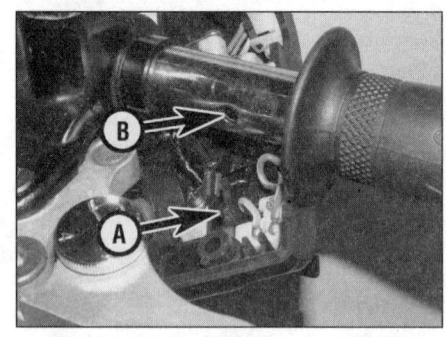

12.5 Locate the pin (A) in the hole (B)

13.3 Carburettor heater relay (arrowed)

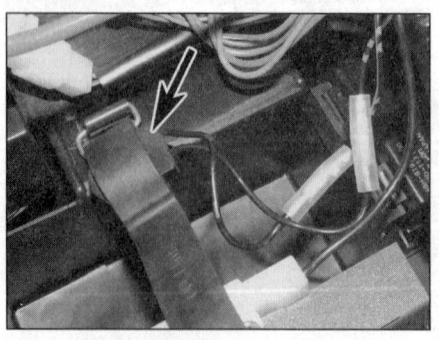

13.4a Remove the thermo switch from its holder . . .

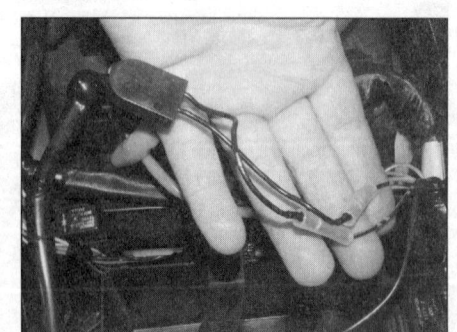

13.4b . . . and disconnect the wiring connectors

Fuel and exhaust systems 3•23

14.1 Slacken the clamp bolt (arrowed)

14.2a Unscrew the bolt . . .

14.2b . . . and remove the silencer

seat (see Chapter 7), then remove it from its holder in the battery strap and unplug the wiring connectors **(see illustrations)**. To properly check the action of the switch you will need a thermometer and a way of isolating the switch in a container that can be warmed up and cooled down, effectively to simulate increasing and decreasing air temperatures. Using a continuity tester or multimeter, connect the positive (+ve) probe to the black wire terminal, and the negative (–ve) probe to the black/red wire terminal. When the air is cool (below 11°C) the meter reading should show continuity, indicating that the switch is closed (ON). As the temperature rises, the meter should continue to show continuity until the temperature reaches 16°C, whereupon it should open and show no continuity (OFF). As the temperature falls again, the meter should continue to show no continuity until the temperature drops to 11°C, whereupon it should close and show continuity (ON). If the meter readings are obtained at different temperatures, or if it remains constantly ON or OFF at all temperatures, then the switch is faulty and must be renewed.

5 If the heaters, the relay and the switch are all good, refer to the *Wiring Diagrams* at the end of Chapter 8 and check the circuits for damaged or broken wiring.

14 Exhaust system – removal and installation

Warning: If the engine has been running the exhaust system will be very hot. Allow the system to cool before carrying out any work.

Silencers

Removal

1 Slacken the clamp bolt securing the silencer to the collector box **(see illustration)**.

2 Unscrew and remove the silencer mounting bolt and its washer, then release the silencer from the collector box **(see illustrations)**. Note the collar fitted in the rubber mounting bush. Check the condition of the bush and renew it if it is damaged, deformed or deteriorated.

3 Check the condition of the sealing rings in the silencers and renew them if they are damaged or deformed. Yamaha recommend always using new ones, but they can be difficult to remove, and unless they are damaged they are re-usable. It is too easy to damage a new one trying to install it to make it worthwhile destroying a good one that is already installed. If necessary, dig the old ones out using a screwdriver, then push the new ones into place **(see illustrations)**.

Installation

4 Make sure the collar is fitted in the rubber mounting bush.

5 Fit the silencer into the collector box, making sure it is pushed fully home. Align the silencer mounting bracket at the rear and install the bolt with its washer, aligning the captive nut in the bracket with it, and tighten it finger-tight.

6 Tighten the clamp bolt to the torque setting specified at the beginning of the Chapter, then tighten the silencer mounting bolt to the specified torque.

7 Run the engine and check that there are no exhaust gas leaks from the system.

Downpipe/collector box assembly

Note: *It is worth spraying some penetrating fluid or WD40 onto the flange nuts and downpipe-to-collector box clamp bolts (if you need to separate them) and allowing it to work its way in before starting as they are prone to seizing.*

Removal

8 Remove the silencers (see above).

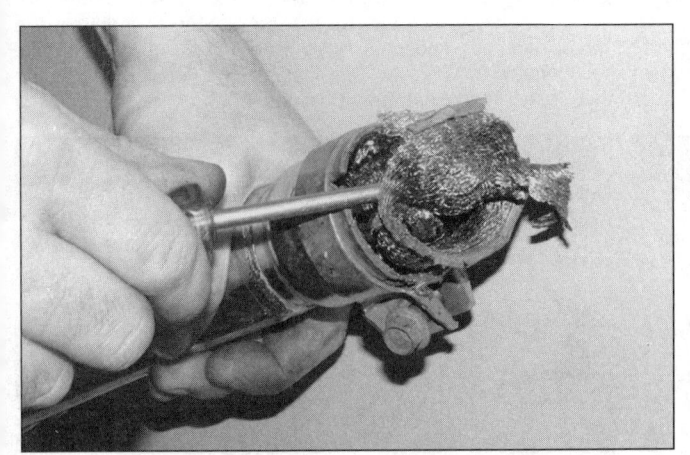

14.3a You will probably have to dig the old sealing ring out

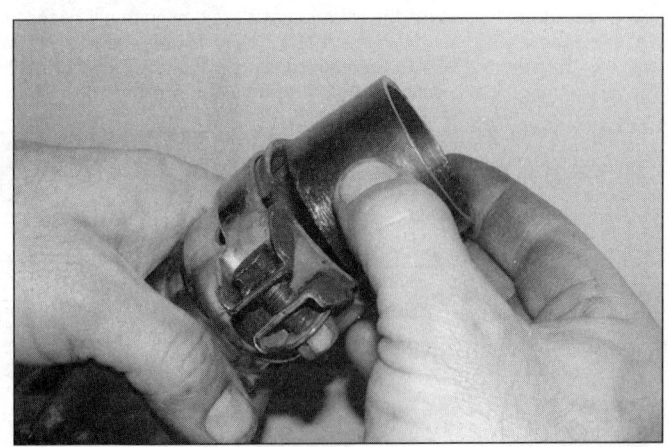

14.3b Fit the new sealing ring carefully as they are easily damaged

3•24 Fuel and exhaust systems

14.9 Unscrew the nuts (arrowed) on each downpipe and draw the flanges off

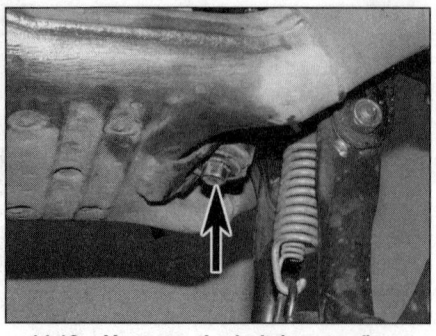

14.10a Unscrew the bolt (arrowed) . . .

14.10b . . . and remove the downpipe assembly

14.11 Remove the old gasket and fit a new one

9 Unscrew the eight downpipe flange nuts and draw the flanges off the studs **(see illustration)**.
10 Supporting the system, unscrew the bolt securing the rear of the collector box, then detach the downpipes from the cylinder head and remove the system **(see illustrations)**. Note the collar fitted in the collector box rubber mounting bushes. Check the condition of the bushes and renew them if they are damaged, deformed or deteriorated.
11 Remove the gasket from each port in the cylinder head and discard them as new ones must be fitted – you may have to dig them out using a screwdriver, so take care not to damage the head **(see illustration)**.
12 If required, slacken the clamp bolts securing the downpipes in the collector box and separate them. Refer to Step 3 regarding the sealing rings in the collector box.

Installation

Note: *Clean all corrosion off the nuts and bolts using a wire brush. It is worth applying a smear of copper grease to all threads to prevent them from seizing in the future.*
13 If separated, fit the downpipes into the box, making sure they are pushed fully home. Align them so they are roughly in the correct position. Do not tighten the clamp bolts yet.
14 Make sure the collar is fitted in the collector box rubber mounting bushes.
15 Fit a new gasket into each of the cylinder head ports. Apply a smear of grease to the gaskets to keep them in place whilst fitting the downpipes if necessary.
16 Manoeuvre the assembly into position so that the head of each downpipe is located in its port in the cylinder head, then install the collector box bolt, but do not yet tighten it fully.
17 Locate the downpipe flanges onto the studs, then fit the nuts and tighten them to the torque setting specified at the beginning of the Chapter. Now tighten the rear bolt to the specified torque. If the downpipes were separated from the collector box, also tighten the clamp bolts to the specified torque.
18 Install the silencers (see above).
19 Run the engine and check that there are no exhaust gas leaks from the system.

15 Fuel gauge and level sender – check, removal and installation

Check

1 The circuit consists of the sender mounted in the fuel tank and the gauge mounted in the instrument panel. If the system malfunctions check first that the battery is fully charged and that the signal circuit fuse is good (see Chapter 8). If they are, remove the sender (see below).
2 Connect the positive (+ve) probe of an ohmmeter to the green terminal on the sender connector, and the negative (-ve) probe to the black terminal. Check the resistance of the sender in both the FULL and EMPTY positions and compare the readings to those specified at the beginning of the Chapter **(see illustrations)**. If the readings are not as specified, renew the sender.
3 If the readings are as specified, connect the sender wiring connector and turn the ignition switch ON. With the sender in the FULL position, the gauge should read FULL, and with the sender in the empty position the gauge should read EMPTY (the gauge needle may not respond immediately – leave it in the position being tested for at least three minutes to accurately check the system).
4 If the gauge responds as described, remove the headlight (see Chapter 8) and disconnect the 9-pin instrument cluster wiring connector **(see illustration)**. Check for voltage to the gauge by connecting the positive (+ve) probe of a voltmeter to the brown terminal on the loom side of the instrument cluster wiring connector, and the

15.2a Check the resistance in the FULL position . . .

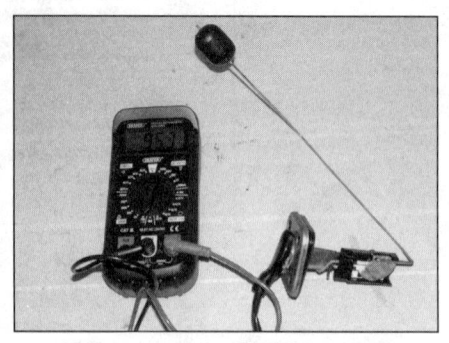

15.2b . . . and the EMPTY position

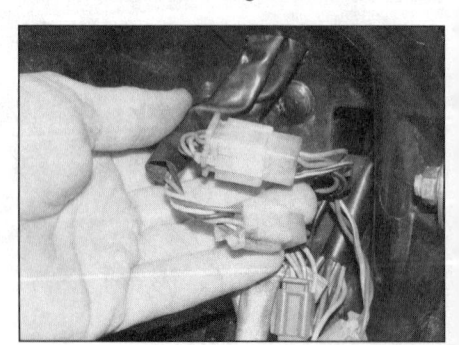

15.4 Disconnect the 9-pin instrument connector

Fuel and exhaust systems 3•25

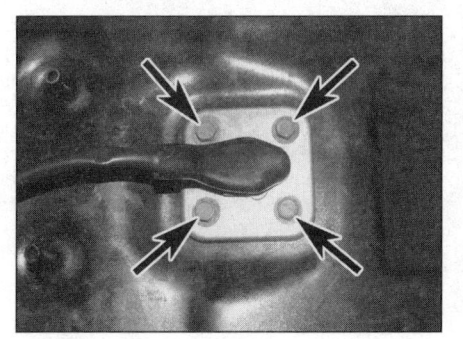

15.9a Unscrew the bolts (arrowed) . . .

15.9b . . . and carefully draw the sender out

15.10a Fit a new gasket . . .

negative (-ve) probe to the black terminal, then turn the ignition switch ON. If no voltage is present, check for continuity to earth in the black wire, then if that is good check all the relevant wiring and wiring connectors in the power circuit to the instrument cluster, and between the sender and the gauge, referring to the *Wiring Diagrams* at the end of Chapter 8. If the wiring and connectors are good, there could be an internal fault in the instrument cluster wiring between the connector and the gauge. If not, renew the gauge.

5 Check that no fuel has entered the float due to a leak, and check that the arm moves up and down smoothly.

Removal and installation

⚠️ **Warning:** *Refer to the precautions given in Section 1 before starting work.*

6 See Chapter 8 for details of the fuel gauge removal and installation.
7 To access the sender, remove the fuel tank (see Section 2).
8 If required, connect a drain hose to the fuel outlet union on the tap and insert its end in a container suitable and large enough for storing the petrol. Turn the fuel tap to the PRI position and allow the tank to drain. When the tank has drained, turn the tap to the ON or RES position. If you don't want to drain the tank, make sure the filler cap is secure, then turn the tank over and lay it on a cushion of rags to protect it and soak up any fuel that may leak.

9 Remove the bolts securing the sender and carefully manoeuvre it out of the tank **(see illustrations)**. Discard the gasket.
10 Fit a new gasket onto the sender then install then sender in the tank with the wiring to the back **(see illustrations)**. Tighten the bolts evenly and a little at a time in a criss-cross pattern to the torque setting specified at the beginning of the Chapter.
11 Install the tank (see Section 2), and check carefully that there are no leaks around the sender before using the bike.

16 Air induction system (AIS) – general information, removal and installation

Note: *The AIS is only fitted on 2002 models onward.*

General information

1 The air induction system uses negative exhaust gas pulses to suck fresh air into the exhaust ports, where it mixes with hot combustion gases. The extra oxygen causes continued combustion, allowing unburnt hydrocarbons to burn off, thereby reducing emissions. Reed valves control the flow of air into the ports and prevent exhaust gases flowing back into the AIS. An air cut-off valve shuts off the flow of air during deceleration, preventing backfiring.
2 Refer to Chapter 1 for routine checks of the system.

3 If the control valve is thought to be faulty, remove it (see below). Yamaha provide no test details for the valve, and it comes as a unit with no individual parts available. However in theory with no vacuum applied to the air cut-off valve union on the top of the control valve, it should be possible to blow air into the hose union from the air filter and it should exit via the reed valves through the unions for the hoses to the cylinder head. If you then apply a vacuum it should not be possible to blow air through. If not, the control valve is faulty. Also it should not be possible to blow air through in the opposite direction via any one of the cylinder head hose unions and for it to exit via the air filter hose union, if you can, then the reed valve for the union that does allow air to pass is faulty.
4 The tests described above should give a good indication of the control valve's condition, but as there are no specifications for the vacuum required to open the air cut-off valve and the pressure required to open the reed valves, a valve assembly that does not behave as described should not automatically be condemned as faulty. Take it to a Yamaha dealer for testing, or substitute it with a known good one.

Removal

5 When removing the engine or valve cover, release the clamps and detach the hoses from the control valve unions, then slacken the clamps and detach the pipes from the unions on the cylinder head **(see illustrations)**.

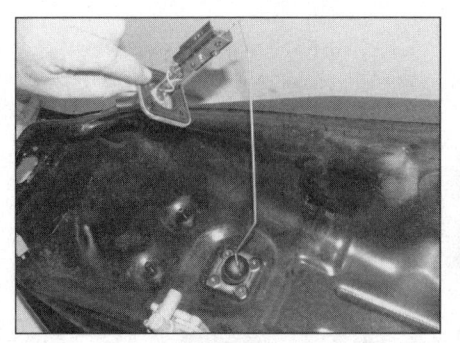

15.10b . . . then carefully install the sender

16.5a Detach the hoses from the valve (arrowed)

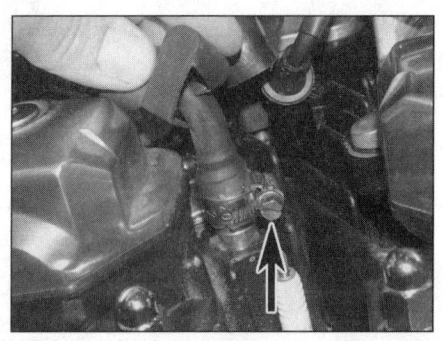

16.5b Slacken the clamp screw (arrowed) on each pipe and detach them from their unions

3•26 Fuel and exhaust systems

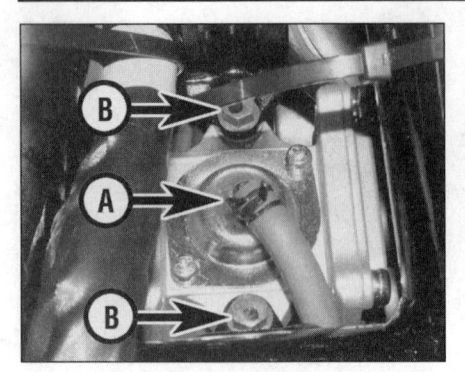

16.6 Control valve vacuum hose union (A) and mounting bolts (B)

Remove the hoses and pipes, noting how they fit. Remove the sealing collars from the cylinder head unions and renew them if they are deformed or damaged.

6 To remove the control valve, release the clamps securing the air inlet hose, the vacuum hose, and the outlet hoses and detach them from their unions, noting which fits where **(see illustration 16.5a)**. Unscrew the two bolts securing the control valve and remove it **(see illustration)**.

7 To remove the reed valves, first remove the control valve. Undo the side cover screws and remove the cover, then lift the reed valves out – there are two valves per cover on each side. Clean off any carbon build-up, and check that the maximum amount of bend in the reed is 0.2 mm.

8 To remove the air cut-off valve, first remove the control valve. Undo the two air cut-off valve screws, then withdraw the valve from the housing.

9 To renew any hoses or pipes, release the clamps securing them and disconnect them at each end, referring to Step 5 if disconnecting the pipes from the cylinder head.

Installation

10 Reassemble the system, making sure all the hoses and pipes are correctly and securely connected at each end and held by their clamps, and are correctly routed.

Chapter 4
Ignition system

Contents

Clutch switch – check and renewal .... see Chapter 8
General information 1
Ignition (main) switch – check, removal and installation .see Chapter 8
Ignition control unit – check, removal and installation 5
Ignition HT coil assembly – check, removal and installation 3
Ignition system – check 2
Ignition timing – general information and check 6
Neutral switch – check and renewal .... see Chapter 8
Pick-up coil – check, removal and installation 4
Sidestand switch – check and renewal .... see Chapter 8
Spark plugs – check .... see Chapter 1
Starter circuit cut-off relay – check and renewal .... see Chapter 8
Throttle position sensor – check, adjustment, removal
 and installation 7

Degrees of difficulty

| Easy, suitable for novice with little experience | Fairly easy, suitable for beginner with some experience | Fairly difficult, suitable for competent DIY mechanic | Difficult, suitable for experienced DIY mechanic | Very difficult, suitable for expert DIY or professional |

Specifications

General information
Cylinder numbering .... 1 to 4 from left to right
Spark plugs .... see Chapter 1

Ignition timing
At idle .... 5° BTDC @ 1050 rpm
Full advance .... 50° BTDC @ 5000 rpm

Pick-up coil
Resistance
 1995 to 1998 models .... 304 to 456 ohms @ 20°C
 1999 models onwards .... 248 to 372 ohms @ 20°C

Ignition HT coils
Primary winding resistance .... 1.9 to 2.9 ohms @ 20°C
Secondary winding resistance (without plug caps) .... 9.5 to 14.3 K-ohms @ 20°C
Spark plug cap resistance .... approx. 10 K-ohms @ 20°C
Minimum spark gap (see Section 2) .... 6 mm

Throttle position sensor
XJR1200
 Maximum resistance .... 5.0 ± 1.5 K-ohms
 Resistance range .... Zero to 5.0 ± 1.5 K-ohms
XJR1300
 Maximum resistance .... 5.0 ± 1.0 K-ohms
 Resistance range .... Zero to 5.0 ± 1.0 K-ohms

Torque wrench settings
Pick-up coil baseplate screws .... 4 Nm
Pick-up coil cover screws .... 7 Nm

1 General information

All models are fitted with a fully transistorised electronic ignition system, which due to its lack of mechanical parts is totally maintenance free. The system comprises a trigger, pick-up coil, ignition control unit and ignition HT coils (refer to the wiring diagrams at the end of Chapter 8 for details). All models are fitted with two HT coils. A throttle position sensor mounted on the right-hand end of the carburettors provides throttle opening information to the ignition control unit.

The ignition trigger, which is on the left-hand end of the crankshaft, magnetically operates the pick-up coil as the crankshaft rotates. The pick-up coil sends a signal to the ignition control unit which then supplies the ignition HT coils with the power necessary to produce a spark at the plugs. Each HT coil works on the 'wasted spark' principle with each spark plug sparking twice for every cycle of the engine; once on the compression stroke and once on the exhaust stroke.

The system incorporates an electronic advance system controlled by signals from the ignition trigger and pick-up coil and the throttle position sensor.

4•2 Ignition system

The system also incorporates a safety interlock circuit which will cut the ignition if the sidestand is extended whilst the engine is running and in gear, or if a gear is selected whilst the engine is running and the sidestand is extended. It also prevents the engine from being started if the engine is in gear unless the clutch lever is pulled in and the sidestand is up.

Because of their nature, the individual ignition system components can be checked but not repaired. If ignition system troubles occur, and the faulty component can be isolated, the only cure for the problem is to renew the part. Keep in mind that most electrical parts, once purchased, cannot be returned. To avoid unnecessary expense, make very sure the faulty component has been positively identified before buying a replacement part.

Note that there is no provision for adjusting the ignition timing on these models.

2 Ignition system – check

Warning: The energy levels in electronic systems can be very high. On no account should the ignition be switched on whilst the plugs or plug caps are being held. Shocks from the HT circuit can be most unpleasant. Secondly, it is vital that the engine is not turned over or run with any of the plug caps removed, and that the plugs are soundly earthed (grounded) when the system is checked for sparking. The ignition system components can be seriously damaged if the HT circuit becomes isolated.

1 As no means of adjustment is available, any failure of the system can be traced to failure of a system component or a simple wiring fault. Of the two possibilities, the latter is by far the most likely. In the event of failure, check the system in a logical fashion, as described below.

2 Working on one cylinder at a time, pull the cap off the spark plug **(see illustration)**. Fit a spare spark plug that is known to be good into the cap and lay the plug against the cylinder head with the threads contacting it. If necessary, hold the spark plug with an insulated tool.

Warning: Do not remove any of the spark plugs from the engine to perform this check – atomised fuel being pumped out of the open spark plug hole could ignite, causing severe injury! Make sure the plugs are securely held against the engine – if they are not earthed when the engine is turned over, the ignition control unit could be damaged.

3 Check that the kill switch is in the 'RUN' position and the transmission is in neutral, then turn the ignition switch ON and turn the engine over on the starter motor. If the system is in good condition a regular, fat blue spark should be evident at the plug electrodes. If the spark appears thin or yellowish, or is non-existent, further investigation will be necessary. Turn the ignition off and repeat the test for each spark plug lead in turn.

4 The ignition system must be able to produce a spark which is capable of jumping a particular size gap. Yamaha specify that a healthy system should produce a spark capable of jumping at least 6 mm. A simple testing tool can be made to test the minimum gap across which the spark will jump **(see Tool Tip)** or alternatively it is possible to buy an ignition spark gap tester tool, most of which are adjustable to alter the gap.

5 Connect one of the spark plug caps from one coil to the protruding electrode on the test tool, and clip the tool to a good earth (ground) on the engine or frame. Check that the kill switch is in the 'RUN' position, turn the ignition switch ON and turn the engine over on the starter motor. If the system is in good condition a regular, fat blue spark should be seen to jump the gap between the nail ends. Repeat the test for the other cap from that coil, then test the other coil. If the test results are good the entire ignition system can be considered good. If the spark appears thin or yellowish, or is non-existent, further investigation will be necessary.

6 Ignition faults can be divided into two categories, namely those where the ignition system has failed completely, and those which are due to a partial failure. The likely faults are listed below, starting with the most probable source of failure. Work through the list systematically, referring to the subsequent sections for full details of the necessary checks and tests. **Note:** *Before checking the following items ensure that the battery is fully charged and that all fuses are in good condition.*

a) *Loose, corroded or damaged wiring connections, broken or shorted wiring between any of the component parts of the ignition system (see Chapter 8).*
b) *Faulty HT lead or spark plug cap, faulty spark plug, dirty, worn or corroded plug electrodes, or incorrect gap between electrodes.*
c) *Faulty ignition (main) switch or engine kill switch (see Chapter 8).*
d) *Faulty neutral, clutch or sidestand switch, or starter circuit cut-off relay (see Chapter 8).*
e) *Faulty pick-up coil or damaged trigger.*
f) *Faulty ignition HT coil(s).*
g *Faulty throttle position sensor.*
h) *Faulty ignition control unit.*

7 If the above checks don't reveal the cause of the problem, have the ignition system tested by a Yamaha dealer.

3 Ignition HT coil assembly – check, removal and installation

Check

1 Remove the fuel tank (see Chapter 3). Check the coils visually for cracks and other damage.
2 Disconnect the battery negative (–ve) lead.
3 The coils are mounted under the main frame tube – they can be tested in situ, but remove them as described below to improve access if required. If you do not remove them, pull the caps off the spark plugs.
4 Measure the primary winding resistance with an ohmmeter or multimeter as follows. Disconnect the primary circuit electrical connectors from the coil being tested **(see illustration)**. Set the meter to the ohms x 1 scale and measure the resistance between

TOOL TiP

A simple spark gap testing tool can be made from a block of wood, a large alligator clip and two nails, one of which is fashioned so that a spark plug cap or bare HT lead end can be connected to its end. Make sure the gap between the two nail ends is the same as specified

2.2 Pull the cap off the spark plug

3.4a Disconnect the primary circuit connectors from the coil

Ignition system 4•3

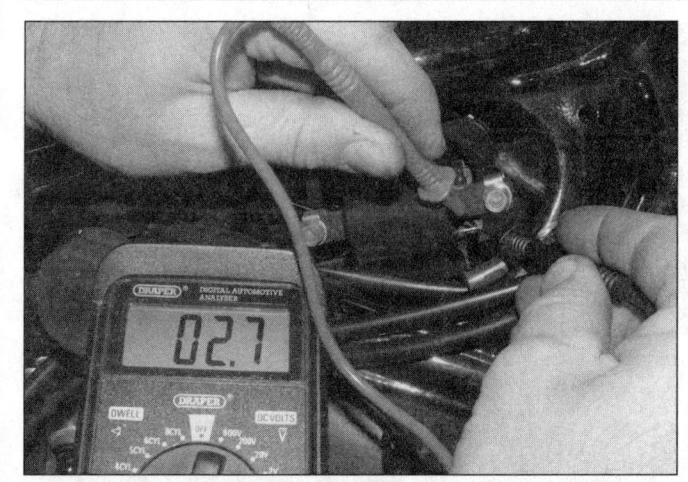

3.4b To test the coil primary winding resistance, connect the multimeter leads between the primary circuit terminals

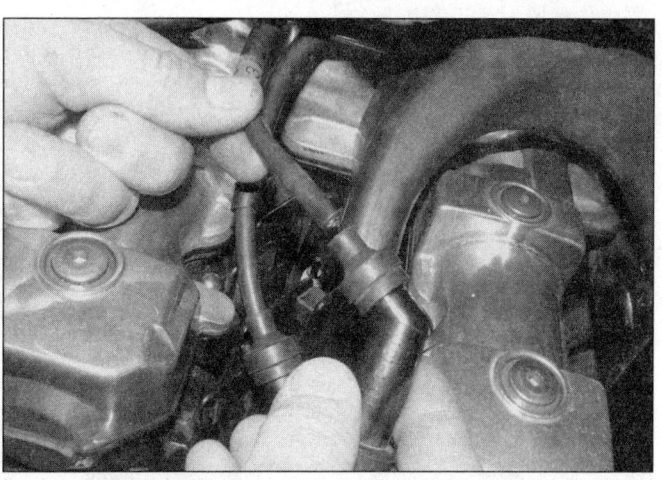

3.5a Thread the cap off the end of the lead

3.5b To test the coil secondary winding resistance, insert the multimeter probes into the HT lead ends

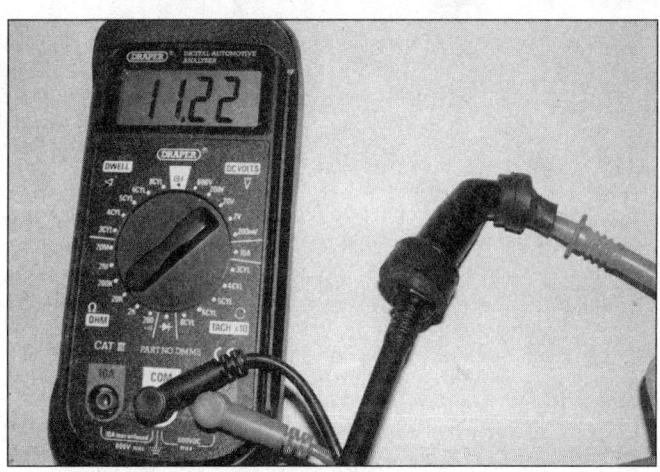

3.6 Measuring the resistance of the spark plug cap

the terminals on the coil (**see illustration**). If the reading obtained is not within the range shown in the Specifications, it is likely that the coil is defective.

5 Measure the secondary winding resistance with an ohmmeter or multimeter as follows. Unscrew the spark plug caps from the HT leads on the coil being tested (**see illustration**). Set the meter to the K-ohm scale. Connect one meter probe to one HT lead end and the other probe to the other lead end (**see illustration**). If the reading obtained is not within the range shown in the Specifications, it is likely that the coil is defective.

6 If the reading is as specified, measure the resistance of the spark plug cap by connecting the meter probes between the HT lead socket in the cap and the spark plug contact in the cap (**see illustration**). If the reading obtained is not as specified, renew the spark plug cap.

7 If either coil is confirmed to be faulty, it must be renewed; the coils are sealed units and cannot therefore be repaired.

Removal

8 The coils are mounted under the main frame tube. Remove the fuel tank (see Chapter 3). Disconnect the battery negative (–ve) lead (see Chapter 8). Mark the locations of all wires and leads before disconnecting them.

9 Disconnect the primary circuit electrical connectors from each coil (see illustration 3.4a). Pull all the caps off the spark plugs.

10 Note the routing of the HT leads. Unscrew the nuts and withdraw the bolts securing the coils to the frame and each other and remove them, noting the mounting dampers (**see illustration**).

Installation

11 Installation is the reverse of removal. Make sure the mounting dampers are installed, and the wiring connectors and HT leads are securely connected.

3.10 Coil assembly mounting bolts (arrowed)

4 Pick-up coil – check, removal and installation

Check

1 Remove the seat (see Chapter 7). Disconnect the battery negative (–ve) lead.
2 Trace the wiring from the pick-up coil on the left-hand side of the engine and disconnect it at the white 2-pin connector on

4•4 Ignition system

4.2 Disconnect the pick-up coil wiring connector (arrowed)

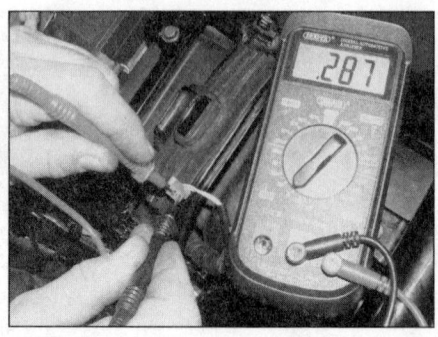

4.4 Measuring pick-up coil resistance

4.7 Undo the screws (arrowed) and remove the cover and gasket

4.8 Undo the screws (arrowed) and remove the pick-up coil assembly

4.9a Install the pick-up coil assembly . . .

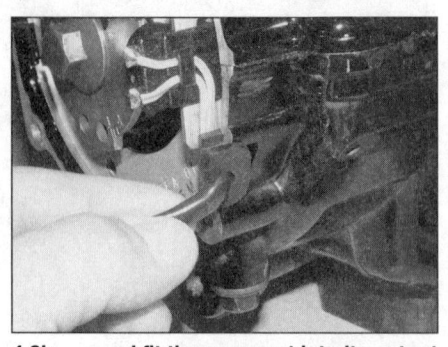

4.9b . . . and fit the grommet into its cutout

the top of the air filter housing **(see illustration)**. Perform the following check(s).

3 Using an ohmmeter check for continuity between each of the connector terminals on the coil side of the connector and earth (ground). If there is continuity between any of the connector terminals and earth (ground) then the pick-up coil is faulty.

4 Using a multimeter set to the ohms x 100 scale, connect the positive (+ve) probe to the white/red wire terminal on the pick-up coil side of the connector and the negative (-ve) probe to the white/green wire terminal and measure the resistance **(see illustration)**. If the reading is different to that specified at the beginning of the chapter, first check the connector and the wiring between the connector and the coil itself (see below to access it). If the wiring is good, renew the pick-up coil.

Removal

5 Remove the seat (see Chapter 7). Disconnect the battery negative (–ve) lead.
6 Trace the wiring from the pick-up coil on the left-hand side of the engine and disconnect it at the white 2-pin connector on the top of the air filter housing **(see illustration 4.2)**. Feed the wiring back to the coil, noting its routing and releasing it from any clips or ties.
7 Undo the pick-up coil cover screws on the left-hand side of the engine and remove the cover and its gasket **(see illustration)**. Discard the gasket.

8 Undo the pick-up coil baseplate screws and remove the plate with the coil attached, freeing the wiring grommet from the crankcase as you do **(see illustration)**. There is no need to separate the coil from the plate as they come as an assembly.

Installation

9 Fit the pick-up coil baseplate assembly, then apply threadlock to its screws and tighten them to the specified torque **(see illustration)**. Smear some sealant onto the wiring grommet and press it into its cutout **(see illustration)**.
10 Fit the pick-up coil cover using a new gasket and tighten the screws to the specified torque **(see illustrations)**.

4.10a Locate the gasket . . .

4.10b . . . and install the cover

Ignition system 4•5

5.3a Ignition control unit – 1999 model

5.3b Ignition control unit – 2002 model

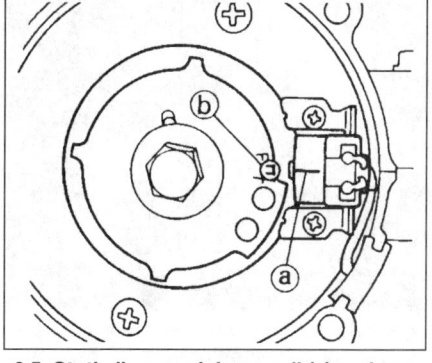

6.5 Static line on pick-up coil (a) and two lines next to F Mark (b)

11 Route the wiring back up to the connector, securing it with any clips or ties previously released and making sure it is correctly routed, and reconnect it. Install the seat (see Chapter 7).

5 Ignition control unit – check, removal and installation

Check

1 If the tests shown in the preceding or following Sections have failed to isolate the cause of an ignition fault, it is possible that the ignition control unit itself is faulty. No test details are available with which the unit can be tested. The only way to test the unit is to substitute it with one which is know to be in good condition.

Removal

2 Remove the seat and left-hand side panel (see Chapter 7). Disconnect the battery negative (–ve) lead.
3 Disconnect the wiring connector(s) from the ignition control unit (see illustrations).
4 Remove the screws securing the ignition control unit, noting the earth wire, and remove the unit.

Installation

5 Installation is the reverse of removal. Do not forget to secure the earth wire with the rear screw. Make sure the wiring connectors are correctly and securely connected.

6 Ignition timing – general information and check

General information

1 Since no provision exists for adjusting the ignition timing and since no component is subject to mechanical wear, there is no need for regular checks: only if investigating a fault such as a loss of power or a misfire need the ignition timing be checked.
2 The timing is checked dynamically (engine running) using a stroboscopic lamp. The inexpensive neon lamps should be adequate in theory, but in practice may produce a pulse of such low intensity that the timing mark remains indistinct. If possible, one of the more precise xenon tube lamps should be used, powered by an external source of the appropriate voltage. **Note:** *Do not use the machine's own battery as an incorrect reading may result from stray impulses within the machine's electrical system.*

Check

3 Warm the engine up to normal operating temperature then stop it.
4 Undo the pick-up coil cover screws on the left-hand side of the engine and remove the cover and its gasket (see illustration 4.7). Discard the gasket.
5 The marks on the timing rotor which indicate the firing range at idle speed for the No. 1 cylinder are two lines next to an 'F' (see illustration). The static timing mark with which this should align is the horizontal line on the pick-up coil.

> **HAYNES HiNT** *The timing marks can be highlighted with white paint to make them more visible under the stroboscope light.*

6 Connect the timing light to the No. 1 cylinder HT lead as described in the manufacturer's instructions.
7 Start the engine and aim the light at the static timing mark.
8 With the machine idling at the specified speed, the static timing mark should point between the lines next to the 'F'.
9 Slowly increase the engine speed whilst observing the lines – they should move clockwise, increasing in relation to the engine speed until it reaches full advance (no identification mark).
10 As already stated, there is no means of adjustment of the ignition timing on these machines. If the ignition timing is incorrect, or suspected of being incorrect, one of the ignition system components is at fault, and the system must be tested as described in the preceding Sections of this Chapter.
11 When the check is complete, fit the pick-up coil cover using a new gasket and tighten the screws to the specified torque (see illustrations 4.10a and b).

7 Throttle position sensor – check, adjustment, removal and installation

1 The throttle position sensor (TPS) is mounted on the outside of the right-hand carburettor and is keyed to the throttle shaft. The sensor provides the ignition control unit with information on throttle position and rate of opening or closing.
2 On XJR1300 models, when the ignition is first switched ON, or while the engine is running, the throttle position sensor performs its own self-diagnosis. If a fault occurs, the tachometer will be seen to display zero rpm for 3 seconds, then 3000 rpm for 2.5 seconds, then the actual engine speed for 3 seconds, whereupon it will repeat the cycle until the engine is switched off. Note that the motorcycle can be ridden even though a fault has been diagnosed, though a difference in performance will be noticed.

Check

3 The throttle sensor is mounted on the outside of the right-hand carburettor (see illustrations). It is accessible with the fuel tank in place, though on 2002 models onward the wiring connector may be difficult to

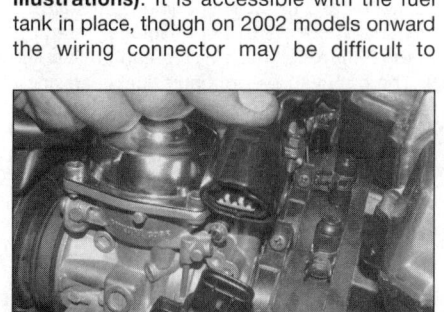

7.3a Throttle position sensor (arrowed) with wiring connector disconnected – 1995 to 2001 models

4•6 Ignition system

7.3b Throttle position sensor (arrowed) – 2002-on models

7.4 Throttle position sensor wiring connector (arrowed) – 2002-on models

access. Remove the fuel tank if required (see Chapter 3).

4 Make sure the ignition is switched OFF, then on 1995 to 2001 models disconnect the wiring connector from the sensor **(see illustration 7.3a)**, and on 2002-on models trace the wiring from the sensor and disconnect it at the connector **(see illustration)**.

5 Using an ohmmeter or multimeter set to the K-ohms range, measure the sensor maximum resistance by connecting the meter probes between the blue and black/blue wire terminals on the sensor. Now measure the resistance range by connecting the meter probes between the yellow and black/blue wire terminals on the sensor, and slowly opening the throttle from fully closed to fully open. If the readings obtained differ greatly from those specified at the beginning of the Chapter, renew the sensor. When checking the resistance range, it is important that there is a smooth and constant change in the resistance as the throttle is opened rather than the figures themselves being accurately as specified.

6 If the readings were as specified, remove the left-hand side panel (see Chapter 7) and disconnect the ignition control unit wiring connector(s) **(see illustration 5.3a or b)**. Using a multimeter or a continuity tester, check for continuity between the terminals on the wiring loom side of the sensor wiring connector and the corresponding terminals on the ignition control unit connector(s), referring to the *Wiring Diagrams* at the end of Chapter 8. There should be continuity between each terminal. If not, this is probably due to a damaged or broken wire between the connectors; pinched or broken wires can usually be repaired. Also check the connectors for loose or corroded terminals, and check the sensor itself for cracks and other damage. If the wiring and connectors are good, check the adjustment of the sensor as described below.

7 If the sensor is suspected of being faulty, take it to a Yamaha dealer for further testing. If it is confirmed to be faulty, it must be renewed; the sensor is a sealed unit and cannot therefore be repaired. If the sensor is good, the fault could lie in the ignition control unit.

Adjustment

Note: *The sensor mounting screws are a special type of Torx screw for security. Unfortunately this means that a special tool (available from any good tool shop) is needed to unscrew them.*

XJR1200

8 Before adjusting the sensor, check the idle speed and carburettor synchronisation (see Chapter 1).

9 Turn the ignition switch ON, then disconnect the sensor wiring connector **(see illustration 7.3a)**. Using an ohmmeter or multimeter set to the K-ohms range, connect the meter probes between the yellow and black/blue wire terminals on the sensor side of the connector. The sensor must be adjusted so that the minimum resistance reading, i.e. with the throttle fully closed (idle position), is between 0.12 and 0.16 x the maximum reading obtained in Step 5. For example, if the maximum reading was 5.0 K-ohms, then the minimum reading required is between 5 x 0.12 and 5 x 0.16, which is 600 to 800 ohms.

10 Slacken the sensor mounting screws and rotate the sensor until the reading is as calculated above, then tighten the screws evenly and a little at a time. If it cannot be adjusted to within the range, or if no reading is obtained, check it as described above.

XJR1300

11 Before adjusting the sensor, check the idle speed and carburettor synchronisation (see Chapter 1).

12 Turn the ignition switch ON, then disconnect and reconnect the sensor wiring connector **(see illustration 7.3a or 7.4)**. This sets the ignition control unit to sensor adjustment mode. If on 2002 models onward the wiring connector is difficult to access, remove the fuel tank (see Chapter 3).

13 Slacken the sensor mounting screws and rotate the sensor until the tachometer needle reads 5000 rpm. If the tachometer reads either 1000 rpm or 10,000 rpm, the angle of the sensor is either too narrow or too wide. Adjust it as required until the reading is 5000 rpm, then tighten the screws evenly and a little at a time. If it cannot be adjusted to within the range, or if no reading is obtained, check it as described above. Start the engine or turn the ignition switch OFF to reset the mode.

Removal and installation

Note: *The sensor mounting screws are a special type of Torx screw for security. Unfortunately this means that a special tool (available from any good tool shop) is needed to unscrew them.*

14 The throttle sensor is mounted on the outside of the right-hand carburettor **(see illustration 7.3a or b)**. It is accessible with the fuel tank in place, though on 2002 models onward the wiring connector may be difficult to access. Remove the fuel tank if required (see Chapter 3).

15 Make sure the ignition is switched OFF, then on 1995 to 2001 models disconnect the wiring connector from the sensor **(see illustration 7.3a)**, and on 2002 models onward trace the wiring from the sensor and disconnect it at the connector **(see illustration 7.4)**.

16 Undo the sensor mounting screws and remove the sensor, noting how it fits. Retrieve the washer and seal (not fitted on 2002-on models).

17 Install the sensor and lightly tighten the screws, then connect the wiring connector and adjust the sensor as described above until the correct reading is obtained. On completion, tighten the screws evenly and a little at a time.

Chapter 5
Frame, suspension and final drive

Contents

Drive chain – removal, cleaning and installation 15
Drive chain and sprockets – check, adjustment
  and lubrication . . . . .see Chapter 1
Footrests, brake pedal and gearchange lever – removal
  and installation 3
Forks – disassembly, inspection and reassembly 8
Forks – oil renewal 7
Forks – removal and installation 6
Frame – inspection and repair 2
General information 1
Handlebars and levers – removal and installation 5
Handlebar switches – check . . . . .see Chapter 8
Handlebar switches – removal and installation . . . . . . .see Chapter 8
Rear shock absorbers – removal, inspection and
  installation 11
Rear sprocket coupling/rubber damper – removal, inspection
  and installation 17
Sprockets – check, removal and installation 16
Sidestand and centrestand – check and lubrication . . . .see Chapter 1
Sidestand and centrestand – removal and installation 4
Sidestand switch – check and replacement . . . . .see Chapter 8
Steering head bearings – check and adjustment . . . . . .see Chapter 1
Steering head bearings – inspection, removal and installation 10
Steering head bearings – lubrication . . . . .see Chapter 1
Steering stem – removal and installation 9
Suspension – adjustment 12
Suspension – check . . . . .see Chapter 1
Swingarm – inspection, bearing check and renewal 14
Swingarm – removal and installation 13
Swingarm bearings – lubrication . . . . .see Chapter 1

Degrees of difficulty

Easy, suitable for novice with little experience	Fairly easy, suitable for beginner with some experience	Fairly difficult, suitable for competent DIY mechanic	Difficult, suitable for experienced DIY mechanic	Very difficult, suitable for expert DIY or professional

Specifications

Front forks
Fork oil type . . . . 10W fork oil
Fork oil capacity
  XJR1200 . . . . 555 cc
  XJR1300 . . . . 538 cc
Fork oil level*
  XJR1200 . . . . 121 mm
  XJR1300 . . . . 137 mm
Fork spring free length
  XJR1200
    Standard . . . . 398.5 mm
    Service limit . . . . 387 mm
  XJR1300
    Standard . . . . 407.3 mm
    Service limit . . . . 395 mm
Fork tube runout limit . . . . 0.2 mm

*Oil level is measured from the top of the tube with the fork spring removed and the leg fully compressed.

Final drive

Drive chain slack and lubricant	see Chapter 1
Drive chain	
XJR1200	
Type	532ZLV.KAI/DAIDO
Length	110 links
XJR1300	
Type	50ZVM/DAIDO
Length	110 links
Sprocket sizes	
Front (engine) sprocket	
1995 to 2001 models	17T
2002 models onward	18T
Rear (wheel) sprocket	
1995 to 2001 models	38T
2002 models onward	39T

Torque settings

Brake torque arm nuts	23 Nm
Centrestand pivot bolt nuts	
XJR1200	56 Nm
XJR1300	41 Nm
Clutch master cylinder clamp bolts	10 Nm
Clutch release cylinder bolts	10 Nm
Footrest bracket bolts	28 Nm
Fork damper rod bolt	30 Nm
Fork top bolt	23 Nm
Fork yokes	
Bottom yoke fork clamp bolts	23 Nm
Top yoke fork clamp bolt	30 Nm
Front brake master cylinder clamp bolts	10 Nm
Front footrest holder bolt	55 Nm
Front sprocket cover bolts	10 Nm
Front sprocket nut	85 Nm
Handlebar clamp bolts	23 Nm
Handlebar end-weights	26 Nm
Handlebar holder nuts	
XJR1200 models	35 Nm
XJR1300 models	40 Nm
Rear sprocket nuts	60 Nm
Shock absorber lower mounting bolt nut	30 Nm
Shock absorber upper mounting bolt	23 Nm
Sidestand pivot bolt and nut	40 Nm
Steering head bearing adjuster nut	
Initial setting	52 Nm
Final setting	18 Nm
Steering stem nut	110 Nm
Swingarm pivot bolt nut	125 Nm

1 General information

The engine is mounted in a duplex cradle-type tubular steel frame.

Front suspension is provided by conventional 43 mm oil-damped telescopic forks. On XJR1200 models the forks are not adjustable. On XJR1300 models the forks are adjustable for spring pre-load.

At the rear, a box-section aluminium swingarm acts on twin shock absorbers with piggyback reservoirs. The shock absorbers are adjustable for spring pre-load. Öhlins rear shock absorbers with distinctive yellow springs are fitted to the XJR1300SP and 2002-on standard XJR1300 models.

The drive to the rear wheel is by chain and sprockets.

2 Frame – inspection and repair

1 The frame should not require attention unless accident damage has occurred. In most cases, frame renewal is the only satisfactory remedy for such damage. A few frame specialists have the jigs and other equipment necessary for straightening the frame to the required standard of accuracy, but even then there is no simple way of assessing to what extent it may have been over stressed.

2 After the machine has accumulated a lot of miles, the frame should be examined closely for signs of cracking or splitting at the welded joints. Loose engine mount bolts can cause ovaling or fracturing of the mounting tabs. Minor damage can often be repaired by welding, depending on the extent and nature of the damage.

3 Remember that a frame which is out of alignment will cause handling problems. If misalignment is suspected as the result of an accident, it will be necessary to strip the machine completely so the frame can be thoroughly checked.

Frame, suspension and final drive 5•3

3 Footrests, brake pedal and gearchange lever – removal and installation

Footrests

Removal

1 The front footrests come as an assembly with their holders, which also form the pivots for the brake pedal and gearchange lever. Unscrew the holder bolt on the inside of the footrest bracket, then withdraw the footrest from the pedal or lever, noting the wave washer, and allow the pedal or lever to dangle **(see illustrations)**.

2 To remove the rear footrests, on 1995 to 2000 models, unscrew the nut and withdraw the pivot bolt, then remove the footrest, noting how the detent plates, ball and spring are fitted, and taking care not to let the spring and ball ping out **(see illustration)**.

3 On 2001 models onward, remove the split pin from the bottom of the pivot pin, then withdraw the pin and remove the footrest, noting how the detent plates, ball and spring are fitted, and taking care not to let the spring and ball ping out.

4 On all footrests the rubbers can be removed and new ones fitted by undoing the two screws on the bottom of the footrest **(see illustration)**.

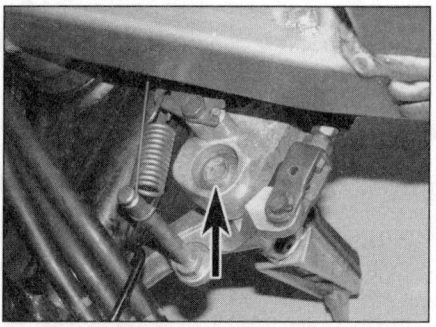

Installation

5 Installation is the reverse of removal.
● Do not omit the wave washer that fits between the brake pedal or gearchange lever and the footrest bracket.
● Apply grease to the brake pedal or gear lever pivot.
● Make sure the footrest holder locates correctly in the bracket. Tighten the footrest holder bolt to the torque setting specified at the beginning of the Chapter.
● Check the operation of the rear brake light switch (see Chapter 1, Section 9).

Brake pedal

Removal

6 Remove the split pin and washer from the clevis pin securing the brake pedal to the master cylinder pushrod **(see illustration)**. Withdraw the clevis pin and separate the pushrod from the pedal **(see illustration)**.

7 Unhook the brake pedal return spring and the brake light switch spring from the bar on the pedal **(see illustration)**.

8 Remove the footrest (see Step 1) and slide the pedal off its pivot on the holder.

Installation

9 Installation is the reverse of removal, noting the following:
● Do not omit the wave washer that fits between the brake pedal and the footrest bracket.
● Apply grease to the pedal pivot.
● Make sure the footrest holder locates correctly in the bracket. Tighten the footrest holder bolt to the torque setting specified at the beginning of the Chapter.
● Use a new split pin on the clevis pin securing the brake pedal to the master cylinder pushrod.
● Check the operation of the rear brake light switch (see Chapter 1, Section 9).

Gearchange lever

Removal

10 Slacken the gearchange lever linkage rod locknuts, then unscrew the rod and separate it from the lever and the arm (the rod is reverse-threaded on one end and so will simultaneously unscrew from both lever and arm when turned in the one direction) **(see**

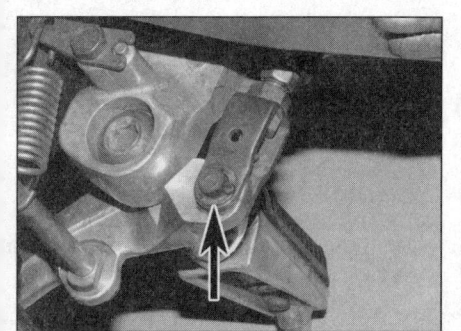

3.1a Right-hand footrest holder bracket (arrowed)

3.1b Left-hand footrest holder bracket (arrowed)

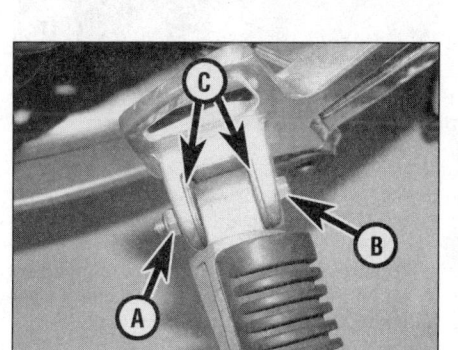

3.2 Unscrew the nut (A) and withdraw the bolt (B), noting the detent assembly (C)

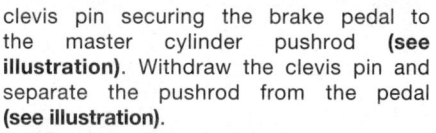

3.4 Footrest rubber retaining screws (arrowed)

3.6a Remove the split pin and washer (arrowed) . . .

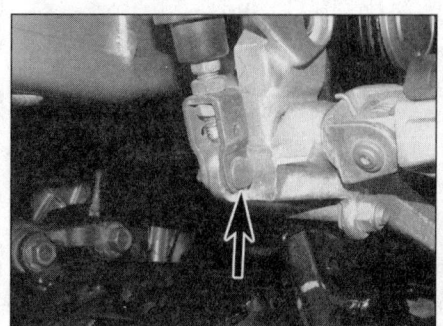

3.6b . . . and withdraw the clevis pin (arrowed)

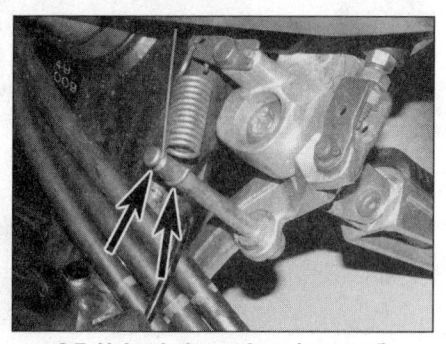

3.7 Unhook the springs (arrowed)

5•4 Frame, suspension and final drive

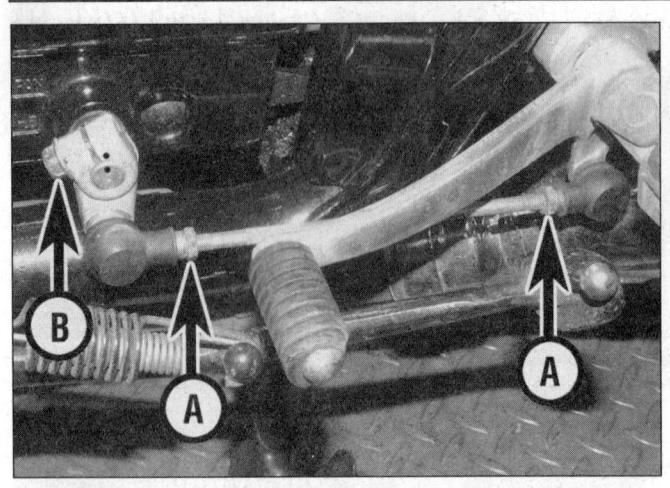

3.10 Slacken the locknuts (A) and thread the rod out of the lever and arm. Linkage arm pinch bolt (B) - note the alignment punch marks

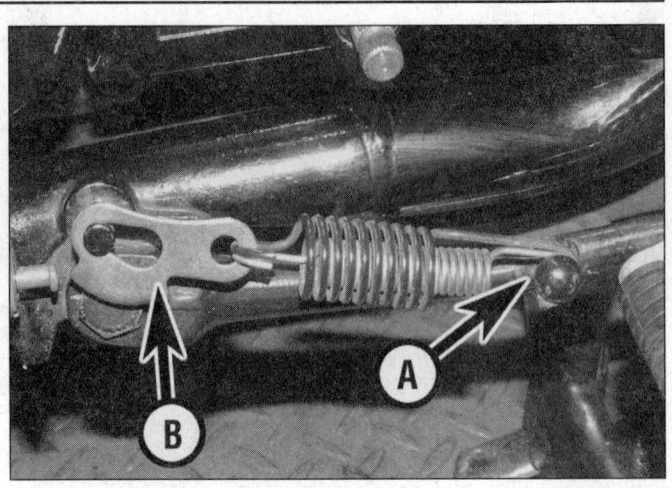

4.2 Unhook the springs (A) and remove the link plate (B)

illustration). Note how far the rod is threaded into the lever and arm as this determines the height of the lever relative to the footrest.

11 Remove the footrest (see Step 1) and slide the lever off its pivot on the holder.

12 To remove the linkage arm, note the alignment of the punch mark on the gearchange shaft end with that on the arm, then unscrew the pinch bolt and slide the arm off the shaft **(see illustration 3.10)**. If no marks are visible make your own so that the arm can be returned to its original position.

Installation

13 Installation is the reverse of removal, noting the following:
- If the linkage arm was removed, align the punch mark on the arm with the punch mark on the end of the gearchange shaft.
- Do not omit the wave washer that fits between the gearchange lever and the footrest bracket.
- Apply grease to the gear lever pivot.
- Make sure the footrest holder locates correctly in the bracket. Tighten the footrest holder bolt to the torque setting specified at the beginning of the Chapter.
- Adjust the gear lever height as required by screwing the linkage rod in or out of the lever and arm. Tighten the locknuts securely.

4 Sidestand and centrestand – removal and installation

Sidestand

Removal

1 The sidestand is bolted to a bracket on the frame. Springs anchored between them ensure the stand is held in the retracted or extended position. Support the bike on the centrestand.

2 Unhook the stand springs and remove the sidestand switch link plate, noting how it fits **(see illustration)**.

3 Unscrew the nut from the pivot bolt, then unscrew the bolt and remove the stand **(see illustration)**.

Installation

4 Apply grease to the pivot bolt shank. Tighten the bolt and nut to the torque setting specified at the beginning of the Chapter.

5 Reconnect the springs and link plate and check that they hold the stand securely up when not in use – an accident is almost certain to occur if the stand extends while the machine is in motion. Make sure the link plate locates against the sidestand switch plunger and actuates it correctly.

Centrestand

Removal

6 The centrestand is bolted to brackets on the frame. Springs anchored between them ensure the stand is held in the retracted or extended position. Support the bike on the sidestand.

7 Unhook the stand springs **(see illustration)**.

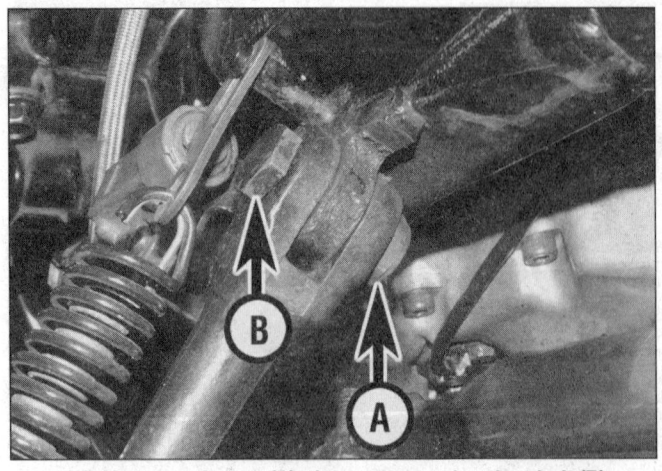

4.3 Unscrew the nut (A), then unscrew the pivot bolt (B)

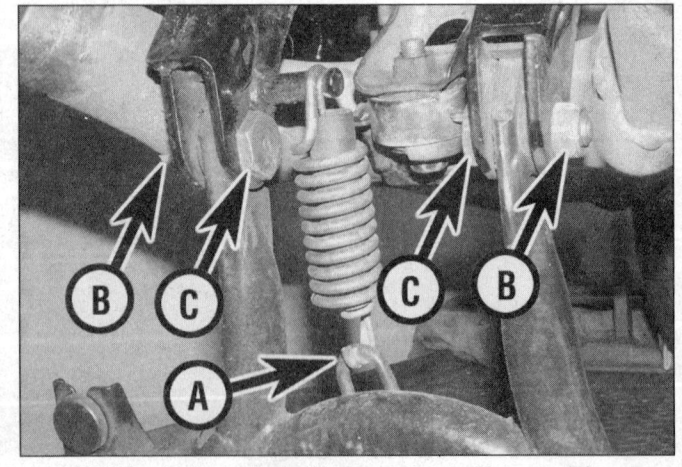

4.7 Unhook the springs (A), then unscrew the nuts (B) and withdraw the bolts (C)

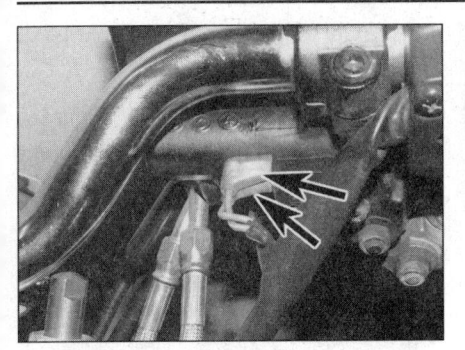

Frame, suspension and final drive 5•5

5.2a Disconnect the wiring connectors (arrowed)

5.2b Note how the clamp surfaces align with the punch mark (arrowed)

5.2c Master cylinder clamp bolts (arrowed)

8 Unscrew the nut from each pivot bolt, then withdraw the bolts and remove the stand.

Installation

9 Apply grease to the pivot bolt shanks and tighten the nuts to the torque setting specified at the beginning of the Chapter.

10 Reconnect the springs and check that they hold the stand securely up when not in use – an accident is almost certain to occur if the stand extends while the machine is in motion.

5.3a Disconnect the wiring connector (A) and unscrew the master cylinder clamp bolts (B) . . .

5.3b . . . noting how the clamp surfaces align with the punch mark (arrowed)

5 Handlebars and levers – removal and installation

Handlebars

Removal

Note: *The handlebars can be displaced from the top yoke without having to remove the individual assemblies from them – follow Step 8 only. If you do this, cover the instrument cluster with some rag and lay the handlebar assembly on it.*

1 Remove the rear view mirrors (see Chapter 7).
2 Disconnect the wiring connectors from the brake light switch **(see illustration)**. Note how the front brake master cylinder assembly clamp mating surfaces align with the punch mark on the handlebars, then unscrew the two bolts and position the assembly clear, making sure no strain is placed on the hydraulic hose(s) **(see illustrations)**. Keep the master cylinder reservoir upright to prevent possible fluid leakage.
3 Disconnect the wiring connector from the clutch switch **(see illustration)**. Note how the clutch master cylinder assembly clamp mating surfaces align with the punch mark on the handlebars, then unscrew the two bolts and position the assembly clear, making sure no strain is placed on the hydraulic hose **(see illustration)**. Keep the master cylinder reservoir upright to prevent possible fluid leakage. Note the plastic collar that fits between the master cylinder and switch housing.
4 Refer to Chapter 3, Sections 11 and 12, and detach the throttle cables from the twistgrip and the choke cable from the lever (except 1995 models). The choke cable procedure incorporates detaching the handlebar switch housing. Create slack in the throttle cables as necessary using the adjusters (see Chapter 1) to avoid having to detach the cable ends from the throttle cam on the carburettor. Refer to Chapter 8 and displace the right-hand switch housing. On 1995 models (without a choke cable), refer to Chapter 8 and displace the left-hand switch housing.
5 Remove the blanking cap from the right handlebar end-weight, then unscrew the weight from the end of the handlebar and slide the throttle twistgrip off the end.
6 Remove the blanking cap from the left handlebar end-weight, then unscrew the weight from the end of the handlebar and peel off the grip. If the grip has been glued on, you will probably have to slit it with a knife to remove it.
7 If the handlebar holders are being removed from the top yoke, slacken the nuts securing them on the underside of the yoke whilst the handlebars are still in place.
8 Carefully prise the blanking caps out of the handlebar clamp bolts **(see illustration)**. Note how the punch mark on the handlebar aligns with the top mating surface of the holder **(see illustration)**. Support the handlebars, then unscrew the bolts and remove the clamps and the handlebars, noting the arrow on each

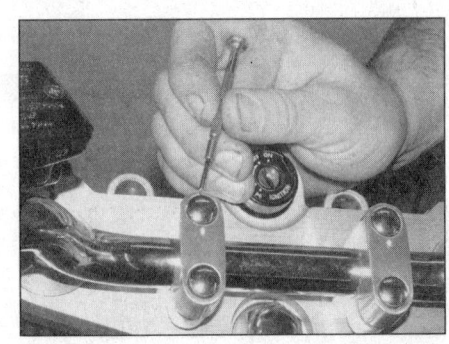

5.8a Carefully remove the blanking caps

5.8b Note the alignment of the punch mark (arrowed) with the holder . . .

5•6 Frame, suspension and final drive

5.8c ... then unscrew the bolts (arrowed) ...

5.8d ... and remove the clamps, noting the arrow

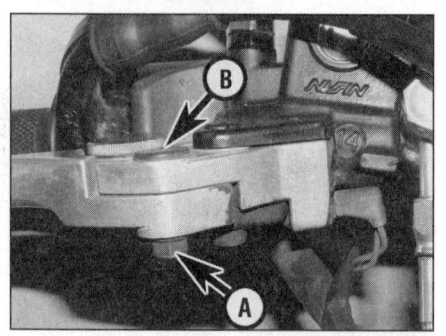

5.11a Unscrew the nut (A), then unscrew the bolt (B)

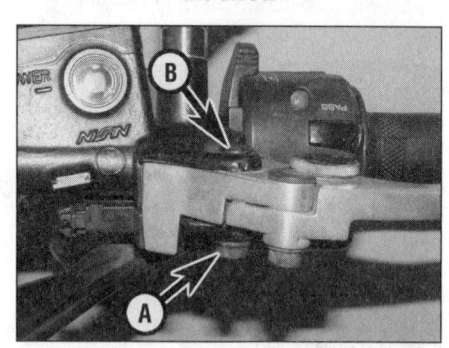

5.11b Unscrew the nut (A), then unscrew the bolt (B)

clamp which points to the front **(see illustrations)**.

9 If required, unscrew the nuts on the handlebar holder bolts, then draw the holders out of the top yoke.

Installation

10 Installation is the reverse of removal, noting the following.
- If removed, tighten the handlebar holder nuts after the handlebars are installed, and tighten them to the torque setting specified at the beginning of the Chapter.
- Fit the left-hand clamp first, with the arrow pointing to the front, then align the punch mark on the back of the handlebar with the mating surface of the left-hand holder **(see illustrations 5.8d and b)**. Make sure the handlebars are central in the clamps – the roughened surface can be used to align them.
- Fit the right-hand clamp with the arrows pointing forwards, then tighten the front bolts first, then the rear bolts, so that the gap between holder and clamp is at the back, and tighten them to the specified torque setting.
- Apply some grease to the throttle twistgrip section of the handlebar.
- Make sure the front brake and clutch master cylinder assembly clamps are installed with the UP mark facing up **(see illustration 5.2c)**. Align the top mating surfaces of the clamp with the punch mark on the top of the handlebar, then tighten the top bolt first, then the bottom bolt, to the specified torque setting **(see illustration 5.2b)**. Do not forget the plastic collar that fits between the clutch master cylinder and the left-hand switch housing.
- Make sure the pin in each switch housing locates in its hole in the handlebar.
- When installing the handlebar end-weights, use some non-permanent thread locking compound on the screws. If new grips are being fitted, secure them using a suitable adhesive.
- Do not forget to reconnect the front brake light switch and clutch switch wiring connectors.

Handlebar levers

11 To remove the front brake lever or clutch lever, unscrew the nut on the underside of the lever bracket **(see illustrations)**. Unscrew the pivot bolt and remove the lever.

12 Installation is the reverse of removal. Apply grease to the pivot bolt shaft and the contact areas between the lever and its bracket. Apply silicone grease to the tip of the master cylinder pushrod.

6 Forks – removal and installation

Removal

1 Remove the front wheel (see Chapter 6). Tie the front brake calipers and hoses back so that they are out of the way.

2 Remove the front mudguard (see Chapter 7).

3 Measure and note the amount of protrusion (if any) of the fork tube above the top surface of the top yoke – measure up to the top rim of the tube itself, do not include the top bolt.

4 Working on one fork at a time, slacken the fork clamp bolt in the top yoke **(see illustration)**. If the fork is to be disassembled, or if the fork oil is being changed, it is advisable to slacken the fork top bolt now while the fork is held by the bottom yoke **(see illustration 6.9)**. On XJR1300 models, first note the spring pre-load setting, then set it to its minimum amount (see Section 12).

> **HAYNES HINT** Slackening the fork clamp bolts in the top yoke before slackening the fork top bolts releases pressure on the top bolt. This makes it much easier to remove and helps to preserve the threads.

5 Slacken the fork clamp bolts in the bottom yoke, and remove the fork by twisting it and pulling it downwards **(see illustrations)**.

6.4 Slacken the clamp bolt (arrowed) in the top yoke

6.5a Slacken the clamp bolts (arrowed) in the bottom yoke ...

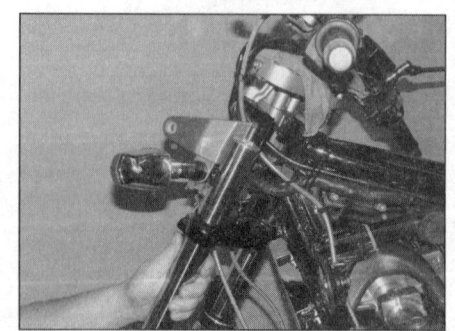

6.5b ... and draw the fork down out of the yokes

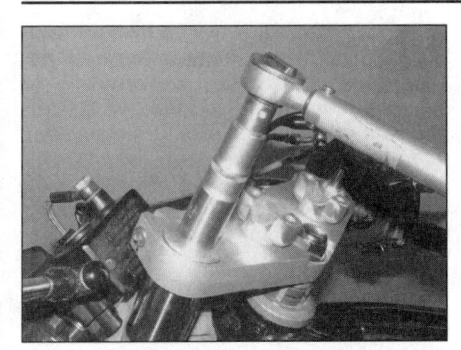

Frame, suspension and final drive 5•7

6.9 If slackened, tighten the fork top bolt to the specified torque

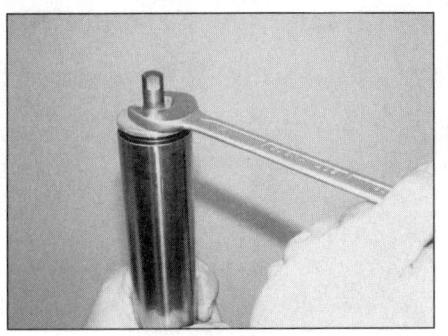

7.3a Thread the top bolt out of the tube

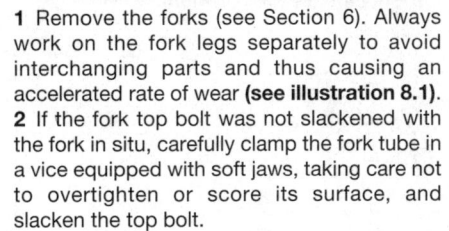

7.3b On XJR1300 models remove the adjuster plate

HAYNES HiNT *If the fork legs are seized in the yokes, spray the area with penetrating oil and allow time for it to soak in before trying again.*

Installation

6 Remove all traces of corrosion from the fork tube and the yokes. Slide the fork up through the bottom yoke and into the top yoke, making sure all cables, hoses and wiring are routed on the correct side of the fork.

7 Set the amount of protrusion of the top of the fork tube (not the top of the fork top bolt) above the top yoke as noted on removal. Make sure it is the same on both sides.

8 Tighten the fork clamp bolts in the bottom yoke to the torque setting specified at the beginning of the Chapter **(see illustration 6.5a)**.

9 If the fork has been dismantled or if the fork oil was changed, and if not already done, tighten the fork top bolt to the specified torque setting – note that to apply a torque wrench it is necessary to displace the handlebars (see Section 5), so alternatively tighten the bolt securely using a ring spanner **(see illustration)**.

10 Tighten the fork clamp bolt in the top yoke to the specified torque **(see illustration 6.4)**.

11 On XJR1300 models, set the spring pre-load as required (see Section 12).

12 Install the front mudguard (see Chapter 7), and the front wheel (see Chapter 6).

13 Check the operation of the front forks and brakes before taking the machine out on the road.

7 Forks – oil renewal

1 Remove the forks (see Section 6). Always work on the fork legs separately to avoid interchanging parts and thus causing an accelerated rate of wear **(see illustration 8.1)**.

2 If the fork top bolt was not slackened with the fork in situ, carefully clamp the fork tube in a vice equipped with soft jaws, taking care not to overtighten or score its surface, and slacken the top bolt.

3 Unscrew the fork top bolt from the top of the fork tube **(see illustration)**. On XJR1300 models, remove the pre-load adjuster plate **(see illustration)**.

⚠ **Warning: The fork spring is pressing on the fork top bolt (via the spacer) with considerable pressure. Unscrew the bolt very carefully, keeping a downward pressure on it and release it slowly as it is likely to spring clear. It is advisable to wear some form of eye and face protection when carrying out this operation.**

4 Slide the fork tube down into the slider and remove the spacer, the spring seat and the spring from the tube **(see illustrations)**. Note which way up the spring fits.

5 Invert the fork over a suitable container and pump the fork tube vigorously to expel as much oil as possible **(see illustration)**. Support the fork upside down in the container for a while to allow as much oil as possible to drain, and pump the fork again.

6 Slowly pour in the specified quantity of the specified grade of fork oil and pump the fork at least ten times to distribute it evenly **(see illustration)**. Fully compress the fork tube into the slider and measure the oil level, and make any adjustment by adding more or tipping some out until the oil is at the level specified

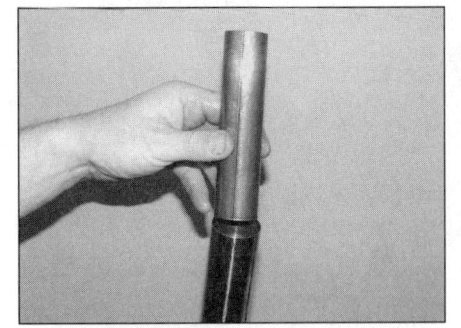

7.4a Remove the spacer . . .

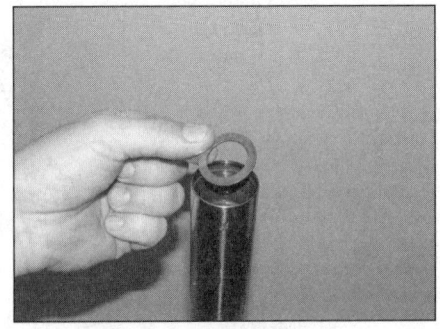

7.4b . . . the spring seat . . .

7.4c . . . and the spring

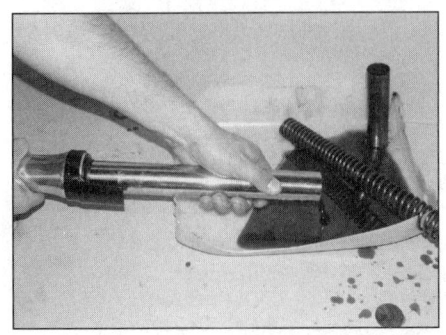

7.5 Invert the fork over a container and pump the tube to expel the oil

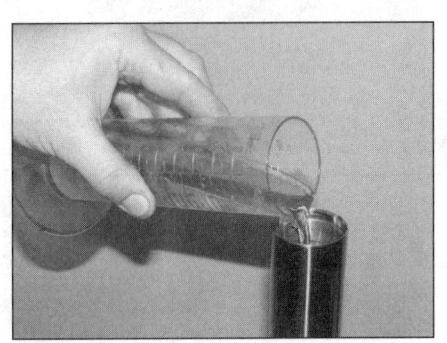

7.6a Pour the oil into the top of the tube

5

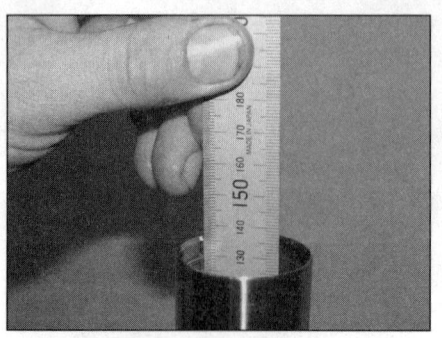

5•8 Frame, suspension and final drive

7.6b Measure the oil level and adjust if necessary

7.8 Fit a new O-ring onto the top bolt then thread it into the fork tube

at the beginning of the Chapter **(see illustration)**.

7 Pull the fork tube out of the slider as far as possible then install the spring with its closer wound coils at the bottom, the spring seat and the spacer. On XJR1300 models, fit the pre-load adjuster plate onto the top of the spacer.

8 Fit a new O-ring smeared with fork fluid onto the fork top bolt and thread the bolt into the fork tube **(see illustration)**.

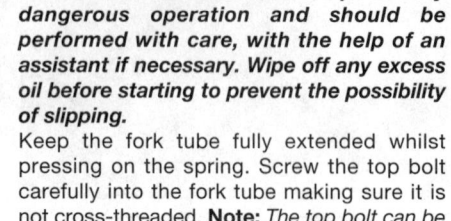

> **Warning:** It will be necessary to compress the spring by pressing it down using the top bolt to engage the threads of the top bolt with the fork tube. This is a potentially dangerous operation and should be performed with care, with the help of an assistant if necessary. Wipe off any excess oil before starting to prevent the possibility of slipping.

Keep the fork tube fully extended whilst pressing on the spring. Screw the top bolt carefully into the fork tube making sure it is not cross-threaded. **Note:** *The top bolt can be tightened to the specified torque setting at this stage if the tube is held between the padded jaws of a vice, but do not risk distorting the tube by doing so. A better method is to tighten the top bolt when the fork has been installed in the bike and is securely held in the bottom yoke.*

> **TOOL TIP** *Use a ratchet-type tool when installing the fork top bolt. This makes it unnecessary to remove the tool from the bolt whilst threading it in making it easier to maintain a downward pressure on the spring.*

9 Install the forks (see Section 6).

8 Forks – disassembly, inspection and reassembly

Disassembly

1 Remove the forks (see Section 6). Always dismantle the fork legs separately to avoid interchanging parts and thus causing an accelerated rate of wear. Store all components in separate, clearly marked containers **(see illustration)**.

2 Before dismantling the fork, it is advisable to slacken the damper rod bolt now as there is less chance of the damper rotating with it (due to the pressure of the spring). Compress the fork tube in the slider so that the spring exerts maximum pressure on the damper rod head, then have an assistant slacken the bolt in the base of the fork slider **(see illustration)**. If this

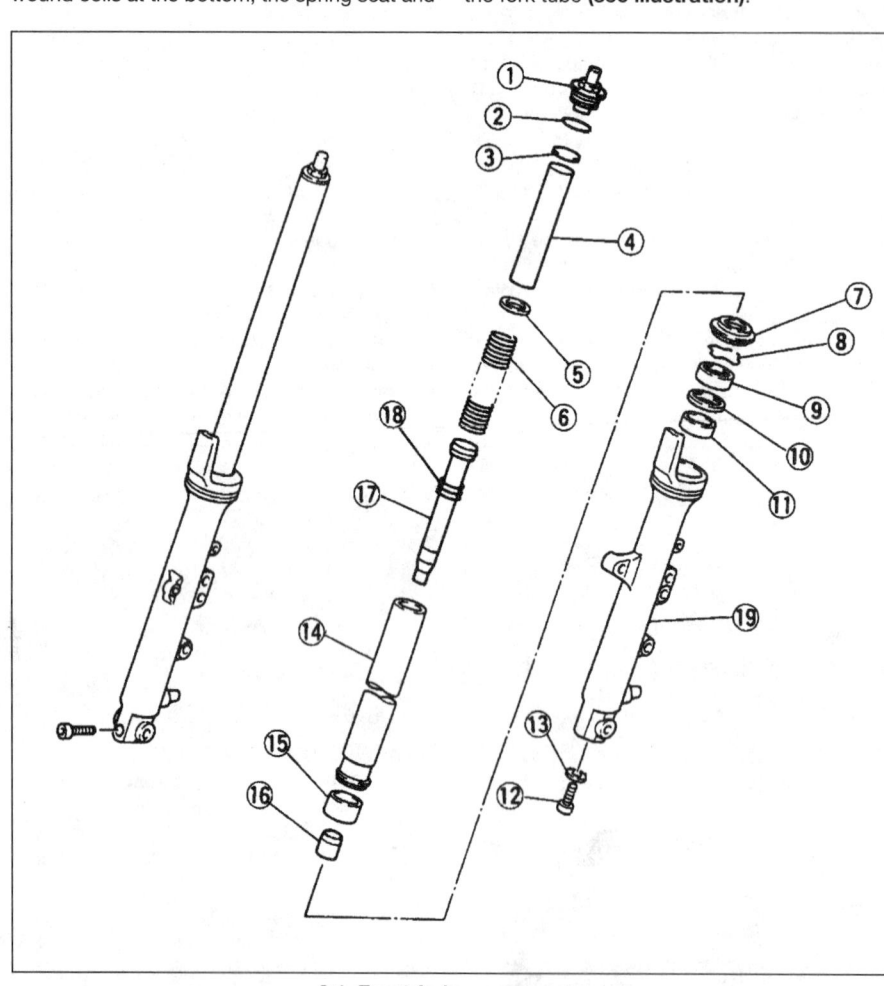

8.1 Front fork components

1 Top bolt	7 Dust seal	14 Fork tube
2 O-ring	8 Retaining clip	15 Bottom bush
3 Pre-load adjuster plate (XJR1300)	9 Oil seal	16 Damper rod seat
4 Spacer	10 Washer	17 Damper rod
5 Spring seat	11 Top bush	18 Rebound spring
6 Spring	12 Damper rod bolt	19 Slider
	13 Sealing washer	

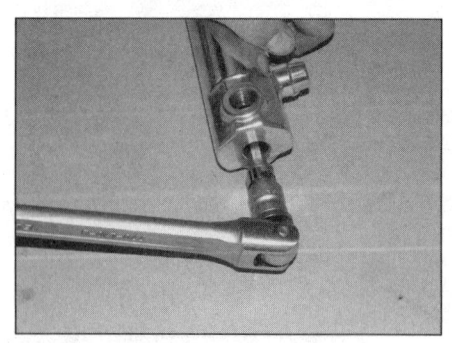

8.2 Slacken the damper rod bolt

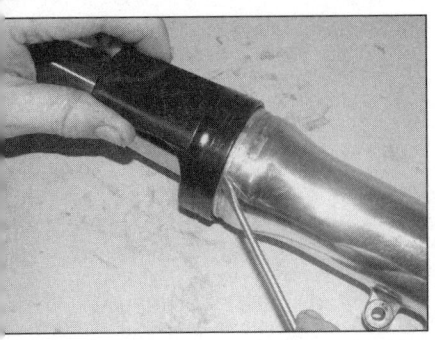

Frame, suspension and final drive 5•9

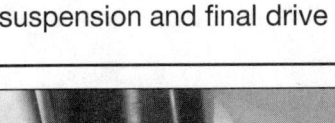

8.7a Where fitted, remove the protector

8.7b Prise out the dust seal using a flat-bladed screwdriver

8.8 Prise out the retaining clip using a flat-bladed screwdriver

method fails to slacken the damper rod, note that a Yamaha service tool can be obtained to hold the damper rod head – see Step 9.

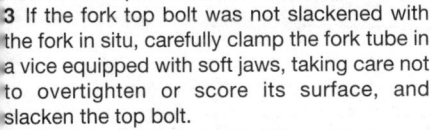

3 If the fork top bolt was not slackened with the fork in situ, carefully clamp the fork tube in a vice equipped with soft jaws, taking care not to overtighten or score its surface, and slacken the top bolt.

4 Unscrew the fork top bolt from the top of the fork tube (see illustration 7.3a). On XJR1300 models, remove the pre-load adjuster plate (see illustration 7.3b).

⚠ **Warning:** *The fork spring is pressing on the fork top bolt (via the spacer) with considerable pressure. Unscrew the bolt very carefully, keeping a downward pressure on it and release it slowly as it is likely to spring clear. It is advisable to wear some form of eye and face protection when carrying out this operation.*

5 Slide the fork tube down into the slider and remove the spacer, the spring seat and the spring from the tube (see illustrations 7.4a, b and c). Note which way up the spring fits.

6 Invert the fork over a suitable container and pump the fork tube vigorously to expel as much oil as possible (see illustration 7.5). Support the fork upside down in the container for a while to allow as much oil as possible to drain, and pump the fork again.

7 On 1998-on models, remove the fork protector, noting how it fits (see illustration). Carefully prise out the dust seal from the top of the slider to gain access to the oil seal

8.9a Unscrew and remove the damper rod bolt . . .

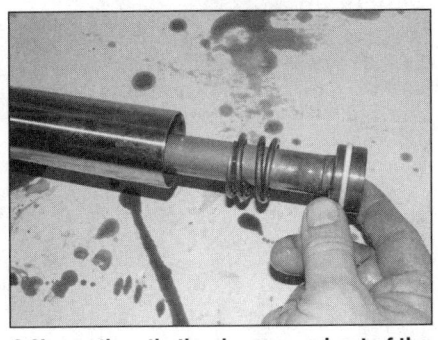

retaining clip (see illustration). Discard the dust seal as a new one must be used.

8 Slide the fork tube fully into slider to prevent accidental damage to its working surface, then carefully remove the retaining clip (see illustration).

9 Remove the previously slackened damper rod bolt and its copper sealing washer from the bottom of the slider (see illustration). Discard the sealing washer as a new one must be used on reassembly. If it was not possible to slacken the bolt as described above, a Yamaha service tool (Pt. Nos. 90890-01327 and 90890-01326) can be used to engage the head of the damper rod and hold it steady whilst the bolt is removed. Invert the fork and tip the damper rod out of the top of the tube (see illustration).

10 To separate the tube from the slider it is

8.9b . . . then tip the damper rod out of the fork

necessary to displace the oil seal and top bush. The bottom bush does not pass through the top bush, and this can be used to good effect. Push the tube gently inwards until it stops against the damper seat. Take care not to do this forcibly or the seat may be damaged. Now pull the tube sharply outwards until the bottom bush strikes the top bush (see illustration). Repeat this operation until the top bush and seal are tapped out of the slider.

11 With the tube removed, slide off the oil seal, washer and top bush, noting which way up they fit (see illustration). Discard the oil seal as a new one must be used.

Caution: *Do not remove the bottom bush from the tube unless it is to be renewed.*

12 Tip the damper rod seat out of the slider – you may have to push it from the bottom via the damper bolt hole (see illustration).

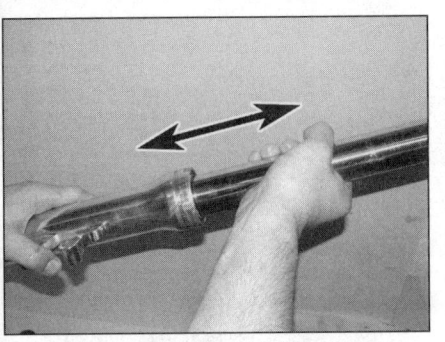

8.10 To separate the fork tube from the slider, pull them apart firmly several times . . .

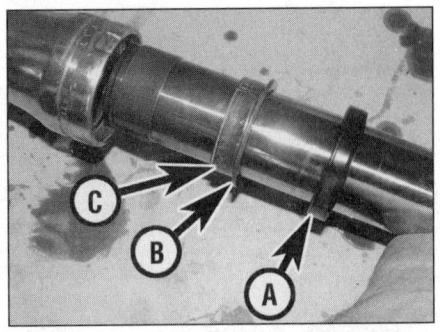

8.11 . . . the slide hammer effect will displace the oil seal and bush. Slide the oil seal (A), washer (B) and top bush (C) off the top of the tube

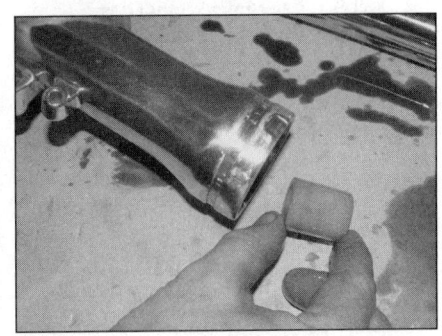

8.12 Tip the damper rod seat out of the slider

5

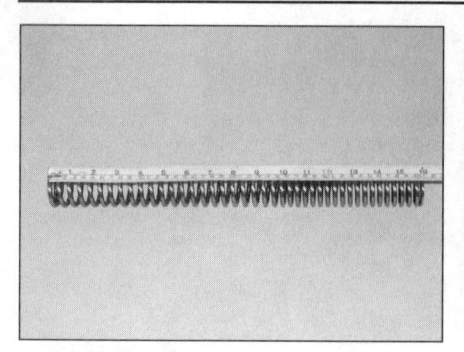

5•10 Frame, suspension and final drive

8.15 Check the spring free length

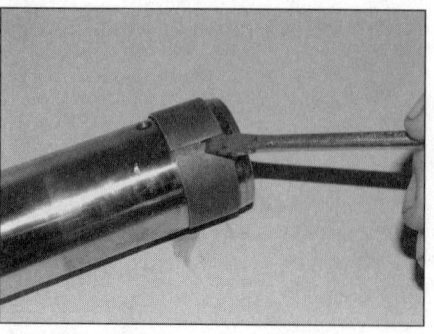

8.16 Carefully lever the ends apart and slide the bush off

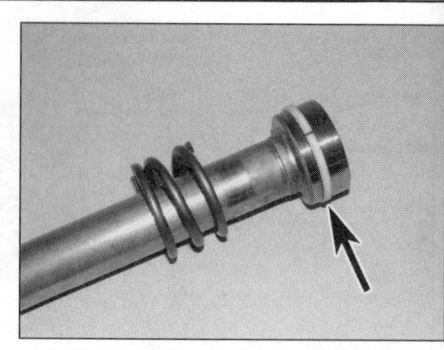

8.17 Check the damper rod, rebound spring and piston ring (arrowed)

Inspection

13 Clean all parts in solvent and blow them dry with compressed air, if available. Check the fork tube for score marks, scratches, flaking of the chrome finish and excessive or abnormal wear. Look for dents in the tube and renew the tube in both forks if any are found. Check the fork seal seat for nicks, gouges and scratches. If damage is evident, leaks will occur. Also check the oil seal washer for damage or distortion and renew it if necessary.

14 Check the fork tube for runout using V-blocks and a dial gauge. If the amount of runout exceeds the service limit specified, the tube should be renewed.

⚠️ **Warning: If the tube is bent or exceeds the runout limit, it should not be straightened; renew it.**

15 Check the springs (the main spring and the rebound spring on the damper rod) for cracks and other damage. Measure the main spring free length and compare the measurement to the specifications at the beginning of the Chapter **(see illustration)**. If it is defective or sagged below the service limit, renew the main springs in both forks. Never renew only one spring.

16 Examine the working surfaces of the two bushes; if worn or scuffed they must be renewed – they are worn if the grey Teflon coating has rubbed off to reveal the copper surface. To remove the bottom bush from the fork tube, prise it apart at the slit using a flat-bladed screwdriver and slide it off. Make sure the new one seats properly **(see illustration)**.

17 Check the damper rod and its piston ring for damage and wear, and renew them if necessary **(see illustration)**. Do not remove the ring from the top of the rod unless it is being renewed.

Reassembly

18 If removed, fit the piston ring into the groove in the damper rod head, then slide the rebound spring onto the rod **(see illustration 8.17)**. Insert the damper rod into the top of the fork tube and slide it down so that it projects fully from the bottom of the tube **(see illustration)**. Fit the damper rod seat onto the bottom of the damper **(see illustrations)**.

19 Oil the fork tube and bottom bush with the specified fork oil and insert the assembly into the slider **(see illustration)**. Fit a new copper sealing washer onto the damper rod bolt and apply a few drops of a suitable non-permanent thread locking compound, then install the bolt into the bottom of the slider **(see illustrations)**. Tighten the bolt to the

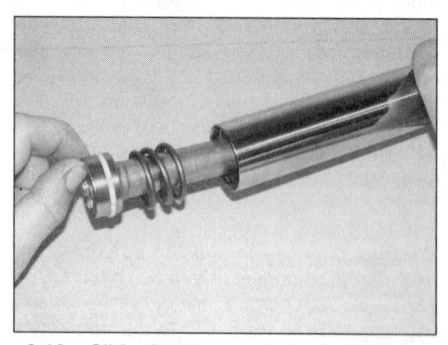

8.18a Slide the damper rod into the tube and all the way down so that it projects from the bottom

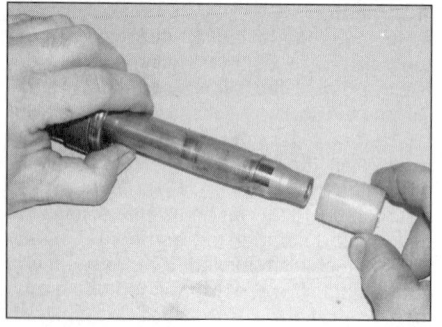

8.18b Fit the seat onto the rod . . .

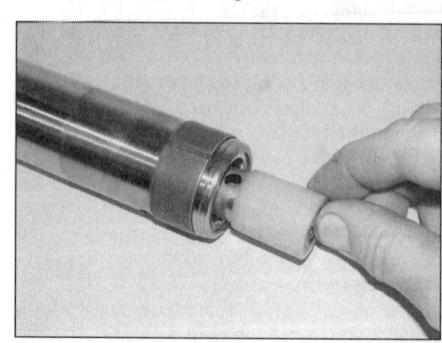

8.18c . . . then push the rod back into the tube

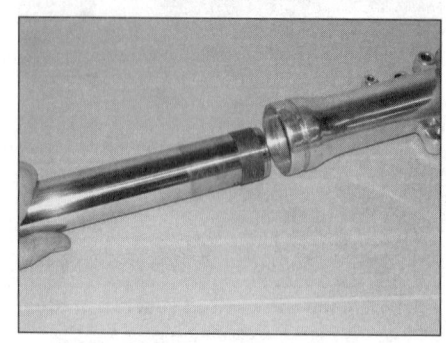

8.19a Slide the tube into the slider

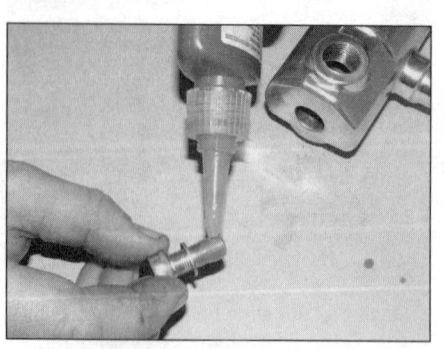

8.19b Apply threadlock to the bolt and fit a new sealing washer . . .

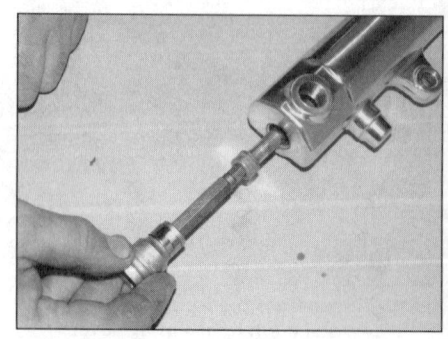

8.19c . . . thread it into the damper rod . . .

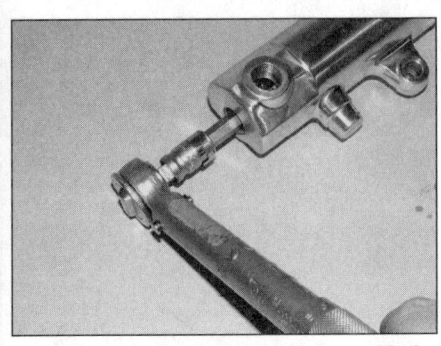

Frame, suspension and final drive 5•11

8.19d ...and tighten it to the specified torque

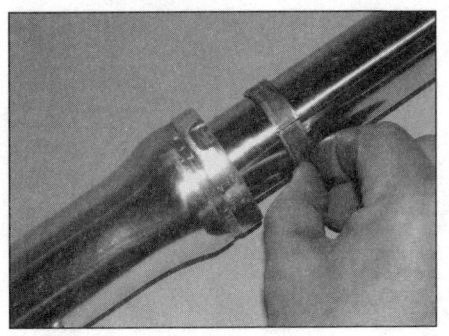

8.20a Install the top bush...

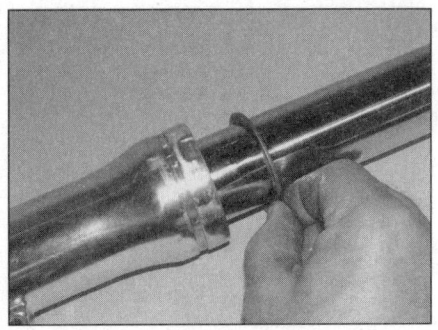

8.20b ...followed by the washer

specified torque setting **(see illustration)**. If the damper rod rotates inside the tube, temporarily install the fork spring, spring seat, spacer and top bolt (see Steps 26 and 27) and compress the fork to hold the damper rod. Alternatively, a long metal bar or length of wood doweling (such as a broom handle) pressed hard into the damper rod head quite often suffices. Otherwise, wait until the fork is fully reassembled before tightening the bolt.

20 Push the fork tube fully into the slider, then oil the top bush and slide it down over the tube **(see illustration)**. Press the bush squarely into its recess in the slider as far as possible, then install the oil seal washer **(see illustration)**. Use either the Yamaha service tool (Pt. Nos. 90890-01367 and 90890-01364), or a suitable piece of plastic tubing to tap the bush fully into place; the tubing must be slightly larger in diameter than the fork tube and slightly smaller in diameter than the bush recess in the slider. Take care not to scratch the fork tube during this operation; wind insulating tape around the exposed length of tube, and push the tube fully into the slider so that any

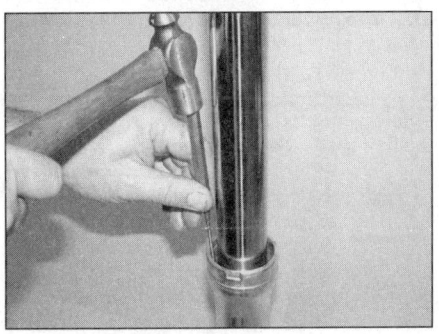

8.20c A drift can be used to tap the bush into place

accidental scratching is confined to the area above the oil seal. A drift or punch can be used, but this does not help the bush enter squarely, and the angle narrows as the bush gets deeper and makes it more difficult to make a good contact with a hammer **(see illustration)**. If using a drift or punch, wrap tape around it to prevent it scratching the tube.

21 Remove the washer to check the bush is seated fully and squarely in its recess in the

8.21 Remove the washer and check the bush is fully home

slider, then wipe the recess clean and refit the washer **(see illustration)**.

22 Smear the lips of the new oil seal with fork oil and slide it over the tube so that its markings face upwards **(see illustration)**. Press the seal into the slider, then drive it fully into place as described in Step 20 until the retaining clip groove is visible above it **(see illustration)**.

23 Once the seal is correctly seated, fit the retaining clip, making sure it is

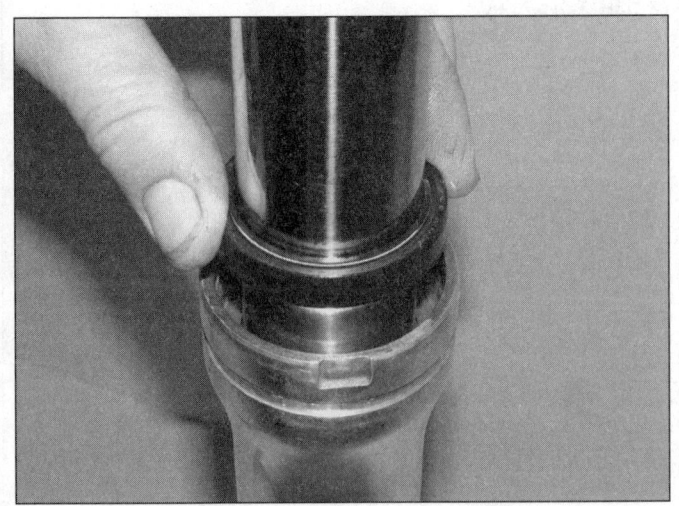

8.22a Smear the new oil seal with clean fork oil then slide it down the tube

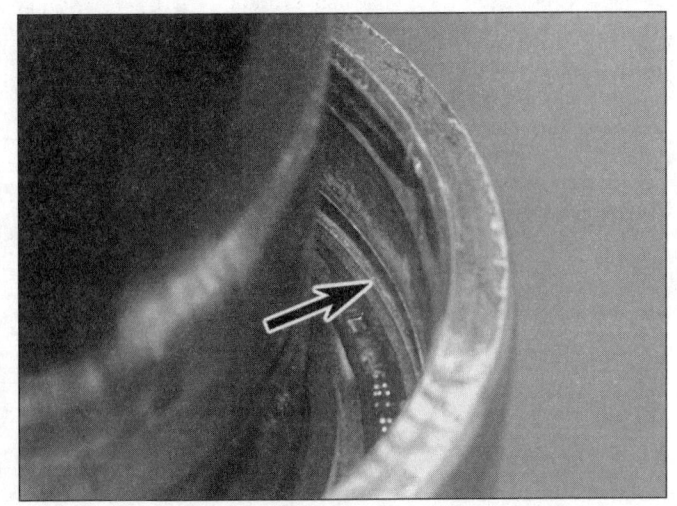

8.22b Press the seal into the top of the slider then drive it in as described until the groove (arrowed) is visible

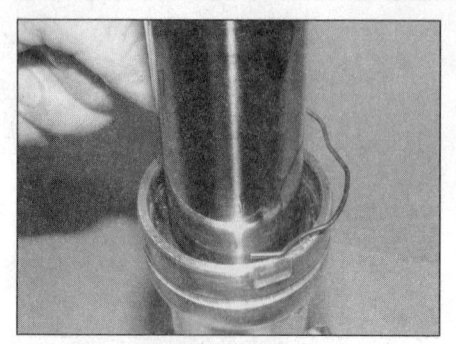

5•12 Frame, suspension and final drive

8.23 Install the retaining clip . . .

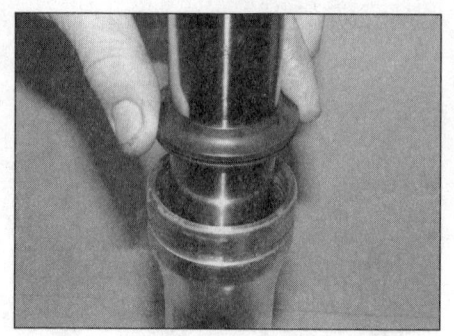

8.24a . . . followed by the dust seal . . .

8.24b . . . which can be pressed in using your fingers

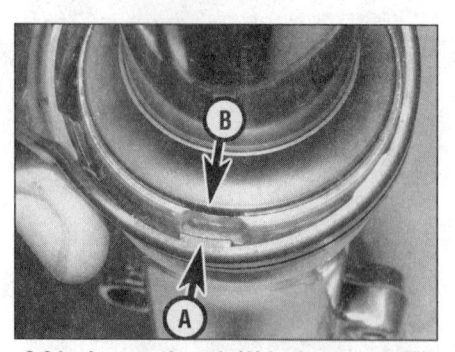

8.24c Locate the tab (A) in the groove (B)

correctly located in its groove **(see illustration)**.

24 Lubricate the lips of the new dust seal then slide it down the fork tube and press it into position **(see illustrations)**. On 1998-on models, fit the fork protector, locating its tab in the groove in the top of the fork slider **(see illustration)**.

25 Slowly pour in the specified quantity and grade of fork oil and pump the fork at least ten times to distribute it evenly **(see illustration 7.6a)**. Fully compress the fork tube into the slider and measure the oil level, and make any adjustment by adding more or tipping some out until it is at the level specified at the beginning of the Chapter **(see illustration 7.6b)**.

26 Pull the fork tube out of the slider as far as possible then install the spring with its closer wound coils at the bottom, the spring seat and the spacer **(see illustrations 7.4c, b and a)**. On XJR1300 models, fit the pre-load adjuster plate onto the top of the spacer **(see illustration 7.3b)**.

27 Fit a new O-ring smeared with fork fluid onto the fork top bolt and thread the bolt into the fork tube **(see illustration 7.8)**.

> **Warning:** *It will be necessary to compress the spring by pressing it down using the top bolt to engage the threads of the top bolt with the fork tube. This is a potentially dangerous operation and should be performed with care, using an assistant if necessary. Wipe off any excess oil before starting to prevent the possibility of slipping.*

Keep the fork tube fully extended whilst pressing on the spring. Screw the top bolt carefully into the fork tube making sure it is not cross-threaded. **Note:** *The top bolt can be tightened to the specified torque setting at this stage if the tube is held between the padded jaws of a vice, but do not risk distorting the tube by doing so. A better method is to tighten the top bolt when the fork has been installed in the bike and is securely held in the bottom yoke.*

TOOL TiP *Use a ratchet-type tool when installing the fork top bolt. This makes it unnecessary to remove the tool from the bolt whilst threading it in making it easier to maintain a downward pressure on the spring.*

28 If the damper rod bolt requires tightening (see Step 19), clamp the fork slider between the padded jaws of a vice and have an assistant compress the tube into the slider so that maximum spring pressure is placed on the damper rod head – tighten the damper rod bolt to the specified torque setting **(see illustration 8.19d)**.

29 Install the forks (see Section 6).

9 Steering stem – removal and installation

Removal

1 Remove the fuel tank (see Chapter 3). This will prevent the possibility of damage should a tool slip.

2 Remove the headlight assembly and the instrument cluster (see Chapter 8). Note how the headlight adjuster bracket bolts also secure the headlight and instrument cluster bracket to the bottom yoke, and note the brake hose guide arrangement **(see illustration)**.

3 Remove the front wheel (see Chapter 6). Tie the front brake calipers and hoses aside so that they are out of the way.

4 Remove the front mudguard (see Chapter 7).

5 Remove the front forks (see Section 6).

6 Displace the handlebars and lay them on some rag across the frame behind the steering head (see Section 5).

7 Unscrew the steering stem nut, and on 1997-on models remove the washer – the washer sits in a recess in the yoke and needs to be helped out with a small screwdriver or a magnet, or alternatively tip it out of the yoke after it has been lifted off **(see illustration)**.

8 Ease the top yoke up and off the steering stem and either remove it or position it clear, using a rag to protect other components **(see illustration opposite)**.

9 Remove the tabbed lockwasher, noting how it fits, then unscrew and remove the locknut, if required using either a C-spanner, a peg spanner or a drift located in one of the notches, though it should only be finger-tight

9.2 Unscrew the bolts (arrowed) and displace the bracket

9.7 Unscrew the steering stem nut

Frame, suspension and final drive 5•13

9.8 Ease the top yoke up and off the forks

9.9a Remove the lockwasher . . .

9.9b . . . then unscrew the locknut . . .

(see illustrations). Remove the rubber washer (see illustration).

10 Supporting the bottom yoke, unscrew the adjuster nut using either a C-spanner, a peg-spanner or a drift located in one of the notches, then remove the adjuster nut and the bearing cover from the steering stem (see illustrations).

11 Gently lower the bottom yoke and steering stem out of the frame (see illustration). Take care not to strain or knock the brake hoses.

12 Remove the inner race and bearing from the top of the steering head (see illustrations 9.15b and a). Remove the rubber washer from half-way up the steering stem and the bearing and seal from the base (see illustrations 9.14d, c and b).

13 Remove all traces of old grease from the bearings and races and check them for wear or damage as described in Section 10. **Note:** *Do not attempt to remove the outer races from the steering head or the inner race from the steering stem unless they are to be renewed.*

Installation

14 Smear a liberal quantity of multi-purpose grease onto the bearing races, and work some grease well into both the upper and lower bearings (see illustration). Also smear the grease seal lip, using a new seal if necessary. Fit the seal and lower bearing onto the base of the

9.9c . . . and remove the rubber washer

9.10a Unscrew the adjuster nut . . .

9.10b . . . and remove the bearing cover . . .

9.11 . . . then draw the bottom yoke/ steering stem out of the steering head

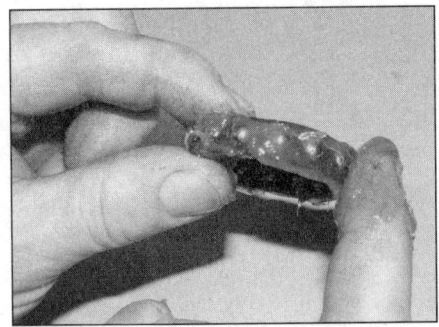

9.14a Grease the bearings and races

9.14b Fit the seal around the inner race . . .

9.14c . . . then fit the bearing

5•14 Frame, suspension and final drive

9.14d Slide the rubber washer onto the stem

9.15a Fit the upper bearing . . .

9.15b . . . and the inner race

9.16 Tighten the locknut as described so the notches align

9.17a Fit the washer (where applicable) . . .

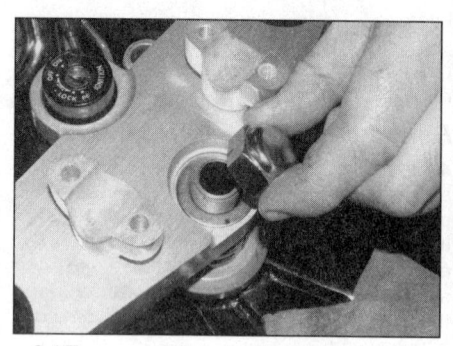

9.17b . . . and the steering stem nut . . .

steering stem **(see illustrations)**. Fit the rubber washer onto its ledge on the stem **(see illustration)**.
15 Carefully lift the steering stem/bottom yoke up through the steering head. Fit the upper bearing and the inner race into the top of the steering head, then fit the bearing cover **(see illustrations and 9.10b)**. Thread the adjuster nut onto the steering stem and adjust the bearings as described in Chapter 1 **(see illustration 9.10a)**.
Caution: Take great care not to overtighten the bearings as this will cause premature failure.
16 When the bearings are correctly adjusted install the rubber washer and the locknut **(see illustrations 9.9c and b)**. Tighten the locknut finger-tight, then tighten it further until its notches align with those in the adjuster nut, but make sure it is not so tight that the rubber

washer starts to be squeezed out the side **(see illustration)**. Install the tabbed lockwasher so that the tabs fit into the notches in both the locknut and adjuster nut **(see illustration 9.9a)**.
17 Fit the top yoke onto the steering stem, then install the washer (1997-on models) and steering stem nut and tighten it finger-tight **(see illustrations)**. Temporarily install one of the forks to align the top and bottom yokes, and secure it by tightening the bottom yoke clamp bolts only **(see illustrations 6.5b and a)**. Now tighten the steering stem nut to the torque setting specified at the beginning of the Chapter **(see illustration)**.
18 Install the remaining components in a reverse of the removal procedure.
19 Carry out a final check of the steering head bearing freeplay as described in Chapter 1, and if necessary re-adjust.

10 Steering head bearings – inspection, removal and installation

Inspection

1 Remove the steering stem (see Section 9).
2 Remove all traces of old grease from the bearings and races and check them for wear or damage.
3 The outer races should be polished and free from indentations **(see illustrations)**. Inspect the bearing balls for signs of wear, damage or discoloration, and examine the ball retainer cage for signs of cracks or splits. If there are any signs of wear on any of the above components both upper and lower bearing assemblies must be renewed as a set. Only remove the outer races in the steering

9.17c . . . and tighten the nut to the specified torque

10.3a Check the upper bearing outer race . . .

10.3b . . . and the lower bearing outer race

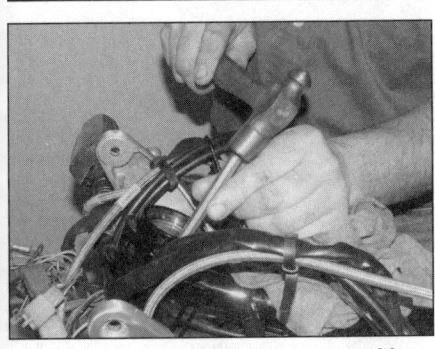

Frame, suspension and final drive 5•15

10.4a Drive the bearing races out with a brass drift . . .

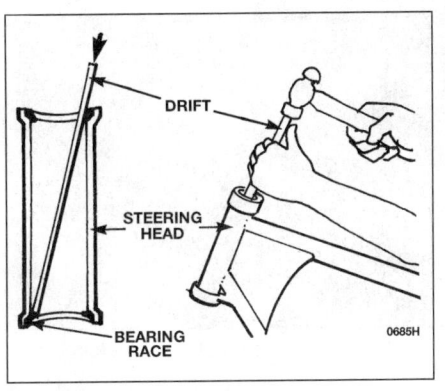

10.4b . . . locating it as shown

head and the lower bearing inner race on the steering stem if they need to be renewed – do not re-use them once they have been removed.

Removal and installation

4 The outer races are an interference fit in the steering head and can be tapped from position with a suitable drift **(see illustrations)**. Tap firmly and evenly around each race to ensure that it is driven out squarely. It may prove advantageous to curve the end of the drift slightly to improve access.
5 Alternatively, the races can be removed using a slide-hammer type bearing extractor; these can often be hired from tool shops.
6 The new outer races can be pressed into the head using a drawbolt arrangement **(see illustration)**, or by using a large diameter tubular drift. Ensure that the drawbolt washer or drift (as applicable) bears only on the outer edge of the race and does not contact the working surface. Alternatively, have the races installed by a Yamaha dealer equipped with the bearing race installation tools.

> **HAYNES HINT**
> *Installation of new bearing outer races is made much easier if the races are left overnight in the freezer. This causes them to contract slightly making them a looser fit. Alternatively, use a freeze spray.*

7 The lower bearing inner race should only be removed from the steering stem if a new one is being fitted **(see illustration)**. To remove the race, use two screwdrivers placed on opposite sides to work it free, using blocks of wood to improve leverage and protect the yoke, or tap under it using a cold chisel. If the steering stem is placed on its side on a hard surface, thread a suitable nut onto the top to prevent the threads being damaged. If the race is firmly in place it will be necessary to use a puller, or in extreme circumstances to split the race using an angle grinder **(see illustration)**. Take the steering stem to a Yamaha dealer if required.
8 Fit the new lower race onto the steering stem. A length of tubing with an internal diameter slightly larger than the steering stem will be needed to tap the new race into position **(see illustration)**.
9 Install the steering stem (see Section 9).

11 Rear shock absorbers – removal, inspection and installation

> **Warning:** *Do not attempt to disassemble this shock absorbers. They are nitrogen-charged under high pressure. Improper disassembly could result in serious injury. Instead, take the shocks to a Yamaha dealer or suspension specialist*

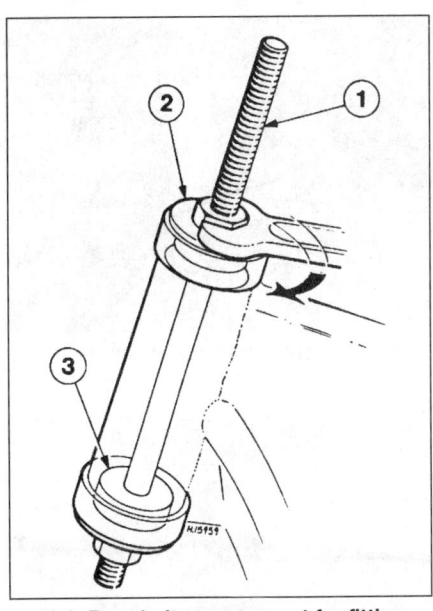

10.6 Drawbolt arrangement for fitting steering stem bearing races

1 Long bolt or threaded bar
2 Thick washer
3 Guide for lower race

with the proper equipment to do the job. If new shock absorbers have been fitted, note that the old shocks must be taken to a Yamaha dealer or suspension specialist for dispersal of the nitrogen gas.

Note: *On XJR1300 models, the upper mounting bolt on each shock absorber is a special type of Torx bolt for security. Unfortunately this means that a special tool (available from any good tool shop) is needed to unscrew them.*

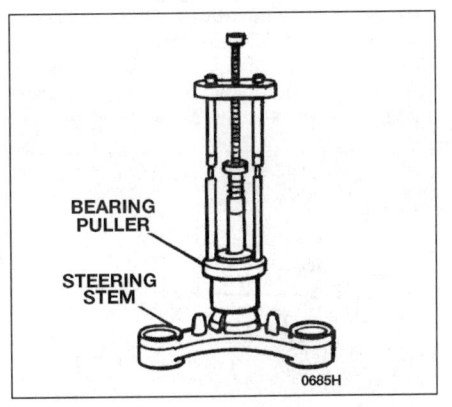

Removal

1 Support the motorcycle on its centrestand. If both shocks are being removed, place a support under the rear wheel or swingarm so that it does not drop when the shocks are removed, but also making sure that the weight of the machine is off the rear suspension so that the shocks are not compressed. Make a

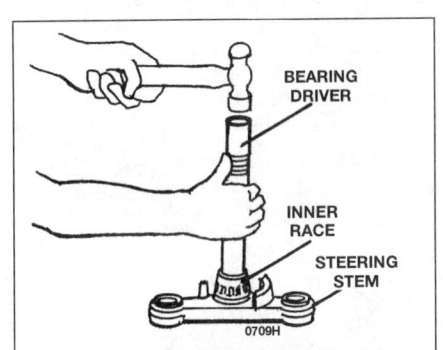

10.7a Remove the lower bearing inner race (arrowed) . . .

10.7b . . . using a puller if necessary

10.8 Drive the new race on using a suitable bearing driver or a length of pipe that bears only against its inner edge and not on its working surface

5•16 Frame, suspension and final drive

11.3a Unscrew the nut and withdraw the bolt ...

11.3b ... then pivot the shock back

11.4 Unscrew the upper mounting bolt and remove the shock

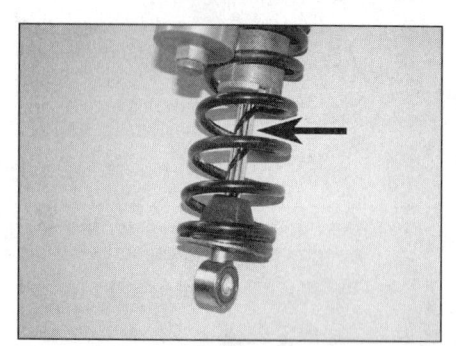

11.6 Check the damper rod (arrowed) as described

note of which side the bolts go in from, and make a note of which way round the shock absorbers fit.
2 Remove the exhaust silencers (see Chapter 3).
3 Unscrew the nut and withdraw the bolt securing the bottom of the shock absorber to the swingarm, then pivot the shock back out of its mount **(see illustrations)**.
4 Unscrew the shock absorber upper mounting bolt, noting the washer (XJR1200) or bungee hook (XJR1300), and on XJR1300SP models the washer that fits on the inside between the mount and the frame, and remove the shock **(see illustration)**.

Inspection

5 Inspect the shock absorber for obvious physical damage and the coil spring for looseness, cracks or signs of fatigue.
6 Inspect the damper rod for signs of bending, pitting and oil leakage **(see illustration)**.
7 Inspect the pivot hardware at the top and bottom of the shock for wear or damage.
8 The top and bottom mount bushes are available for certain models – check with a Yamaha dealer. No other individual components are available for the shock absorbers, so if either shock is worn or damaged they must be renewed as a pair. Note that it is worth seeking advice from a suspension specialist on the possibility of overhauling the shock absorbers, particularly in the case of Öhlins shocks.

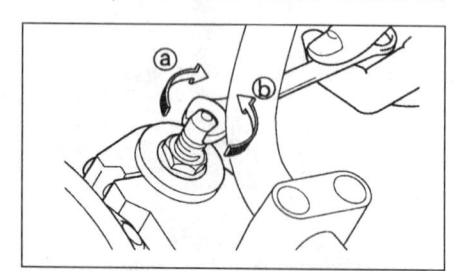

Installation

9 Installation is the reverse of removal. Apply multi-purpose grease to the shock absorber pivot points. Install the shock absorber with the reservoir at the back. Do not tighten the upper bolt until the lower bolt is in position. Tighten the nut and bolt to the torque settings specified at the beginning of the Chapter.

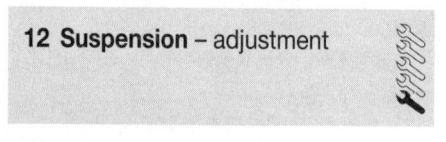

12 Suspension – adjustment

Front forks

1 On XJR1200 models the front forks are not adjustable.
2 On XJR1300 models the front forks are adjustable for spring pre-load. Pre-load is adjusted using a suitable spanner on the flats of the adjuster **(see illustration)**. Turn the adjuster clockwise to increase pre-load and anti-clockwise to decrease it. The amount of pre-load is indicated by grooves on the adjuster **(see illustration)**. There are seven grooves – if all seven are visible the spring pre-load is at a minimum, and at a maximum with only one groove showing. The standard position is with the 5th groove aligned with the top of the hex on the fork bolt. Always make sure both adjusters are set equally.

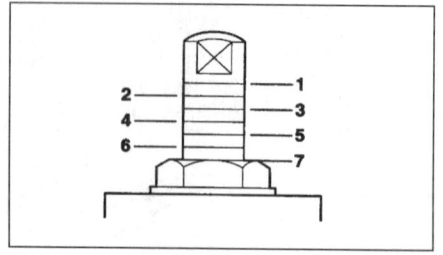

Rear shock absorber

3 On all models the shock absorbers are adjustable for spring pre-load.
4 Pre-load is adjusted using two suitable C-spanners (they are provided in the toolkit supplied with the bike) on the adjuster mechanism on the top of each shock absorber. Locate one C-spanner in the notches in the top ring and use it to counter-hold the shock to prevent it twisting on its mounts. Locate the other C-spanner in the notches in the adjuster ring, then turn it to the right to increase pre-load and to the left to decrease it **(see illustration)**.

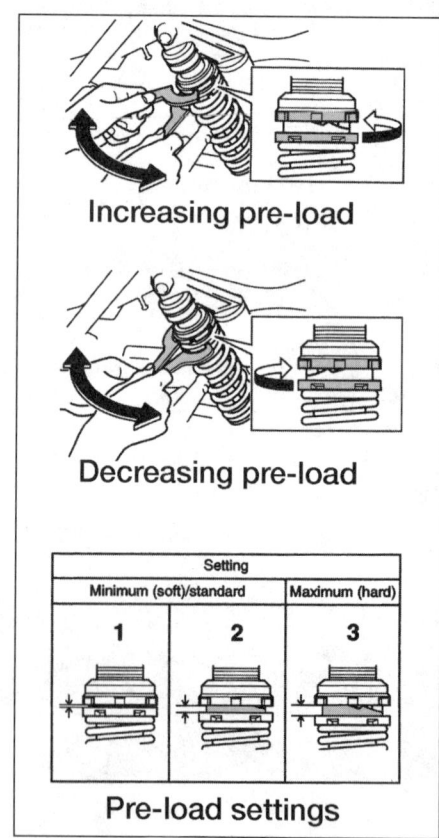

Increasing pre-load

Decreasing pre-load

Pre-load settings

Setting		
Minimum (soft/standard)		Maximum (hard)
1	2	3

12.2a Adjusting fork pre-load – A to increase, B to decrease

12.2b Fork pre-load adjuster grooves – XJR1300 models

12.4 Adjusting rear pre-load

Frame, suspension and final drive 5•17

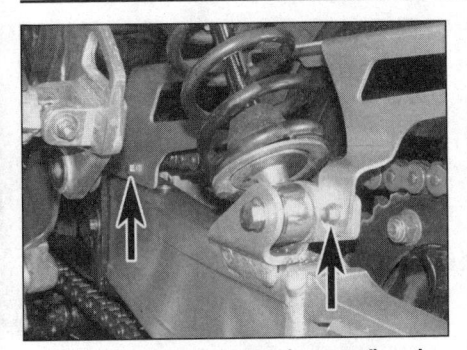

13.4 Unscrew the bolts (arrowed) and remove the chainguard

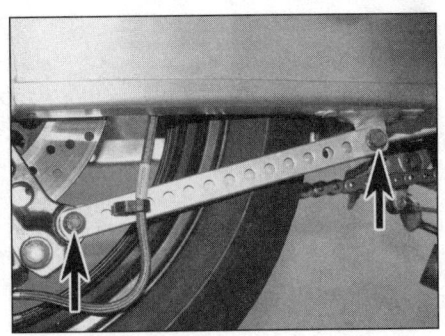

13.5a Brake torque arm bolts (arrowed)

13.5b Brake hose guide bolts (arrowed)

5 The amount of pre-load is indicated by the gap between the top ring and the adjuster ring. There are three positions – the number 1 position, where there is no gap between them, provides minimum pre-load, and the number 3 position, where the gap is largest, provides the maximum. The standard setting is on number 1 or 2.

13 Swingarm – removal and installation

Removal

1 Remove the exhaust silencers (see Chapter 3).
2 Remove the rear wheel (see Chapter 6).
3 Unhook the brake light switch spring from its hook on the pedal, then swing it up and tape or hook it onto something to keep it clear of the swingarm **(see illustration 3.7)**.
4 Undo the screws securing the chainguard to the swingarm and remove the guard, noting how it locates **(see illustration)**.
5 On XJR1200 models remove the split pin from the brake torque arm front mounting bolt. On all models unscrew the nut and withdraw the bolt securing the brake torque arm to the swingarm **(see illustration)**. Unscrew the brake hose guide bolts and displace the guides **(see illustration)**. Loop the rear brake caliper assembly over the swingarm and secure it clear.
6 Unscrew the nut and withdraw the bolt securing the bottom of each shock absorber to the swingarm, then pivot the shock back out of its mount **(see illustrations 11.3a and b)**.
7 Remove the blanking cap from each end of the swingarm pivot **(see illustration)**. Unscrew the nut on the left-hand end of the pivot bolt and remove the washer where fitted **(see illustration)**. Push the pivot bolt end into the swingarm so that the head of the bolt is clear of the frame on the right-hand side and can be grasped.
8 Support the swingarm and withdraw the pivot bolt from the right-hand side **(see illustration)**. Manoeuvre the swingarm out of the frame, noting how the drive chain routes around the front **(see illustration)**.
9 If required, unscrew the bolt securing the chain slider to the swingarm, noting the washer and spacer, and remove it, noting how it fits **(see illustration)**. If the chain slider is badly worn or damaged it should be renewed.
10 Inspect all pivot components for wear or damage as described in Section 14.

Installation

11 If removed, install the chain slider, making sure it locates correctly.
12 Remove the dust cap from each side of the swingarm pivot noting any shim(s) (they are fitted as required according to tolerances by the manufacturer), then withdraw the

13.7a Remove the blanking cap from each side

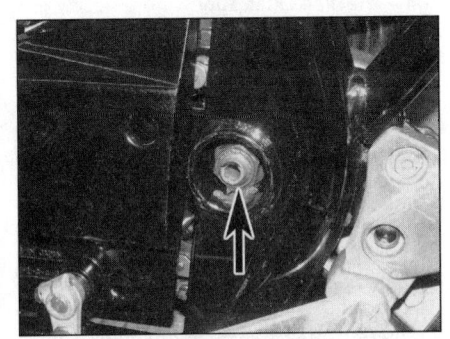

13.7b Unscrew the nut (arrowed) and remove the washer if fitted

13.8a Withdraw the pivot bolt . . .

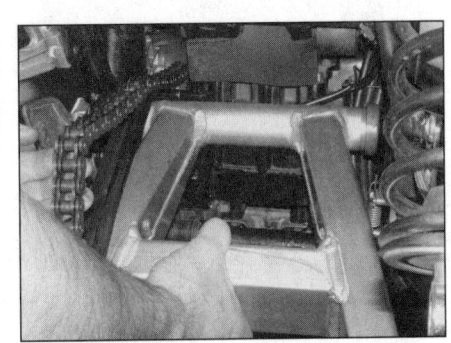

13.8b . . . and remove the swingarm

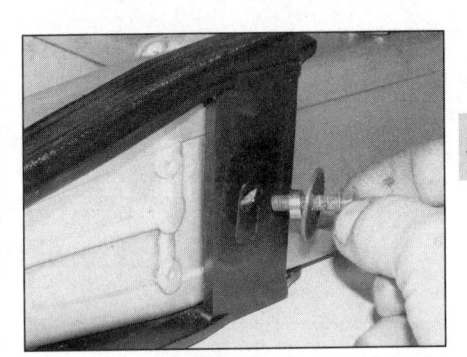

13.9 Remove the chain slider if required

5•18 Frame, suspension and final drive

13.12a Remove the dust cap . . .

13.12b . . . and withdraw the spacer

13.13a Locate the swingarm in the frame, looping the chain around the front then slide the pivot bolt through . . .

spacer **(see illustrations)**. Check the condition of the rubber seals fitted in each pivot cap and renew the caps if the rubber is damaged, deformed or deteriorated. Where water has found its way into the bearings there is likely to be corrosion on both the bearings and end sections of the spacer. Renew corroded or worn parts (see Section 14). Clean off all old grease, then lubricate the bearings, spacer, caps and the pivot bolt with multi-purpose grease. Insert the spacer, then fit the shim(s) and dust caps.

13 Offer up the swingarm and have an assistant hold it in place. Make sure the drive chain is looped over the front of the swingarm. Slide the pivot bolt through from the right-hand side and push it all the way through, locating the flats on the head in the cutout in the frame **(see illustrations)**.

14 Fit the nut, with its washer (where fitted) onto the left-hand end of the bolt and tighten it to the torque setting specified at the beginning of the Chapter **(see illustration)**. Move the swingarm up and down – it should move smoothly and freely. If it is tight, slacken the nut, then tighten it again to the specified torque. Fit the blanking caps.

15 Locate the bottom of each shock absorber in its mounting, then fit the bolt and tighten the nut to the specified torque setting.

16 Loop the brake caliper assembly over the swingarm so the hose is correctly routed around it. Locate the torque arm onto its mount, then fit the bolt and tighten the nut finger-tight only at this stage. Locate the brake hose guides and tighten the bolts securely.

17 Install the chainguard, making sure it locates correctly, and tighten the bolts securely.

18 Hook the brake light switch spring onto its lug on the brake pedal.

19 Install the rear wheel (see Chapter 6) and the silencers (see Chapter 3). Now tighten the nut on the brake torque arm front bolt to the specified torque setting. On XJR1200 models fit a new split pin into the bolt and secure its ends.

20 Check and adjust the drive chain slack (see Chapter 1). Check the operation of the rear suspension and brake before taking the machine on the road.

14 Swingarm – inspection, bearing check and renewal

Inspection

1 Remove the swingarm (see Section 13).
2 Thoroughly clean the swingarm, removing all traces of dirt, corrosion and grease.
3 Inspect the swingarm closely, looking for obvious signs of wear such as heavy scoring, and cracks or distortion due to accident damage. Any damaged or worn component must be renewed.
4 Check the swingarm pivot bolt for straightness by rolling it on a flat surface such as a piece of plate glass (first wipe off all old grease and remove any corrosion using fine emery cloth). If the pivot bolt is bent, renew it.

Bearing check and renewal

5 Remove the dust cap from each side of the swingarm pivot noting any shim(s) (they are fitted as required according to tolerances by the manufacturer), then withdraw the spacer **(see illustrations 13.12a and b)**.

6 Check the condition of the bearings – a needle roller bearing is fitted on each side **(see illustration)**. Where water has found its way into the bearings there is likely to be corrosion on both the bearings and end sections of the spacer. Renew any corroded or worn parts. Slip the spacer back into its bearing and check that there is not an excessive amount of freeplay between the two components. If the bearings do not run smoothly and freely or if there is excessive freeplay, they must be renewed. Refer to *Tools and Workshop Tips* (Section 5) in the Reference section for more information on bearings.

7 Worn bearings can be driven out of their bores, but note that removal will destroy them; new bearings should be obtained before work commences. The new bearings should be pressed or drawn into their bores rather than driven into position. In the absence of a press, a suitable drawbolt tool can be made up as described in *Tools and Workshop Tips* in the Reference section. A central spacer separates the two bearings –

13.13b . . . locating the flats in the cutout

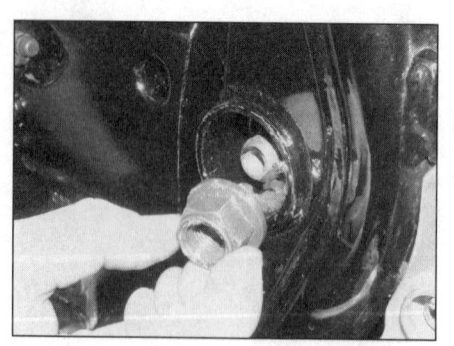

13.14 Fit the nut and tighten it to the specified torque

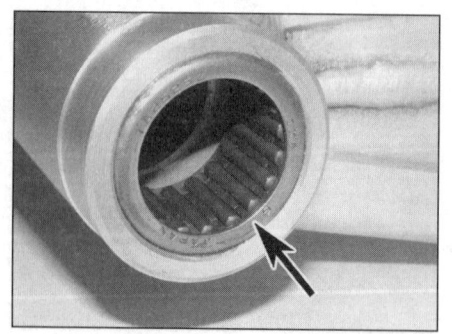

14.6 Check each needle bearing (arrowed) as described

Frame, suspension and final drive 5•19

remove it if required, but do not forget to fit it before installing the second bearing.

8 Check the condition of the rubber seals fitted in each pivot cap and renew the caps if the rubber is damaged, deformed or deteriorated. Clean off all old grease, then lubricate the bearings, spacer, caps and the pivot bolt with multi-purpose grease. Insert the spacer, then fit the shim(s) and dust caps.

15 Drive chain – removal, cleaning and installation

Note: *Inspect the drive chain to determine whether it has a soft joining link (its pin ends will be deeply centre punched rather than peened over as all other chain links). If a soft link is fitted, the chain can be split and rejoined using a new soft link – this must be done using the correct tool (see 'Chains' in the Tools and Workshop Tips section in Reference). If a soft link is not fitted, the chain is effectively endless, and can only be removed as described below. The original equipment drive chain fitted is an endless chain, and the swingarm must be removed to free the chain.*

⚠ **Warning:** *NEVER install a drive chain which uses a clip-type master (split) link.*

Removal

1 If the sprockets are also being renewed, slacken the front sprocket nut before removing the rear wheel so that the rear brake can be used to stop the sprocket turning (see Section 16).
2 Remove the swingarm (see Section 13), then remove the chain.

Cleaning

3 Soak the chain in kerosene (paraffin) for approximately five or six minutes, then clean it using a soft brush.
Caution: *Don't use gasoline (petrol), solvent or other cleaning fluids which might damage its internal sealing properties. Don't use high-pressure water. Remove the chain, wipe it off, then blow dry it with compressed air immediately.*

16.1 Unscrew the bolt and slide the arm off the shaft, noting the punch marks

The entire process shouldn't take longer than ten minutes – if it does, the O-rings in the chain rollers could be damaged.

Installation

4 Installation is the reverse of removal. On completion adjust and lubricate the chain following the procedures described in Section 1.

16 Sprockets – check, removal and installation

Check

1 Unscrew the gearchange lever linkage arm pinch bolt and slide the arm off the shaft, noting how the punch mark on the shaft aligns with that on the arm **(see illustration)**. If no mark is visible, make your own before removing the arm so that it can be correctly aligned with the shaft on installation.
2 Displace the clutch release cylinder – there is no need to detach the clutch hose (see Chapter 2).
3 Unscrew the front sprocket cover bolts and remove the cover **(see illustration)**. Discard the gasket and sealing ring as new ones must be used. Remove the dowels if they are loose.
4 Check the wear pattern on both sprockets (see Chapter 1, Section 1). If the sprocket teeth are worn excessively, renew the chain and both sprockets as a set. Whenever the sprockets are inspected, the drive chain

16.3 Unscrew the bolts and remove the cover

should be inspected also (see Chapter 1). If you are renewing the chain, renew the sprockets as well.
5 Adjust and lubricate the chain following the procedures described in Chapter 1.

Removal and installation

Front sprocket

> **HAYNES HINT:** *Keep your old front sprocket as it can be used along with a holding tool to lock the transmission input shaft should you ever need to remove the clutch (see Chapter 2).*

6 Unscrew the gearchange lever linkage arm pinch bolt and slide the arm off the shaft, noting how the punch mark on the shaft aligns with that on the arm **(see illustration 16.1)**. If no mark is visible, make your own before removing the arm so that it can be correctly aligned with the shaft on installation.
7 Displace the clutch release cylinder – there is no need to detach the clutch hose (see Chapter 2).
8 Unscrew the front sprocket cover bolts and remove the cover **(see illustration 16.3)**. Discard the gasket and sealing ring as new ones must be used. Remove the dowels if they are loose.
9 Bend down the tabs on the sprocket nut lockwasher **(see illustration)**. Engage first gear, then have an assistant apply the rear brake hard. Unscrew the sprocket nut and remove the washer **(see illustration)**. Note

16.9a Bend down the lockwasher tabs . . .

16.9b . . . then unscrew the nut . . .

16.9c . . . and remove the washer

5•20 Frame, suspension and final drive

16.11a Slide the sprocket off the shaft . . .

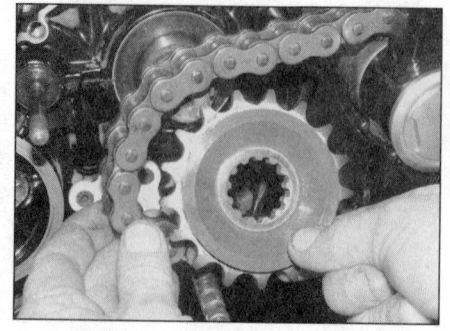

16.11b . . . and out of the chain

16.13 Bend the lockwasher tabs up against the nut

that Yamaha recommend that a new washer should be used as a matter of course.
10 Fully slacken the drive chain as described in Chapter 1. If the rear sprocket is being renewed as well, remove the rear wheel now to give full slack.
11 Slide the sprocket off the shaft then disengage the chain from it **(see illustrations)**.
12 Fit the new sprocket into the chain, making sure the marked side is facing out, the slide the sprocket onto the shaft. Install the rear wheel if removed (see Chapter 6). Take up the slack in the chain.
13 Fit the new lockwasher onto the shaft. Fit the nut and tighten it to the specified torque setting, applying the rear brake to prevent the sprocket turning. Bend the lockwasher tabs up onto the nut **(see illustration)**.
14 If removed, fit the sprocket cover dowels into the crankcase. Fit a new gasket onto the

dowels **(see illustration)**. Smear the new sealing ring with grease to keep it in place and locate it on the crankcase or cover **(see illustration)**. Fit the sprocket cover and tighten its bolts to the specified torque setting. Adjust and lubricate the chain following the procedure in Chapter 1.
15 Install the clutch release cylinder (see Chapter 2).
16 Slide the gearchange lever linkage arm onto the shaft, aligning the punch mark on the shaft with that on the arm **(see illustration 16.1)**. Tighten the pinch bolt securely.

Rear sprocket

17 Remove the rear wheel (see Chapter 6).
18 Unscrew the nuts securing the sprocket to the hub assembly, and remove the washers **(see illustration)**. Remove the sprocket, noting which way round it fits.
19 Fit the sprocket onto the hub with the

stamped mark facing out. Install the nuts with their washers, and tighten the nuts evenly and in a criss-cross sequence to the torque setting specified at the beginning of the Chapter.
20 Install the rear wheel (see Chapter 6).

17 Rear sprocket coupling/ rubber dampers – removal, inspection and installation

1 Remove the rear wheel (see Chapter 6).
Caution: Do not lay the wheel down on the disc as it could become warped. Lay the wheel on wooden blocks so that the disc is off the ground.
2 Lift the sprocket coupling away from the wheel leaving the rubber dampers in position **(see illustration)**. Note the spacer inside the coupling – it should be a tight fit but remove it if it is likely to drop out. Check the coupling for cracks or any obvious signs of damage. Also check the sprocket studs for wear or damage.
3 Lift the rubber damper segments from the wheel, noting how they fit, and check them for cracks, hardening and general deterioration **(see illustration)**. Renew them as a set if necessary.
4 Checking and renewal procedures for the sprocket coupling bearing are described in Chapter 6.
5 Installation is the reverse of removal. Smear some grease or spray some light oil (such as WD40) over the rubbers to making fitting the coupling easier if required. Make sure the spacer is still correctly installed in the coupling, or install it if it was removed.
6 Install the rear wheel (see Chapter 6).

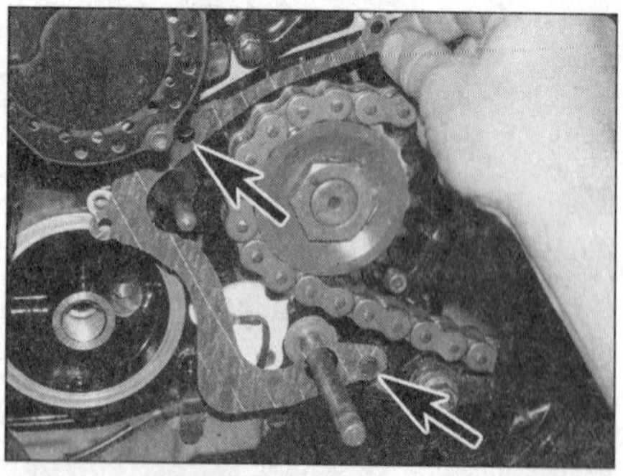

16.14a Locate the new gasket onto the dowels (arrowed) . . .

16.14b . . . and fit a new sealing ring

16.18 Rear sprocket nuts (arrowed)

17.2 Lift the sprocket coupling out of the wheel

17.3 Check the rubber dampers

Chapter 6
Brakes, wheels and tyres

Contents

Brake discs (front and rear) – inspection, removal and installation . . 3	Rear brake caliper – removal, inspection and installation 5
Brake fluid level check . . . . see *Daily (pre-ride) checks*	Rear brake master cylinder – removal, inspection and installation . . 7
Brake light switches . . . . .see Chapter 8	Rear wheel – removal and installation 13
Brake pads (front and rear) – renewal 2	Tyres – general information and fitting new tyres 15
Brake pad wear check . . . . .see Chapter 1	Tyres – pressure, tread depth and
Brake hoses and unions – inspection, removal and installation 8	condition . . . . .see *Daily (pre-ride) checks*
Brake system – bleeding and fluid renewal 9	Wheels – general check . . . . .see Chapter 1
Brake system check . . . . .see Chapter 1	Wheel bearings – check . . . . .see Chapter 1
Front brake calipers – removal, inspection and installation 4	Wheel bearings – removal, inspection and installation 14
Front brake master cylinder – removal, inspection and installation . 6	Wheels – alignment check 11
Front wheel – removal and installation 12	Wheels – inspection and repair 10
General information 1	

Degrees of difficulty

Easy, suitable for novice with little experience	**Fairly easy,** suitable for beginner with some experience	**Fairly difficult,** suitable for competent DIY mechanic	**Difficult,** suitable for experienced DIY mechanic	**Very difficult,** suitable for expert DIY or professional

Specifications

Brakes

Brake fluid type	DOT 4
Front caliper bore ID	
XJR1200	32.1 mm
XJR1300	
Upper bore	30.20 mm
Lower bore	27.00 mm
Front disc thickness	
XJR1200	
Standard	4.0 mm
Service limit	3.5 mm
XJR1300	
Standard	5.0 mm
Service limit	4.5 mm
Front disc maximum runout	0.20 mm
Front master cylinder bore ID	
XJR1200	15.875 mm
XJR1300	14.0 mm
Rear caliper bore ID	42.85 mm
Rear disc thickness	
Standard	5.0 mm
Service limit	4.5 mm
Rear disc maximum runout	0.15 mm
Rear master cylinder bore ID	12.7 mm

6•2 Brakes, wheels and tyres

Wheels

Rim size
- Front .... 17 x MT3.50
- Rear .... 17 x MT5.50

Wheel runout (max)
- XJR1200
  - Axial (side-to-side) .... 2.0 mm
  - Radial (out-of-round) .... 2.0 mm
- XJR1300
  - Axial (side-to-side) .... 0.5 mm
  - Radial (out-of-round) .... 1.0 mm

Tyres

Tyre pressures .... see *Daily (pre-ride) checks*
Tyre sizes*
- XJR1200
  - Front .... 130/70ZR17 tubeless
  - Rear .... 170/60ZR17 tubeless
- XJR1300
  - Front .... 120/70ZR17 (58W) tubeless
  - Rear .... 180/55ZR17 (73W) tubeless

Refer to the owners handbook, the tyre information label, or your dealer for approved tyre brands.

Torque wrench settings

Bleed valves	6 Nm
Brake hose banjo bolts	30 Nm
Brake torque arm nuts	23 Nm
Front brake caliper mounting bolts	
XJR1200	35 Nm
XJR1300	40 Nm
Front brake disc bolts	20 Nm
Front brake master cylinder clamp bolts	10 Nm
Front wheel axle	73 Nm
Front wheel axle clamp bolt	19 Nm
Rear brake caliper mounting bolts	
XJR1200	35 Nm
XJR1300	40 Nm
Rear brake disc bolts	20 Nm
Rear brake master cylinder mounting bolts	23 Nm
Rear wheel axle nut	150 Nm

1 General information

All models are fitted with cast alloy wheels designed for tubeless tyres only. Both front and rear brakes are hydraulically operated disc brakes.

The front brakes are twin opposed-piston calipers. The rear brake is a single opposed-piston caliper.

Caution: *Disc brake components rarely require disassembly. Do not disassemble components unless absolutely necessary. If a hydraulic brake line is loosened, the entire system must be disassembled, drained, cleaned and then properly filled and bled upon reassembly. Do not use solvents on internal brake components. Solvents will cause the seals to swell and distort. Use only clean brake fluid or denatured alcohol for cleaning. Use care when working with brake fluid as it can injure your eyes and it will damage painted surfaces and plastic parts.*

2 Brake pads (front and rear) – renewal

Warning: *The dust created by the brake system may contain asbestos, which is harmful to your health. Never blow it out with compressed air and don't inhale any of it. An approved filtering mask should be worn when working on the brakes. Do not, under any circumstances, use petroleum-based solvents to clean brake parts. Use clean brake fluid, brake cleaner or denatured alcohol only.*

Front

Note: *If the pad pins have not been previously greased and have not been removed for a while, they could well be very difficult to withdraw. If this is the case, they will have to be driven out using a suitable drift or punch. To do this you will have to remove the caliper (see Section 4), as otherwise the shock could distort the disc. If you apply penetrating fluid this will help, but make sure none gets on the pads.*

1 Displace the brake caliper (see Section 4). There is no need to disconnect the brake hose. Note that Yamaha recommend using a new pad spring when new pads are installed.

2 On XJR1200 models, prise off the brake pad cover using a flat-bladed screwdriver **(see illustration 4.5a)**. Pull the retaining clips out of the pad pins. Look into the caliper and note how the pad spring fits. Withdraw the pad pins using a suitable pair of pliers and remove the pad spring. Withdraw the pads from the caliper body. Where fitted and if required, remove the anti-chatter shim from the back of each pad, noting how they fit.

3 On XJR1300 models, pull the retaining clip out of each end of the pad pin **(see**

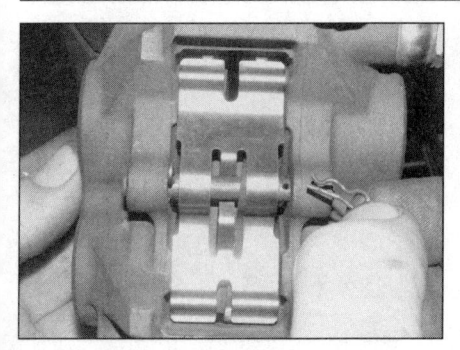

Brakes, wheels and tyres 6•3

2.3a Remove the retaining clips . . .

2.3b . . . then withdraw the pad pin . . .

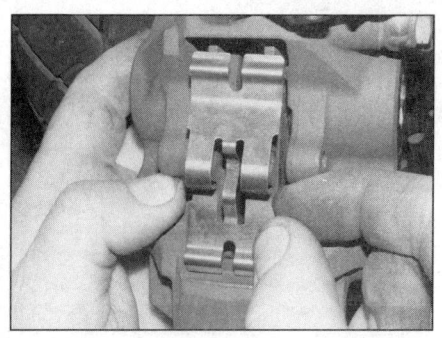

2.3c . . . and remove the pad spring

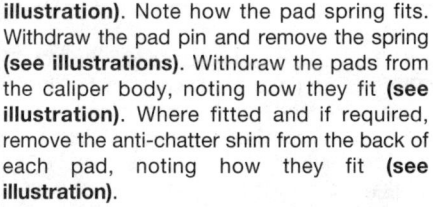

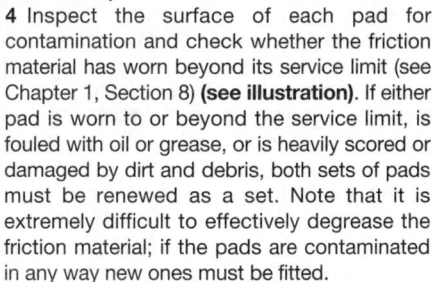

2.3d Lift the pads out of the caliper . . .

2.3e . . . and remove the shim, where fitted

illustration). Note how the pad spring fits. Withdraw the pad pin and remove the spring (see illustrations). Withdraw the pads from the caliper body, noting how they fit (see illustration). Where fitted and if required, remove the anti-chatter shim from the back of each pad, noting how they fit (see illustration).

4 Inspect the surface of each pad for contamination and check whether the friction material has worn beyond its service limit (see Chapter 1, Section 8) (see illustration). If either pad is worn to or beyond the service limit, is fouled with oil or grease, or is heavily scored or damaged by dirt and debris, both sets of pads must be renewed as a set. Note that it is extremely difficult to effectively degrease the friction material; if the pads are contaminated in any way new ones must be fitted.

5 If the pads are in good condition clean them carefully, using a fine wire brush which is completely free of oil and grease to remove all traces of road dirt and corrosion. Using a pointed instrument, clean out the grooves in the friction material and dig out any embedded particles of foreign matter (see illustration 2.4). Any areas of glazing can be removed using a very fine flat file, but pad renewal is suggested as a cure. Spray with a dedicated brake cleaner to remove any dust. It is also worth spraying the inside of the caliper to remove any dust there, and also to spray the discs.

6 Check the condition of the brake discs (see Section 3).

7 Remove all traces of corrosion from the pad pin(s). Check for signs of damage and renew if necessary.

8 If new pads are being fitted, push the pistons back into the caliper to create room – you can use your hands to do this, or use a piece of wood as leverage, or place the old pads back in the caliper and use a metal bar or a screwdriver inserted between them, or use grips and a rag or card to protect the caliper body (see illustration). Alternatively obtain a proper piston-pushing tool from a good tool supplier (see illustration). It may be necessary to remove the master cylinder reservoir cap and diaphragm and siphon out some fluid (see Daily (pre-ride) checks). If the pistons are difficult to push back, attach a length of clear hose to the bleed valve and place the open end in a suitable container, then open the valve and try again (see illustration 9.5a or b). Take great care not to draw any air into the system. If in doubt, bleed the brake afterwards (see Section 9).

9 Smear the backs of the pads and shims (where fitted) and the shank of the pad pin(s) with copper-based grease, making sure that none gets on the front or sides of the pads.

10 Where fitted and if removed, fit the shim onto the back of each pad, making sure any arrow points in the normal direction of disc rotation (see illustration 2.3e).

11 On XJR1200 models, insert the pads into the caliper so that the friction material of each pad faces the disc (see illustration 4.5a). Insert one of the pad pins, making sure it passes through the hole in each pad. When fitting the pad spring, make sure the longer outer tangs on the spring point forward in the direction of normal disc rotation. Hook one

2.4 Check the pads as described

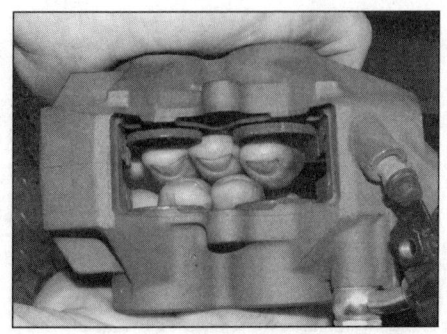

2.8a Push the pistons back into the caliper using one of the methods described . . .

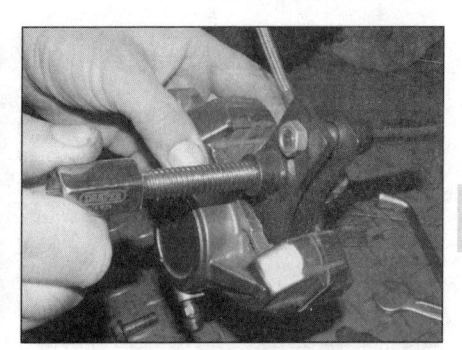

2.8b . . . here a commercially available special tool is being used

6•4 Brakes, wheels and tyres

2.17a Remove the pad cover

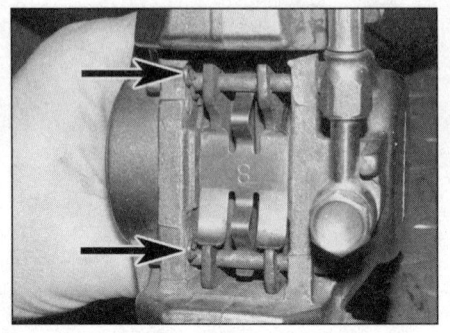

2.17b Remove the retaining clips (arrowed) . . .

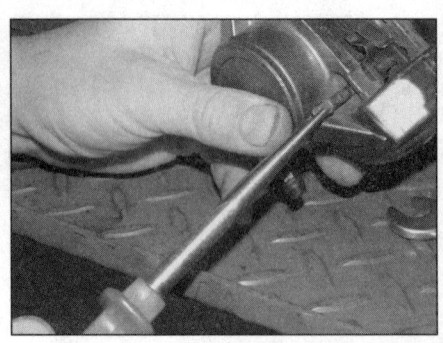

2.17c . . . then withdraw the pad pin and remove the pad spring . . .

end of the pad spring under the installed pin. Insert the other pad pin, pressing down on the spring end so that the pin fits over it. Fit the retaining clips, using new ones if the old ones are damaged or deformed – if necessary, rotate the pad pins to align their holes correctly.

12 On XJR1300 models, fit the pads into the caliper so that the friction material of each pad faces the disc **(see illustration 2.3d)**. Fit the pad spring onto the pads, making sure the arrow points in the direction of normal disc rotation **(see illustration 2.3c)**. Insert the pad retaining pin through the hole in the outer pad, then press down on the pad spring and push the pin through the spring and the hole in the inner pad **(see illustration 2.3b)**. Fit the retaining clips, using new ones if the old ones are damaged or deformed – if necessary, rotate the pad pin to align its holes correctly **(see illustration 2.3a)**.

13 Install the brake caliper (see Section 4).
14 Top up the master cylinder reservoir if necessary (see *Daily (pre-ride) checks*), and refit the diaphragm, plate and reservoir cover.
15 Repeat the pad renewal procedure on the other front caliper – never renew the pads in one caliper only. When complete, operate the brake lever several times to bring the pads into contact with the disc. Check the operation of the brake before riding the motorcycle.

Rear

Note: *If the pad pins have not been previously greased and have not been removed for a while, they could well be very difficult to withdraw. If this is the case, they will have to be driven out from the back of the caliper. To do this you will have to remove the caliper (see Section 5), as otherwise the shock could distort the disc. If you apply penetrating fluid this will help, but make sure none gets on the pads.*

16 Displace the brake caliper (see Section 5). There is no need to disconnect the brake hose. Note that Yamaha recommend using a new pad spring when new pads are installed.
17 On 1995 to 2001 models remove the brake pad cover – use a flat-bladed screwdriver to release its clips if necessary **(see illustration)**. On all models, remove the pad pin retaining clips, then withdraw the pad pins from the caliper using a suitable pair of pliers and noting how they fit through the pad spring **(see illustrations)**. Remove the pad spring, noting how it fits. Withdraw the pads from the caliper body **(see illustration)**. If required and where fitted, remove the anti-chatter shim from the back of each pad, noting how it fits.
18 Refer to Steps 4 to 9 above, applying the instructions to the rear brake.
19 If removed, fit the anti-chatter shim onto the back of each pad with the arrow pointing in the direction of normal disc rotation. Insert the pads into the caliper so that the friction material of each pad is facing the disc **(see illustration)**. Insert one of the pad pins, making sure it passes through the hole in each pad **(see illustration)**. When fitting the pad spring, make sure the longer outer tangs on the spring point forward in the direction of normal disc rotation. Hook one end of the pad spring under the installed pin **(see illustration)**. Insert the other pad pin, pressing down on the spring end so that the pin fits over it **(see illustration)**. Fit the retaining clips,

2.17d . . . and lift the pads out of the caliper

2.19a Fit the pads into the caliper . . .

2.19b . . . and insert one of the pins

2.19c Locate the correct end of the spring under the pin . . .

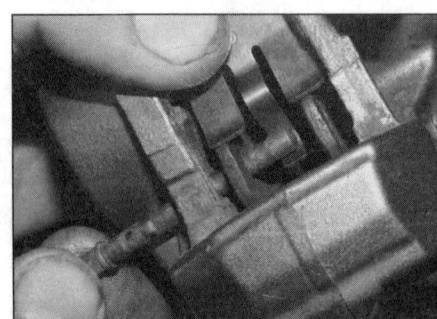

2.19d . . . then press down the other end and insert the other pin over it

Brakes, wheels and tyres 6•5

2.19e Secure the pins with the clips . . .

2.19f . . . then fit the cover

3.3 Checking disc thickness

using new ones if the old ones are damaged or deformed – if necessary, rotate the pad pins to align their holes correctly **(see illustration)**. Check that everything is correctly installed **(see illustration 2.17b)**. On 1995 to 2001 models fit the caliper cover **(see illustration)**.
20 Install the brake caliper (see Section 5).
21 Top up the rear master cylinder reservoir if necessary (see *Daily (pre-ride) checks*).
22 Operate the brake pedal several times to bring the pads into contact with the disc. Check the operation of the brake before riding the motorcycle.

3 Brake discs (front and rear) – inspection, removal and installation

Warning: *The dust created by the brake system may contain asbestos, which is harmful to your health. Never blow it out with compressed air and don't inhale any of it. An approved filtering mask should be worn when working on the brakes. Do not, under any circumstances, use petroleum-based solvents to clean brake parts. Use clean brake fluid, brake cleaner or denatured alcohol only.*

Inspection

1 Visually inspect the surface of the disc for score marks and other damage. Light scratches are normal after use and won't affect brake operation, but deep grooves and heavy score marks will reduce braking efficiency and accelerate pad wear. If a disc is badly grooved it must be machined or renewed.
2 To check disc runout, position the bike on its centrestand so that the wheel being checked is off the ground. Mount a dial gauge to a fork leg or on the swingarm, according to wheel, with the plunger on the gauge touching the surface of the disc about 10 mm (1/2 in) from the outer edge. Rotate the wheel and watch the gauge needle, comparing the reading with the limit listed in the Specifications at the beginning of the Chapter. If the runout is greater than the service limit, check the wheel bearings for play (see Chapter 1). If the bearings are worn, renew them (see Section 14) and repeat this check. It is also worth removing the disc (see below) and checking for built-up corrosion (see Step 6) as this will cause runout. If the runout is still excessive, the disc will have to be renewed, although machining by an engineer may be possible.
3 The disc must not be machined or allowed to wear down to a thickness less than the service limit as listed in this Chapter's Specifications and as sometimes marked on the disc itself. Check the thickness of the disc using a micrometer **(see illustration)**. If the thickness of the disc is less than the service limit, it must be renewed. In the case of the front wheel, always renew the discs as pair.

Removal

4 Remove the wheel (see Section 12 or 13).
Caution: *Do not lay the wheel down and allow it to rest on the disc – the disc could become warped. Set the wheel on wood blocks so the disc doesn't support the weight of the wheel.*
5 Mark the relationship of the disc to the wheel, so it can be installed in the same position. Unscrew the disc retaining bolts, loosening them a little at a time in a criss-cross pattern to avoid distorting the disc, then remove the disc from the wheel **(see illustrations)**.

Installation

6 Before installing the disc, make sure there is no dirt or corrosion where the disc seats on the hub, particularly right in the angle of the seat, as this will not allow the disc to sit flat when it is bolted down and it will appear to be

3.5a Front disc bolts (arrowed)

3.5b Rear disc bolts (arrowed)

6•6 Brakes, wheels and tyres

4.1 Brake hose banjo bolt (arrowed)

4.2 Brake hose holder bolt (arrowed)

4.3 Brake caliper mounting bolts (arrowed)

warped when checked or when applying the brake.

7 Install the disc on the wheel, making sure the directional arrow is on the outside and pointing in the direction of normal (i.e. forward) rotation. Also note any R or L marking on the front discs that denotes on which side of the wheel it must be mounted. Align the previously applied matchmarks (if you're reinstalling the original disc).

8 Apply a suitable non-permanent thread locking compound to the threads of the disc bolts, and tighten them evenly in a criss-cross pattern to the torque setting specified at the beginning of the Chapter. Clean off all grease from the brake disc(s) using acetone or brake system cleaner. If a new brake disc has been installed, remove any protective coating from its working surfaces.

9 Install the wheel (see Section 12 or 13). Note that when installing a new disc always fit new brake pads (see Section 2).

10 Operate the brake lever/pedal several times to bring the pads into contact with the disc. Check the operation of the brakes carefully before riding the bike.

4 Front brake calipers – removal, inspection and installation

⚠ **Warning:** *If a caliper indicates the need for an overhaul (usually due to leaking fluid or sticky operation), all old brake fluid should be flushed from the system. Also, the dust created by the brake system may contain asbestos, which is harmful to your health. Never blow it out with compressed air and don't inhale any of it. An approved filtering mask should be worn when working on the brakes. Do not, under any circumstances, use petroleum-based solvents to clean brake parts. Use the specified clean brake fluid, dedicated brake cleaner or denatured alcohol only, as described. Use care when working with brake fluid as it can injure your eyes and it will damage painted surfaces and plastic parts.*

Removal

1 If the caliper is just being displaced and not completely removed or overhauled, do not disconnect the brake hose. If the caliper is being completely removed or overhauled, unscrew the brake hose banjo bolt and detach the hose, noting its alignment with the caliper **(see illustration)**. Either plug the hose using another suitable short piece of hose fitted through the eye of the banjo bolt (it must be a fairly tight fit to seal it properly), clamp it using a hose clamp, or wrap a plastic bag tightly around to minimise fluid loss and prevent dirt entering the system. Discard the sealing washers as new ones must be used on installation. **Note:** *If you are planning to overhaul the caliper and don't have a source of compressed air to blow out the pistons, just loosen the banjo bolt at this stage and retighten it lightly. The bike's hydraulic system can then be used to force the pistons out of the body once the pads have been removed. Disconnect the hose once the pistons have been sufficiently displaced.*

2 If the caliper is just being displaced unscrew the bolt securing the brake hose holder to the front fork **(see illustration)**.

3 Unscrew the caliper mounting bolts and slide the caliper off the disc **(see illustration)**.

4 If the caliper is being overhauled, remove the brake pads (see Section 2).

Inspection

5 Clean the exterior of the caliper with denatured alcohol or brake system cleaner **(see illustrations)**.

6 Using a flat piece of wood, block the pistons on one side of the caliper in their bores and displace the opposite pistons either by pumping them out by operating the front brake lever, or by forcing them out using

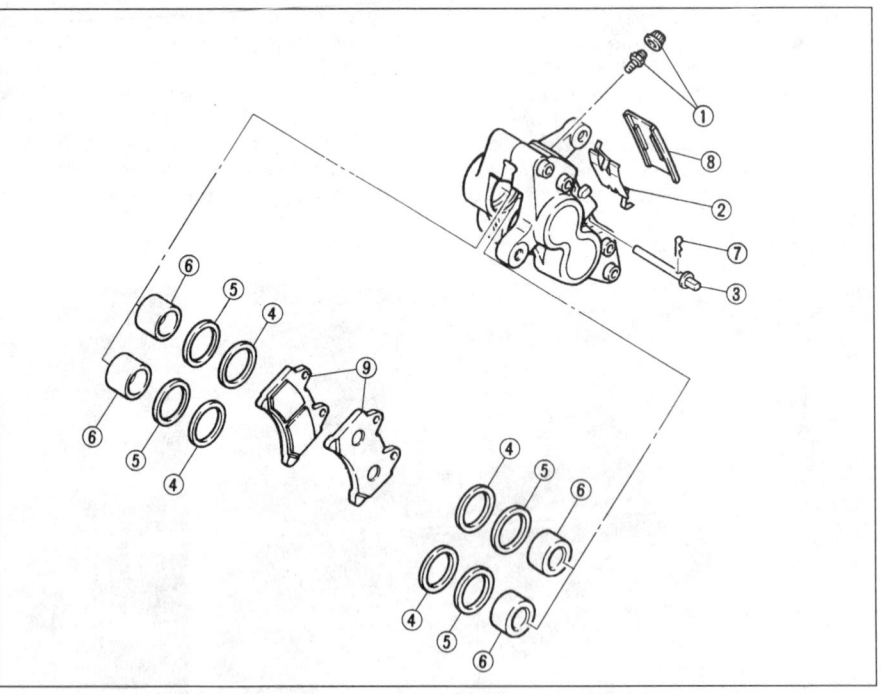

4.5a Front brake caliper components – XJR1200 models

1 Bleed valve and cap	4 Dust seals	7 Retaining clips
2 Pad spring	5 Piston seals	8 Brake pad cover
3 Pad pins	6 Pistons	9 Brake pads

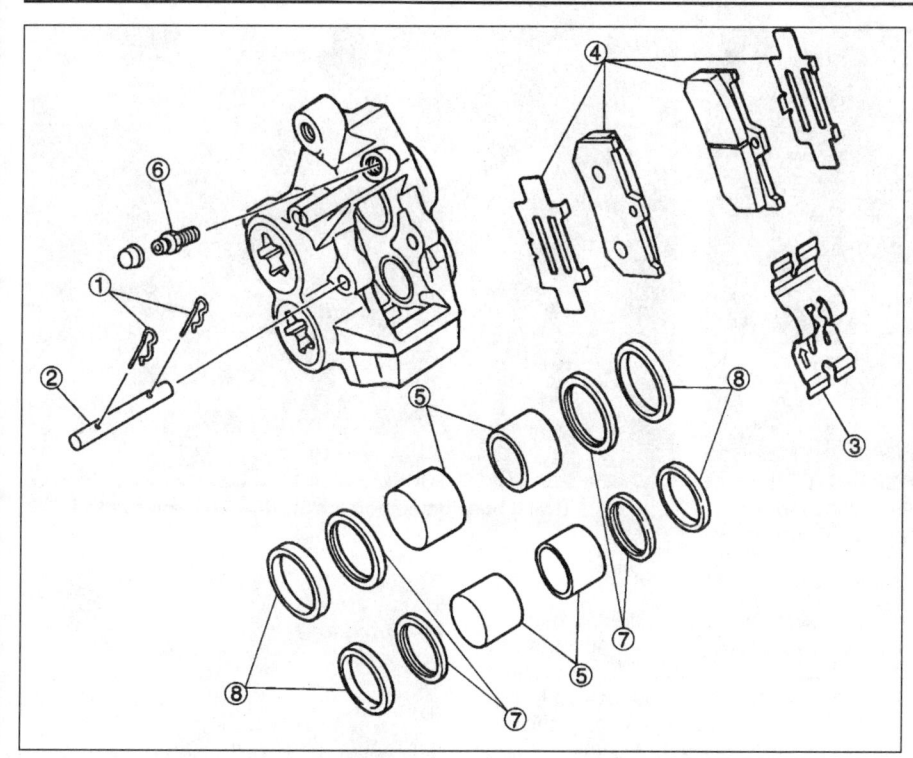

Brakes, wheels and tyres 6•7

4.5b Front brake caliper components – XJR1300 models

1. Retaining clips
2. Pad pin
3. Pad spring
4. Brake pads and shims
5. Pistons
6. Bleed valve
7. Dust seals
8. Piston seals

compressed air **(see illustration)**. Remove the seals (see Steps 7 and 8) from the bore of the displaced pistons, then reinstall the pistons and block them using the wood. Now displace the pistons from the other side using the same method. Remove the wood and all the pistons. Mark each piston head and caliper body with a felt marker to ensure that the pistons can be matched to their original bores on reassembly. If the compressed air method is used, direct the air into the fluid inlet to force the pistons out of the body. Use only low pressure to ease the pistons out and make sure both pistons on the side concerned are displaced at the same time. If the air pressure is too high and the pistons are forced out, the caliper and/or pistons may be damaged.

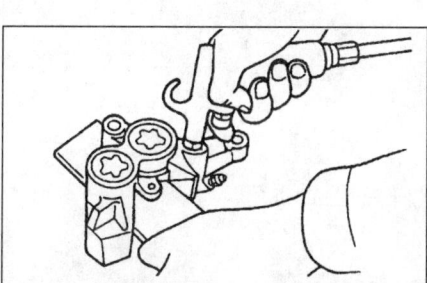

4.6 Hold the wood firmly against the pistons in the lower half of the caliper and apply compressed air to release the pistons in the upper half

⚠️ *Warning: Never place your fingers in front of the pistons in an attempt to catch or protect them when applying compressed air, as serious injury could result.*

Caution: Do not try to remove the pistons by levering them out, or by using pliers or any other grips. On XJR1300 models do not attempt to remove the caliper bore plugs on the outside of the caliper. Do not unscrew the caliper body joining bolts and separate the caliper halves.

7 Remove the dust seal from each caliper bore using a wooden or plastic tool. Discard them as new ones must be used on installation. If a metal tool is being used, take great care not to damage the bores.

4.15 Slide the caliper onto the disc and install the bolts

8 Remove and discard the piston seals in the same way.

9 Clean the pistons and bores with clean brake fluid of the specified type. If compressed air is available, use it to dry the parts thoroughly (make sure it's filtered and unlubricated).

Caution: Do not, under any circumstances, use a petroleum-based solvent to clean brake parts.

10 Inspect the caliper bores and pistons for signs of corrosion, nicks and burrs and loss of plating. If surface defects are present, the caliper assembly must be renewed. If the necessary measuring equipment is available, compare the dimensions of the caliper bores to those specified at the beginning of the Chapter, and install a new caliper if necessary. If the caliper is in bad shape the master cylinder should also be checked.

11 Lubricate the new piston seals with clean brake fluid and install them in their grooves in the caliper bores. On XJR1300 models note that two sizes of bore and piston are used (see Specifications), and care must therefore be taken to ensure that the correct size seals are fitted to the correct bores. The same applies when fitting the new dust seals and pistons.

12 Lubricate the new dust seals with clean brake fluid and install them in their grooves in the caliper bores.

13 Lubricate the pistons with clean brake fluid and install them closed-end first into the caliper bores. Using your thumbs, push the pistons all the way in, making sure they enter the bore squarely.

Installation

14 If removed, install the brake pads (see Section 2).

15 If necessary, push the pistons a little way back into the caliper using hand pressure on the pads or a piece of wood as leverage. Slide the caliper onto the brake disc, making sure the pads sit squarely over the disc **(see illustration)**. Install the caliper mounting bolts and tighten them to the torque setting specified at the beginning of the Chapter.

16 Fit the brake hose holder onto the front fork and tighten the bolt.

17 If removed, connect the brake hose to the caliper, using new sealing washers on each side of the fitting. Align the hose as noted on removal **(see illustration 4.1)**. Tighten the banjo bolt to the torque setting specified at the beginning of the Chapter. Top up the master cylinder reservoir with DOT 4 fluid (see *Daily (pre-ride) checks*) and bleed the hydraulic system as described in Section 9.

18 Check that there are no fluid leaks and thoroughly test the operation of the brake before riding the motorcycle.

6•8 Brakes, wheels and tyres

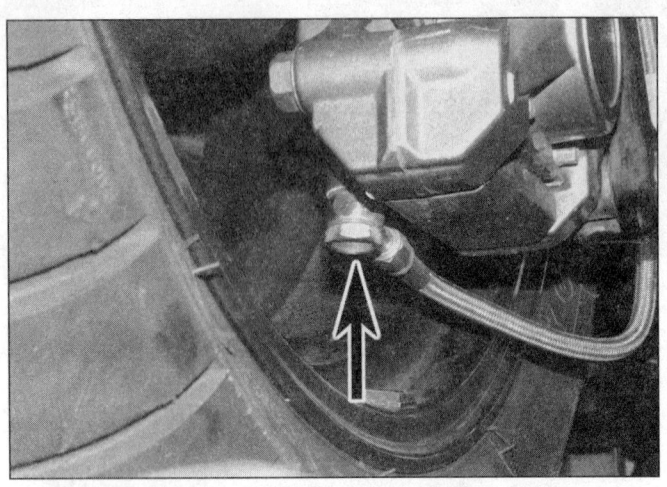

5.1a Brake hose banjo bolt (arrowed) – 1995 to 2001 models

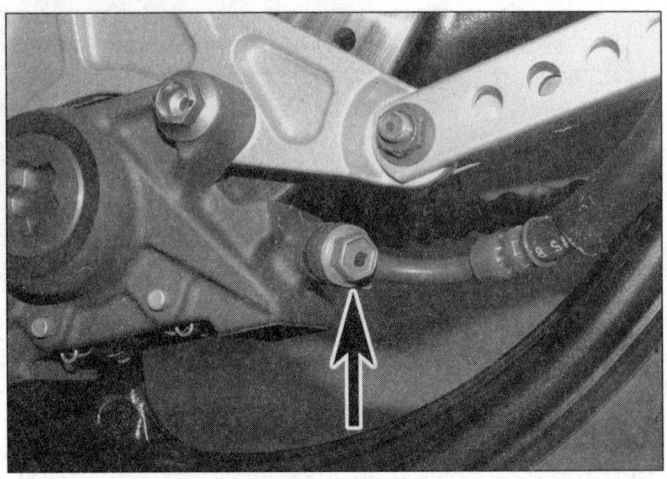

5.1b Brake hose banjo bolt (arrowed) – 2002-on models

5 Rear brake caliper – removal, inspection and installation

Warning: *If a caliper indicates the need for an overhaul (usually due to leaking fluid or sticky operation), all old brake fluid should be flushed from the system. Also, the dust created by the brake system may contain asbestos, which is harmful to your health. Never blow it out with compressed air and don't inhale any of it. An approved filtering mask should be worn when working on the brakes. Do not, under any circumstances, use petroleum-based solvents to clean brake parts. Use the specified clean brake fluid, dedicated brake cleaner or denatured alcohol only, as described. Use care when working with brake fluid as it can injure your eyes and it will damage painted surfaces and plastic parts.*

Removal

1 If the caliper is just being displaced and not completely removed or overhauled, do not disconnect the brake hose. If the caliper is being completely removed or overhauled, unscrew the brake hose banjo bolt and detach the hose, noting its alignment with the caliper **(see illustrations)**. Either plug the hose using another suitable short piece of hose fitted through the eye of the banjo bolt (it must be a fairly tight fit to seal it properly), clamp it using a hose clamp, or wrap a plastic bag tightly around to minimise fluid loss and prevent dirt entering the system. Discard the sealing washers as new ones must be used on installation. **Note:** *If you are planning to overhaul the caliper and don't have a source of compressed air to blow out the pistons, just loosen the banjo bolt at this stage and retighten it lightly. The bike's hydraulic system can then be used to force the pistons out of the body once the pads have been removed. Disconnect the hose once the pistons have been sufficiently displaced.*

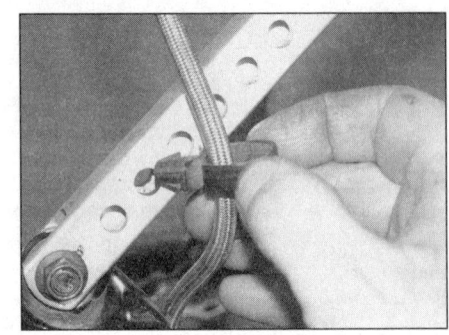

5.2 Release the guide from the torque arm as described

2 If required, on 1995 and 1996 models, remove the split pin from the bolt securing the brake torque arm to the caliper bracket, then unscrew the nut and draw the brake hose guide off. On 1997 models onward release the guide from the torque arm by pressing its locating ears together and pulling it out **(see illustration)**.

3 Unscrew the caliper mounting bolts and slide the caliper off the disc **(see illustrations)**.

5.3a Rear caliper mounting bolts (arrowed) – 1995 to 2001 models

5.3b Rear caliper mounting bolts (arrowed) – 2002-on models

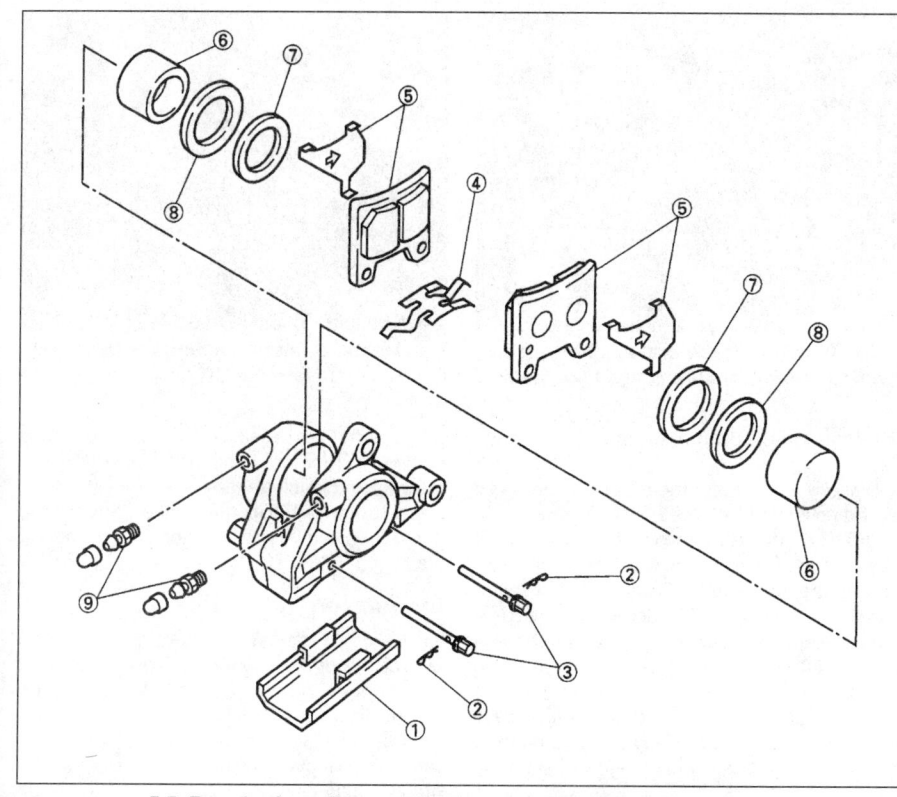

Brakes, wheels and tyres 6•9

5.5 Rear brake caliper components – 1995 to 2001 type shown

1 Pad cover
2 Retaining clips
3 Pad pins
4 Pad spring
5 Brake pads and anti-chatter shims
6 Pistons
7 Dust seals
8 Piston seals
9 Bleed valves

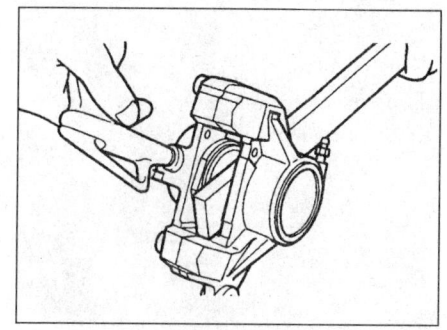

5.6 Hold the wood firmly against the piston in one half of the caliper and apply compressed air to release the piston in the opposite half

4 If the caliper is being overhauled, remove the brake pads (see Section 2).

Inspection

5 Clean the exterior of the caliper with denatured alcohol or brake system cleaner **(see illustration)**.

6 Using a flat piece of wood, block the piston on one side of the caliper in its bore and displace the opposite piston either by pumping it out by operating the brake pedal, or by forcing it out using compressed air **(see illustration)**. Remove the seals (see Steps 7 and 8) from the bore of the displaced piston, then reinstall the piston and block it using the wood. Now displace the piston from the other side using the same method. Remove the wood and the pistons. Mark each piston head and caliper body with a felt marker to ensure that the pistons can be matched to their original bores on reassembly. If the compressed air method is used, direct the air into the fluid inlet to force the pistons out of the body. Use only low pressure to ease the pistons out. If the air pressure is too high and the pistons are forced out, the caliper and/or pistons may be damaged.

⚠ **Warning: Never place your fingers in front of the pistons in an attempt to catch or protect them when applying compressed air, as serious injury could result.**

Caution: Do not try to remove the pistons by levering them out, or by using pliers or any other grips. Do not unscrew the caliper body joining bolts and separate the caliper halves. On 2002 models onward do not attempt to remove the caliper bore plugs on the outside of the caliper.

7 Remove the dust seal from each caliper bore using a wooden or plastic tool. Discard them as new ones must be used on installation. If a metal tool is being used, take great care not to damage the bores.

8 Remove and discard the piston seals in the same way.

9 Clean the pistons and bores with clean brake fluid of the specified type. If compressed air is available, use it to dry the parts thoroughly (make sure it's filtered and unlubricated).

Caution: Do not, under any circumstances, use a petroleum-based solvent to clean brake parts.

10 Inspect the caliper bores and pistons for signs of corrosion, nicks and burrs and loss of plating. If surface defects are present, the caliper assembly must be renewed. If the necessary measuring equipment is available, compare the dimensions of the caliper bores to those specified at the beginning of the Chapter, and install a new caliper if necessary. If the caliper is in bad shape the master cylinder should also be checked.

11 Lubricate the new piston seals with clean brake fluid and install them in their grooves in the caliper bores.

12 Lubricate the new dust seals with clean brake fluid and install them in their grooves in the caliper bores.

13 Lubricate the pistons with clean brake fluid and install them closed-end first into the caliper bores. Using your thumbs, push the pistons all the way in, making sure they enter the bore squarely.

Installation

14 If removed, install the brake pads (see Section 2).

15 If necessary, push the pistons a little way back into the caliper using hand pressure on the pads or a piece of wood as leverage. Slide the caliper onto the brake disc, making sure the pads sit squarely over the disc **(see illustration)**. Install the caliper mounting bolts and tighten them to the torque setting specified at the beginning of the Chapter.

16 On 1995 and 1996 models fit the brake hose guide onto the torque arm bolt, then fit the nut and tighten it to the specified torque setting. Fit a new split pin into the bolt. On later models fit the guide back into the arm **(see illustration 5.2)**.

17 If removed, connect the brake hose to the caliper, using new sealing washers on each side of the fitting. Align the hose as noted on removal **(see illustration 5.1a or b)**. Tighten the banjo bolt to the torque setting specified at the beginning of the Chapter. Top up the

5.15 Slide the caliper onto the disc and install the bolts

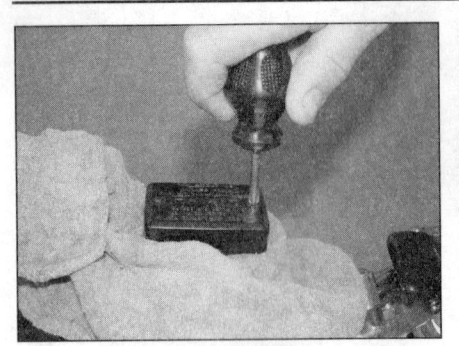

6•10 Brakes, wheels and tyres

6.4 Slacken the reservoir cover screws

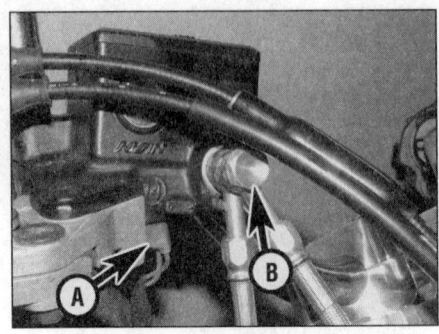

6.6 Disconnect the brake light switch wiring connectors (A). Brake hose banjo bolt (B)

6.8 Master cylinder clamp bolts (arrowed). Note the UP mark

master cylinder reservoir with DOT 4 brake fluid (see *Daily (pre-ride) checks*) and bleed the hydraulic system as described in Section 9.

18 Check that there are no fluid leaks and thoroughly test the operation of the brake before riding the motorcycle.

6 Front brake master cylinder – removal, inspection and installation

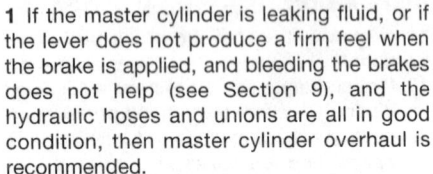

1 If the master cylinder is leaking fluid, or if the lever does not produce a firm feel when the brake is applied, and bleeding the brakes does not help (see Section 9), and the hydraulic hoses and unions are all in good condition, then master cylinder overhaul is recommended.

2 Before disassembling the master cylinder, read through the entire procedure and make sure that you have the correct rebuild kit. Also, you will need some new DOT 4 brake fluid, some clean rags and internal circlip pliers. **Note:** *To prevent damage to the paint from spilled brake fluid, always cover the fuel tank when working on the master cylinder.*

⚠ **Warning:** *Disassembly, overhaul and reassembly of the brake master cylinder must be done in a spotlessly clean work area to avoid contamination and possible failure of the brake hydraulic system components. Do not, under any circumstances, use petroleum-based solvents to clean brake parts. Use the specified clean brake fluid, dedicated brake cleaner or denatured alcohol only, as described. Use care when working with brake fluid as it can injure your eyes and it will damage painted surfaces and plastic parts.*

Removal

Note: *If the master cylinder is being displaced from the handlebar and not being removed completely or overhauled, follow Steps 6 and 8 only.*

3 Remove the rear view mirror (see Chapter 7).
4 Loosen, but do not remove, the screws holding the reservoir cover in place **(see illustration)**.

5 Remove the front brake lever (see Chapter 5).
6 Disconnect the electrical connectors from the brake light switch **(see illustration)**.
7 Unscrew the brake hose banjo bolt and separate the hose(s) from the master cylinder, noting the alignment. Discard the sealing washers as they must be renewed. Either plug the hose(s) using another suitable short piece of hose fitted through the eye(s) of the banjo union(s) (the hose must be a fairly tight fit to seal it properly), clamp it/them using a hose clamp, or wrap a plastic bag tightly around to minimise fluid loss and prevent dirt entering the system.
8 Unscrew the master cylinder clamp bolts, then lift the master cylinder and reservoir away from the handlebar, noting how the mating surfaces of the clamp align with the punch mark on the top of the handlebar **(see illustration)**.

Caution: *Do not tip the master cylinder upside down or brake fluid will run out.*

9 Remove the reservoir cover, diaphragm plate and rubber diaphragm. Drain the brake fluid from the reservoir into a suitable container. Wipe any remaining fluid out of the reservoir with a clean rag.
10 If required undo the brake light switch screw and remove the switch, noting how it fits.

Inspection

11 Carefully remove the dust boot from the end of the master cylinder and from around the piston, noting how it locates **(see illustration)**.
12 Push the piston in and, using circlip pliers, remove the circlip from its groove in the master cylinder and slide out the piston assembly and the spring, noting how they fit. If they are difficult to remove, apply low pressure compressed air to the fluid outlet. Lay the parts out in order as you remove them to prevent confusion during reassembly.
13 Clean all parts with clean brake fluid or denatured alcohol. If compressed air is available, use it to dry the parts thoroughly (make sure it's filtered and unlubricated).

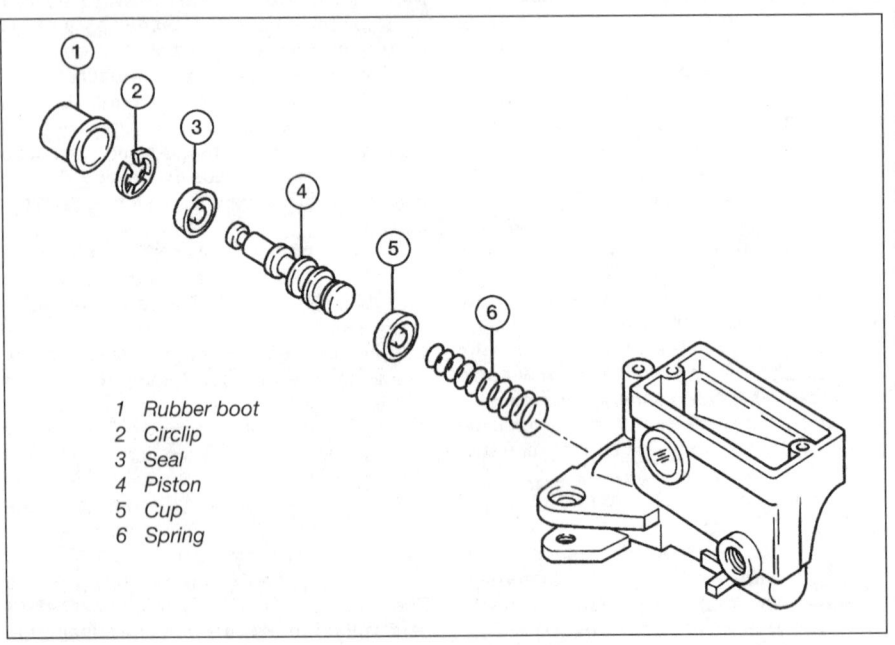

1 Rubber boot
2 Circlip
3 Seal
4 Piston
5 Cup
6 Spring

6.11 Front master cylinder components

Brakes, wheels and tyres 6•11

6.21 Align the clamp mating surfaces with the punch mark (arrowed) on the top of the handlebar

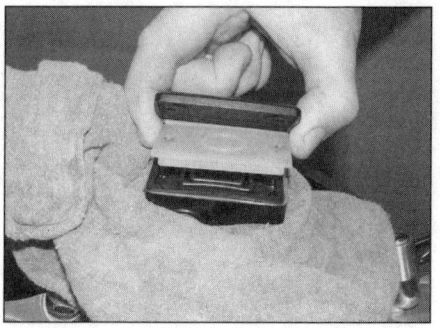

6.25 Make sure the diaphragm is correctly seated before fitting the plate and cover

Caution: Do not, under any circumstances, use a petroleum-based solvent to clean brake parts.

14 Check the master cylinder bore for corrosion, scratches, nicks and score marks. If the necessary measuring equipment is available, compare the diameter of the bore to that given in the Specifications Section of this Chapter. If damage or wear is evident, the master cylinder must be renewed. If the master cylinder is in poor condition, then the calipers should be checked as well. Check that the fluid inlet and outlet ports in the master cylinder are clear.

15 The dust boot, circlip, piston, seal, cup and spring are included in the rebuild kit. Use all of the new parts, regardless of the apparent condition of the old ones. Assemble and install them according to the layout of the old ones.

16 Lubricate the cup, seal and piston with clean brake fluid.

17 Fit the spring and piston assembly into the master cylinder, with the wide end of the spring going in first. Make sure the lips on the cup and seal do not turn inside out when they enter the bore. Depress the piston and install the new circlip, making sure that it locates in the groove in the master cylinder.

18 Apply some silicone grease to the inside of the rubber dust boot, then install it, making sure it is seated properly in the groove in the master cylinder and around the piston.

19 Inspect the reservoir rubber diaphragm and renew it if it is damaged or deteriorated.

Installation

20 If removed, locate the brake light switch on the underside of the master cylinder and secure it with the screw.

21 Attach the master cylinder to the handlebar and fit the clamp, with its UP mark facing up **(see illustration 6.8)**. Align the top mating surfaces of the clamp with the punch mark on the top of the handlebar, then tighten the top bolt first, then the bottom bolt, to the torque setting specified at the beginning of the Chapter **(see illustration)**.

22 Connect the brake hose(s) to the master cylinder, using new sealing washers on each side of the union(s), and aligning the hose(s) as noted on removal **(see illustration 6.6)**. Note that on the double hose fitting used on 1995 to 1998 and 2002-on models, there is a sealing washer on each side of the unions, making three washers in all. Tighten the banjo bolt to the torque setting specified at the beginning of the Chapter.

23 Install the brake lever (see Chapter 5). Connect the brake light switch wiring.

24 Fill the fluid reservoir with new DOT 4 brake fluid as described in *Daily (pre-ride) checks*. Refer to Section 9 of this Chapter and bleed the air from the system.

25 Fit the rubber diaphragm, making sure it is correctly seated, the diaphragm plate and the cover onto the reservoir **(see illustration)**.

26 Install the rear view mirror (see Chapter 7).

27 Check the operation of the front brake and brake light before riding the motorcycle.

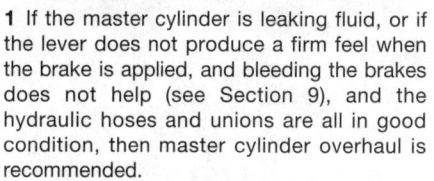

7 Rear brake master cylinder – removal, inspection and installation

1 If the master cylinder is leaking fluid, or if the lever does not produce a firm feel when the brake is applied, and bleeding the brakes does not help (see Section 9), and the hydraulic hoses and unions are all in good condition, then master cylinder overhaul is recommended.

2 Before disassembling the master cylinder, read through the entire procedure and make sure that you have the correct rebuild kit. Also, you will need some new DOT 4 brake fluid, some clean rags and internal circlip pliers. **Note:** *To prevent damage to the paint from spilled brake fluid, always cover the surrounding components when working on the master cylinder.*

⚠️ **Warning:** *Disassembly, overhaul and reassembly of the brake master cylinder must be done in a spotlessly clean work area to avoid contamination and possible failure of the brake hydraulic system components. Do not, under any circumstances, use petroleum-based solvents to clean brake parts. Use the specified clean brake fluid, dedicated brake cleaner or denatured alcohol only, as described. Use care when working with brake fluid as it can injure your eyes and it will damage painted surfaces and plastic parts.*

Removal

3 If available, fit a brake hose clamp onto the master cylinder reservoir hose. Detach the hose from the union on the master cylinder, being prepared to catch any drops of fluid with a rag **(see illustration)**. If a clamp is not available, allow the reservoir to drain into a suitable container. If you do this, you may have to remove the right-hand side panel (see Chapter 7), undo the reservoir mounting screw and displace the reservoir, then unscrew the cap and remove the diaphragm plate and diaphragm to act as a vent **(see illustrations)**. Refit the diaphragm, plate and cover afterwards and remount the reservoir.

7.3a Reservoir hose clamp (arrowed)

7.3b Undo the screw and displace the reservoir . . .

7.3c . . . and remove the cap, plate and diaphragm

6•12 Brakes, wheels and tyres

7.4 Brake hose banjo bolt (arrowed)

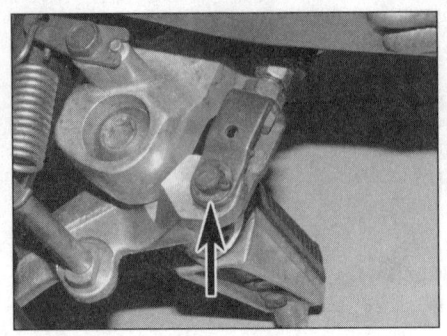

7.5a Remove the split pin and washer (arrowed) ...

7.5b ... then withdraw the clevis pin (arrowed)

4 Unscrew the brake hose banjo bolt and separate the hose from the master cylinder, noting its alignment **(see illustration)**. Discard the two sealing washers as they must be renewed. Either plug the hose using another suitable short piece of hose fitted through the eye of the banjo union (it must be a fairly tight fit to seal it properly), clamp it using a hose clamp, or wrap a plastic bag tightly around to minimise fluid loss and prevent dirt entering the system.

5 Remove the split pin and washer from the clevis pin securing the brake pedal to the master cylinder pushrod, then remove the clevis pin and separate the pedal from the pushrod **(see illustrations)**.

6 Unscrew the two bolts securing the master cylinder to the bracket and remove the master cylinder **(see illustration)**.

Inspection

7 If required, mark the position of the clevis locknut on the pushrod, then slacken the locknut and thread the clevis and its base nut off the pushrod **(see illustration)**.

8 Dislodge the rubber dust boot from the base of the master cylinder and from around the pushrod, noting how it locates, and slide it down the pushrod **(see illustration)**.

9 Push the pushrod in and, using circlip pliers, remove the circlip from its groove in the master cylinder and slide out the pushrod, piston assembly and the spring, noting how they fit. If they are difficult to remove, apply low pressure compressed air to the fluid outlet. Lay the parts out in the proper order to prevent confusion during reassembly.

10 If required, remove the fluid reservoir hose union from the master cylinder. Discard the bush as a new one must be used. Inspect the reservoir hose for cracks or splits and renew it if necessary.

11 Clean all of the parts with clean brake fluid or denatured alcohol.

Caution: Do not, under any circumstances, use a petroleum-based solvent to clean brake parts. If compressed air is available, use it to dry the parts thoroughly (make sure it's filtered and unlubricated).

12 Check the master cylinder bore for corrosion, scratches, nicks and score marks. If the necessary measuring equipment is available, compare the diameter of the bore to that given in the Specifications Section of this Chapter. If damage or wear is evident, the master cylinder must be renewed. If the master cylinder is in poor condition, then the caliper should be checked as well.

13 The dust boot, pushrod, circlip, piston, seal, cup and spring are included in the rebuild kit. Use all of the new parts, regardless of the apparent condition of the old ones. Assemble and install them according to the layout of the old ones.

14 Lubricate the cup, seal and piston with clean brake fluid.

15 Fit the spring and piston assembly into the master cylinder. Make sure the lips on the cup and seal do not turn inside out when they enter the bore.

16 Apply some silicone grease to the end of the pushrod and fit it into the master cylinder. Depress the pushrod, then install the new circlip, making sure it is properly seated in the groove.

17 Install the rubber dust boot, making sure it is seated properly in the groove in the master cylinder and around the pushrod.

18 If removed, fit the fluid reservoir hose union using a new a bush.

19 If removed, thread the clevis locknut, the clevis and its base nut onto the master cylinder pushrod end **(see illustration 7.7)**. Position the clevis as noted on removal, then tighten the clevis locknut securely.

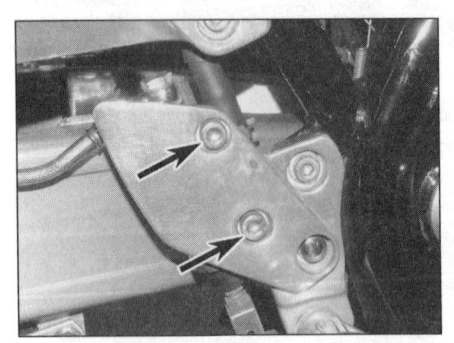

7.6 Master cylinder mounting bolts (arrowed)

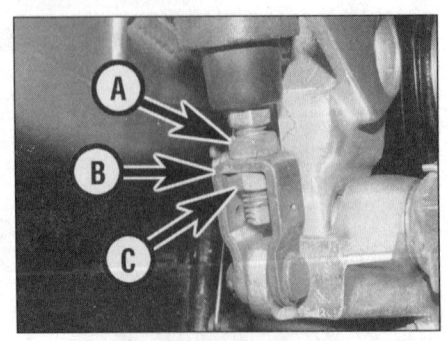

7.7 Locknut (A), clevis (B), base nut (C)

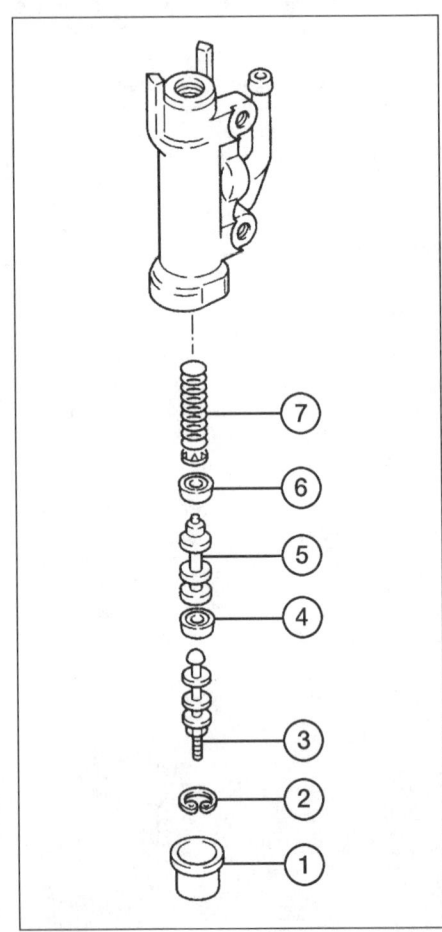

7.8 Rear master cylinder components

1 Rubber boot
2 Circlip
3 Pushrod
4 Seal
5 Piston
6 Cup
7 Spring

Brakes, wheels and tyres 6•13

Installation

20 Fit the master cylinder onto the footrest bracket and tighten its mounting bolts to the torque setting specified at the beginning of the Chapter.
21 Align the brake pedal with the master cylinder pushrod clevis, then slide in the clevis pin, fit the washer and secure it using a new split pin, bending its ends securely **(see illustrations 7.5b and a)**.
22 Connect the brake hose to the master cylinder, using a new sealing washer on each side of the union. Align the hose as noted on removal and tighten the banjo bolt to the specified torque setting **(see illustration 7.4)**.
23 Connect the reservoir hose to the union on the master cylinder and secure it with the clip. Check that the hose is secure at the reservoir end as well. If the clips have weakened, use new ones. If used on removal, release the hose clamp.
24 Fill the fluid reservoir with new DOT 4 brake fluid (see *Daily (pre-ride) checks*) and bleed the system following the procedure in Section 9.
25 Check the operation of the brake and brake light carefully before riding the motorcycle.

8 Brake hoses and unions – inspection, removal and installation

Inspection

1 Brake hose condition should be checked regularly and the hoses renewed at the specified interval (see Chapter 1).
2 Twist and flex the rubber hoses while looking for cracks, bulges and seeping fluid **(see illustration)**. Check extra carefully around the areas where the hoses connect with the banjo fittings, as these are common areas for hose failure.
3 Inspect the banjo union fittings connected to the brake hoses, and on 1999 to 2001 models the hose splitter (bolted to the bottom yoke) for the front brake system. If the fittings are rusted, scratched or cracked, renew them.

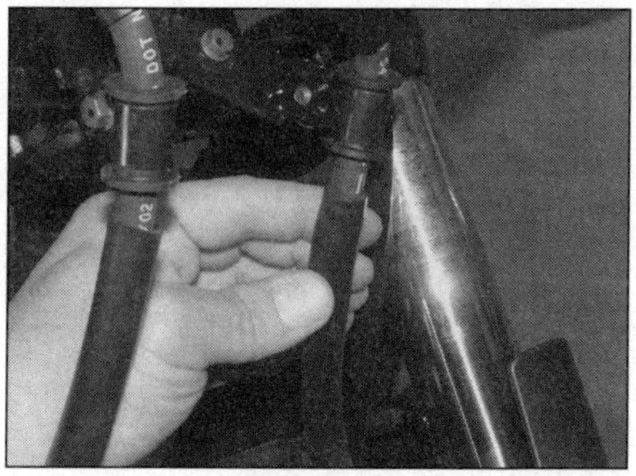

8.2 Check the brake hoses for cracks and signs of deterioration

Renewal

> **Warning:** Use care when working with brake fluid as it can injure your eyes and it will damage painted surfaces and plastic parts.

4 The brake hoses have banjo union fittings on each end. Cover the surrounding area with plenty of rags and unscrew the banjo bolt at each end of the hose, noting its alignment **(see illustrations 4.1, 5.1a or b, 6.6 and 7.4)**. Free the hoses from any clips or guides and remove them. Discard the sealing washers as new ones must be used. Note that on the front master cylinder double hose fitting on 1995 to 1998 and 2002-on models there is a sealing washer on each side of the unions, making three washers in all.
5 Position the new hose, making sure it isn't twisted or otherwise strained, and abut the tab on the hose union with the lug on the component casting, where present. Otherwise align the hose as noted on removal. Install the hose banjo bolts using new sealing washers on both sides of the unions. Tighten the banjo bolts to the torque setting specified at the beginning of this Chapter.
6 Make sure the hoses are correctly aligned and routed clear of all moving components. Flush the old brake fluid from the system, refill with new DOT 4 brake fluid (see *Daily (pre-ride) checks*) and bleed the air from the system (see Section 9). Check the operation of the brakes carefully before riding the motorcycle.

9 Brake system – bleeding and fluid renewal

> **Warning:** Use care when working with brake fluid as it can injure your eyes and it will damage painted surfaces and plastic parts.

Bleeding air from the system

1 Bleeding the brakes is simply the process of removing all the air bubbles from the brake fluid reservoirs, the hoses and the brake calipers. Bleeding is necessary whenever a brake system hydraulic connection is loosened, when a component or hose is renewed, or when the master cylinder or caliper is overhauled. Leaks in the system may also allow air to enter, but leaking brake fluid will reveal their presence and warn you of the need for repair.
2 To bleed the brakes, you will need some new DOT 4 brake fluid, a length of clear vinyl or plastic tubing, a small container partially filled with clean brake fluid, some rags and a ring spanner to fit the brake caliper bleed valves.
3 Cover the fuel tank, front mudguard, tail light cover and other painted components to prevent damage in the event that brake fluid is spilled.
4 Remove the reservoir cover or cap, diaphragm plate and diaphragm (see *Daily (pre-ride) checks*) and slowly pump the brake lever or pedal a few times, until no air bubbles can be seen floating up from the holes in the bottom of the reservoir. Doing this bleeds the air from the master cylinder end of the line. Loosely refit the reservoir cover.
5 Pull the dust cap off the bleed valve **(see illustrations)**. Attach one end of the clear vinyl or plastic tubing to the bleed valve and submerge the other end in the brake fluid in the container **(see illustration)**. Note that the rear caliper has two bleed valves.
6 Remove the reservoir cap or cover and check the fluid level. Do not allow the fluid level to drop below the lower mark during the bleeding process.

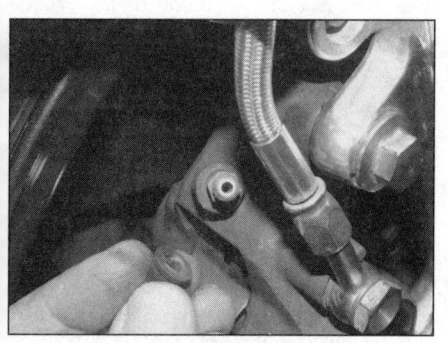

9.5a Front brake caliper bleed valve

9.5b Rear brake caliper bleed valve

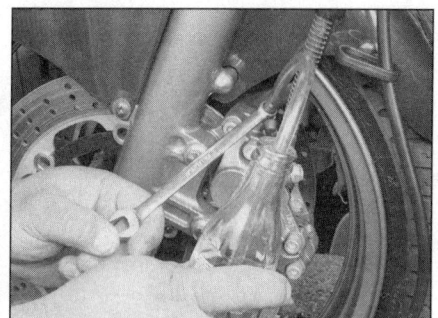

9.5c To bleed the brakes, you need a spanner, a short section of clear tubing, and a clear container half-filled with brake fluid

6•14 Brakes, wheels and tyres

7 Carefully pump the brake lever or pedal three or four times and hold it in (front) or down (rear) while opening the caliper bleed valve. When the valve is opened, brake fluid will flow out of the caliper into the clear tubing and the lever will move toward the handlebar or the pedal will move down.

8 Retighten the bleed valve, then release the brake lever or pedal gradually. Repeat the process until no air bubbles are visible in the brake fluid leaving the caliper and the lever or pedal is firm when applied. On completion, disconnect the bleeding equipment, then tighten the bleed valve to the torque setting specified at the beginning of the chapter and install the dust cap. Repeat the procedure on the other caliper (front brake) or other bleed valve on the caliper (rear brake).

9 Install the diaphragm, plate and cover or cap assembly, wipe up any spilled brake fluid and check the entire system for leaks.

> **HAYNES HiNT** *If it's not possible to produce a firm feel to the lever or pedal the fluid my be aerated. Let the brake fluid in the system stabilise for a few hours and then repeat the procedure when the tiny bubbles in the system have settled out. Also check to make sure that there are no 'high-spots' in the brake hose in which an air bubble can become trapped – this will occur most often in an incorrectly mounted hose union, but can also arise through bleeding the brakes while some of the brake system components are at such an angle to encourage this. Reversing the angle or displacing and moving the offending component around will normally dislodge any trapped air.*

Fluid renewal

10 Changing the brake fluid is a similar process to bleeding the brakes and requires the same materials plus a suitable tool for siphoning the fluid out of the hydraulic reservoir. Also ensure that the container is large enough to take all the old fluid when it is flushed out of the system.

11 Cover the fuel tank, front mudguard, tail light cover and other painted components to prevent damage in the event that brake fluid is spilled.

12 Pull the dust cap off the bleed valve **(see illustrations 9.5a or b)**. Attach one end of the clear vinyl or plastic tubing to the bleed valve and submerge the other end in the brake fluid in the container **(see illustration 9.5c)**.

13 Remove the reservoir cover or cap, diaphragm plate and diaphragm (see *Daily (pre-ride) checks*) and siphon the old fluid out of the reservoir. Fill the reservoir with new brake fluid.

14 Carefully pump the brake lever or pedal three or four times and hold it in (front) or down (rear) while opening the caliper bleed valve. When the valve is opened, brake fluid will flow out of the caliper into the clear tubing and the lever will move toward the handlebar or the pedal will move down.

15 Retighten the bleed valve, then release the brake lever or pedal gradually. Keep the reservoir topped-up with new fluid to above the LOWER level at all times or air may enter the system and greatly increase the length of the task. Repeat the process until new fluid can be seen emerging from the bleed valve.

> **HAYNES HiNT** *Old brake fluid is invariably much darker in colour than new fluid, making it easy to see when all old fluid has been expelled from the system.*

16 Disconnect the hose, then tighten the bleed valve to the specified torque setting and install the dust cap.

17 Top-up the reservoir, install the diaphragm, diaphragm plate and cap, and wipe up any spilled brake fluid. Check the entire system for fluid leaks.

18 Check the operation of the brakes before riding the motorcycle.

10 Wheels – inspection and repair

1 Position the motorcycle on its centrestand. When checking the front wheel, support the bike so that it is raised off the ground. Clean the wheels thoroughly to remove mud and dirt that may interfere with the inspection procedure or mask defects. Make a general check of the wheels (see Chapter 1) and tyres (see *Daily (pre-ride) checks*).

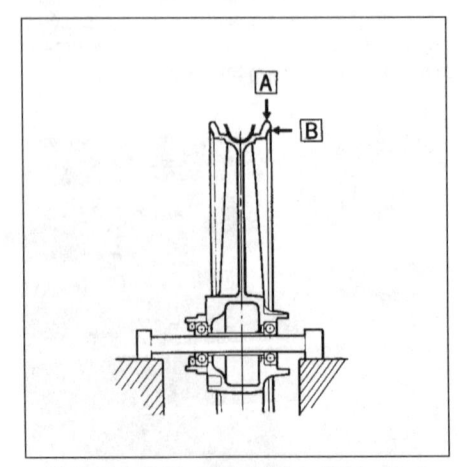

10.2 Check the wheel for radial (out-of-round) runout (A) and axial (side-to-side) runout (B)

2 To check axial (side-to-side) runout, attach a dial gauge to the fork slider or the swingarm and position its stem against the side of the rim **(see illustration)**. Spin the wheel slowly and check the amount of runout at the rim. To accurately check radial (out of round) runout with the dial gauge, remove the wheel from the machine, and the tyre from the wheel. With the axle clamped in a vice and the dial gauge positioned on the top of the rim, rotate the wheel and check the runout.

3 An easier, though slightly less accurate, method is to attach a stiff wire pointer to the fork slider or the swingarm and position the end a fraction of an inch from the wheel (where the wheel and tyre join). If the wheel is true, the distance from the pointer to the rim will be constant as the wheel is rotated.

4 Visually inspect the wheels for cracks, flat spots on the rim, and other damage. Look very closely for dents in the area where the tyre bead contacts the rim. Dents in this area may prevent complete sealing of the tyre against the rim, which leads to deflation of the tyre over a period of time.

5 If damage is evident, or if runout in either direction is excessive, the wheel will have to be renewed. Never attempt to repair a damaged cast alloy wheel. **Note:** *If wheel runout is excessive, check the wheel bearings and axle very carefully before renewing the wheel.*

11 Wheels – alignment check

1 Misalignment of the wheels, which may be due to a cocked rear wheel or a bent frame or fork yokes, can cause strange and possibly serious handling problems. If the frame or yokes are at fault, repair by a frame specialist or renewal of the damaged parts is the only alternative.

2 To check the alignment you will need an assistant, a length of string or a perfectly straight piece of wood and a ruler. A plumb bob or other suitable weight will also be required.

3 Place the bike on its centrestand. Measure the width of both tyres at their widest points. Subtract the smaller measurement from the larger measurement, then divide the difference by two. The result is the amount of offset that should exist between the front and rear tyres on both sides.

4 If a string is used, have your assistant hold one end of it about halfway between the floor and the rear axle, touching the rear sidewall of the tyre.

5 Run the other end of the string forward and pull it tight so that it is roughly parallel to the

Brakes, wheels and tyres 6•15

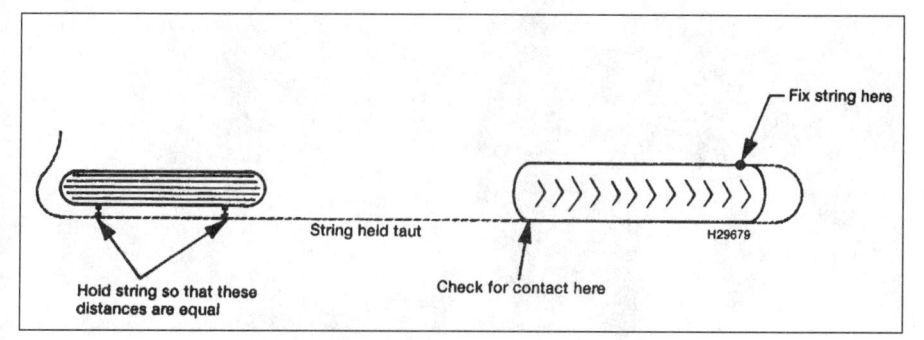

11.5 Wheel alignment check using string

floor **(see illustration)**. Slowly bring the string into contact with the front sidewall of the rear tyre, then turn the front wheel until it is parallel with the string. Measure the distance from the front tyre sidewall to the string.

6 Repeat the procedure on the other side of the motorcycle. The distance from the front tyre sidewall to the string should be equal on both sides.

7 As previously mentioned, a perfectly straight length of wood or metal bar may be substituted for the string **(see illustration)**. The procedure is the same.

8 If the distance between the string and tyre is greater on one side, or if the rear wheel appears to be cocked, refer to Chapter 1 and check that the chain adjuster markings are in the same position on each side of the swingarm.

9 If the front-to-back alignment is correct, the wheels still may be out of alignment vertically.

10 Using a plumb bob, or other suitable weight, and a length of string, check the rear wheel to make sure it is vertical. To do this, hold the string against the tyre upper sidewall and allow the weight to settle just off the floor. When the string touches both the upper and lower tyre sidewalls and is perfectly straight, the wheel is vertical. If it is not, place thin spacers under one leg of the stand until it is.

11 Once the rear wheel is vertical, check the front wheel in the same manner. If both wheels are not perfectly vertical, the frame and/or major suspension components are bent.

12 Front wheel – removal and installation

Removal

1 Position the motorcycle on its centrestand and support it so that the front wheel is off the ground. Always make sure the motorcycle is properly supported.

2 Displace the front brake calipers (see Section 4). Support the calipers with a cable tie or a bungee cord so that no strain is placed on their hydraulic hoses. There is no need to disconnect the hoses from the calipers. **Note:** *Do not operate the front brake lever with the calipers removed.*

3 Unscrew the knurled ring securing the speedometer cable to the drive housing and detach it, noting how it locates **(see illustration)**.

4 Slacken the axle clamp bolt on the bottom of the right-hand fork, then unscrew the axle **(see illustration)**.

5 Support the wheel, then withdraw the axle from the right-hand side, using a drift to tap it out if necessary, and carefully lower the wheel **(see illustration)**.

6 Remove the speedometer drive housing from the left-hand side of the wheel, noting how it fits, and the spacer from the right-hand

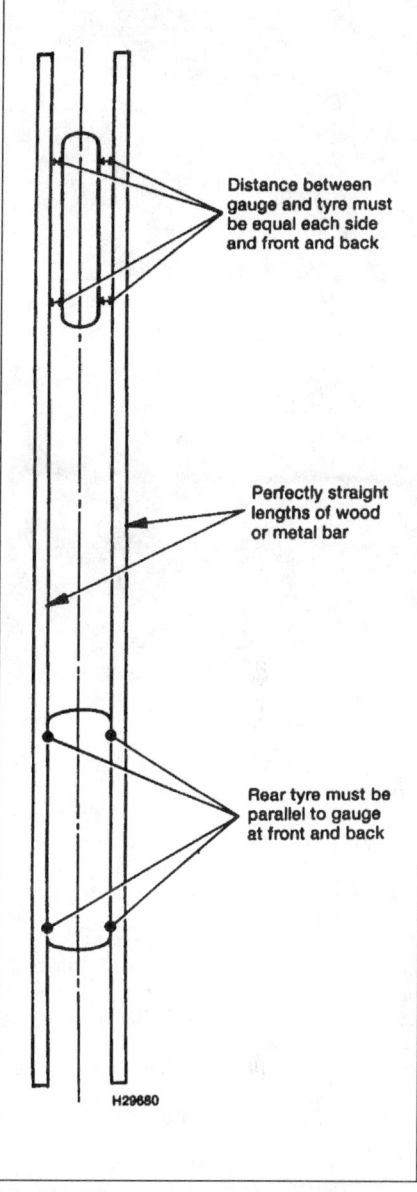

11.7 Wheel alignment check using a straight edge

12.3 Unscrew the ring and detach the cable

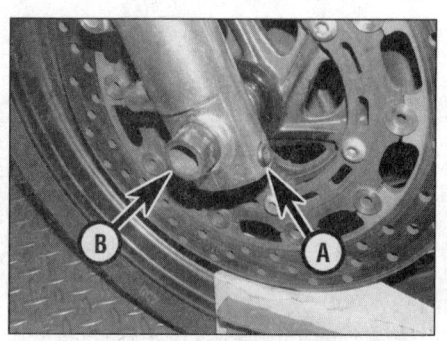

12.4 Slacken the axle clamp bolts (A), then unscrew the axle (B)

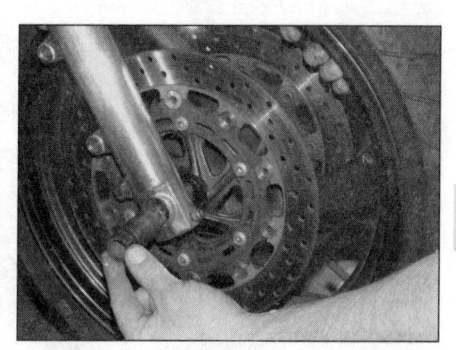

12.5 Withdraw the axle and remove the wheel

6•16 Brakes, wheels and tyres

12.6a Remove the speedometer drive housing ...

12.6b ... and the spacer

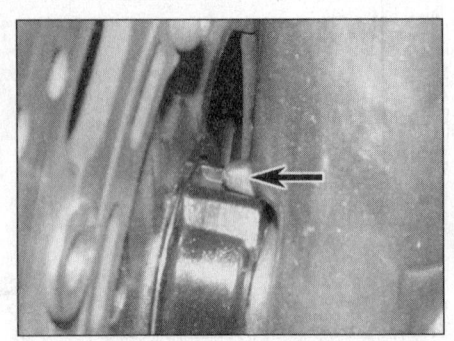

12.11a Make sure the lug (arrowed) locates between the stoppers on the drive housing

12.11b Tighten the axle to the specified torque

12.15 Make sure the inner cable end locates correctly before tightening the ring

side, noting which way round it fits **(see illustrations)**.
Caution: Don't lay the wheel down and allow it to rest on a disc – the disc could become warped. Set the wheel on wood blocks so the disc doesn't support the weight of the wheel.
7 Check that the axle is straight by rolling it on a flat surface such as a piece of plate glass (first wipe off all old grease and remove any corrosion using wire wool). If the equipment is available, place the axle in V-blocks and check it for runout using a dial gauge. If the axle is bent, renew it.
8 Check the condition of the wheel bearings (see Section 14).

Installation

9 Apply a smear of grease to the inside of the speedometer drive housing and the wheel spacer, and also to the outside where they fit into the wheel. Also apply a thin coat of grease to the axle.
10 Manoeuvre the wheel into position between the fork sliders. Fit the speedometer drive housing into the left-hand side of the wheel, locating the drive plate tabs into its cutouts **(see illustration 12.6a)**. Fit the spacer into the right-hand side, with its narrow end on the inside **(see illustration 12.6b)**.
11 Lift the wheel into place, making sure the drive housing and spacer remain in position, and that the housing is positioned so that the lug on the bottom of the fork is between the stoppers on the housing **(see illustration)**. Slide the axle in from the right-hand side and tighten it to the torque setting specified at the beginning of the Chapter **(see illustration)**. Check that the wheel spins freely.
12 Lower the front wheel to the ground, then install the brake calipers (see Section 4).
13 Apply the front brake a few times to bring the pads back into contact with the discs. Move the motorcycle off its stand, apply the front brake and pump the front forks a few times to settle all components in position.
14 Now tighten the axle clamp bolt on the bottom of the right-hand fork to the specified torque setting.
15 Connect the speedometer cable to the drive housing, making sure it locates correctly, and tighten the knurled ring to secure it **(see illustration)**.
16 Check for correct operation of the brakes before riding the motorcycle.

13 Rear wheel –
removal and installation

Removal

1 Position the motorcycle its centrestand so that the wheel is off the ground.
2 On XJR1200 models remove the split pin from the bolt securing the brake torque arm to the rear brake caliper. On all models slacken the nut on the bolt securing the brake torque arm to the rear brake caliper **(see illustration)**.
3 Unscrew the axle nut and remove the washer and left-hand chain adjustment marker **(see illustration)**.
4 Support the wheel (a good way to do this is to slide your foot part way under it) then withdraw the axle along with the adjustment marker from the right-hand side **(see illustration)**. Gently lower the wheel to the

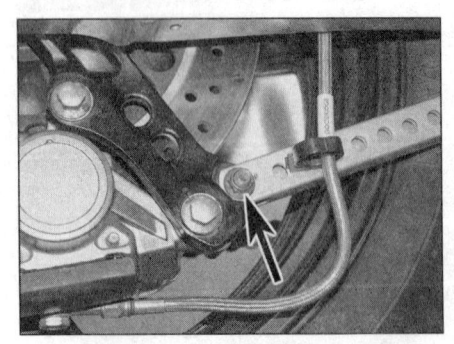

13.2 Slacken the nut (arrowed)

13.3 Unscrew the nut and remove the washer and marker

13.4a Withdraw the axle and lower the wheel ...

Brakes, wheels and tyres 6•17

13.4b ... and disengage the chain from the sprocket

13.5a Remove the spacer from the right-hand side ...

13.5b ... and from the left-hand side, noting which fits where

ground, making sure no strain is placed on the brake hose as the caliper lowers with it, then disengage the chain from the sprocket and draw the wheel back so the disc is clear of the caliper and remove the wheel **(see illustration)**. Note how the axle passes through the caliper mounting bracket.

5 Remove the spacer from each side of the wheel, noting which fits where **(see illustrations)**.

Caution: *Do not lay the wheel down and allow it to rest on the disc or the sprocket – they could become warped. Set the wheel on wood blocks so the disc or the sprocket doesn't support the weight of the wheel. Do not operate the brake pedal with the wheel removed.*

6 Check that the axle is straight by rolling it on a flat surface such as a piece of plate glass (first wipe off all old grease and remove any corrosion using wire wool). If the equipment is available, place the axle in V-blocks and check for runout using a dial gauge. If the axle is bent, renew it.

7 Check the condition of the grease seals and wheel bearings (see Section 14).

Installation

8 Apply a smear of grease to the inside of the wheel spacers, and also to the outside where they fit into the wheel. Fit the narrow diameter spacer into the right-hand side of the wheel, and the wider spacer into the left-hand side **(see illustrations 13.5a and b)**.

9 Push the pistons a little way back into the brake caliper using hand pressure or a piece of wood on the pads as leverage.

10 Slide the right-hand adjustment marker onto the axle, making sure it is the right way round.

11 Manoeuvre the wheel so that it is in between the ends of the swingarm and move it forward so that the brake disc slides into the caliper, making sure the pads sit squarely on each side of the disc **(see illustration)**. Engage the drive chain with the sprocket **(see illustration 13.4b)**.

12 Lift the wheel into position, making sure the caliper stays on the disc and the caliper bracket is correctly aligned with the wheel and the swingarm, and the spacers remain correctly in place in the wheel, then slide the axle through from the right, making sure it passes through the caliper mounting bracket **(see illustration 13.4a)**.

13 Push the axle all the way through, locating the adjustment marker horizontally in the swingarm and the axle head flats in the cutout in the adjustment marker **(see illustration)**. Check that everything is correctly aligned, then fit the left-hand side adjustment marker, again locating it horizontally in the swingarm, the washer and the axle nut, but do not tighten it yet **(see illustrations)**. If it is difficult to insert the axle due to the tension of the drive chain, back off the chain adjusters (see Chapter 1).

14 Adjust the chain slack as described in Chapter 1.

15 Tighten the axle nut to the torque setting specified at the beginning of the Chapter **(see illustration)**.

16 Tighten the brake torque arm nut to the specified torque setting. On XJR1200 models, fit a new split pin into the bolt and bend its ends securely.

17 Operate the brake pedal several times to bring the pads into contact with the disc. Check the operation of the rear brake carefully before riding the bike.

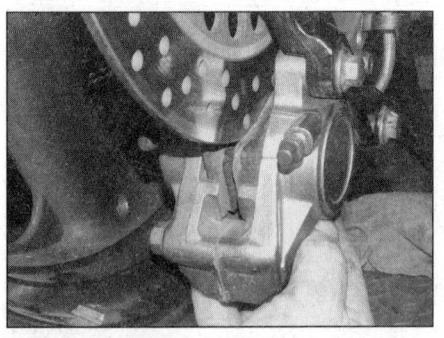

13.11 Make sure the disc slots squarely between the brake pads

13.13a Make sure the axle head and adjustment marker locate correctly ...

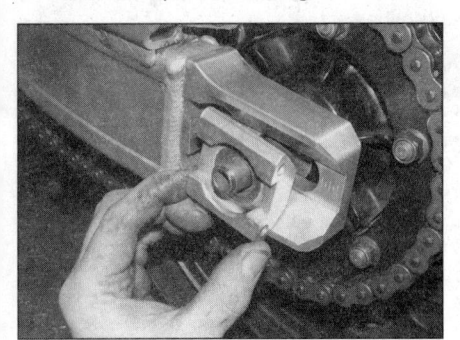

13.13b ... then fit the left-hand marker ...

13.13c ... the washer and the nut

13.15 Tighten the axle nut to the specified torque

6•18 Brakes, wheels and tyres

14.3a Lever out the grease seals...

14.3b ... and the retainer plate...

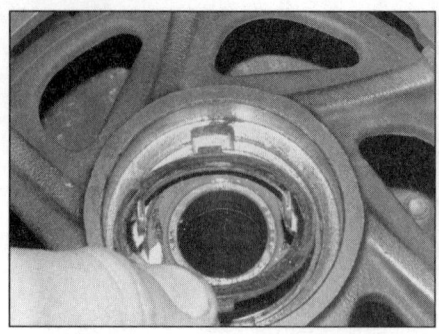

14.3c ... and remove the drive plate

14 Wheel bearings – removal, inspection and installation

Front wheel bearings

Note: *Always renew the wheel bearings in pairs. Never renew the bearings individually. Avoid using a high pressure cleaner on the wheel bearing area.*

1 Remove the front wheel (see Section 12).
2 Set the wheel on blocks so as not to allow the weight to rest on the brake disc.
3 Lever out the grease seal on each side of the wheel using a flat-bladed screwdriver, taking care not to damage the rim of the hub **(see illustration)**. Discard the seals if they are damaged or deteriorated. Lever out the retainer plate on the left-hand side of the wheel and remove the speedometer drive

> **HAYNES HiNT** *Position a piece of wood against the wheel to prevent the screwdriver shaft damaging it when levering the grease seal out.*

plate, noting how it fits **(see illustrations)**.
4 Using a metal rod (preferably a brass drift punch) inserted through the centre of the upper bearing, tap evenly around the inner race of the lower bearing to drive it from the hub **(see illustrations)**. The bearing spacer will also come out.

14.4a Knock out the bearings using a drift...

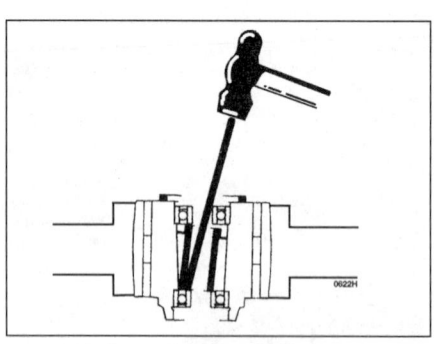

14.4b ... locating it as shown

14.9 A socket can be used to drive in the bearing

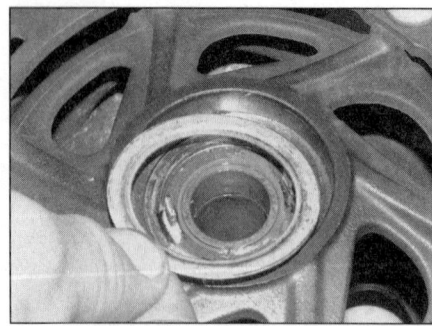

14.11 Press the retainer plate onto the drive plate

5 Lay the wheel on its other side so that the remaining bearing faces down. Drive the bearing out of the wheel using the same technique as above.
6 If the bearings are of the unsealed type or are only sealed on one side, clean them with a high flash-point solvent (one which won't leave any residue) and blow them dry with compressed air (don't let the bearings spin as you dry them). Apply a few drops of oil to the bearing. **Note:** *If the bearing is sealed on both sides don't attempt to clean it.*

> **HAYNES HiNT** *Refer to Tools and Workshop Tips (Section 5) for more information about bearings.*

7 Hold the outer race of the bearing and rotate the inner race – if the bearing doesn't turn smoothly, has rough spots or is noisy, renew it.
8 If the bearing is good and can be re-used, wash it in solvent once again and dry it, then pack the bearing with grease.
9 Thoroughly clean the hub area of the wheel. Install the left-hand bearing into the recess in the hub, with the marked or sealed side facing outwards. Using the old bearing (if new ones are being fitted), a bearing driver or a socket large enough to contact only the outer race of the bearing, drive it in until it's completely seated **(see illustration)**.
10 Turn the wheel over and install the bearing spacer. Drive the other bearing into place as described above.
11 Fit the speedometer drive plate into the left-hand side of the wheel, with the drive tabs facing out and aligning the flat tabs with the cutouts in the hub **(see illustration 14.3c)**. Press the retainer plate onto the drive plate **(see illustration)**.
12 Apply a smear of lithium based grease to the lips of the seals, then press them into the wheel, using a seal or bearing driver or a suitable socket to drive them into place if necessary **(see illustration)**. As the seals sit flush with the top surface of their housing, using a piece of wood as shown will automatically set them flush without the risk of

Brakes, wheels and tyres 6•19

14.12a Press or drive the seal into place

14.12b Using a piece of wood as shown automatically sets the seal flush

14.14 Removing the sprocket coupling

setting them too deep and having to lever them out again **(see illustration)**. When the wheel is installed the speedometer drive housing will automatically set its seal deeper if needs be.
13 Clean off all grease from the brake discs using acetone or brake system cleaner then install the wheel (see Section 12).

Rear wheel bearings

Note: *Always renew the wheel bearings in pairs. Never renew the bearings individually. Avoid using a high pressure cleaner on the wheel bearing area.*

14 Remove the rear wheel (see Section 13). Lift the sprocket coupling out of the left-hand side of the wheel, taking care not to lose its inner spacer if it is loose **(see illustration)**.
15 Set the wheel on blocks so as not to allow the weight of the wheel to rest on the brake disc.
16 Lever out the grease seal on the right-hand side of the wheel using a flat-bladed screwdriver, taking care not to damage the rim of the hub **(see illustration 14.3a)**. Discard the seal as a new one should be used.

> **HAYNES HiNT** Position a piece of wood against the wheel to prevent the screwdriver shaft damaging it when levering the grease seal out.

17 Using a metal rod (preferably a brass drift punch) inserted through the centre of the right-hand bearing, tap evenly around the inner race of the left-hand bearing to drive it from the hub **(see illustrations 14.4a and b)**. The bearing spacer will also come out.

18 Lay the wheel on its other side so that the remaining bearing faces down. Drive the bearing out of the wheel using the same technique as above.
19 Refer to Steps 6 to 8 above and check the bearings.
20 Thoroughly clean the hub area of the wheel. First install the right-hand bearing into its recess in the hub, with the marked or sealed side facing outwards. Using the old bearing (if new ones are being fitted), a bearing driver or a socket large enough to contact only the outer race of the bearing, drive it in squarely until it's completely seated **(see illustration 14.21)**.
21 Turn the wheel over and install the bearing spacer. Drive the left-hand side bearing into place as described above **(see illustration)**.
22 Apply a smear of grease to the lips of the new grease seal, and press it into the right-hand side of the wheel, using a seal or bearing driver, a suitable socket or a flat piece of wood to drive it into place if necessary **(see illustration 14.12a)**. As the seal sits flush with the top surface of the housing, using a piece of wood as shown will automatically set it flush without the risk of setting it too deep and having to lever it out again **(see illustration 14.12b)**.
23 Clean off all grease from the brake disc using acetone or brake system cleaner. Fit the sprocket coupling assembly onto the wheel making sure its spacer is in place. Install the wheel (see Section 13).

Sprocket coupling bearing

24 Remove the rear wheel (see Section 13). Lift the sprocket coupling out of the wheel,

14.21 A socket can be used to drive in the bearing

taking care not to lose its inner spacer if it is loose **(see illustration 14.14)**.
25 Using a flat-bladed screwdriver, lever out the grease seal from the outside of the coupling **(see illustration)**.

> **HAYNES HiNT** Position a piece of wood against the sprocket coupling to prevent the screwdriver shaft damaging it when levering the grease seal out.

26 Remove the spacer from the inside of the coupling bearing, noting which way round it fits. The spacer could be a tight fit and may have to be driven out from the outside using a suitable socket or piece of tubing **(see illustration)**. Support the coupling on blocks of wood to do this.
27 Support the coupling on blocks of wood and drive the bearing out from the inside using a bearing driver or socket **(see illustration)**.

14.25 Lever out the grease seal

14.26 Remove the spacer from inside the coupling

14.27 A socket can be used to drive the bearing out . . .

6•20 Brakes, wheels and tyres

14.29 ... and to drive the new one in

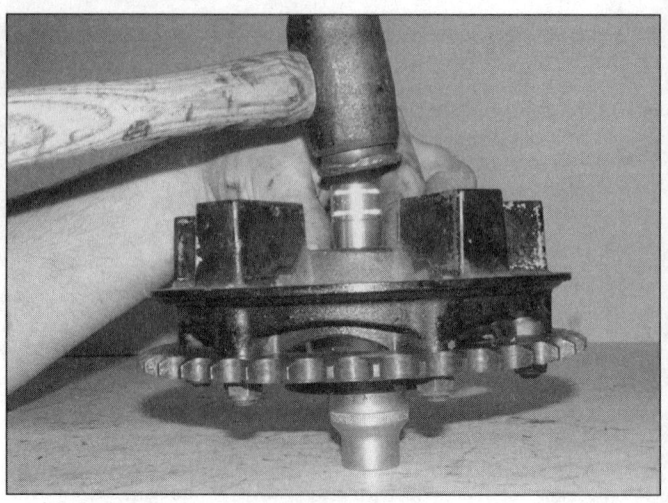

14.30 Support the bearing using a socket when driving the spacer into it

28 Refer to Steps 6 to 8 above and check the bearing.
29 Thoroughly clean the bearing recess then fit the bearing into the coupling, with the marked or sealed side facing out. Using the old bearing (if a new one is being fitted), a bearing driver or a socket large enough to contact only the outer race of the bearing, drive it in until it is completely seated **(see illustration)**.
30 Fit the spacer into the inside of the coupling, making sure it is the correct way round and fits squarely into the bearing. Drive it into place if it is tight, supporting the bearing inner race on a suitable socket as you do to prevent it from being damaged or driven out at the same time **(see illustration)**.
31 Apply a smear of grease to the lips of the new seal, and press it into the coupling, using a seal or bearing driver, a suitable socket or a flat piece of wood to drive it into place if necessary **(see illustration)**. As the seal sits flush with the top surface of their housing, using a piece of wood as shown will automatically set it flush without the risk of setting it too deep and having to lever it out again **(see illustration)**.
32 Check the sprocket coupling/rubber dampers (see Chapter 5).
33 Fit the sprocket coupling into the wheel, then install the wheel (see Section 13).

15 Tyres – general information and fitting new tyres

General information
1 The wheels fitted to all models are designed to take tubeless tyres only. Tyre sizes are given in the Specifications at the beginning of this chapter, in the owners handbook supplied with the machine or on the tyre information label attached to the machine.
2 Refer to the *Daily (pre-ride) checks* listed at the beginning of this manual for tyre maintenance.

Fitting new tyres
3 Ensure that front and rear tyre types are compatible, the correct size and correct speed rating; if necessary seek advice from a Yamaha dealer or tyre fitting specialist **(see illustration)**.
4 It is recommended that tyres are fitted by a motorcycle tyre specialist rather than attempted in the home workshop. This is particularly relevant in the case of tubeless tyres because the force required to break the seal between the wheel rim and tyre bead is substantial, and is usually beyond the capabilities of an individual working with normal tyre levers. Additionally, the specialist will be able to balance the wheels after tyre fitting.
5 Note that punctured tubeless tyres can in some cases be repaired. Yamaha recommend that such repairs are carried out only by an authorised dealer.

14.31a Press or drive the seal into the coupling

14.31b Using a piece of wood as shown automatically sets the seal flush

Brakes, wheels and tyres 6•21

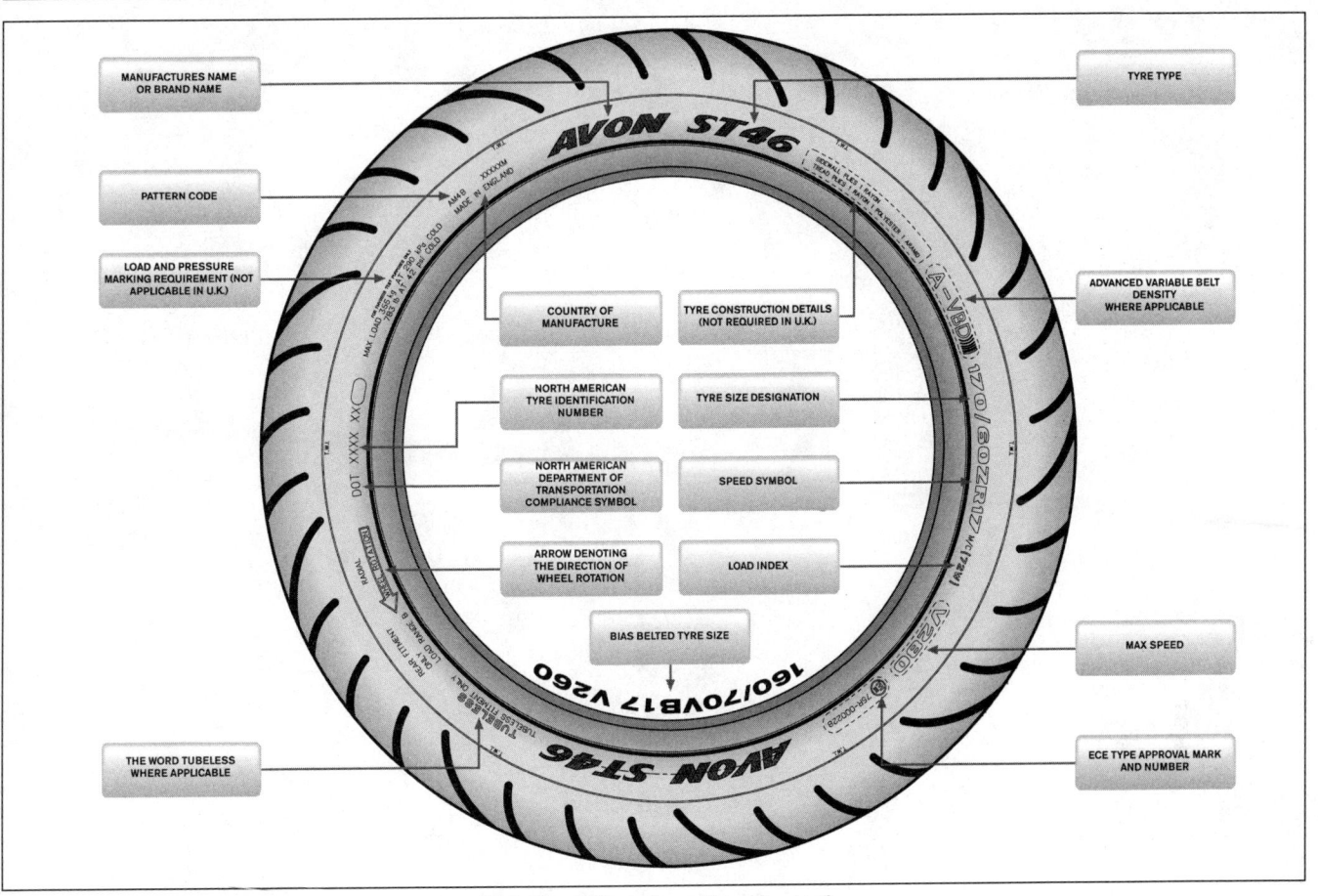

15.3 Tyre sidewall markings (typical)

Notes

Chapter 7
Bodywork

Contents

Front mudguard – removal and installation	5	Seat – removal and installation	2
General information	1	Side panels – removal and installation	3
Rear view mirrors – removal and installation	6	Tail light cover – removal and installation	4

Degrees of difficulty

Easy, suitable for novice with little experience	Fairly easy, suitable for beginner with some experience	Fairly difficult, suitable for competent DIY mechanic	Difficult, suitable for experienced DIY mechanic	Very difficult, suitable for expert DIY or professional

1 General information

This Chapter covers the procedures necessary to remove and install the body parts. Since many service and repair operations on these motorcycles require the removal of body parts, the procedures are grouped here and referred to from other Chapters.

In the case of damage to the body parts, it is usually necessary to remove the broken component and replace it with a new (or used) one. The material that the body panels are composed of doesn't lend itself to conventional repair techniques. There are however some shops that specialise in 'plastic welding', so it may be worthwhile seeking the advice of one of these specialists before consigning an expensive component to the bin.

7•2 Bodywork

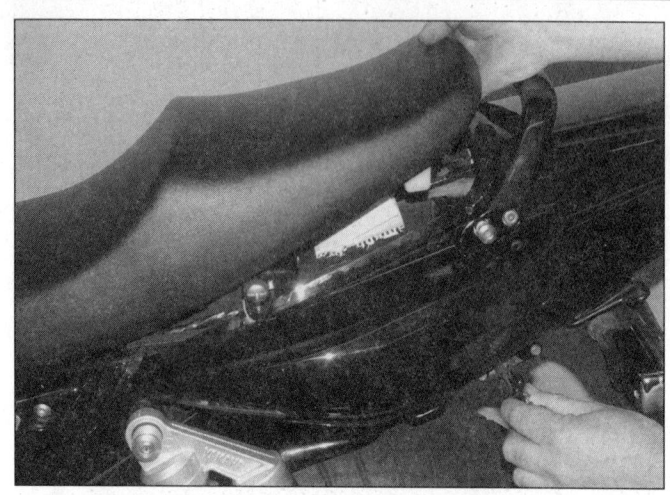

2.1 Turn the key and draw the seat up and back

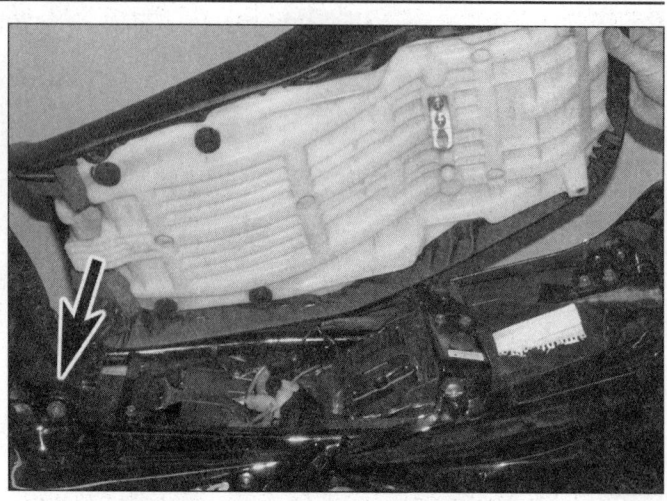

2.2 The tab locates under the tank bracket

2 Seat – removal and installation

Removal

1 Insert the ignition key into the seat lock located on the left-hand side panel and turn it clockwise to unlock the seat **(see illustration)**. Remove the seat by lifting the back and drawing it back, noting how the tab at the front locates under the tank bracket, and how the latch engages in the lock.

Installation

2 Installation is the reverse of removal. Make sure the tab locates correctly **(see illustration)**. Push down on the rear of the seat to engage the latch.

3 Side panels – removal and installation

Removal

1 Remove the seat (see Section 2).
2 On 1995 to 2001 models, undo the screw and the bolt on the top of the panel, noting the washer with the bolt, then carefully pull the bottom of the panel away to free the peg from the grommet **(see illustrations)**.
3 On 2002 models onward, unscrew the bolt on the bottom of the panel, then carefully pull the top of the panel away to free the pegs from the grommets **(see illustrations)**.

Installation

4 Installation is the reverse of removal.

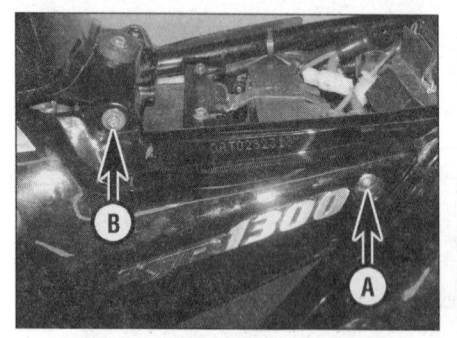

3.2a Undo the screw (A) and the bolt (B) . . .

3.2b . . . then release the peg (C) from the grommet (D)

3.3a Unscrew the bolt (arrowed) . . .

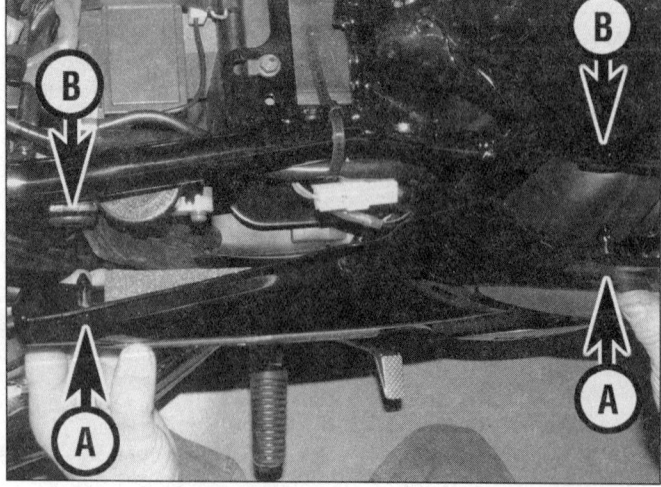

3.3b . . . then release the pegs (A) from the grommets (B)

Bodywork 7•3

4.2a Unscrew the two bolts (arrowed) on each side . . .

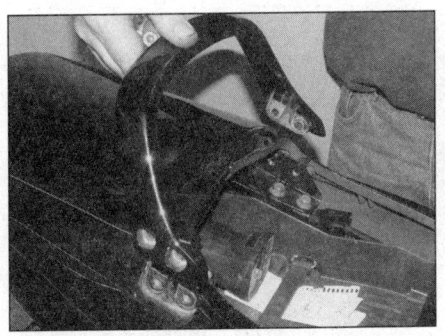

4.2b . . . and remove the grab-rail

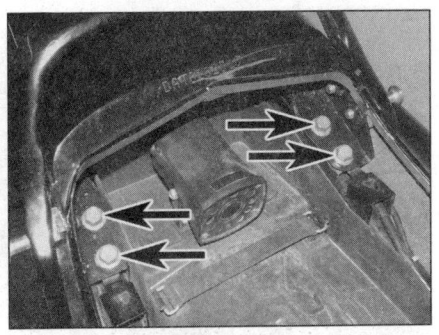

4.2c Slacken the bolts (arrowed) if the grab-rail is tight

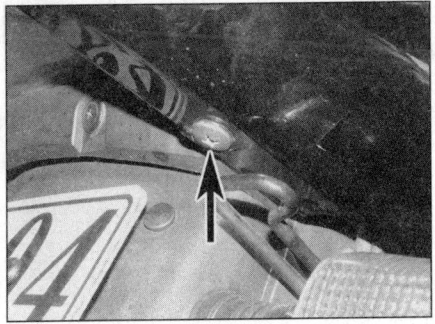

4.3a Undo the screw (arrowed) on each underside . . .

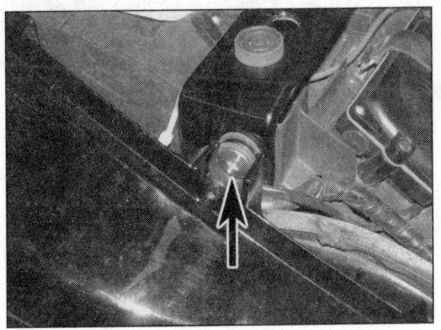

4.3b . . . and the screw (arrowed) on each side . . .

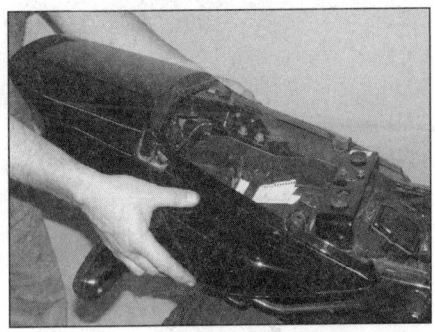

4.4 . . . and carefully draw the cover off

4 Tail light cover – removal and installation

Removal

1 Remove the seat (see Section 2).
2 Unscrew the four pillion grab-rail bolts, noting which fit where, and remove it **(see illustrations)**. If it is tight in its mount, or if it is difficult to install later, slacken the four bolts securing the bracket to the rear sub-frame **(see illustration)**.
3 Undo the two screws on the underside of the cowling and the screw on each side **(see illustrations)**.
4 Carefully draw the cover back off the tail light **(see illustration)**.

Installation

5 Installation is the reverse of removal. If slackened, do not forget to tighten the bolts securing the grab-rail bracket to the sub-frame **(see illustration 4.2c)**.

5 Front mudguard – removal and installation

Removal

1 To improve access, remove the front wheel (see Chapter 6).
2 Unscrew the two bolts on each side and draw the mudguard forwards **(see illustrations)**. Note the brackets on the inside

5.2a Unscrew the bolts (arrowed) . . .

5.2b . . . and remove the mudguard

7

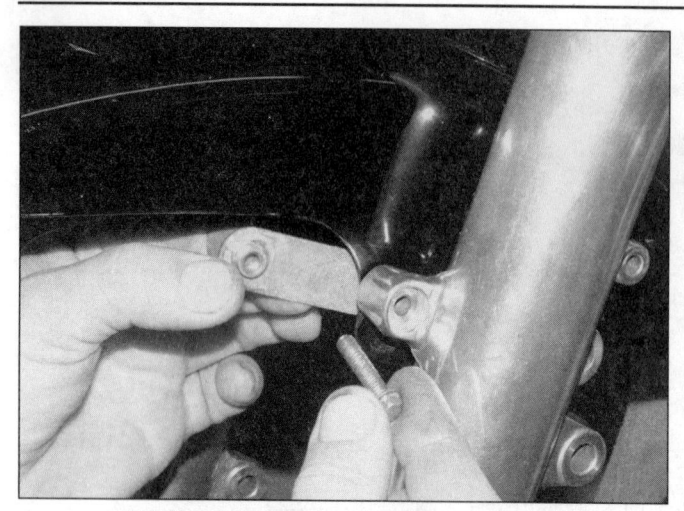

7•4 Bodywork

5.3 Make sure the brackets locate correctly

6.1 Slacken the locknut (arrowed) then unscrew the mirror

of the mudguard and remove them if they are loose.

Installation

3 Installation is the reverse of removal. If removed, fit the brackets to the inside of the mudguard **(see illustration)**.

6 Rear view mirrors – removal and installation

Removal

1 The mirrors simply screw into the handlebar mounting – slacken the locknut on the base of the stem then unscrew the mirror **(see illustration)**.

Installation

2 Installation is the reverse of removal. The position of the mirror can be adjusted by slackening the locknut, moving the mirror as required, then tightening the nut.

Chapter 8
Electrical system

Contents

Alternator/regulator/rectifier – check, removal, inspection and installation 32	Ignition (main) switch – check, removal and installation 18
Battery – charging 4	Ignition system components . . . . see Chapter 4
Battery – removal, installation, inspection and maintenance 3	Instrument and warning light bulbs – renewal 17
Brake light switches – check, removal and installation 14	Instrument cluster – removal and installation 15
Brake/tail light bulb – renewal 9	Instruments – check, removal and installation 16
Charging system testing – general information and precautions . . . 30	Lighting system – check 6
Charging system – leakage and output test 31	Neutral switch – check, removal and installation 21
Clutch switch – check and renewal 23	Oil level sensor and relay – check and renewal 26
Electrical system – fault finding 2	Sidestand switch – check, removal and installation 22
Fuel pump and relay . . . . .see Chapter 3	Speedometer cable – renewal 16
Fuses – check and renewal 5	Starter circuit cut-off relay – check, removal and installation 24
General information 1	Starter motor – disassembly, inspection and reassembly 29
Handlebar switches – check 19	Starter motor – removal and installation 28
Handlebar switches – removal and installation 20	Starter relay – check and renewal 27
Headlight aim – check and adjustment . . . . .see Chapter 1	Tail light assembly – removal and installation 10
Headlight assembly – removal and installation 8	Turn signal assemblies – removal and installation 13
Headlight bulb and sidelight bulb – renewal 7	Turn signal bulbs – renewal 12
Horns – check, removal and installation 25	Turn signal circuit – check 11

Degrees of difficulty

Easy, suitable for novice with little experience	Fairly easy, suitable for beginner with some experience	Fairly difficult, suitable for competent DIY mechanic	Difficult, suitable for experienced DIY mechanic	Very difficult, suitable for expert DIY or professional

Specifications

Battery

Capacity	12V, 12Ah
Type	
XJR1200	YTX14-BS
XJR1300	GT12-B4
Charge condition	
Fully charged	12.8V
Half-charged	12.4V
Discharged	12V or less
Charging time	until fully charged (12.8V) (see Text)
Current leakage	1 mA (max)

Alternator

Nominal output	
XJR1200	12V, 28A @ 3000 rpm
XJR1300	13.5V, 28A @ 3000 rpm
Rotor coil resistance	
XJR1200	2.76 to 3.05 ohms @ 20°C
XJR1300	2.8 to 3.0 ohms @ 20°C
Stator coil resistance	0.19 to 0.21 ohms @ 20°C
Brush length	
Standard	13.7 mm
Service limit (min)	4.7 mm

Regulator/rectifier
Regulated voltage output (no load) .... 14.2 to 14.8 V

Starter circuit cut-off relay
Cut-off relay coil resistance .... 8.2 ohms @ 20°C
Oil level sensor resistor
   XJR1200 .... 202 to 248 ohms @ 20°C
   XJR1300 .... 162 to 198 ohms @ 20°C

Starter relay
Resistance .... 4.2 to 4.6 ohms @ 20°C

Starter motor
XJR1200
   Brush length
      Standard .... 12.5 mm
      Service limit (min) .... 5 mm
   Commutator diameter
      Standard .... 28 mm
      Service limit (min) .... 27 mm
   Mica depth .... 1.6 mm
XJR1300
   Brush length
      Standard .... 10 mm
      Service limit (min) .... 5 mm
   Commutator diameter
      Standard .... 28 mm
      Service limit (min) .... 27 mm
   Mica depth .... 0.7 mm

Fuses
1995 to 2001 models
   Main 30A
   Headlight 15A
   Signal (turn signals, horn, brake light, warning lights etc) 15A
   Ignition 7.5A
   Spares 30A, 15A, 7.5A
2002 models onward
   Main 40A
   Headlight 15A
   Signal (horn, brake light, warning lights etc) 15A
   Turn signals 15A
   Ignition 15A
   Spares 40A, 15A

Bulbs
Headlight .... 60/55W halogen x 1
Sidelight .... 4W x 1
Brake/tail light .... 21/5W x 2
Turn signal lights .... 21W x 4
Instrument illumination .... 1.7W x 4
Warning lights
   Neutral 1.7W
   High beam 1.7W
   Oil level 1.7W
   Turn signal .... 1.7W x 2

Torque wrench settings
Alternator mounting bolts .... 25 Nm
Fork clamp bolts (top yoke) .... 30 Nm
Oil level sensor bolts .... 10 Nm
Starter motor bolts .... 10 Nm
Steering stem nut .... 110 Nm

Electrical system 8•3

1 General information

All models have a 12-volt electrical system charged by a three-phase alternator with an integral regulator/rectifier.

The regulator maintains the charging system output within the specified range to prevent overcharging, and the rectifier converts the ac (alternating current) output of the alternator to dc (direct current) to power the lights and other components and to charge the battery. The alternator rotor is mounted in the top of the crankcase and is driven off the crankshaft by a Hy-Vo chain.

The starter motor is mounted on the top of the crankcase. The starting system includes the motor, the battery, the starter circuit cut-off relay and the various switches and wires. If the engine kill switch in the RUN position and the ignition (main) switch is ON, the starter relay allows the starter motor to operate only if the transmission is in neutral (neutral switch on) or, if the transmission is in gear, if the clutch lever is pulled into the handlebar and the sidestand is up.

Note: *Keep in mind that electrical parts, once purchased, cannot be returned. To avoid unnecessary expense, make very sure the faulty component has been positively identified before buying a new part.*

2 Electrical system – fault finding

Warning: To prevent the risk of short circuits, the ignition (main) switch must always be OFF and the battery negative (–ve) terminal should be disconnected before any of the bike's other electrical components are disturbed. Don't forget to reconnect the terminal securely once work is finished or if battery power is needed for circuit testing.

1 A typical electrical circuit consists of an electrical component, the switches, relays, etc. related to that component and the wiring and connectors that link the component to the battery and the frame. To aid in locating a problem in any electrical circuit, and to guide you with the wiring colour codes and connectors, refer to the *Wiring Diagrams* at the end of this Chapter.

2 Before tackling any troublesome electrical circuit, first study the wiring diagram (see end of Chapter) thoroughly to get a complete picture of what makes up that individual circuit. Trouble spots, for instance, can often be narrowed down by noting if other components related to that circuit are operating properly or not. If several components or circuits fail at one time, chances are the fault lies in the fuse or earth (ground) connection, as several circuits often are routed through the same fuse and earth (ground) connections.

3 Electrical problems often stem from simple causes, such as loose or corroded connections or a blown fuse. Prior to any electrical fault finding, always visually check the condition of the fuse, wires and connections in the problem circuit. Intermittent failures can be especially frustrating, since you can't always duplicate the failure when it's convenient to test. In such situations, a good practice is to clean all connections in the affected circuit, whether or not they appear to be good. All of the connections and wires should also be wiggled to check for looseness which can cause intermittent failure.

4 If testing instruments are going to be utilised, use the wiring diagram to plan where you will make the necessary connections in order to accurately pinpoint the trouble spot.

5 The basic tools needed for electrical fault finding include a battery and bulb test circuit or a continuity tester, a test light, and a jumper wire. A multimeter capable of reading volts, ohms and amps is a very useful alternative and performs the functions of all of the above, and is necessary for performing more extensive tests and checks where specific voltage, current or resistance values are needed.

HAYNES HINT: *Refer to Fault Finding Equipment in the Reference section for details of how to use electrical test equipment.*

3 Battery – removal, installation, inspection and maintenance

Caution: *Be extremely careful when handling or working around the battery. The electrolyte is very caustic and an explosive gas (hydrogen) is given off when the battery is charging.*

Removal and installation

1 Remove the seat (see Chapter 7).
2 Unscrew the negative (–ve) terminal bolt first and disconnect the lead from the battery **(see illustration)**. Lift up the insulating cover to access the positive (+ve) terminal, then unscrew the bolt and disconnect the lead.
3 Release the battery strap and remove the battery from the bike **(see illustrations)**.
4 On installation, clean the battery terminals and lead ends with a wire brush or knife, and emery paper. Reconnect the leads, connecting the positive (+ve) terminal first.

HAYNES HINT: *Battery corrosion can be kept to a minimum by applying a layer of petroleum jelly or dielectric grease to the terminals after the cables have been connected.*

5 Install the seat (see Chapter 7).

Inspection and maintenance

6 The battery fitted on all models is of the maintenance-free (sealed) type, therefore requiring no specific maintenance. However, the following checks should still be regularly performed.

7 Check the battery terminals and leads for tightness and corrosion. If corrosion is evident, unscrew the terminal bolts and disconnect the leads from the battery, disconnecting the negative (–ve) terminal first, and clean the terminals and lead ends with a wire brush or knife, and emery paper. Reconnect the leads, connecting the negative (–ve) terminal last, and apply a thin coat of petroleum jelly or dielectric grease to the connections to slow further corrosion.

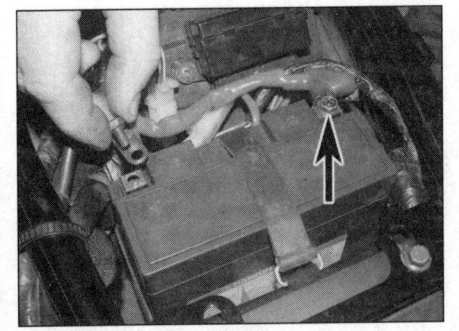

3.2 Disconnect the negative terminal first, then the positive (arrowed)

3.3a Release the strap . . .

3.3b . . . and lift the battery out of its box

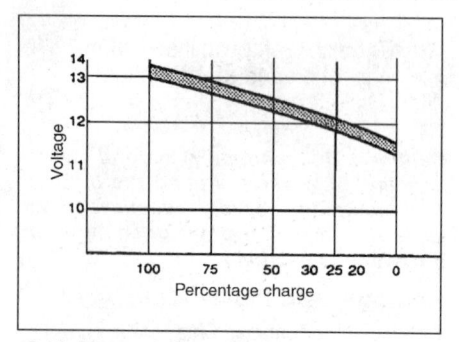

8•4 Electrical system

3.11 Measure the voltage and assess the condition of the battery from the chart

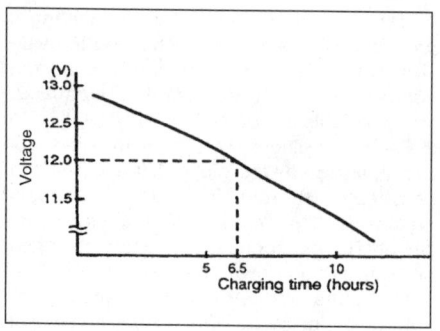

4.1 Measure the voltage to determine the charging time required

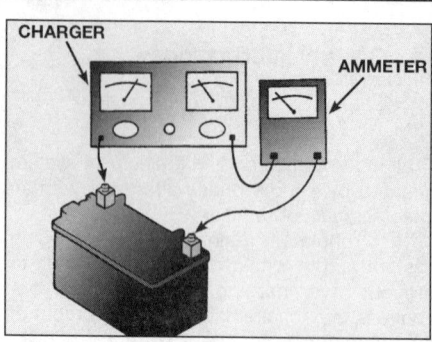

4.2 If the charger doesn't have ammeter built in, connect one in series as shown. DO NOT connect the ammeter between the battery terminals or it will be ruined

8 Keep the battery case clean to prevent current leakage, which can discharge the battery over a period of time (especially when it sits unused). Wash the outside of the case with a solution of baking soda and water. Rinse the battery thoroughly, then dry it.

9 Look for cracks in the case and renew the battery if any are found. If acid has been spilled on the frame or battery box, neutralise it with a baking soda and water solution, dry thoroughly, then touch up any damaged paint.

10 If the motorcycle sits unused for long periods of time, disconnect the leads from the battery terminals, negative (–ve) terminal first. Refer to Section 4 and charge the battery once every month to six weeks.

11 Assess the condition of the battery by measuring the voltage across the battery terminals – connect the voltmeter positive (+ve) probe to the battery positive (+ve) terminal, and the negative (–ve) probe to the battery negative (–ve) terminal and compare the figure obtained against the chart **(see illustration)**. When fully charged there should be 12.8 volts (or more) present. If the voltage falls below 12.3 volts the battery must be removed, disconnecting the negative (–ve) terminal first, and recharged as described in Section 4.

4 Battery – charging

Caution: Be extremely careful when handling or working around the battery.

The electrolyte is very caustic and an explosive gas (hydrogen) is given off when the battery is charging.

1 Remove the battery (see Section 3). If not already done, refer to Section 3, Step 11, and check the open circuit voltage of the battery. Refer to the chart and read off the charging time required according to the voltage reading taken **(see illustration)**.

2 Connect the charger to the battery, making sure that the positive (+ve) lead on the charger is connected to the positive (+ve) terminal on the battery, and the negative (–ve) lead is connected to the negative (–ve) terminal. The battery should be charged for the specified time, or until the voltage across the terminals reaches 12.8V (allow the battery to stabilise for 30 minutes after charging before taking a voltage reading). Exceeding this can cause the battery to overheat, buckling the plates and rendering it useless. Few owners will have access to an expensive current controlled charger, so if a normal domestic charger is used check that after a possible initial peak, the charge rate falls to a safe level consistant with that marked on the battery case **(see illustration)**. If the battery becomes hot during charging **stop**. Further charging will cause damage. **Note:** *In emergencies the battery can be charged at a higher rate of around 3.0 amps for a period of 1 hour. However, this is not recommended and the low amp charge is by far the safer method of charging the battery.*

3 If the recharged battery discharges rapidly when left disconnected it is likely that an internal short caused by physical damage or sulphation has occurred. A new battery will be required. A sound item will tend to lose its charge at about 1% per day.

4 Install the battery (see Section 3).

5 If the motorcycle sits unused for long periods of time, charge the battery once every month to six weeks and leave it disconnected.

5 Fuses – check and renewal

1 The electrical system is protected by fuses of different ratings. All the fuses are housed in the fusebox, which is located under the seat.

2 To access the fuses, remove the seat (see Chapter 7) and unclip the fusebox lid **(see illustration)**.

3 The fuses can be removed and checked visually. If you can't pull the fuse out with your fingertips, use a suitable pair of pliers **(see illustration)**. A blown fuse is easily identified by a break in the element **(see illustration)**, or can be tested for continuity using an ohmmeter or continuity tester – if there is no continuity, it has blown. Each fuse is clearly marked with its rating and must only be replaced by a fuse of the same rating. A spare fuse of each rating is housed in the fusebox. If a spare fuse is used, always obtain another so that a spare is available at all times.

⚠ **Warning: Never put in a fuse of a higher rating or bridge the terminals with any other**

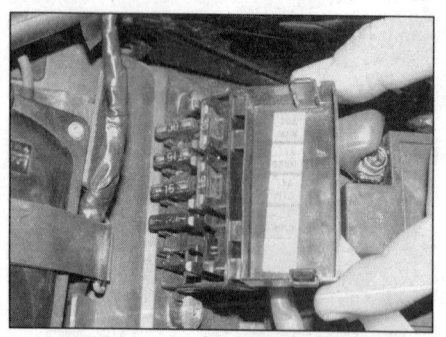

5.2 Unclip the lid to access the fusebox fuses

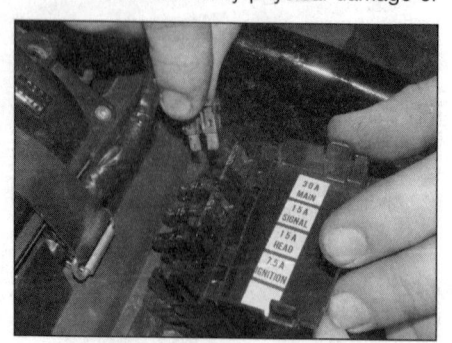

5.3a Remove the fuse and check it

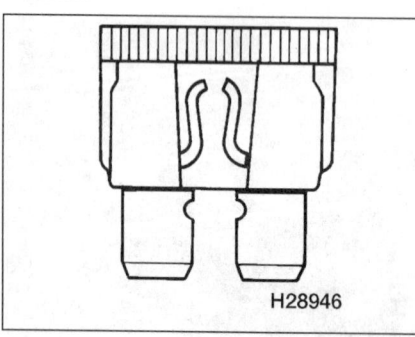

5.3b A blown fuse can be identified by a break in its element

Electrical system 8•5

substitute, however temporary it may be. Serious damage may be done to the circuit, or a fire may start.

4 If a fuse blows, be sure to check the wiring circuit very carefully for evidence of a short-circuit. Look for bare wires and chafed, melted or burned insulation. If the fuse is renewed before the cause is located, the new fuse will blow immediately.

5 Occasionally a fuse will blow or cause an open-circuit for no obvious reason. Corrosion of the fuse ends and fusebox terminals may occur and cause poor fuse contact. If this happens, remove the corrosion with a wire brush or emery paper, then spray the fuse end and terminals with electrical contact cleaner.

6 Lighting system – check

1 The battery provides power for operation of the headlight, tail light, brake light, turn signals and instrument cluster lights. If none of the lights operate, always check battery voltage before proceeding. Low battery voltage indicates either a faulty battery or a defective charging system. Refer to Section 3 for battery checks and Sections 30 and 31 for charging system tests. Also, check the condition of the fuses (see Section 5). When checking for a blown filament in a bulb, it is advisable to back up a visual check with a continuity test of the filament as it is not always apparent that a bulb has blown. When testing for continuity, remember that on tail light and turn signal bulbs it is often the metal body of the bulb which is the ground or earth. Note that if there is more than one problem at the same time, it is likely to be a fault relating to a multi-function component, such as one of the fuses governing more than one circuit, or the ignition switch.

Headlight

2 If the headlight fails to work, check the bulb first (see Section 7), then the headlight fuse (see Section 5), and the wiring connector, then check for battery voltage at the yellow (HI beam) and/or green (LO beam) wire terminal on the supply side of the headlight wiring connector, with the ignition switch and light switch ON. If voltage is present, check for continuity between the black wire terminal and earth (ground). If there is no continuity, check the earth (ground) circuit for an open or poor connection.

3 If no voltage is indicated, check the wiring between the headlight, light switches and the ignition switch, then check the switches themselves.

Tail light

4 If the tail light fails to work, check the bulb and the bulb terminals and wiring connector first (see Section 9), then the headlight fuse, then check for battery voltage at the blue/red wire terminal on the supply side of the tail light wiring connector, with the ignition switch and light switch ON. If voltage is present, check for continuity between the wiring connector terminals on the tail light side of the wiring connector and the corresponding terminals in the bulbholder. If voltage and continuity are present, check for continuity between the black wire terminal on the supply side of the tail light wiring connector and earth (ground). If there is no continuity, check the earth (ground) circuit for an open or poor connection.

5 If no voltage is indicated, check the wiring between the tail light, the light switch and the ignition switch, then check the switches themselves.

Sidelight

6 If the sidelight fails to work, check the bulb and the bulb terminals and wiring connector first (see Section 7), then the headlight fuse, then check for battery voltage at the blue/red wire terminal on the supply side of the sidelight wiring connector, with the ignition switch and light switch ON. If voltage is present, check for continuity between the wiring connector terminals on the sidelight side of the wiring connector and the corresponding terminals in the bulbholder. If voltage and continuity are present, check for continuity between the black wire terminal on the supply side of the sidelight wiring connector and earth (ground). If there is no continuity, check the earth (ground) circuit for an open or poor connection.

7 If no voltage is indicated, check the wiring between the sidelight, the light switch and the ignition switch, then check the switches themselves.

Brake light

8 If the brake light fails to work, check the bulb(s) and the bulb terminals and wiring connector first (see Section 9), then the signal fuse, then check for battery voltage at the yellow wire terminal on the supply side of the tail light wiring connector, with the ignition switch ON and the brake lever or pedal applied. If voltage is present, check for continuity between the wiring connector terminals on the tail light side of the wiring connector and the corresponding terminals in the bulbholder. If voltage and continuity are present, check for continuity between the black wire terminal on the supply side of the tail light wiring connector and earth (ground). If there is no continuity, check the earth (ground) circuit for an open or poor connection.

9 If no voltage is indicated, check the brake light switches (see Section 14), then the wiring between the tail light and the switches.

Instrument and warning lights

10 See Section 17.

Turn signal lights

11 If one light fails to work, check the bulb and the bulb terminals first, then the wiring connectors (see Section 12). If none of the turn signals work, first check the signal fuse (1995 to 2001 models) or turn signal fuse (2002-on models).

12 If the fuse is good, see Section 11 for the turn signal circuit check.

7 Headlight bulb and sidelight bulb – renewal

⚠ *Warning: Allow the bulb time to cool before removing it if the headlight has just been on.*

Headlight

Note: *The headlight bulb is of the quartz-halogen type. Do not touch the bulb glass as skin acids will shorten the bulb's service life. If the bulb is accidentally touched, it should be wiped carefully when cold with a rag soaked in methylated spirit and dried before fitting.*

1 Undo the screw on each side of the headlight rim **(see illustration)**. Pull the bottom of the rim out of the shell then release the tab at the top, noting how it locates **(see illustration)**.

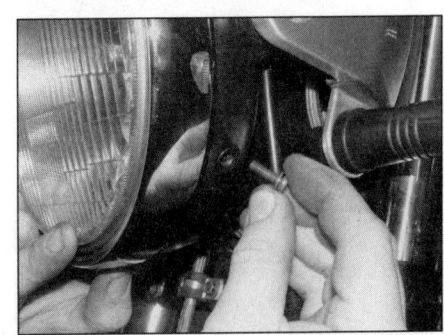

7.1a Undo the screw on each side . . .

7.1b . . . and draw the rim out of the shell as described

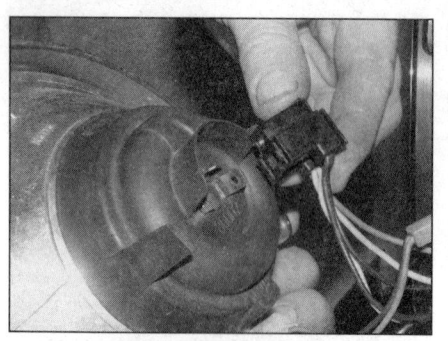

8•6 Electrical system

7.2a Disconnect the headlight wiring connector...

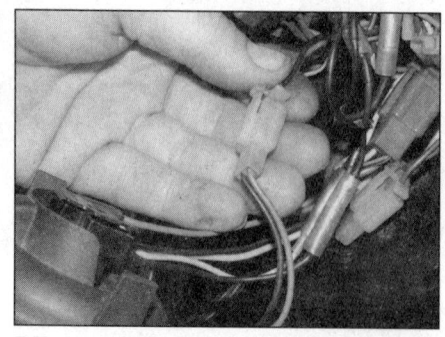

7.2b ...and the sidelight wiring connector

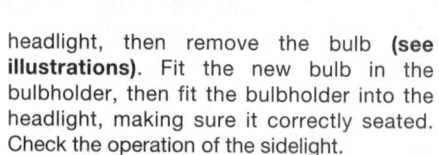

7.3a Remove the dust cover

2 Disconnect the headlight and sidelight wiring connectors **(see illustrations)**.
3 Remove the rubber dust cover, noting how it fits **(see illustration)**. Release the bulb retaining clip, noting how it fits, then remove the bulb **(see illustrations)**.
4 Fit the new bulb, bearing in mind the information in the **Note** above. Make sure the tabs on the bulb fit correctly in the slots in the bulb housing, and secure it in position with the retaining clip.
5 Install the dust cover, making sure it is correctly seated and with the 'TOP' mark at the top **(see illustration 7.3a)**. Connect the headlight and sidelight wiring connectors.
6 Check the operation of the headlight and sidelight.
7 Locate the tab on the top of the headlight rim behind the protrusion on the shell, then push the bottom of the rim in **(see illustration)**. Make sure it is correctly seated all the way round then install the screws.

> **HAYNES HiNT** *Always use a paper towel or dry cloth when handling new bulbs to prevent injury if the bulb should break and to increase bulb life.*

Sidelight

8 Undo the screw on each side of the headlight rim **(see illustration 7.1a)**. Pull the bottom of the rim out of the shell then release the tab at the top, noting how it locates **(see illustration 7.1b)**.
9 Disconnect the headlight and sidelight wiring connectors **(see illustrations 7.2a and b)**.
10 Pull the sidelight bulbholder out of the headlight, then remove the bulb **(see illustrations)**. Fit the new bulb in the bulbholder, then fit the bulbholder into the headlight, making sure it correctly seated. Check the operation of the sidelight.
11 Connect the headlight and sidelight wiring connectors. Check the operation of the headlight and sidelight.
12 Locate the tab on the top of the headlight rim behind the protrusion on the shell, then push the bottom of the rim in **(see illustration 7.7)**. Make sure it is correctly seated all the way round then install the screws.

8 Headlight assembly – removal and installation

Removal

1 Undo the screw on each side of the headlight rim **(see illustration 7.1a)**. Pull the bottom of the rim out of the shell then release the tab at the top, noting how it locates **(see illustration 7.1b)**.
2 Disconnect the headlight and sidelight wiring connectors **(see illustrations 7.2a and b)**.
3 Make a note of the routing of all the wiring into the headlight shell (i.e. which hole it enters via), and the location of the wiring connectors. Release the wiring from the clips and disconnect the connectors.
4 Unscrew the two bolts securing the

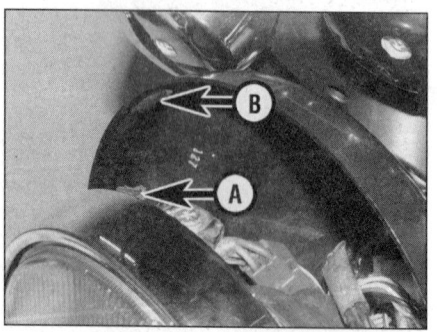

7.3b Release the clip...

7.3c ...and remove the bulb

7.7 Locate the tab (A) behind the protrusion (B)

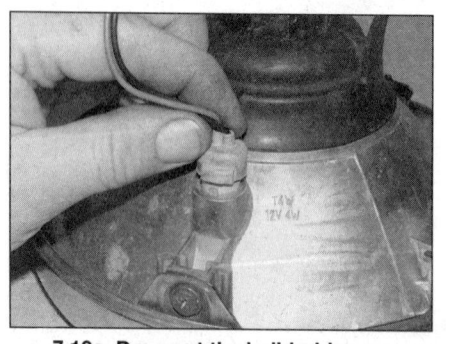

7.10a Draw out the bulbholder...

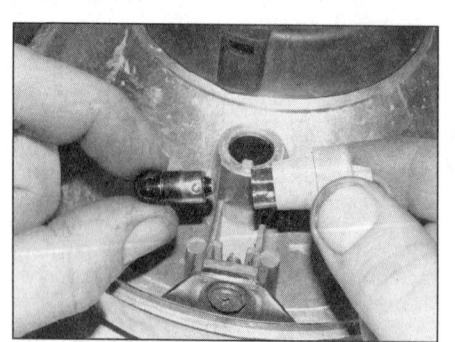

7.10b ...and remove the bulb

Electrical system 8•7

8.4a Unscrew the bracket bolts (arrowed)

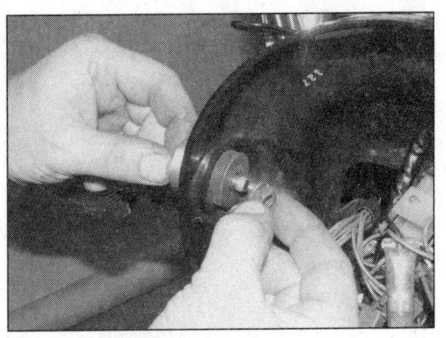

8.4b Unscrew the nut and withdraw the bolt on each side . . .

8.4c . . . then remove the shell and feed the wiring connectors out the back

headlight beam height adjuster bracket to the bottom yoke, noting the brake hose holders or splitter (according to model) **(see illustration)**. Support the shell, then unscrew the two nuts, withdraw the bolts and remove the shell from between the brackets, feeding the wiring out of the back of the shell as you do **(see illustration)**. Note the collars in the rubber mounts. Check the rubber mounts for damage, deformation and deterioration and renew them if necessary.

Installation

5 Installation is the reverse of removal. Make sure all the wiring is correctly routed, connected and secured – feed the ignition switch and instrument cluster wiring through the top hole in the shell; feed the right-hand handlebar switch wiring through the right-hand hole; feed the left-hand handlebar switch and main loom wiring through the left-hand hole. Check the operation of the headlight and sidelight. Check the headlight aim (see Chapter 1).

9 Brake/tail light bulb – renewal

1 Remove the seat (see Chapter 7). For best access also remove the tail light cover (see Chapter 7), though this should not be necessary if you have small hands.
2 Turn the bulbholder anti-clockwise and withdraw it from the tail light **(see illustration)**. Push the bulb into the holder and twist it anti-clockwise to remove it **(see illustration)**.
3 Check the socket terminals for corrosion and clean them if necessary. Line up the pins of the new bulb with the slots in the socket, then push the bulb in and turn it clockwise until it locks into place. **Note:** *The pins on the bulb are offset so it can only be installed one way. It is a good idea to use a paper towel or dry cloth when handling the new bulb to prevent injury if the bulb should break and to increase bulb life.*
4 Fit the bulbholder into the tail light and turn it clockwise to secure it, then install the cover if removed and the seat (see Chapter 7).

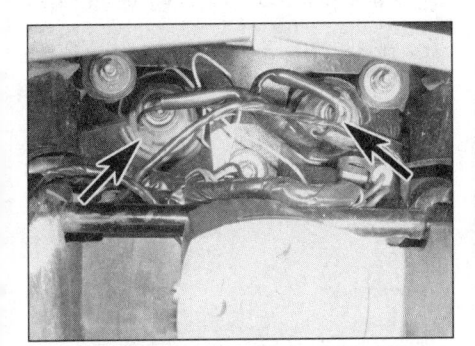

10 Tail light assembly – removal and installation

Removal

1 Remove the seat and the tail light cover (see Chapter 7). Either remove the bulbholders from the tail light by turning them anti-clockwise **(see illustration)** or disconnect the tail light assembly wiring connector **(see illustration)**.
2 Undo the nuts securing the tail light and remove it **(see illustration)**. Note the arrangement of the washers, collars and rubber mounts. Check the rubber mounts for damage, deformation and deterioration and renew them if necessary.

Installation

3 Installation is the reverse of removal. Check the operation of the tail light and the brake light.

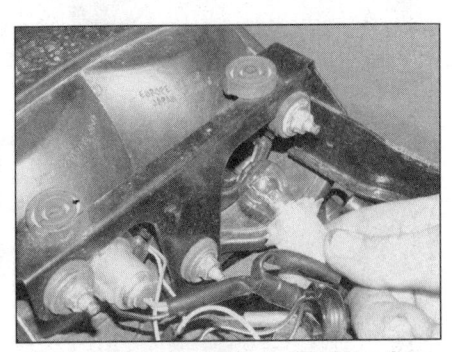

9.2a Release the relevant bulbholder from the tail light (arrows) . . .

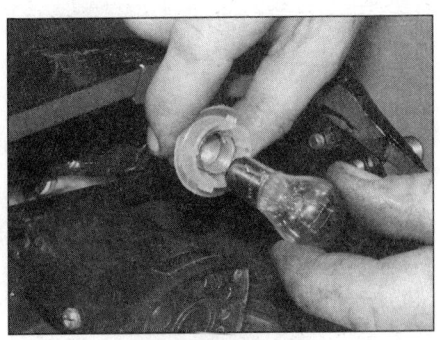

9.2b . . . then release the bulb from the holder

10.1a Either release the bulbholders from the tail light . . .

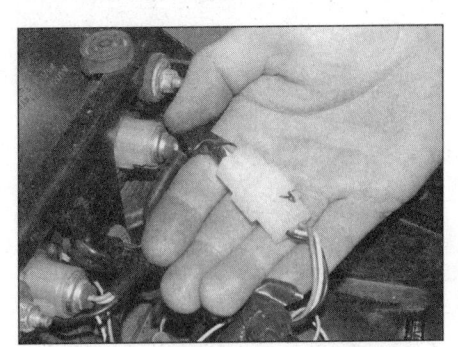

10.1b . . . or disconnect the wiring connector

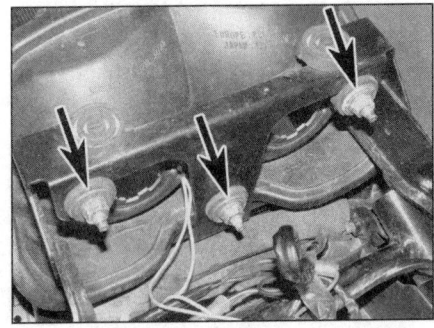

10.2 Tail light mounting nuts (arrowed)

8

8•8 Electrical system

11.3 Turn signal relay (arrowed)

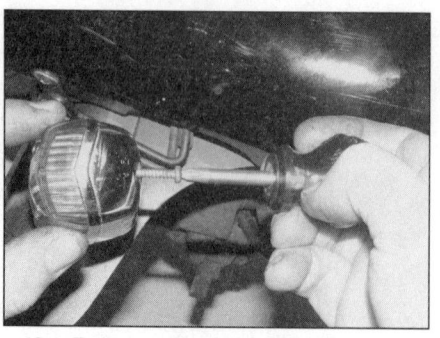

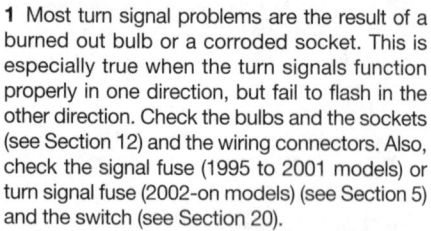

12.1 Remove the screw and detach the lens . . .

12.2 . . . and remove the bulb

11 Turn signal circuit – check

1 Most turn signal problems are the result of a burned out bulb or a corroded socket. This is especially true when the turn signals function properly in one direction, but fail to flash in the other direction. Check the bulbs and the sockets (see Section 12) and the wiring connectors. Also, check the signal fuse (1995 to 2001 models) or turn signal fuse (2002-on models) (see Section 5) and the switch (see Section 20).
2 The battery provides power for operation of the turn signal lights, so if they do not operate, also check the battery voltage. Low battery voltage indicates either a faulty battery or a defective charging system. Refer to Section 3 for battery checks and Sections 30 and 31 for charging system tests.

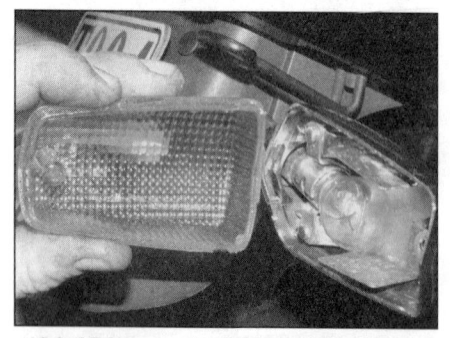

12.3 Make sure the tab locates correctly when fitting the lens

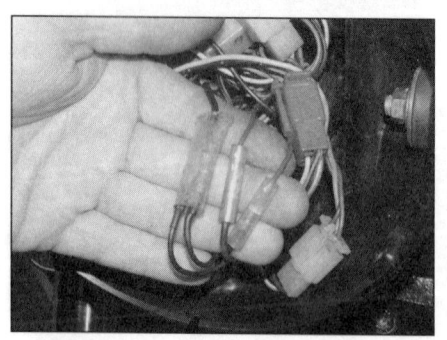

3 If the bulbs, sockets, connectors, fuse, switch and battery are good, check the turn signal relay, which is mounted behind the left-hand side panel **(see illustration)**. Remove the panel for access (see Chapter 7).
4 Check for voltage at the brown wire in the relay wiring connector with the ignition ON. If no voltage is present, using the appropriate wiring diagram at the end of this Chapter check the wiring between the relay and the ignition (main) switch. If voltage was present, check for voltage at the brown/white wire with the ignition ON, and with the switch turned to either LEFT or RIGHT. If no voltage is present, renew the relay. If voltage was present, check the wiring between the relay, turn signal switch and turn signal lights for continuity. Turn the ignition OFF when the check is complete.

12 Turn signal bulbs – renewal

1 Remove the screw securing the turn signal lens and remove the lens, noting how it fits **(see illustration)**.
2 Push the bulb into the holder and twist it anti-clockwise to remove it **(see illustration)**. Check the socket terminals for corrosion and clean them if necessary. Line up the pins of the new bulb with the slots in the socket, then push the bulb in and turn it clockwise until it locks into place.
3 Fit the lens onto the holder, making sure the tab locates correctly **(see illustration)**. Do not

overtighten the screw as the lens or threads could be damaged.

13 Turn signal assemblies – removal and installation

Front
Removal
1 Refer to Section 7, Steps 1 and 2 and remove the headlight from the shell.
2 Trace the wiring from the turn signal and disconnect it at the connectors **(see illustration)**. Feed the wiring out the back of the headlight shell and through to the turn signal, noting its routing.
3 Pull back the rubber boot on the inside of the turn signal bracket. Support the turn signal, then unscrew the nut **(see illustration)**. Draw the nut off the wiring, then remove the turn signal, taking care not to snag the connector as you draw it through the bracket.

Installation
4 Installation is the reverse of removal. Make sure the wiring is correctly routed and securely connected. Check the operation of the turn signals.

Rear
Removal
5 Remove the seat (see Chapter 7).
6 Trace the wiring back from the turn signal and disconnect it at the connectors **(see illustration)**.

13.2 Disconnect the turn signal wiring connectors

13.3 Front turn signal mounting nut (arrowed)

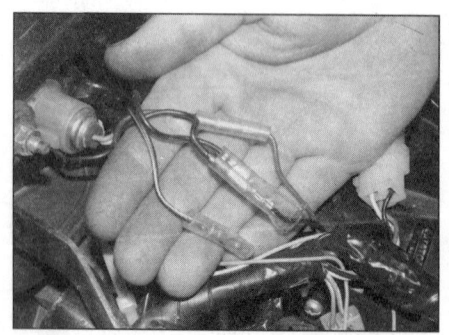

13.6 Disconnect the turn signal wiring connectors

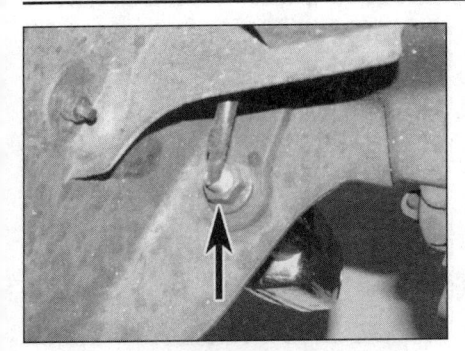

Electrical system 8•9

13.7 Rear turn signal mounting nut (arrowed)

14.2 Front brake switch wiring connectors (arrowed)

14.3 Rear brake switch wiring connector

14.6 Front brake switch mounting screw (arrowed)

14.9a Unhook the spring (arrowed) from the bar on the brake pedal ...

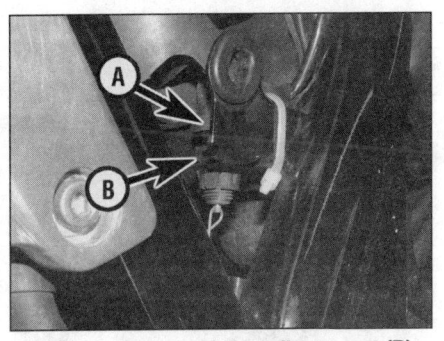

14.9b ... then hold the adjuster nut (B) and unscrew the switch (A)

7 Unscrew the nut securing the turn signal to the inside of the mudguard **(see illustration)**. Remove the turn signal from the mudguard, taking care not to snag the wiring as you pull it through.

Installation

8 Installation is the reverse of removal. Make sure the wiring is correctly routed and securely connected. Check the operation of the turn signals.

14 Brake light switches – check, removal and installation

Check

1 Before checking the switches, check the brake light circuit (see Section 6, Step 8).
2 The front brake light switch is mounted on the underside of the brake master cylinder. Disconnect the wiring connectors from the switch **(see illustration)**. Using a continuity tester, connect the probes to the terminals of the switch. With the brake lever at rest, there should be no continuity. With the brake lever applied, there should be continuity. If the switch does not behave as described, renew it.
3 The rear brake light switch is mounted on the inside of the frame on the right-hand side, above the brake pedal. Remove the right-hand side panel to access the wiring connector (see Chapter 7). Trace the wiring from the switch and disconnect it at the connector **(see illustration)**. Using a continuity tester, connect the probes to the terminals on the switch side of the wiring connector. With the brake pedal at rest, there should be no continuity. With the brake pedal applied, there should be continuity. If the switch does not behave as described, renew it. Check first, however, that the switch is correctly adjusted as described in Step 10.
4 If the switches are good, check for voltage at the brown wire terminal on the connector with the ignition switch ON – there should be battery voltage. If there's no voltage present, check the wiring between the switch and the ignition switch (see the *Wiring Diagrams* at the end of this Chapter).

Removal and installation

Front brake light switch

5 The switch is mounted on the underside of the brake master cylinder. Disconnect the wiring connectors from the switch **(see illustration 14.2)**.
6 Remove the single screw and washers securing the switch to the bottom of the master cylinder and remove the switch **(see illustration)**.
7 Installation is the reverse of removal. The switch isn't adjustable.

Rear brake light switch

8 The switch is mounted on the inside of the frame on the right-hand side, above the brake pedal. Remove the right-hand side panel to access the wiring connector (see Chapter 7). Trace the wiring from the switch and disconnect it at the connector **(see illustration 14.3)**. Free the wiring from any clips or ties and feed it through the switch.

9 Detach the lower end of the switch spring from the brake pedal, then unscrew and remove the switch **(see illustrations)**.
10 Installation is the reverse of removal. Make sure the brake light is activated just before the rear brake pedal takes effect. If adjustment is necessary, hold the switch and turn the adjuster nut on the switch body until the brake light is activated when required.

15 Instrument cluster – removal and installation

Removal

1 Refer to Section 7, Steps 1 and 2 and remove the headlight from the shell.
2 Trace the wiring from the instrument cluster and disconnect it at the connectors **(see illustration)**.

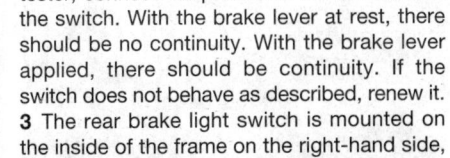

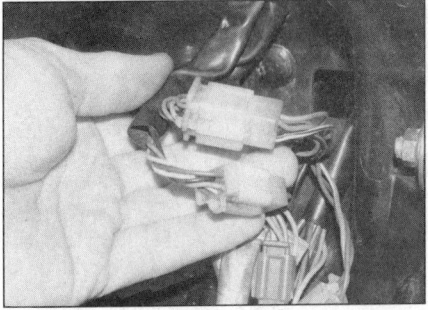

15.2 Disconnect the instrument cluster wiring connectors

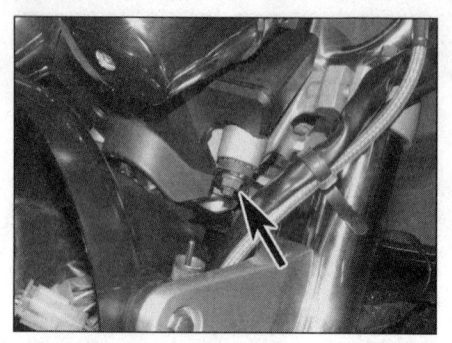

8•10 Electrical system

15.4a Unscrew the nut (arrowed) on each side . . .

3 Unscrew the knurled ring securing the speedometer cable and detach it **(see illustration 16.11)**.
4 Unscrew the nuts securing the cluster and

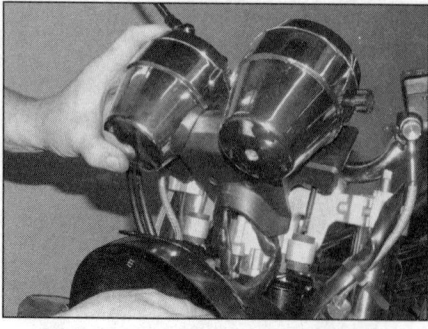

15.4b . . . then lift the cluster away, feeding the wiring out of the headlight as you do

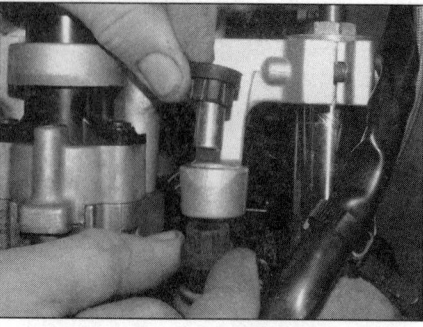

lift it off the stay, feeding the wiring out the back of the shell as you do **(see illustrations)**. Note the collar fitted in the rubber mounts.

15.5a Check the mounting rubbers and make sure the collar is installed

Installation

5 Installation is the reverse of removal. Check the rubber mounting grommets for cracks and deterioration and renew them if necessary **(see illustration)**. Feed the wiring through the top hole in the headlight shell **(see illustration)**.

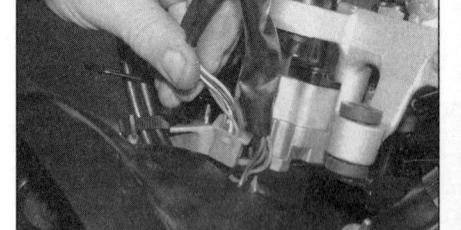

15.5b Feed the wiring through the top hole in the shell

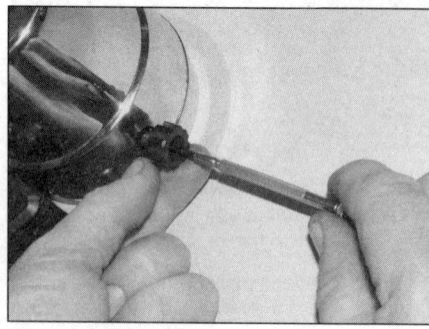

16.3 Undo the screw and remove the knob

16 Instruments and speedometer cable – check, removal and installation

Speedometer

Check

1 Special instruments are required to properly check the operation of this meter. If it is believed to be faulty, take the motorcycle to a Yamaha dealer for assessment. Before doing this, make sure that the fault is not due to a faulty cable or drive gear, either at the front wheel or at the instruments.

Removal and installation

2 Remove the instrument cluster (see Section 15).
3 Undo the screw in the centre of the odometer trip knob and remove the knob **(see illustration)**.
4 Undo each chrome cover screw on the back of the cluster and remove the covers **(see illustrations)**.
5 Undo the two screws securing the rear cover and remove it **(see illustrations)**.
6 Unscrew the nuts securing the mounting bracket and remove it **(see illustrations)**.

16.4a Undo the screws (arrowed) . . .

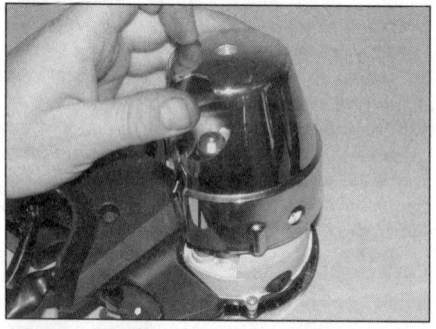

16.4b . . . and remove the chrome covers

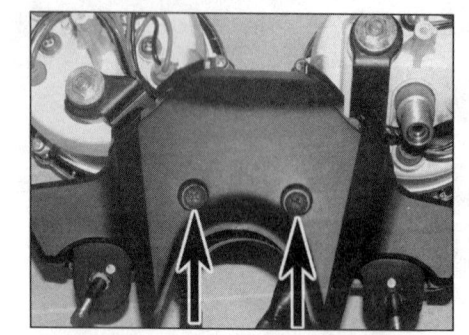

16.5a Undo the screws (arrowed) . . .

16.5b . . . and remove the rear cover

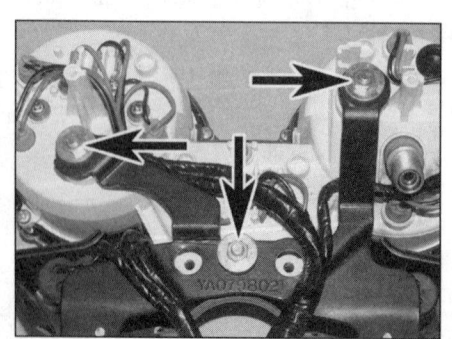

16.6a Unscrew the nuts (arrowed) . . .

Electrical system 8•11

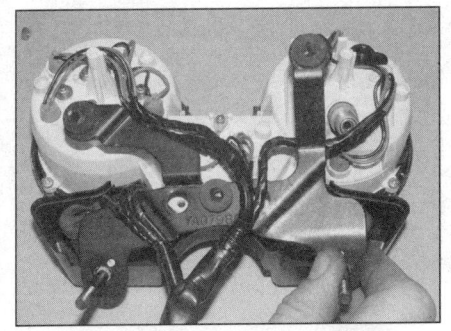

16.6b ... and remove the bracket

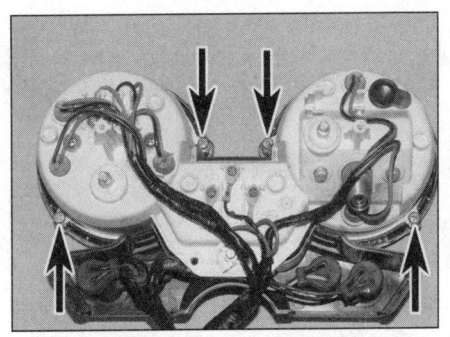

16.7a Undo the screws (arrowed) ...

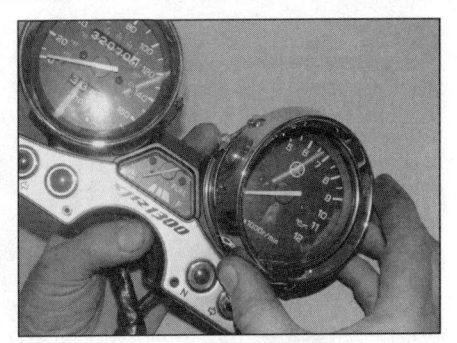

16.7b ... and remove the rims ...

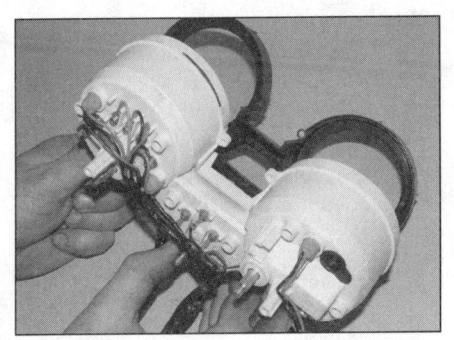

16.7c ... and the front cover ...

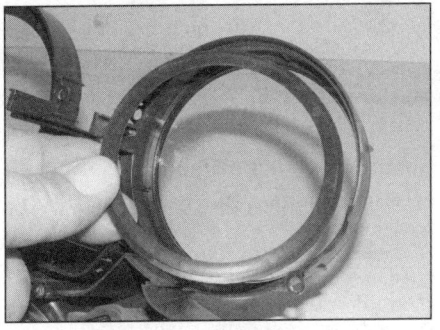

16.7d ... noting the seals

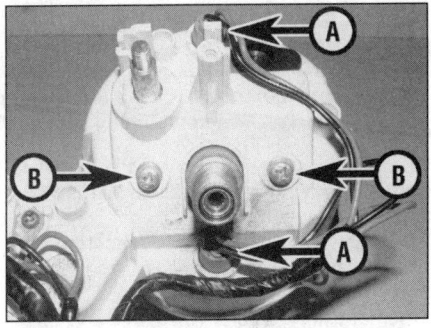

16.8 Withdraw the bulbholders (A), then undo the speedometer screws (B)

7 Undo the four screws securing the chrome rims and the front cover and remove them, noting the rubber seals that fit in the cover **(see illustrations)**.
8 Carefully pull the speedometer bulbholders out of the casing **(see illustration)**. Undo the two screws securing the speedometer to the casing. Carefully withdraw the speedometer from the front.
9 Installation is the reverse of removal. Make sure the front cover seals are in good condition, and that the cover locates correctly **(see illustration)**. Use new seals if necessary.

Speedometer cable

10 Unscrew the knurled ring securing the speedometer cable to the drive housing on the front wheel and detach it, noting how it locates **(see illustration)**.
11 Unscrew the knurled ring securing the speedometer cable to the speedometer and detach it **(see illustration)**. Withdraw the cable, noting its routing.
12 Check that the inner cable rotates freely in the outer cable and that the outer cable is free from bends, kinks and damage.
13 The operation of the speedometer drive can be checked by placing the bike on its centrestand and supporting it so that the front wheel is off the ground. With the cable disconnected from the drive unit housing, spin the front wheel and check that the drive tab inside the housing rotates. If not, remove the front wheel and check the drive unit (see Chapter 6).
14 Installation is the reverse of removal. Unless a new cable is being fitted, lubricate the inner cable, but avoid the top six inches which go into the speedometer head. Make sure the cable is correctly routed.

Tachometer

Check

15 Special instruments are required to properly check the operation of this meter. If it is believed to be faulty, take the motorcycle to a Yamaha dealer for assessment.

Removal and installation

16 Remove the instrument cluster (see Section 15).
17 Undo the screw in the centre of the odometer trip knob and remove the knob **(see illustration 16.3)**.
18 Undo each chrome cover screw on the back of the cluster and remove the covers **(see illustrations 16.4a and b)**.
19 Undo the two screws securing the rear cover and remove it **(see illustrations 16.5a and b)**.

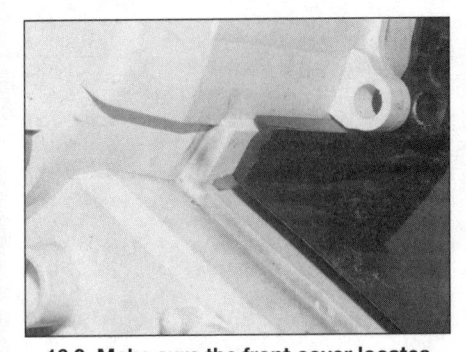

16.9 Make sure the front cover locates correctly

16.10 Detach the cable from the drive housing ...

16.11 ... and from the speedometer, and withdraw it

8

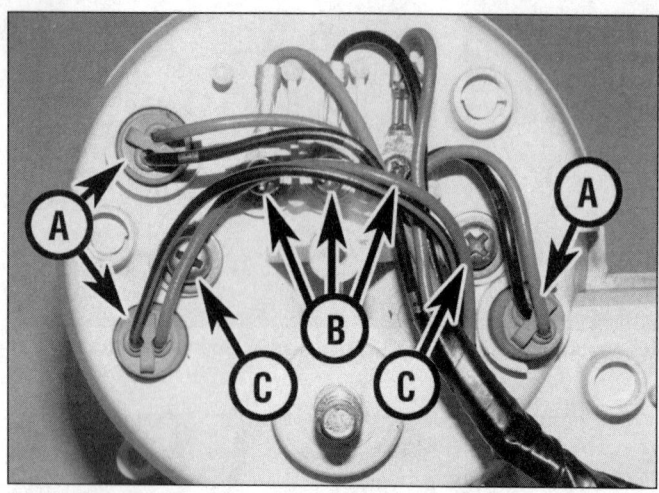

8•12 Electrical system

16.22 Tachometer bulbholders (A), wiring connector screws (B) and mounting screws (C)

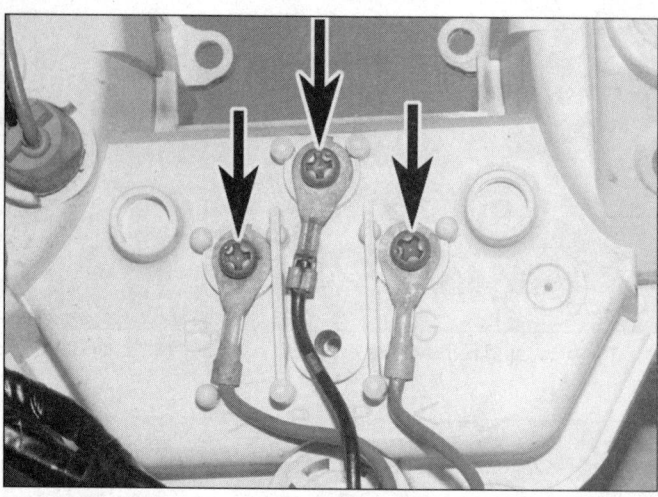

16.33 Fuel gauge wiring and mounting screws (arrowed)

20 Unscrew the nuts securing the mounting bracket and remove it **(see illustrations 16.6a and b)**.
21 Undo the four screws securing the chrome rims and the front cover and remove them, noting the rubber seals that fit in the cover **(see illustrations 16.7a, b, c and d)**.
22 Carefully pull the tachometer bulbholders out of the casing **(see illustration)**.
23 Undo the screws securing the wiring connectors and detach them, noting which fits where **(see illustration 16.22)**. Undo the two screws securing the tachometer to the casing. Carefully withdraw the tachometer from the front.
24 Installation is the reverse of removal. Make sure the wiring is correctly connected. As you look at the back of the casing, the brown wire is for the right-hand terminal, the black for the middle terminal, and the grey for the left-hand terminal – colour code letters are stamped into the casing to remove any doubt **(see illustration 16.22)**.
25 Make sure the front cover seals are in good condition, and that the cover locates correctly **(see illustration 16.9)**. Use new seals if necessary.

Fuel gauge

Check

26 See Chapter 3.

Removal and installation

27 Remove the instrument cluster (see Section 15).
28 Undo the screw in the centre of the odometer trip knob and remove the knob **(see illustration 16.3)**.
29 Undo each chrome cover screw on the back of the cluster and remove the covers **(see illustrations 16.4a and b)**.
30 Undo the two screws securing the rear cover and remove it **(see illustrations 16.5a and b)**.
31 Unscrew the nuts securing the mounting bracket and remove it **(see illustrations 16.6a and b)**.
32 Undo the four screws securing the chrome rims and the front cover and remove them, noting the rubber seals that fit in the cover **(see illustrations 16.7a, b, c and d)**.
33 Undo the screws securing the wiring connectors and detach them, noting which fits where – note that these screws also secure the gauge to the casing, so take care not to let it drop out the front **(see illustration)**. Carefully withdraw the gauge from the front.
34 Installation is the reverse of removal. Make sure the wiring is correctly connected. As you look at the back of the casing, the green wire is for the right-hand terminal, the black for the middle terminal, and the brown for the left-hand terminal – colour code letters are stamped into the casing to remove any doubt.
35 Make sure the front cover seals are in good condition, and that the cover locates correctly **(see illustration 16.9)**. Use new seals if necessary.

17 Instrument and warning light bulbs – renewal

Instrument bulbs

1 If renewing a speedometer bulb, undo the screw in the centre of the odometer trip knob and remove the knob **(see illustration 16.3)**.
2 For either instrument, undo the chrome cover screw on the back of the cluster and remove the cover – you will need an angled screwdriver to do this, otherwise you will have to remove the instrument cluster (see Section 15) **(see illustrations)**.
3 Carefully pull the bulbholder out of the instrument casing, then pull the bulb out of the bulbholder **(see illustrations)**.
4 If the socket contacts are dirty or corroded, scrape them clean and spray with electrical contact cleaner before a new bulb is installed.

17.2a Unscrew the cover screw . . .

17.2b . . . and remove the cover

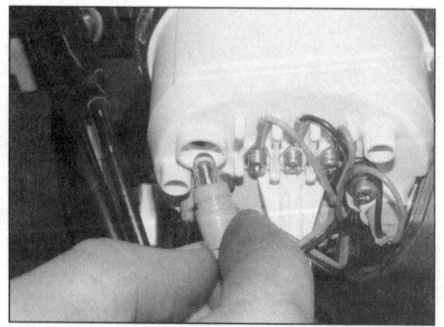

17.3a Pull out the bulbholder . . .

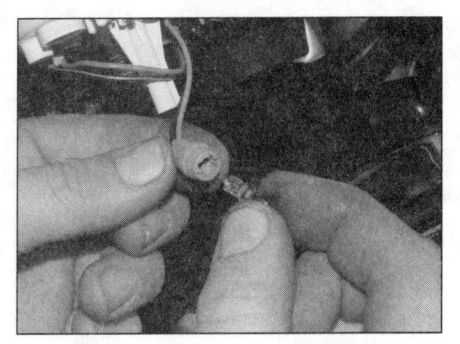

Electrical system 8•13

17.3b . . . and remove the bulb

17.7 Carefully lever out the lens . . .

17.8 . . . and remove the bulb as described

5 Carefully push the new bulb into the holder and push the holder into the casing.
6 Install the cover, trip knob and instrument cluster as required.

Warning light bulbs

7 Carefully prise the relevant lens out of the panel on the front of the instrument cluster **(see illustration)**.
8 Carefully pull the bulb out of the bulbholder – as the bulb is recessed and the holder is small, you will need either a pair of tweezers with small rubber caps fitted to provide some grip, or a suitable size of some wiring shrink-wrap which can be pushed over the bulb **(see illustration)**.
9 If the socket contacts are dirty or corroded, scrape them clean and spray with electrical contact cleaner before a new bulb is installed.
10 Carefully push the new bulb into the holder – if you used shrink-wrap to remove the bulb, use it again to install it, pushing the bulb home using a hex key or small rod inserted into the wrap **(see illustration)**.
11 Fit the lens, making sure its rim locates correctly in the holder – smear some oil onto the rim to ease its entry.

18 Ignition (main) switch – check, removal and installation

⚠️ **Warning:** To prevent the risk of short circuits, remove the seat and disconnect the battery negative (–ve) lead before making any ignition (main) switch checks.

Check

1 Refer to Section 7, Steps 1 and 2 and remove the headlight from the shell.
2 Trace the wiring from the base of the ignition switch and disconnect it at the connectors **(see illustration)**. Make the checks on the switch side of the connectors.
3 Using an ohmmeter or a continuity tester, check the continuity of the connector terminal pairs (see the *Wiring Diagrams* at the end of this Chapter). Continuity should exist between the terminals connected by a solid line on the diagram when the switch key is turned to the indicated position.
4 If the switch fails any of the tests, renew it.

Removal

5 Remove the fuel tank (see Chapter 3) and the instrument cluster (see Section 15). *Note: Although it is not strictly necessary to remove the fuel tank, doing so will prevent the possibility of damage should a tool slip.*
6 Trace the wiring from the base of the ignition switch and disconnect it at the connectors **(see illustration 18.2)**.
7 Displace the handlebars from the top yoke and lay them on some rag across the frame behind the steering head (see Chapter 5).
8 Slacken the fork clamp bolts in the top yoke **(see illustration)**.
9 Unscrew the steering stem nut, and on 1997-on models remove the washer – the washer sits in a recess in the yoke and needs to be helped out with a small screwdriver or a magnet, or alternatively tip it out of the yoke after it has been lifted off.
10 Gently ease the top yoke up and off the steering stem and fork tubes and remove it **(see illustration)**.
11 Two shear-head bolts mount the ignition switch to the underside of the top yoke **(see illustration)**. The heads of the bolts must be

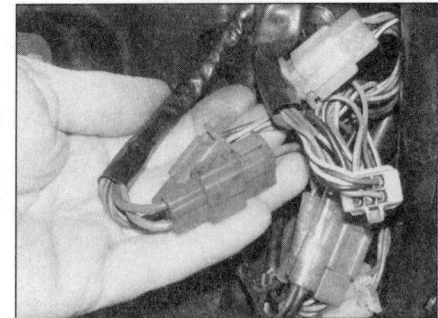

17.10 Carefully push the new bulb into its socket

18.2 Disconnect the ignition switch wiring connectors

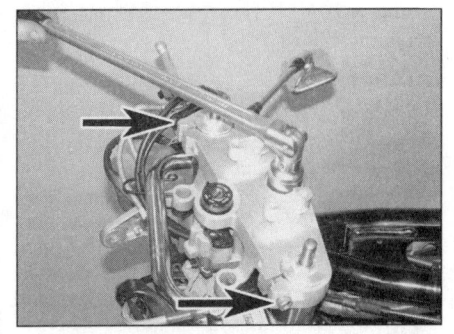

18.8 Slacken the fork clamp bolts (arrowed), then unscrew the steering stem nut

18.10 Ease the yoke up off the steering stem and forks

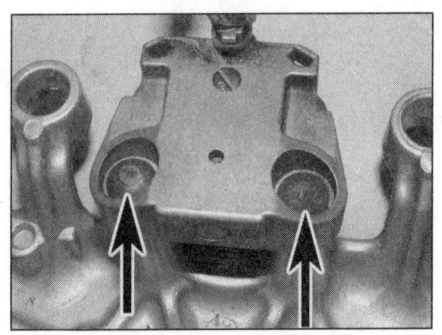

18.11 Ignition switch bolts (arrowed)

8

8•14 Electrical system

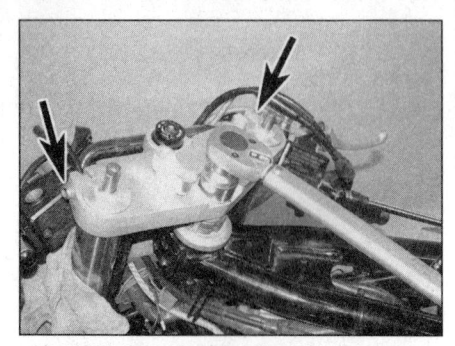

18.12 Tighten the steering stem nut then the fork clamp bolts (arrowed) to the specified torque settings

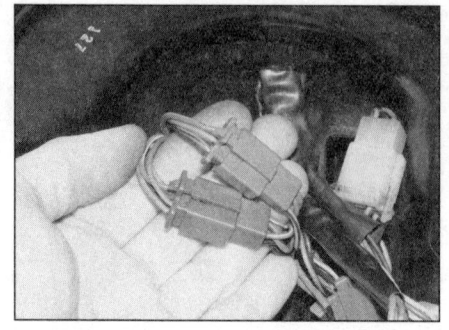

19.4a Right-hand switch connectors

19.4b Left-hand switch connectors

drifted round using a suitable punch or drift, or drilled off, before the switch can be removed. Mount the yoke in a vice equipped with soft jaws and padded out with rags to do this. Remove the bolts and withdraw the switch from the top yoke.

Installation

12 Installation is the reverse of removal. Obtain new shear-head bolts from a Yamaha dealer and tighten them until their heads shear off. Make sure wiring connectors are securely connected and correctly routed. Tighten the steering stem nut to the specified torque setting before tightening the fork clamp bolts, then tighten the clamp bolts to the specified torque setting **(see illustration)**.

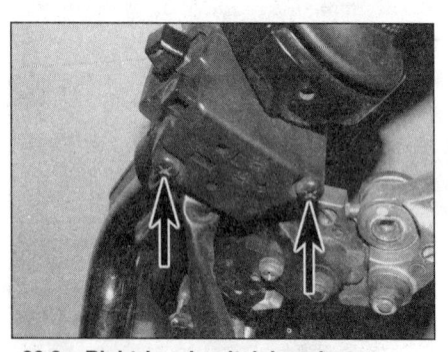

20.3a Right-hand switch housing screws (arrowed) - 1996-on type shown

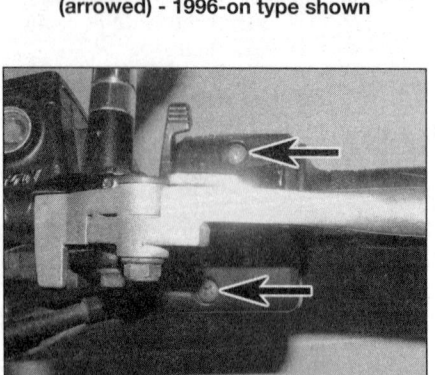

20.3b Left-hand switch housing screws (arrowed) - 1996-on type shown

19 Handlebar switches – check

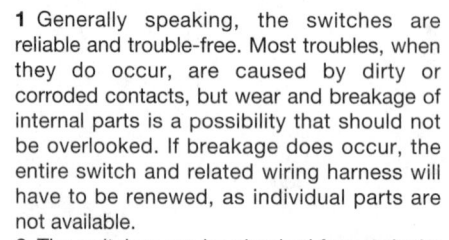

1 Generally speaking, the switches are reliable and trouble-free. Most troubles, when they do occur, are caused by dirty or corroded contacts, but wear and breakage of internal parts is a possibility that should not be overlooked. If breakage does occur, the entire switch and related wiring harness will have to be renewed, as individual parts are not available.

2 The switches can be checked for continuity using an ohmmeter or a continuity test light. Always disconnect the battery negative (–ve) cable, which will prevent the possibility of a short circuit, before making the checks (see Section 3).

3 Refer to Section 7, Steps 1 and 2 and remove the headlight from the shell.

4 Trace the wiring from the switch housing being checked and disconnect it at the connectors **(see illustrations)**. Make the checks on the switch side of the connectors.

5 Check for continuity between the terminals of the switch connector with the switch in the various positions (i.e. switch off – no continuity, switch on – continuity) – see the *wiring diagrams* at the end of this Chapter. Continuity should exist between the terminals connected by a solid line on the diagram when the switch is in the indicated position.

6 If the continuity check indicates a problem

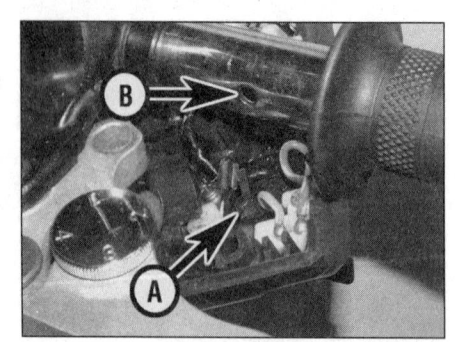

20.4 Locate the pin (A) the hole (B)

exists, refer to Section 20, displace the switch housing and spray the switch contacts with electrical contact cleaner (there is no need to remove the switch completely). If they are accessible, the contacts can be scraped clean with a knife or polished with crocus cloth. If switch components are damaged or broken, it will be obvious when the switch is disassembled.

20 Handlebar switches – removal and installation

Removal

1 If the switch is to be removed from the bike, rather than just displaced from the handlebar, refer to Section 7, Steps 1 and 2 and remove the headlight from the shell. Trace the wiring from the switch housing and disconnect it at the connectors **(see illustration 19.4a or b)**. Work back along the harness, freeing it from all clips and ties, and feed it out of the shell, noting its routing.

2 Disconnect the wiring connectors from the brake light switch (if removing the right-hand switch) or the clutch switch (if removing the left-hand switch) **(see illustration 14.2 or 23.2)**.

3 Unscrew the handlebar switch screws and free the switch from the handlebar by separating the halves **(see illustrations)**. On all except 1995 models, when removing the left-hand switch, remove the choke cable lever, noting how it fits.

Installation

4 Installation is the reverse of removal. On all except 1995 models, refer to Chapter 3 for installation of the choke cable if required. Make sure the locating pin in the switch housing locates in the hole in the handlebar **(see illustration)**. Make sure the wiring connectors are correctly routed and securely connected – the wiring from the right-hand switch routes through the right-hand hole in the headlight shell, and the left-hand switch wiring routes through the left-hand hole.

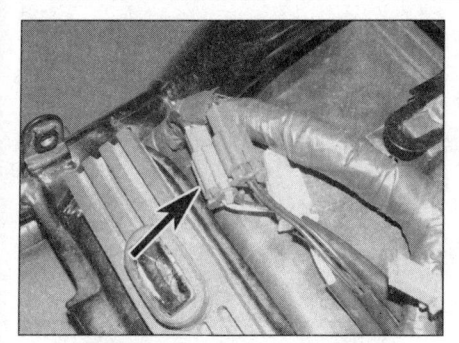

Electrical system 8•15

21.2 Disconnect the neutral switch/oil level sensor wiring connector

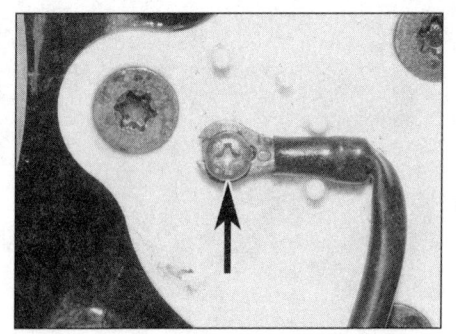

21.4 Slacken the screw (arrowed) and detach the connector

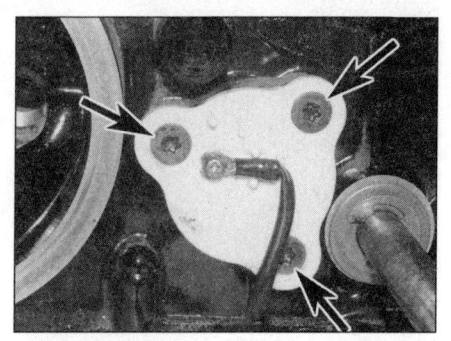

21.9 Neutral switch screws (arrowed)

21 Neutral switch – check, removal and installation

Check

1 Before checking the electrical circuit, check the bulb (see Section 17) and signal fuse (see Section 5).
2 The switch is located on the left-hand side of the engine below the front sprocket. Make sure the transmission is in neutral. To access the neutral switch/oil level sensor wiring connector, remove the fuel tank (see Chapter 3). Trace the wiring from the switch and disconnect it at the brown connector **(see illustration)**.
3 With the connector disconnected and the ignition switched ON, the neutral light should be out. If not, the wire between the instrument cluster and connector must be earthed (grounded) at some point.
4 Check for continuity between the light blue wire terminal on the switch side of the wiring connector and the crankcase. With the transmission in neutral, there should be continuity. With the transmission in gear, there should be no continuity. If the tests prove otherwise, remove the front sprocket cover (see Chapter 5, Section 16), then slacken the screw securing the wiring terminal to the switch and detach it **(see illustration)**. Check for continuity in the wiring between the connector and the terminal. If the wiring is good, check for continuity between the terminal screw on the switch side and the crankcase. With the transmission in neutral, there should be continuity. With the transmission in gear, there should be no continuity. If the tests prove otherwise, remove the switch and check its contact on the inner face, and also check the contact plunger and spring in the end of the selector drum, and renew whichever is faulty.
5 If the continuity tests prove the switch is good, refer to Section 7, Steps 1 and 2 and remove the headlight from the shell. Trace the wiring from the instrument cluster and disconnect it at the 6-pin connector **(see illustration 15.2)**. Check for voltage (with the ignition ON) at the brown wire terminal on the wiring loom side of the connector. If there's no voltage present, check the wire between the connector and signal fuse (see the *Wiring Diagrams* at the end of this Chapter). If the voltage is good, check the wiring between the connector and the bulbholder, then check the starter circuit cut-off relay and other components in the starter circuit as described in the relevant sections of this Chapter. If all components are good, check the wiring between the various components (see the *Wiring Diagrams* at the end of this Chapter).

Removal

6 The switch is located in the left-hand side of the transmission casing below the front sprocket. Make sure the transmission is in neutral.
7 Remove the front sprocket cover (see Chapter 5, Section 16, following the relevant Steps).
8 Undo the single screw securing the wiring connector to the switch **(see illustration 21.4)**.
9 Undo the Torx screws securing the switch and detach it from the casing **(see illustration)**. Discard the O-ring, as a new one must be used.

Installation

10 Fit a new O-ring onto the switch, then install the switch and tighten its screws securely **(see illustrations)**.
11 Attach the wiring connector and secure it with the screw. Check the operation of the neutral light.
12 Install the front sprocket cover (see Chapter 5, Section 16, following the relevant Steps).

22 Sidestand switch – check, removal and installation

Check

1 The sidestand switch is mounted on the frame just ahead of the sidestand. The switch is part of the safety circuit which prevents or stops the engine running if the transmission is in gear whilst the sidestand is down, and prevents the engine from starting if the transmission is in gear unless the sidestand is up, and unless the clutch is pulled in.
2 To access the wiring connector, remove the fuel tank (see Chapter 3). Trace the wiring from the switch and disconnect it at the blue connector **(see illustration)**.

21.10a Fit a new O-ring ...

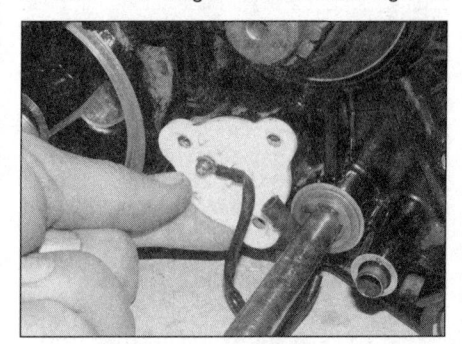

21.10b ... then install the switch

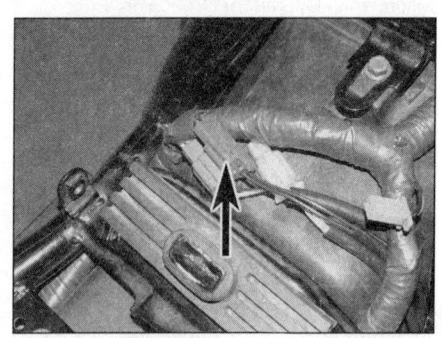

22.2 Sidestand switch wiring connector

8

8•16 Electrical system

22.7 The sidestand switch is secured by two screws (arrowed)

23.2 Clutch switch wiring connector (A) and mounting screw (B)

24.2 Starter circuit cut-off relay (arrowed) – 2002-on models

3 Check the operation of the switch using an ohmmeter or continuity test light. Connect the meter probes to the terminals on the switch side of the connector. With the sidestand up there should be continuity (zero resistance) between the terminals, and with the stand down there should be no continuity (infinite resistance).
4 If the switch does not perform as expected, it is defective and must be renewed.
5 If the switch is good, check the starter circuit cut-off relay and other components in the starter circuit as described in the relevant sections of this Chapter. If all components are good, check the wiring between the various components (see the *Wiring Diagrams* at the end of this Chapter).

Removal and installation

6 The sidestand switch is mounted on the frame just ahead of the sidestand. Remove the fuel tank (see Chapter 3). Trace the wiring from the switch and disconnect it at the connector **(see illustration 22.2)**. Feed the wiring down to the switch, freeing it from any clips and ties, noting its correct routing.
7 Undo the screws securing the switch and remove it, noting how it fits **(see illustration)**.
8 Fit the new switch, making sure the plunger locates correctly, and tighten the screws securely.
9 Make sure the wiring is correctly routed up to the connector and retained by the clips and ties.
10 Reconnect the wiring connector and check the operation of the switch as described in Chapter 1, Section 14.
11 Install the fuel tank (see Chapter 3).

23 Clutch switch – check, removal and installation

Check

1 The clutch switch is mounted on the underside of the clutch lever bracket. The switch is part of the safety circuit which prevents or stops the engine running if the transmission is in gear whilst the sidestand is down, and prevents the engine from starting if the transmission is in gear unless the sidestand is up and the clutch lever is pulled in. The switch isn't adjustable.
2 To check the switch, disconnect the wiring connector **(see illustration)**. Connect the probes of an ohmmeter or a continuity test light to the two switch terminals. With the clutch lever pulled in, continuity should be indicated. With the clutch lever out, no continuity (infinite resistance) should be indicated.
3 If the switch is good, check the starter circuit cut-off relay and other components in the starter circuit as described in the relevant sections of this Chapter. If all components are good, check the wiring between the various components (see the *Wiring Diagrams* at the end of this Chapter).

Removal and installation

4 The clutch switch is mounted on the underside of the clutch lever bracket.
5 Disconnect the wiring connector **(see illustration 23.2)**, then remove the screw and detach the switch.
6 Installation is the reverse of removal.

24 Starter circuit cut-off relay – check, removal and installation

Check

1 The starter circuit cut-off relay is part of the safety circuit which prevents or stops the engine running if the transmission is in gear whilst the sidestand is down, and prevents the engine from starting if the transmission is in gear unless the sidestand is up and the clutch lever is pulled in.
2 The starter circuit cut-off relay and its diodes are contained within the relay assembly, on 1995 to 2001 models mounted under the frame rail behind the rear brake master cylinder reservoir – remove the seat and right-hand side panel for access (see Chapter 7), then displace the starter relay (see Section 27) **(see illustration 27.2a)**. On 2002 models onward the relay is easier to get at – just remove the seat and it is accessible **(see illustration)**.
3 Remove the relay (see below). Refer to the wiring diagram for your model (see end of chapter) and the following procedures:
4 To check the operation of the relay, connect a meter set to the ohms x 100 range, or a continuity tester, between the blue and blue/white wire terminals of the relay on XJR1200 models, and between the blue/white and black wire terminals on XJR1300 models. No continuity should be shown. Using jumper wires now connect a fully charged 12V battery to the relay's red/black and black/yellow wire terminals (positive (+ve) lead to red/black and negative (–ve) lead to black/yellow). The meter should show continuity with battery voltage applied.
5 To check the cut-off relay coil resistance, connect a meter set to the ohms x 100 range between the black/yellow and red/black wire terminals of the relay. The figure given in the Specifications at the beginning of this chapter should be obtained.
6 The diodes contained within the relay assembly can be checked by performing a continuity test. Refer to the appropriate wiring diagram at the end of this chapter and connect the meter (set to the ohms function) or continuity tester across the wire terminals for the diode being tested. The diode should show continuity in one direction and no continuity when the meter or tester probes are reversed. If the diode shows the same condition in both directions it should be considered faulty.
7 If the cut-off relay and diodes are proved good, yet the starting system fault still exists check all other components in the starting circuit (i.e. the neutral switch, side stand switch, clutch switch, starter switch and starter relay) as described in the relevant sections of this Chapter. If all components are good, check the wiring between the various components (see *Wiring Diagrams* at the end of this Chapter).

Removal and installation

8 The starter circuit cut-off relay and its diodes are contained within the relay assembly, on 1995 to 2001 models mounted under the frame rail behind the rear brake master cylinder reservoir – remove the seat and right-hand side panel for access (see

Chapter 7), then displace the starter relay (see Section 27) **(see illustration 27.2a)**. On 2002 models onward the relay is easier to get at – just remove the seat and it is accessible **(see illustration 24.2)**.
9 Displace the relay from its mount and disconnect the wiring connector.
10 Installation is the reverse of removal.

25 Horns – check, removal and installation

Check

1 If a horn doesn't work, first check the signal fuse (see Section 5) and the battery (see Section 3).
2 A horn is mounted on each frame downtube above each end of the oil cooler.
3 Unplug the wiring connectors from the horn **(see illustration)**. Using two jumper wires, apply battery voltage directly to the terminals on the horn. If the horn sounds, check the switch (see Section 19) and the wiring between the horns and the switch, and between the switch and earth (see *Wiring Diagrams* at the end of this Chapter). Also check for battery voltage at each brown wire terminal with the ignition ON.
4 If a horn doesn't sound, renew it.

Removal and installation

5 A horn is mounted on each frame downtube above each end of the oil cooler.
6 Unplug the wiring connectors from the horn **(see illustration 25.3)**. Unscrew the bolt securing the horn and remove it from the bike.
7 Install the horn and securely tighten the bolt. Connect the wiring connectors.

26 Oil level sensor and relay – check, removal and installation

Check

1 With the ignition switch ON and the kill switch in the 'RUN' position, the oil level warning light should come on for a few seconds, then go out, indicating that the oil level is good. If the light does not come on, check the bulb (see Section 17) and the signal fuse (see Section 5). If the light stays on, check the oil level (see *Daily (pre-ride) checks*). If the oil level is good, check the sensor and relay (see Steps 3 and 4).
2 Start the engine. The oil level warning light should come on briefly, and then go out. If the light stays on, stop the engine immediately and check the oil level. If the light does not come on, check the bulb (see Section 17).
3 To check the sensor, remove it from the

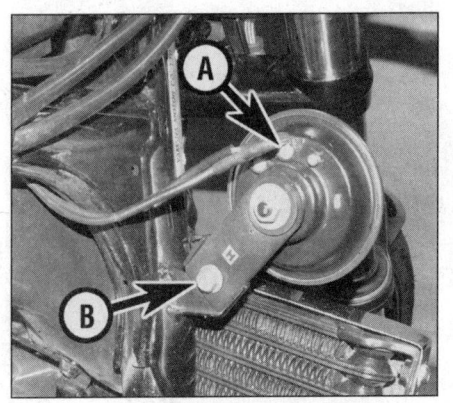

25.3 Horn wiring connectors (A) and mounting bolt (B)

sump (see below). Connect one probe of an ohmmeter or continuity tester to the sensor wire and the other probe to its base. With the sensor in its normal installed position (wiring at the bottom), there should be continuity. Turn the sensor upside down. There should be no continuity. If either condition does not occur, renew the sensor.
4 To check the relay, remove the left-hand side panel (see Chapter 7), then release the relay from its holder and disconnect the wiring connector **(see illustration)**. Set a multimeter to the ohms x 1 scale and connect the positive (+ve) probe to the red/blue wire terminal, and the negative (–ve) probe to the black terminal. There should be no continuity. Leaving the meter connected, and using a fully-charged 12 volt battery and two insulated jumper wires, connect the battery positive (+ve) lead to the brown wire terminal, and the negative (–ve) lead to the black/red wire terminal. There should now be continuity shown on the meter. If the relay doesn't behave as stated, renew it.
5 If the sensor and relay are good, check all the wiring between the sensor, the relay and the warning light, referring to the wiring diagram at the end of this Chapter for your model.
6 A resistor is fitted inside the starter circuit cut-off relay assembly to stabilise the signals

26.4 Oil level sensor relay (arrowed)

to the oil level warning light, thus preventing it flickering when cornering or braking hard. If there is a fault in the warning light operation which is not due to a faulty bulb or relay, the resistor value can be checked as follows.
7 Refer to Section 24 and remove the relay. Using a multimeter set to the ohms x 100 range, connect its positive probe (+ve) to the black/red wire terminal and the negative (–ve) probe to the red/blue wire terminal on the relay. The value obtained should be similar to that given in the Specifications at the beginning of this chapter. If no continuity (infinite resistance) is indicated the resistor is open-circuit and the relay assembly should be renewed.

Removal

8 Drain the engine oil (see Chapter 1).
9 Trace the wiring back from the sensor and disconnect it at the single bullet connector **(see illustration)**. Free it from its clamp. Unscrew the two bolts securing the sensor to the bottom of the sump and withdraw it, being prepared to catch any residual oil **(see illustration)**. Discard the O-ring as a new one must be used.
10 To remove the relay, remove the left-hand side panel (see Chapter 7), then release the relay from its holder and disconnect the wiring connector **(see illustration 26.4)**.

26.9a Disconnect the bullet connector (arrowed) ...

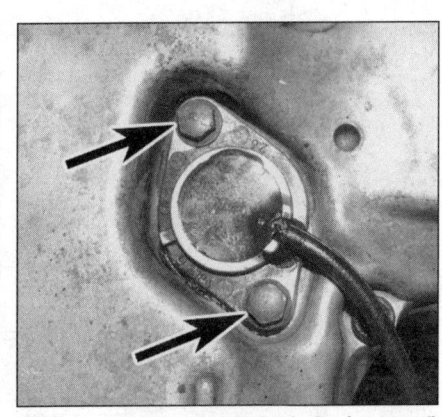

26.9b ... then unscrew the bolts (arrowed) and remove the sensor

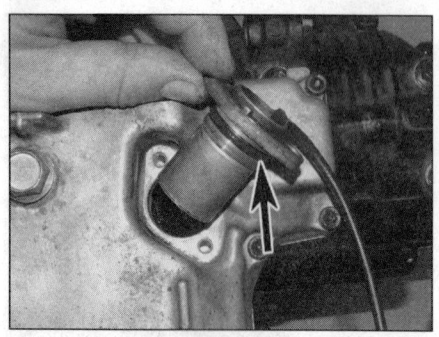

8•18 Electrical system

26.11 Fit a new O-ring (arrowed) before installing the sensor

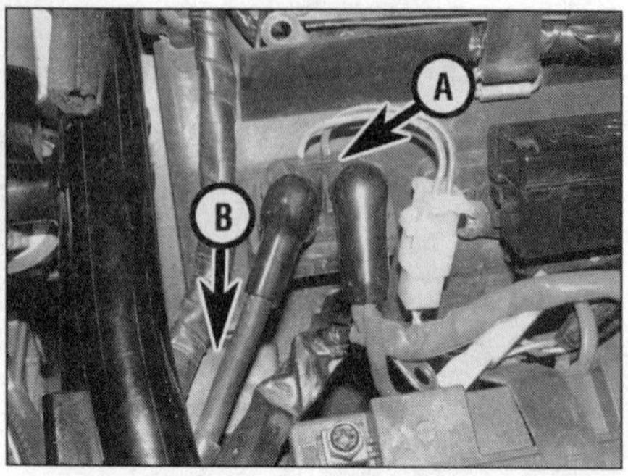

27.2 Starter relay (A). Starter circuit cut-off relay (B) - 1995 to 2001 models

Installation

11 Fit a new O-ring onto the sensor, then fit the sensor into the sump **(see illustration)**. Tighten its bolts to the torque setting specified at the beginning of the Chapter.
12 Connect the wiring at the connector and check the operation of the sensor (see Steps above). Secure the wiring in its clamp.
13 Fill the engine with the specified type and quantity of oil (see Chapter 1).
14 Fit the relay into its holder and connect the wiring connector.

27 Starter relay – check and renewal

Check

1 If the starter circuit is faulty, first check the main fuse and ignition fuse (see Section 5).
2 Remove the seat (see Chapter 7). The starter relay is located behind the battery **(see illustration)**. With the ignition switch ON, the engine kill switch in the 'RUN' position, and the transmission in neutral, press the starter switch. The relay should be heard to click. If the relay doesn't click, switch off the ignition and remove the relay as described below; test it as follows.
3 Set a multimeter to the ohms x 1 scale and connect it across the relay's starter motor and battery lead terminals. Using a fully-charged 12 volt battery and two insulated jumper wires, connect the positive (+ve) terminal of the battery to the red/white wire terminal on the relay wiring connector, and the negative (–ve) terminal to the blue/white wire terminal on the connector **(see illustration)**. At this point the relay should be heard to click and the multimeter read zero ohms (continuity). If this is the case the relay is proved good. If the relay does not click when battery voltage is applied and indicates no continuity (infinite resistance) across its terminals, it is faulty and must be renewed.
4 The relay's coil winding resistance can be measured by connecting the multimeter (set to the ohms x 1 scale) across the blue/white and red/white terminals of the connector **(see illustration)**. The reading obtained should be as given in the Specifications at the beginning of this Chapter. If infinite resistance is indicated the relay coil is open-circuit and the relay must be renewed.
5 If the relay is good, check for battery voltage at the red/white wire terminal on the loom side of the relay wiring connector when the starter button is pressed. If voltage is present, check the other components after the relay in the starter circuit and the wiring between them as described in the relevant sections of this Chapter. If no voltage was present, check the wiring between the various components before the relay in the circuit (see *Wiring Diagrams* at the end of this Chapter).

Renewal

6 Remove the seat (see Chapter 7). The starter relay is located behind the battery **(see illustration 27.2)**. Disconnect the battery negative (–ve) lead before removing the starter relay **(see illustration 3.2)**.
7 Disconnect the relay wiring connector **(see illustration)**. Unscrew the two bolts securing

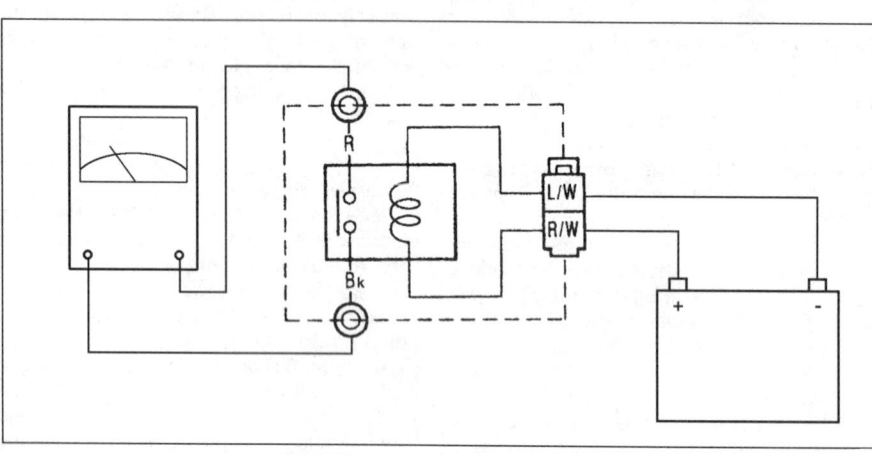

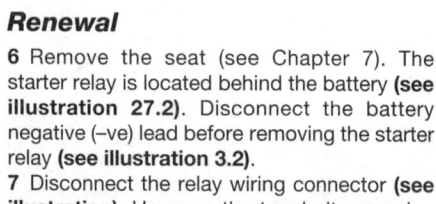

27.3 Starter relay operation test
R - red, Bk - black, L/W - blue/white, R/W - red/white

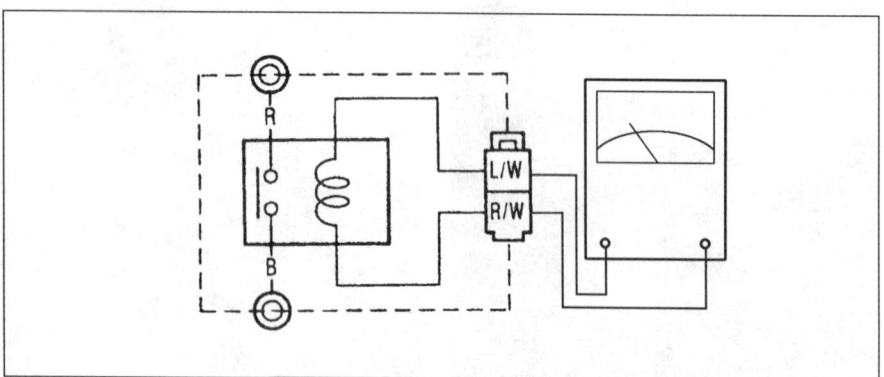

27.4 Starter relay coil test
R - red, Bk - black, L/W - blue/white, R/W - red/white

27.7a Disconnect the relay wiring connector (arrowed)

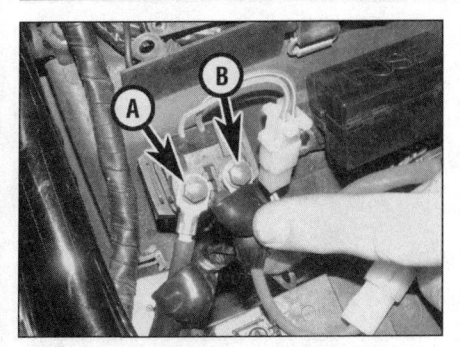

Electrical system 8•19

27.7b Starter motor lead (A), battery lead (B)

27.7c Lift the relay off its mounts

the starter motor and battery leads to the relay and detach the leads **(see illustration)**. Remove the relay with its rubber sleeve from its mounting lugs on the frame **(see illustration)**.

8 Installation is the reverse of removal. Make sure the terminal bolts are securely tightened. Connect the battery negative (–ve) lead last.

28 Starter motor – removal and installation

Removal

1 Remove the seat (see Chapter 7).

Disconnect the battery negative (–ve) lead **(see illustration 3.2)**. The starter motor is mounted on the crankcase, behind the cylinder block.

2 Peel back the rubber terminal cover and unscrew the nut securing the lead to the starter motor **(see illustration)**. Detach the lead.

3 Unscrew the two bolts securing the starter motor **(see illustration)**. Draw the starter motor out of the crankcase and remove it from the machine **(see illustration)**.

4 Remove the O-ring on the end of the starter motor and discard it as a new one must be used.

Installation

5 Fit a new O-ring onto the end of the starter motor, making sure it is seated in its groove, and smear it with grease **(see illustration)**.

6 Manoeuvre the motor into position and slide it into the crankcase. Ensure that the starter motor teeth mesh correctly with those of the starter idle/reduction gear. Install the mounting bolts and tighten them to the torque setting specified at the beginning of the Chapter.

7 Connect the lead to the starter motor and secure it with the nut **(see illustration)**. Make sure the rubber cover is correctly seated over the terminal.

8 Connect the battery negative (–ve) lead and install the seat.

29 Starter motor – disassembly, inspection and reassembly

Disassembly

1 Remove the starter motor (see Section 28).

2 Note the alignment marks between the main housing and the front and rear covers, or make your own if they aren't clear.

3 Unscrew the two long bolts and withdraw them from the starter motor **(see illustration)**.

4 Wrap some insulating tape around the teeth on the end of the starter motor shaft – this will protect the oil seal from damage as the front

28.2 Pull back the rubber cover and unscrew the terminal nut (arrowed)

28.3a Unscrew the bolts (arrowed) . . .

28.3b . . . and remove the starter motor

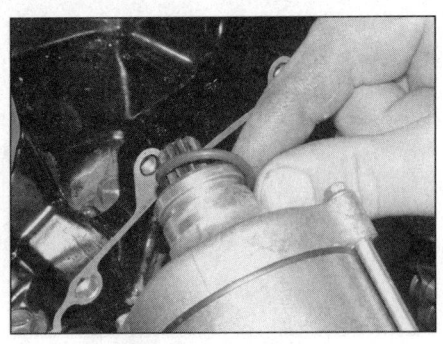

28.5 Fit a new O-ring

28.7 Connect the lead and secure it with the nut

29.3 Unscrew and remove the two long bolts

8•20 Electrical system

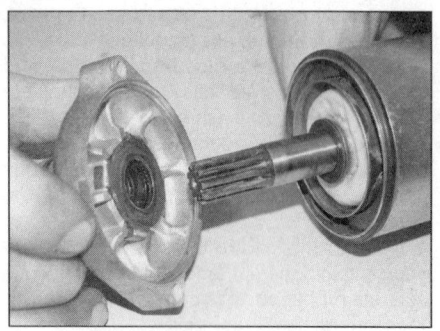

29.4a Remove the front cover . . .

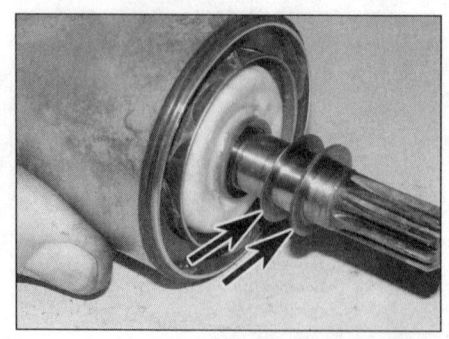

29.4b . . . and slide the shims (arrowed) off the shaft

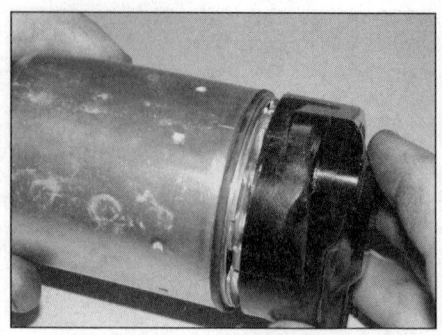

29.5a Remove the rear cover . . .

29.5b . . . and slide the shims (arrowed) off the shaft

29.6 Withdraw the armature from the housing

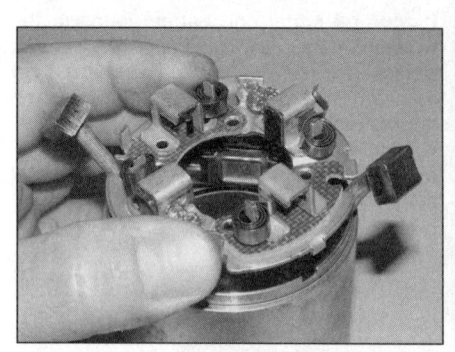

29.7 Slide the insulated brushes out and remove the brushplate from the main housing

cover is removed. Remove the front cover from the motor **(see illustration)**. Remove the cover O-ring from the main housing and discard it as a new one must be used. Remove the shims from the front end of the armature shaft or the inside of the front cover, noting their correct fitted locations **(see illustration)**. Also remove the tabbed thrust washer from the front cover **(see illustration 29.21b)**.

5 Remove the rear cover from the motor **(see illustration)**. Remove the cover O-ring from the main housing and discard it as a new one must be used. Remove the shims from the rear end of the armature shaft or from inside the rear cover **(see illustration)**.

6 Withdraw the armature from the main housing, noting that you will have to pull it out against the attraction of the magnets **(see illustration)**.

7 Slide the brushes with the yellow insulated wires out of their housings. Remove the brushplate assembly from the main housing, noting how it locates **(see illustration)**.

8 Noting the correct fitted location of each component, unscrew the terminal nut and remove it along with its washer, the one large and two small insulating washers and the O-ring **(see illustration)**. Withdraw the terminal bolt, then remove the insulated brush assembly from the brushplate seat, noting how it fits **(see illustration 29.16d)**. Remove the insulator and the brushplate seat **(see illustrations 29.16b and a)**. Check the condition of the O-ring and renew it if it is damaged, deformed or deteriorated.

Inspection

9 The parts of the starter motor that are most likely to require attention are the brushes. Measure the length of each brush and compare the results to the length listed in this Chapter's Specifications **(see illustration)**. If any of the brushes are worn beyond the service limit, renew the brush assemblies. If the brushes are not worn excessively, nor cracked, chipped, or otherwise damaged, they may be re-used.

10 Inspect the commutator bars on the armature for scoring, scratches and discoloration. The commutator can be cleaned and polished with crocus cloth, but do not use sandpaper or emery paper. After cleaning, wipe away any residue with a cloth soaked in electrical system cleaner or denatured alcohol. Measure the diameter of the commutator and compare it to the specifications **(see illustration)**. If it has worn below the service limit, renew the starter motor. Measure the depth of the insulating

29.8 Unscrew the nut and remove the washers and O-ring

29.9 Measure the brush length

29.10a Measure the diameter of the commutator . . .

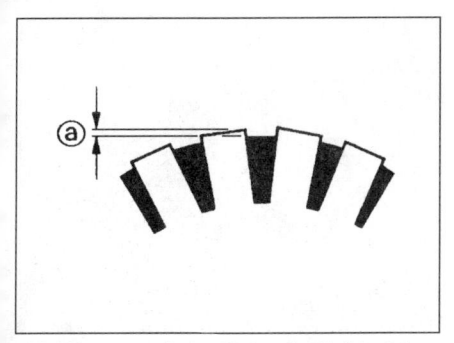

Electrical system 8•21

29.10b ... and check the depth (a) of the mica below the bars

29.11a Continuity should exist between the commutator bars

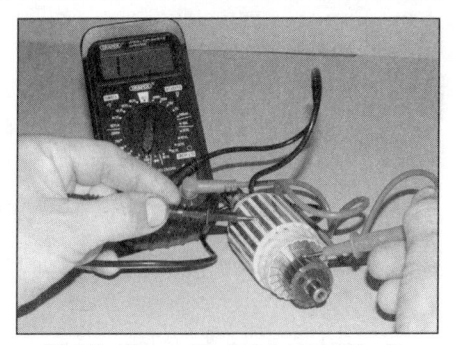

29.11b There should be no continuity between the commutator bars and the armature shaft

mica below the surface of the commutator bars **(see illustration)**. If the mica is less than the depth specified, scrape it away using a suitably shaped hacksaw blade until the specified depth is reached.

11 Using an ohmmeter or a continuity test light, check for continuity between the commutator bars **(see illustration)**. Continuity should exist between each bar and all of the others. Also, check for continuity between the commutator bars and the armature **(see illustration)**. There should be no continuity (infinite resistance) between the commutator and the shaft. If the checks indicate otherwise, the armature is defective.

12 Check for continuity between the un-insulated brushes and the brushplate – there should be continuity. When the starter motor has been assembled check for continuity between the terminal bolt and the housing. There should be no continuity (infinite resistance).

13 Check the front end of the armature shaft for worn, cracked, chipped and broken teeth. If the shaft is damaged or worn, renew the starter motor.

14 Inspect the end covers for signs of cracks or wear. Inspect the magnets in the main housing and the housing itself for cracks.

15 Inspect the front cover oil seal for signs of damage and renew it if necessary **(see illustration)**. Check the needle bearing in the front cover and the bush in the rear cover for wear and damage – they are not listed as being available separately so if any is found new covers must be fitted **(see illustration)**.

Reassembly

16 Fit the brushplate seat and insulator into the main housing **(see illustrations)**. Fit the insulated brush assembly, locating the arms into the brushplate seat **(see illustration)**. Insert the terminal bolt, then fit the O-ring, small and large insulating washers, plain washer and nut onto the bolt and tighten the nut **(see illustrations)**. Use a new O-ring if necessary.

29.15a Check the seal and bearing in the front cover ...

29.15b ... and the bush in the rear cover

29.16a Fit the brushplate seat ...

29.16b ... and the insulator

29.16c Locate the brush assembly ...

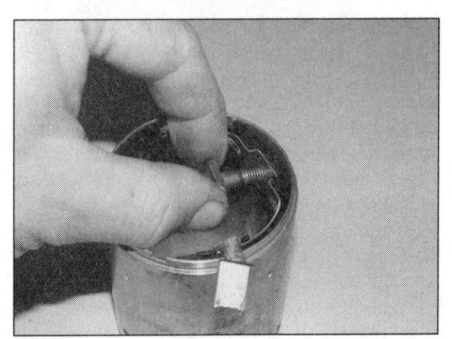

29.16d ... then insert the terminal bolt ...

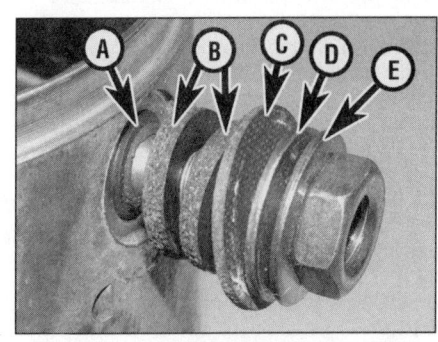

29.16e ... and fit the O-ring (A), small insulating washers (B), large insulating washer (C), plain washer (D) and nut (E)

8

8•22 Electrical system

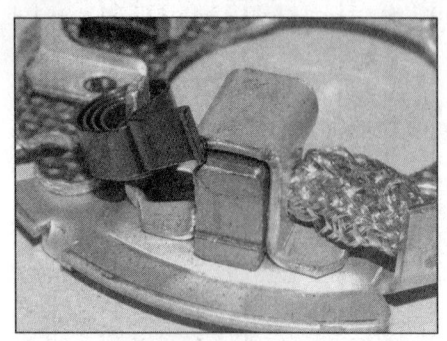

29.17a Locate each brush spring onto the top of its housing

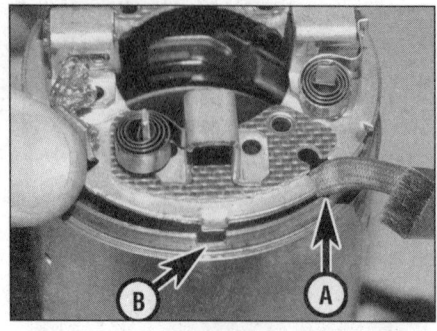

29.17b Fit the brushplate, locating the insulated wires (A) and the tab (B) correctly

29.18 Slide the brushes into their housings

29.19 Locate the spring ends onto the brushes

29.20a Fit a new O-ring

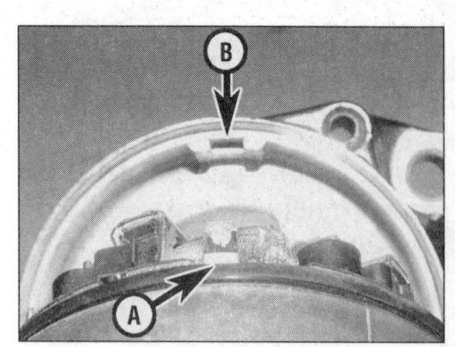

29.20b Locate the tab (A) in the slot (B) in the rear cover

29.21a Fit a new O-ring

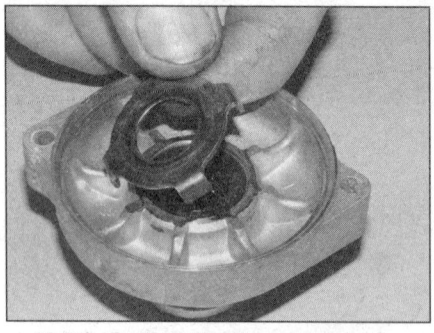

29.21b Fit the tabbed washer into the cover

29.22 Install the two long bolts and tighten them

17 Place each brush spring end onto the top of its brush housing – this allows the brushes to be slid right in so they do not foul the commutator bars when the armature is installed **(see illustration)**. Fit the brushplate assembly onto the main housing, locating the insulated brush wires in the cutouts and making sure the tab on the plate locates in the cutout in the housing **(see illustration)**.
18 Fit each insulated brush into its housing and slide them fully in **(see illustration)**.
19 Insert the armature into the main housing, noting that it will be forcibly drawn in by the attraction of the magnets **(see illustration 29.6)**. Locate each brush spring end onto its brush **(see illustration)**. Check that each brush is securely pressed against the commutator and is free to move in its housing.
20 Slide the shims onto the rear end of the armature **(see illustration 29.5b)**, then fit a new rear cover O-ring **(see illustration)**. Fit the rear cover onto the housing, aligning the marks noted or made earlier **(see illustration 29.5a)**, and locating the tab on the housing in the slot in the cover **(see illustration)**.
21 Fit a new front cover O-ring **(see illustration)**. Slide the shims onto the front of the armature **(see illustration 29.4b)**. Apply a smear of grease to the lips of the front cover oil seal. Fit the tabbed washer onto the cover **(see illustration)**, making sure the tabs locate correctly, then install the cover, aligning the marks made on removal **(see illustration 29.4a)**. Remove the protective tape from the shaft end.
22 Check the alignment marks made on removal are correctly aligned, then install the long bolts and tighten them securely **(see illustration)**.
23 Install the starter motor (see Section 28).

30 Charging system testing –
general information and precautions

1 If the performance of the charging system is suspect, the system as a whole should be checked first, followed by testing of the individual components. **Note:** *Before beginning the checks, make sure the battery is fully charged and that all system connections are clean and tight.*
2 Checking the output of the charging system and the performance of the various components within the charging system requires the use of a multimeter (with voltage, current and resistance checking facilities).
3 When making the checks, follow the procedures carefully to prevent incorrect

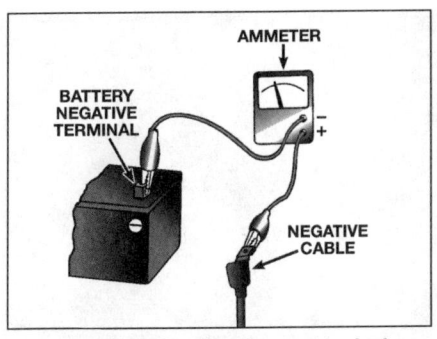

Electrical system 8•23

31.3 Checking the charging system leakage rate - connect the ammeter as shown

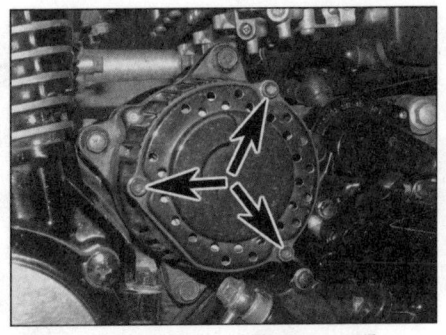

32.1a Unscrew the bolts (arrowed) ...

32.1b ... and remove the cover

connections or short circuits, as irreparable damage to electrical system components may result if short circuits occur.
4 If a multimeter is not available, the job of checking the charging system should be left to a Yamaha dealer or automotive electrician.

31 Charging system – leakage and output test

1 If the charging system of the machine is thought to be faulty, remove the seat (see Chapter 7) and perform the following checks.

Leakage test

Caution: Always connect an ammeter in series, never in parallel with the battery, otherwise it will be damaged. Do not turn the ignition ON or operate the starter motor when the ammeter is connected – a sudden surge in current will blow the meter's fuse.

2 Make sure the ignition switch is OFF. Remove the seat (see Chapter 7) and disconnect the lead from the battery negative (–ve) terminal **(see illustration 3.2)**.
3 Set the multimeter to the Amps function and connect its negative (–ve) probe to the battery negative (–ve) terminal, and positive (+ve) probe to the disconnected negative (–ve) lead **(see illustration)**. Always set the meter to a high amps range initially and then bring it down to the mA (milli Amps) range; if there is a

high current flow in the circuit it may blow the meter's fuse.
4 No current flow should be indicated. If current leakage is indicated (generally greater than 0.1 mA), there is a short circuit in the wiring. Using the wiring diagrams at the end of this Chapter, systematically disconnect individual electrical components, checking the meter each time until the source is identified.
5 If no leakage is indicated, disconnect the meter and connect the negative (–ve) lead to the battery, tightening it securely.

> **HAYNES HINT** *If an alarm or immobiliser is fitted, its current drain should be taken into account when checking for current leakage.*

Output test

6 Start the engine and warm it up to normal operating temperature. Remove the seat (see Chapter 7).
7 To check the regulated voltage output, allow the engine to idle and connect a multimeter set to the 0 to 20 volts DC scale (voltmeter) across the terminals of the battery (positive (+ve) lead to battery positive (+ve) terminal, negative (–ve) lead to battery negative (–ve) terminal). Slowly increase the engine speed to 3000 rpm and note the reading obtained. The regulated voltage should be as specified at the beginning of the Chapter. If the voltage is outside these limits,

check the alternator/regulator/rectifier (see Section 32).

> **HAYNES HINT** *Clues to a faulty regulator are constantly blowing bulbs, with brightness varying considerably with engine speed, and battery overheating.*

32 Alternator/regulator/rectifier – check, removal, inspection and installation

Check

1 Undo the alternator end cover bolts and remove the cover **(see illustrations)**.
2 Undo the screws securing the brush holder, noting the lead secured by the bottom screw, and remove the holder, noting how it fits **(see illustration)**. Inspect the holder for any signs of damage. Measure the length of the brushes and compare the results to the service limit in this Chapter's Specifications **(see illustration)**. Push the brushes into the holder and check they move freely **(see illustration)**. If the brushes are not worn excessively, nor cracked, chipped, or otherwise damaged, they may be re-used. Otherwise, renew the brushholder assembly – the brushes are not available separately. Clean the slip rings (the rings on the shaft which contact the brushes) with a rag moistened with some solvent.

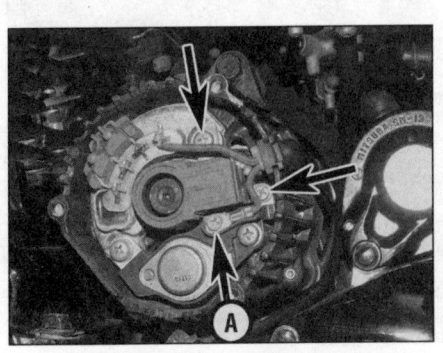

32.2a Undo the screws (arrowed) and remove the brush holder ...

32.2b ... and measure the brushes

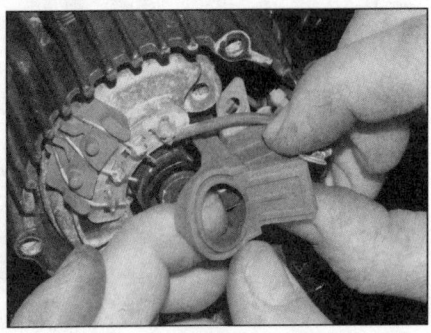

32.2c Push the brushes in and check they move freely

8•24 Electrical system

32.3 Checking rotor coil resistance

32.4 Checking stator coil resistance

3 To check the rotor coil resistance, first remove the brush holder (see above), then set a multimeter to the ohms x 1 (ohmmeter) scale and measure the resistance between the slip rings (the rings on the shaft which contact the brushes) and compare the reading to the Specifications **(see illustration)**. If it is higher than specified, renew the rotor.

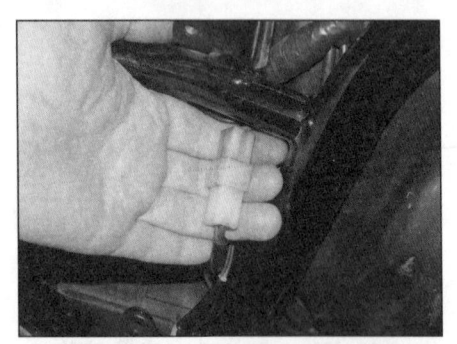

32.8 Alternator wiring connector

4 To check the stator coil resistance, set a multimeter to the ohms x 1 (ohmmeter) scale and measure the resistance between each of the white wires coming out of the left-hand side of the alternator, taking a total of three readings, then check for continuity between each terminal and ground (earth) **(see illustration)**. If the stator coil windings are in good condition the three readings should be within the range shown in the Specifications at the beginning of the Chapter, and there should be no continuity (infinite resistance) between any of the terminals and ground (earth). If not, the alternator stator coil assembly is faulty and should be renewed.

5 Check for continuity between the slip rings and the armature housing. There should be no continuity (infinite resistance). If there is continuity, renew the rotor.

6 Yamaha do not provide any test Specifications for the regulator and rectifier. If none of the checks made here or in other Sections of the Chapter reveal any faults, then take the assembly to a Yamaha dealer for further tests. Individual components are available.

Removal

7 Remove the right-hand side panel (see Chapter 7).
8 Trace the wiring from the alternator/regulator/rectifier and disconnect it at the connector **(see illustration)**. Feed the wiring back to the alternator assembly, noting its routing and releasing it from any clips or ties.
9 Unscrew the three bolts securing the alternator assembly to the crankcase and withdraw it **(see illustrations)**. Discard the O-ring as a new one must be used.

Inspection

10 Undo the alternator end cover bolts and remove the cover **(see illustrations 32.1a and b)**.
11 Undo the screws securing the brush

32.9a Unscrew the bolts (arrowed) . . .

32.9b . . . and remove the alternator

Electrical system 8•25

holder, noting the lead secured by the bottom screw, and remove the holder, noting how it fits **(see illustration 32.2a)**.

12 To remove the regulator, undo the two screws securing it, noting the washers **(see illustration)**. Note that one of the screws also secures the rectifier.

13 The rectifier should only be removed if it is faulty as it is possible for the diodes within to be damaged by the heat transferred when unsoldering the wires from the terminals. To remove the rectifier, unsolder the three wires and bend them straight, then undo the two screws securing it, noting the washers. Note that one of the screws also secures the rectifier. Lift the wire guide off then remove the rectifier.

14 To access the rotor assembly and bearings, unscrew the two nuts securing the rear cover and remove the cover. Draw the rotor out of the main housing/stator assembly. To access the bearing in the rear cover undo the four screws and remove the bearing cover. The other bearing will either be on the end of the rotor or in the main housing. Refer to *Tools and Workshop Tips* in the Reference Section for information on bearing checks and removal methods. Discard the oil seal in the rear cover as a new one must be fitted.

15 Reassemble the alternator in a reverse of the above procedure. Take care not to leave the soldering iron in contact with the rectifier terminals for too long when soldering the rectifier wires.

Installation

16 Installation is the reverse of removal. Use a new O-ring **(see illustration)**. Apply a suitable non-permanent threadlock to the alternator lower bolt **(see illustration)**. Tighten the alternator bolts to the torque setting specified at the beginning of the Chapter.

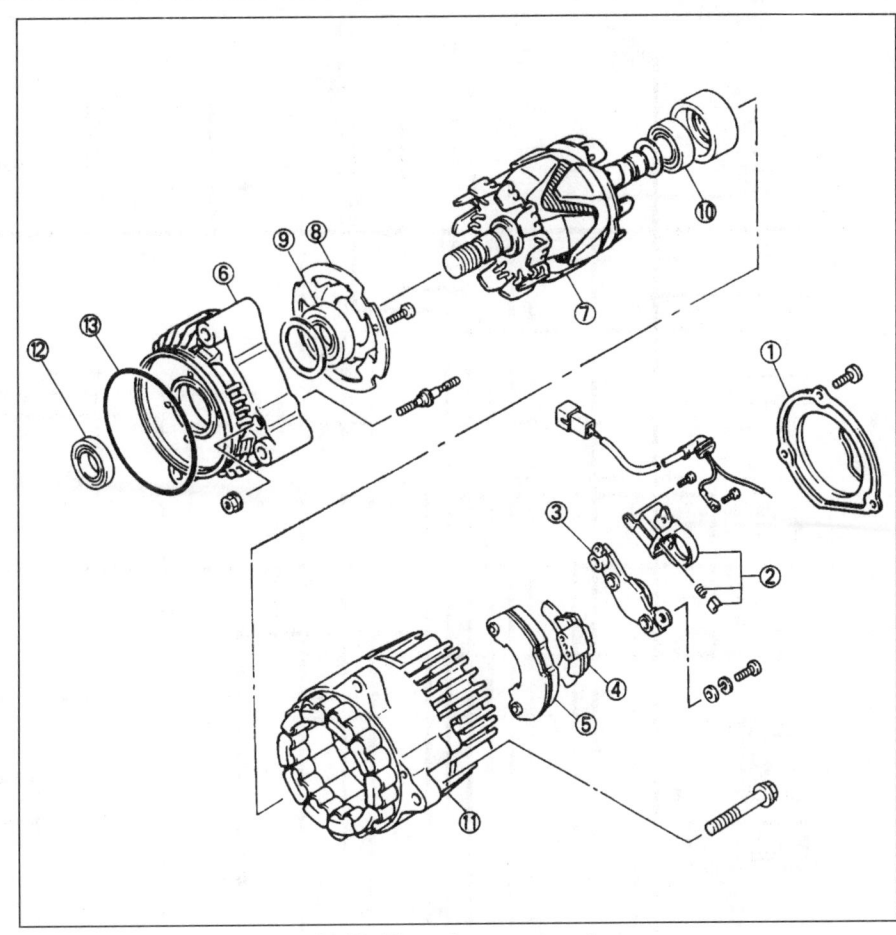

32.12 Alternator components

1 End cover
2 Brush holder
3 Regulator
4 Wire guide
5 Rectifier
6 Rear cover
7 Rotor
8 Bearing cover
9 Bearing
10 Bearing
11 Stator
12 Seal
13 O-ring

32.16a Fit a new O-ring into the groove . . .

32.16b . . . and apply threadlock to the lower bolt

8•26 Electrical system

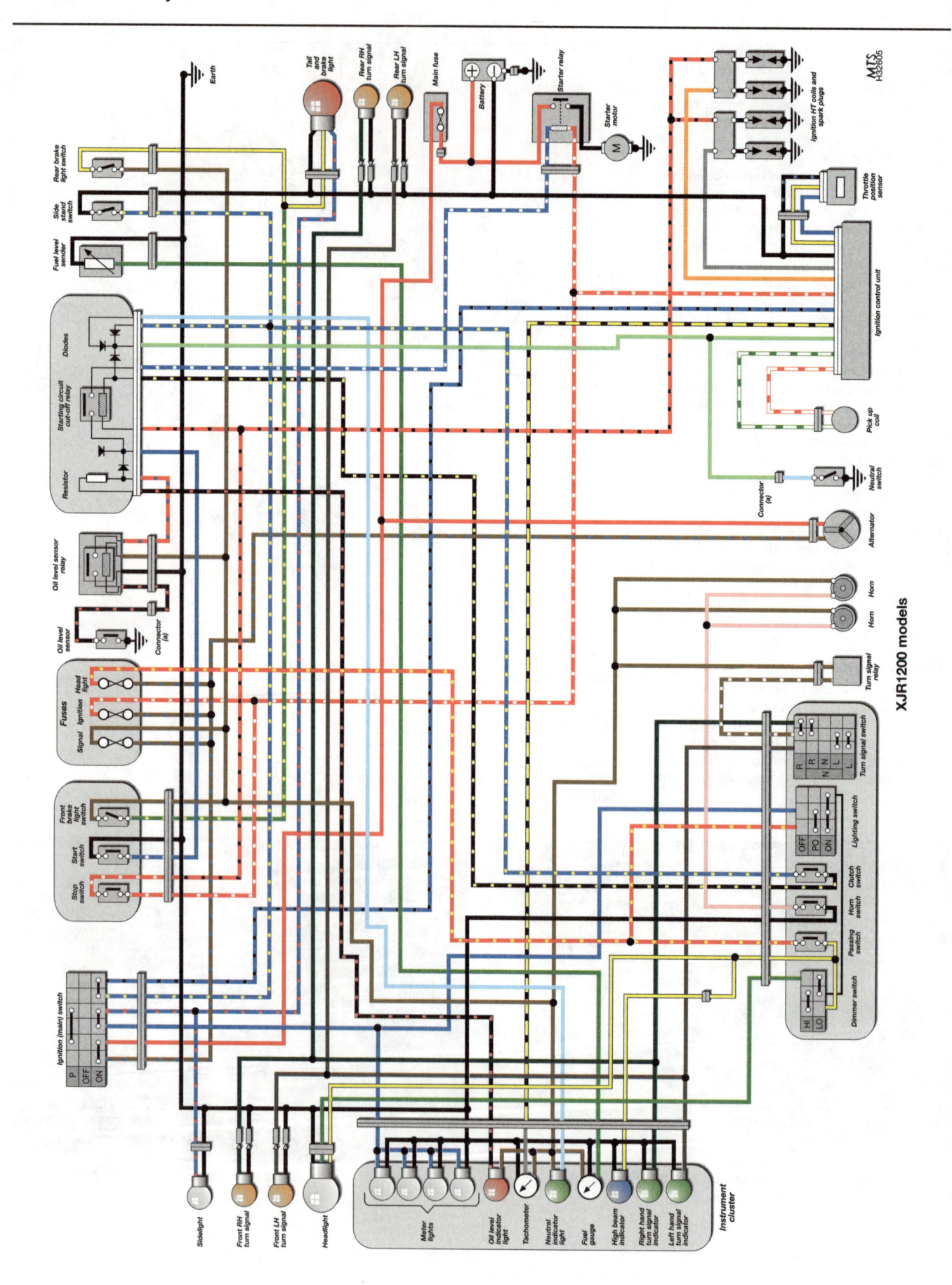

XJR1200 models

Electrical system 8•27

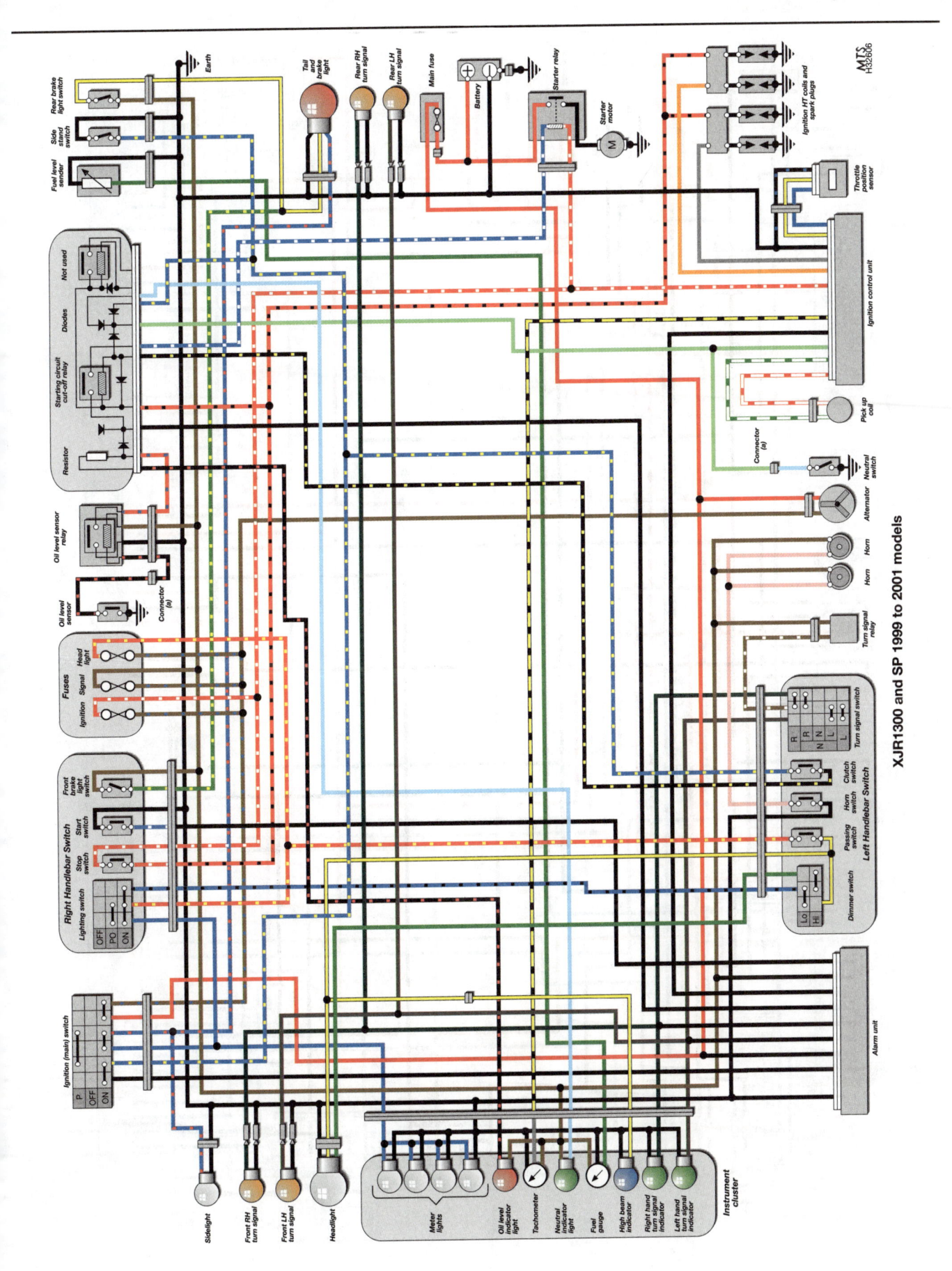

8•28 Electrical system

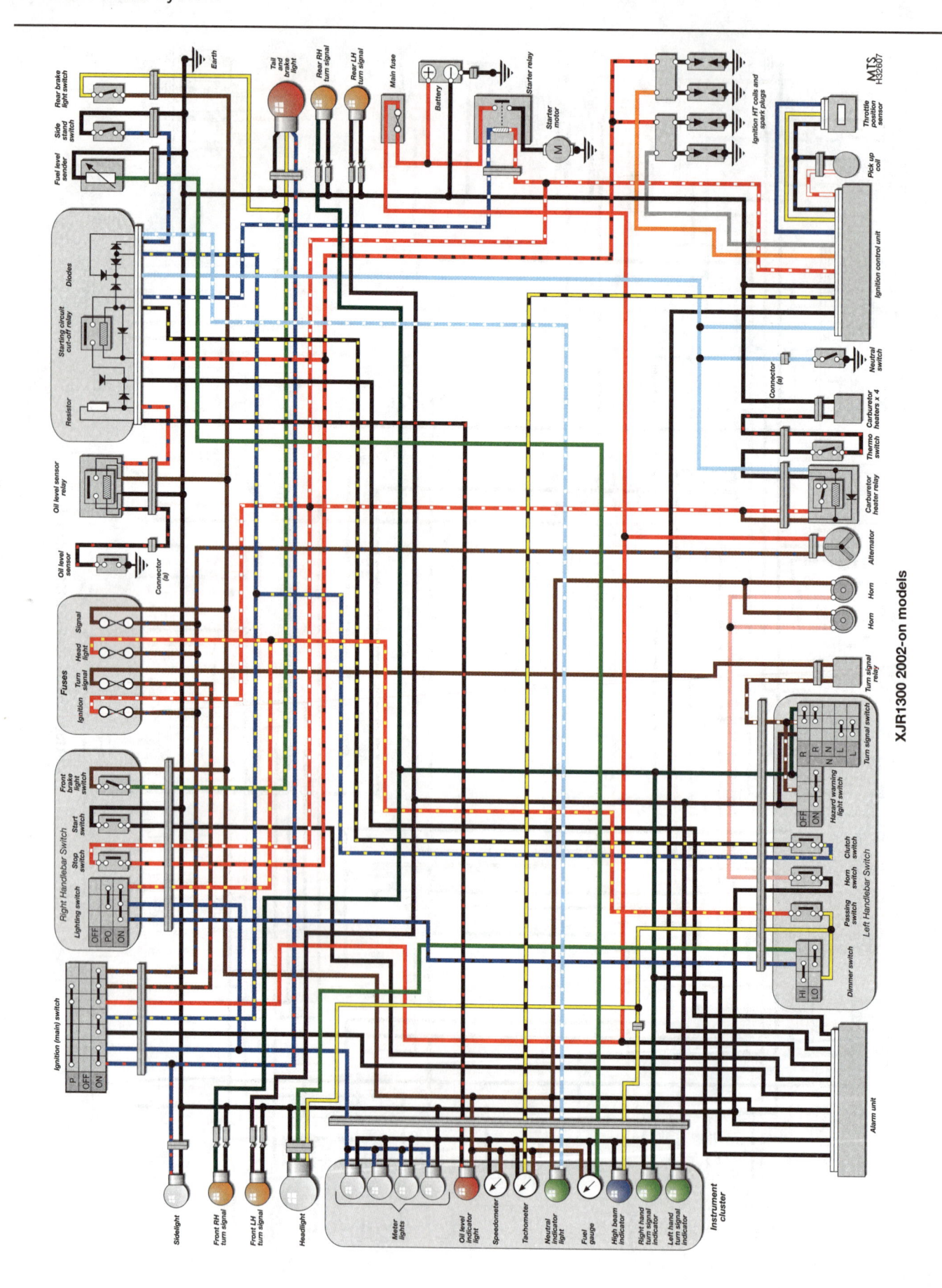

XJR1300 2002-on models

Reference

Tools and Workshop Tips — REF•2
- Building up a tool kit and equipping your workshop ● Using tools ● Understanding bearing, seal, fastener and chain sizes and markings ● Repair techniques

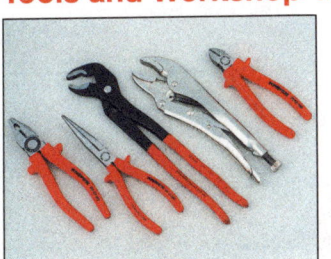

Security — REF•20
- Locks and chains ● U-locks ● Disc locks ● Alarms and immobilisers ● Security marking systems ● Tips on how to prevent bike theft

Lubricants and fluids — REF•23
- Engine oils ● Transmission (gear) oils ● Coolant/anti-freeze ● Fork oils and suspension fluids ● Brake/clutch fluids ● Spray lubes, degreasers and solvents

Conversion Factors — REF•26
34 Nm x 0.738 = 25 lbf ft
- Formulae for conversion of the metric (SI) units used throughout the manual into Imperial measures

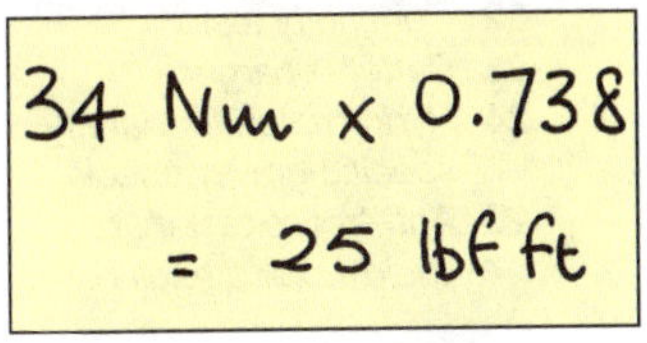

MOT Test Checks — REF•27
- A guide to the UK MOT test ● Which items are tested ● How to prepare your motorcycle for the test and perform a pre-test check

Storage — REF•32
- How to prepare your motorcycle for going into storage and protect essential systems ● How to get the motorcycle back on the road

Fault Finding — REF•35
- Common faults and their likely causes ● How to check engine cylinder compression ● How to make electrical tests and use test meters

Technical Terms Explained — REF•48
- Component names, technical terms and common abbreviations explained

Index — REF•52

REF•2 Tools and Workshop Tips

Buying tools

A toolkit is a fundamental requirement for servicing and repairing a motorcycle. Although there will be an initial expense in building up enough tools for servicing, this will soon be offset by the savings made by doing the job yourself. As experience and confidence grow, additional tools can be added to enable the repair and overhaul of the motorcycle. Many of the specialist tools are expensive and not often used so it may be preferable to hire them, or for a group of friends or motorcycle club to join in the purchase.

As a rule, it is better to buy more expensive, good quality tools. Cheaper tools are likely to wear out faster and need to be renewed more often, nullifying the original saving.

> **Warning:** To avoid the risk of a poor quality tool breaking in use, causing injury or damage to the component being worked on, always aim to purchase tools which meet the relevant national safety standards.

The following lists of tools do not represent the manufacturer's service tools, but serve as a guide to help the owner decide which tools are needed for this level of work. In addition, items such as an electric drill, hacksaw, files, soldering iron and a workbench equipped with a vice, may be needed. Although not classed as tools, a selection of bolts, screws, nuts, washers and pieces of tubing always come in useful.

For more information about tools, refer to the Haynes *Motorcycle Workshop Practice TechBook* (Bk. No. 3470).

Manufacturer's service tools

Inevitably certain tasks require the use of a service tool. Where possible an alternative tool or method of approach is recommended, but sometimes there is no option if personal injury or damage to the component is to be avoided. Where required, service tools are referred to in the relevant procedure.

Service tools can usually only be purchased from a motorcycle dealer and are identified by a part number. Some of the commonly-used tools, such as rotor pullers, are available in aftermarket form from mail-order motorcycle tool and accessory suppliers.

Maintenance and minor repair tools

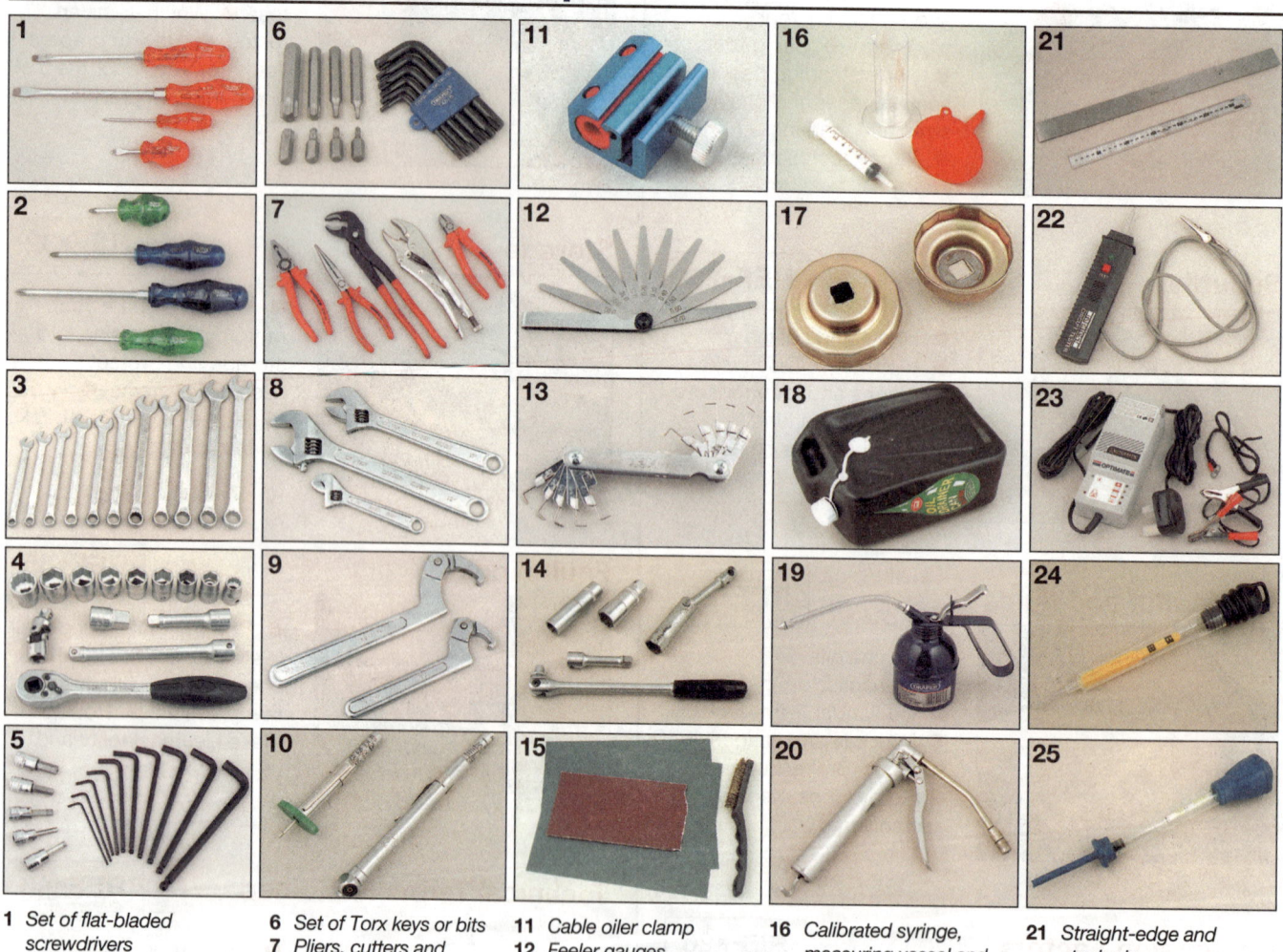

1. Set of flat-bladed screwdrivers
2. Set of Phillips head screwdrivers
3. Combination open-end and ring spanners
4. Socket set (3/8 inch or 1/2 inch drive)
5. Set of Allen keys or bits
6. Set of Torx keys or bits
7. Pliers, cutters and self-locking grips (Mole grips)
8. Adjustable spanners
9. C-spanners
10. Tread depth gauge and tyre pressure gauge
11. Cable oiler clamp
12. Feeler gauges
13. Spark plug gap measuring tool
14. Spark plug spanner or deep plug sockets
15. Wire brush and emery paper
16. Calibrated syringe, measuring vessel and funnel
17. Oil filter adapters
18. Oil drainer can or tray
19. Pump type oil can
20. Grease gun
21. Straight-edge and steel rule
22. Continuity tester
23. Battery charger
24. Hydrometer (for battery specific gravity check)
25. Anti-freeze tester (for liquid-cooled engines)

Tools and Workshop Tips REF•3

Repair and overhaul tools

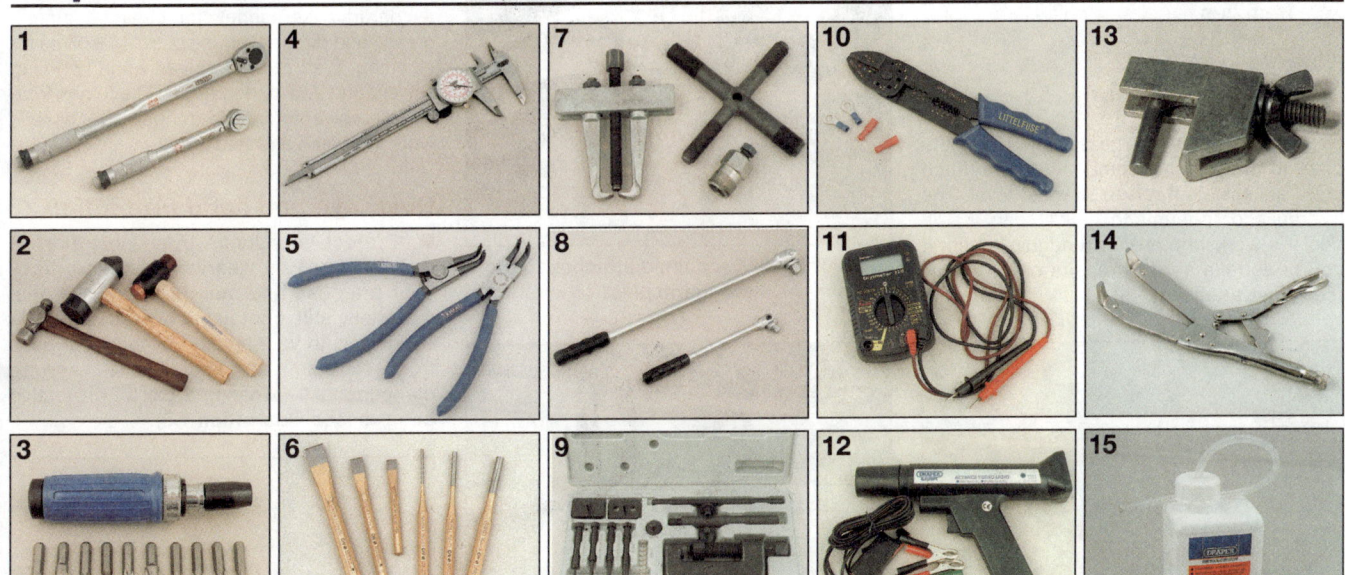

1 Torque wrench (small and mid-ranges)
2 Conventional, plastic or soft-faced hammers
3 Impact driver set
4 Vernier gauge
5 Circlip pliers (internal and external, or combination)
6 Set of cold chisels and punches
7 Selection of pullers
8 Breaker bars
9 Chain breaking/riveting tool set
10 Wire stripper and crimper tool
11 Multimeter (measures amps, volts and ohms)
12 Stroboscope (for dynamic timing checks)
13 Hose clamp (wingnut type shown)
14 Clutch holding tool
15 One-man brake/clutch bleeder kit

Specialist tools

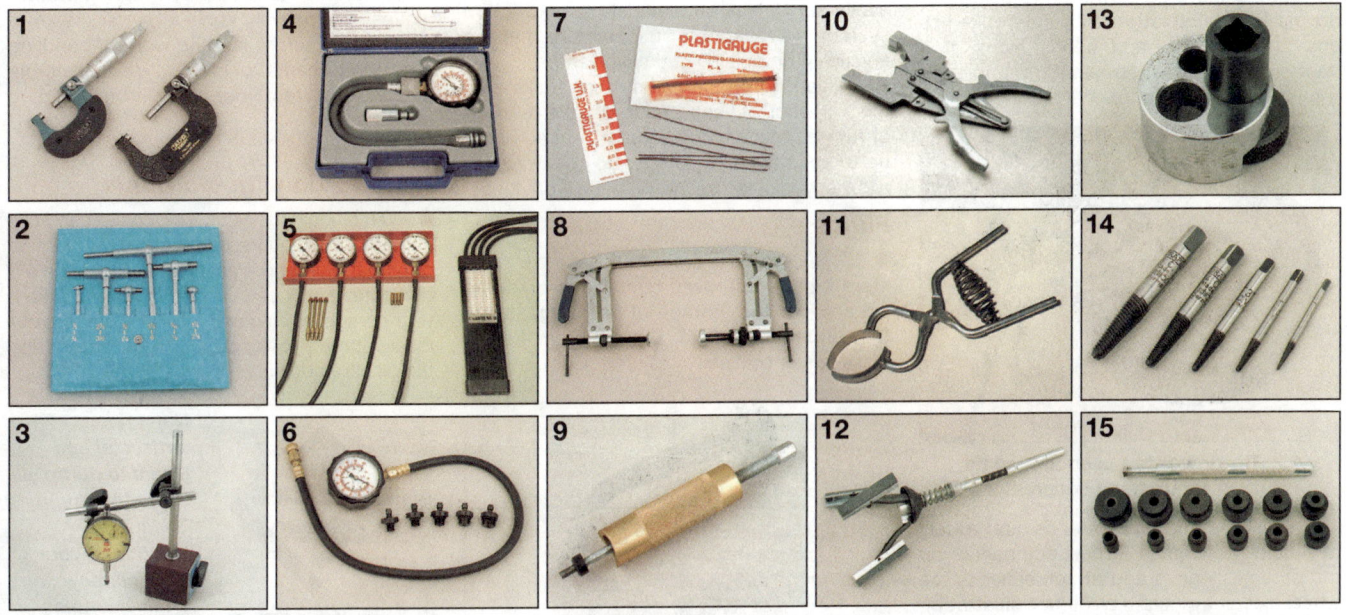

1 Micrometers (external type)
2 Telescoping gauges
3 Dial gauge
4 Cylinder compression gauge
5 Vacuum gauges (left) or manometer (right)
6 Oil pressure gauge
7 Plastigauge kit
8 Valve spring compressor (4-stroke engines)
9 Piston pin drawbolt tool
10 Piston ring removal and installation tool
11 Piston ring clamp
12 Cylinder bore hone (stone type shown)
13 Stud extractor
14 Screw extractor set
15 Bearing driver set

REF•4 Tools and Workshop Tips

1 Workshop equipment and facilities

The workbench

● Work is made much easier by raising the bike up on a ramp - components are much more accessible if raised to waist level. The hydraulic or pneumatic types seen in the dealer's workshop are a sound investment if you undertake a lot of repairs or overhauls **(see illustration 1.1)**.

1.1 Hydraulic motorcycle ramp

● If raised off ground level, the bike must be supported on the ramp to avoid it falling. Most ramps incorporate a front wheel locating clamp which can be adjusted to suit different diameter wheels. When tightening the clamp, take care not to mark the wheel rim or damage the tyre - use wood blocks on each side to prevent this.

● Secure the bike to the ramp using tie-downs **(see illustration 1.2)**. If the bike has only a sidestand, and hence leans at a dangerous angle when raised, support the bike on an auxiliary stand.

1.2 Tie-downs are used around the passenger footrests to secure the bike

● Auxiliary (paddock) stands are widely available from mail order companies or motorcycle dealers and attach either to the wheel axle or swingarm pivot **(see illustration 1.3)**. If the motorcycle has a centrestand, you can support it under the crankcase to prevent it toppling whilst either wheel is removed **(see illustration 1.4)**.

1.3 This auxiliary stand attaches to the swingarm pivot

1.4 Always use a block of wood between the engine and jack head when supporting the engine in this way

Fumes and fire

● Refer to the Safety first! page at the beginning of the manual for full details. Make sure your workshop is equipped with a fire extinguisher suitable for fuel-related fires (Class B fire - flammable liquids) - it is not sufficient to have a water-filled extinguisher.

● Always ensure adequate ventilation is available. Unless an exhaust gas extraction system is available for use, ensure that the engine is run outside of the workshop.

● If working on the fuel system, make sure the workshop is ventilated to avoid a build-up of fumes. This applies equally to fume build-up when charging a battery. Do not smoke or allow anyone else to smoke in the workshop.

Fluids

● If you need to drain fuel from the tank, store it in an approved container marked as suitable for the storage of petrol (gasoline) **(see illustration 1.5)**. Do not store fuel in glass jars or bottles.

1.5 Use an approved can only for storing petrol (gasoline)

● Use proprietary engine degreasers or solvents which have a high flash-point, such as paraffin (kerosene), for cleaning off oil, grease and dirt - never use petrol (gasoline) for cleaning. Wear rubber gloves when handling solvent and engine degreaser. The fumes from certain solvents can be dangerous - always work in a well-ventilated area.

Dust, eye and hand protection

● Protect your lungs from inhalation of dust particles by wearing a filtering mask over the nose and mouth. Many frictional materials still contain asbestos which is dangerous to your health. Protect your eyes from spouts of liquid and sprung components by wearing a pair of protective goggles **(see illustration 1.6)**.

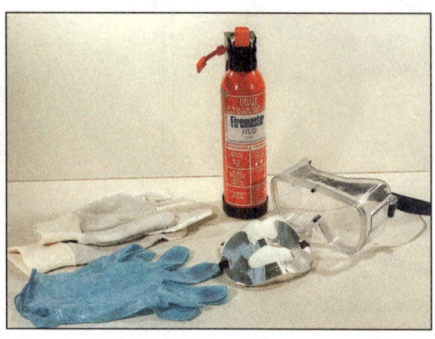

1.6 A fire extinguisher, goggles, mask and protective gloves should be at hand in the workshop

● Protect your hands from contact with solvents, fuel and oils by wearing rubber gloves. Alternatively apply a barrier cream to your hands before starting work. If handling hot components or fluids, wear suitable gloves to protect your hands from scalding and burns.

What to do with old fluids

● Old cleaning solvent, fuel, coolant and oils should not be poured down domestic drains or onto the ground. Package the fluid up in old oil containers, label it accordingly, and take it to a garage or disposal facility. Contact your local authority for location of such sites or ring the oil care hotline.

OIL CARE
OIL BANK LINE
0800 66 33 66
www.oilbankline.org.uk

Note: It is antisocial and illegal to dump oil down the drain. To find the location of your local oil recycling bank, call this number free.

In the USA, note that any oil supplier must accept used oil for recycling.

Tools and Workshop Tips REF•5

2 Fasteners - screws, bolts and nuts

Fastener types and applications

Bolts and screws

● Fastener head types are either of hexagonal, Torx or splined design, with internal and external versions of each type **(see illustrations 2.1 and 2.2)**; splined head fasteners are not in common use on motorcycles. The conventional slotted or Phillips head design is used for certain screws. Bolt or screw length is always measured from the underside of the head to the end of the item **(see illustration 2.11)**.

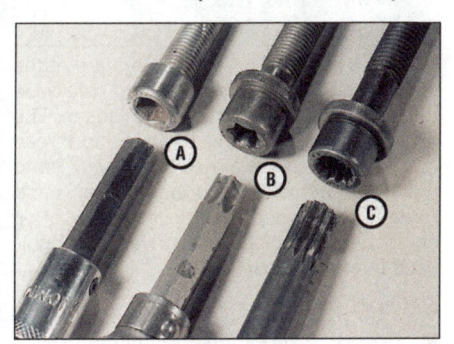

2.1 Internal hexagon/Allen (A), Torx (B) and splined (C) fasteners, with corresponding bits

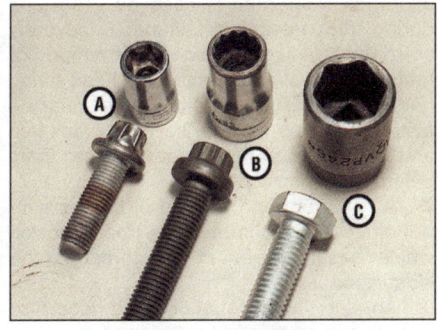

2.2 External Torx (A), splined (B) and hexagon (C) fasteners, with corresponding sockets

● Certain fasteners on the motorcycle have a tensile marking on their heads, the higher the marking the stronger the fastener. High tensile fasteners generally carry a 10 or higher marking. Never replace a high tensile fastener with one of a lower tensile strength.

Washers (see illustration 2.3)

● Plain washers are used between a fastener head and a component to prevent damage to the component or to spread the load when torque is applied. Plain washers can also be used as spacers or shims in certain assemblies. Copper or aluminium plain washers are often used as sealing washers on drain plugs.

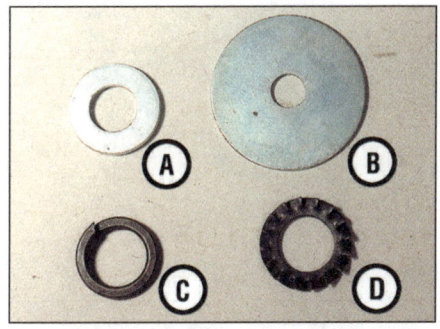

2.3 Plain washer (A), penny washer (B), spring washer (C) and serrated washer (D)

● The split-ring spring washer works by applying axial tension between the fastener head and component. If flattened, it is fatigued and must be renewed. If a plain (flat) washer is used on the fastener, position the spring washer between the fastener and the plain washer.

● Serrated star type washers dig into the fastener and component faces, preventing loosening. They are often used on electrical earth (ground) connections to the frame.

● Cone type washers (sometimes called Belleville) are conical and when tightened apply axial tension between the fastener head and component. They must be installed with the dished side against the component and often carry an OUTSIDE marking on their outer face. If flattened, they are fatigued and must be renewed.

● Tab washers are used to lock plain nuts or bolts on a shaft. A portion of the tab washer is bent up hard against one flat of the nut or bolt to prevent it loosening. Due to the tab washer being deformed in use, a new tab washer should be used every time it is disturbed.

● Wave washers are used to take up endfloat on a shaft. They provide light springing and prevent excessive side-to-side play of a component. Can be found on rocker arm shafts.

Nuts and split pins

● Conventional plain nuts are usually six-sided **(see illustration 2.4)**. They are sized by thread diameter and pitch. High tensile nuts carry a number on one end to denote their tensile strength.

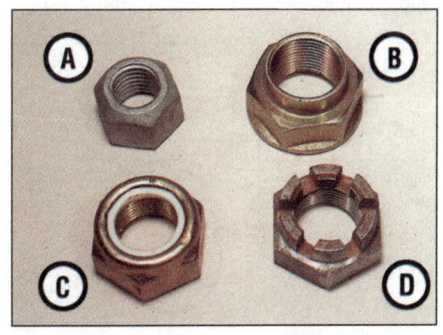

2.4 Plain nut (A), shouldered locknut (B), nylon insert nut (C) and castellated nut (D)

● Self-locking nuts either have a nylon insert, or two spring metal tabs, or a shoulder which is staked into a groove in the shaft - their advantage over conventional plain nuts is a resistance to loosening due to vibration. The nylon insert type can be used a number of times, but must be renewed when the friction of the nylon insert is reduced, ie when the nut spins freely on the shaft. The spring tab type can be reused unless the tabs are damaged. The shouldered type must be renewed every time it is disturbed.

● Split pins (cotter pins) are used to lock a castellated nut to a shaft or to prevent slackening of a plain nut. Common applications are wheel axles and brake torque arms. Because the split pin arms are deformed to lock around the nut a new split pin must always be used on installation - always fit the correct size split pin which will fit snugly in the shaft hole. Make sure the split pin arms are correctly located around the nut **(see illustrations 2.5 and 2.6)**.

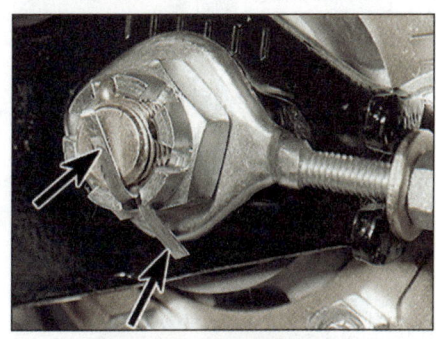

2.5 Bend split pin (cotter pin) arms as shown (arrows) to secure a castellated nut

2.6 Bend split pin (cotter pin) arms as shown to secure a plain nut

Caution: If the castellated nut slots do not align with the shaft hole after tightening to the torque setting, tighten the nut until the next slot aligns with the hole - never slacken the nut to align its slot.

● R-pins (shaped like the letter R), or slip pins as they are sometimes called, are sprung and can be reused if they are otherwise in good condition. Always install R-pins with their closed end facing forwards **(see illustration 2.7)**.

REF•6 Tools and Workshop Tips

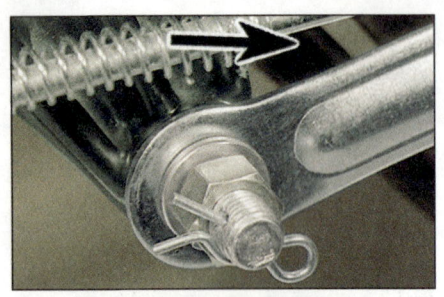

2.7 Correct fitting of R-pin. Arrow indicates forward direction

Circlips (see illustration 2.8)

- Circlips (sometimes called snap-rings) are used to retain components on a shaft or in a housing and have corresponding external or internal ears to permit removal. Parallel-sided (machined) circlips can be installed either way round in their groove, whereas stamped circlips (which have a chamfered edge on one face) must be installed with the chamfer facing away from the direction of thrust load **(see illustration 2.9)**.

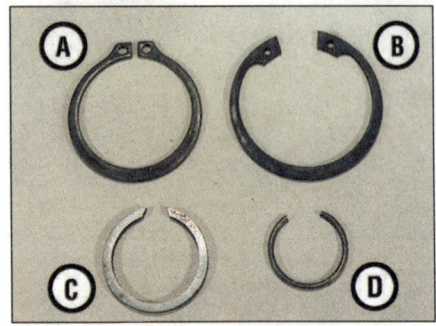

2.8 External stamped circlip (A), internal stamped circlip (B), machined circlip (C) and wire circlip (D)

- Always use circlip pliers to remove and install circlips; expand or compress them just enough to remove them. After installation, rotate the circlip in its groove to ensure it is securely seated. If installing a circlip on a splined shaft, always align its opening with a shaft channel to ensure the circlip ends are well supported and unlikely to catch **(see illustration 2.10)**.

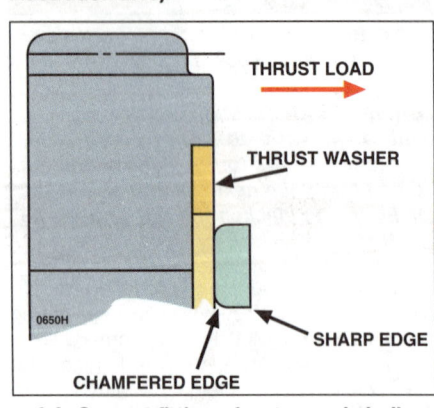

2.9 Correct fitting of a stamped circlip

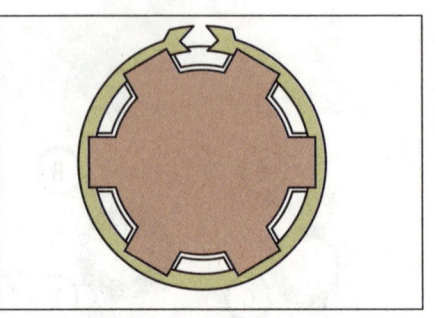

2.10 Align circlip opening with shaft channel

- Circlips can wear due to the thrust of components and become loose in their grooves, with the subsequent danger of becoming dislodged in operation. For this reason, renewal is advised every time a circlip is disturbed.
- Wire circlips are commonly used as piston pin retaining clips. If a removal tang is provided, long-nosed pliers can be used to dislodge them, otherwise careful use of a small flat-bladed screwdriver is necessary. Wire circlips should be renewed every time they are disturbed.

Thread diameter and pitch

- Diameter of a male thread (screw, bolt or stud) is the outside diameter of the threaded portion **(see illustration 2.11)**. Most motorcycle manufacturers use the ISO (International Standards Organisation) metric system expressed in millimetres, eg M6 refers to a 6 mm diameter thread. Sizing is the same for nuts, except that the thread diameter is measured across the valleys of the nut.
- Pitch is the distance between the peaks of the thread **(see illustration 2.11)**. It is expressed in millimetres, thus a common bolt size may be expressed as 6.0 x 1.0 mm (6 mm thread diameter and 1 mm pitch). Generally pitch increases in proportion to thread diameter, although there are always exceptions.
- Thread diameter and pitch are related for conventional fastener applications and the accompanying table can be used as a guide. Additionally, the AF (Across Flats), spanner or socket size dimension of the bolt or nut **(see illustration 2.11)** is linked to thread and pitch specification. Thread pitch can be measured with a thread gauge **(see illustration 2.12)**.

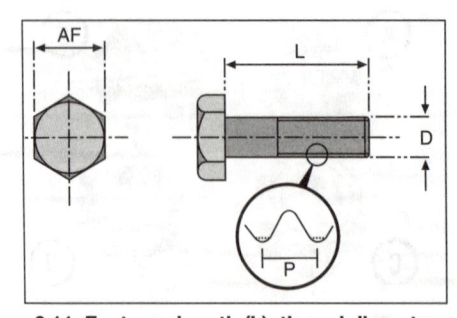

2.11 Fastener length (L), thread diameter (D), thread pitch (P) and head size (AF)

2.12 Using a thread gauge to measure pitch

AF size	Thread diameter x pitch (mm)
8 mm	M5 x 0.8
8 mm	M6 x 1.0
10 mm	M6 x 1.0
12 mm	M8 x 1.25
14 mm	M10 x 1.25
17 mm	M12 x 1.25

- The threads of most fasteners are of the right-hand type, ie they are turned clockwise to tighten and anti-clockwise to loosen. The reverse situation applies to left-hand thread fasteners, which are turned anti-clockwise to tighten and clockwise to loosen. Left-hand threads are used where rotation of a component might loosen a conventional right-hand thread fastener.

Seized fasteners

- Corrosion of external fasteners due to water or reaction between two dissimilar metals can occur over a period of time. It will build up sooner in wet conditions or in countries where salt is used on the roads during the winter. If a fastener is severely corroded it is likely that normal methods of removal will fail and result in its head being ruined. When you attempt removal, the fastener thread should be heard to crack free and unscrew easily - if it doesn't, stop there before damaging something.
- A smart tap on the head of the fastener will often succeed in breaking free corrosion which has occurred in the threads **(see illustration 2.13)**.
- An aerosol penetrating fluid (such as WD-40) applied the night beforehand may work its way down into the thread and ease removal. Depending on the location, you may be able to make up a Plasticine well around the fastener head and fill it with penetrating fluid.

2.13 A sharp tap on the head of a fastener will often break free a corroded thread

Tools and Workshop Tips

• If you are working on an engine internal component, corrosion will most likely not be a problem due to the well lubricated environment. However, components can be very tight and an impact driver is a useful tool in freeing them **(see illustration 2.14)**.

2.14 Using an impact driver to free a fastener

• Where corrosion has occurred between dissimilar metals (eg steel and aluminium alloy), the application of heat to the fastener head will create a disproportionate expansion rate between the two metals and break the seizure caused by the corrosion. Whether heat can be applied depends on the location of the fastener - any surrounding components likely to be damaged must first be removed **(see illustration 2.15)**. Heat can be applied using a paint stripper heat gun or clothes iron, or by immersing the component in boiling water - wear protective gloves to prevent scalding or burns to the hands.

2.15 Using heat to free a seized fastener

• As a last resort, it is possible to use a hammer and cold chisel to work the fastener head unscrewed **(see illustration 2.16)**. This will damage the fastener, but more importantly extreme care must be taken not to damage the surrounding component.

Caution: Remember that the component being secured is generally of more value than the bolt, nut or screw - when the fastener is freed, do not unscrew it with force, instead work the fastener back and forth when resistance is felt to prevent thread damage.

2.16 Using a hammer and chisel to free a seized fastener

Broken fasteners and damaged heads

• If the shank of a broken bolt or screw is accessible you can grip it with self-locking grips. The knurled wheel type stud extractor tool or self-gripping stud puller tool is particularly useful for removing the long studs which screw into the cylinder mouth surface of the crankcase or bolts and screws from which the head has broken off **(see illustration 2.17)**. Studs can also be removed by locking two nuts together on the threaded end of the stud and using a spanner on the lower nut **(see illustration 2.18)**.

2.17 Using a stud extractor tool to remove a broken crankcase stud

2.18 Two nuts can be locked together to unscrew a stud from a component

• A bolt or screw which has broken off below or level with the casing must be extracted using a screw extractor set. Centre punch the fastener to centralise the drill bit, then drill a hole in the fastener **(see illustration 2.19)**. Select a drill bit which is approximately half to three-quarters the

2.19 When using a screw extractor, first drill a hole in the fastener . . .

diameter of the fastener and drill to a depth which will accommodate the extractor. Use the largest size extractor possible, but avoid leaving too small a wall thickness otherwise the extractor will merely force the fastener walls outwards wedging it in the casing thread.

• If a spiral type extractor is used, thread it anti-clockwise into the fastener. As it is screwed in, it will grip the fastener and unscrew it from the casing **(see illustration 2.20)**.

2.20 . . . then thread the extractor anti-clockwise into the fastener

• If a taper type extractor is used, tap it into the fastener so that it is firmly wedged in place. Unscrew the extractor (anti-clockwise) to draw the fastener out.

> ⚠ *Warning: Stud extractors are very hard and may break off in the fastener if care is not taken - ask an engineer about spark erosion if this happens.*

• Alternatively, the broken bolt/screw can be drilled out and the hole retapped for an oversize bolt/screw or a diamond-section thread insert. It is essential that the drilling is carried out squarely and to the correct depth, otherwise the casing may be ruined - if in doubt, entrust the work to an engineer.

• Bolts and nuts with rounded corners cause the correct size spanner or socket to slip when force is applied. Of the types of spanner/socket available always use a six-point type rather than an eight or twelve-point type - better grip

REF•8 Tools and Workshop Tips

2.21 Comparison of surface drive ring spanner (left) with 12-point type (right)

is obtained. Surface drive spanners grip the middle of the hex flats, rather than the corners, and are thus good in cases of damaged heads **(see illustration 2.21)**.

● Slotted-head or Phillips-head screws are often damaged by the use of the wrong size screwdriver. Allen-head and Torx-head screws are much less likely to sustain damage. If enough of the screw head is exposed you can use a hacksaw to cut a slot in its head and then use a conventional flat-bladed screwdriver to remove it. Alternatively use a hammer and cold chisel to tap the head of the fastener around to slacken it. Always replace damaged fasteners with new ones, preferably Torx or Allen-head type.

> **HAYNES HiNT**
>
> *A dab of valve grinding compound between the screw head and screwdriver tip will often give a good grip.*

Thread repair

● Threads (particularly those in aluminium alloy components) can be damaged by overtightening, being assembled with dirt in the threads, or from a component working loose and vibrating. Eventually the thread will fail completely, and it will be impossible to tighten the fastener.

● If a thread is damaged or clogged with old locking compound it can be renovated with a thread repair tool (thread chaser) **(see illustrations 2.22 and 2.23)**; special thread

2.22 A thread repair tool being used to correct an internal thread

2.23 A thread repair tool being used to correct an external thread

chasers are available for spark plug hole threads. The tool will not cut a new thread, but clean and true the original thread. Make sure that you use the correct diameter and pitch tool. Similarly, external threads can be cleaned up with a die or a thread restorer file **(see illustration 2.24)**.

2.24 Using a thread restorer file

● It is possible to drill out the old thread and retap the component to the next thread size. This will work where there is enough surrounding material and a new bolt or screw can be obtained. Sometimes, however, this is not possible - such as where the bolt/screw passes through another component which must also be suitably modified, also in cases where a spark plug or oil drain plug cannot be obtained in a larger diameter thread size.

● The diamond-section thread insert (often known by its popular trade name of Heli-Coil) is a simple and effective method of renewing the thread and retaining the original size. A kit can be purchased which contains the tap, insert and installing tool **(see illustration 2.25)**. Drill out the damaged thread with the size drill specified **(see illustration 2.26)**. Carefully retap the thread **(see illustration 2.27)**. Install the

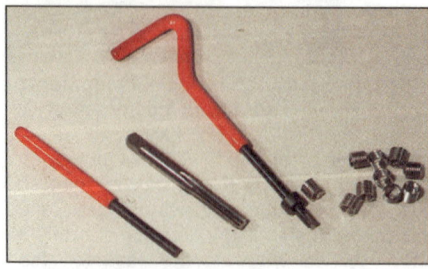

2.25 Obtain a thread insert kit to suit the thread diameter and pitch required

2.26 To install a thread insert, first drill out the original thread . . .

2.27 . . . tap a new thread . . .

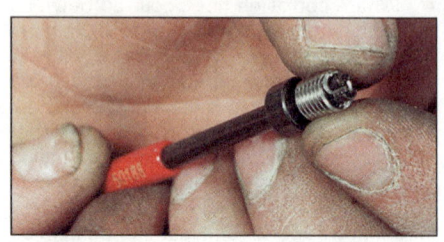

2.28 . . . fit insert on the installing tool . . .

2.29 . . . and thread into the component . . .

2.30 . . . break off the tang when complete

insert on the installing tool and thread it slowly into place using a light downward pressure **(see illustrations 2.28 and 2.29)**. When positioned between a 1/4 and 1/2 turn below the surface withdraw the installing tool and use the break-off tool to press down on the tang, breaking it off **(see illustration 2.30)**.

● There are epoxy thread repair kits on the market which can rebuild stripped internal threads, although this repair should not be used on high load-bearing components.

Tools and Workshop Tips REF•9

Thread locking and sealing compounds

● Locking compounds are used in locations where the fastener is prone to loosening due to vibration or on important safety-related items which might cause loss of control of the motorcycle if they fail. It is also used where important fasteners cannot be secured by other means such as lockwashers or split pins.

● Before applying locking compound, make sure that the threads (internal and external) are clean and dry with all old compound removed. Select a compound to suit the component being secured - a non-permanent general locking and sealing type is suitable for most applications, but a high strength type is needed for permanent fixing of studs in castings. Apply a drop or two of the compound to the first few threads of the fastener, then thread it into place and tighten to the specified torque. Do not apply excessive thread locking compound otherwise the thread may be damaged on subsequent removal.

● Certain fasteners are impregnated with a dry film type coating of locking compound on their threads. Always renew this type of fastener if disturbed.

● Anti-seize compounds, such as copper-based greases, can be applied to protect threads from seizure due to extreme heat and corrosion. A common instance is spark plug threads and exhaust system fasteners.

3 Measuring tools and gauges

Feeler gauges

● Feeler gauges (or blades) are used for measuring small gaps and clearances **(see illustration 3.1)**. They can also be used to measure endfloat (sideplay) of a component on a shaft where access is not possible with a dial gauge.

● Feeler gauge sets should be treated with care and not bent or damaged. They are etched with their size on one face. Keep them clean and very lightly oiled to prevent corrosion build-up.

3.1 Feeler gauges are used for measuring small gaps and clearances - thickness is marked on one face of gauge

● When measuring a clearance, select a gauge which is a light sliding fit between the two components. You may need to use two gauges together to measure the clearance accurately.

Micrometers

● A micrometer is a precision tool capable of measuring to 0.01 or 0.001 of a millimetre. It should always be stored in its case and not in the general toolbox. It must be kept clean and never dropped, otherwise its frame or measuring anvils could be distorted resulting in inaccurate readings.

● External micrometers are used for measuring outside diameters of components and have many more applications than internal micrometers. Micrometers are available in different size ranges, eg 0 to 25 mm, 25 to 50 mm, and upwards in 25 mm steps; some large micrometers have interchangeable anvils to allow a range of measurements to be taken. Generally the largest precision measurement you are likely to take on a motorcycle is the piston diameter.

● Internal micrometers (or bore micrometers) are used for measuring inside diameters, such as valve guides and cylinder bores. Telescoping gauges and small hole gauges are used in conjunction with an external micrometer, whereas the more expensive internal micrometers have their own measuring device.

External micrometer

Note: *The conventional analogue type instrument is described. Although much easier to read, digital micrometers are considerably more expensive.*

● Always check the calibration of the micrometer before use. With the anvils closed (0 to 25 mm type) or set over a test gauge (for

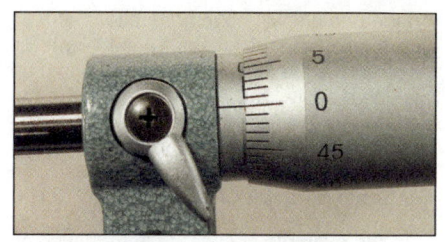

3.2 Check micrometer calibration before use

the larger types) the scale should read zero **(see illustration 3.2)**; make sure that the anvils (and test piece) are clean first. Any discrepancy can be adjusted by referring to the instructions supplied with the tool. Remember that the micrometer is a precision measuring tool - don't force the anvils closed, use the ratchet (4) on the end of the micrometer to close it. In this way, a measured force is always applied.

● To use, first make sure that the item being measured is clean. Place the anvil of the micrometer (1) against the item and use the thimble (2) to bring the spindle (3) lightly into contact with the other side of the item **(see illustration 3.3)**. Don't tighten the thimble down because this will damage the micrometer - instead use the ratchet (4) on the end of the micrometer. The ratchet mechanism applies a measured force preventing damage to the instrument.

● The micrometer is read by referring to the linear scale on the sleeve and the annular scale on the thimble. Read off the sleeve first to obtain the base measurement, then add the fine measurement from the thimble to obtain the overall reading. The linear scale on the sleeve represents the measuring range of the micrometer (eg 0 to 25 mm). The annular scale

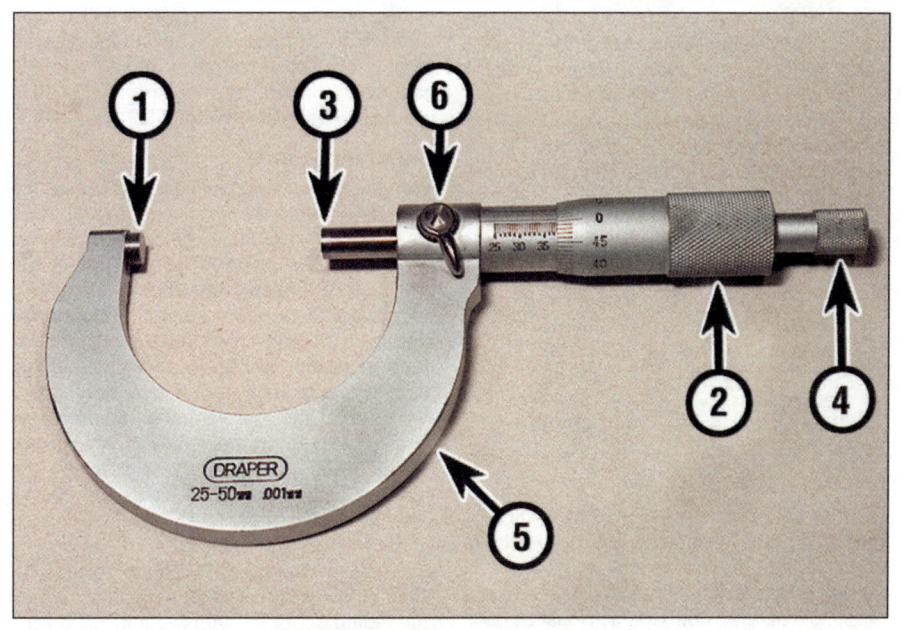

3.3 Micrometer component parts

| 1 Anvil | 3 Spindle | 5 Frame |
| 2 Thimble | 4 Ratchet | 6 Locking lever |

REF•10 Tools and Workshop Tips

on the thimble will be in graduations of 0.01 mm (or as marked on the frame) - one full revolution of the thimble will move 0.5 mm on the linear scale. Take the reading where the datum line on the sleeve intersects the thimble's scale. Always position the eye directly above the scale otherwise an inaccurate reading will result.

In the example shown the item measures 2.95 mm (see illustration 3.4):

Linear scale	2.00 mm
Linear scale	0.50 mm
Annular scale	0.45 mm
Total figure	**2.95 mm**

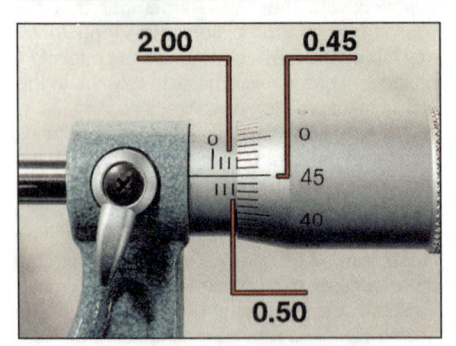

3.4 Micrometer reading of 2.95 mm

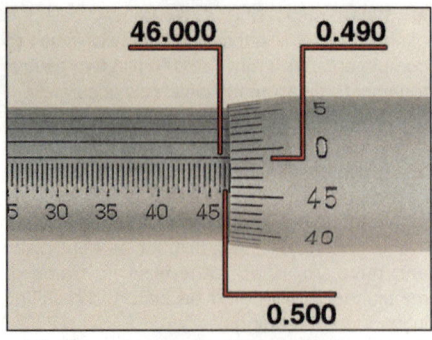

3.5 Micrometer reading of 46.99 mm on linear and annular scales . . .

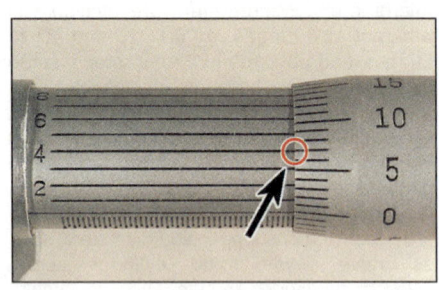

3.6 . . . and 0.004 mm on vernier scale

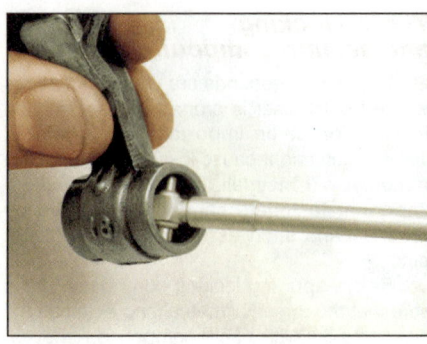

3.7 Expand the telescoping gauge in the bore, lock its position . . .

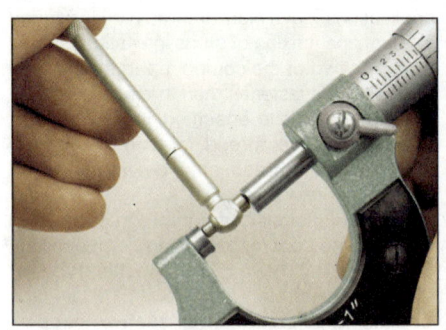

3.8 . . . then measure the gauge with a micrometer

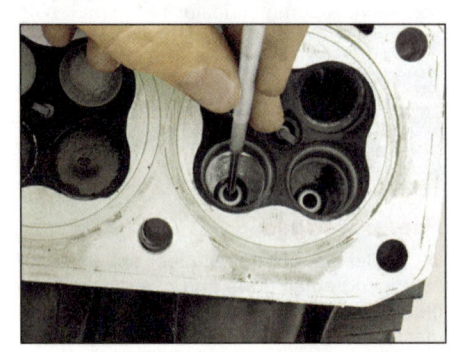

3.9 Expand the small hole gauge in the bore, lock its position . . .

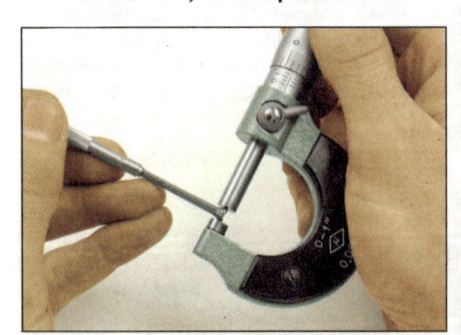

3.10 . . . then measure the gauge with a micrometer

Most micrometers have a locking lever (6) on the frame to hold the setting in place, allowing the item to be removed from the micrometer.

● Some micrometers have a vernier scale on their sleeve, providing an even finer measurement to be taken, in 0.001 increments of a millimetre. Take the sleeve and thimble measurement as described above, then check which graduation on the vernier scale aligns with that of the annular scale on the thimble **Note:** *The eye must be perpendicular to the scale when taking the vernier reading - if necessary rotate the body of the micrometer to ensure this.* Multiply the vernier scale figure by 0.001 and add it to the base and fine measurement figures.

In the example shown the item measures 46.994 mm (see illustrations 3.5 and 3.6):

Linear scale (base)	46.000 mm
Linear scale (base)	00.500 mm
Annular scale (fine)	00.490 mm
Vernier scale	00.004 mm
Total figure	**46.994 mm**

Internal micrometer

● Internal micrometers are available for measuring bore diameters, but are expensive and unlikely to be available for home use. It is suggested that a set of telescoping gauges and small hole gauges, both of which must be used with an external micrometer, will suffice for taking internal measurements on a motorcycle.

● Telescoping gauges can be used to measure internal diameters of components. Select a gauge with the correct size range, make sure its ends are clean and insert it into the bore. Expand the gauge, then lock its position and withdraw it from the bore (see illustration 3.7). Measure across the gauge ends with a micrometer (see illustration 3.8).

● Very small diameter bores (such as valve guides) are measured with a small hole gauge. Once adjusted to a slip-fit inside the component, its position is locked and the gauge withdrawn for measurement with a micrometer (see illustrations 3.9 and 3.10).

Vernier caliper

Note: *The conventional linear and dial gauge type instruments are described. Digital types are easier to read, but are far more expensive.*

● The vernier caliper does not provide the precision of a micrometer, but is versatile in being able to measure internal and external diameters. Some types also incorporate a depth gauge. It is ideal for measuring clutch plate friction material and spring free lengths.

● To use the conventional linear scale vernier, slacken off the vernier clamp screws (1) and set its jaws over (2), or inside (3), the item to be measured (see illustration 3.11). Slide the jaw into contact, using the thumbwheel (4) for fine movement of the sliding scale (5) then tighten the clamp screws (1). Read off the main scale (6) where the zero on the sliding scale (5) intersects it, taking the whole number to the left of the zero; this provides the base measurement. View along the sliding scale and select the division which lines up exactly with any of the divisions on the main scale, noting that the divisions usually represents 0.02 of a millimetre. Add this fine measurement to the base measurement to obtain the total reading.

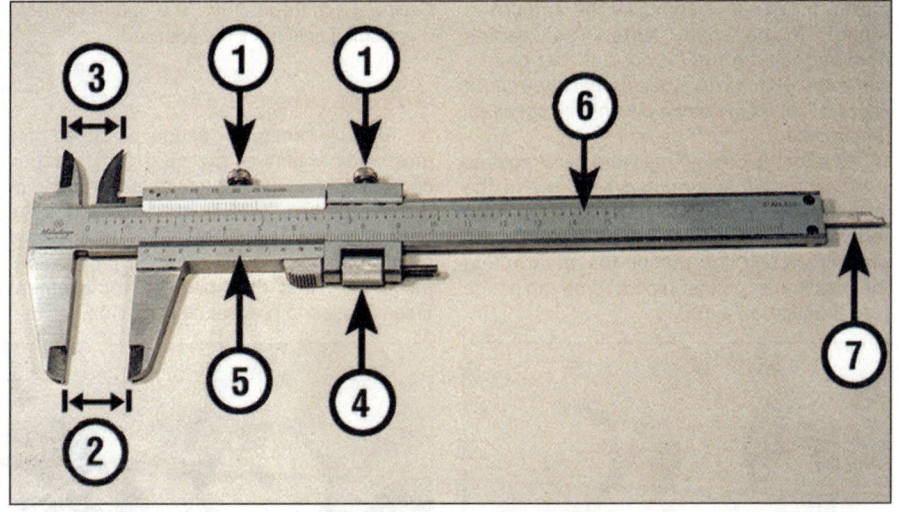

Tools and Workshop Tips REF•11

3.11 Vernier component parts (linear gauge)

1 Clamp screws
2 External jaws
3 Internal jaws
4 Thumbwheel
5 Sliding scale
6 Main scale
7 Depth gauge

In the example shown the item measures 55.92 mm **(see illustration 3.12)**:

Base measurement	55.00 mm
Fine measurement	00.92 mm
Total figure	**55.92 mm**

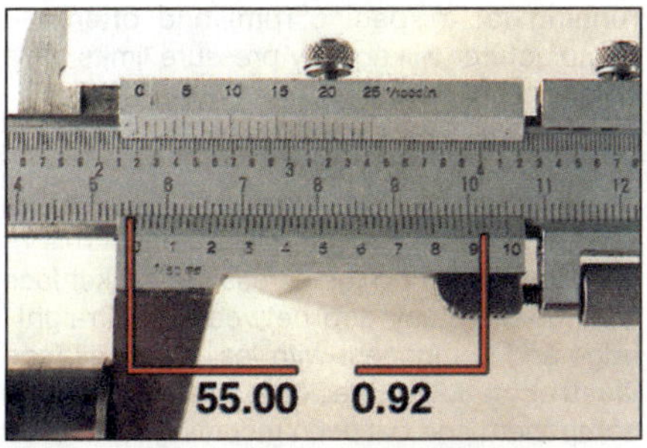

3.12 Vernier gauge reading of 55.92 mm

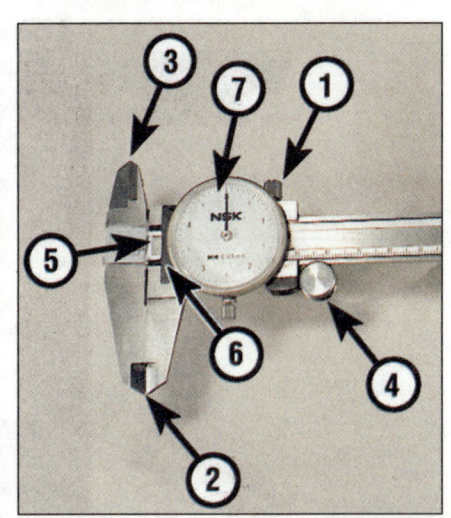

● Some vernier calipers are equipped with a dial gauge for fine measurement. Before use, check that the jaws are clean, then close them fully and check that the dial gauge reads zero. If necessary adjust the gauge ring accordingly. Slacken the vernier clamp screw (1) and set its jaws over (2), or inside (3), the item to be measured **(see illustration 3.13)**. Slide the jaws into contact, using the thumbwheel (4) for fine movement. Read off the main scale (5) where the edge of the sliding scale (6) intersects it, taking the whole number to the left of the zero; this provides the base measurement. Read off the needle position on the dial gauge (7) scale to provide the fine measurement; each division represents 0.05 of a millimetre. Add this fine measurement to the base measurement to obtain the total reading.

In the example shown the item measures 55.95 mm **(see illustration 3.14)**:

Base measurement	55.00 mm
Fine measurement	00.95 mm
Total figure	**55.95 mm**

3.13 Vernier component parts (dial gauge)

1 Clamp screw
2 External jaws
3 Internal jaws
4 Thumbwheel
5 Main scale
6 Sliding scale
7 Dial gauge

3.14 Vernier gauge reading of 55.95 mm

Plastigauge

● Plastigauge is a plastic material which can be compressed between two surfaces to measure the oil clearance between them. The width of the compressed Plastigauge is measured against a calibrated scale to determine the clearance.

● Common uses of Plastigauge are for measuring the clearance between crankshaft journal and main bearing inserts, between crankshaft journal and big-end bearing inserts, and between camshaft and bearing surfaces. The following example describes big-end oil clearance measurement.

● Handle the Plastigauge material carefully to prevent distortion. Using a sharp knife, cut a length which corresponds with the width of the bearing being measured and place it carefully across the journal so that it is parallel with the shaft **(see illustration 3.15)**. Carefully install both bearing shells and the connecting rod. Without rotating the rod on the journal tighten its bolts or nuts (as applicable) to the specified torque. The connecting rod and bearings are then disassembled and the crushed Plastigauge examined.

3.15 Plastigauge placed across shaft journal

● Using the scale provided in the Plastigauge kit, measure the width of the material to determine the oil clearance **(see illustration 3.16)**. Always remove all traces of Plastigauge after use using your fingernails.

Caution: Arriving at the correct clearance demands that the assembly is torqued correctly, according to the settings and sequence (where applicable) provided by the motorcycle manufacturer.

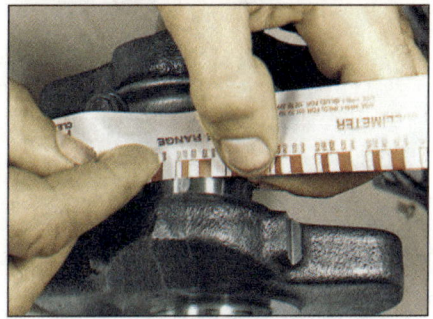

3.16 Measuring the width of the crushed Plastigauge

REF•12 Tools and Workshop Tips

Dial gauge or DTI (Dial Test Indicator)

● A dial gauge can be used to accurately measure small amounts of movement. Typical uses are measuring shaft runout or shaft endfloat (sideplay) and setting piston position for ignition timing on two-strokes. A dial gauge set usually comes with a range of different probes and adapters and mounting equipment.

● The gauge needle must point to zero when at rest. Rotate the ring around its periphery to zero the gauge.

● Check that the gauge is capable of reading the extent of movement in the work. Most gauges have a small dial set in the face which records whole millimetres of movement as well as the fine scale around the face periphery which is calibrated in 0.01 mm divisions. Read off the small dial first to obtain the base measurement, then add the measurement from the fine scale to obtain the total reading.

In the example shown the gauge reads 1.48 mm **(see illustration 3.17)**:

Base measurement	1.00 mm
Fine measurement	0.48 mm
Total figure	**1.48 mm**

3.17 Dial gauge reading of 1.48 mm

● If measuring shaft runout, the shaft must be supported in vee-blocks and the gauge mounted on a stand perpendicular to the shaft. Rest the tip of the gauge against the centre of the shaft and rotate the shaft slowly whilst watching the gauge reading **(see illustration 3.18)**. Take several measurements along the length of the shaft and record the maximum gauge reading as the amount of runout in the shaft. **Note:** *The reading obtained will be total runout at that point - some manufacturers specify that the runout figure is halved to compare with their specified runout limit.*

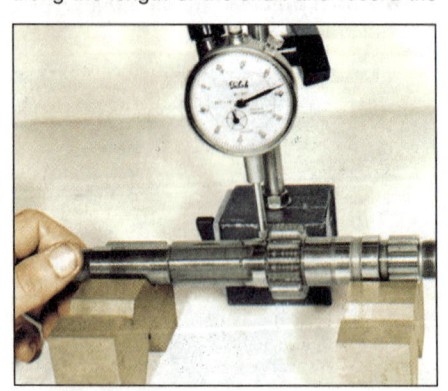

● Endfloat (sideplay) measurement requires that the gauge is mounted securely to the surrounding component with its probe touching the end of the shaft. Using hand pressure, push and pull on the shaft noting the maximum endfloat recorded on the gauge **(see illustration 3.19)**.

3.19 Using a dial gauge to measure shaft endfloat

● A dial gauge with suitable adapters can be used to determine piston position BTDC on two-stroke engines for the purposes of ignition timing. The gauge, adapter and suitable length probe are installed in the place of the spark plug and the gauge zeroed at TDC. If the piston position is specified as 1.14 mm BTDC, rotate the engine back to 2.00 mm BTDC, then slowly forwards to 1.14 mm BTDC.

Cylinder compression gauges

● A compression gauge is used for measuring cylinder compression. Either the rubber-cone type or the threaded adapter type can be used. The latter is preferred to ensure a perfect seal against the cylinder head. A 0 to 300 psi (0 to 20 Bar) type gauge (for petrol/gasoline engines) will be suitable for motorcycles.

● The spark plug is removed and the gauge either held hard against the cylinder head (cone type) or the gauge adapter screwed into the cylinder head (threaded type) **(see illustration 3.20)**. Cylinder compression is measured with the engine turning over, but not running - carry out the compression test as described in *Fault Finding Equipment*. The gauge will hold the reading until manually released.

Oil pressure gauge

● An oil pressure gauge is used for measuring engine oil pressure. Most gauges come with a set of adapters to fit the thread of the take-off point **(see illustration 3.21)**. If the take-off point specified by the motorcycle manufacturer is an external oil pipe union, make sure that the specified replacement union is used to prevent oil starvation.

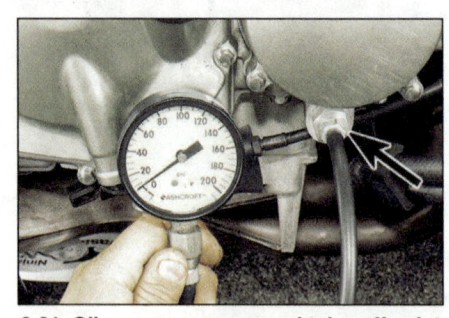

3.21 Oil pressure gauge and take-off point adapter (arrow)

● Oil pressure is measured with the engine running (at a specific rpm) and often the manufacturer will specify pressure limits for a cold and hot engine.

Straight-edge and surface plate

● If checking the gasket face of a component for warpage, place a steel rule or precision straight-edge across the gasket face and measure any gap between the straight-edge and component with feeler gauges **(see illustration 3.22)**. Check diagonally across the component and between mounting holes **(see illustration 3.23)**.

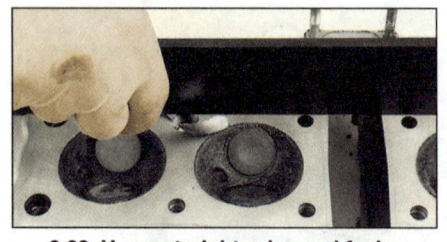

3.22 Use a straight-edge and feeler gauges to check for warpage

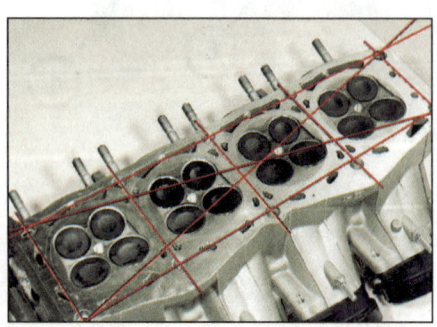

3.18 Using a dial gauge to measure shaft runout

3.20 Using a rubber-cone type cylinder compression gauge

3.23 Check for warpage in these directions

Tools and Workshop Tips REF•13

- Checking individual components for warpage, such as clutch plain (metal) plates, requires a perfectly flat plate or piece or plate glass and feeler gauges.

4 Torque and leverage

What is torque?

- Torque describes the twisting force about a shaft. The amount of torque applied is determined by the distance from the centre of the shaft to the end of the lever and the amount of force being applied to the end of the lever; distance multiplied by force equals torque.
- The manufacturer applies a measured torque to a bolt or nut to ensure that it will not slacken in use and to hold two components securely together without movement in the joint. The actual torque setting depends on the thread size, bolt or nut material and the composition of the components being held.
- Too little torque may cause the fastener to loosen due to vibration, whereas too much torque will distort the joint faces of the component or cause the fastener to shear off. Always stick to the specified torque setting.

Using a torque wrench

- Check the calibration of the torque wrench and make sure it has a suitable range for the job. Torque wrenches are available in Nm (Newton-metres), kgf m (kilograms-force metre), lbf ft (pounds-feet), lbf in (inch-pounds). Do not confuse lbf ft with lbf in.
- Adjust the tool to the desired torque on the scale (see illustration 4.1). If your torque wrench is not calibrated in the units specified, carefully convert the figure (see *Conversion Factors*). A manufacturer sometimes gives a torque setting as a range (8 to 10 Nm) rather than a single figure - in this case set the tool midway between the two settings. The same torque may be expressed as 9 Nm ± 1 Nm. Some torque wrenches have a method of locking the setting so that it isn't inadvertently altered during use.

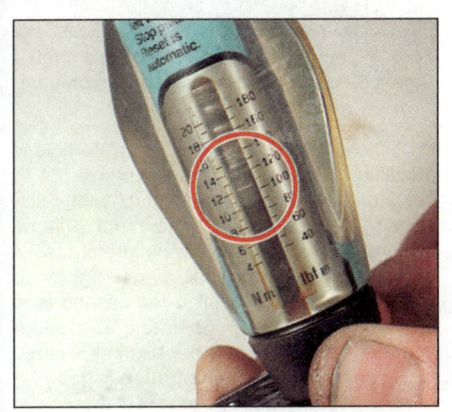

- Install the bolts/nuts in their correct location and secure them lightly. Their threads must be clean and free of any old locking compound. Unless specified the threads and flange should be dry - oiled threads are necessary in certain circumstances and the manufacturer will take this into account in the specified torque figure. Similarly, the manufacturer may also specify the application of thread-locking compound.
- Tighten the fasteners in the specified sequence until the torque wrench clicks, indicating that the torque setting has been reached. Apply the torque again to double-check the setting. Where different thread diameter fasteners secure the component, as a rule tighten the larger diameter ones first.
- When the torque wrench has been finished with, release the lock (where applicable) and fully back off its setting to zero - do not leave the torque wrench tensioned. Also, do not use a torque wrench for slackening a fastener.

Angle-tightening

- Manufacturers often specify a figure in degrees for final tightening of a fastener. This usually follows tightening to a specific torque setting.
- A degree disc can be set and attached to the socket (see illustration 4.2) or a protractor can be used to mark the angle of movement on the bolt/nut head and the surrounding casting (see illustration 4.3).

4.2 Angle tightening can be accomplished with a torque-angle gauge . . .

4.1 Set the torque wrench index mark to the setting required, in this case 12 Nm

4.3 . . . or by marking the angle on the surrounding component

Loosening sequences

- Where more than one bolt/nut secures a component, loosen each fastener evenly a little at a time. In this way, not all the stress of the joint is held by one fastener and the components are not likely to distort.
- If a tightening sequence is provided, work in the REVERSE of this, but if not, work from the outside in, in a criss-cross sequence (see illustration 4.4).

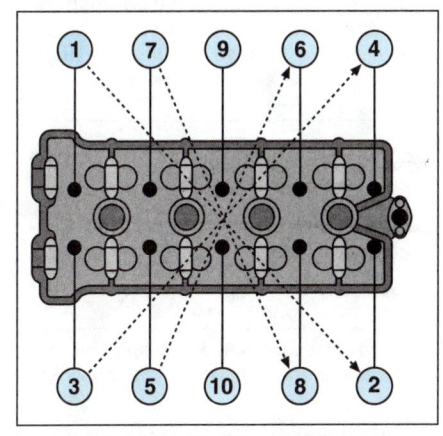

4.4 When slackening, work from the outside inwards

Tightening sequences

- If a component is held by more than one fastener it is important that the retaining bolts/nuts are tightened evenly to prevent uneven stress build-up and distortion of sealing faces. This is especially important on high-compression joints such as the cylinder head.
- A sequence is usually provided by the manufacturer, either in a diagram or actually marked in the casting. If not, always start in the centre and work outwards in a criss-cross pattern (see illustration 4.5). Start off by securing all bolts/nuts finger-tight, then set the torque wrench and tighten each fastener by a small amount in sequence until the final torque is reached. By following this practice,

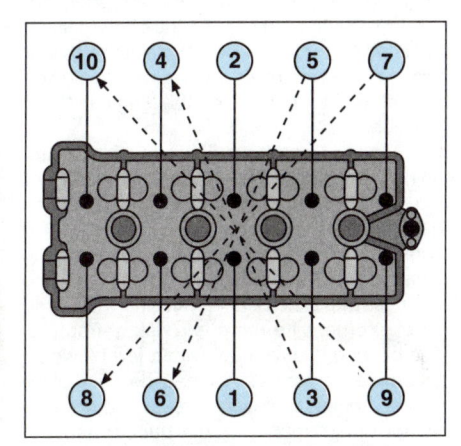

4.5 When tightening, work from the inside outwards

Tools and Workshop Tips

the joint will be held evenly and will not be distorted. Important joints, such as the cylinder head and big-end fasteners often have two- or three-stage torque settings.

Applying leverage

● Use tools at the correct angle. Position a socket wrench or spanner on the bolt/nut so that you pull it towards you when loosening. If this can't be done, push the spanner without curling your fingers around it **(see illustration 4.6)** - the spanner may slip or the fastener loosen suddenly, resulting in your fingers being crushed against a component.

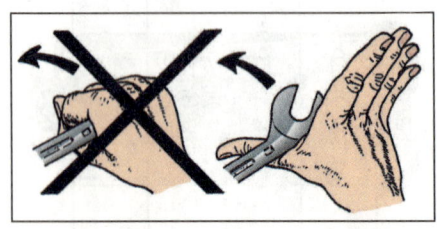

4.6 If you can't pull on the spanner to loosen a fastener, push with your hand open

● Additional leverage is gained by extending the length of the lever. The best way to do this is to use a breaker bar instead of the regular length tool, or to slip a length of tubing over the end of the spanner or socket wrench.
● If additional leverage will not work, the fastener head is either damaged or firmly corroded in place (see *Fasteners*).

5 Bearings

Bearing removal and installation
Drivers and sockets

● Before removing a bearing, always inspect the casing to see which way it must be driven out - some casings will have retaining plates or a cast step. Also check for any identifying markings on the bearing and if installed to a certain depth, measure this at this stage. Some roller bearings are sealed on one side - take note of the original fitted position.
● Bearings can be driven out of a casing using a bearing driver tool (with the correct size head) or a socket of the correct diameter. Select the driver head or socket so that it contacts the outer race of the bearing, not the balls/rollers or inner race. Always support the casing around the bearing housing with wood blocks, otherwise there is a risk of fracture. The bearing is driven out with a few blows on the driver or socket from a heavy mallet. Unless access is severely restricted (as with wheel bearings), a pin-punch is not recommended unless it is moved around the bearing to keep it square in its housing.

● The same equipment can be used to install bearings. Make sure the bearing housing is supported on wood blocks and line up the bearing in its housing. Fit the bearing as noted on removal - generally they are installed with their marked side facing outwards. Tap the bearing squarely into its housing using a driver or socket which bears only on the bearing's outer race - contact with the bearing balls/rollers or inner race will destroy it **(see illustrations 5.1 and 5.2)**.
● Check that the bearing inner race and balls/rollers rotate freely.

5.1 Using a bearing driver against the bearing's outer race

5.2 Using a large socket against the bearing's outer race

Pullers and slide-hammers

● Where a bearing is pressed on a shaft a puller will be required to extract it **(see illustration 5.3)**. Make sure that the puller clamp or legs fit securely behind the bearing and are unlikely to slip out. If pulling a bearing

5.3 This bearing puller clamps behind the bearing and pressure is applied to the shaft end to draw the bearing off

off a gear shaft for example, you may have to locate the puller behind a gear pinion if there is no access to the race and draw the gear pinion off the shaft as well **(see illustration 5.4)**.

Caution: Ensure that the puller's centre bolt locates securely against the end of the shaft and will not slip when pressure is applied. Also ensure that puller does not damage the shaft end.

5.4 Where no access is available to the rear of the bearing, it is sometimes possible to draw off the adjacent component

● Operate the puller so that its centre bolt exerts pressure on the shaft end and draws the bearing off the shaft.
● When installing the bearing on the shaft, tap only on the bearing's inner race - contact with the balls/rollers or outer race with destroy the bearing. Use a socket or length of tubing as a drift which fits over the shaft end **(see illustration 5.5)**.

5.5 When installing a bearing on a shaft use a piece of tubing which bears only on the bearing's inner race

● Where a bearing locates in a blind hole in a casing, it cannot be driven or pulled out as described above. A slide-hammer with knife-edged bearing puller attachment will be required. The puller attachment passes through the bearing and when tightened expands to fit firmly behind the bearing **(see illustration 5.6)**. By operating the slide-hammer part of the tool the bearing is jarred out of its housing **(see illustration 5.7)**.
● It is possible, if the bearing is of reasonable weight, for it to drop out of its housing if the casing is heated as described opposite. If this

Tools and Workshop Tips   REF•15

5.6 Expand the bearing puller so that it locks behind the bearing . . .

5.7 . . . attach the slide hammer to the bearing puller

method is attempted, first prepare a work surface which will enable the casing to be tapped face down to help dislodge the bearing - a wood surface is ideal since it will not damage the casing's gasket surface. Wearing protective gloves, tap the heated casing several times against the work surface to dislodge the bearing under its own weight **(see illustration 5.8)**.

5.8 Tapping a casing face down on wood blocks can often dislodge a bearing

● Bearings can be installed in blind holes using the driver or socket method described above.

Drawbolts

● Where a bearing or bush is set in the eye of a component, such as a suspension linkage arm or connecting rod small-end, removal by drift may damage the component. Furthermore, a rubber bushing in a shock absorber eye cannot successfully be driven out of position. If access is available to a engineering press, the task is straightforward. If not, a drawbolt can be fabricated to extract the bearing or bush.

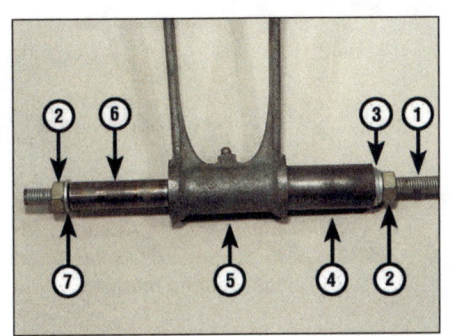

5.9 Drawbolt component parts assembled on a suspension arm

1 Bolt or length of threaded bar
2 Nuts
3 Washer (external diameter greater than tubing internal diameter)
4 Tubing (internal diameter sufficient to accommodate bearing)
5 Suspension arm with bearing
6 Tubing (external diameter slightly smaller than bearing)
7 Washer (external diameter slightly smaller than bearing)

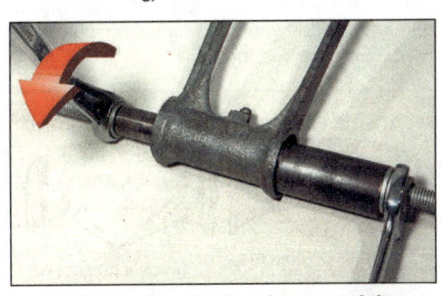

5.10 Drawing the bearing out of the suspension arm

● To extract the bearing/bush you will need a long bolt with nut (or piece of threaded bar with two nuts), a piece of tubing which has an internal diameter larger than the bearing/bush, another piece of tubing which has an external diameter slightly smaller than the bearing/bush, and a selection of washers **(see illustrations 5.9 and 5.10)**. Note that the pieces of tubing must be of the same length, or longer, than the bearing/bush.
● The same kit (without the pieces of tubing) can be used to draw the new bearing/bush back into place **(see illustration 5.11)**.

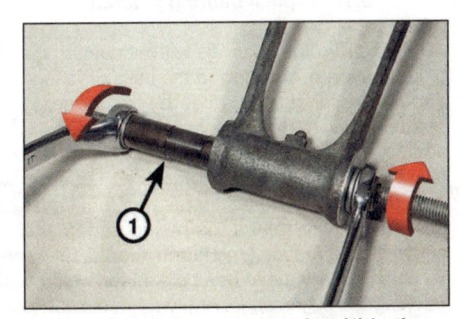

5.11 Installing a new bearing (1) in the suspension arm

Temperature change

● If the bearing's outer race is a tight fit in the casing, the aluminium casing can be heated to release its grip on the bearing. Aluminium will expand at a greater rate than the steel bearing outer race. There are several ways to do this, but avoid any localised extreme heat (such as a blow torch) - aluminium alloy has a low melting point.
● Approved methods of heating a casing are using a domestic oven (heated to 100°C) or immersing the casing in boiling water **(see illustration 5.12)**. Low temperature range localised heat sources such as a paint stripper heat gun or clothes iron can also be used **(see illustration 5.13)**. Alternatively, soak a rag in boiling water, wring it out and wrap it around the bearing housing.

> ⚠ **Warning: All of these methods require care in use to prevent scalding and burns to the hands. Wear protective gloves when handling hot components.**

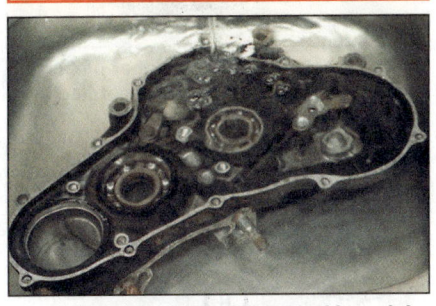

5.12 A casing can be immersed in a sink of boiling water to aid bearing removal

5.13 Using a localised heat source to aid bearing removal

● If heating the whole casing note that plastic components, such as the neutral switch, may suffer - remove them beforehand.
● After heating, remove the bearing as described above. You may find that the expansion is sufficient for the bearing to fall out of the casing under its own weight or with a light tap on the driver or socket.
● If necessary, the casing can be heated to aid bearing installation, and this is sometimes the recommended procedure if the motorcycle manufacturer has designed the housing and bearing fit with this intention.

REF•16 Tools and Workshop Tips

- Installation of bearings can be eased by placing them in a freezer the night before installation. The steel bearing will contract slightly, allowing easy insertion in its housing. This is often useful when installing steering head outer races in the frame.

Bearing types and markings

- Plain shell bearings, ball bearings, needle roller bearings and tapered roller bearings will all be found on motorcycles **(see illustrations 5.14 and 5.15)**. The ball and roller types are usually caged between an inner and outer race, but uncaged variations may be found.

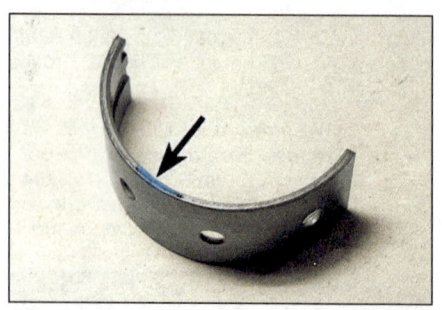

5.14 Shell bearings are either plain or grooved. They are usually identified by colour code (arrow)

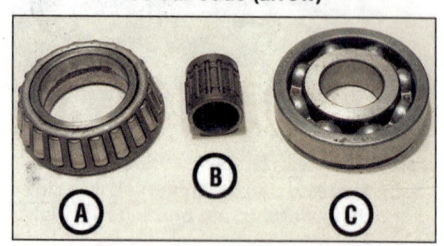

5.15 Tapered roller bearing (A), needle roller bearing (B) and ball journal bearing (C)

- Shell bearings (often called inserts) are usually found at the crankshaft main and connecting rod big-end where they are good at coping with high loads. They are made of a phosphor-bronze material and are impregnated with self-lubricating properties.
- Ball bearings and needle roller bearings consist of a steel inner and outer race with the balls or rollers between the races. They require constant lubrication by oil or grease and are good at coping with axial loads. Taper roller bearings consist of rollers set in a tapered cage set on the inner race; the outer race is separate. They are good at coping with axial loads and prevent movement along the shaft - a typical application is in the steering head.
- Bearing manufacturers produce bearings to ISO size standards and stamp one face of the bearing to indicate its internal and external diameter, load capacity and type **(see illustration 5.16)**.
- Metal bushes are usually of phosphor-bronze material. Rubber bushes are used in suspension mounting eyes. Fibre bushes have also been used in suspension pivots.

5.16 Typical bearing marking

Bearing fault finding

- If a bearing outer race has spun in its housing, the housing material will be damaged. You can use a bearing locking compound to bond the outer race in place if damage is not too severe.
- Shell bearings will fail due to damage of their working surface, as a result of lack of lubrication, corrosion or abrasive particles in the oil **(see illustration 5.17)**. Small particles of dirt in the oil may embed in the bearing material whereas larger particles will score the bearing and shaft journal. If a number of short journeys are made, insufficient heat will be generated to drive off condensation which has built up on the bearings.

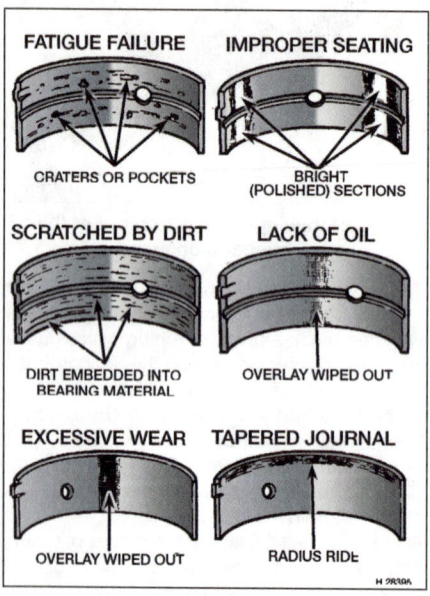

5.17 Typical bearing failures

- Ball and roller bearings will fail due to lack of lubrication or damage to the balls or rollers. Tapered-roller bearings can be damaged by overloading them. Unless the bearing is sealed on both sides, wash it in paraffin (kerosene) to remove all old grease then allow it to dry. Make a visual inspection looking to dented balls or rollers, damaged cages and worn or pitted races **(see illustration 5.18)**.
- A ball bearing can be checked for wear by listening to it when spun. Apply a film of light oil to the bearing and hold it close to the ear - hold the outer race with one hand and spin the inner race with the other hand **(see illustration 5.19)**. The bearing should be almost silent when spun; if it grates or rattles it is worn.

5.18 Example of ball journal bearing with damaged balls and cages

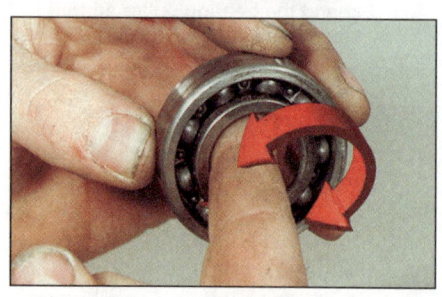

5.19 Hold outer race and listen to inner race when spun

6 Oil seals

Oil seal removal and installation

- Oil seals should be renewed every time a component is dismantled. This is because the seal lips will become set to the sealing surface and will not necessarily reseal.
- Oil seals can be prised out of position using a large flat-bladed screwdriver **(see illustration 6.1)**. In the case of crankcase seals, check first that the seal is not lipped on the inside, preventing its removal with the crankcases joined.

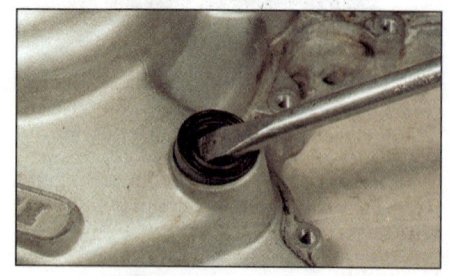

6.1 Prise out oil seals with a large flat-bladed screwdriver

- New seals are usually installed with their marked face (containing the seal reference code) outwards and the spring side towards the fluid being retained. In certain cases, such as a two-stroke engine crankshaft seal, a double lipped seal may be used due to there being fluid or gas on each side of the joint.

Tools and Workshop Tips REF•17

● Use a bearing driver or socket which bears only on the outer hard edge of the seal to install it in the casing - tapping on the inner edge will damage the sealing lip.

Oil seal types and markings

● Oil seals are usually of the single-lipped type. Double-lipped seals are found where a liquid or gas is on both sides of the joint.
● Oil seals can harden and lose their sealing ability if the motorcycle has been in storage for a long period - renewal is the only solution.
● Oil seal manufacturers also conform to the ISO markings for seal size - these are moulded into the outer face of the seal (see illustration 6.2).

6.2 These oil seal markings indicate inside diameter, outside diameter and seal thickness

7 Gaskets and sealants

Types of gasket and sealant

● Gaskets are used to seal the mating surfaces between components and keep lubricants, fluids, vacuum or pressure contained within the assembly. Aluminium gaskets are sometimes found at the cylinder joints, but most gaskets are paper-based. If the mating surfaces of the components being joined are undamaged the gasket can be installed dry, although a dab of sealant or grease will be useful to hold it in place during assembly.
● RTV (Room Temperature Vulcanising) silicone rubber sealants cure when exposed to moisture in the atmosphere. These sealants are good at filling pits or irregular gasket faces, but will tend to be forced out of the joint under very high torque. They can be used to replace a paper gasket, but first make sure that the width of the paper gasket is not essential to the shimming of internal components. RTV sealants should not be used on components containing petrol (gasoline).
● Non-hardening, semi-hardening and hard setting liquid gasket compounds can be used with a gasket or between a metal-to-metal joint. Select the sealant to suit the application: universal non-hardening sealant can be used on virtually all joints; semi-hardening on joint faces which are rough or damaged; hard setting sealant on joints which require a permanent bond and are subjected to high temperature and pressure. **Note:** *Check first if the paper gasket has a bead of sealant impregnated in its surface before applying additional sealant.*
● When choosing a sealant, make sure it is suitable for the application, particularly if being applied in a high-temperature area or in the vicinity of fuel. Certain manufacturers produce sealants in either clear, silver or black colours to match the finish of the engine. This has a particular application on motorcycles where much of the engine is exposed.
● Do not over-apply sealant. That which is squeezed out on the outside of the joint can be wiped off, whereas an excess of sealant on the inside can break off and clog oilways.

Breaking a sealed joint

● Age, heat, pressure and the use of hard setting sealant can cause two components to stick together so tightly that they are difficult to separate using finger pressure alone. Do not resort to using levers unless there is a pry point provided for this purpose (see illustration 7.1) or else the gasket surfaces will be damaged.
● Use a soft-faced hammer (see illustration 7.2) or a wood block and conventional hammer to strike the component near the mating surface. Avoid hammering against cast extremities since they may break off. If this method fails, try using a wood wedge between the two components.

Caution: If the joint will not separate, double-check that you have removed all the fasteners.

7.1 If a pry point is provided, apply gently pressure with a flat-bladed screwdriver

7.2 Tap around the joint with a soft-faced mallet if necessary - don't strike cooling fins

Removal of old gasket and sealant

● Paper gaskets will most likely come away complete, leaving only a few traces stuck on

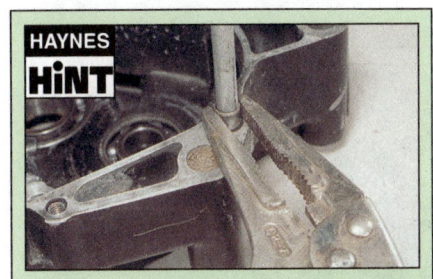

> **HAYNES HiNT**
>
> *Most components have one or two hollow locating dowels between the two gasket faces. If a dowel cannot be removed, do not resort to gripping it with pliers - it will almost certainly be distorted. Install a close-fitting socket or Phillips screwdriver into the dowel and then grip the outer edge of the dowel to free it.*

the sealing faces of the components. It is imperative that all traces are removed to ensure correct sealing of the new gasket.
● Very carefully scrape all traces of gasket away making sure that the sealing surfaces are not gouged or scored by the scraper (see illustrations 7.3, 7.4 and 7.5). Stubborn deposits can be removed by spraying with an aerosol gasket remover. Final preparation of

7.3 Paper gaskets can be scraped off with a gasket scraper tool . . .

7.4 . . . a knife blade . . .

7.5 . . . or a household scraper

REF•18 Tools and Workshop Tips

7.6 Fine abrasive paper is wrapped around a flat file to clean up the gasket face

7.7 A kitchen scourer can be used on stubborn deposits

8.1 Tighten the chain breaker to push the pin out of the link . . .

8.2 . . . withdraw the pin, remove the tool . . .

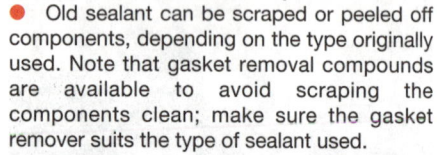

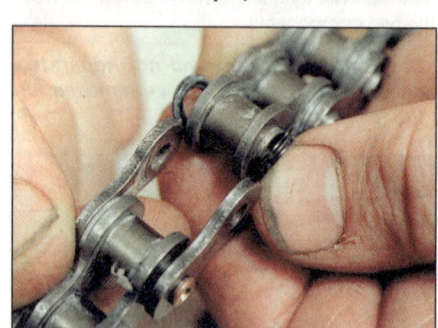

8.3 . . . and separate the chain link

8.4 Insert the new soft link, with O-rings, through the chain ends . . .

8.5 . . . install the O-rings over the pin ends . . .

8.6 . . . followed by the sideplate

8.7 Push the sideplate into position using a clamp

the gasket surface can be made with very fine abrasive paper or a plastic kitchen scourer **(see illustrations 7.6 and 7.7)**.

● Old sealant can be scraped or peeled off components, depending on the type originally used. Note that gasket removal compounds are available to avoid scraping the components clean; make sure the gasket remover suits the type of sealant used.

8 Chains

Breaking and joining final drive chains

● Drive chains for all but small bikes are continuous and do not have a clip-type connecting link. The chain must be broken using a chain breaker tool and the new chain securely riveted together using a new soft rivet-type link. Never use a clip-type connecting link instead of a rivet-type link, except in an emergency. Various chain breaking and riveting tools are available, either as separate tools or combined as illustrated in the accompanying photographs - read the instructions supplied with the tool carefully.

> **Warning:** The need to rivet the new link pins correctly cannot be overstressed - loss of control of the motorcycle is very likely to result if the chain breaks in use.

● Rotate the chain and look for the soft link. The soft link pins look like they have been deeply centre-punched instead of peened over like all the other pins **(see illustration 8.9)** and its sideplate may be a different colour. Position the soft link midway between the sprockets and assemble the chain breaker tool over one of the soft link pins **(see illustration 8.1)**. Operate the tool to push the pin out through the chain **(see illustration 8.2)**. On an O-ring chain, remove the O-rings **(see illustration 8.3)**. Carry out the same procedure on the other soft link pin.

> **Caution: Certain soft link pins (particularly on the larger chains) may require their ends to be filed or ground off before they can be pressed out using the tool.**

● Check that you have the correct size and strength (standard or heavy duty) new soft link - do not reuse the old link. Look for the size marking on the chain sideplates **(see illustration 8.10)**.

● Position the chain ends so that they are engaged over the rear sprocket. On an O-ring chain, install a new O-ring over each pin of the link and insert the link through the two chain ends **(see illustration 8.4)**. Install a new O-ring over the end of each pin, followed by the sideplate (with the chain manufacturer's marking facing outwards) **(see illustrations 8.5 and 8.6)**. On an unsealed chain, insert the link through the two chain ends, then install the sideplate with the chain manufacturer's marking facing outwards.

● Note that it may not be possible to install the sideplate using finger pressure alone. If using a joining tool, assemble it so that the plates of the tool clamp the link and press the sideplate over the pins **(see illustration 8.7)**. Otherwise, use two small sockets placed over

Tools and Workshop Tips REF•19

8.8 Assemble the chain riveting tool over one pin at a time and tighten it fully

8.9 Pin end correctly riveted (A), pin end unriveted (B)

the rivet ends and two pieces of the wood between a G-clamp. Operate the clamp to press the sideplate over the pins.
● Assemble the joining tool over one pin (following the maker's instructions) and tighten the tool down to spread the pin end securely **(see illustrations 8.8 and 8.9)**. Do the same on the other pin.

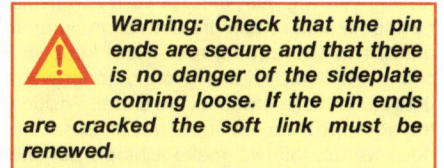

> **Warning: Check that the pin ends are secure and that there is no danger of the sideplate coming loose. If the pin ends are cracked the soft link must be renewed.**

Final drive chain sizing

● Chains are sized using a three digit number, followed by a suffix to denote the chain type **(see illustration 8.10)**. Chain type is either standard or heavy duty (thicker sideplates), and also unsealed or O-ring/X-ring type.
● The first digit of the number relates to the pitch of the chain, ie the distance from the centre of one pin to the centre of the next pin **(see illustration 8.11)**. Pitch is expressed in eighths of an inch, as follows:

8.10 Typical chain size and type marking

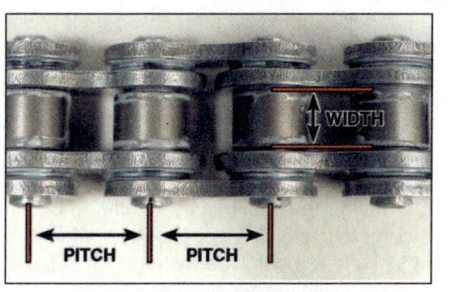

8.11 Chain dimensions

> Sizes commencing with a 4 (eg 428) have a pitch of 1/2 inch (12.7 mm)
> Sizes commencing with a 5 (eg 520) have a pitch of 5/8 inch (15.9 mm)
> Sizes commencing with a 6 (eg 630) have a pitch of 3/4 inch (19.1 mm)

● The second and third digits of the chain size relate to the width of the rollers, again in imperial units, eg the 525 shown has 5/16 inch (7.94 mm) rollers **(see illustration 8.11)**.

9 Hoses

Clamping to prevent flow

● Small-bore flexible hoses can be clamped to prevent fluid flow whilst a component is worked on. Whichever method is used, ensure that the hose material is not permanently distorted or damaged by the clamp.
a) A brake hose clamp available from auto accessory shops **(see illustration 9.1)**.
b) A wingnut type hose clamp **(see illustration 9.2)**.
c) Two sockets placed each side of the hose and held with straight-jawed self-locking grips **(see illustration 9.3)**.
d) Thick card each side of the hose held between straight-jawed self-locking grips **(see illustration 9.4)**.

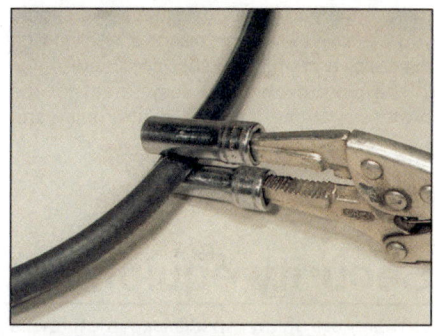

9.1 Hoses can be clamped with an automotive brake hose clamp . . .

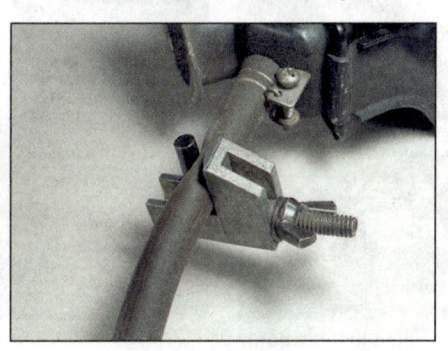

9.2 . . . a wingnut type hose clamp . . .

9.3 . . . two sockets and a pair of self-locking grips . . .

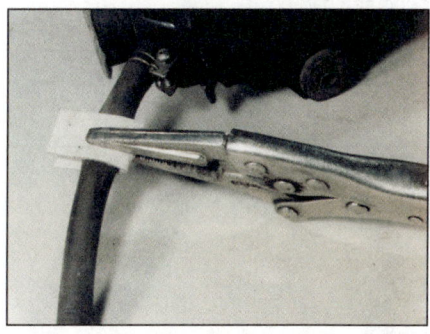

9.4 . . . or thick card and self-locking grips

Freeing and fitting hoses

● Always make sure the hose clamp is moved well clear of the hose end. Grip the hose with your hand and rotate it whilst pulling it off the union. If the hose has hardened due to age and will not move, slit it with a sharp knife and peel its ends off the union **(see illustration 9.5)**.
● Resist the temptation to use grease or soap on the unions to aid installation; although it helps the hose slip over the union it will equally aid the escape of fluid from the joint. It is preferable to soften the hose ends in hot water and wet the inside surface of the hose with water or a fluid which will evaporate.

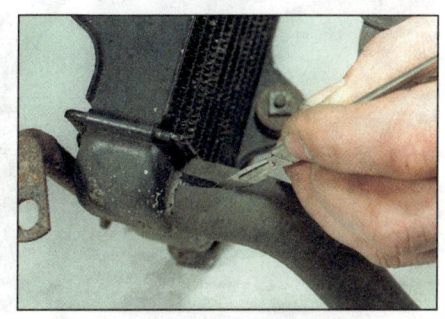

9.5 Cutting a coolant hose free with a sharp knife

REF•20 Security

Introduction

In less time than it takes to read this introduction, a thief could steal your motorcycle. Returning only to find your bike has gone is one of the worst feelings in the world. Even if the motorcycle is insured against theft, once you've got over the initial shock, you will have the inconvenience of dealing with the police and your insurance company.

The motorcycle is an easy target for the professional thief and the joyrider alike and the official figures on motorcycle theft make for depressing reading; on average a motorcycle is stolen every 16 minutes in the UK!

Motorcycle thefts fall into two categories, those stolen 'to order' and those taken by opportunists. The thief stealing to order will be on the look out for a specific make and model and will go to extraordinary lengths to obtain that motorcycle. The opportunist thief on the other hand will look for easy targets which can be stolen with the minimum of effort and risk.

Whilst it is never going to be possible to make your machine 100% secure, it is estimated that around half of all stolen motorcycles are taken by opportunist thieves. Remember that the opportunist thief is always on the look out for the easy option: if there are two similar motorcycles parked side-by-side, they will target the one with the lowest level of security. By taking a few precautions, you can reduce the chances of your motorcycle being stolen.

Security equipment

There are many specialised motorcycle security devices available and the following text summarises their applications and their good and bad points.

Once you have decided on the type of security equipment which best suits your needs, we recommended that you read one of the many equipment tests regularly carried out by the motorcycle press. These tests compare the products from all the major manufacturers and give impartial ratings on their effectiveness, value-for-money and ease of use.

No one item of security equipment can provide complete protection. It is highly recommended that two or more of the items described below are combined to increase the security of your motorcycle (a lock and chain plus an alarm system is just about ideal). The more security measures fitted to the bike, the less likely it is to be stolen.

Lock and chain

Pros: *Very flexible to use; can be used to secure the motorcycle to almost any immovable object. On some locks and chains, the lock can be used on its own as a disc lock (see below).*

Cons: *Can be very heavy and awkward to carry on the motorcycle, although some types will be supplied with a carry bag which can be strapped to the pillion seat.*

● Heavy-duty chains and locks are an excellent security measure **(see illustration 1)**. Whenever the motorcycle is parked, use the lock and chain to secure the machine to a solid, immovable object such as a post or railings. This will prevent the machine from being ridden away or being lifted into the back of a van.

● When fitting the chain, always ensure the chain is routed around the motorcycle frame or swingarm **(see illustrations 2 and 3)**. Never merely pass the chain around one of the wheel rims; a thief may unbolt the wheel and lift the rest of the machine into a van, leaving you with just the wheel! Try to avoid having excess chain free, thus making it difficult to use cutting tools, and keep the chain and lock off the ground to prevent thieves attacking it with a cold chisel. Position the lock so that its lock barrel is facing downwards; this will make it harder for the thief to attack the lock mechanism.

1 Ensure the lock and chain you buy is of good quality and long enough to shackle your bike to a solid object

2 Pass the chain through the bike's frame, rather than just through a wheel . . .

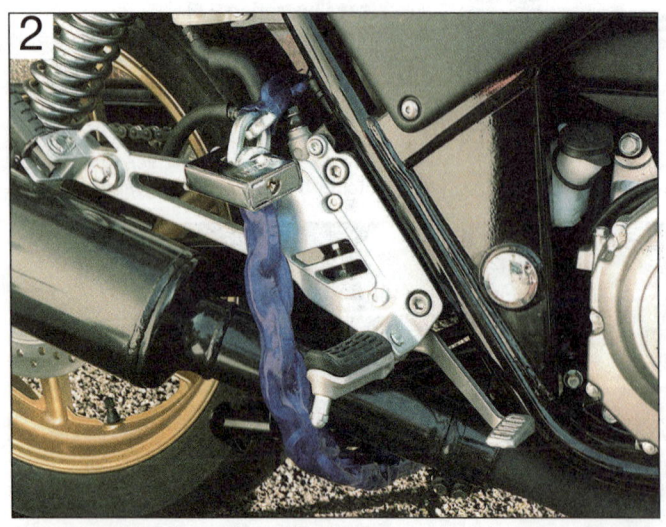

3 . . . and loop it around a solid object

Security REF•21

U-locks

Pros: *Highly effective deterrent which can be used to secure the bike to a post or railings. Most U-locks come with a carrier which allows the lock to be easily carried on the bike.*

Cons: *Not as flexible to use as a lock and chain.*

● These are solid locks which are similar in use to a lock and chain. U-locks are lighter than a lock and chain but not so flexible to use. The length and shape of the lock shackle limit the objects to which the bike can be secured **(see illustration 4)**.

U-locks can be used to secure the bike to a solid object – ensure you purchase one which is long enough

Disc locks

Pros: *Small, light and very easy to carry; most can be stored underneath the seat.*

Cons: *Does not prevent the motorcycle being lifted into a van. Can be very embarrassing if you forget to remove the lock before attempting to ride off!*

● Disc locks are designed to be attached to the front brake disc. The lock passes through one of the holes in the disc and prevents the wheel rotating by jamming against the fork/brake caliper **(see illustration 5)**. Some are equipped with an alarm siren which sounds if the disc lock is moved; this not only acts as a theft deterrent but also as a handy reminder if you try to move the bike with the lock still fitted.

● Combining the disc lock with a length of cable which can be looped around a post or railings provides an additional measure of security **(see illustration 6)**.

A typical disc lock attached through one of the holes in the disc

Alarms and immobilisers

Pros: *Once installed it is completely hassle-free to use. If the system is 'Thatcham' or 'Sold Secure-approved', insurance companies may give you a discount.*

Cons: *Can be expensive to buy and complex to install. No system will prevent the motorcycle from being lifted into a van and taken away.*

● Electronic alarms and immobilisers are available to suit a variety of budgets. There are three different types of system available: pure alarms, pure immobilisers, and the more expensive systems which are combined alarm/immobilisers **(see illustration 7)**.

● An alarm system is designed to emit an audible warning if the motorcycle is being tampered with.

● An immobiliser prevents the motorcycle being started and ridden away by disabling its electrical systems.

● When purchasing an alarm/immobiliser system, check the cost of installing the system unless you are able to do it yourself. If the motorcycle is not used regularly, another consideration is the current drain of the system. All alarm/immobiliser systems are powered by the motorcycle's battery; purchasing a system with a very low current drain could prevent the battery losing its charge whilst the motorcycle is not being used.

A disc lock combined with a security cable provides additional protection

A typical alarm/immobiliser system

REF•22 Security

Indelible markings can be applied to most areas of the bike – always apply the manufacturer's sticker to warn off thieves

Chemically-etched code numbers can be applied to main body panels . . .

. . . again, always ensure that the kit manufacturer's sticker is applied in a prominent position

Security marking kits

Pros: *Very cheap and effective deterrent. Many insurance companies will give you a discount on your insurance premium if a recognised security marking kit is used on your motorcycle.*

Cons: *Does not prevent the motorcycle being stolen by joyriders.*

● There are many different types of security marking kits available. The idea is to mark as many parts of the motorcycle as possible with a unique security number **(see illustrations 8, 9 and 10)**. A form will be included with the kit to register your personal details and those of the motorcycle with the kit manufacturer. This register is made available to the police to help them trace the rightful owner of any motorcycle or components which they recover should all other forms of identification have been removed. Always apply the warning stickers provided with the kit to deter thieves.

Ground anchors, wheel clamps and security posts

Pros: *An excellent form of security which will deter all but the most determined of thieves.*

Cons: *Awkward to install and can be expensive.*

● Whilst the motorcycle is at home, it is a good idea to attach it securely to the floor or a solid wall, even if it is kept in a securely locked garage. Various types of ground anchors, security posts and wheel clamps are available for this purpose **(see illustration 11)**. These security devices are either bolted to a solid concrete or brick structure or can be cemented into the ground.

Permanent ground anchors provide an excellent level of security when the bike is at home

Security at home

A high percentage of motorcycle thefts are from the owner's home. Here are some things to consider whenever your motorcycle is at home:

✔ Where possible, always keep the motorcycle in a securely locked garage. Never rely solely on the standard lock on the garage door, these are usual hopelessly inadequate. Fit an additional locking mechanism to the door and consider having the garage alarmed. A security light, activated by a movement sensor, is also a good investment.

✔ Always secure the motorcycle to the ground or a wall, even if it is inside a securely locked garage.

✔ Do not regularly leave the motorcycle outside your home, try to keep it out of sight wherever possible. If a garage is not available, fit a motorcycle cover over the bike to disguise its true identity.

✔ It is not uncommon for thieves to follow a motorcyclist home to find out where the bike is kept. They will then return at a later date. Be aware of this whenever you are returning home on your motorcycle. If you suspect you are being followed, do not return home, instead ride to a garage or shop and stop as a precaution.

✔ When selling a motorcycle, do not provide your home address or the location where the bike is normally kept. Arrange to meet the buyer at a location away from your home. Thieves have been known to pose as potential buyers to find out where motorcycles are kept and then return later to steal them.

Security away from the home

As well as fitting security equipment to your motorcycle here are a few general rules to follow whenever you park your motorcycle.

✔ Park in a busy, public place.

✔ Use car parks which incorporate security features, such as CCTV.

✔ At night, park in a well-lit area, preferably directly underneath a street light.

✔ Engage the steering lock.

✔ Secure the motorcycle to a solid, immovable object such as a post or railings with an additional lock. If this is not possible, secure the bike to a friend's motorcycle. Some public parking places provide security loops for motorcycles.

✔ Never leave your helmet or luggage attached to the motorcycle. Take them with you at all times.

Lubricants and fluids

A wide range of lubricants, fluids and cleaning agents is available for motor-cycles. This is a guide as to what is available, its applications and properties.

Four-stroke engine oil

- Engine oil is without doubt the most important component of any four-stroke engine. Modern motorcycle engines place a lot of demands on their oil and choosing the right type is essential. Using an unsuitable oil will lead to an increased rate of engine wear and could result in serious engine damage. Before purchasing oil, always check the recommended oil specification given by the manufacturer. The manufacturer will state a recommended 'type or classification' and also a specific 'viscosity' range for engine oil.
- The oil 'type or classification' is identified by its API (American Petroleum Institute) rating. The API rating will be in the form of two letters, e.g. SG. The S identifies the oil as being suitable for use in a petrol (gasoline) engine (S stands for spark ignition) and the second letter, ranging from A to J, identifies the oil's performance rating. The later this letter, the higher the specification of the oil; for example API SG oil exceeds the requirements of API SF oil. **Note:** *On some oils there may also be a second rating consisting of another two letters, the first letter being C, e.g. API SF/CD. This rating indicates the oil is also suitable for use in a diesel engines (the C stands for compression ignition) and is thus of no relevance for motorcycle use.*
- The 'viscosity' of the oil is identified by its SAE (Society of Automotive Engineers) rating. All modern engines require multigrade oils and the SAE rating will consist of two numbers, the first followed by a W, e.g. 10W/40. The first number indicates the viscosity rating of the oil at low temperatures (W stands for winter – tested at –20ºC) and the second number represents the viscosity of the oil at high temperatures (tested at 100ºC). The lower the number, the thinner the oil. For example an oil with an SAE 10W/40 rating will give better cold starting and running than an SAE 15W/40 oil.
- As well as ensuring the 'type' and 'viscosity' of the oil match the recommendations, another consideration to make when buying engine oil is whether to purchase a standard mineral-based oil, a semi-synthetic oil (also known as a synthetic blend or synthetic-based oil) or a fully-synthetic oil. Although all oils will have a similar rating and viscosity, their cost will vary considerably; mineral-based oils are the cheapest, the fully-synthetic oils the most expensive with the semi-synthetic oils falling somewhere in-between. This decision is very much up to the owner, but it should be noted that modern synthetic oils have far better lubricating and cleaning qualities than traditional mineral-based oils and tend to retain these properties for far longer. Bearing in mind the operating conditions inside a modern, high-revving motorcycle engine it is highly recommended that a fully synthetic oil is used. The extra expense at each service could save you money in the long term by preventing premature engine wear.
- As a final note always ensure that the oil is specifically designed for use in motorcycle engines. Engine oils designed primarily for use in car engines sometimes contain additives or friction modifiers which could cause clutch slip on a motorcycle fitted with a wet-clutch.

Two-stroke engine oil

- Modern two-stroke engines, with their high power outputs, place high demands on their oil. If engine seizure is to be avoided it is essential that a high-quality oil is used. Two-stroke oils differ hugely from four-stroke oils. The oil lubricates only the crankshaft and piston(s) (the transmission has its own lubricating oil) and is used on a total-loss basis where it is burnt completely during the combustion process.
- The Japanese have recently introduced a classification system for two-stroke oils, the JASO rating. This rating is in the form of two letters, either FA, FB or FC – FA is the lowest classification and FC the highest. Ensure the oil being used meets or exceeds the recommended rating specified by the manufacturer.
- As well as ensuring the oil rating matches the recommendation, another consideration to make when buying engine oil is whether to purchase a standard mineral-based oil, a semi-synthetic oil (also known as a synthetic blend or synthetic-based oil) or a fully-synthetic oil. The cost of each type of oil varies considerably; mineral-based oils are the cheapest, the fully-synthetic oils the most expensive with the semi-synthetic oils falling somewhere in-between. This decision is very much up to the owner, but it should be noted that modern synthetic oils have far better lubricating properties and burn cleaner than traditional mineral-based oils. It is therefore recommended that a fully synthetic oil is used. The extra expense could save you money in the long term by preventing premature engine wear, engine performance will be improved, carbon deposits and exhaust smoke will be reduced.

Lubricants and fluids

- Always ensure that the oil is specifically designed for use in an injector system. Many high quality two-stroke oils are designed for competition use and need to be pre-mixed with fuel. These oils are of a much higher viscosity and are not designed to flow through the injector pumps used on road-going two-stroke motorcycles.

Transmission (gear) oil

- On a two-stroke engine, the transmission and clutch are lubricated by their own separate oil bath which must be changed in accordance with the Maintenance Schedule.
- Although the engine and transmission units of most four-strokes use a common lubrication supply, there are some exceptions where the engine and gearbox have separate oil reservoirs and a dry clutch is used.
- Motorcycle manufacturers will either recommend a monograde transmission oil or a four-stroke multigrade engine oil to lubricate the transmission.
- Transmission oils, or gear oils as they are often called, are designed specifically for use in transmission systems. The viscosity of these oils is represented by an SAE number, but the scale of measurement applied is different to that used to grade engine oils. As a rough guide a SAE90 gear oil will be of the same viscosity as an SAE50 engine oil.

Shaft drive oil

- On models equipped with shaft final drive, the shaft drive gears are will have their own oil supply. The manufacturer will state a recommended 'type or classification' and also a specific 'viscosity' range in the same manner as for four-stroke engine oil.
- Gear oil classification is given by the number which follows the API GL (GL standing for gear lubricant) rating, the higher the number, the higher the specification of the oil, e.g. API GL5 oil is a higher specification than API GL4 oil. Ensure the oil meets or exceeds the classification specified and is of the correct viscosity. The viscosity of gear oils is also represented by an SAE number but the scale of measurement used is different to that used to grade engine oils. As a rough guide an SAE90 gear oil will be of the same viscosity as an SAE50 engine oil.
- If the use of an EP (Extreme Pressure) gear oil is specified, ensure the oil purchased is suitable.

Fork oil and suspension fluid

- Conventional telescopic front forks are hydraulic and require fork oil to work. To ensure the forks function correctly, the fork oil must be changed in accordance with the Maintenance Schedule.
- Fork oil is available in a variety of viscosities, identified by their SAE rating; fork oil ratings vary from light (SAE 5) to heavy (SAE 30). When purchasing fork oil, ensure the viscosity rating matches that specified by the manufacturer.
- Some lubricant manufacturers also produce a range of high-quality suspension fluids which are very similar to fork oil but are designed mainly for competition use. These fluids may have a different viscosity rating system which is not to be confused with the SAE rating of normal fork oil. Refer to the manufacturer's instructions if in any doubt.

Brake and clutch fluid

- All disc brake systems and some clutch systems are hydraulically operated. To ensure correct operation, the hydraulic fluid must be changed in accordance with the Maintenance Schedule.
- Brake and clutch fluid is classified by its DOT rating with most motorcycle manufacturers specifying DOT 3 or 4 fluid. Both fluid types are glycol-based and can be mixed together without adverse effect; DOT 4 fluid exceeds the requirements of DOT 3 fluid. Although it is safe to use DOT 4 fluid in a system designed for use with DOT 3 fluid, never use DOT 3 fluid in a system which specifies the use of DOT 4 as this will adversely affect the system's performance. The type required for the system will be marked on the fluid reservoir cap.
- Some manufacturers also produce a DOT 5 hydraulic fluid. DOT 5 hydraulic fluid is silicone-based and is not compatible with the glycol-based DOT 3 and 4 fluids. Never mix DOT 5 fluid with DOT 3 or 4 fluid as this will seriously affect the performance of the hydraulic system.

Coolant/antifreeze

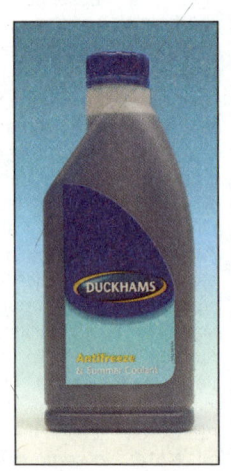

- When purchasing coolant/antifreeze, always ensure it is suitable for use in an aluminium engine and contains corrosion inhibitors to prevent possible blockages of the internal coolant passages of the system. As a general rule, most coolants are designed to be used neat and should not be diluted whereas antifreeze can be mixed with distilled water to provide a coolant solution of the required strength. Refer to the manufacturer's instructions on the bottle.
- Ensure the coolant is changed in accordance with the Maintenance Schedule.

Chain lube

- Chain lube is an aerosol-type spray lubricant specifically designed for use on motorcycle final drive chains. Chain lube has two functions, to minimise friction between the final drive chain and sprockets and to prevent corrosion of the chain. Regular use of a good-quality chain lube will extend the life of the drive chain and sprockets and thus maximise the power being transmitted from the transmission to the rear wheel.
- When using chain lube, always allow some time for the solvents in the lube to evaporate before riding the motorcycle. This will minimise the amount of lube which will

Lubricants and fluids

'fling' off from the chain when the motorcycle is used. If the motorcycle is equipped with an 'O-ring' chain, ensure the chain lube is labelled as being suitable for use on 'O-ring' chains.

Degreasers and solvents

● There are many different types of solvents and degreasers available to remove the grime and grease which accumulate around the motorcycle during normal use. Degreasers and solvents are usually available as an aerosol-type spray or as a liquid which you apply with a brush. Always closely follow the manufacturer's instructions and wear eye protection during use. Be aware that many solvents are flammable and may give off noxious fumes; take adequate precautions when using them (see Safety First!).

● For general cleaning, use one of the many solvents or degreasers available from most motorcycle accessory shops. These solvents are usually applied then left for a certain time before being washed off with water.

Brake cleaner is a solvent specifically designed to remove all traces of oil, grease and dust from braking system components. Brake cleaner is designed to evaporate quickly and leaves behind no residue.

Carburettor cleaner is an aerosol-type solvent specifically designed to clear carburettor blockages and break down the hard deposits and gum often found inside carburettors during overhaul.

Contact cleaner is an aerosol-type solvent designed for cleaning electrical components. The cleaner will remove all traces of oil and dirt from components such as switch contacts or fouled spark plugs and then dry, leaving behind no residue.

Gasket remover is an aerosol-type solvent designed for removing stubborn gaskets from engine components during overhaul. Gasket remover will minimise the amount of scraping required to remove the gasket and therefore reduce the risk of damage to the mating surface.

Spray lubricants

● Aerosol-based spray lubricants are widely available and are excellent for lubricating lever pivots and exposed cables and switches. Try to use a lubricant which is of the dry-film type as the fluid evaporates, leaving behind a dry-film of lubricant. Lubricants which leave behind an oily residue will attract dust and dirt which will increase the rate of wear of the cable/lever.

● Most lubricants also act as a moisture dispersant and a penetrating fluid. This means they can also be used to 'dry out' electrical components such as wiring connectors or switches as well as helping to free seized fasteners.

Greases

● Grease is used to lubricate many of the pivot-points. A good-quality multi-purpose grease is suitable for most applications but some manufacturers will specify the use of specialist greases for use on components such as swingarm and suspension linkage bushes. These specialist greases can be purchased from most motorcycle (or car) accessory shops; commonly specified types include molybdenum disulphide grease, lithium-based grease, graphite-based grease, silicone-based grease and high-temperature copper-based grease.

Gasket sealing compounds

● Gasket sealing compounds can be used in conjunction with gaskets, to improve their sealing capabilities, or on their own to seal metal-to-metal joints. Depending on their type, sealing compounds either set hard or stay relatively soft and pliable.

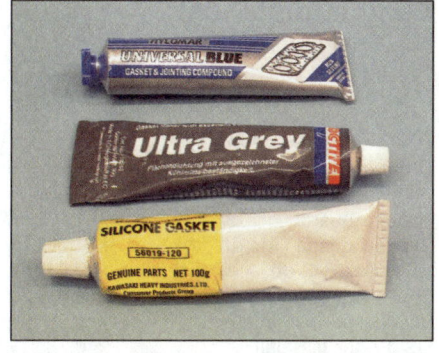

● When purchasing a gasket sealing compound, ensure that it is designed specifically for use on an internal combustion engine. General multi-purpose sealants available from DIY stores may appear visibly similar but they are not designed to withstand the extreme heat or contact with fuel and oil encountered when used on an engine (see 'Tools and Workshop Tips' for further information).

Thread locking compound

● Thread locking compounds are used to secure certain threaded fasteners in position to prevent them from loosening due to vibration. Thread locking compounds can be purchased from most motorcycle (and car) accessory shops. Ensure the threads of the both components are completely clean and dry before sparingly applying the locking compound (see 'Tools and Workshop Tips' for further information).

Fuel additives

● Fuel additives which protect and clean the fuel system components are widely available. These additives are designed to remove all traces of deposits that build up on the carburettors/injectors and prevent wear, helping the fuel system to operate more efficiently. If a fuel additive is being used, check that it is suitable for use with your motorcycle, especially if your motorcycle is equipped with a catalytic converter.

● Octane boosters are also available. These additives are designed to improve the performance of highly-tuned engines being run on normal pump-fuel and are of no real use on standard motorcycles.

Conversion Factors

Length (distance)
Inches (in)	x 25.4	= Millimetres (mm)	x 0.0394	=	Inches (in)
Feet (ft)	x 0.305	= Metres (m)	x 3.281	=	Feet (ft)
Miles	x 1.609	= Kilometres (km)	x 0.621	=	Miles

Volume (capacity)
Cubic inches (cu in; in^3)	x 16.387	= Cubic centimetres (cc; cm^3)	x 0.061	=	Cubic inches (cu in; in^3)
Imperial pints (Imp pt)	x 0.568	= Litres (l)	x 1.76	=	Imperial pints (Imp pt)
Imperial quarts (Imp qt)	x 1.137	= Litres (l)	x 0.88	=	Imperial quarts (Imp qt)
Imperial quarts (Imp qt)	x 1.201	= US quarts (US qt)	x 0.833	=	Imperial quarts (Imp qt)
US quarts (US qt)	x 0.946	= Litres (l)	x 1.057	=	US quarts (US qt)
Imperial gallons (Imp gal)	x 4.546	= Litres (l)	x 0.22	=	Imperial gallons (Imp gal)
Imperial gallons (Imp gal)	x 1.201	= US gallons (US gal)	x 0.833	=	Imperial gallons (Imp gal)
US gallons (US gal)	x 3.785	= Litres (l)	x 0.264	=	US gallons (US gal)

Mass (weight)
Ounces (oz)	x 28.35	= Grams (g)	x 0.035	=	Ounces (oz)
Pounds (lb)	x 0.454	= Kilograms (kg)	x 2.205	=	Pounds (lb)

Force
Ounces-force (ozf; oz)	x 0.278	= Newtons (N)	x 3.6	=	Ounces-force (ozf; oz)
Pounds-force (lbf; lb)	x 4.448	= Newtons (N)	x 0.225	=	Pounds-force (lbf; lb)
Newtons (N)	x 0.1	= Kilograms-force (kgf; kg)	x 9.81	=	Newtons (N)

Pressure
Pounds-force per square inch (psi; lbf/in^2; lb/in^2)	x 0.070	= Kilograms-force per square centimetre (kgf/cm^2; kg/cm^2)	x 14.223	=	Pounds-force per square inch (psi; lbf/in^2; lb/in^2)
Pounds-force per square inch (psi; lbf/in^2; lb/in^2)	x 0.068	= Atmospheres (atm)	x 14.696	=	Pounds-force per square inch (psi; lbf/in^2; lb/in^2)
Pounds-force per square inch (psi; lbf/in^2; lb/in^2)	x 0.069	= Bars	x 14.5	=	Pounds-force per square inch (psi; lbf/in^2; lb/in^2)
Pounds-force per square inch (psi; lbf/in^2; lb/in^2)	x 6.895	= Kilopascals (kPa)	x 0.145	=	Pounds-force per square inch (psi; lbf/in^2; lb/in^2)
Kilopascals (kPa)	x 0.01	= Kilograms-force per square centimetre (kgf/cm^2; kg/cm^2)	x 98.1	=	Kilopascals (kPa)
Millibar (mbar)	x 100	= Pascals (Pa)	x 0.01	=	Millibar (mbar)
Millibar (mbar)	x 0.0145	= Pounds-force per square inch (psi; lbf/in^2; lb/in^2)	x 68.947	=	Millibar (mbar)
Millibar (mbar)	x 0.75	= Millimetres of mercury (mmHg)	x 1.333	=	Millibar (mbar)
Millibar (mbar)	x 0.401	= Inches of water (inH$_2$O)	x 2.491	=	Millibar (mbar)
Millimetres of mercury (mmHg)	x 0.535	= Inches of water (inH$_2$O)	x 1.868	=	Millimetres of mercury (mmHg)
Inches of water (inH$_2$O)	x 0.036	= Pounds-force per square inch (psi; lbf/in^2; lb/in^2)	x 27.68	=	Inches of water (inH$_2$O)

Torque (moment of force)
Pounds-force inches (lbf in; lb in)	x 1.152	= Kilograms-force centimetre (kgf cm; kg cm)	x 0.868	=	Pounds-force inches (lbf in; lb in)
Pounds-force inches (lbf in; lb in)	x 0.113	= Newton metres (Nm)	x 8.85	=	Pounds-force inches (lbf in; lb in)
Pounds-force inches (lbf in; lb in)	x 0.083	= Pounds-force feet (lbf ft; lb ft)	x 12	=	Pounds-force inches (lbf in; lb in)
Pounds-force feet (lbf ft; lb ft)	x 0.138	= Kilograms-force metres (kgf m; kg m)	x 7.233	=	Pounds-force feet (lbf ft; lb ft)
Pounds-force feet (lbf ft; lb ft)	x 1.356	= Newton metres (Nm)	x 0.738	=	Pounds-force feet (lbf ft; lb ft)
Newton metres (Nm)	x 0.102	= Kilograms-force metres (kgf m; kg m)	x 9.804	=	Newton metres (Nm)

Power
Horsepower (hp)	x 745.7	= Watts (W)	x 0.0013	=	Horsepower (hp)

Velocity (speed)
Miles per hour (miles/hr; mph)	x 1.609	= Kilometres per hour (km/hr; kph)	x 0.621	=	Miles per hour (miles/hr; mph)

Fuel consumption*
Miles per gallon (mpg)	x 0.354	= Kilometres per litre (km/l)	x 2.825	=	Miles per gallon (mpg)

Temperature

Degrees Fahrenheit = (°C x 1.8) + 32   Degrees Celsius (Degrees Centigrade; °C) = (°F - 32) x 0.56

It is common practice to convert from miles per gallon (mpg) to litres/100 kilometres (l/100km), where mpg x l/100 km = 282

MOT Test Checks REF•27

About the MOT Test

In the UK, all vehicles more than three years old are subject to an annual test to ensure that they meet minimum safety requirements. A current test certificate must be issued before a machine can be used on public roads, and is required before a road fund licence can be issued. Riding without a current test certificate will also invalidate your insurance.

For most owners, the MOT test is an annual cause for anxiety, and this is largely due to owners not being sure what needs to be checked prior to submitting the motorcycle for testing. The simple answer is that a fully roadworthy motorcycle will have no difficulty in passing the test.

This is a guide to getting your motorcycle through the MOT test. Obviously it will not be possible to examine the motorcycle to the same standard as the professional MOT tester, particularly in view of the equipment required for some of the checks. However, working through the following procedures will enable you to identify any problem areas before submitting the motorcycle for the test.

It has only been possible to summarise the test requirements here, based on the regulations in force at the time of printing. Test standards are becoming increasingly stringent, although there are some exemptions for older vehicles. More information about the MOT test can be obtained from the TSO publications, *How Safe is your Motorcycle* and *The MOT Inspection Manual for Motorcycle Testing*.

Many of the checks require that one of the wheels is raised off the ground. If the motorcycle doesn't have a centre stand, note that an auxiliary stand will be required. Additionally, the help of an assistant may prove useful.

Certain exceptions apply to machines under 50 cc, machines without a lighting system, and Classic bikes - if in doubt about any of the requirements listed below seek confirmation from an MOT tester prior to submitting the motorcycle for the test.

Check that the frame number is clearly visible.

> **HAYNES HiNT** *If a component is in borderline condition, the tester has discretion in deciding whether to pass or fail it. If the motorcycle presented is clean and evidently well cared for, the tester may be more inclined to pass a borderline component than if the motorcycle is scruffy and apparently neglected.*

Electrical System

Lights, turn signals, horn and reflector

✔ With the ignition on, check the operation of the following electrical components. **Note:** The electrical components on certain small-capacity machines are powered by the generator, requiring that the engine is run for this check.

a) Headlight and tail light. Check that both illuminate in the low and high beam switch positions.
b) Position lights. Check that the front position (or sidelight) and tail light illuminate in this switch position.
c) Turn signals. Check that all flash at the correct rate, and that the warning light(s) function correctly. Check that the turn signal switch works correctly.
d) Hazard warning system (where fitted). Check that all four turn signals flash in this switch position.
e) Brake stop light. Check that the light comes on when the front and rear brakes are independently applied. Models first used on or after 1st April 1986 must have a brake light switch on each brake.
f) Horn. Check that the sound is continuous and of reasonable volume.

✔ Check that there is a red reflector on the rear of the machine, either mounted separately or as part of the tail light lens.
✔ Check the condition of the headlight, tail light and turn signal lenses.

Headlight beam height

✔ The MOT tester will perform a headlight beam height check using specialised beam setting equipment **(see illustration 1)**. This equipment will not be available to the home mechanic, but if you suspect that the headlight is incorrectly set or may have been maladjusted in the past, you can perform a rough test as follows.
✔ Position the bike in a straight line facing a brick wall. The bike must be off its stand, upright and with a rider seated. Measure the height from the ground to the centre of the headlight and mark a horizontal line on the wall at this height. Position the motorcycle 3.8 metres from the wall and draw a vertical line up the wall central to the centreline of the motorcycle. Switch to dipped beam and check that the beam pattern falls slightly lower than the horizontal line and to the left of the vertical line **(see illustration 2)**.

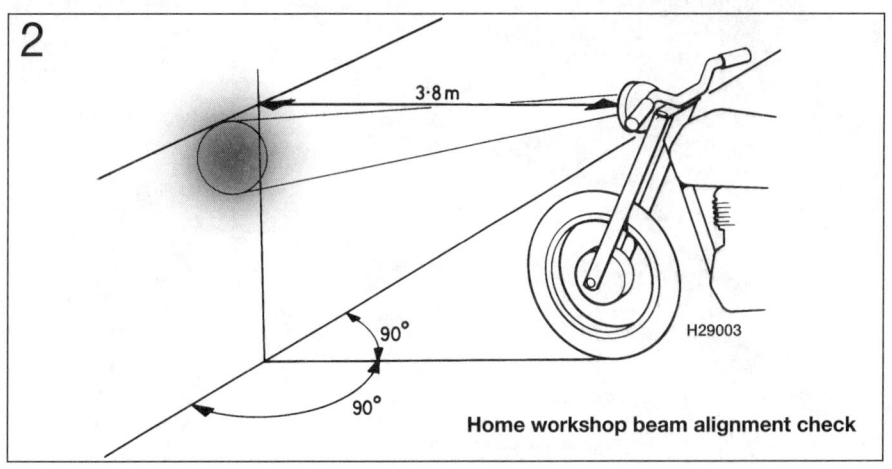

1

Headlight beam height checking equipment

2

Home workshop beam alignment check

REF•28 MOT Test Checks

Exhaust System and Final Drive

Exhaust

✔ Check that the exhaust mountings are secure and that the system does not foul any of the rear suspension components.
✔ Start the motorcycle. When the revs are increased, check that the exhaust is neither holed nor leaking from any of its joints. On a linked system, check that the collector box is not leaking due to corrosion.
✔ Note that the exhaust decibel level ("loudness" of the exhaust) is assessed at the discretion of the tester. If the motorcycle was first used on or after 1st January 1985 the silencer must carry the BSAU 193 stamp, or a marking relating to its make and model, or be of OE (original equipment) manufacture. If the silencer is marked NOT FOR ROAD USE, RACING USE ONLY or similar, it will fail the MOT.

Final drive

✔ On chain or belt drive machines, check that the chain/belt is in good condition and does not have excessive slack. Also check that the sprocket is securely mounted on the rear wheel hub. Check that the chain/belt guard is in place.
✔ On shaft drive bikes, check for oil leaking from the drive unit and fouling the rear tyre.

Steering and Suspension

Steering

✔ With the front wheel raised off the ground, rotate the steering from lock to lock. The handlebar or switches must not contact the fuel tank or be close enough to trap the rider's hand. Problems can be caused by damaged lock stops on the lower yoke and frame, or by the fitting of non-standard handlebars.
✔ When performing the lock to lock check, also ensure that the steering moves freely without drag or notchiness. Steering movement can be impaired by poorly routed cables, or by overtight head bearings or worn bearings. The tester will perform a check of the steering head bearing lower race by mounting the front wheel on a surface plate, then performing a lock to lock check with the weight of the machine on the lower bearing (see illustration 3).
✔ Grasp the fork sliders (lower legs) and attempt to push and pull on the forks (see illustration 4). Any play in the steering head bearings will be felt. Note that in extreme cases, wear of the front fork bushes can be misinterpreted for head bearing play.
✔ Check that the handlebars are securely mounted.
✔ Check that the handlebar grip rubbers are secure. They should by bonded to the bar left end and to the throttle cable pulley on the right end.

Front wheel mounted on a surface plate for steering head bearing lower race check

Front suspension

✔ With the motorcycle off the stand, hold the front brake on and pump the front forks up and down (see illustration 5). Check that they are adequately damped.

Checking the steering head bearings for freeplay

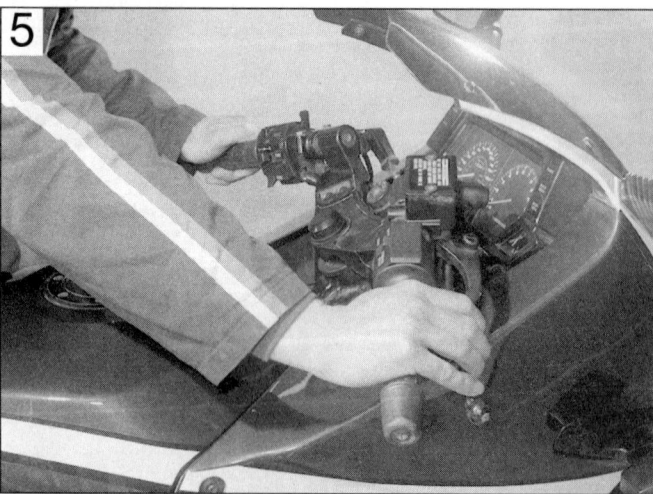

Hold the front brake on and pump the front forks up and down to check operation

MOT Test Checks REF•29

Inspect the area around the fork dust seal for oil leakage (arrow)

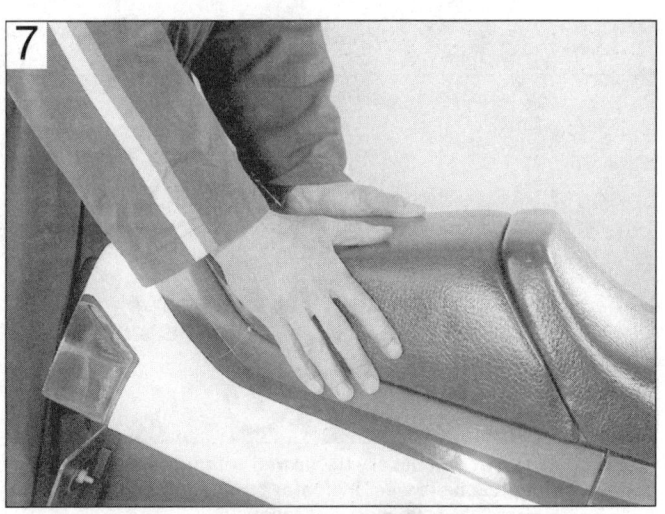

Bounce the rear of the motorcycle to check rear suspension operation

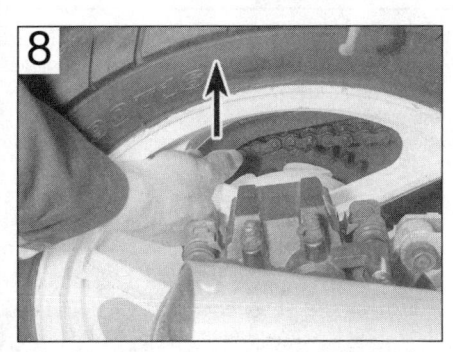

Checking for rear suspension linkage play

✔ Inspect the area above and around the front fork oil seals **(see illustration 6)**. There should be no sign of oil on the fork tube (stanchion) nor leaking down the slider (lower leg). On models so equipped, check that there is no oil leaking from the anti-dive units.

✔ On models with swingarm front suspension, check that there is no freeplay in the linkage when moved from side to side.

Rear suspension

✔ With the motorcycle off the stand and an assistant supporting the motorcycle by its handlebars, bounce the rear suspension **(see illustration 7)**. Check that the suspension components do not foul on any of the cycle parts and check that the shock absorber(s) provide adequate damping.

✔ Visually inspect the shock absorber(s) and check that there is no sign of oil leakage from its damper. This is somewhat restricted on certain single shock models due to the location of the shock absorber.

✔ With the rear wheel raised off the ground, grasp the wheel at the highest point and attempt to pull it up **(see illustration 8)**. Any play in the swingarm pivot or suspension linkage bearings will be felt as movement.
Note: *Do not confuse play with actual suspension movement.* Failure to lubricate suspension linkage bearings can lead to bearing failure **(see illustration 9)**.

✔ With the rear wheel raised off the ground, grasp the swingarm ends and attempt to move the swingarm from side to side and forwards and backwards - any play indicates wear of the swingarm pivot bearings **(see illustration 10)**.

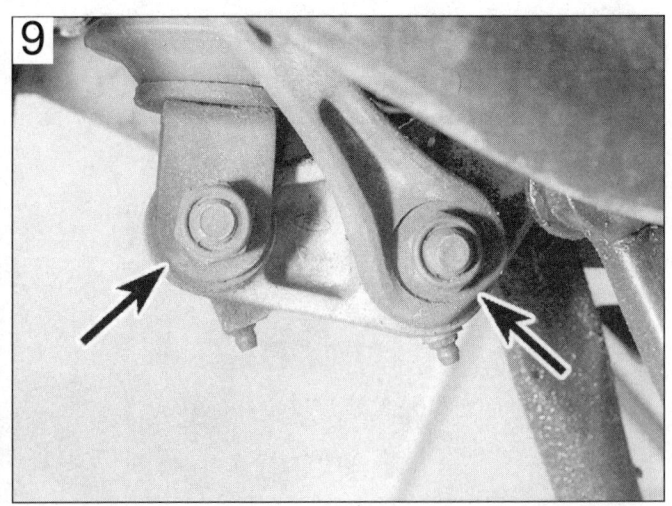

Worn suspension linkage pivots (arrows) are usually the cause of play in the rear suspension

Grasp the swingarm at the ends to check for play in its pivot bearings

REF•30 MOT Test Checks

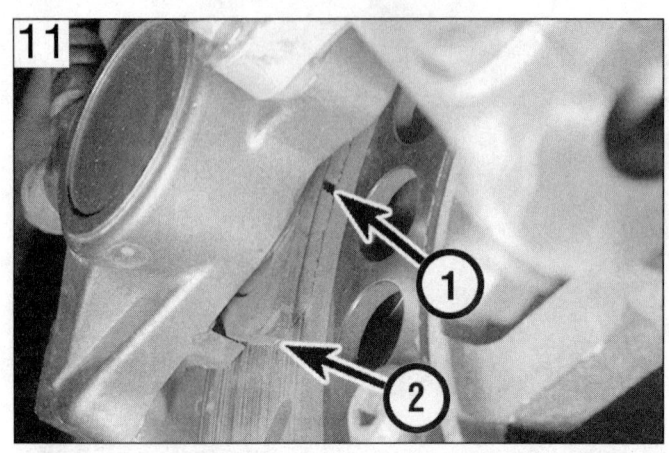

Brake pad wear can usually be viewed without removing the caliper. Most pads have wear indicator grooves (1) and some also have indicator tangs (2)

On drum brakes, check the angle of the operating lever with the brake fully applied. Most drum brakes have a wear indicator pointer and scale.

Brakes, Wheels and Tyres

Brakes

✔ With the wheel raised off the ground, apply the brake then free it off, and check that the wheel is about to revolve freely without brake drag.

✔ On disc brakes, examine the disc itself. Check that it is securely mounted and not cracked.

✔ On disc brakes, view the pad material through the caliper mouth and check that the pads are not worn down beyond the limit **(see illustration 11)**.

✔ On drum brakes, check that when the brake is applied the angle between the operating lever and cable or rod is not too great **(see illustration 12)**. Check also that the operating lever doesn't foul any other components.

✔ On disc brakes, examine the flexible hoses from top to bottom. Have an assistant hold the brake on so that the fluid in the hose is under pressure, and check that there is no sign of fluid leakage, bulges or cracking. If there are any metal brake pipes or unions, check that these are free from corrosion and damage. Where a brake-linked anti-dive system is fitted, check the hoses to the anti-dive in a similar manner.

✔ Check that the rear brake torque arm is secure and that its fasteners are secured by self-locking nuts or castellated nuts with split-pins or R-pins **(see illustration 13)**.

✔ On models with ABS, check that the self-check warning light in the instrument panel works.

✔ The MOT tester will perform a test of the motorcycle's braking efficiency based on a calculation of rider and motorcycle weight. Although this cannot be carried out at home, you can at least ensure that the braking systems are properly maintained. For hydraulic disc brakes, check the fluid level, lever/pedal feel (bleed of air if its spongy) and pad material. For drum brakes, check adjustment, cable or rod operation and shoe lining thickness.

Wheels and tyres

✔ Check the wheel condition. Cast wheels should be free from cracks and if of the built-up design, all fasteners should be secure. Spoked wheels should be checked for broken, corroded, loose or bent spokes.

✔ With the wheel raised off the ground, spin the wheel and visually check that the tyre and wheel run true. Check that the tyre does not foul the suspension or mudguards.

✔ With the wheel raised off the ground, grasp the wheel and attempt to move it about the axle (spindle) **(see illustration 14)**. Any play felt here indicates wheel bearing failure.

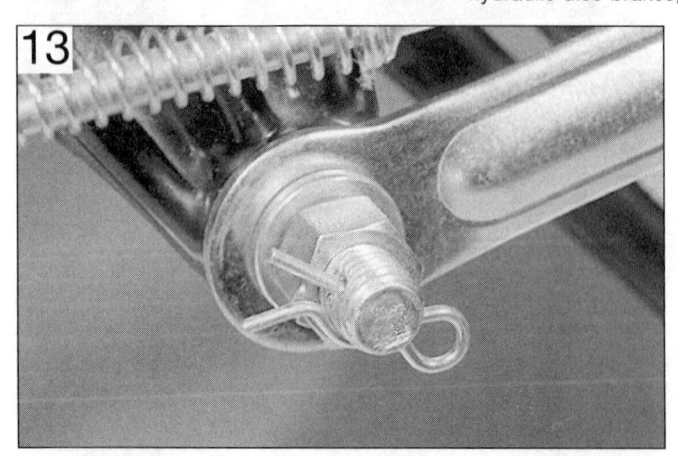

Brake torque arm must be properly secured at both ends

Check for wheel bearing play by trying to move the wheel about the axle (spindle)

MOT Test Checks REF•31

Checking the tyre tread depth

Tyre direction of rotation arrow can be found on tyre sidewall

Castellated type wheel axle (spindle) nut must be secured by a split pin or R-pin

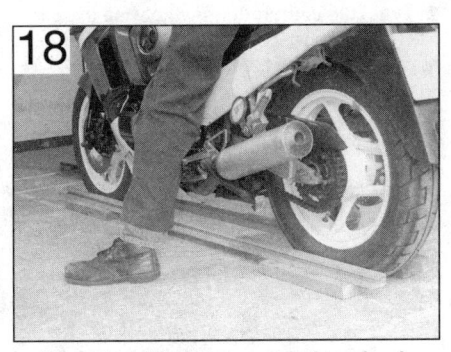

Two straightedges are used to check wheel alignment

✔ Check the tyre tread depth, tread condition and sidewall condition **(see illustration 15)**.
✔ Check the tyre type. Front and rear tyre types must be compatible and be suitable for road use. Tyres marked NOT FOR ROAD USE, COMPETITION USE ONLY or similar, will fail the MOT.

✔ If the tyre sidewall carries a direction of rotation arrow, this must be pointing in the direction of normal wheel rotation **(see illustration 16)**.
✔ Check that the wheel axle (spindle) nuts (where applicable) are properly secured. A self-locking nut or castellated nut with a split-pin or R-pin can be used **(see illustration 17)**.
✔ Wheel alignment is checked with the motorcycle off the stand and a rider seated. With the front wheel pointing straight ahead, two perfectly straight lengths of metal or wood and placed against the sidewalls of both tyres **(see illustration 18)**. The gap each side of the front tyre must be equidistant on both sides. Incorrect wheel alignment may be due to a cocked rear wheel (often as the result of poor chain adjustment) or in extreme cases, a bent frame.

General checks and condition

✔ Check the security of all major fasteners, bodypanels, seat, fairings (where fitted) and mudguards.
✔ Check that the rider and pillion footrests, handlebar levers and brake pedal are securely mounted.
✔ Check for corrosion on the frame or any load-bearing components. If severe, this may affect the structure, particularly under stress.

Sidecars

A motorcycle fitted with a sidecar requires additional checks relating to the stability of the machine and security of attachment and swivel joints, plus specific wheel alignment (toe-in) requirements. Additionally, tyre and lighting requirements differ from conventional motorcycle use. Owners are advised to check MOT test requirements with an official test centre.

Storage

Preparing for storage

Before you start

If repairs or an overhaul is needed, see that this is carried out now rather than left until you want to ride the bike again.

Give the bike a good wash and scrub all dirt from its underside. Make sure the bike dries completely before preparing for storage.

Engine

● Remove the spark plug(s) and lubricate the cylinder bores with approximately a teaspoon of motor oil using a spout-type oil can **(see illustration 1)**. Reinstall the spark plug(s). Crank the engine over a couple of times to coat the piston rings and bores with oil. If the bike has a kickstart, use this to turn the engine over. If not, flick the kill switch to the OFF position and crank the engine over on the starter **(see illustration 2)**. If the nature on the ignition system prevents the starter operating with the kill switch in the OFF position, remove the spark plugs and fit them back in their caps; ensure that the plugs are earthed (grounded) against the cylinder head when the starter is operated **(see illustration 3)**.

Warning: It is important that the plugs are earthed (grounded) away from the spark plug holes otherwise there is a risk of atomised fuel from the cylinders igniting.

HAYNES HINT: *On a single cylinder four-stroke engine, you can seal the combustion chamber completely by positioning the piston at TDC on the compression stroke.*

● Drain the carburettor(s) otherwise there is a risk of jets becoming blocked by gum deposits from the fuel **(see illustration 4)**.

● If the bike is going into long-term storage, consider adding a fuel stabiliser to the fuel in the tank. If the tank is drained completely, corrosion of its internal surfaces may occur if left unprotected for a long period. The tank can be treated with a rust preventative especially for this purpose. Alternatively, remove the tank and pour half a litre of motor oil into it, install the filler cap and shake the tank to coat its internals with oil before draining off the excess. The same effect can also be achieved by spraying WD40 or a similar water-dispersant around the inside of the tank via its flexible nozzle.

● Make sure the cooling system contains the correct mix of antifreeze. Antifreeze also contains important corrosion inhibitors.

● The air intakes and exhaust can be sealed off by covering or plugging the openings. Ensure that you do not seal in any condensation; run the engine until it is hot

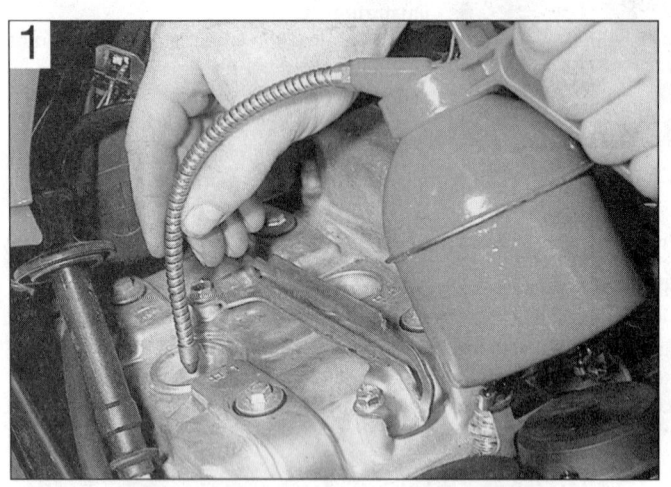

Squirt a drop of motor oil into each cylinder

Flick the kill switch to OFF...

...and ensure that the metal bodies of the plugs (arrows) are earthed against the cylinder head

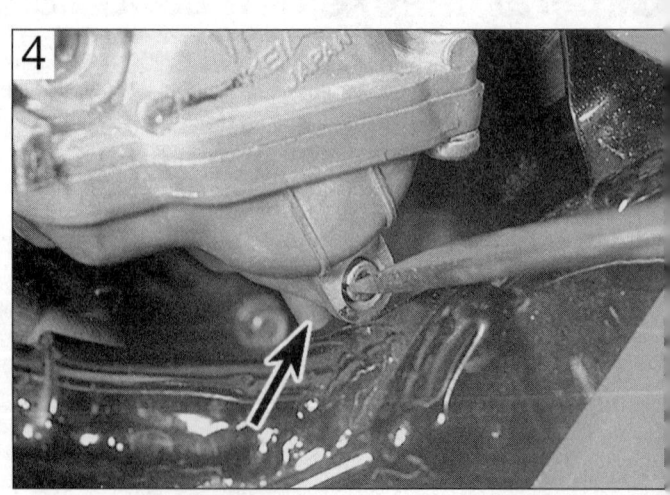

Connect a hose to the carburettor float chamber drain stub (arrow) and unscrew the drain screw

Storage   REF•33

Exhausts can be sealed off with a plastic bag

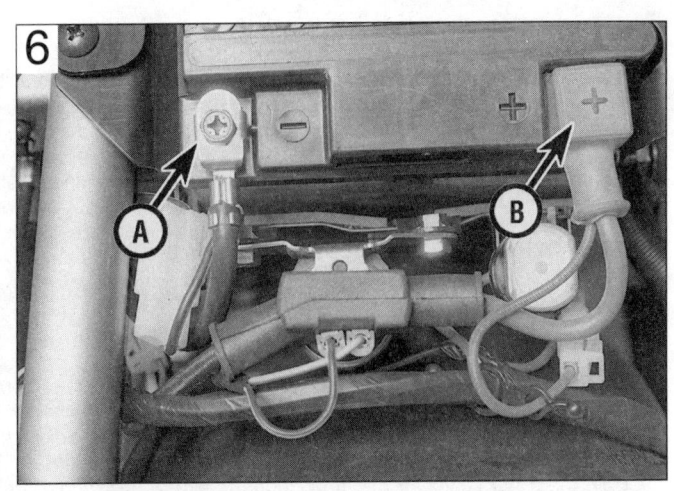

Disconnect the negative lead (A) first, followed by the positive lead (B)

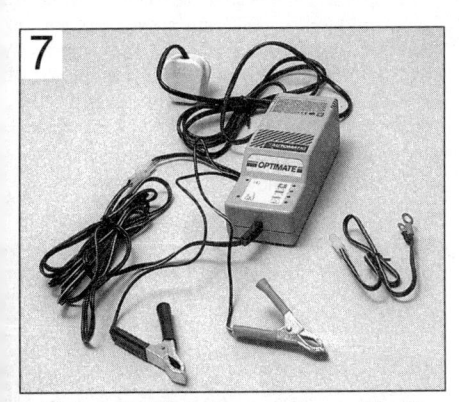

Use a suitable battery charger - this kit also assess battery condition

then switch off and allow to cool. Tape a piece of thick plastic over the silencer end(s) **(see illustration 5)**. Note that some advocate pouring a tablespoon of motor oil into the silencer(s) before sealing them off.

Battery

● Remove it from the bike - in extreme cases of cold the battery may freeze and crack its case **(see illustration 6)**.

● Check the electrolyte level and top up if necessary (conventional refillable batteries). Clean the terminals.
● Store the battery off the motorcycle and away from any sources of fire. Position a wooden block under the battery if it is to sit on the ground.
● Give the battery a trickle charge for a few hours every month **(see illustration 7)**.

Tyres

● Place the bike on its centrestand or an auxiliary stand which will support the motorcycle in an upright position. Position wood blocks under the tyres to keep them off the ground and to provide insulation from damp. If the bike is being put into long-term storage, ideally both tyres should be off the ground; not only will this protect the tyres, but will also ensure that no load is placed on the steering head or wheel bearings.
● Deflate each tyre by 5 to 10 psi, no more or the beads may unseat from the rim, making subsequent inflation difficult on tubeless tyres.

Pivots and controls

● Lubricate all lever, pedal, stand and footrest pivot points. If grease nipples are fitted to the rear suspension components, apply lubricant to the pivots.
● Lubricate all control cables.

Cycle components

● Apply a wax protectant to all painted and plastic components. Wipe off any excess, but don't polish to a shine. Where fitted, clean the screen with soap and water.
● Coat metal parts with Vaseline (petroleum jelly). When applying this to the fork tubes, do not compress the forks otherwise the seals will rot from contact with the Vaseline.
● Apply a vinyl cleaner to the seat.

Storage conditions

● Aim to store the bike in a shed or garage which does not leak and is free from damp.
● Drape an old blanket or bedspread over the bike to protect it from dust and direct contact with sunlight (which will fade paint). This also hides the bike from prying eyes. Beware of tight-fitting plastic covers which may allow condensation to form and settle on the bike.

Getting back on the road

Engine and transmission

● Change the oil and replace the oil filter. If this was done prior to storage, check that the oil hasn't emulsified - a thick whitish substance which occurs through condensation.
● Remove the spark plugs. Using a spout-type oil can, squirt a few drops of oil into the cylinder(s). This will provide initial lubrication as the piston rings and bores comes back into contact. Service the spark plugs, or fit new ones, and install them in the engine.

● Check that the clutch isn't stuck on. The plates can stick together if left standing for some time, preventing clutch operation. Engage a gear and try rocking the bike back and forth with the clutch lever held against the handlebar. If this doesn't work on cable-operated clutches, hold the clutch lever back against the handlebar with a strong elastic band or cable tie for a couple of hours **(see illustration 8)**.
● If the air intakes or silencer end(s) were blocked off, remove the bung or cover used.
● If the fuel tank was coated with a rust

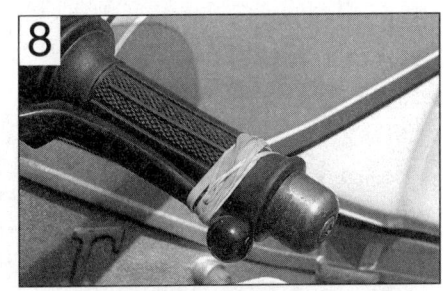

Hold clutch lever back against the handlebar with elastic bands or a cable tie

Storage

preventative, oil or a stabiliser added to the fuel, drain and flush the tank and dispose of the fuel sensibly. If no action was taken with the fuel tank prior to storage, it is advised that the old fuel is disposed of since it will go off over a period of time. Refill the fuel tank with fresh fuel.

Frame and running gear

- Oil all pivot points and cables.
- Check the tyre pressures. They will definitely need inflating if pressures were reduced for storage.
- Lubricate the final drive chain (where applicable).
- Remove any protective coating applied to the fork tubes (stanchions) since this may well destroy the fork seals. If the fork tubes weren't protected and have picked up rust spots, remove them with very fine abrasive paper and refinish with metal polish.
- Check that both brakes operate correctly. Apply each brake hard and check that it's not possible to move the motorcycle forwards, then check that the brake frees off again once released. Brake caliper pistons can stick due to corrosion around the piston head, or on the sliding caliper types, due to corrosion of the slider pins. If the brake doesn't free after repeated operation, take the caliper off for examination. Similarly drum brakes can stick due to a seized operating cam, cable or rod linkage.
- If the motorcycle has been in long-term storage, renew the brake fluid and clutch fluid (where applicable).
- Depending on where the bike has been stored, the wiring, cables and hoses may have been nibbled by rodents. Make a visual check and investigate disturbed wiring loom tape.

Battery

- If the battery has been previously removal and given top up charges it can simply be reconnected. Remember to connect the positive cable first and the negative cable last.
- On conventional refillable batteries, if the battery has not received any attention, remove it from the motorcycle and check its electrolyte level. Top up if necessary then charge the battery. If the battery fails to hold a charge and a visual checks show heavy white sulphation of the plates, the battery is probably defective and must be renewed. This is particularly likely if the battery is old. Confirm battery condition with a specific gravity check.
- On sealed (MF) batteries, if the battery has not received any attention, remove it from the motorcycle and charge it according to the information on the battery case - if the battery fails to hold a charge it must be renewed.

Starting procedure

- If a kickstart is fitted, turn the engine over a couple of times with the ignition OFF to distribute oil around the engine. If no kickstart is fitted, flick the engine kill switch OFF and the ignition ON and crank the engine over a couple of times to work oil around the upper cylinder components. If the nature of the ignition system is such that the starter won't work with the kill switch OFF, remove the spark plugs, fit them back into their caps and earth (ground) their bodies on the cylinder head. Reinstall the spark plugs afterwards.
- Switch the kill switch to RUN, operate the choke and start the engine. If the engine won't start don't continue cranking the engine - not only will this flatten the battery, but the starter motor will overheat. Switch the ignition off and try again later. If the engine refuses to start, go through the fault finding procedures in this manual. **Note:** *If the bike has been in storage for a long time, old fuel or a carburettor blockage may be the problem. Gum deposits in carburettors can block jets - if a carburettor cleaner doesn't prove successful the carburettors must be dismantled for cleaning.*
- Once the engine has started, check that the lights, turn signals and horn work properly.
- Treat the bike gently for the first ride and check all fluid levels on completion. Settle the bike back into the maintenance schedule.

Fault Finding REF•35

This Section provides an easy reference-guide to the more common faults that are likely to afflict your machine. Obviously, the opportunities are almost limitless for faults to occur as a result of obscure failures, and to try and cover all eventualities would require a book. Indeed, a number have been written on the subject.

Successful troubleshooting is not a mysterious 'black art' but the application of a bit of knowledge combined with a systematic and logical approach to the problem. Approach any troubleshooting by first accurately identifying the symptom and then checking through the list of possible causes, starting with the simplest or most obvious and progressing in stages to the most complex.

Take nothing for granted, but above all apply liberal quantities of common sense.

The main symptom of a fault is given in the text as a major heading below which are listed the various systems or areas which may contain the fault. Details of each possible cause for a fault and the remedial action to be taken are given, in brief, in the paragraphs below each heading. Further information should be sought in the relevant Chapter.

1 Engine doesn't start or is difficult to start
- [ ] Starter motor doesn't rotate
- [ ] Starter motor rotates but engine does not turn over
- [ ] Starter works but engine won't turn over (seized)
- [ ] No fuel flow
- [ ] Engine flooded
- [ ] No spark or weak spark
- [ ] Compression low
- [ ] Stalls after starting
- [ ] Rough idle

2 Poor running at low speed
- [ ] Spark weak
- [ ] Fuel/air mixture incorrect
- [ ] Compression low
- [ ] Poor acceleration

3 Poor running or no power at high speed
- [ ] Firing incorrect
- [ ] Fuel/air mixture incorrect
- [ ] Compression low
- [ ] Knocking or pinking
- [ ] Miscellaneous causes

4 Overheating
- [ ] Engine overheats
- [ ] Firing incorrect
- [ ] Fuel/air mixture incorrect
- [ ] Compression too high
- [ ] Engine load excessive
- [ ] Lubrication inadequate
- [ ] Miscellaneous causes

5 Clutch problems
- [ ] Clutch slipping
- [ ] Clutch not disengaging completely

6 Gearchanging problems
- [ ] Doesn't go into gear, or lever doesn't return
- [ ] Jumps out of gear
- [ ] Overselects

7 Abnormal engine noise
- [ ] Knocking or pinking
- [ ] Piston slap or rattling
- [ ] Valve noise
- [ ] Other noise

8 Abnormal driveline noise
- [ ] Clutch noise
- [ ] Transmission noise
- [ ] Final drive noise

9 Abnormal frame and suspension noise
- [ ] Front end noise
- [ ] Shock absorber noise
- [ ] Brake noise

10 Excessive exhaust smoke
- [ ] White smoke
- [ ] Black smoke
- [ ] Brown smoke

11 Poor handling or stability
- [ ] Handlebar hard to turn
- [ ] Handlebar shakes or vibrates excessively
- [ ] Handlebar pulls to one side
- [ ] Poor shock absorbing qualities

12 Braking problems
- [ ] Brakes are spongy, don't hold
- [ ] Brake lever or pedal pulsates
- [ ] Brakes drag

13 Electrical problems
- [ ] Battery dead or weak
- [ ] Battery overcharged

Fault Finding

1 Engine doesn't start or is difficult to start

Starter motor doesn't rotate

- ☐ Engine kill switch OFF.
- ☐ Fuse blown. Check main fuse and ignition circuit fuse (see Chapter 8).
- ☐ Battery voltage low. Check and recharge battery (see Chapter 8).
- ☐ Starter motor defective. Make sure the wiring to the starter is secure. Make sure the starter relay clicks when the start button is pushed. If the relay clicks, then the fault is in the wiring or motor.
- ☐ Starter relay faulty. Check it according to the procedure in Chapter 8.
- ☐ Starter switch not contacting. The contacts could be wet, corroded or dirty. Disassemble and clean the switch (see Chapter 8).
- ☐ Wiring open or shorted. Check all wiring connections and harnesses to make sure that they are dry, tight and not corroded. Also check for broken or frayed wires that can cause a short to ground (earth) (see wiring diagram, Chapter 8).
- ☐ Ignition (main) switch defective. Check the switch according to the procedure in Chapter 8. Renew the switch if it is defective.
- ☐ Engine kill switch defective. Check for wet, dirty or corroded contacts. Clean or renew the switch as necessary (see Chapter 8).
- ☐ Faulty neutral, sidestand or clutch switch, or starter circuit cut-off relay. Check the wiring to each switch and the switch itself according to the procedures in Chapter 8, and check the relay.

Starter motor rotates but engine does not turn over

- ☐ Starter clutch defective. Inspect and repair or renew (see Chapter 2).
- ☐ Damaged idler or starter gears. Inspect and renew the damaged parts (see Chapter 2).

Starter works but engine won't turn over (seized)

- ☐ Seized engine caused by one or more internally damaged components. Failure due to wear, abuse or lack of lubrication. Damage can include seized valves, followers, camshafts, pistons, crankshaft, connecting rod bearings, or transmission gears or bearings. Refer to Chapter 2 for engine disassembly.

No fuel flow

- ☐ No fuel in tank.
- ☐ Fuel tank breather hose obstructed.
- ☐ Fuel tap filter clogged. Remove the tap and clean it and the filter (see Chapter 3). On XJR1300 models also check the in-line filter.
- ☐ Fuel tap vacuum hose split or detached. Check the hose.
- ☐ Fuel tap diaphragm split. Remove the tap and check the diaphragm (see Chapter 3).
- ☐ Fuel line clogged. Pull the fuel line loose and carefully blow through it.
- ☐ Float needle valve filter clogged. For all of the valves to be clogged, either a very bad batch of fuel with an unusual additive has been used, or some other foreign material has entered the tank. After a machine has been stored for many months without running, the fuel turns to a varnish-like liquid and forms deposits on the inlet needle valves and jets. The carburettors should be removed and overhauled if draining the float chambers doesn't solve the problem.

Engine flooded

- ☐ Float height too high. Check as described in Chapter 3.
- ☐ Float needle valve worn or stuck open. A piece of dirt, rust or other debris can cause the valve to seat improperly, causing excess fuel to be admitted to the float chamber. In this case, the float chamber should be cleaned and the needle valve and seat inspected. If the needle and seat are worn, then the leaking will persist and the parts should be renewed (see Chapter 3).
- ☐ Starting technique incorrect. Under normal circumstances (i.e., if all the carburettor functions are sound) the machine should start with little or no throttle. When the engine is cold, the choke should be operated and the engine started without opening the throttle. When the engine is at operating temperature, only a very slight amount of throttle should be necessary. If the engine is flooded, disconnect the vacuum hose (according to model – see Chapter 3) and hold the throttle open while cranking the engine. This will allow additional air to reach the cylinders. Remember to attach the vacuum hose afterwards.

No spark or weak spark

- ☐ Ignition switch OFF.
- ☐ Engine kill switch turned to the OFF position.
- ☐ Battery voltage low. Check and recharge the battery as necessary (see Chapter 8).
- ☐ Spark plugs dirty, defective or worn out. Locate reason for fouled plugs using the spark plug condition chart on the inside rear cover and follow the plug maintenance procedures in Chapter 1.
- ☐ Spark plug caps or HT leads faulty. Check condition. Renew either or both components if cracks or deterioration are evident (see Chapter 4).
- ☐ Spark plug caps not making good contact. Make sure that the plug caps fit snugly over the plug ends.
- ☐ Ignition control unit defective. Take the unit to a Yamaha dealer for testing (see Chapter 4).
- ☐ Pick-up coil defective. Check the unit (see Chapter 4).
- ☐ Ignition HT coils defective. Check the coils (see Chapter 4).
- ☐ Ignition (main) switch or kill switch shorted. This is usually caused by water, corrosion, damage or excessive wear. The switches can be disassembled and cleaned with electrical contact cleaner. If cleaning does not help, renew the switches (see Chapter 8).
- ☐ Wiring shorted or broken between:
  a) Ignition (main) switch and engine kill switch (or blown ignition fuse)
  b) Ignition control unit and engine kill switch
  c) Ignition control unit and ignition HT coils
  d) Ignition HT coils and spark plugs
  e) Ignition control unit and pick-up coil
- ☐ Make sure that all wiring connections are clean, dry and tight. Look for chafed and broken wires (Chapters 4 and 8).

Compression low

- ☐ Spark plugs loose. Remove the plugs and inspect their threads. Reinstall and tighten to the specified torque (see Chapter 1).
- ☐ Cylinder head not sufficiently tightened down. If the cylinder head is suspected of being loose, then there's a chance that the gasket or head is damaged if the problem has persisted for any length of time. The head nuts should be tightened to the proper torque in the correct sequence (see Chapter 2).
- ☐ Improper valve clearance. This means that the valve is not closing completely and compression pressure is leaking past the valve. Check and adjust the valve clearances (see Chapter 1).
- ☐ Cylinder and/or piston worn. Excessive wear will cause compression pressure to leak past the rings. This is usually accompanied by worn rings as well. A top-end overhaul is necessary (see Chapter 2).
- ☐ Piston rings worn, weak, broken, or sticking. Broken or sticking piston rings usually indicate a lubrication or carburation problem that causes excess carbon deposits or seizures to form on the pistons and rings. Top-end overhaul is necessary (see Chapter 2).
- ☐ Piston ring-to-groove clearance excessive. This is caused by excessive wear of the piston ring lands. Piston renewal is necessary (see Chapter 2).
- ☐ Cylinder head gasket damaged. If the head is allowed to become loose, or if excessive carbon build-up on the piston crown and combustion chamber causes extremely high compression, the head gasket may leak. Retorquing the head is not always sufficient to restore the seal, so gasket renewal is necessary (see Chapter 2).

# Fault Finding REF•37

1 Engine doesn't start or is difficult to start (continued)

- Cylinder head warped. This is caused by overheating or improperly tightened head nuts. Machine shop resurfacing or head renewal is necessary (see Chapter 2).
- Valve spring broken or weak. Caused by component failure or wear; the springs must be renewed (see Chapter 2).
- Valve not seating properly. This is caused by a bent valve (from over-revving or improper valve adjustment), burned valve or seat (improper carburation) or an accumulation of carbon deposits on the seat (from carburation or lubrication problems). The valves must be cleaned and/or renewed and the seats serviced if possible (see Chapter 2).

Stalls after starting

- Improper choke action. Make sure the choke linkage shaft is getting a full stroke and staying in the out position (see Chapter 3).
- Ignition malfunction (see Chapter 4).
- Carburettor malfunction (see Chapter 3).
- Fuel contaminated. The fuel can be contaminated with either dirt or water, or can change chemically if the machine is allowed to sit for several months or more. Drain the tank and float chambers (see Chapter 3).
- Intake air leak. Check for loose carburettor-to-intake manifold connections, loose or missing vacuum gauge adapter caps or hoses, or loose carburettor tops (see Chapter 3).
- Engine idle speed incorrect. Turn idle adjusting screw until the engine idles at the specified rpm (see Chapter 1).

Rough idle

- Ignition malfunction (see Chapter 4).
- Idle speed incorrect (see Chapter 1).
- Carburettors not synchronised. Adjust carburettors with vacuum gauge or manometer set as described in Chapter 1.
- Carburettor malfunction (see Chapter 3).
- Fuel contaminated. The fuel can be contaminated with either dirt or water, or can change chemically if the machine is allowed to sit for several months or more. Drain the tank and float chambers (see Chapter 3).
- Intake air leak. Check for loose carburettor-to-intake manifold connections, loose or missing vacuum gauge adapter caps or hoses, or loose carburettor tops (see Chapter 3).
- Air filter clogged. Renew the air filter element (see Chapter 1).

2 Poor running at low speeds

Spark weak

- Battery voltage low. Check and recharge battery (see Chapter 8).
- Spark plugs fouled, defective or worn out. Refer to Chapter 1 for spark plug maintenance.
- Spark plug cap or HT lead defective. Refer to Chapters 1 and 4 for details on the ignition system.
- Spark plug caps not making contact. Make sure they are securely pushed on to the plugs.
- Incorrect spark plugs. Wrong type, heat range or cap configuration. Check and install correct plugs listed in Chapter 1.
- Ignition control unit defective (see Chapter 4).
- Pick-up coil defective (see Chapter 4).
- Ignition HT coils defective (see Chapter 4).

Fuel/air mixture incorrect

- Pilot screws out of adjustment (see Chapter 3).
- Pilot jet or air passage clogged. Remove and overhaul the carburettors (see Chapter 3).
- Air bleed holes clogged. Remove carburettor and blow out all passages (see Chapter 3).
- Air filter clogged, poorly sealed or missing (see Chapter 1).
- Air filter housing poorly sealed. Look for cracks, holes or loose clamps and renew or repair defective parts.
- Fuel level too high or too low. Check the fuel level or float height (see Chapter 3).
- Fuel tank breather hose obstructed.
- Carburettor intake manifolds loose. Check for cracks, breaks, tears or loose clamps. Renew the rubber intake manifold joints if split or perished.

Compression low

- Spark plugs loose. Remove the plugs and inspect their threads. Reinstall and tighten to the specified torque (see Chapter 1).
- Cylinder head not sufficiently tightened down. If the cylinder head is suspected of being loose, then there's a chance that the gasket and head are damaged if the problem has persisted for any length of time. The head nuts should be tightened to the proper torque in the correct sequence (see Chapter 2).
- Improper valve clearance. This means that the valve is not closing completely and compression pressure is leaking past the valve. Check and adjust the valve clearances (see Chapter 1).
- Cylinder and/or piston worn. Excessive wear will cause compression pressure to leak past the rings. This is usually accompanied by worn rings as well. A top end overhaul is necessary (see Chapter 2).
- Piston rings worn, weak, broken, or sticking. Broken or sticking piston rings usually indicate a lubrication or carburation problem that causes excess carbon deposits or seizures to form on the pistons and rings. Top-end overhaul is necessary (see Chapter 2).
- Piston ring-to-groove clearance excessive. This is caused by excessive wear of the piston ring lands. Piston renewal is necessary (see Chapter 2).
- Cylinder head gasket damaged. If the head is allowed to become loose, or if excessive carbon build-up on the piston crown and combustion chamber causes extremely high compression, the head gasket may leak. Retorquing the head is not always sufficient to restore the seal, so gasket renewal is necessary (see Chapter 2).
- Cylinder head warped. This is caused by overheating or improperly tightened head nuts. Machine shop resurfacing or head renewal is necessary (see Chapter 2).
- Valve spring broken or weak. Caused by component failure or wear; the springs must be renewed (see Chapter 2).
- Valve not seating properly. This is caused by a bent valve (from over-revving or improper valve adjustment), burned valve or seat (improper carburation) or an accumulation of carbon deposits on the seat (from carburation, lubrication problems). The valves must be cleaned and/or renewed and the seats serviced if possible (see Chapter 2).

Poor acceleration

- Carburettors leaking or dirty. Overhaul the carburettors (see Chapter 3).
- Timing not advancing. The pick-up coil or the ignition control unit may be defective. If so, they must be renewed, as they can't be repaired.
- Carburettors not synchronised. Adjust them with a vacuum gauge set or manometer (see Chapter 1).
- Engine oil viscosity too high. Using a heavier oil than that recommended in Chapter 1 can damage the oil pump or lubrication system and cause drag on the engine.
- Brakes dragging. Usually caused by debris which has entered the brake piston seals, or from a warped disc or bent axle. Repair as necessary (see Chapter 6).
- Fuel flow rate insufficient. Check the filters (Chapters 1 and 3).

3 Poor running or no power at high speed

Firing incorrect
- [ ] Air filter restricted. Clean or renew filter (see Chapter 1).
- [ ] Spark plugs fouled, defective or worn out. See Chapter 1 for spark plug maintenance.
- [ ] Spark plug caps or HT leads defective. See Chapters 1 and 4 for details of the ignition system.
- [ ] Spark plug caps not in good contact (see Chapter 4).
- [ ] Incorrect spark plugs. Wrong type, heat range or cap configuration. Check and install correct plugs listed in Chapter 1.
- [ ] Ignition control unit defective (see Chapter 4).
- [ ] Ignition HT coils defective (see Chapter 4).

Fuel/air mixture incorrect
- [ ] Main jet clogged. Dirt, water or other contaminants can clog the main jets. Clean the fuel tap filter, the in-line filter (XJR1300), the float chamber area, float needle valve filter and the jets and carburettor orifices (see Chapter 3).
- [ ] Main jet wrong size. The standard jetting is for sea level atmospheric pressure and oxygen content.
- [ ] Air bleed holes clogged. Remove and overhaul carburettors (see Chapter 3).
- [ ] Air filter clogged, poorly sealed, or missing (see Chapter 1).
- [ ] Air filter housing poorly sealed. Look for cracks, holes or loose clamps, and renew or repair defective parts.
- [ ] Fuel level too high or too low. Check the fuel level or float height (see Chapter 3).
- [ ] Fuel tank breather hose obstructed.
- [ ] Carburettor intake manifolds loose. Check for cracks, breaks, tears or loose clamps. Renew the rubber intake manifolds if they are split or perished (see Chapter 3).

Compression low
- [ ] Spark plugs loose. Remove the plugs and inspect their threads. Reinstall and tighten to the specified torque (see Chapter 1).
- [ ] Cylinder head not sufficiently tightened down. If the cylinder head is suspected of being loose, then there's a chance that the gasket and head are damaged if the problem has persisted for any length of time. The head nuts should be tightened to the proper torque in the correct sequence (see Chapter 2).
- [ ] Improper valve clearance. This means that the valve is not closing completely and compression pressure is leaking past the valve. Check and adjust the valve clearances (see Chapter 1).
- [ ] Cylinder and/or piston worn. Excessive wear will cause compression pressure to leak past the rings. This is usually accompanied by worn rings as well. A top-end overhaul is necessary (see Chapter 2).
- [ ] Piston rings worn, weak, broken, or sticking. Broken or sticking piston rings usually indicate a lubrication or carburation problem that causes excess carbon deposits or seizures to form on the pistons and rings. Top-end overhaul is necessary (see Chapter 2).
- [ ] Piston ring-to-groove clearance excessive. This is caused by excessive wear of the piston ring lands. Piston renewal is necessary (see Chapter 2).
- [ ] Cylinder head gasket damaged. If the head is allowed to become loose, or if excessive carbon build-up on the piston crown and combustion chamber causes extremely high compression, the head gasket may leak. Retorquing the head is not always sufficient to restore the seal, so gasket renewal is necessary (see Chapter 2).
- [ ] Cylinder head warped. This is caused by overheating or improperly tightened head nuts. Machine shop resurfacing or head renewal is necessary (see Chapter 2).
- [ ] Valve spring broken or weak. Caused by component failure or wear; the springs must be renewed (see Chapter 2).
- [ ] Valve not seating properly. This is caused by a bent valve (from over-revving or improper valve adjustment), burned valve or seat (improper carburation) or an accumulation of carbon deposits on the seat (from carburation or lubrication problems). The valves must be cleaned and/or renewed and the seats serviced if possible (see Chapter 2).

Knocking or pinking
- [ ] Carbon build-up in combustion chamber. Use of a fuel additive that will dissolve the adhesive bonding the carbon particles to the crown and chamber is the easiest way to remove the build-up. Otherwise, the cylinder head will have to be removed and decarbonised (see Chapter 2).
- [ ] Incorrect or poor quality fuel. Old or improper grades of fuel can cause detonation. This causes the piston to rattle, thus the knocking or pinking sound. Drain old fuel and always use the recommended fuel grade.
- [ ] Spark plug heat range incorrect. Uncontrolled detonation indicates the plug heat range is too hot. The plug in effect becomes a glow plug, raising cylinder temperatures. Install the proper heat range plug (see Chapter 1).
- [ ] Improper air/fuel mixture. This will cause the cylinders to run hot, which leads to detonation. Clogged jets or an air leak can cause this imbalance. See Chapter 4.

Miscellaneous causes
- [ ] Throttle valve doesn't open fully. Adjust the throttle grip freeplay (see Chapter 1).
- [ ] Clutch slipping. May be caused by loose or worn clutch components. Refer to Chapter 2 for clutch overhaul procedures.
- [ ] Timing not advancing.
- [ ] Engine oil viscosity too high. Using a heavier oil than the one recommended in Chapter 1 can damage the oil pump or lubrication system and cause drag on the engine.
- [ ] Brakes dragging. Usually caused by debris which has entered the brake piston seals, or from a warped disc or bent axle. Repair as necessary.
- [ ] Fuel flow rate insufficient. Check the filters (Chapters 1 and 3).

Fault Finding REF•39

4 Overheating

Firing incorrect
- [ ] Spark plugs fouled, defective or worn out. See Chapter 1 for spark plug maintenance.
- [ ] Incorrect spark plugs.
- [ ] Ignition control unit defective (see Chapter 4).
- [ ] Faulty ignition HT coils (see Chapter 4).

Fuel/air mixture incorrect
- [ ] Main jet clogged. Dirt, water and other contaminants can clog the main jets. Clean the fuel tap filter, the in-line filter (XJR1300), the float valve filter, the float chamber area and the jets and carburettor orifices (see Chapter 3).
- [ ] Main jet wrong size. The standard jetting is for sea level atmospheric pressure and oxygen content.
- [ ] Air filter clogged, poorly sealed or missing (see Chapter 1).
- [ ] Air filter housing poorly sealed. Look for cracks, holes or loose clamps and renew or repair.
- [ ] Fuel level too low. Check the fuel level and float height (see Chapter 3).
- [ ] Fuel tank breather hose obstructed.
- [ ] Carburettor intake manifolds loose. Check for cracks, breaks, tears or loose clamps. Renew the rubber intake manifold joints if split or perished.

Compression too high
- [ ] Carbon build-up in combustion chamber. Use of a fuel additive that will dissolve the adhesive bonding the carbon particles to the piston crown and chamber is the easiest way to remove the build-up. Otherwise, the cylinder head will have to be removed and decarbonised (see Chapter 2).
- [ ] Improperly machined head surface or installation of incorrect gasket during engine assembly.

Engine load excessive
- [ ] Clutch slipping. Can be caused by damaged, loose or worn clutch components. Refer to Chapter 2 for overhaul procedures.
- [ ] Engine oil level too high. The addition of too much oil will cause pressurisation of the crankcase and inefficient engine operation. Check Specifications and drain to proper level (see Chapter 1).
- [ ] Engine oil viscosity too high. Using a heavier oil than the one recommended in Chapter 1 can damage the oil pump or lubrication system as well as cause drag on the engine.
- [ ] Brakes dragging. Usually caused by debris which has entered the brake piston seals, or from a warped disc or bent axle. Repair as necessary.

Lubrication inadequate
- [ ] Engine oil level too low. Friction caused by intermittent lack of lubrication or from oil that is overworked can cause overheating. The oil provides a definite cooling function in the engine. Check the oil level (see *Daily (pre-ride) checks*).
- [ ] Poor quality engine oil or incorrect viscosity or type. Oil is rated not only according to viscosity but also according to type. Some oils are not rated high enough for use in this engine. Check the Specifications section and change to the correct oil (see *Daily (pre-ride) checks*).

Miscellaneous causes
- [ ] Modification to exhaust system. Most aftermarket exhaust systems cause the engine to run leaner, which make them run hotter. When installing an accessory exhaust system, always rejet the carburettors.

5 Clutch problems

Clutch slipping
- [ ] Clutch fluid level too high. Check and adjust level (see *Daily (pre-ride) checks*).
- [ ] Friction plates worn or warped. Overhaul the clutch assembly (see Chapter 2).
- [ ] Plain plates warped (see Chapter 2).
- [ ] Clutch diaphragm spring broken or weak. An old or heat-damaged (from slipping clutch) spring should be renewed (see Chapter 2).
- [ ] Clutch release mechanism defective. Renew any defective parts (see Chapter 2).
- [ ] Clutch centre or housing unevenly worn. This causes improper engagement of the plates. Renew the damaged or worn parts (see Chapter 2).

Clutch not disengaging completely
- [ ] Clutch fluid level too low. Check and adjust level (see *Daily (pre-ride) checks*).
- [ ] Air in hydraulic release system. Bleed the system (see Chapter 2).
- [ ] Clutch plates warped or damaged. This will cause clutch drag, which in turn will cause the machine to creep. Overhaul the clutch assembly (see Chapter 2).
- [ ] Engine oil deteriorated. Old, thin, worn out oil will not provide proper lubrication for the plates, causing the clutch to drag. Renew the oil and filter (see Chapter 1).
- [ ] Engine oil viscosity too high. Using a heavier oil than recommended can cause the plates to stick together, putting a drag on the engine. Change to the correct weight oil (see *Daily (pre-ride) checks*).
- [ ] Clutch housing seized on input shaft. Lack of lubrication, severe wear or damage can cause the collar to seize on the shaft. Overhaul of the clutch, and perhaps transmission, may be necessary to repair the damage (see Chapter 2).
- [ ] Clutch release mechanism defective. Overhaul the master and release (slave) cylinders (see Chapter 2). Check the hose for bulges and leaks.
- [ ] Loose clutch centre nut. Causes housing and centre misalignment putting a drag on the engine. Engagement adjustment continually varies. Overhaul the clutch assembly (see Chapter 2).

6 Gearchanging problems

Doesn't go into gear or lever doesn't return
- [ ] Clutch not disengaging. See above.
- [ ] Selector fork(s) bent or seized. Often caused by dropping the machine or from lack of lubrication. Overhaul the transmission (see Chapter 2).
- [ ] Gear(s) stuck on shaft. Most often caused by a lack of lubrication or excessive wear in transmission bearings and bushes. Overhaul the transmission (see Chapter 2).
- [ ] Selector drum binding. Caused by lubrication failure or excessive wear. Renew the drum and bearing (see Chapter 2).
- [ ] Gearchange centralising spring weak or broken (see Chapter 2).
- [ ] Gearchange lever broken. Splines stripped out of linkage arm or shaft, caused by allowing the lever to get loose or from dropping the machine. Renew necessary parts (see Chapter 2).
- [ ] Gearchange mechanism stopper arm broken or worn. Full engagement and rotary movement of selector drum results. Renew the arm (see Chapter 2).
- [ ] Stopper arm spring broken. Allows arm to float, causing sporadic gearchange operation. Renew spring (see Chapter 2).

Jumps out of gear
- [ ] Selector fork(s) worn. Overhaul the transmission (see Chapter 2).
- [ ] Gear groove(s) worn. Overhaul the transmission (see Chapter 2).
- [ ] Gear dogs or dog slots worn or damaged. The gears should be inspected and renewed. No attempt should be made to service the worn parts.

Overselects
- [ ] Stopper arm spring weak or broken (see Chapter 2).
- [ ] Gearchange shaft centralising spring locating pin broken or distorted (see Chapter 2).

7 Abnormal engine noise

Knocking or pinking
- [ ] Carbon build-up in combustion chamber. Use of a fuel additive that will dissolve the adhesive bonding the carbon particles to the piston crown and chamber is the easiest way to remove the build-up. Otherwise, the cylinder head will have to be removed and decarbonised (see Chapter 2).
- [ ] Incorrect or poor quality fuel. Old or improper fuel can cause detonation. This causes the pistons to rattle, thus the knocking or pinking sound. Drain the old fuel and always use the recommended grade fuel (see Chapter 4).
- [ ] Spark plug heat range incorrect. Uncontrolled detonation indicates that the plug heat range is too hot. The plug in effect becomes a glow plug, raising cylinder temperatures. Install the proper heat range plug (see Chapter 1).
- [ ] Improper air/fuel mixture. This will cause the cylinders to run hot and lead to detonation. Clogged jets or an air leak can cause this imbalance. See Chapter 4.

Piston slap or rattling
- [ ] Cylinder-to-piston clearance excessive. Caused by improper assembly. Inspect and overhaul top-end parts (see Chapter 2).
- [ ] Connecting rod bent. Caused by over-revving, trying to start a badly flooded engine or from ingesting a foreign object into the combustion chamber. Renew the damaged parts (see Chapter 2).
- [ ] Piston pin or piston pin bore worn or seized from wear or lack of lubrication. Renew damaged parts (see Chapter 2).
- [ ] Piston ring(s) worn, broken or sticking. Overhaul the top-end (see Chapter 2).
- [ ] Piston seizure damage. Usually from lack of lubrication or overheating. Renew the pistons and rebore the cylinder block (XJR1200) or renew the cylinder block (XJR1300), as necessary (see Chapter 2).
- [ ] Connecting rod upper or lower end clearance excessive. Caused by excessive wear or lack of lubrication. Renew worn parts.

Valve noise
- [ ] Incorrect valve clearances. Adjust the clearances by referring to Chapter 1.
- [ ] Valve spring broken or weak. Check and renew weak valve springs (see Chapter 2).
- [ ] Camshaft or cylinder head worn or damaged. Lack of lubrication at high rpm is usually the cause of damage. Insufficient oil or failure to change the oil at the recommended intervals are the chief causes. Since there are no renewable bearings in the head, the head itself will have to be renewed if there is excessive wear or damage (see Chapter 2).

Other noise
- [ ] Cylinder head gasket leaking.
- [ ] Exhaust pipe leaking at cylinder head connection. Caused by improper fit of pipe(s) or loose exhaust flange. All exhaust fasteners should be tightened evenly and carefully. Failure to do this will lead to a leak.
- [ ] Crankshaft runout excessive. Caused by a bent crankshaft (from over-revving) or damage from an upper cylinder component failure.
- [ ] Engine mounting bolts loose. Tighten all engine mount bolts (see Chapter 2).
- [ ] Engine mounting dampers deteriorated or worn (see Chapter 2).
- [ ] Crankshaft bearings worn (see Chapter 2).
- [ ] Cam chain worn or tensioner faulty. Check according to the procedure in Chapter 2.

Fault Finding REF•41

8 Abnormal driveline noise

Clutch noise
- [ ] Clutch housing/friction plate clearance excessive (see Chapter 2).
- [ ] Loose or damaged clutch pressure plate and/or bolts (see Chapter 2).

Transmission noise
- [ ] Bearings worn. Also includes the possibility that the shafts are worn. Overhaul the transmission (see Chapter 2).
- [ ] Gears worn or chipped (see Chapter 2).
- [ ] Metal chips jammed in gear teeth. Probably pieces from a broken clutch, gear or selector mechanism that were picked up by the gears. This will cause early bearing failure (see Chapter 2).
- [ ] Engine oil level too low. Causes a howl from transmission. Also affects engine power and clutch operation (see *Daily (pre-ride) checks*).

Final drive noise
- [ ] Chain not adjusted properly (see Chapter 1).
- [ ] Front or rear sprocket loose. Tighten fasteners (see Chapter 5).
- [ ] Sprockets worn. Renew sprockets (see Chapter 5).
- [ ] Rear sprocket warped. Renew sprockets (see Chapter 5).
- [ ] Loose or worn rear wheel or sprocket coupling bearings. Check and renew as needed (see Chapter 6).

9 Abnormal frame and suspension noise

Front end noise
- [ ] Low fluid level or improper viscosity oil in forks. This can sound like spurting and is usually accompanied by irregular fork action (see Chapter 5).
- [ ] Spring weak or broken. Makes a clicking or scraping sound. Fork oil, when drained, will have a lot of metal particles in it (see Chapter 5).
- [ ] Steering head bearings loose or damaged. Clicks when braking. Check and adjust or renew as necessary (Chapters 1 and 5).
- [ ] Fork yokes loose. Make sure all clamp bolts are tightened to the specified torque (see Chapter 5).
- [ ] Fork tube bent. Good possibility if machine has been dropped. Renew tube (see Chapter 5).
- [ ] Front axle or axle clamp bolt loose. Tighten them to the specified torque (see Chapter 6).
- [ ] Loose or worn wheel bearings. Check and renew as needed (see Chapter 6).

Shock absorber noise
- [ ] Fluid level incorrect. Indicates a leak caused by defective seal. Shock will be covered with oil. Renew shock or seek advice on repair from a Yamaha dealer or suspension specialist (see Chapter 5).
- [ ] Defective shock absorber with internal damage. This is in the body of the shock and can't be remedied. The shocks must be renewed as a pair (see Chapter 5).
- [ ] Bent or damaged shock body. Renew the shocks as a pair (see Chapter 5).
- [ ] Loose or worn shock absorber mountings. Check and renew as necessary (see Chapter 5).

Brake noise
- [ ] Squeal caused by pad shim not installed or positioned correctly (where fitted) (see Chapter 6).
- [ ] Squeal caused by dust on brake pads. Usually found in combination with glazed pads. Clean using brake cleaning solvent (see Chapter 6).
- [ ] Contamination of brake pads. Oil, brake fluid or dirt causing brake to chatter or squeal. Renew pads (see Chapter 6).
- [ ] Pads glazed. Caused by excessive heat from prolonged use or from contamination. Do not use sandpaper, emery cloth, carborundum cloth or any other abrasive to roughen the pad surfaces as abrasives will stay in the pad material and damage the disc. A very fine flat file can be used, but pad renewal is suggested as a cure (see Chapter 6).
- [ ] Disc warped. Can cause a chattering, clicking or intermittent squeal. Usually accompanied by a pulsating lever and uneven braking. Renew the disc (see Chapter 6).
- [ ] Loose or worn wheel bearings. Check and renew as needed (see Chapter 6).

10 Excessive exhaust smoke

White smoke
- [ ] Piston oil ring worn. The ring may be broken or damaged, causing oil from the crankcase to be pulled past the piston into the combustion chamber. Renew the rings (see Chapter 2).
- [ ] Cylinders worn, cracked, or scored. Caused by overheating or oil starvation. Check the cylinder block and lubrication system (see Chapter 2).
- [ ] Valve oil seal damaged or worn. Renew oil seals (see Chapter 2).
- [ ] Valve guide worn. Perform a complete valve job (see Chapter 2).
- [ ] Engine oil level too high, which causes the oil to be forced past the rings. Drain oil to the proper level (see *Daily (pre-ride) checks*).
- [ ] Head gasket broken between oil return and cylinder. Causes oil to be pulled into the combustion chamber. Renew the head gasket and check the head for warpage (see Chapter 2).
- [ ] Abnormal crankcase pressurisation, which forces oil past the rings. Clogged breather is usually the cause.

Black smoke
- [ ] Air filter clogged. Clean or renew the element (see Chapter 1).
- [ ] Main jet too large or loose. Compare the jet size to the Specifications (see Chapter 3).
- [ ] Choke cable (1996-on models) or linkage shaft stuck, causing fuel to be pulled through choke circuit (see Chapter 3).
- [ ] Fuel level too high. Check the fuel level and adjust the float height(s) as necessary (see Chapter 3).
- [ ] Float needle valve held off needle seat. Clean the float chambers and fuel line and renew the needles and seats if necessary (see Chapter 3).

Brown smoke
- [ ] Main jet too small or clogged. Lean condition caused by wrong size main jet or by a restricted orifice. Clean float chambers and jets and compare jet size to Specifications (see Chapter 3).
- [ ] Fuel flow insufficient – float needle valve stuck closed due to chemical reaction with old fuel; fuel level incorrect; restricted fuel line, blocked float valve, blocked in-line fuel filter (XJR1300) or blocked fuel tap filter (see Chapter 3).
- [ ] Carburettor intake manifold clamps loose (see Chapter 3).
- [ ] Air filter poorly sealed or not installed (see Chapter 1).

Fault Finding

11 Poor handling or stability

Handlebar hard to turn
- [ ] Steering head bearing adjuster nut too tight. Check adjustment as described in Chapter 1.
- [ ] Bearings damaged. Roughness can be felt as the bars are turned from side-to-side. Renew bearings and races (see Chapter 5).
- [ ] Races dented or worn. Denting results from wear in only one position (e.g., straight ahead), from a collision or hitting a pothole or from dropping the machine. Renew races and bearings (see Chapter 5)
- [ ] Steering stem lubrication inadequate. Causes are grease getting hard from age or being washed out by high pressure car washes. Disassemble steering head and repack bearings (see Chapter 5).
- [ ] Steering stem bent. Caused by a collision, hitting a pothole or by dropping the machine. Renew damaged part. Don't try to straighten the steering stem (see Chapter 5).
- [ ] Front tyre air pressure too low (see Chapter 1).

Handlebar shakes or vibrates excessively
- [ ] Tyres worn or out of balance (see Chapter 6).
- [ ] Swingarm bearings worn. Renew worn bearings (see Chapter 5).
- [ ] Wheel rim(s) warped or damaged. Inspect wheels for runout (see Chapter 6).
- [ ] Wheel bearings worn. Worn front or rear wheel bearings can cause poor tracking. Worn front bearings will cause wobble (see Chapter 6).
- [ ] Handlebar clamp bolts loose (see Chapter 5).
- [ ] Fork yoke bolts loose. Tighten them to the specified torque (see Chapter 5).
- [ ] Engine mounting bolts loose or rubber mountings worn. Will cause excessive vibration with increased engine rpm (see Chapter 2).

Handlebar pulls to one side
- [ ] Frame bent. Definitely suspect this if the machine has been dropped. May or may not be accompanied by cracking near the bend. Renew the frame (see Chapter 5).
- [ ] Wheels out of alignment. Caused by improper location of axle spacers or from bent steering stem or frame (see Chapter 6).
- [ ] Swingarm bent or twisted. Caused by age (metal fatigue) or impact damage. Renew the arm (see Chapter 5).
- [ ] Steering stem bent. Caused by impact damage or by dropping the motorcycle. Renew the steering stem (see Chapter 5).
- [ ] Fork tube bent. Disassemble the forks and renew the damaged parts (see Chapter 5).
- [ ] Fork oil level uneven. Check and add or drain as necessary (see Chapter 5).

Poor shock absorbing qualities
- [ ] Too hard:
  a) Fork oil level excessive (see Chapter 5).
  b) Fork oil viscosity too high. Use a lighter oil (see the Specifications in Chapter 5).
  c) Fork tube bent. Causes a harsh, sticking feeling (see Chapter 5).
  d) Fork internal damage (see Chapter 5).
  e) Rear shock shaft or body bent or damaged (see Chapter 5).
  f) Rear shock internal damage.
  g) Tyre pressure too high (see Chapter 1).
- [ ] Too soft:
  a) Fork or rear shock oil insufficient and/or leaking (see Chapter 5).
  b) Fork oil level too low (see Chapter 5).
  c) Fork oil viscosity too light (see Chapter 5).
  d) Fork spring weak or broken (see Chapter 5).
  e) Rear shock internal damage or leakage (see Chapter 5).

12 Braking problems

Brakes are spongy, don't hold
- [ ] Air in brake line. Caused by inattention to master cylinder fluid level or by leakage. Locate problem and bleed brakes (see Chapter 6).
- [ ] Pad or disc worn (Chapters 1 and 6).
- [ ] Brake fluid leak. See paragraph 1.
- [ ] Contaminated pads. Caused by contamination with oil, grease, brake fluid, etc. Renew pads. Clean disc thoroughly with brake cleaner (see Chapter 6).
- [ ] Brake fluid deteriorated. Fluid is old or contaminated. Drain system, replenish with new fluid and bleed the system (see Chapter 6).
- [ ] Master cylinder internal parts worn or damaged causing fluid to bypass (see Chapter 6).
- [ ] Master cylinder bore scratched by foreign material or broken spring. Repair or renew master cylinder (see Chapter 6).
- [ ] Disc warped. Renew disc (see Chapter 6).

Brake lever or pedal pulsates
- [ ] Disc warped. Renew disc (see Chapter 6).
- [ ] Axle bent. Renew axle (see Chapter 6).
- [ ] Brake caliper bolts loose (see Chapter 6).
- [ ] Wheel warped or otherwise damaged (see Chapter 6).
- [ ] Wheel bearings damaged or worn (see Chapter 6).

Brakes drag
- [ ] Master cylinder piston seized. Caused by wear or damage to piston or cylinder bore (see Chapter 6).
- [ ] Lever balky or stuck. Check pivot and lubricate (see Chapter 6).
- [ ] Brake caliper piston seized in bore. Caused by wear or ingestion of dirt past deteriorated seal (see Chapter 6).
- [ ] Brake pad damaged. Pad material separated from backing plate. Usually caused by faulty manufacturing process or from contact with chemicals. Renew pads (see Chapter 6).
- [ ] Pads improperly installed (see Chapter 6).

Fault Finding   REF•43

13 Electrical problems

Battery dead or weak

- [ ] Battery faulty. Caused by sulphated plates which are shorted through sedimentation. Also, broken battery terminal making only occasional contact (see Chapter 8).
- [ ] Battery cables making poor contact (see Chapter 8).
- [ ] Load excessive. Caused by addition of high wattage lights or other electrical accessories.
- [ ] Ignition (main) switch defective. Switch either grounds (earths) internally or fails to shut off system. Renew the switch (see Chapter 8).
- [ ] Regulator/rectifier defective (see Chapter 8).
- [ ] Alternator stator coil open or shorted (see Chapter 8).
- [ ] Wiring faulty. Wiring grounded (earthed) or connections loose in ignition, charging or lighting circuits (see Chapter 8).

Battery overcharged

- [ ] Regulator/rectifier defective. Overcharging is noticed when battery gets excessively warm (see Chapter 8).
- [ ] Battery defective. Renew battery (see Chapter 8).
- [ ] Battery amperage too low, wrong type or size. Install manufacturer's specified amp-hour battery to handle charging load (see Chapter 8).

REF•44 Fault Finding Equipment

Checking engine compression

● Low compression will result in exhaust smoke, heavy oil consumption, poor starting and poor performance. A compression test will provide useful information about an engine's condition and if performed regularly, can give warning of trouble before any other symptoms become apparent.
● A compression gauge will be required, along with an adapter to suit the spark plug hole thread size. Note that the screw-in type gauge/adapter set up is preferable to the rubber cone type.
● Before carrying out the test, first check the valve clearances as described in Chapter 1.

1 Run the engine until it reaches normal operating temperature, then stop it and remove the spark plug(s), taking care not to scald your hands on the hot components.
2 Install the gauge adapter and compression gauge in No. 1 cylinder spark plug hole (see illustration 1).

Screw the compression gauge adapter into the spark plug hole, then screw the gauge into the adapter

3 On kickstart-equipped motorcycles, make sure the ignition switch is OFF, then open the throttle fully and kick the engine over a couple of times until the gauge reading stabilises.
4 On motorcycles with electric start only, the procedure will differ depending on the nature of the ignition system. Flick the engine kill switch (engine stop switch) to OFF and turn the ignition switch ON; open the throttle fully and crank the engine over on the starter motor for a couple of revolutions until the gauge reading stabilises. If the starter will not operate with the kill switch OFF, turn the ignition switch OFF and refer to the next paragraph.
5 Install the spark plugs back into their suppressor caps and arrange the plug electrodes so that their metal bodies are earthed (grounded) against the cylinder head; this is essential to prevent damage to the ignition system as the engine is spun over (see illustration 2). Position the plugs well

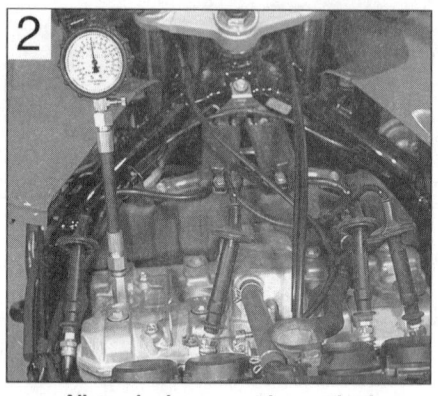

All spark plugs must be earthed (grounded) against the cylinder head

away from the plug holes otherwise there is a risk of atomised fuel escaping from the combustion chambers and igniting. As a safety precaution, cover the top of the valve cover with rag. Now turn the ignition switch ON and kill switch ON, open the throttle fully and crank the engine over on the starter motor for a couple of revolutions until the gauge reading stabilises.
6 After one or two revolutions the pressure should build up to a maximum figure and then stabilise. Take a note of this reading and on multi-cylinder engines repeat the test on the remaining cylinders.
7 The correct pressures are given in Chapter 1 Specifications. If the results fall within the specified range and on multi-cylinder engines all are relatively equal, the engine is in good condition. If there is a marked difference between the readings, or if the readings are lower than specified, inspection of the top-end components will be required.
8 Low compression pressure may be due to worn cylinder bores, pistons or rings, failure of the cylinder head gasket, worn valve seals, or poor valve seating.
9 To distinguish between cylinder/piston wear and valve leakage, pour a small quantity of oil into the bore to temporarily seal the piston rings, then repeat the compression tests (see illustration 3). If the readings show

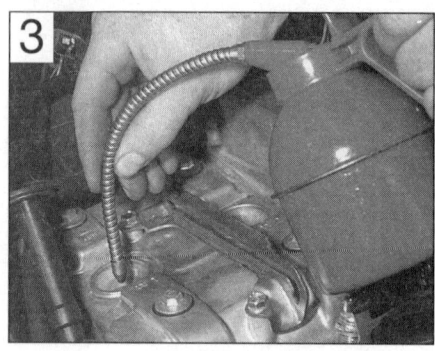

Bores can be temporarily sealed with a squirt of motor oil

a noticeable increase in pressure this confirms that the cylinder bore, piston, or rings are worn. If, however, no change is indicated, the cylinder head gasket or valves should be examined.
10 High compression pressure indicates excessive carbon build-up in the combustion chamber and on the piston crown. If this is the case the cylinder head should be removed and the deposits removed. Note that excessive carbon build-up is less likely with the used on modern fuels.

Checking battery open-circuit voltage

⚠ *Warning: The gases produced by the battery are explosive - never smoke or create any sparks in the vicinity of the battery. Never allow the electrolyte to contact your skin or clothing - if it does, wash it off and seek immediate medical attention.*

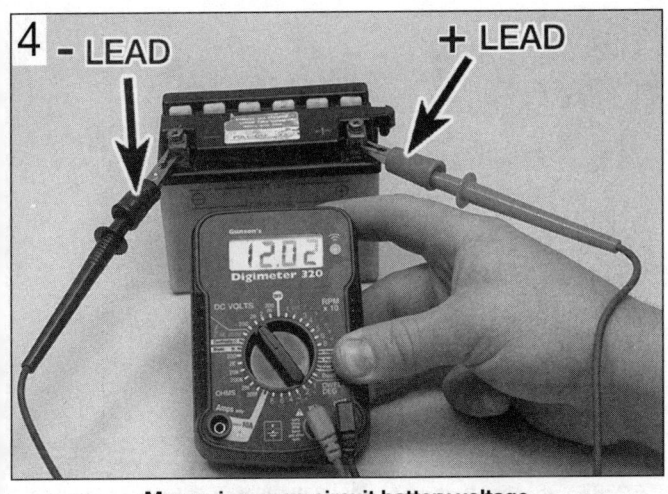

Fault Finding Equipment REF•45

Measuring open-circuit battery voltage

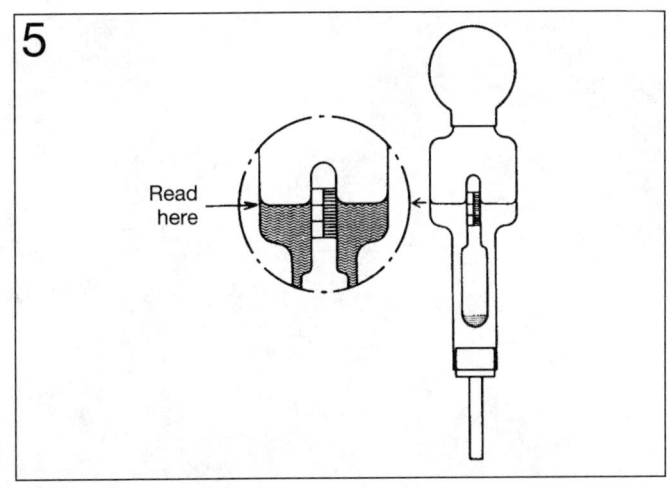

Float-type hydrometer for measuring battery specific gravity

- Before any electrical fault is investigated the battery should be checked.
- You'll need a dc voltmeter or multimeter to check battery voltage. Check that the leads are inserted in the correct terminals on the meter, red lead to positive (+ve), black lead to negative (-ve). Incorrect connections can damage the meter.
- A sound fully-charged 12 volt battery should produce between 12.3 and 12.6 volts across its terminals (12.8 volts for a maintenance-free battery). On machines with a 6 volt battery, voltage should be between 6.1 and 6.3 volts.

1 Set a multimeter to the 0 to 20 volts dc range and connect its probes across the battery terminals. Connect the meter's positive (+ve) probe, usually red, to the battery positive (+ve) terminal, followed by the meter's negative (-ve) probe, usually black, to the battery negative terminal (-ve) **(see illustration 4)**.

2 If battery voltage is low (below 10 volts on a 12 volt battery or below 4 volts on a six volt battery), charge the battery and test the voltage again. If the battery repeatedly goes flat, investigate the motorcycle's charging system.

Checking battery specific gravity (SG)

⚠ *Warning: The gases produced by the battery are explosive - never smoke or create any sparks in the vicinity of the battery. Never allow the electrolyte to contact your skin or clothing - if it does, wash it off and seek immediate medical attention.*

- The specific gravity check gives an indication of a battery's state of charge.
- A hydrometer is used for measuring specific gravity. Make sure you purchase one which has a small enough hose to insert in the aperture of a motorcycle battery.
- Specific gravity is simply a measure of the electrolyte's density compared with that of water. Water has an SG of 1.000 and fully-charged battery electrolyte is about 26% heavier, at 1.260.
- Specific gravity checks are not possible on maintenance-free batteries. Testing the open-circuit voltage is the only means of determining their state of charge.

1 To measure SG, remove the battery from the motorcycle and remove the first cell cap. Draw some electrolyte into the hydrometer and note the reading **(see illustration 5)**. Return the electrolyte to the cell and install the cap.

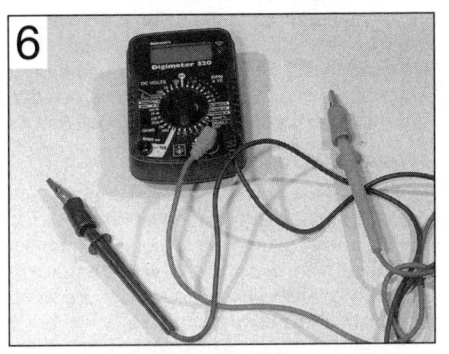

2 The reading should be in the region of 1.260 to 1.280. If SG is below 1.200 the battery needs charging. Note that SG will vary with temperature; it should be measured at 20°C (68°F). Add 0.007 to the reading for every 10°C above 20°C, and subtract 0.007 from the reading for every 10°C below 20°C. Add 0.004 to the reading for every 10°F above 68°F, and subtract 0.004 from the reading for every 10°F below 68°F.

3 When the check is complete, rinse the hydrometer thoroughly with clean water.

Checking for continuity

- The term continuity describes the uninterrupted flow of electricity through an electrical circuit. A continuity check will determine whether an **open-circuit** situation exists.
- Continuity can be checked with an ohmmeter, multimeter, continuity tester or battery and bulb test circuit **(see illustrations 6, 7 and 8)**.

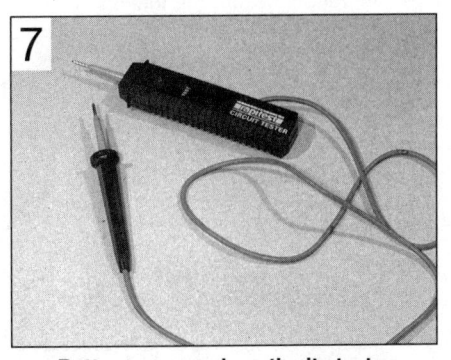

Digital multimeter can be used for all electrical tests

Battery-powered continuity tester

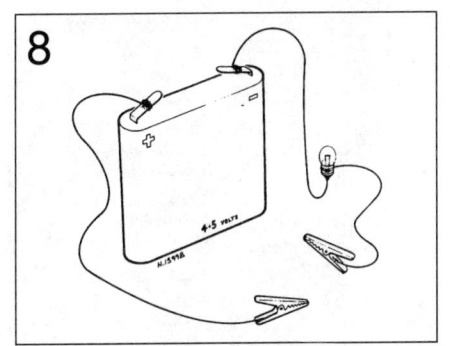

Battery and bulb test circuit

REF•46 Fault Finding Equipment

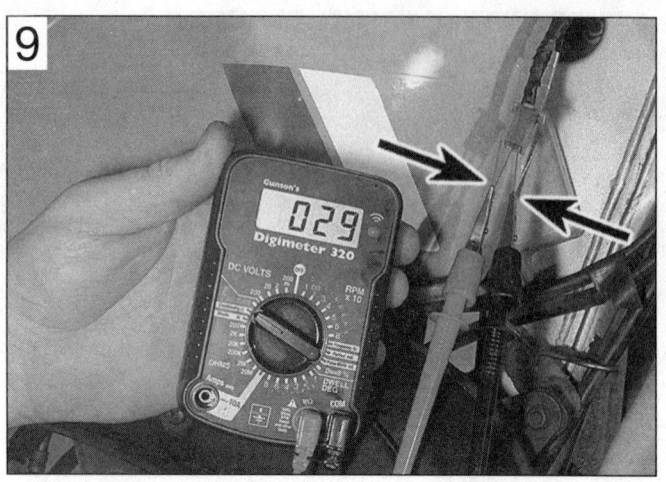

Continuity check of front brake light switch using a meter - note split pins used to access connector terminals

Continuity check of rear brake light switch using a continuity tester

- All of these instruments are self-powered by a battery, therefore the checks are made with the ignition OFF.
- As a safety precaution, always disconnect the battery negative (-ve) lead before making checks, particularly if ignition switch checks are being made.
- If using a meter, select the appropriate ohms scale and check that the meter reads infinity (∞). Touch the meter probes together and check that meter reads zero; where necessary adjust the meter so that it reads zero.
- After using a meter, always switch it OFF to conserve its battery.

Switch checks

1 If a switch is at fault, trace its wiring up to the wiring connectors. Separate the wire connectors and inspect them for security and condition. A build-up of dirt or corrosion here will most likely be the cause of the problem - clean up and apply a water dispersant such as WD40.

2 If using a test meter, set the meter to the ohms x 10 scale and connect its probes across the wires from the switch (see illustration 9). Simple ON/OFF type switches, such as brake light switches, only have two wires whereas combination switches, like the ignition switch, have many internal links. Study the wiring diagram to ensure that you are connecting across the correct pair of wires. Continuity (low or no measurable resistance - 0 ohms) should be indicated with the switch ON and no continuity (high resistance) with it OFF.

3 Note that the polarity of the test probes doesn't matter for continuity checks, although care should be taken to follow specific test procedures if a diode or solid-state component is being checked.

4 A continuity tester or battery and bulb circuit can be used in the same way. Connect its probes as described above (see illustration 10). The light should come on to indicate continuity in the ON switch position, but should extinguish in the OFF position.

Wiring checks

- Many electrical faults are caused by damaged wiring, often due to incorrect routing or chaffing on frame components.
- Loose, wet or corroded wire connectors can also be the cause of electrical problems, especially in exposed locations.

1 A continuity check can be made on a single length of wire by disconnecting it at each end and connecting a meter or continuity tester across both ends of the wire (see illustration 11).

2 Continuity (low or no resistance - 0 ohms) should be indicated if the wire is good. If no continuity (high resistance) is shown, suspect a broken wire.

Checking for voltage

- A voltage check can determine whether current is reaching a component.
- Voltage can be checked with a dc voltmeter, multimeter set on the dc volts scale, test light or buzzer (see illustrations 12 and 13). A meter has the advantage of being able to measure actual voltage.
- When using a meter, check that its leads are inserted in the correct terminals on the meter, red to positive (+ve), black to negative (-ve). Incorrect connections can damage the meter.
- A voltmeter (or multimeter set to the dc volts scale) should always be connected in parallel (across the load). Connecting it in series will destroy the meter.
- Voltage checks are made with the ignition ON.

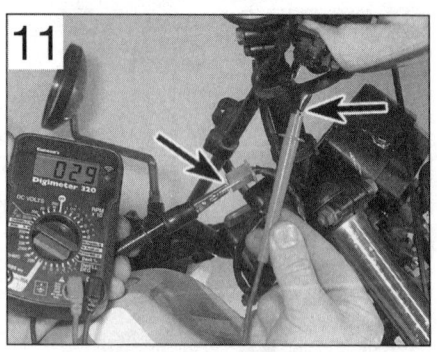

Continuity check of front brake light switch sub-harness

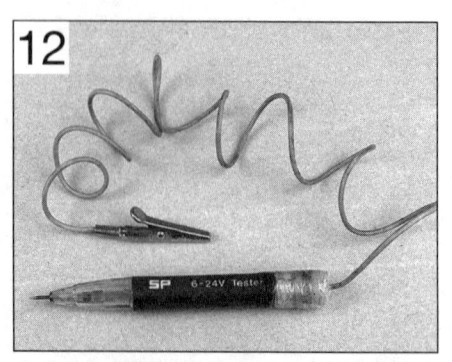

A simple test light can be used for voltage checks

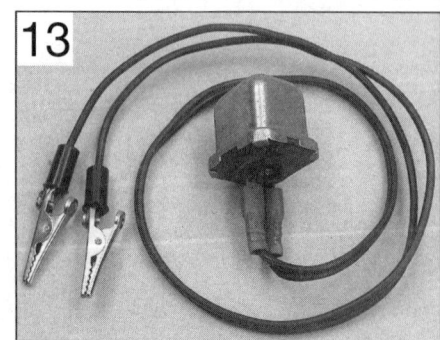

A buzzer is useful for voltage checks

Fault Finding Equipment REF•47

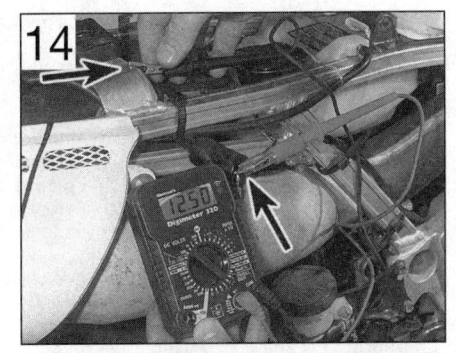

Checking for voltage at the rear brake light power supply wire using a meter . . .

1 First identify the relevant wiring circuit by referring to the wiring diagram at the end of this manual. If other electrical components share the same power supply (ie are fed from the same fuse), take note whether they are working correctly - this is useful information in deciding where to start checking the circuit.

2 If using a meter, check first that the meter leads are plugged into the correct terminals on the meter (see above). Set the meter to the dc volts function, at a range suitable for the battery voltage. Connect the meter red probe (+ve) to the power supply wire and the black probe to a good metal earth (ground) on the motorcycle's frame or directly to the battery negative (-ve) terminal **(see illustration 14)**. Battery voltage should be shown on the meter

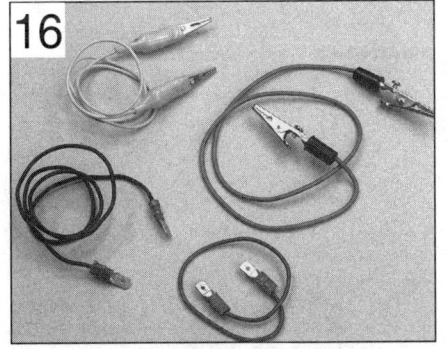

A selection of jumper wires for making earth (ground) checks

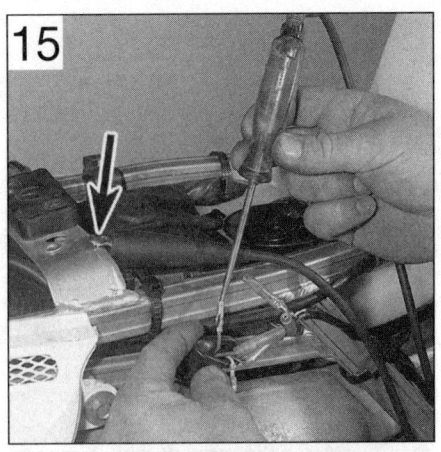

. . . or a test light - note the earth connection to the frame (arrow)

with the ignition switched ON.

3 If using a test light or buzzer, connect its positive (+ve) probe to the power supply terminal and its negative (-ve) probe to a good earth (ground) on the motorcycle's frame or directly to the battery negative (-ve) terminal **(see illustration 15)**. With the ignition ON, the test light should illuminate or the buzzer sound.

4 If no voltage is indicated, work back towards the fuse continuing to check for voltage. When you reach a point where there is voltage, you know the problem lies between that point and your last check point.

Checking the earth (ground)

- Earth connections are made either directly to the engine or frame (such as sensors, neutral switch etc. which only have a positive feed) or by a separate wire into the earth circuit of the wiring harness. Alternatively a short earth wire is sometimes run directly from the component to the motorcycle's frame.
- Corrosion is often the cause of a poor earth connection.
- If total failure is experienced, check the security of the main earth lead from the negative (-ve) terminal of the battery and also the main earth (ground) point on the wiring harness. If corroded, dismantle the connection and clean all surfaces back to bare metal.

1 To check the earth on a component, use an insulated jumper wire to temporarily bypass its earth connection **(see illustration 16)**. Connect one end of the jumper wire between the earth terminal or metal body of the component and the other end to the motorcycle's frame.

2 If the circuit works with the jumper wire installed, the original earth circuit is faulty. Check the wiring for open-circuits or poor connections. Clean up direct earth connections, removing all traces of corrosion and remake the joint. Apply petroleum jelly to the joint to prevent future corrosion.

Tracing a short-circuit

- A short-circuit occurs where current shorts to earth (ground) bypassing the circuit components. This usually results in a blown fuse.

- A short-circuit is most likely to occur where the insulation has worn through due to wiring chafing on a component, allowing a direct path to earth (ground) on the frame.

1 Remove any bodypanels necessary to access the circuit wiring.

2 Check that all electrical switches in the circuit are OFF, then remove the circuit fuse and connect a test light, buzzer or voltmeter (set to the dc scale) across the fuse terminals. No voltage should be shown.

3 Move the wiring from side to side whilst observing the test light or meter. When the test light comes on, buzzer sounds or meter shows voltage, you have found the cause of the short. It will usually shown up as damaged or burned insulation.

4 Note that the same test can be performed on each component in the circuit, even the switch.

Technical Terms Explained

A

ABS (Anti-lock braking system) A system, usually electronically controlled, that senses incipient wheel lockup during braking and relieves hydraulic pressure at wheel which is about to skid.
Aftermarket Components suitable for the motorcycle, but not produced by the motorcycle manufacturer.
Allen key A hexagonal wrench which fits into a recessed hexagonal hole.
Alternating current (ac) Current produced by an alternator. Requires converting to direct current by a rectifier for charging purposes.
Alternator Converts mechanical energy from the engine into electrical energy to charge the battery and power the electrical system.
Ampere (amp) A unit of measurement for the flow of electrical current. Current = Volts ÷ Ohms.
Ampere-hour (Ah) Measure of battery capacity.
Angle-tightening A torque expressed in degrees. Often follows a conventional tightening torque for cylinder head or main bearing fasteners **(see illustration)**.

Angle-tightening cylinder head bolts

Antifreeze A substance (usually ethylene glycol) mixed with water, and added to the cooling system, to prevent freezing of the coolant in winter. Antifreeze also contains chemicals to inhibit corrosion and the formation of rust and other deposits that would tend to clog the radiator and coolant passages and reduce cooling efficiency.
Anti-dive System attached to the fork lower leg (slider) to prevent fork dive when braking hard.
Anti-seize compound A coating that reduces the risk of seizing on fasteners that are subjected to high temperatures, such as exhaust clamp bolts and nuts.
API American Petroleum Institute. A quality standard for 4-stroke motor oils.
Asbestos A natural fibrous mineral with great heat resistance, commonly used in the composition of brake friction materials. Asbestos is a health hazard and the dust created by brake systems should never be inhaled or ingested.
ATF Automatic Transmission Fluid. Often used in front forks.
ATU Automatic Timing Unit. Mechanical device for advancing the ignition timing on early engines.
ATV All Terrain Vehicle. Often called a Quad.
Axial play Side-to-side movement.
Axle A shaft on which a wheel revolves. Also known as a spindle.

B

Backlash The amount of movement between meshed components when one component is held still. Usually applies to gear teeth.
Ball bearing A bearing consisting of a hardened inner and outer race with hardened steel balls between the two races.
Bearings Used between two working surfaces to prevent wear of the components and a build-up of heat. Four types of bearing are commonly used on motorcycles: plain shell bearings, ball bearings, tapered roller bearings and needle roller bearings.
Bevel gears Used to turn the drive through 90°. Typical applications are shaft final drive and camshaft drive **(see illustration)**.

Bevel gears are used to turn the drive through 90°

BHP Brake Horsepower. The British measurement for engine power output. Power output is now usually expressed in kilowatts (kW).
Bias-belted tyre Similar construction to radial tyre, but with outer belt running at an angle to the wheel rim.
Big-end bearing The bearing in the end of the connecting rod that's attached to the crankshaft.
Bleeding The process of removing air from an hydraulic system via a bleed nipple or bleed screw.
Bottom-end A description of an engine's crankcase components and all components contained there-in.
BTDC Before Top Dead Centre in terms of piston position. Ignition timing is often expressed in terms of degrees or millimetres BTDC.
Bush A cylindrical metal or rubber component used between two moving parts.
Burr Rough edge left on a component after machining or as a result of excessive wear.

C

Cam chain The chain which takes drive from the crankshaft to the camshaft(s).
Canister The main component in an evaporative emission control system (California market only); contains activated charcoal granules to trap vapours from the fuel system rather than allowing them to vent to the atmosphere.
Castellated Resembling the parapets along the top of a castle wall. For example, a castellated wheel axle or spindle nut.
Catalytic converter A device in the exhaust system of some machines which converts certain pollutants in the exhaust gases into less harmful substances.
Charging system Description of the components which charge the battery, ie the alternator, rectifier and regulator.
Circlip A ring-shaped clip used to prevent endwise movement of cylindrical parts and shafts. An internal circlip is installed in a groove in a housing; an external circlip fits into a groove on the outside of a cylindrical piece such as a shaft. Also known as a snap-ring.
Clearance The amount of space between two parts. For example, between a piston and a cylinder, between a bearing and a journal, etc.
Coil spring A spiral of elastic steel found in various sizes throughout a vehicle, for example as a springing medium in the suspension and in the valve train.
Compression Reduction in volume, and increase in pressure and temperature, of a gas, caused by squeezing it into a smaller space.
Compression damping Controls the speed the suspension compresses when hitting a bump.
Compression ratio The relationship between cylinder volume when the piston is at top dead centre and cylinder volume when the piston is at bottom dead centre.
Continuity The uninterrupted path in the flow of electricity. Little or no measurable resistance.
Continuity tester Self-powered bleeper or test light which indicates continuity.
Cp Candlepower. Bulb rating commonly found on US motorcycles.
Crossply tyre Tyre plies arranged in a criss-cross pattern. Usually four or six plies used, hence 4PR or 6PR in tyre size codes.
Cush drive Rubber damper segments fitted between the rear wheel and final drive sprocket to absorb transmission shocks **(see illustration)**.

Cush drive rubbers dampen out transmission shocks

D

Degree disc Calibrated disc for measuring piston position. Expressed in degrees.
Dial gauge Clock-type gauge with adapters for measuring runout and piston position. Expressed in mm or inches.
Diaphragm The rubber membrane in a master cylinder or carburettor which seals the upper chamber.
Diaphragm spring A single sprung plate often used in clutches.
Direct current (dc) Current produced by a dc generator.

Technical Terms Explained REF•49

Decarbonisation The process of removing carbon deposits - typically from the combustion chamber, valves and exhaust port/system.
Detonation Destructive and damaging explosion of fuel/air mixture in combustion chamber instead of controlled burning.
Diode An electrical valve which only allows current to flow in one direction. Commonly used in rectifiers and starter interlock systems.
Disc valve (or rotary valve) A induction system used on some two-stroke engines.
Double-overhead camshaft (DOHC) An engine that uses two overhead camshafts, one for the intake valves and one for the exhaust valves.
Drivebelt A toothed belt used to transmit drive to the rear wheel on some motorcycles. A drivebelt has also been used to drive the camshafts. Drivebelts are usually made of Kevlar.
Driveshaft Any shaft used to transmit motion. Commonly used when referring to the final driveshaft on shaft drive motorcycles.

E

Earth return The return path of an electrical circuit, utilising the motorcycle's frame.
ECU (Electronic Control Unit) A computer which controls (for instance) an ignition system, or an anti-lock braking system.
EGO Exhaust Gas Oxygen sensor. Sometimes called a Lambda sensor.
Electrolyte The fluid in a lead-acid battery.
EMS (Engine Management System) A computer controlled system which manages the fuel injection and the ignition systems in an integrated fashion.
Endfloat The amount of lengthways movement between two parts. As applied to a crankshaft, the distance that the crankshaft can move side-to-side in the crankcase.
Endless chain A chain having no joining link. Common use for cam chains and final drive chains.
EP (Extreme Pressure) Oil type used in locations where high loads are applied, such as between gear teeth.
Evaporative emission control system Describes a charcoal filled canister which stores fuel vapours from the tank rather than allowing them to vent to the atmosphere. Usually only fitted to California models and referred to as an EVAP system.
Expansion chamber Section of two-stroke engine exhaust system so designed to improve engine efficiency and boost power.

F

Feeler blade or gauge A thin strip or blade of hardened steel, ground to an exact thickness, used to check or measure clearances between parts.
Final drive Description of the drive from the transmission to the rear wheel. Usually by chain or shaft, but sometimes by belt.
Firing order The order in which the engine cylinders fire, or deliver their power strokes, beginning with the number one cylinder.
Flooding Term used to describe a high fuel level in the carburettor float chambers, leading to fuel overflow. Also refers to excess fuel in the combustion chamber due to incorrect starting technique.

Free length The no-load state of a component when measured. Clutch, valve and fork spring lengths are measured at rest, without any preload.
Freeplay The amount of travel before any action takes place. The looseness in a linkage, or an assembly of parts, between the initial application of force and actual movement. For example, the distance the rear brake pedal moves before the rear brake is actuated.
Fuel injection The fuel/air mixture is metered electronically and directed into the engine intake ports (indirect injection) or into the cylinders (direct injection). Sensors supply information on engine speed and conditions.
Fuel/air mixture The charge of fuel and air going into the engine. See **Stoichiometric ratio**.
Fuse An electrical device which protects a circuit against accidental overload. The typical fuse contains a soft piece of metal which is calibrated to melt at a predetermined current flow (expressed as amps) and break the circuit.

G

Gap The distance the spark must travel in jumping from the centre electrode to the side electrode in a spark plug. Also refers to the distance between the ignition rotor and the pickup coil in an electronic ignition system.
Gasket Any thin, soft material - usually cork, cardboard, asbestos or soft metal - installed between two metal surfaces to ensure a good seal. For instance, the cylinder head gasket seals the joint between the block and the cylinder head.
Gauge An instrument panel display used to monitor engine conditions. A gauge with a movable pointer on a dial or a fixed scale is an analogue gauge. A gauge with a numerical readout is called a digital gauge.
Gear ratios The drive ratio of a pair of gears in a gearbox, calculated on their number of teeth.
Glaze-busting see **Honing**
Grinding Process for renovating the valve face and valve seat contact area in the cylinder head.
Gudgeon pin The shaft which connects the connecting rod small-end with the piston. Often called a piston pin or wrist pin.

H

Helical gears Gear teeth are slightly curved and produce less gear noise that straight-cut gears. Often used for primary drives.

Installing a Helicoil thread insert in a cylinder head

Helicoil A thread insert repair system. Commonly used as a repair for stripped spark plug threads **(see illustration)**.
Honing A process used to break down the glaze on a cylinder bore (also called glaze-busting). Can also be carried out to roughen a rebored cylinder to aid ring bedding-in.
HT (High Tension) Description of the electrical circuit from the secondary winding of the ignition coil to the spark plug.
Hydraulic A liquid filled system used to transmit pressure from one component to another. Common uses on motorcycles are brakes and clutches.
Hydrometer An instrument for measuring the specific gravity of a lead-acid battery.
Hygroscopic Water absorbing. In motorcycle applications, braking efficiency will be reduced if DOT 3 or 4 hydraulic fluid absorbs water from the air - care must be taken to keep new brake fluid in tightly sealed containers.

I

lbf ft Pounds-force feet. An imperial unit of torque. Sometimes written as ft-lbs.
lbf in Pound-force inch. An imperial unit of torque, applied to components where a very low torque is required. Sometimes written as in-lbs.
IC Abbreviation for Integrated Circuit.
Ignition advance Means of increasing the timing of the spark at higher engine speeds. Done by mechanical means (ATU) on early engines or electronically by the ignition control unit on later engines.
Ignition timing The moment at which the spark plug fires, expressed in the number of crankshaft degrees before the piston reaches the top of its stroke, or in the number of millimetres before the piston reaches the top of its stroke.
Infinity (∞) Description of an open-circuit electrical state, where no continuity exists.
Inverted forks (upside down forks) The sliders or lower legs are held in the yokes and the fork tubes or stanchions are connected to the wheel axle (spindle). Less unsprung weight and stiffer construction than conventional forks.

J

JASO Quality standard for 2-stroke oils.
Joule The unit of electrical energy.
Journal The bearing surface of a shaft.

K

Kickstart Mechanical means of turning the engine over for starting purposes. Only usually fitted to mopeds, small capacity motorcycles and off-road motorcycles.
Kill switch Handebar-mounted switch for emergency ignition cut-out. Cuts the ignition circuit on all models, and additionally prevent starter motor operation on others.
km Symbol for kilometre.
kmh Abbreviation for kilometres per hour.

L

Lambda (λ) sensor A sensor fitted in the exhaust system to measure the exhaust gas oxygen content (excess air factor).

Technical Terms Explained

Lapping see **Grinding**.
LCD Abbreviation for Liquid Crystal Display.
LED Abbreviation for Light Emitting Diode.
Liner A steel cylinder liner inserted in a aluminium alloy cylinder block.
Locknut A nut used to lock an adjustment nut, or other threaded component, in place.
Lockstops The lugs on the lower triple clamp (yoke) which abut those on the frame, preventing handlebar-to-fuel tank contact.
Lockwasher A form of washer designed to prevent an attaching nut from working loose.
LT Low Tension Description of the electrical circuit from the power supply to the primary winding of the ignition coil.

M

Main bearings The bearings between the crankshaft and crankcase.
Maintenance-free (MF) battery A sealed battery which cannot be topped up.
Manometer Mercury-filled calibrated tubes used to measure intake tract vacuum. Used to synchronise carburettors on multi-cylinder engines.
Micrometer A precision measuring instrument that measures component outside diameters **(see illustration)**.

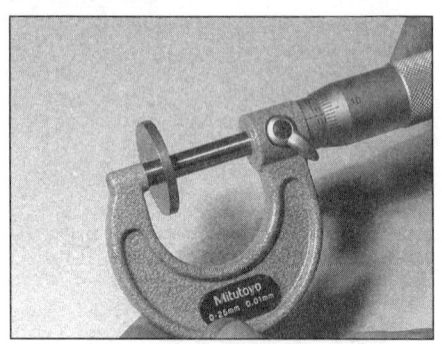

Tappet shims are measured with a micrometer

MON (Motor Octane Number) A measure of a fuel's resistance to knock.
Monograde oil An oil with a single viscosity, eg SAE80W.
Monoshock A single suspension unit linking the swingarm or suspension linkage to the frame.
mph Abbreviation for miles per hour.
Multigrade oil Having a wide viscosity range (eg 10W40). The W stands for Winter, thus the viscosity ranges from SAE10 when cold to SAE40 when hot.
Multimeter An electrical test instrument with the capability to measure voltage, current and resistance. Some meters also incorporate a continuity tester and buzzer.

N

Needle roller bearing Inner race of caged needle rollers and hardened outer race. Examples of uncaged needle rollers can be found on some engines. Commonly used in rear suspension applications and in two-stroke engines.
Nm Newton metres.
NOx Oxides of Nitrogen. A common toxic pollutant emitted by petrol engines at higher temperatures.

O

Octane The measure of a fuel's resistance to knock.
OE (Original Equipment) Relates to components fitted to a motorcycle as standard or replacement parts supplied by the motorcycle manufacturer.
Ohm The unit of electrical resistance. Ohms = Volts ÷ Current.
Ohmmeter An instrument for measuring electrical resistance.
Oil cooler System for diverting engine oil outside of the engine to a radiator for cooling purposes.
Oil injection A system of two-stroke engine lubrication where oil is pump-fed to the engine in accordance with throttle position.
Open-circuit An electrical condition where there is a break in the flow of electricity - no continuity (high resistance).
O-ring A type of sealing ring made of a special rubber-like material; in use, the O-ring is compressed into a groove to provide the sealing action.
Oversize (OS) Term used for piston and ring size options fitted to a rebored cylinder.
Overhead cam (sohc) engine An engine with single camshaft located on top of the cylinder head.
Overhead valve (ohv) engine An engine with the valves located in the cylinder head, but with the camshaft located in the engine block or crankcase.
Oxygen sensor A device installed in the exhaust system which senses the oxygen content in the exhaust and converts this information into an electric current. Also called a Lambda sensor.

P

Plastigauge A thin strip of plastic thread, available in different sizes, used for measuring clearances. For example, a strip of Plastigauge is laid across a bearing journal. The parts are assembled and dismantled; the width of the crushed strip indicates the clearance between journal and bearing.
Polarity Either negative or positive earth (ground), determined by which battery lead is connected to the frame (earth return). Modern motorcycles are usually negative earth.
Pre-ignition A situation where the fuel/air mixture ignites before the spark plug fires. Often due to a hot spot in the combustion chamber caused by carbon build-up. Engine has a tendency to 'run-on'.
Pre-load (suspension) The amount a spring is compressed when in the unloaded state. Preload can be applied by gas, spacer or mechanical adjuster.
Premix The method of engine lubrication on older two-stroke engines. Engine oil is mixed with the petrol in the fuel tank in a specific ratio. The fuel/oil mix is sometimes referred to as "petroil".
Primary drive Description of the drive from the crankshaft to the clutch. Usually by gear or chain.
PS Pfedestärke - a German interpretation of BHP.
PSI Pounds-force per square inch. Imperial measurement of tyre pressure and cylinder pressure measurement.
PTFE Polytetrafluroethylene. A low friction substance.
Pulse secondary air injection system A process of promoting the burning of excess fuel present in the exhaust gases by routing fresh air into the exhaust ports.

Q

Quartz halogen bulb Tungsten filament surrounded by a halogen gas. Typically used for the headlight **(see illustration)**.

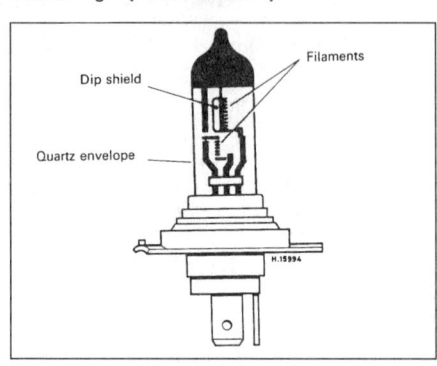

Quartz halogen headlight bulb construction

R

Rack-and-pinion A pinion gear on the end of a shaft that mates with a rack (think of a geared wheel opened up and laid flat). Sometimes used in clutch operating systems.
Radial play Up and down movement about a shaft.
Radial ply tyres Tyre plies run across the tyre (from bead to bead) and around the circumference of the tyre. Less resistant to tread distortion than other tyre types.
Radiator A liquid-to-air heat transfer device designed to reduce the temperature of the coolant in a liquid cooled engine.
Rake A feature of steering geometry - the angle of the steering head in relation to the vertical **(see illustration)**.

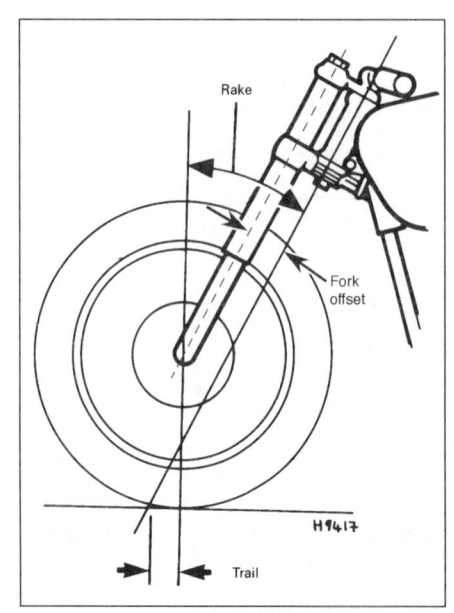

Steering geometry

Technical Terms Explained

Rebore Providing a new working surface to the cylinder bore by boring out the old surface. Necessitates the use of oversize piston and rings.
Rebound damping A means of controlling the oscillation of a suspension unit spring after it has been compressed. Resists the spring's natural tendency to bounce back after being compressed.
Rectifier Device for converting the ac output of an alternator into dc for battery charging.
Reed valve An induction system commonly used on two-stroke engines.
Regulator Device for maintaining the charging voltage from the generator or alternator within a specified range.
Relay A electrical device used to switch heavy current on and off by using a low current auxiliary circuit.
Resistance Measured in ohms. An electrical component's ability to pass electrical current.
RON (Research Octane Number) A measure of a fuel's resistance to knock.
rpm revolutions per minute.
Runout The amount of wobble (in-and-out movement) of a wheel or shaft as it's rotated. The amount a shaft rotates 'out-of-true'. The out-of-round condition of a rotating part.

S

SAE (Society of Automotive Engineers) A standard for the viscosity of a fluid.
Sealant A liquid or paste used to prevent leakage at a joint. Sometimes used in conjunction with a gasket.
Service limit Term for the point where a component is no longer useable and must be renewed.
Shaft drive A method of transmitting drive from the transmission to the rear wheel.
Shell bearings Plain bearings consisting of two shell halves. Most often used as big-end and main bearings in a four-stroke engine. Often called bearing inserts.
Shim Thin spacer, commonly used to adjust the clearance or relative positions between two parts. For example, shims inserted into or under tappets or followers to control valve clearances. Clearance is adjusted by changing the thickness of the shim.
Short-circuit An electrical condition where current shorts to earth (ground) bypassing the circuit components.
Skimming Process to correct warpage or repair a damaged surface, eg on brake discs or drums.
Slide-hammer A special puller that screws into or hooks onto a component such as a shaft or bearing; a heavy sliding handle on the shaft bottoms against the end of the shaft to knock the component free.
Small-end bearing The bearing in the upper end of the connecting rod at its joint with the gudgeon pin.
Spalling Damage to camshaft lobes or bearing journals shown as pitting of the working surface.
Specific gravity (SG) The state of charge of the electrolyte in a lead-acid battery. A measure of the electrolyte's density compared with water.
Straight-cut gears Common type gear used on gearbox shafts and for oil pump and water pump drives.
Stanchion The inner sliding part of the front forks, held by the yokes. Often called fork tube.
Stoichiometric ratio The optimum chemical air/fuel ratio for a petrol engine, said to be 14.7 parts of air to 1 part of fuel.
Sulphuric acid The liquid (electrolyte) used in a lead-acid battery. Poisonous and extremely corrosive.
Surface grinding (lapping) Process to correct a warped gasket face, commonly used on cylinder heads.

T

Tapered-roller bearing Tapered inner race of caged needle rollers and separate tapered outer race. Examples of taper roller bearings can be found on steering heads.
Tappet A cylindrical component which transmits motion from the cam to the valve stem, either directly or via a pushrod and rocker arm. Also called a cam follower.
TCS Traction Control System. An electronically-controlled system which senses wheel spin and reduces engine speed accordingly.
TDC Top Dead Centre denotes that the piston is at its highest point in the cylinder.
Thread-locking compound Solution applied to fastener threads to prevent slackening. Select type to suit application.
Thrust washer A washer positioned between two moving components on a shaft. For example, between gear pinions on gearshaft.
Timing chain See **Cam Chain**.
Timing light Stroboscopic lamp for carrying out ignition timing checks with the engine running.
Top-end A description of an engine's cylinder block, head and valve gear components.
Torque Turning or twisting force about a shaft.
Torque setting A prescribed tightness specified by the motorcycle manufacturer to ensure that the bolt or nut is secured correctly. Undertightening can result in the bolt or nut coming loose or a surface not being sealed. Overtightening can result in stripped threads, distortion or damage to the component being retained.
Torx key A six-point wrench.
Tracer A stripe of a second colour applied to a wire insulator to distinguish that wire from another one with the same colour insulator. For example, Br/W is often used to denote a brown insulator with a white tracer.
Trail A feature of steering geometry. Distance from the steering head axis to the tyre's central contact point.
Triple clamps The cast components which extend from the steering head and support the fork stanchions or tubes. Often called fork yokes.
Turbocharger A centrifugal device, driven by exhaust gases, that pressurises the intake air. Normally used to increase the power output from a given engine displacement.
TWI Abbreviation for Tyre Wear Indicator. Indicates the location of the tread depth indicator bars on tyres.

U

Universal joint or U-joint (UJ) A double-pivoted connection for transmitting power from a driving to a driven shaft through an angle. Typically found in shaft drive assemblies.
Unsprung weight Anything not supported by the bike's suspension (ie the wheel, tyres, brakes, final drive and bottom (moving) part of the suspension).

V

Vacuum gauges Clock-type gauges for measuring intake tract vacuum. Used for carburettor synchronisation on multi-cylinder engines.
Valve A device through which the flow of liquid, gas or vacuum may be stopped, started or regulated by a moveable part that opens, shuts or partially obstructs one or more ports or passageways. The intake and exhaust valves in the cylinder head are of the poppet type.
Valve clearance The clearance between the valve tip (the end of the valve stem) and the rocker arm or tappet/follower. The valve clearance is measured when the valve is closed. The correct clearance is important - if too small the valve won't close fully and will burn out, whereas if too large noisy operation will result.
Valve lift The amount a valve is lifted off its seat by the camshaft lobe.
Valve timing The exact setting for the opening and closing of the valves in relation to piston position.
Vernier caliper A precision measuring instrument that measures inside and outside dimensions. Not quite as accurate as a micrometer, but more convenient.
VIN Vehicle Identification Number. Term for the bike's engine and frame numbers.
Viscosity The thickness of a liquid or its resistance to flow.
Volt A unit for expressing electrical "pressure" in a circuit. Volts = current x ohms.

W

Water pump A mechanically-driven device for moving coolant around the engine.
Watt A unit for expressing electrical power. Watts = volts x current.
Wear limit see **Service limit**
Wet liner A liquid-cooled engine design where the pistons run in liners which are directly surrounded by coolant **(see illustration)**.

Wet liner arrangement

Wheelbase Distance from the centre of the front wheel to the centre of the rear wheel.
Wiring harness or loom Describes the electrical wires running the length of the motorcycle and enclosed in tape or plastic sheathing. Wiring coming off the main harness is usually referred to as a sub harness.
Woodruff key A key of semi-circular or square section used to locate a gear to a shaft. Often used to locate the alternator rotor on the crankshaft.
Wrist pin Another name for gudgeon or piston pin.

Index

Note: *References throughout this index are in the form - "Chapter number" • "Page number"*

A

Air filter – 1•11
Air filter housing – 3•5
Air induction system (AIS) – 1•12, 3•25
Alternator
    brushes – 1•25
    check, removal, inspection and installation – 8•23
    drive shaft – 2•50

B

Battery
    charging – 8•4
    check, inspection and maintenance – 1•16, 8•3, REF•44
    removal and installation – 8•3
    specifications – 8•1
Bleeding
    brakes – 6•13
    clutch – 2•38
Brake lights
    bulb check – 8•5
    bulb renewal – 8•7
    switch adjustment (rear) – 1•15
    switches – 8•9
Brakes
    bleeding – 6•13
    calipers – 6•6, 6•8
    check – 1•14
    discs – 6•5
    fault finding – REF•42
    fluid level check – 0•14
    fluid renewal – 1•26, 6•14
    hoses and unions – 1•26, 6•13
    lever – 5•6
    master cylinders – 6•10, 6•11
    pads – 1•14, 6•2
    pedal height adjustment – 1•15
    pedal removal and installation – 5•3
    seal renewal – 1•26
    specifications – 6•1
Bulbs
    brake/tail light – 8•7
    headlight – 8•5
    instrument – 8•12
    sidelight – 8•6
    turn signal – 8•8
    warning light – 8•13
    wattages – 8•2

C

Cables
    choke – 1•17, 3•21
    lubrication – 1•17
    speedometer – 8•11
    throttle – 1•16, 3•20
Calipers (brake) – 6•6, 6•8
Cam chain – 2•13
Cam chain tensioner – 2•12
Cam chain tensioner blades and guides – 2•14
Camshafts – 2•15
Carburettors
    float height/fuel level check – 3•15
    heater system – 3•22
    idle fuel/air mixture adjustment – 3•5
    idle speed adjustment – 1•9
    overhaul – 3•5, 3•7, 3•15
    removal and installation – 3•6
    separation and joining – 3•12
    specifications – 3•1
    synchronisation – 1•10
Centrestand – 1•16, 1•17, 5•4
Chain (cam) – 2•13
Chain (final drive) – 1•7, 5•2, 5•9
Charging system – 8•22
Choke cable
    check and adjustment – 1•17
    removal and installation – 3•21
Clutch
    fault finding – REF•39
    overhaul – 2•29
    specifications – 2•4
Clutch lever – 5•6
Clutch release mechanism
    bleeding – 2•38
    check – 1•15
    fluid level check – 0•15
    fluid renewal – 1•26
    hose renewal – 1•26
    master cylinder – 2•35
    release cylinder – 2•36
    seal renewal – 1•26
    specifications – 2•4
Clutch switch – 8•16
Connecting rods – 2•49, 2•54
Control unit (ignition) – 4•4
Conversion factors – REF•26
Crankcases – 2•46, 2•48
Crankshaft – 2•52
Cush drive – 5•20
Cylinder compression check – 1•26, REF•44
Cylinder block – 2•24
Cylinder head – 2•19, 2•20

Index

D

Dimensions – 0•11
Discs (brake) – 6•5

E

Electrical system
  alternator – 1•25, 8•23
  battery – 1•16, 8•3, 8•4
  brake light switches – 8•9
  brake/tail light – 8•7
  clutch switch – 8•16
  fault finding – 8•3, REF•43
  fuel gauge and level sender – 3•24
  fuses – 8•4
  handlebar switches – 8•14
  headlight – 1•26, 8•5, 8•6
  horns – 8•17
  instrument cluster – 8•9, 8•10, 8•12
  lighting system – 8•5
  neutral switch – 8•15
  oil level sensor and relay – 8•17
  regulator/rectifier – 8•25
  sidestand switch – 8•15
  specifications – 8•1
  starter circuit cut-off relay – 8•16
  starter motor – 8•19
  starter relay – 8•18
  turn signals – 8•8
  wiring diagrams – 8•26
Engine
  cam chain – 2•13
  cam chain tensioner – 2•12
  cam chain tensioner blade and guides – 2•14
  camshafts – 2•15
  connecting rods – 2•54
  crankcases – 2•46, 2•48
  crankshaft – 2•52
  cylinder block – 2•24
  cylinder compression check – 1•26, REF•44
  cylinder head – 2•19, 2•20
  fault finding – REF•36, REF•40
  followers – 2•15
  idle speed – 1•9
  main and connecting rod bearings – 2•49
  oil change – 1•13
  oil cooler – 2•11
  oil level check – 0•13
  oil level sensor and relay – 8•17
  oil and filter change – 1•20
  oil pressure check – 1•26
  oil pressure relief valves – 2•44
  oil pump – 2•41
  oil strainer – 2•44
  oil sump – 2•44
  piston rings – 2•28
  pistons – 2•26
  removal and installation – 2•6
  running-in – 2•64
  specifications – 2•2
  valve clearances – 1•21
  valve cover – 2•12
  valves – 2•20
Engine number – 0•12
Exhaust system – 3•23

F

Fault finding – REF•35 *et seq*
Filter
  air – 1•10
  fuel – 1•13
  oil – 1•20
Final drive chain
  adjustment – 1•7
  checks – 0•16, 1•7
  lubrication – 1•8
  removal, cleaning and installation – 5•19
  specifications – 5•2
Final drive sprockets
  checks – 1•7, 5•19
  removal and installation – 5•19
  sizes – 5•2
Float height/fuel level check – 3•15
Followers – 2•15
Footrests – 5•3
Frame – 5•2
Frame number – 0•12
Front brake
  calipers – 6•6
  discs – 6•5
  fluid level check – 0•14
  fluid renewal – 1•26, 6•14
  hoses and unions – 1•26, 6•13
  lever – 5•6
  master cylinder – 6•10
  pads – 1•14, 6•2
  specifications – 6•1
Front forks
  check – 1•18
  oil renewal – 1•27, 5•7
  overhaul – 5•8
  removal and installation – 5•6
  specifications – 5•1
Front mudguard – 7•3
Front sprocket – 5•20
Front wheel
  bearings – 6•18
  removal and installation – 6•15
Fuel system
  carburettors – 1•10, 3•5, 3•6, 3•7, 3•12, 3•15, 3•22
  filters – 1•12
  gauge and level sender – 3•24, 8•12
  hose renewal – 1•27
  tank – 3•3, 3•5
  tap – 3•4
Fuses
  check and renewal – 8•4
  ratings – 8•2

G

Gearbox – 2•56, 2•57
Gearchange
  fault finding – REF•40
  lever – 5•3
  mechanism – 2•38

Index

H

Handlebar levers – 5•6
Handlebar switches – 8•14
Handlebars – 5•5
Headlight
  aim – 1•26
  bulb – 8•5
  check – 8•5
  unit – 8•6
Heater system (carburettor) – 3•22
Horns – 8•17
HT coils – 4•3

I

Idle fuel/air mixture adjustment – 3•5
Idle speed – 1•9
Ignition (main) switch – 8•13
Ignition system
  check – 4•2
  HT coils – 4•3
  ignition control unit – 4•4
  pick-up coil – 4•3
  throttle position sensor – 4•5
  timing – 4•5
Instrument cluster – 8•9, 8•10, 8•12

L

Legal checks – 0•16
Lubricants and fluids – 1•2, REF•23

M

Main bearings – 2•49, 2•52
Maintenance procedures – 1•5 *et seq*
Maintenance schedule – 1•3, 1•4
Master cylinder
  clutch – 2•35
  front brake – 6•10
  rear brake – 6•11
Mirrors – 7•4
Model development – 0•10
MOT test – REF•27
Mudguard (front) – 7•3

N

Neutral switch – 8•15

O

Oil (engine/transmission)
  change – 1•13
  filter change – 1•20
  level check – 0•13
  types – 1•2

Oil (front forks) – 1•27, 5•7
Oil cooler – 2•11
Oil level sensor and relay – 8•17
Oil pump – 2•41
Oil pressure check – 1•26
Oil pressure relief valves – 2•44
Oil strainer – 2•44
Oil sump – 2•44

P

Pads (brake) – 1•14, 6•2
Performance data – 0•10
Pick-up coil – 4•3
Piston rings – 2•28
Pistons – 2•26
Pressure relief valves – 2•44
Pump (oil) – 2•41

R

Rear brake
  caliper – 6•8
  disc – 6•5
  fluid level check – 0•14
  fluid renewal – 1•26, 6•14
  hoses and unions – 1•26, 6•13
  master cylinder – 6•11
  pads – 1•14, 6•4
  pedal height adjustment – 1•15
  pedal removal and installation – 5•3
  specifications – 6•1
Rear suspension
  adjustment – 5•16
  checks – 1•18
  shock absorbers – 5•15
  swingarm – 5•17, 5•18
Rear sprocket – 5•20, 6•19
Rear view mirrors – 7•4
Rear wheel
  bearings – 6•19
  removal and installation – 6•16
  sprocket coupling – 5•20, 6•19
Regulator/rectifier – 8•25
Release cylinder (clutch) – 2•36
Rubber dampers (sprocket coupling) – 5•20
Running-in – 2•64

S

Safety – 0•9, 0•16
Seat – 7•2
Security – REF•20
Selector drum and forks – 2•62
Side panels – 7•2
Sidelight – 8•6
Sidestand – 1•16, 1•17, 5•4
Sidestand switch – 8•15
Spark plugs – 1•9

Specifications
 brakes – 6•1
 clutch – 2•4
 electrical system – 8•1
 engine – 2•2
 final drive – 5•2
 front forks – 5•1
 fuel system – 3•1
 general – 0•11
 ignition system – 4•1
 routine maintenance and servicing – 1•2
 transmission – 2•4
Speedometer – 8•10
Speedometer cable – 8•11
Sprocket coupling – 5•20, 6•19
Sprockets
 checks – 1•7, 5•19
 removal and installation – 5•19
 sizes – 5•2
Starter circuit cut-off relay – 8•16
Starter clutch and idle/reduction gear – 2•50
Starter motor – 8•19
Starter relay – 8•18
Steering checks – 0•16
Steering head bearings
 check and adjustment – 1•19
 re-greasing – 1•21
 renewal – 5•14
Steering stem – 5•12
Storage – REF•32
Sump – 2•44
Suspension
 adjustment – 5•16
 checks – 0•16, 1•18
 fault finding – REF•41
 front forks – 1•27, 5•6, 5•7, 5•8
 rear shocks – 5•15
 specifications – 5•1
 swingarm – 5•17, 5•18
Swingarm
 bearings – 1•21, 5•18
 check – 1•18
 removal and installation – 5•17

T

Tachometer – 8•11

Tail light – 8•7
Tail light cover – 7•3
Tank (fuel) – 3•3, 3•5
Tap (fuel) – 3•4
Tensioner (cam chain) – 2•12
Tensioner blade (cam chain) – 2•14
Throttle cables
 adjustment – 1•16
 removal and installation – 3•20
Throttle position sensor – 4•5
Timing (ignition) – 4•5
Timing (valve) – 2•17
Tools – REF•2
Torque wrench settings – 1•2, 2•4, 3•2, 4•1, 5•2, 6•2, 8•2
Transmission
 gearshafts – 2•56, 2•57
 selector drum and forks – 2•62
 specifications – 2•4
Turn signals – 8•8
Tyres
 general information and fitting – 6•20
 pressures and tread depth – 0•16
 sizes – 6•2

V

Valve clearances – 1•21
Valve cover – 2•12
Valves – 2•20

W

Warning light bulbs – 8•13
Weights – 0•11
Wheel bearings
 check – 1•16
 renewal – 6•18
Wheels
 alignment – 6•14
 bearings – 1•16, 6•18
 inspection and repair – 1•16, 6•14
 removal and installation – 6•15, 6•16
 sizes – 6•2
Wiring diagrams – 8•26

Haynes Motorcycle Manuals – The Complete List

Title	Book No
BMW	
BMW 2-valve Twins (70 - 96)	0249
BMW K100 & 75 2-valve Models (83 - 96)	1373
BMW R850 & R1100 4-valve Twins (93 - 97)	3466
BSA	
BSA Bantam (48 - 71)	0117
BSA Unit Singles (58 - 72)	0127
BSA Pre-unit Singles (54 - 61)	0326
BSA A7 & A10 Twins (47 - 62)	0121
BSA A50 & A65 Twins (62 - 73)	0155
DUCATI	
Ducati MK III & Desmo Singles (69 - 76)	0445
Ducati 600, 750 & 900 2-valve V-Twins (91 - 96)	3290
Ducati 748, 916 & 996 4-valve V-Twins (94 - 01)	3756
HARLEY-DAVIDSON	
Harley-Davidson Sportsters (70 - 01)	0702
Harley-Davidson Big Twins (70 - 99)	0703
HONDA	
Honda NB, ND, NP & NS50 Melody (81 - 85)	◊ 0622
Honda NE/NB50 Vision & SA50 Vision Met-in (85 - 95)	◊ 1278
Honda MB, MBX, MT & MTX50 (80 - 93)	0731
Honda C50, C70 & C90 (67 - 99)	0324
Honda XR80R & XR100R (85 - 96)	2218
Honda XL/XR 80, 100, 125, 185 & 200 2-valve Models (78 - 87)	0566
Honda H100 & H100S Singles (80 - 92)	◊ 0734
Honda CB/CD125T & CM125C Twins (77 - 88)	◊ 0571
Honda CG125 (76 - 00)	◊ 0433
Honda NS125 (86 - 93)	◊ 3056
Honda MBX/MTX125 & MTX200 (83 - 93)	◊ 1132
Honda CD/CM185 200T & CM250C 2-valve Twins (77 - 85)	0572
Honda XL/XR 250 & 500 (78 - 84)	0567
Honda XR250L, XR250R & XR400R (86 - 01)	2219
Honda CB250 & CB400N Super Dreams (78 - 84)	◊ 0540
Honda CR Motocross Bikes (86 - 01)	2222
Honda Elsinore 250 (73 - 75)	0217
Honda CBR400RR Fours (88 - 99)	3552
Honda VFR400 (NC30) & RVF400 (NC35) V-Fours (89 - 98)	3496
Honda CB500 (93 - 01)	3753
Honda CB400 & CB550 Fours (73 - 77)	0262
Honda CX/GL500 & 650 V-Twins (78 - 86)	0442
Honda CBX550 Four (82 - 86)	◊ 0940
Honda XL600R & XR600R (83 - 00)	2183
Honda XL600/650V Transalp & XRV750 Africa Twin (87 - 02)	3919
Honda CBR600F1 & 1000F Fours (87 - 96)	1730
Honda CBR600F2 & F3 Fours (91 - 98)	2070
Honda CBR600F4 (99 - 02)	3911
Honda CB600F Hornet (98 - 02)	3915
Honda CB650 sohc Fours (78 - 84)	0665
Honda NTV600/650/Deauville V-Twins (88 - 01)	3243
Honda Shadow VT600 & 750 (USA) (88 - 00)	2312
Honda CB750 sohc Four (69 - 79)	0131
Honda V45/65 Sabre & Magna (82 - 88)	0820
Honda VFR750 & 700 V-Fours (86 - 97)	2101
Honda VFR800 V-Fours (97 - 01)	3703
Honda VTR1000 (FireStorm, Super Hawk) & XL1000V (Varadero) (97 - 00)	3744
Honda CB750 & CB900 dohc Fours (78 - 84)	0535
Honda CBR900RR FireBlade (92 - 99)	2161
Honda CBR900RR FireBlade (00 - 03)	4060
Honda CBR1100XX Super Blackbird (97 - 02)	3901
Honda ST1100 Pan European V-Fours (90 - 01)	3384
Honda Shadow VT1100 (USA) (85 - 98)	2313
Honda GL1000 Gold Wing (75 - 79)	0309

Title	Book No
Honda GL1100 Gold Wing (79 - 81)	0669
Honda Gold Wing 1200 (USA) (84 - 87)	2199
Honda Gold Wing 1500 (USA) (88 - 00)	2225
KAWASAKI	
Kawasaki AE/AR 50 & 80 (81 - 95)	1007
Kawasaki KC, KE & KH100 (75 - 99)	1371
Kawasaki KMX125 & 200 (86 - 02)	◊ 3046
Kawasaki 250, 350 & 400 Triples (72 - 79)	0134
Kawasaki 400 & 440 Twins (74 - 81)	0281
Kawasaki 400, 500 & 550 Fours (79 - 91)	0910
Kawasaki EN450 & 500 Twins (Ltd/Vulcan) (85 - 93)	2053
Kawasaki EX & ER500 (GPZ500S & ER-5) Twins (87 - 99)	2052
Kawasaki ZX600 (Ninja ZX-6, ZZ-R600) Fours (90 - 00)	2146
Kawasaki ZX-6R Ninja Fours (95 - 98)	3541
Kawasaki ZX600 (GPZ600R, GPX600R, Ninja 600R & RX) & ZX750 (GPX750R, Ninja 750R) Fours (85 - 97)	1780
Kawasaki 650 Four (76 - 78)	0373
Kawasaki Vulcan 700/750 & 800 (85 - 01)	2457
Kawasaki 750 Air-cooled Fours (80 - 91)	0574
Kawasaki ZR550 & 750 Zephyr Fours (90 - 97)	3382
Kawasaki ZX750 (Ninja ZX-7 & ZXR750) Fours (89 - 96)	2054
Kawasaki Ninja ZX-7R & ZX-9R (ZX750P, ZX900B/C/D/E) (94 - 00)	3721
Kawasaki 900 & 1000 Fours (73 - 77)	0222
Kawasaki ZX900, 1000 & 1100 Liquid-cooled Fours (83 - 97)	1681
MOTO GUZZI	
Moto Guzzi 750, 850 & 1000 V-Twins (74 - 78)	0339
MZ	
MZ ETZ Models (81 - 95)	◊ 1680
NORTON	
Norton 500, 600, 650 & 750 Twins (57 - 70)	0187
Norton Commando (68 - 77)	0125
PEUGEOT	
Peugeot Speedfight, Trekker & Vivacity Scooters (96 - 02)	3920
PIAGGIO	
Piaggio (Vespa) Scooters (91 - 98)	3492
SUZUKI	
Suzuki GT, ZR & TS50 (77 - 90)	◊ 0799
Suzuki TS50X (84 - 00)	◊ 1599
Suzuki 100, 125, 185 & 250 Air-cooled Trail bikes (79 - 89)	0797
Suzuki GP100 & 125 Singles (78 - 93)	◊ 0576
Suzuki GS, GN, GZ & DR125 Singles (82 - 99)	◊ 0888
Suzuki 250 & 350 Twins (68 - 78)	0120
Suzuki GT250X7, GT200X5 & SB200 Twins (78 - 83)	◊ 0469
Suzuki GS/GSX250, 400 & 450 Twins (79 - 85)	0736
Suzuki GS500 Twin (89 - 02)	3238
Suzuki GS550 (77 - 82) & GS750 Fours (76 - 79)	0363
Suzuki GS/GSX550 4-valve Fours (83 - 88)	1133
Suzuki SV650 (99 - 02)	3912
Suzuki GSX-R600 & 750 (96 - 99)	3553
Suzuki GSX-R600 (01 - 02), GSX-R750 (00 - 02) & GSX-R1000 (01 - 02)	3986
Suzuki GSF600 & 1200 Bandit Fours (95 - 01)	3367
Suzuki GS850 Fours (78 - 88)	0536
Suzuki GS1000 Four (77 - 79)	0484
Suzuki GSX-R750, GSX-R1100 (85 - 92), GSX600F, GSX750F, GSX1100F (Katana) Fours (88 - 96)	2055
Suzuki GSX600/750F & GSX750 (98 - 02)	3987
Suzuki GS/GSX1000, 1100 & 1150 4-valve Fours (79 - 88)	0737
TRIUMPH	
Triumph Tiger Cub & Terrier (52 - 68)	0414
Triumph 350 & 500 Unit Twins (58 - 73)	0137
Triumph Pre-Unit Twins (47 - 62)	0251
Triumph 650 & 750 2-valve Unit Twins (63 - 83)	0122
Triumph Trident & BSA Rocket 3 (69 - 75)	0136
Triumph Fuel Injected Triples (97 - 00)	3755
Triumph Triples & Fours (carburettor engines) (91 - 99)	2162

Title	Book No
VESPA	
Vespa P/PX125, 150 & 200 Scooters (78 - 95)	0707
Vespa Scooters (59 - 78)	0126
YAMAHA	
Yamaha DT50 & 80 Trail Bikes (78 - 95)	◊ 0800
Yamaha T50 & 80 Townmate (83 - 95)	◊ 1247
Yamaha YB100 Singles (73 - 91)	◊ 0474
Yamaha RS/RXS100 & 125 Singles (74 - 95)	0331
Yamaha RD & DT125LC (82 - 87)	◊ 0887
Yamaha TZR125 (87 - 93) & DT125R (88 - 02)	◊ 1655
Yamaha TY50, 80, 125 & 175 (74 - 84)	◊ 0464
Yamaha XT & SR125 (82 - 02)	1021
Yamaha Trail Bikes (81 - 00)	2350
Yamaha 250 & 350 Twins (70 - 79)	0040
Yamaha XS250, 360 & 400 sohc Twins (75 - 84)	0378
Yamaha RD250 & 350LC Twins (80 - 82)	0803
Yamaha RD350 YPVS Twins (83 - 95)	1158
Yamaha RD400 Twin (75 - 79)	0333
Yamaha XT, TT & SR500 Singles (75 - 83)	0342
Yamaha XZ550 Vision V-Twins (82 - 85)	0821
Yamaha FJ, FZ, XJ & YX600 Radian (84 - 92)	2100
Yamaha XJ600S (Diversion, Seca II) & XJ600N Fours (92 - 99)	2145
Yamaha YZF600R Thundercat & FZS600 Fazer (96 - 01)	3702
Yamaha YZF-R6 (98 - 02)	3900
Yamaha 650 Twins (70 - 83)	0341
Yamaha XJ650 & 750 Fours (80 - 84)	0738
Yamaha XS750 & 850 Triples (76 - 85)	0340
Yamaha TDM850, TRX850 & XTZ750 (89 - 99)	3540
Yamaha YZF750R & YZF1000R Thunderace (93 - 00)	3720
Yamaha FZR600, 750 & 1000 Fours (87 - 96)	2056
Yamaha XV V-Twins (81 - 96)	0802
Yamaha XJ900F Fours (83 - 94)	3239
Yamaha XJ900S Diversion (94 - 01)	3739
Yamaha YZF-R1 (98 - 01)	3754
Yamaha FJ1100 & 1200 Fours (84 - 96)	2057
Yamaha XJR1200 & 1300 (95 - 03)	3981
ATVs	
Honda ATC70, 90, 110, 185 & 200 (71 - 85)	0565
Honda TRX300 Shaft Drive ATVs (88 - 00)	2125
Honda TRX300EX & TRX400EX ATVs (93 - 99)	2318
Honda Foreman 400 and 450 ATVs (95 - 02)	2465
Kawasaki Bayou 220/300 & Prairie 300 ATVs (86 - 01)	2351
Polaris ATVs (85 to 97)	2302
Yamaha YT, YFM, YTM & YTZ ATVs (80 - 85)	1154
Yamaha YFS200 Blaster ATV (88 - 98)	2317
Yamaha YFB250 Timberwolf ATV (92 - 96)	2217
Yamaha YFM350 (ER and Big Bear) ATVs (87 - 99)	2126
Yamaha Warrior and Banshee ATVs (87 - 99)	2314
ATV Basics	10450
MOTORCYCLE TECHBOOKS	
Motorcycle Basics TechBook (2nd Edition)	3515
Motorcycle Electrical TechBook (3rd Edition)	3471
Motorcycle Fuel Systems TechBook	3514
Motorcycle Workshop Practice TechBook (2nd Edition)	3470

◊ = not available in the USA   **Bold type** = Superbike

The manuals on this page are available through good motorcycle dealers and accessory shops. In case of difficulty, contact: **Haynes Publishing** (UK) +44 1963 442030   (USA) +1 805 498 6703 (FR) +33 1 47 17 66 29   (SV) +46 18 124016 (Australia/New Zealand) +61 3 9763 8100

Preserving Our Motoring Heritage

The Model J Duesenberg Derham Tourster. Only eight of these magnificent cars were ever built – this is the only example to be found outside the United States of America

Almost every car you've ever loved, loathed or desired is gathered under one roof at the Haynes Motor Museum. Over 300 immaculately presented cars and motorbikes represent every aspect of our motoring heritage, from elegant reminders of bygone days, such as the superb Model J Duesenberg to curiosities like the bug-eyed BMW Isetta. There are also many old friends and flames. Perhaps you remember the 1959 Ford Popular that you did your courting in? The magnificent 'Red Collection' is a spectacle of classic sports cars including AC, Alfa Romeo, Austin Healey, Ferrari, Lamborghini, Maserati, MG, Riley, Porsche and Triumph.

A Perfect Day Out

Each and every vehicle at the Haynes Motor Museum has played its part in the history and culture of Motoring. Today, they make a wonderful spectacle and a great day out for all the family. Bring the kids, bring Mum and Dad, but above all bring your camera to capture those golden memories for ever. You will also find an impressive array of motoring memorabilia, a comfortable 70 seat video cinema and one of the most extensive transport book shops in Britain. The Pit Stop Cafe serves everything from a cup of tea to wholesome, home-made meals or, if you prefer, you can enjoy the large picnic area nestled in the beautiful rural surroundings of Somerset.

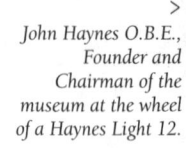

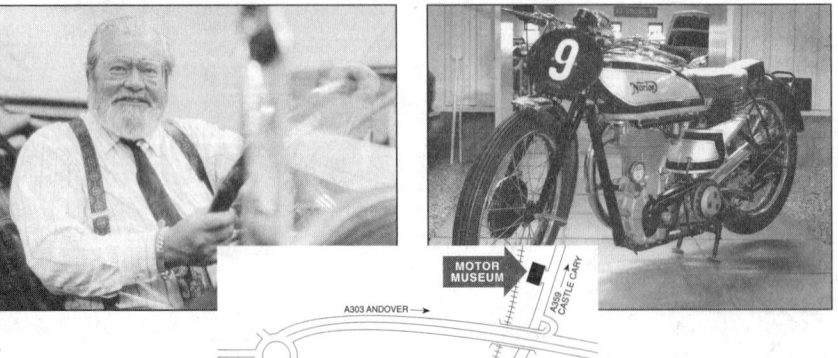

John Haynes O.B.E., Founder and Chairman of the museum at the wheel of a Haynes Light 12.

The 1936 490cc sohc-engined International Norton – well known for its racing success

The Museum is situated on the A359 Yeovil to Frome road at Sparkford, just off the A303 in Somerset. It is about 40 miles south of Bristol, and 25 minutes drive from the M5 intersection at Taunton.
Open 9.30am - 5.30pm (10.00am - 4.00pm Winter) 7 days a week, *except Christmas Day, Boxing Day and New Years Day*
Special rates available for schools, coach parties and outings Charitable Trust No. 292048